3 x CARLIN
AN ORGY of GEORGE

3x CARLIN
AN ORGY of GEORGE

George Carlin

HYPERION

NEW YORK

ISBN 978-1-4013-0243-6

CONTENTS

brain droppings

GEORGE CARLIN

 HYPERION

NEW YORK

This book is dedicated to my big brother Patrick,
who was kind enough to teach me attitude.

ACKNOWLEDGMENTS

I would like to acknowledge the invaluable assistance and direction I received from my (very first) editor in assembling this book. Laurie Abkemeier took the many disparate items I turned in and somehow fashioned a coherent book. Her calm, professional style also helped keep my inner maniac somewhat in check. Somewhat. Thank you, Laurie.

This would also be a good time to acknowledge and express gratitude for the wise and careful guidance my career has received over the past 15 years from Jerry Hamza. His judgment, generosity, and belief in my career's long-term potential have helped me reach a level I never expected. It isn't often a performer can say his manager is also his best friend. I can. By the way, it helps a little that Jerry's inner maniac is even weirder than mine.

And finally, a sincere thank you to my first boss in radio, Joe Monroe, who, when I was 18, told me always to write down my ideas and save them. He also gave me my start. Thanks, buddy.

"There is a vitality, a life force, a quickening that is translated through you into action, and because there is only one of you in all time, this expression is unique. And if you block it, it will never exist through any other medium and be lost. The world will not have it. It is not your business to determine how good it is, nor how valuable it is, nor how it compares with other expressions. It is your business to keep it yours clearly and directly, to keep the channel open. You do not even have to believe in yourself or your work. You have to keep yourself open and aware directly to the urges that motivate you. Keep the channel open. . . .

"No artist is pleased. . . . [There is no] satisfaction whatever at any time. There is only a queer, divine dissatisfaction, a blessed unrest that keeps us marching and makes us more alive than the others."

—Martha Graham to Agnes de Mille, *Martha: The Life and Work of Martha Graham*

"We shall never understand one another until we reduce the language to seven words."

—Kahlil Gibran, *Sand and Foam*

PREFACE

For a long time, my stand-up material has drawn from three sources. The first is the English language: words, phrases, sayings, and the ways we speak. The second source, as with most comedians, has been what I think of as the "little world," those things we all experience every day: driving, food, pets, relationships, and idle thoughts. The third area is what I call the "big world": war, politics, race, death, and social issues. Without having actually measured, I would say this book reflects that balance very closely.

The first two areas will speak for themselves, but concerning the "big world," let me say a few things.

I'm happy to tell you there is very little in this world that I believe in. Listening to the comedians who comment on political, social, and cultural issues, I notice most of their material reflects an underlying belief that somehow things were better once and that with just a little effort we could set them right again. They're looking for solutions, and rooting for particular results, and I think that necessarily limits the tone and substance of what they say. They're talented and funny people, but they're nothing more than cheerleaders attached to a specific, wished-for outcome.

I don't feel so confined. I frankly don't give a fuck how it all turns out in this country—or anywhere else, for that matter. I think the human game was up a long time ago (when the high priests and traders took over), and now we're just playing out the string. And that is, of course, precisely what I find so amusing: the slow circling of the drain by a once promising species, and the sappy, ever-more-desperate belief in this country that there is actually some sort of "American Dream," which has merely been misplaced.

The decay and disintegration of this culture is astonishingly amusing if you are emotionally detached from it. I have always viewed it from a safe distance, knowing I don't belong; it doesn't include me, and it never has. No matter how you care to define it, **I do not identify with the local group.** Planet, species, race, nation, state, religion, party, union, club, association, neighborhood improvement committee; I have no interest in any of it. I love and treasure individuals as I meet them, I loathe and despise the groups they identify with and belong to.

So, if you read something in this book that sounds like advocacy of a particular political point of view, please reject the notion. My interest in "issues" is merely to point out how badly we're doing, not to suggest a way we might do better. Don't confuse me with those who cling to hope. I enjoy describing how things are, I have no interest in how they "ought to be." And I certainly have no interest in fixing them. I sincerely believe that if you think there's a solution, you're part of the problem. My motto: Fuck Hope!

P.S. Lest you wonder, personally, I am a joyful individual with a long, happy marriage and a close and loving family. My career has turned out better than I ever dreamed, and it continues to expand. I am a personal optimist but a skeptic about all else. What may sound to some like anger is really nothing more than sympathetic contempt. I view my species with a combination of wonder and pity, and I root for its destruction. And please don't confuse my point of view with cynicism; the real cynics are the ones who tell you everything's gonna be all right.

P.P.S. By the way, if, by some chance, you folks do manage to straighten things out and make everything better, I still don't wish to be included.

PEOPLE AHEAD OF ME ON LINE

Here's something I can do without: People ahead of me on the supermarket line who are paying for an inexpensive item by credit card or personal check. People! Take my word for this: Tic Tacs is not a major purchase. And, I get just as discouraged when a guy who's buying a simple jar of spaghetti sauce tries to pay with a letter of credit from the Bank of Liechtenstein. Folks, carry some fuckin' money around, will ya? It comes in handy! No one should be borrowing money from a bank at 18 percent interest to buy a loaf of bread.

And what about these cretins at the airport gift shop who think somehow they're in the Mall of America? It's an airport! I'm standin' there with one newspaper and a pack of gum; I gotta get to my plane. Why does the genetic defective ahead of me choose this moment to purchase a complete set of dishes and a new fall wardrobe? What is this, fuckin' Macy's? And of course, the clerk lady has to carefully wrap each dish separately, but she's working real fast—because she's eighty-nine!! Plus she's from Sri Lanka. The rural part. And now dishman wants to know if it's okay to use Turkish traveler's checks. You know what I do? I steal things. Fuck 'em! I grab a handful of candy bars and six magazines and head for the gate. My attitude? It wasn't their stuff to begin with.

PEOPLE WHO SHOULD BE PHASED OUT

❏ Guys who always harmonize the last few notes of "Happy Birthday."

❏ People over 40 who can't put on reading glasses without making self-conscious remarks about their advancing age.

❏ Guys who wink when they're kidding.

❏ Men who propose marriage on the giant TV screen at a sports stadium.

❏ Guys in their fifties who flash me the peace sign and really mean it.

❏ People with a small patch of natural white hair who think it makes them look interesting.

❏ Guys with creases in their jeans.

❏ People who know a lot of prayers by heart.

❏ People who move their lips—when *I'm* talking!

❏ Guys who want to shake my hand even though we just saw each other an hour ago.

❏ A celebrity couple who adopt a Third-World baby and call it Rain Forest.

❏ Guys who wear suits all day and think an earring makes them cool at night.

❏ Old people who tell me what the weather used to be where they used to live.

☐ Men who have one long, uninterrupted eyebrow.

☐ Guys who wink and give me the peace sign simultaneously.

✖ People who say, "Knock knock," when entering a room and, "Beep beep," when someone is in their path.

☐ Fat guys who laugh at everything.

☐ People who have memorized a lot of TV-show theme songs and are really proud of it.

✖ Women who think it's cute to have first names consisting solely of initials.

☐ People who give their house or car a name.

☐ People who give their genitals a name.

☐ Guys who can juggle, but only a little bit.

☐ Actors who drive race cars.

✖ Men who wear loafers without socks. Especially if they have creases in their jeans.

☐ Athletes and coaches who give more than a hundred percent.

☐ Guys who still smell like their soap in the late afternoon.

✖ Blind people who don't want any help.

✖ Guys who wear their watches on the inside of their wrists.

✖ Any man who wears a suit and tie to a ballgame.

✖ Guys who flash me the thumbs-up sign. Especially if they're winking and making the peace sign with the other hand.

SEVEN THINGS I'M TIRED OF

I'm gettin' tired of guys who smoke pipes. When are they gonna outlaw this shit? Guy with a fuckin' pipe! It's an arrogant thing to place a burning barrier between you and the rest of the world. It's supposed to imply thoughtfulness or intelligence. It's not intelligent to stand around with a controlled fire sticking out of your mouth. I say, "Hey, professor! You want somethin' hot to suck on? Call me! I'll give ya somethin' to put in your mouth!" I think these pipe-smokers oughta just move to the next level and go ahead and suck a dick. There's nothing wrong with suckin' dicks. Men do it, women do it; can't be all bad if everybody's doin' it. I say, Drop the pipe, and go to the dick! That's my advice. I'm here to help.

I'm also sick of car alarms. Not the screeching and beeping; that doesn't bother me. It's just the idea of a car alarm that I find offensive. Especially the ones that talk to you: "Move away! Move away!" "Ohhhh? Really!" That's when I reach for my sharpest key. And I put a deep gouge in that paint job, all the way 'round the car. Three hundred and sixty degrees. I might even make two trips around, if I don't have a luncheon appointment that day. And then I walk away slowly, unconcerned about the screeching and beeping, because I know that no one takes car alarms seriously. Car alarms are a Yuppie-boomer conceit, and they're responsible for most of the carjacking that's going on. Car alarms and The Club have have made it harder for thieves to steal parked cars, and so instead they're stealing cars with people in them, and people are dying. And it's all because these selfish, boomer degenerates can't stand to part with their personal property. Fuck boomers, and fuck their pussified car alarms!

I'm also sick of having to look at bearded guys who don't know how to trim the lower edges of their beards, where they extend back toward the neck. They trim too far up toward the chin, leaving a glaring, fleshy strip where there ought to be hair. Guys, you need to let the beard extend far enough back under your chin, so it reaches the point where your neck begins. Then, from the fold or angle that forms between your jaw and neck, you shave downward. If you don't have that fold; if you have a fat, fleshy pouch under your jaw with no definition, you shouldn't be trimming your beard at all. You should let it grow long and bushy, so it covers that goofy-looking pouch.

And I've just about had it with all these geeky fucks who walk around listening to Walkmans. What are these jack-offs telling us? They're too good to participate in daily life? They're sealing themselves off? Big fuckin' loss. And what is it they're listening to that's so compelling? I think a person has to be fairly uncomfortable with his thoughts to have the need to block them out while simply walking around. I'd love to know how many of these obviously disturbed people become suicides.

I've also grown weary of reading about clouds in a book. Doesn't this piss you off? You're reading a nice story, and suddenly the writer has to stop and describe the clouds. Who cares? I'll bet you anything I can write a decent novel, with a good, entertaining story, and never once mention the clouds. Really! Every book you read, if there's an outdoor scene, an open window, or even a door slightly ajar, the writer has to say, "As Bo and Velma walked along the shore, the clouds hung ponderously on the horizon like steel-gray, loosely formed gorilla turds." I'm not interested. Skip the clouds and get to the fucking. The only story I know of where clouds were important was Noah's Ark.

And I don't appreciate being put on hold and being forced to listen to someone else's radio. I don't even listen to my own radio, why should I have to pay money to call some company and listen to theirs? And it's always that same shit, soft rock! That sucky, non-threatening, easy-listening pussy music. Soft rock is an oxymoron. Furthermore, it's not rock, and it's not even music. It's just soft.

I'm tired of being unable to buy clothing that doesn't have writing and printing all over it. Insipid sayings, pseudo-wisdom, cute slogans, team logos, designer names, brand trademarks, small-business ego trips; the marketing pigs and advertising swine have turned us all into walking billboards. You see some asshole walkin' by, and he's got on a fruity Dodger hat and a Hard Rock Cafe T-shirt. Of course you can't see the shirt if he's wearing his hot-shit Chicago Bulls jacket. The one that only 50 million other loser jock-sniffers own. And since this cretinous sports fan/consumer zombie is completely for sale to anyone, he rounds out his ensemble with FedEx sneakers, ValuJet socks, *Wall Street Journal* sweatpants, a Starbucks jock strap, and a Microsoft condom with Bill Gates's head on the end of it. No one in this country owns his personal appearance anymore. America has become a nation of obedient consumers, actively participating in their own degradation.

A FEW THINGS I LIKE

{ } A guy who doesn't know what he's doing and won't admit it.

{ } A permanently disfigured gun collector.

{ } A whole lotta people tap dancing at once.

{ } When a big hole opens up in the ground.

{ } The third week in February.

{ } Guys who say "cock-a-roach."

{ } A woman with no feet, because she's not always nagging you to take her dancing.

KEEP IT CLEAN

I never wash my hands after using a public restroom. Unless something gets on me. Otherwise, I figure I'm as clean as when I walked in. Besides, the sink is usually filthier than I am. I'm convinced that many of the men I see frantically washing up do not do the same thing at home. Americans are obsessed with appearances and have an unhealthy fixation on cleanliness. Relax, boys. It's only your dick. If it's so dirty that after handling it you need to wash your hands, you may as well just go ahead and scrub your dick while you're at it. Tell the truth. Wouldn't you like to see some guy trying to dry his genitals with one of those forced-air blowing machines that are mounted four feet off the ground?

G.C.'S GUIDE TO DINING OUT

RESTAURANTS

There are certain clues that tell you how much a restaurant will cost. If the word *cuisine* appears in the advertising, it will be expensive. If they use the word *food*, it will be moderately priced. However, if the sign says *eats*, even though you'll save some money on food, your medical bills may be quite high.

I don't like trendy food. When I hear, "sauteed boneless panda groin," I know I'm in the wrong place. There's such a thing as pretentious food. Puree of woodchuck, marinated bat nipples, weasel chops, porcupine cacciatore. Or fried eagle. A guy said to me recently, "C'mon, we'll go to Baxter's, they have really great fried eagle." I'm thinkin' to myself, "Do I really wanna know this guy?"

However, if you *are* going to dine with pretentious people, here are some items you can order that are sure to impress: deep-dish moose balls, diced yak, badger gumbo, gorilla fondue, filet of hyena, jackal tartare, rack of prairie dog, free-range mole en brochette, wolf noodle soup, loin of chipmunk, curried woodpecker, stir-fried weasel, penguin scallopini, sweet-and-sour loon heads, whale chowder, toasted snail penises, koala flambé, wombat souvlaki, grenadine of mule, and candied goat anus.

Then, at the other end of the spectrum, there is the decidedly nontrendy restaurant, where the special sometimes is simply "meat." Big sign in the window: "Today's special: Meat."

"I'll have the meat."

"Would you like sauce with that?"

"What kind of sauce would that be?"

"That would be meat sauce."

It's similar to a fish sandwich. Have you ever seen these
places that feature "fish sandwiches"? I always think, "Well,
that's kind of general." I mean, I wouldn't order something
called a "meat sandwich," would you?" At least not without
a couple of follow-up questions: "Does anyone know where
this meat came from?" "Are any of the waitresses missing?"

DEALING WITH THE WAITER

I think when you eat out you should have a little fun;
it's good for digestion. Simple things. After the waiter recites
a long list of specials, ask him if they serve cow feet.

But act really interested in the specials. When he says,
"Today we have goat-cheese terrine with arugula juice,
sautéed cod with capers and baby vegetables, coastal shrimp
cooked in spiced carrot juice, roast free-range chicken with
ginger and chickpea fries, and duck breast in truffle juice,"
act like you're completely involved. Say, "The cod. What is
the cod sautéed in?" "A blend of canola and tomato oils."
(No hurry here.) "Ahhh, yes! [pointing thoughtfully at the
waiter] I'll have the grilled cheese sandwich."

Even some low-end places are pretentious. The menu
can't merely say "cheeseburger." They have to get wordy. So,

go along with them. When you order your food use their language. But you must look right at the waiter; no fair reading from the menu. Look him in the eye and say, "I'll have the succulent, fresh-ground, government-inspected, choice, all-beef, six-ounce patty on your own award-winning sesame-seed bun, topped with a generous slice of Wisconsin's finest Grade-A cheddar cheese made from only premium milk and poured from large, galvanized steel cans, having originally been extracted from a big, fat, smelly, champion blue-ribbon cow with a brain disease."

Continue that style with other items: Instead of asking for a glass of water, say you'd like a "cylindrical, machine-blown, clear drinking vessel filled with nature's own color-less, odorless, extra-wet, liquid water."

Have fun. Be difficult. Order unusual things: a chopped corn sandwich. Rye potato chips. Filet of bone with diced peas. Peanut butter and jellyfish. Ask for a glass of skim water. Insist on fried milk. Chocolate orange juice. Order a grilled gorgonzola cheese sandwich on whole-wheat ladyfingers. Then top the whole thing off with a bowl of food coloring and a large glass of saturated fat.

Issue special instructions. Ask for the French toast, medium rare. Get a pizza with no toppings, hold the crust. Tell 'em you want eggs: "Fry the whites and poach the yolks." Order a basket of poppy seed rolls and tell them to scrape off the seeds and put them in a separate bowl and heat them to 200 degrees. Keep them busy.

Tell your waiter you want to make a substitution: "Instead of my napkin, I'll have the lobster tails." See what he says. Ask him if the garnish is free. If it is, tell him all you're having is a large plate of garnish.

If they have a salad bar, ask how many times you can go back. If they say as many times as you like, ask for a lawn bag. Come back the next day with a small truck. Tell them you weren't quite finished eating the night before. You're actually within your legal rights, because, technically, no one is ever finished eating.

Ask him if the chef would mind preparing a dish that's not on the menu. Then describe something simple but unusual. Like half a coconut filled with egg whites. When the waiter comes back and says, "Yes, the chef said he will be delighted to make that for you," tell him, "Well, never mind, I don't like that anymore."

Giving the waiter your drink order can be fun. If you're alone, show the guy you're a real man. "Gimme a glass of napalm and paint thinner straight up." Be an individualist; order a gin and hot chocolate. If you're with a date, be sophisticated. Say, "I'll have a rum and goat juice with a twist of cucumber on dry ice." Always order your date's drink; that's very romantic. Especially if you're trying to get laid. "The lady will have a martini, a glass of wine, two zombies, and a beer. And do you have any quaaludes?"

By the way, if your date is complaining of constipation, order her a prune margarita with a twist of Feenamint.

When the food arrives, change your mind. Say, "I've changed my mind, waiter. Instead of the roast suckling pig, I believe I'll have a half order of Kellogg's Product 19."

And always, when the food arrives, send something back. It's considered very sophisticated. But make sure you use colorful language. Tell him, "Waiter, this veal tastes like the inside front panel of Ferdinand Magellan's shorts. And I'm referring to the first voyage."

Show him you're a man of new ideas. When he comes with the pepper mill, refuse the pepper, but tell him to sprinkle some dandruff on your food.

Actually, the pepper mill can be a source of great fun. Keep the waiter going on the pepper mill for a long time. Disturbingly long. Like, for about fifteen minutes. Until everyone in the restaurant is really uncomfortable. Then, when your food and silverware are completely covered with a thin layer of ground pepper, say, "Okay, stop! That's perfect!" Then, a few minutes later, call the waiter over and tell him, "This food has way too much pepper on it!"

Now that you have your food, the waiter can begin to ask you if everything is all right. "Is everything all right?" "Yes. Thank you. Good-bye!" Some waiters are very persistent. I had one call me at home the following day. "Did the food stay down?"

Usually, when they ask me if everything is all right, I'll tell them the truth. I say, "Well, I had a problem with the peas. I received 143 peas. Of them, 36 were overcooked, 27 were undercooked, and 18 were not quite the same color as the others."

Or I'll tell them more than they really want to know. "No, everything is not all right. I'm going through a period of upheaval. I have a rogue polyp in my bowel, my wife ran off with a periodontist, and my son has been arrested for defe-cating in a mall."

And always fill out the "How did we do?" card. It's very helpful to the owner. "Everything was wonderful, except the waiter had some vomit on his shoes and a tiny snot on the end of his nose. It was small, but it was definitely a snot."

I hope these pointers and suggestions will enhance your next experience dining out. Tell 'em George sent you.

FOOD TERMS

BREADSTICKS:

If drumsticks are for playing drums, you'd think breadsticks would be for playing bread, wouldn't you? "Would you like some breadsticks?" "No thank you. I don't play bread; I play drums. Perhaps I'll have a drum roll."

SHELLED PEANUTS:

Why don't shelled peanuts have shells? If you're clothed, you have clothes, so if you're shelled, you should have shells. You'd think they'd call peanuts without shells, "unshelled" peanuts, wouldn't you? Same goes for pitted prunes.

And boned chicken. I ask you, Where are the bones? I can't find them. In my opinion, it ought to be called *de*-boned chicken.

And what about semi-boneless ham? What's going on? Does it have only half a bone? Or does "semi-boneless ham" mean that some complete object that is not entirely a bone has been removed from the ham?

WAFFLE IRON:

Why on earth would you want to iron a waffle? Wouldn't that just flatten out all the little squares? No, I believe waffles should be dry cleaned. Pancakes, of course, should always be ironed.

OPENING YOUR OWN RESTAURANT

Everyone thinks they have a really good idea for a restaurant but I've heard some terrible schemes. I even had a few myself.

My first idea was: All You Can Eat for 60 Cents. That didn't work. So I went the other way: All You Can Eat for $1500. That didn't work either. Then I made my fatal mistake: All You Can Eat for Free. Closed after one meal.

My next idea was The Used Footwear Restaurant. Our slogan was, How Would You Like to Enjoy a Nice Hot Meal Eaten Out of Someone Else's Used Footwear? Somehow, it didn't work. Although, after I sold it, it became the very successful fast-food franchise, Beef in a Brogan.

Chili Alley was my favorite, and a lot of people got a kick out of it. It was a drive-through chili restaurant. And you didn't even have to slow down. You could drive through at speeds up to 40 miles an hour, and we would shoot the chili at you from a shotgun. Just two dollars. Both barrels, three-fifty. Dry cleaning extra.

Vinny's House of Toast. This was great. My partner Vinny and I tried to come up with 101 different ways to serve toast. Eventually, we could only settle on three. The first item was . . . toast. Basically, an order of toast. With something on it—butter, margarine, jelly, whatever. The second thing we came up with was . . . a double order of toast. That would be, of course, twice as much toast, along with double the butter, margarine, jelly, whatever. The only other thing we

24

could think of was something I liked a lot: a toast sandwich. Usually on toast. We also tried Toast on a Bun, but the public wasn't ready. Too high-concept.

Then there was Bombs Away. This was an idea that should have worked. Patrons were seated on the ground floor; the kitchen was on the balcony. When your order was ready, you stood under the balcony holding a plate, and the chef dropped your food while everyone yelled, "Bombs away!" It worked great with steak and chops. But the idea began to unravel when we tried things like soup and creamed spinach. Peas were a definite problem, too.

My last unsuccessful attempt was The Top of the Schmuck. It was a ten-story statue of a schmuck wearing a cowboy hat, with a revolving restaurant in the hatband. The problem was, it rotated way too fast. People got sick just waiting for a table. But I still think the idea was basically sound.

Bon appétit.

GOBBLE THIS

On Thanksgiving at our house we like variety, so we don't have turkey every year. Last year we had a swan. It was nice; everyone got some neck. Another year we had a seagull. Delicious! It's a little fishy, but at least there's no need to add salt. Two years ago we had a stork. Lots of meat, but, Jesus, the wishbone makes a helluva noise. This year we're expecting a few people over, so we're having a flamingo. And I'm getting the leg that folds up. They say the meat is sweeter and more tender because the flamingo doesn't use it much.

WELL, YA GOTTA LIVE SOMEPLACE

I grew up in New York City and lived there until I was thirty.

At that time, I decided I'd had enough of life in a dynamic, sophisticated city, so I moved to Los Angeles. Actually, I moved there because of the time difference. I was behind in my work, and wanted to pick up the extra three hours. Technically, for the last thirty years I've been living in my own past.

I knew I didn't want to move to the Midwest. I could never live in a place where the outstanding geographic feature is the horizon. The Midwest seems like a nice place to catch up on your sleep.

Another reason I could never live in the Midwest is that it gets really cold there. You've heard of hypothermia and exposure? I could never be comfortable in a place where you can die simply by going out to the mailbox. Living in an area where an open window can cause death seems foolish to me.

Of course, living in the South was never an option—the main problem being they have too much respect for authority; they're soldier-sniffers and cop lovers. I don't respect that, and I could never live with it. There's also way too much religion in the South to be consistent with good mental health.

Still, I love traveling down there, especially when I'm in the mood for a quick trip to the thirteenth century. I'm not someone who buys all that "New South" shit you hear; I judge a place by the number of lynchings they've had, overall. Atlanta even found it necessary to come up with an apologetic civic slogan: Atlanta: The City Too Busy to Hate. I think they're trying to tell us something.

There's also the communications problem. I have trouble understanding Southerners. Some of them sound like they're chewing on a dick. And I really have nothing against them individually; one by one they can be quite charming. But when you take them as a whole, there's some really dangerous genetic material floating around down there.

So, I live in Los Angeles, and it's kind of a goofy place. They have an airport named after John Wayne. That ought to explain it. It has a charming kind of superstitious innocence.

But if you really want to understand life in California, forget the grief clinics and yogaholics. Forget biofeedback, Feldenkrais, neurolinguistic programming, and the Alexander technique.

Disregard spirit guides, centering groups, dream workshops, bioenergetics, pyramid energy, and primal therapy.

Ignore centering, fasting, Rolfing, grounding, channeling, rebirthing, nurturing, self-parenting, and colon cleansing.

And don't even think about polarity work, inversion swings, flower essences, guided synchronicity, harmonic brain wave synergy, and psychocalisthenics.

You also need pay no attention to nude volleyball, spinach therapy, white wine hot tubs, jogging on hot coals, and the people who sing Christmas carols to zoo animals.

Forget all that. The only thing you have to know about California is this: They have traffic school for chocaholics.

Okay?

California is the only place where you might hear someone

say, "Jason can't come to the phone, he's taking his wind lesson."

The problem most New Yorkers have with Los Angeles is that it is fragmented and lacks a vital center. The people have no common experience. Instead, they exude a kind of bemused detachment that renders them intensely uninteresting. The West Coast experience is soft and peripheral, New York is hard and concentrated. California is a small woman saying, "Fuck me." New York is a large man saying, "Fuck you!"

Still, I live in California. But I'm not "laid-back," and I'm certainly not "mellow." I associate those qualities with the comatose. The solar system wasn't formed because matter was laid-back; life didn't arise from the oceans and humans descend from the trees because DNA was mellow. It happened because of something called *energy*.

New York has energy, and all I can say is this: If you can't handle it, stay the fuck out. Living in New York is a character-builder; you must know who you are, what you're doing, where you're going, and how to get there. No bullshit tolerated! New York people are tough and resilient. All the rest of you are varying degrees of soft.

Most outsiders can't handle New York, so they wind up back in Big Loins, Arkansas, badmouthing The City for the rest of their lives. Actually, most of the people who run New York down have never been there. And if they ever went, we would destroy them in nine minutes. People hate New York, because that's where the action is, and they know it's passing them by. Most of the decisions that control people's lives are made in New York City. Not in Washington, not on Pennsylvania

Avenue. In New York City! Madison Avenue and Wall Street. People can't handle that. Pisses 'em off. Fuck 'em!

And I'm really glad the Yankees humiliated the Braves in the World Series. I'm glad the gritty, tough, Third-World, streetwise New York culture triumphed over the soft, suburban, wholesome, white-Christian, tacky mall culture of Atlanta. Overgrown small towns like Atlanta have no business in the major leagues in the first place.

Concerning L.A. versus New York: I have now lived half my life in each of America's two most hated, feared, and envied cities, and you want to know something? There's no comparison. New York even has a better class of assholes. Even the lames in New York have a certain appealing, dangerous quality.

As an example of how hopeless California is, when I first got there, a policeman gave me a ticket for jaywalking. You have to understand the kind of people who live in California. They are willing to stand, passive and inert, on a curb, when absolutely no traffic is coming, or maybe just a little traffic that could easily be dodged. They simply stand there obediently and wait for an electric light to give them permission to proceed. I couldn't believe this cop. I laughed at him. The ticket cost me about twenty dollars in 1966. Since that time, I figure I have jaywalked an additional thousand times or so without being caught. Fuck that lame-ass cop! I've managed to prorate that ticket down to about two cents a jaywalk.

One thing I find appealing in California is the emphasis on driving. I like to drive, I'm skillful at it, and I do it aggressively. And I don't mean I scream at people or flash them the finger. I simply go about my passage swiftly and silently, with a certain deliberate, dark efficiency. In the land of the unassertive, the aggressive man is king.

Of course, in Los Angeles, *everything* is based on driving, even the killings. In New York, most people don't have cars, so if you want to kill a person, you have to take the subway to their house. And sometimes on the way, the train is delayed and you get impatient, so you have to kill someone on the subway. That's why there are so many subway murders; no one has a car. Basically, if more people in New York had cars, the subways would be a lot safer.

I hope you can tell, the Apple is still number one in my heart. I'm so chauvinistic, I even root for New York to raise more money than Los Angeles on the Arthritis Telethon. And we usually do.

California: bordering always on the Pacific and sometimes on the ridiculous. So, why do I live here?

Because the sun goes down a block from my house.

SUN OF GOD

I've begun worshipping the sun for a number of reasons. First of all, unlike some other gods I could mention, I can see the sun. It's there for me every day. And the things it brings me are quite apparent all the time: heat, light, food, a lovely day. There's no mystery, no one asks for money, I don't have to dress up, and there's no boring pageantry. And interestingly enough, I have found that the prayers I offer to the sun and the prayers I formerly offered to "God" are all answered at about the same 50-percent rate.

SMALL TOWNS
You know you're in a small town when:

✖ The restaurant closes at lunch so the waitress can go home and eat.

✖ The mayor's nickname is "Greasy Dick" and besides appearing on the ballot, it also appears on his driver's license.

✖ The fashion boutique/post office is located in one corner of the hardware store between the used milking machines and the pay toilet.

✖ The police station is closed evenings and weekends, but they leave lit the sign that gives the time and temperature.

✖ The newspaper prints the crossword puzzle on the front page above the fold, and prints the answers just below.

✖ The zip code has three digits and features a decimal point.

✖ The Narcotics Anonymous chapter has only one member, and he's strung out on ranch dressing.

A NAME BY ANY OTHER NAME

Whatever happened to Eddie? Where did he go? Seems like he was just here. And where's Billy? And Bobby and Jackie and John? Jimmy, Paul, Vinny, Tom, and Charlie? And Richie? Where did they go?

And where the fuck did Cameron come from? And Jordan and Justin and Shane and Parker? Tucker, Tyler, Taylor, Carter, Flynn, Blake, and Cody? Who let these people in? Brett? Brent? Blair? Cassidy? Where are all these goofy names coming from? Say what you will about the national candidates in 1996, at least they had the decency to be named Bill, Bob, Al, and Jack.

The popularity of first names is perishable; they pass in and out of favor. Occasionally, newspapers will print the most popular names given to babies that year, and they're never the same as years before. You don't run into many little girls named Bertha or Edith. Nor are there a lot of Netties, Effies, Opals, Hopes, or Pearls floatin' around the day care. Ditto Ethel, Nellie, Myrtle, Agatha, and Mabel. And how many expectant parents are praying for a girl so they can name her Blanche, Clara, Agnes, or Lottie? None. You know why? Because most of those women are in nursing homes.

But thanks to the "trendies"—and the sheer passage of time—someday our substandard nursing homes will be filled with Ambers, Kaylas, Tiffanys, Caitlins, Morgans, Courtneys, Whitneys, Cheyennes, Ashleys, Megans, Brittanys, and Heathers. And that's not to overlook Judi, Lori, Suzi, Debi, Keli, and Wendi, and any other name that can conceiveably be spelled with a final "i."

There are even some girls whose names don't end in "y" who can't resist that trend: "Hi, my name is Margaret, but somehow, I spell it with an 'i."

There are women named Faith, Hope, Joy, and Prudence. Why not Despair, Guilt, Rage, and Grief? It seems only right. "Tom, I'd like you to meet the girl of my dreams, Tragedy." These days, Trajedi.

I had an uncle who was embarassed because he had a

woman's name. We told him not to worry, lots of men have women's names: Leslie, Marion, Chris, Dale, Lonnie. We tried to reassure him. But old Uncle Margaret Mary . . . I guess he just couldn't handle it. I don't know why, it never bothered his wife, Turk.

Do you know why hurricanes have names instead of numbers? To keep the killing personal. No one cares about a bunch of people killed by a number. "200 Dead as Number Three Slams Ashore" is not nearly as interesting a headline as "Charlie Kills 200." Death is much more satisfying and entertaining if you personalize it.

Me, I'm still waitin' for Hurricane Ed. Old Ed wouldn't hurt ya, would he? Sounds kinda friendly. "Hell no, we ain't evacuatin'. Ed's comin'!"

Guess the white guy: Odell, Tyrone, Tremaine, and Sparky.

Guess the black girl: Cathy, Joan, Peggy, and Vondella.

First names can even suggest how tough you are. Who would you want on your side in a bar fight? Arnold, Seymour, Jasper, and Percy? Or Nitro, Hacksaw, Rhino, and Skull?

And, guys, which women would you rather run into when you're out drinking: Lillian, Priscilla, and Judith? Or Trixie, Bubbles, and Candy?

The Kennedy family changed William Kennedy Smith's first name in order to influence the outcome of his rape trial. They changed it from Willie to Will because guys named Will hardly ever go to jail, while America's prisons are chock full of Willies. Will is all-American, Willie is . . . well, just ask Michael Dukakis.

Through all these years, I have kept alive my one remaining childhood Catholic fantasy: I'm hoping that someday a new pope will choose the name Corky. Just once in my life, I want to look up at that balcony and see His Holiness, Pope Corky IX. I think you'd have to skip straight to nine to give him a little credibility, don't you? Somehow, Pope Corky the First doesn't command a great deal of authority.

That's because some names are inappropriate in the wrong settings. You won't find many Schuyler Vanderpools blowin' into a harmonica on death row; no one in need of brain surgery is breakin' down the door to see Dr. Lucky Lipshitz; and I'm sure only the most devoted aficionado would pay money to see a ballet dancer named Bruno McNulty.

On the other hand, you'll know that America has relaxed its hopelessly tight asshole if we someday elect a president named Booger. If we ever get a president named Booger, Skeeter, T-Bone, or Downtown President Brown, you'll know that finally this country is a relaxed, comfortable place to live.

The point is, there are emotional values that attach to names; they carry psychological baggage. Just think of the Old West. I'm sure if Billy the Kid's name had been Billy the Schmuck, people wouldn't have been afraid.

"Who's that ridin' into town?"

"Billy the Schmuck."

"Oh. Well, fuck 'im!"

Would anyone have paid to see a Wild West show if the star attraction was Buffalo Shecky?

Using this approach, western movies would have been completely unbelievable:

"Hey, Shemp! Go get Sheriff Quackenbush, there's gonna be trouble. Two-Gun Noodleman and Wild Bill Swackhammer are drunk, and they're lookin' for Deadeye Stoopnagle."

This also applies to the legendary criminals of the thirties. Do you think the police would've spent a lot of time looking for Pretty Boy Heffleflekker?

And what about Jack the Ripper? If his name had been Wally, I don't think people would have been afraid to walk the streets of London. Not if they thought Wally the Ripper was on the loose.

"Who's that? Wally who? Wally the Ripper? Ha-ha-ha-ha! Really? Wally the Ripper, indeed! Ha-ha-ha-ha!"

Religion presents an interesting situation. Jerry Falwell; it's simply an absurd name for a clergyman. The last person in the world I'm going to believe has an inside track with God is some guy named Jerry. Can you imagine the supreme being, in the middle of the night, "Jerry! Wake up. I got some revelations."

On the other hand, the founders of the major religions had names that seem quite suitable. There's still a certain mystery surrounding the names Buddha, Moses, and Mohammed. But the poor Mormons. All they could come up with was Joseph Smith. Not too impressive.

"Listen, Caleb, we got a new religion. You wanna join?"

"Who started it?"

"Joe Smith."

"See ya later."

You can't blame him. I wouldn't follow a guy named Joe Smith halfway across a continent, either.

"C'mon, we're goin' to Utah."

"Why?"

"Joe Smith said that's where we're supposed to be."

"Well, I'm gonna finish this crossword. Why don'tcha drop me a postcard."

In ancient times, the rulers had magnificent names: Alexander the Great. Suppose he had been a less imposing figure, do you think he would have been called Alexander the Marginal? As it is, he had his detractors. You know, people who called him Alexander the Scumbag.

History has given us other impressive names from simpler times: Edward the Fair, Charles the Bold, Catherine the Great. These days, they would be Edward the Abuse Victim, Charles the Underachiever, and Catherine the Recovering Codependent.

And let's not forget the historical figures we never hear of: Tiberius the Wanker and Lucretius the Dog Fucker. Guys like that.

And I'm sure history would not be the same if certain names had been slightly different. For example, World War II would have ended much more quickly if we had been fighting a guy named Skip Hitler.

Suppose there had been a really outstanding eighteenth-century composer who was better than Beethoven, Bach, and Mozart combined. But his name was Joey the Cocksucker. Do you think he would be famous today? "And now, Eugene Ormandy conducts the Philadelphia Orchestra as they perform the Requiem Mass in C-sharp Minor, composed by Joey the Cocksucker."

Some names are embarrassing. We had a guy in our neighborhood, Michael Hunt, who called himself Mickey because the only alternative was Mike Hunt. Of course, some other names are just plain dirty: "Hi, I'm Peter Ball, and this is Dick Cox. We're friends of Randy Bush."

Some people have funny names. They can't help it, but it's hard to keep from laughing when a guy named Elmo Zipaloonie introduces you to his friend El Cunto Prickolini. And if you want funny, you can't beat farmers with names like Orville Pigdicker and Hooter Stumpfuck.

Speaking of funny names, do you realize Howdy Doody's mother and father are known as the Doodys? And Bo Diddley's parents are the Diddleys? How would you like to be at a party and have to introduce the Doodys to the Diddleys? And keep a straight face? "Mr. and Mrs. Doody, I'd like you to meet Mr. and Mrs. Diddley. Mr. Doody, Mr. Diddley; Mrs. Diddley, Mrs. Doody. Mr. Doody, Mrs. Diddley; Mr. Diddley, Mrs. Doody. The Doodys, the Diddleys; the Diddleys, the Doodys." Jesus!

Then, just as you finish all of that, in walks Bo Diddley's brother, Dudley Diddley, and his sisters, Dottie Diddley, Dodie Diddley, and Didi Diddley. And Howdy Doody's sisters, Judy Doody and Trudy Doody. I'd never get through it all. I'd be leanin' over the punchbowl, thinkin', "Please, God, don't let Rootie Kazootie show up."

In Hawaii, I once had the pleasure of meeting Don Ho and his lovely wife, Heidi. Plus his three brothers, Gung, Land, and Hy.

Hospitals often name a new facility after the person who makes the major donation. I grew up with a neighborhood guy who is now extremely wealthy, and I'm hoping someday he'll make a big donation. I just wanna drive past the hospital and see the "No-Balls" Malone Cancer Pavilion.

I've noticed there are a lot of people named Rice, but no one seems to be named Corn.

The artist currently known as The Artist Formerly Known as Prince was presumably trying to shorten his name when he changed it from Prince to an unpronounceable symbol. It didn't work. His name is now five times longer than it was before.

They have Walnut Street and Chestnut Street, but you know what they don't have? Peanut Street. What's wrong with that? And how about some other nuts? Wouldn't you like to live on Pistachio Place? Or Cashew Boulevard? How about a nice big house out on Dry-Roasted Mixed Nuts Lane?

If they have a shoe store called Athlete's Foot, why can't they have a hat store called Ringworm?

There's a planet named Pluto, but we don't have one named Goofy. Goofy would be a good name for this planet. It certainly qualifies.

Just to put a button on this topic: It is said that Indians were sometimes named for the first thing they saw when they were born. Makes you wonder why there aren't more Indians named Hairy Pussy, doesn't it?

And, as Baretta used to say, that's the name of that tune.

THINGS YOU NEVER SEE

- A puppet with a hard-on
- A butterfly with a swastika design
- The Latin word for *douche bag*
- Someone defecating in church
- A junkie with leisure time
- A serial killer with a light-up bow tie
- A mom-and-pop steel mill
- A shot glass full of carrot juice
- A bum with matching luggage
- Really interesting twins
- Condoms with pictures of the saints
- Two homosexuals who own a bait shop
- A pimp with a low profit margin
- A Rolls-Royce that's more than 50 percent primer paint

IT'S YOUR BODY: FEARLESS FASHIONS

I like to look at tattoos on people; I think they're cool. But I would never get one. I always thought it was a bad idea to let some guy draw a picture on me that'll probably never come off. Ya know? I'm conservative on this one. Not only the thing never comes off, but it hurts to put it on, and you gotta pay the guy. Plus if you *do* wanna take it off, it hurts again, and you gotta pay the guy again.

Another reason not to get a tattoo is that a tattoo is positive identification. No one should ever do anything to help the police. In any way. Especially when you may be the object of their interest.

So I never got a tattoo. But I had some good ideas. I was gonna get dotted lines tattooed on all my joints, wherever I bend. With little instructions: "Fold here." "Do not glue."

I also thought about gettin' a necklace of hickeys.

Here's one I almost went through with. I was gonna get my nipples tattooed as radio dials: "volume" and "tuning." And the hair in the middle of my chest was gonna be the speaker. For stereo, I'd raise my arms. Armpit speakers!

I guess the most popular tattoo of all time is MOM. A lot of guys get MOM. No one ever gets POP. You know why? Cause you can't read POP in the mirror. In a mirror, MOM comes out MOM. POP comes out "909." What the fuck is that?

If you guys want to get a MOM tattoo and save a little money, just get two letters done. Get about a one-inch capital *M* tattooed on each cheek of your ass in pink and brown ink. Then when you bend over, it says "Mom." Also, later on if you're havin' sex with your girlfriend, and her parents are in the next room, when you finish up you can just lie on your back, draw your legs up to your chest and silently say, "Wow!"

Here's another good one for guys: at the top of your inner thigh, next to your groin, you put, "In case of emergency, pull handle." Or get your penis tattooed to resemble a candy cane. Great for Christmas blow jobs. But be very careful not to let the tattoo guy bend your penis into a *J* shape.

Get the words, "tote bag" tattooed on your scrotum. Or "Bloomingdale's" might be good. "Cartier" would be more appropriate; a little hairy pouch for your precious jewels.

How about a tattoo of the Three Stooges peering into your asshole? Or a serpent coming out? Or a nice tattoo of Madonna with her hand up your ass? Here's a good one for right next to your asshole: "No gerbils!" Or, "Gerbils welcome." Depending on what puts a smile on your face.

Here would be a great tattoo for right in the middle of your forehead: "I have colored ink in my skin!" Or, "Your message here. Fifty cents." How about, "Yeah, it's a tattoo, you miserable prick! Right in the middle of my forehead. If you don't like it, suck my dick!" This will really keep you from having to deal with that bothersome job market.

And here's a solution to an age old tattoo problem. If your girlfriend's name, say, "Suzie," is tattooed on your arm, and you break up with her, don't have the tattoo removed. Just have the tattoo reworked so it says, "Fuck Suzie."

By the way, you don't actually have to do all these things; they're just suggestions. Think them over first. Sit down, have six or seven vodkas, and give them a few seconds thought.

Besides, you wanna know something? Tattoos are passé. They're yesterday's thing. I'm lookin' for the *next* big thing in body decoration. And I think I may have it.

Everyone's skin has imperfections. It's unavoidable. Pockmarks, wrinkles, bullet holes, scars, blotches, stab wounds, cysts, warts, needle holes, acne pits, enlarged pores.

I think people should see these imperfections and disfigurements as positive things. Flaws and defects can actually be forms of decoration.

Take moles, God's punctuation marks. Moles are great, and they can be useful if you want a really interesting look. The only problem is they're usually randomly placed; they don't represent anything. I think plastic surgeons should offer a new service: rearranging people's moles. Think of your moles as fashion accessories. "God, look at all the moles that guy has!" "Yes, and aren't they nicely arranged?"

There are lots of things you can do with moles: make the double helix, do a happy Hitler face, spell out the name of your bowling team. And how about moles with velcro, so you could change your look every day? Here's something novel. Choose a good size mole on your arm, and tattoo little legs sticking out of the sides. People will constantly be trying to shoo the "bug" off your arm. It's great for picking up girls.

Next, body-piercing. Now, the piercing movement is off to a good start, and I like the idea behind it: self-esteem through self-mutilation. I've always said, when in doubt, punch a hole in yourself. That's fine, but I think the piercing people are missing a good bet. Vital organs. I mean, skin is one thing. That's easy. But how about getting your lungs or kidneys pierced? Why not some lovely diamond studs all over the surface of your liver? Or a couple of nice 18-karat gold rings hanging from your thyroid gland?

But, you know, stuff like this might not be dangerous enough for today's happenin' people. What's really gonna be great is when the ozone layer is completely gone, and everyone has melanomas. Then you'll start to see "fashion skin cancer." It'll probably start in Malibu. People will use their skin cancers to form little designs. Since it's Malibu, a lot of them will do their zodiac sign. Of course, if your sign is Cancer, you'll be in real good shape.

I believe skin cancer will eventually become part of every American's fashion arsenal. "That's a lovely growth, Bambi. Twenty millimeters and right between your eyes. God, I'm so jealous!"

Before I leave this subject, I have two more ideas for the truly avant garde: How about living small, live mammals medically grafted onto your skin? Wouldn't you like to have a prairie dog living in the middle of your chest, sharing your blood supply? How about an adult male Norwegian rat sewn onto the top of your head, keeping an eye on everything?

I think we also might take a page from Africa's book and get into deliberate scarring. Not ritual scars that form coherent designs. Random scarring! Let a bunch of drunks with swords inflict hundreds of small, deep cuts on your skin. Or have a friend throw boiling grease all over you, then sit back and see what develops.

I don't believe the body-decorating trend has reached its peak yet, and as it does, I shall try to be at the forefront, always pointing America toward the hot new look.

SHINE ON

I'm glad sunscreen has been shown to be associated with more skin cancer rather than less. It's not in the mainstream media yet, but the biggest jump in skin cancer has occurred since the advent of sunscreens. That kind of thing makes me happy. The fact that people, in pursuit of a superficial look of health, give themselves a fatal disease. I love it when "reasoning" human beings think they have figured out how to beat something and it comes right back and kicks them in the nuts. God bless the law of unintended consequences. And the irony is impressive: Healthy people, trying to look healthier, make themselves sick. Good!

COOLEST T-SHIRT

I finally escaped what I think of as the "Coolest T-shirt Trap." I realized that no matter how cool I think my T-shirt is, no one else is gonna think so, because everybody thinks *they* have the coolest T-shirt.

There are times when you take fifteen minutes to pick out which shirt to wear, because you're going to a place where there'll be a bunch of guys you've never met; guys you might even secretly want to impress. So you settle on that special black, limited-edition number that your brother brought back from the Middle East. The one that shows Saddam Hussein peeking out of a garbage can, flashing his middle finger and saying, "Ha ha, Mister Bush, you missed me. I was here at home all the time." And you think, "No one has ever seen a shirt like this; this will make them jealous. They'll all want it and wonder where I got it. I'll definitely have the coolest T-shirt."

And then when you get there, no one cares at all. No one even tries to read the writing. And all the other guys turn out to be dorks who will wear any piece of shit that's handed to them. Like "Property of Alcatraz," "No Fear," "Gold's Gym," and "Life Is a Beach." What a letdown.

Personally I haven't worn T-shirts with writing on them for about ten years, but I do own what I consider to be the coolest T-shirt in the world. It's plain white, and inside a kind of faded maroon circle, in an odd, feminine sort of print, it says, "Fuck the Cows." But it's about two sizes too small. Ain't that always the way?

TALKING AND LISTENING

You know how sometimes, at a busy cocktail party, when you're telling a group of people a story, a few of them may become distracted, and you lose their attention? So you concentrate a little harder on the ones who are still listening? You know that feeling? And then, because it's a lively party, a few more of them drift away? And as your audience slowly peels off one by one, after a while you wind up addressing any person you can find who's willing look at you. Even the busboy. And then you realize the busboy doesn't understand English. Isn't that awful?

Sometimes, a person some distance away from you will say something you can't quite understand, so you ask them to repeat it, and you still can't make it out. You try two or three more times without any luck, and by then you're getting embarrassed, so you pretend to understand, and just say, "Yeah!" so you can be done with it. Later, it turns out they said, "We're coming over tonight to remove your wife's ovaries. Will that be all right?"

I CAN'T RECALL

One recent morning there was something I couldn't remember. I sort of knew what it was related to, but I couldn't quite bring it to mind. It seemed like the letter *m* was involved. Then, suddenly, it came to me. That was in the morning. Then, later that afternoon, even though I was able to recall my experience that morning of not being able to remember something, I could no longer remember what the thing was, what it was related to, or what letter of the alphabet had been involved. But what's strange to me is that that morning, the *first* time I couldn't remember it, the thing did eventually come back to me. Later that afternoon, however, in spite of my earlier success, I drew a complete blank. I still don't know what it was, and the nice thing is that a month from now I will have no memory of the incident whatsoever. Unless, of course, something reminds me of it.

A PLACE FOR YOUR STUFF

Hi! How are ya? You got your stuff with you? I'll bet you do. Guys have stuff in their pockets; women have stuff in their purses. Of course, some women have pockets, and some guys have purses. That's okay. There's all different ways of carryin' your stuff.

Then there's all the stuff you have in your car. You got stuff in the trunk. Lotta different stuff: spare tire, jack, tools, old blanket, extra pair of sneakers. Just in case you wind up barefoot on the highway some night.

And you've got other stuff in your car. In the glove box. Stuff you might need in a hurry: flashlight, map, sunglasses, automatic weapon. You know. Just in case you wind up barefoot on the highway some night.

So stuff is important. You gotta take care of your stuff. You gotta have a *place* for your stuff. Everybody's gotta have a place for their stuff. That's what life is all about, tryin' to find a place for your stuff! That's all your house is: a place to keep your stuff. If you didn't have so much stuff, you wouldn't *need* a house. You could just walk around all the time.

A house is just a pile of stuff with a cover on it. You can see that when you're taking off in an airplane. You look down and see all the little piles of stuff. Everybody's got his own little pile of stuff. And they lock it up! That's right! When you leave your house, you gotta lock it up. Wouldn't want somebody to come by and *take* some of your stuff. 'Cause they always take the *good* stuff! They don't bother with that crap you're saving. Ain't nobody interested in your fourth-grade arithmetic papers. *National Geographics*, commemorative plates, your prize collection of Navajo underwear; they're not interested. They just want the good stuff; the shiny stuff; the electronic stuff.

So when you get right down to it, your house is nothing more than a place to keep your stuff . . . while you go out and get . . . *more stuff*. 'Cause that's what this country is all about. Tryin' to get more stuff. Stuff you don't want, stuff you don't need, stuff that's poorly made, stuff that's overpriced. Even stuff you can't afford! Gotta keep on gettin' more stuff. Otherwise someone else might wind up with more stuff. Can't let that happen. Gotta have the most stuff.

So you keep gettin' more and more stuff, and puttin' it in different places. In the closets, in the attic, in the basement, in the garage. And there might even be some stuff you left at your parents' house: baseball cards, comic books, photographs, souvenirs. Actually, your parents threw that stuff out long ago.

So now you got a houseful of stuff. And, even though you might like your house, you gotta move. Gotta get a bigger house. Why? Too much stuff! And that means you gotta move all your stuff. Or maybe, put some of your stuff in storage. Storage! Imagine that. There's a whole industry based on keepin' an eye on other people's stuff.

Or maybe you could sell some of your stuff. Have a yard sale, have a garage sale! Some people drive around all weekend just lookin' for garage sales. They don't have enough of their own stuff, they wanna buy other people's stuff.

Or you could take your stuff to the swap meet, the flea market, the rummage sale, or the auction. There's a lotta ways to get rid of stuff. You can even give your stuff away. The Salvation Army and Goodwill will actually come to your house and pick up your stuff and give it to people who don't have much stuff. It's part of what economists call the Redistribution of Stuff.

OK, enough about your stuff. Let's talk about other people's stuff. Have you ever noticed when you visit someone else's house, you never quite feel at home? You know why? No room for your stuff! Somebody *else's* stuff is all over the place. And what crummy stuff it is! "God! Where'd they get *this* stuff?"

And you know how sometimes when you're visiting someone, you unexpectedly have to stay overnight? It gets real late, and you decide to stay over? So they put you in a bedroom they don't use too often . . . because Grandma died in it eleven years ago! And they haven't moved any of her stuff? Not even the vaporizer?

Or whatever room they put you in, there's usually a dresser or a nightstand, and there's never any room on it for your stuff. Someone else's shit is on the dresser! Have you noticed that their stuff is shit, and your shit is stuff? "Get this shit off of here, so I can put my stuff down!" Crap is also a form of stuff. Crap is the stuff that belongs to the person you just broke up with. "When are you comin' over here to pick up the rest of your crap?"

Now, let's talk about traveling. Sometimes you go on vacation, and you gotta take some of your stuff. Mostly stuff to wear. But which stuff should you take? Can't take all your stuff. Just the stuff you really like; the stuff that fits you well that month. In effect, on vacation, you take a smaller, "second version" of your stuff.

Let's say you go to Honolulu for two weeks. You gotta take two big suitcases of stuff. Two weeks, two big suitcases. That's the stuff you check onto the plane. But you also got your carry-on stuff, plus the stuff you bought in the airport. So now you're all set to go. You got stuff in the overhead rack, stuff under the seat, stuff in the seat pocket, and stuff in your lap. And let's not forget the stuff you're gonna steal from the airline: silverware, soap, blanket, toilet paper, salt and pepper shakers. Too bad those headsets won't work at home.

And so you fly to Honolulu, and you claim your stuff— if the airline didn't drop it in the ocean—and you go to the hotel, and the first thing you do is put away your stuff. There's lots of places in a hotel to put your stuff.

"I'll put some stuff in here, you put some stuff in there. Hey, don't put your stuff in *there*! That's my stuff! Here's another place! Put some stuff in here. And there's another place! Hey, you know what? We've got more places than we've got stuff! We're gonna hafta go out and buy . . . *more stuff!!!*"

Finally you put away all your stuff, but you don't quite feel at ease, because you're a long way from home. Still, you sense that you must be OK, because you do have some of your stuff with you. And so you relax in Honolulu on that basis. That's when your friend from Maui calls and says, "Hey, why don't you come over to Maui for the weekend and spend a couple of nights over here?"

Oh no! Now whaddya bring? Can't bring all this stuff. You gotta bring an even *smaller* version of your stuff. Just enough stuff for a weekend on Maui. The "third version" of your stuff.

And, as you're flyin' over to Maui, you realize that you're really spread out now: You've got stuff all over the world!! Stuff at home, stuff in the garage, stuff at your parents' house (maybe), stuff in storage, stuff in Honolulu, and stuff on the plane. Supply lines are getting longer and harder to maintain!

Finally you get to your friends' place on Maui, and they give you a little room to sleep in, and there's a nightstand. Not much room on it for your stuff, but it's OK because you don't have much stuff now. You got your 8 x 10 autographed picture of Drew Carey, a large can of gorgonzola-flavored Cheez Whiz, a small, unopened packet of brown confetti, a relief map of Corsica, and a family-size jar of peppermint-flavored, petrified egg whites. And you know that even though you're a long way from home, you must be OK because you do have a good supply of peppermint-flavored, petrified egg whites. And so you begin to relax in Maui on that basis. That's when your friend says, "Hey, I think tonight we'll go over to the other side of the island and visit my sister. Maybe spend the night over there."

Oh no! Now whaddya bring? Right! You gotta bring an even smaller version. The "fourth version" of your stuff. Just the stuff you *know* you're gonna need: Money, keys, comb, wallet, lighter, hankie, pen, cigarettes, contraceptives, Vaseline, whips, chains, whistles, dildos, and a book. Just the stuff you *hope* you're gonna need. Actually, your friend's sister probably has her own dildos.

By the way, if you go to the beach while you're visiting the sister, you're gonna have to bring—that's right—an even smaller version of your stuff: the "fifth version." Cigarettes and wallet. That's it. You can always borrow someone's suntan lotion. And then suppose, while you're there on the beach, you decide to walk over to the refreshment stand to get a hot dog? That's right, my friend! Number six! The most important version of your stuff: your wallet! Your wallet contains the only stuff you really can't do without.

Well, by the time you get home you're pretty fed up with your stuff and all the problems it creates. And so about a week later, you clean out the closet, the attic, the basement, the garage, the storage locker, and all the other places you keep your stuff, and you get things down to manageable proportions. Just the right amount of stuff to lead a simple and uncomplicated life. And that's when the phone rings. It's a lawyer. It seems your aunt has died . . . and left you all her stuff. Oh no! Now whaddya do? Right. You do the only thing you can do. The honorable thing. You tell the lawyer to stuff it.

AIR POLLUTION

Think of how much information, in the form of radio energy, there is flying through the air, all around us, all over the world, right now and all the time. AM, FM, UHF, VHF, shortwave radio, television, CB radio, walkie-talkies, cell phones, cordless phones, telephone satellites, microwave relays, faxes, pagers, taxi calls, police, sheriff, hospitals, fire departments, telemetry, navigation, radar, the military, government, financial, legal, medical, the media, etc., etc., etc. Trillions and trillions and trillions and trillions of separate little bits of electronic information flying all around the world through the air at all times. Think of that. Think of how busy the air is. Now realize this: A hundred years ago there was none. None. Silence.

MENTAL BRAIN THOUGHTS

These are the things I think about when I'm sitting home alone and the power goes out:

If something in the future is canceled, what is canceled? What has really happened? Something that didn't occur yet is now never going to occur at all. Does that qualify as an event?

There's a place you've never seen, but for many years you've pictured it in your mind. Then you finally see it. After you leave, do you continue to picture it the old way?

Imagine a place called Moravia; a nonexistent country. See it in your mind. See a few details. OK, now Moravia ceases to exist. Is your picture of the original, nonexistent country different from what it looks like now that it ceases to exist? Why? They're both nonexistent.

OK, picture Moravia again, the original way. Now Moravia is invaded by a neighboring country, Boronia. Picture Boronia. It's completely different from Moravia. Different geography, different ethnic stock, beliefs, way of life, government, everything. See it? Anyway, Boronia invades Moravia and occupies it, and begins to make some changes. Now picture Moravia again. Does it look different? Isn't that weird? It looks a little like Boronia.

Here's another one. You've never been to your friend's place of work, but you've pictured it. Then he changes jobs, but it's a similar job. Do you bother to change your mental picture of where he works? By how much?

Or your friend works at one Wendy's and gets transferred to a different Wendy's. Do you picture a whole new Wendy's? Or do you get lazy and say, "They're all pretty much the same, so I'll just go with the old one."

If a radio station changes its call letters, moves its studio across town, hires all new disk jockeys, and changes the style of music it plays, but keeps the same frequency, is it still the same radio station? Suppose they change only the music?

On a given day, Flight 23 goes from New York to Los Angeles. The following month, Flight 23 goes from New York to Los Angeles again, but the crew is different, the passengers are different and it's a completely different airplane. How can both flights be Flight 23? They can't.

A week has no basis in nature as do days, months, and years. So, birds don't understand weeks or weekdays. They do know enough to come back to the sidewalk café every day for crumbs. But suppose the café is in the business district and closed on weekends? What do the birds think of that? I'll bet they're really glad when Monday rolls around. Unlike the rest of us.

These are just a few of the thoughts that kept me out of the really good schools.

THE GEORGE CARLIN BOOK CLUB— "We've Got Books Out the Ass"

Offer #1: "How-To" Titles

☐ *How to Remove Chewing Gum from Your Bush*

☐ *How to Turn Your Front Lawn into a Cathouse*

☐ *How to Remove an Infected Cyst from a Loved One*

☐ *How to Make Two Small Hats out of a Brassiere*

☐ *How to Make a Brassiere out of Two Small Hats*

☐ *How to Have Really Nice Lymph Glands*

❐ *How to Act Laid-Back During a Grease Fire*

❐ *How to Spot a Creep from Across the Street*

❐ *How to Dance with a Swedish Person*

✖ *How to Induce a Clergyman to Grab You by the Nuts*

❐ *How to Milk a Dog While It's Sleeping*

❐ *How to Get Through College without Books*

❐ *How to Make a Small Salad out of Your Work Pants*

❐ *How to Lure a Weasel into a Cardboard Box*

❐ *How to Filet a Panda*

❐ *How to Get a Tan with a Blow Torch*

❐ *How to Make an Oil Lamp out of Your Genitals*

❐ *How to Style Your Hair with a Bullwhip*

❐ *How to Convert an Old Leather Chair into Twelve Pairs of Shoes*

❐ *How to Achieve Multiple Orgasms with a Pair of Tweezers*

❐ *How to Kill a Rat with a Paper Clip*

❐ *How to Lease Out the Space Inside Your Nose*

❐ *How to Spot Truly Vicious People in Church*

✖ *How to Become a Total Fuckin' Greaseball*

NO ONE EVER WROTE THIS SENTENCE BEFORE

On the Feast of St. Stephen, I was driving my hearse to the wholesale liverwurst outlet when suddenly a hermaphrodite in a piano truck backed out of a crackhouse driveway, and, as my shoes caught fire, I pirouetted across Boris Karloff Boulevard, slapping the truckdriver six times in the loins with a Chattanooga road map, even though he was humming "The Pussycat Song."

Z-Z-Z-Z-Z-Z-Z-Z-Z-Z

People say, "I'm going to sleep now," as if it were nothing. But it's really a bizarre activity. "For the next several hours, while the sun is gone, I'm going to become unconscious, temporarily losing command over everything I know and understand. When the sun returns, I will resume my life."

If you didn't know what sleep was, and you had only seen it in a science fiction movie, you would think it was weird and tell all your friends about the movie you'd seen.

"They had these people, you know? And they would walk around all day and be OK? And then, once a day, usually after dark, they would lie down on these special platforms and become unconscious. They would stop functioning almost completely, except deep in their minds they would have adventures and experiences that were completely impossible in real life. As they lay there, completely vulnerable to their enemies, their only movements were to occasionally shift from one position to another; or, if one of the 'mind adventures' got too real, they would sit up and scream and be glad they weren't unconscious anymore. Then they would drink a lot of coffee."

So, next time you see someone sleeping, make believe you're in a science fiction movie. And whisper, "The creature is regenerating itself."

FUCK THE FARMERS

Can someone please tell me why farmers are always whining and looking for a handout? If it isn't a drought or a flood, it's their bad loans. I was always told farmers were strong, independent people who were too proud to accept help. But sure enough as soon as something goes wrong, they're looking for the government to bail them out. And they're the first ones to complain about city people who live on welfare. Fuck the farmers. They're worrying about losing their land? It wasn't their land to begin with, they stole it from the Indians. Let 'em find out what it feels like to have your land taken away by some square-headed cocksucker who just came over on a boat. They wiped out the bears, the wolves, and the mountain lions; they spoiled the land, poisoned the water table, and they produce tasteless food. Why is it in this capitalist society all businesses are expected to succeed or fail on their own except farming? Why is that?

SMOKE IF YA GOT 'EM

Even though I don't smoke, I'm not one of those fanatics you run into. In fact, I love watching cigarette smokers in their sad little sealed-off areas, sucking away, deep lines in their faces, precancerous lesions taking hold, the posture and body language of petty criminals. You know what you do with these people? Give 'em free cigarettes. Let 'em smoke. Offer them a light! And you hope each one of them gets a small, painful tumor right in the middle of his body so it can grow in six different directions at once. And you pray they get a doctor who doesn't believe in painkillers, and their insurance runs out. I think people should be allowed to enjoy themselves.

BLAME IT ON THE BOSSA NOVA

They try to blame movies and TV for violence in this country. What a load of shit. Long before there were movies and television, Americans killed millions of Indians, enslaved millions of blacks, slaughtered 700,000 of each other in a family feud, and attained the highest murder rate in history. Don't blame Sylvester Stallone. We brought these horrifying genes with us from Europe, and then we gave them our own special twist. American know-how!

Violent American movies like *Die Hard, Terminator,* and *Lethal Weapon* do very well in places like Canada, Japan, and Europe. Very well. Yet these countries do not have nearly the violence of the United States. In 1989, in all of Japan, with a population of 150 million, there were 754 murders. In New York City that year, with a population of only 7.5 million, there were 2,300. It's bred in the bone. Movies and television don't make you violent; all they do is channel the violence more creatively.

Americans even manage to turn positive experiences into violence. Like sports championships. In Detroit, in 1990, the Pistons won the NBA championship: eight people dead. The Chicago Bulls, 1993: nine shot, 1,000 arrested. Montreal, the Canadiens, 1993: 170 injured, 47 police cars vandalized, and $10 million in damages. I'm glad it's happened in a place like Montreal, so these bigoted shit stains who call in on sports-talk shows can't blame it all on the blacks.

I could mention plenty of things that contribute to violence. One is simply the condition of being violent; the predisposition. Everyone knows this is a cranky species. It's especially well known among the other species. And most people can see that the particular strain of critter found in America is especially prone to graceless outbursts, being, as we are, a collection of all the strange and restless castoffs and rolling stones who proved such an ill fit back home. God bless them all, and give them all the guns they want.

Two other things that contribute to violence are religion and government, because they seek to repress and regulate natural impulses like sex and self-gratification. Of course, the two of them will always try to scapegoat movies and television. The truth is, no one knows enough or cares enough to stop the real violence, so their answer is to tone down the pretend violence. It's superstition: "Maybe if we tone down the pretend violence, the real violence will go away. Or not seem so bad."

And maybe the father who forbids his son to watch violent television will not beat the shit out of him when he disobeys.

Maybe.

"HI MOM!"

A man is seated in a football stadium with a small TV set tuned to the game. The sideline camera takes his picture, and his image travels through the lens, out of the camera, to the truck, to the satellite, to a ground station several miles away, back into the air, and to the man's TV set.

He sees himself on the screen. The image travels from his eyes to his brain. His brain sends a signal to his arm to start waving. The image travels to the camera, through the lens, to the truck, to the satellite, to another ground station a thousand miles away where it is retransmitted into the air and picked up by a cable company that sends it to the man's parents' TV set.

The image travels from the screen to his mother's eyes, along the optic nerve to her brain, where it references her memory and recognition takes place. Her brain then sends a series of signals to her lungs, throat, lips, and tongue, and she says, "Look, it's Mike!"

BASEBALL AND FOOTBALL

Baseball is different from any other sport; very different.

For instance, in most sports you score points or goals; in baseball you score runs.

In most sports the ball, or object, is put in play by the offensive team; in baseball the defensive team puts the ball in play, and only the defense is allowed to touch the ball. In fact, in baseball if an offensive player touches the ball intentionally, he's out; sometimes unintentionally, he's out.

Also: In football, basketball, soccer, volleyball, and all sports played with a ball, you score *with* the ball, and without the ball you can't score. In baseball the ball prevents you from scoring.

In most sports the team is run by a coach; in baseball the team is run by a manager; and only in baseball does the manager (or coach) wear the same clothing the players do. If you had ever seen John Madden in his Oakland Raiders football uniform, you would know the reason for this custom.

Now, I've mentioned football. Baseball and football are the two most popular spectator sports in this country. And, as such, it seems they ought to be able to tell us something about ourselves and our values. And maybe how those values have changed over the last 150 years. For those reasons, I enjoy comparing baseball and football:

Baseball is a nineteenth-century pastoral game.
Football is a twentieth-century technological struggle.

Baseball is played on a diamond, in a park. The baseball park!
Football is played on a gridiron, in a stadium, sometimes called Soldier Field or War Memorial Stadium.

Baseball begins in the spring, the season of new life.
Football begins in the fall, when everything is dying.

In football you wear a helmet.
In baseball you wear a cap.

Football is concerned with *downs*. "What down is it?"
Baseball is concerned with *ups*. "Who's up? Are you up? I'm not up! He's up!"

In football you receive a penalty.
In baseball you make an error.

In football the specialist comes in to kick.
In baseball the specialist comes in to relieve somebody.

Football has hitting, clipping, spearing, piling on, personal fouls, late hitting, and unnecessary roughness.
Baseball has the sacrifice.

Football is played in any kind of weather: Rain, snow, sleet, hail, fog . . . can't see the game, don't know if there is a game going on; mud on the field . . . can't read the uniforms, can't read the yard markers, the struggle will continue!

In baseball if it rains, we don't go out to play. "I can't go out! It's raining out!"

Baseball has the seventh-inning stretch.

Football has the two-minute warning.

Baseball has no time limit: "We don't know when it's gonna end!"

Football is rigidly timed, and it will end "even if we have to go to sudden death."

In baseball, during the game, in the stands, there's a kind of picnic feeling. Emotions may run high or low, but there's not that much unpleasantness.

In football, during the game in the stands, you can be sure that at least twenty-seven times you were perfectly capable of taking the life of a fellow human being.

And finally, the objectives of the two games are completely different:

In football the object is for the quarterback, otherwise known as the field general, to be on target with his aerial assault, riddling the defense by hitting his receivers with deadly accuracy in spite of the blitz, even if he has to use the shotgun. With short bullet passes and long bombs, he marches his troops into enemy territory, balancing this aerial assault with a sustained ground attack that punches holes in the forward wall of the enemy's defensive line.

In baseball the object is to go home! And to be safe! "I hope I'll be safe at home!"

ERIN GO FUCK YOURSELF

Being Irish, I guess I should resent the Notre Dame nickname, "The Fighting Irish." After all, how long do you think nicknames like "The Bargaining Jews" or "The Murdering Italians" would last? Only the ironic Irish could be so naively honest. I get the feeling that Notre Dame came real close to naming itself "The Fuckin' Drunken, Thick-skulled, Brawling, Short-dicked Irish."

PLAY BALL!!!

Here's something I don't care about: athlete's families. This is really the bottom of the sports barrel. I'm watchin' a ball-game, and just because some athlete's wife is in the stands, someone thinks they have to put her picture on the screen. And I miss a double steal! Same with a ballplayer's father. Goddamn! "There's his dad, who taught him how to throw the changeup when he was two years old." Fuck him, the sick bastard! His own sports dreams probably crash-landed, so he forced a bunch of shit on his kid, and now the kid's a neurotic athlete. Fuck these athletes' relatives. If they wanna be on TV, let 'em get their own goddamn shows. Let 'em go to cable access.

I also don't care if an athlete's wife had a baby, how she is, how the baby is, how much the baby weighs or what the fuckin' baby's name is. It's got nothin' to do with sports. Leave it out!

And I'm tired of athletes whose children are sick. Healthy men with sick children; how banal. The kid's sick? Talk it over privately. Don't spread it all over television. Have some dignity. And play fuckin' ball!!

Nor do I wanna know about some athlete's crippled little brother or his hemophiliac big sister. The Olympics specialize in this kind of mawkish bullshit. Either his aunt has the clap, or his kid has a forty-pound mole, or his high school buddy overdosed on burritos, etc. Can't sports exist on television without all this embarrassing, maudlin, super-sentimental, tear-jerking bullshit? Keep your personal disasters to yourself, and get in there and score some fuckin' points!

And I don't care for all that middlebrow philosophical bullshit you get from athletes and coaches when someone on the team has a serious illness or dies in an accident. They give you that stuff, "When something like this happens, you realize what's really important. It's only a game." Bullshit! If it's only a game, get the fuck out of the business. You know what's important? The score. Who won. I can get plenty of sad tales somewhere else in this victim-packed society. Fuck all that dewy-eyed sentimental bullshit about people who are sick. And that includes any athlete whose father died a week before the game who says, "This one's for Pop." American bathos. Keep it to yourself. Play ball!

And I shouldn't even have to mention severly injured athletes who are playing on "nothing but heart." Fuck you! Suck it up and get out there, motherfucker.

And they're always tellin' ya that one of these athletes has a tumor. Don't they know that no one gives a fuck? You know when you care about a tumor? When *you* have it! Or someone close to you. Who cares about an athlete? No one cares if a rock star gets a tumor. What's so special about an athlete? By the way, you ever notice you don't hear as much about rock stars getting these tumors as you do about athletes? Maybe the drug life is a little better for us than all that stupid sweaty shit the athletes put themselves through. Just speculating.

And I don't wanna know about sports teams that sew the initials of dead people on their jerseys for one whole season as if it really means something. Leave that mawkish bullshit in the locker room. I don't wanna know who's in mourning. Play ball, you fuckin' grotesque overdeveloped nitwits!

And you can skip tellin' me about the Chevrolet player of the game. A thousand-dollar contribution to a scholarship fund in the athlete's name. Shit. A thousand dollars won't even keep a kid in decent drugs for one semester. Fuck Chevrolet.

And when are they gonna discover that no one cares if an athlete is active in local charities? People don't want to know about some coke-headed, steroid monstrosity who's working to help the National Douche Bag Foundation. Or how much he cares about inner-city kids. Can the cocksucker play ball? Fine. Then suit him up and get him the fuck out there on the field and let him injure someone.

One last thing on this topic. No one, repeat, no one is interested in athletes who can sing or play musical instruments. We already have people to perform these tasks. They're called singers and musicians, and, at last count, it would seem we have quite enough of them. The fact that someone with an IQ triple his age has mastered a few simple chords is unimportant and of monumental disinterest. Play ball!

PASS THE ROLES

I'm surprised that all this shit about role models has persisted as long as it has. Why should a kid need a role model? You know what you tell a kid? "Get the fuck out there, get a job, and make a contribution." Never mind that role model shit. If this country is dependent on things like role models, we're much worse off than I thought.

People say athletes should be role models. I never looked up to an athlete, did you? I liked them. I didn't copy them. Did you ever listen to one of those guys talk? Would you want your kid to turn out like that? Willing to completely subordinate his ego and individuality for the sake of a group whose sole purpose is to compete with other groups? Can't have a mustache? Gotta wear a suit jacket? Shit! If your kid needs a role model and you ain't it, you're both fucked.

SPORTS ROUNDUP

◊ I like sports because I enjoy knowing that many of these macho athletes have to vomit before a big game. Any guy who would take a job where you gotta puke first is my kinda guy.

◊ I read that Monica Seles got stabbed. And although I have nothing against Monica Seles, I'm glad somebody in sports got stabbed. I like the idea of it; it's good entertainment. If we're lucky, it'll spread all through sports. And show business, too! Wouldn't you like to see a guy jump up on stage and stab some famous singer? Especially a real shitty pop singer? Maybe they'll even start stabbing comedians. Fuck it, I'm ready! I never perform without my can of mace. I have a switchblade knife, too. I'll cut your eye out and go right on telling jokes.

In football, I root for the Oakland Raiders because they hire castoffs, outlaws, malcontents, and fuckups, they have lots of penalties, fights, and paybacks, and because Al Davis told the rest of the pig NFL owners to go get fucked. Also, they don't have a lot of Christians kneeling down to pray after touchdowns. Christians are ruining sports. Someday, the Raiders will be strong again, and they will dip the ball in shit and shove it down the throats of the wholesome, white, heartland teams that pray together and don't deliver late hits.

You know the best thing I did for myself during the past five years? I told sports to go take a flying fuck. I was fed up with the way I related to professional sports, so I reordered the relationship on my own terms. I became a little more selective.

I couldn't believe how much time I had wasted watching any old piece of shit ballgame that happened to show up on TV. I must have thought there was some inborn male obligation to tune in and root every time a bunch of sweaty assholes got together to mix it up in a stadium somewhere.

I also realized I was wasting perfectly good emotional energy by sticking with my teams when they were doing poorly. My rooting life was scarcely better than those Cubs fans who think it's a sign of character to feel shitty all the time. It's absurd.

I decided it's not necessary to suffer and feel crappy just because my teams suck. What I do now is cut 'em loose for awhile. I simply let them go about losing, as I go about living my life. Then, when they've improved, and are doing well once again, I get back on board and enjoy their success.

Yeah, I know, I can hear it: diehard, asshole loyal sports fans screaming, "Front-runner!" Goddamn right! Don't be so fuckin' juvenile. Teams are supposed to provide pleasure and entertainment, not depression and disappointment.

It is also completely unnecessary to suffer several days' emotional devastation just because your team loses some big postseason deal like the Super Bowl. Why on earth would you place your happiness and peace of mind in the hands of several dozen strangers? Listen, folks, if they win, fine; if they lose, fuck 'em! Let 'em practice more. As for you, for Chrissakes find something to do! Get your ass down to the massage parlor and spring for a blow job.

If you really want to enjoy sports, do what I did. Become a Harlem Globetrotters fan. There's no losing, no stats, no strikes, no trades, no contract hassles, no postseason, and no annoying media. Just winning, all the time, every night. By the way, I'm just diseased enough to realize it would also be lots of fun to root for the Washington Generals, the team that loses to the Globetrotters every night. At least you wouldn't have to put up with all that annoying, preseason optimism bullshit.

One common American sports gripe I do not share: I am not like those radio call-in, sports-fan asswipes who think athletes are overpaid. I believe the players should get any amount of money they want, and the fans should go fuck themselves. I'm tired of fans whining all that weak shit about how "we pay their salaries" and "without us there would be no games." Bullshit! Fuck you! If you don't want to spend the money, stay the fuck home! And shut your mouth. Sports fans eat shit.

Sports fans rate even lower than the media and the franchise owners on my scale of miserable, shit-eating vermin. Here's the descending hierarchy: athletes, sports media, team owners, fans. Fans on the bottom. Most sports fans are fat, ignorant, beer-soaked, loudmouth, racist, white male cocksuckers, and they're totally unnecessary to the playing of the games.

The athletes are the only people in sports who count; they're the only one who are indispensable. Everyone else is superfluous. Think about it. The entire pro-sports sewer began because groups of men got together and played these games in parks, vacant lots, and gyms simply for the fun of it. No money involved; just personal bets. And if today, all the owners, media, and sports fans suddenly disappeared, the athletes would simply go back to the parks, vacant lots, and gyms and play the games by themselves. No one else is necessary.

Of course, if they did, the usual dull people who lack direction would stand around watching, and some businessman-asshole would get the idea of charging admission and giving the players a tiny percentage of the money, and the whole miserable pool of steaming liquid shit would start all over again.

But in spite of all these negative feelings, I still enjoy watching a good close game played by well-matched teams. Lots of scoring, a few good fights, and then preferably forty innings or an octuple overtime, so that both teams eventually run out of players, and many of them are injured because they're tired.

The score of the game is not the only thing I'm interested in. I also root very hard for slumps, losing streaks, penalties, fights, injuries, team dissension, athletes cracking under pressure, and widespread gambling scandals. An earthquake in a ballpark isn't such a bad thing to me, either. I don't give a shit about the outcome of the game, I'm just looking for an interesting story.

I pray that some year the baseball postseason will include only teams with outdoor stadiums in cold-weather cities. And then I hope there are repeated freak storm systems that keep coming through the Midwest and the East, and all during the playoffs there are constant rainouts and postponements. And I pray for the whole thing to continue for months, so the games are pushed further and further back, and eventually the World Series is played in January. And then I hope it's cold and windy and icy and snowy, and a lot of players get hurt, and the games turn out to be a national disgrace. That's the kind of shit I root for.

Then there are other times when I'm not as positive. And I think to myself, Fuck sports! Fuck sweat, fuck jock itch, and fuck all people who are out of breath. Fuck the players, the sports media, the owners, and above all, the sports fans. Double-fuck the sports fans. Actually, though, to tell you the truth, if I had to endure those owners on the same day-to-day basis as I do the sports fans, I'm sure the owners would quickly work their way to the bottom of my list. Lower than a snake's ballbag. Remember, owners are always rotten people no matter what they own, and no matter where they turn up in life.

In their hatred for the players, the fans often forget that the real insects are the owners; the greedy swine owners who are always pleading poverty. In 1980, Nelson Doubleday paid $21.6 million for the Mets franchise. Today it's worth over $200 million. Where's the risk? And if it's so hard to make money in baseball, why are all these maggot entrepreneur-hustlers around the country so eager to pay $95 million for a last-place expansion team?

I'm not too thrilled with the sports media people, either. The talent is marginal, they bring nothing to the mix, and their palpable envy of the players is actually embarrassing. Many of these media stiffs were failed high school and college athletes and simply not good enough to make the cut. (Obviously, I'm excluding former pro ballplayers.) How dare such also-rans criticize athletes and their play? You wanna know the problem? Athletes get tons of money and pussy, and all the best drugs. The sports media don't. Need any more on that?

Some baseball teams hire "ball girls" to retrieve foul balls that don't go into the stands. But I've noticed many of these women are quite feminine and don't throw very well. These teams are making a mistake. I think they should hire lesbians to do that job. Not femmes, but full-on, bad-ass, 90-mile-an hour bull dykes. The kind you see in hardware stores. I'll tell you one thing, you'd get a lot more good plays and strong return throws out there. And if some fan leaned out of the stands to pick up a foul ball, the "ball dyke" could drag him onto the field and beat the shit out of him for about forty-five minutes. And if any baseball players tried to stop her, she could just deck them, too.

Athletes like that physical shit. When they're pleased with each other they bump chests, butt heads, and bang forearms. Why don't they just punch each other in the fuckin' teeth? Wouldn't that be great? Teammates, I mean. After a touchdown pass, why doesn't the guy who caught the ball just go over and kick the quarterback right in the nuts? Same with a slam dunk in basketball. The guy who scores oughta grab a chair and beat the living shit out of the guy who fed him the ball. For about forty-five minutes. If this type of celebration were more common, the postgame show from the winners' locker room would be a lot livelier.

And I think there should be at least one sport where the object is to kill someone. A team sport. Deathball. Let's face it, athletes are mostly physical freaks with serious personality defects where competition is concerned, and they just love someone to "motivate" them. Well, what greater motivation can there be than trying to avoid being killed? It's a fuckin' natural! And for me, what could be more fun than watching one of these jackoffs motivate his ugly ass into an early grave every game?

Here's another thing: I love losing streaks. I wish some year a baseball team would lose 162 games. I especially like decades-long, postseason losing streaks. In fact, as soon as my teams are out of the running, I start actively rooting for the Cubs, Red Sox, Bills, Broncos, and Vikings to get as far as they can in the postseason so that ultimately they can let the big prize slip away one more time. I think it is an infinitely more interesting news story for a team to repeatedly fail at the highest level than it is for them to finally win. If the Cubs ever win a World Series, the news coverage will be the most boring bunch of shit you can imagine.

And, although I wouldn't wish it on anyone, you'll have to admit it would sure be a lot of fun to see a couple of those chartered planes the athletes fly around in go down in flames. I know it might seem ghoulish to the overly squeamish, but I'd love to read about all the hassles they were having restocking the teams, and it would be fun to see the new lineups. Of course, all the stupid shit on TV about the funerals would be real boring.

P.S. Any professional sports team that has a "fight song" is automatically a bush-league, small-town team. Period.

FUCK YOU, I LIKE THESE KINDS OF JOKES!

Anticlimax: What my uncle was good at.

Chess: The piece movement.

Seersucker: A person who blows clairvoyants.

Passing gear: Clothing worn by light-skinned blacks who wish to be thought of as white.

Outspoken: When you lose a debate.

Hormone: The sound a prostitute makes so you'll think you're a real good fuck.

Drug traffic: Driving to your connection's house.

Sex drive: Similar to drug traffic, but with a different destination.

Douche: A female duke.

Octopus: An eight-sided vagina.

Trampoline: A sexual lubricant popular with sluts.

Parakeet: A keet that takes care of you until the real keet arrives.

Pussyfoot: A rare female birth defect requiring the use of open-toed shoes.

Beer nuts: The official disease of Milwaukee.

Cotton balls: The final stage of beer nuts.

Cowhand: An occupational disability common among dairy farmers.

Woodpecker: A seventeenth-century prosthetic device.

Leatherette: A short sadomasochist.

Cap pistol: A small gun that can be hidden in your hat.

A gay barbarian: Attila the hon.

"LET'S BEAT THEM WITH OUR PURSES!"

The reason for most violence against gays is that heterosexual men are forced to prove that they, themselves, are not gay. It goes like this: Men in strong male subcultures like the police, the military, and sports (and a few other cesspools) bond very strongly. Hunting, fishing, and golfing friendships also produce this unnatural bonding. These guys bond and bond, and get closer and closer, until finally they're just drunk enough to say, "You know, I really love these guys." And that frightens them. So they must quickly add, "But I'm not a queer!"

See the dilemma? Now they have to go out of their way to prove to the world, to their buddies, and to themselves that they don't harbor homoerotic feelings. And it's only a short step from "I"m not a queer" to "In fact, I hate queers!" And another short step to "Let's go kill some queers!" And what they really seek to kill is not the queer outside, it's the queer inside they fear.

Gay bashers are repressed homosexuals attempting to deny the queer inside, but certain signals get past the screen. That's why you see so many policemen with those precious little well-groomed mustaches. You'd see more of those same mustaches on athletes and military men, but those two groups are not allowed to express themselves freely. Military drones and many sheep-like athletes have dress codes and are forbidden to wear facial hair. The idea is to limit and reduce their individuality. These are men who have chosen to allow "the organization" to run their lives. That's why athletes, police, and military men have that rigid unbending body language; they're severely repressed. Guess what they're repressing? And, hey, why do you think they call those police cars "cruisers"?

SIGNS

I have a suggestion that I think would help fight serious crime. Signs. There are lots of signs for minor infractions: No Smoking, Stay Off the Grass, Keep Out, and they seem to work fairly well. I think we should also have signs for major crimes: Murder Strictly Prohibited, No Raping People, Thank You for Not Kidnapping Anyone. It's certainly worth a try. I'm convinced Watergate would never have happened if there had just been a sign in the Oval Office that said, Malfeasance of Office Is Strictly Against the Law, or Thank You for Not Undermining the Constitution.

When you drive through an entrance or exit lane that has one of those signs, Do Not Back Up—Severe Tire Damage, and you're going in the correct direction, don't you sort of worry about it anyway? That maybe they got it wrong? Or somebody turned the sign around? Or some guy on drugs installed the spikes? Or maybe *you're* on drugs, and you think, Am I doing this right? Am I backing up? No, I seem to be going forward. Let's see. Which way are the spikes pointing? Oh, I can't see the spikes anymore. I guess I better back up a little.

Here's a sign I don't like: Authorized Personnel Only. Now, if there's one thing I know about myself, it's that I am definitely not authorized. I wouldn't even know where to go to *get* authorized. Can you do it by mail? Wouldn't baptism sort of authorize you? It doesn't matter; I go through the door anyway. If I get stopped, I say, "Well, I may not be authorized for this, but I am authorized for other things. And your sign doesn't mention which things."

I've got a terrific sign in front of my house that keeps intruders out: Retarded Pit Bull High on Angel Dust. No one's come over the wall yet. Except a couple of retarded guys who were high on angel dust.

DO, TAKE, HAVE, GIVE

People used to *take* drugs, now they *do* drugs. Some people don't do *drugs*, they do *lunch*. Instead of taking *drugs*, they take *meetings*. They used to *have* meetings. Now, instead of having *meetings*, they have *relationships*. Some people who don't do drugs but have a relationship will take a meeting while they do lunch.

People used to *get* sex, now they *have* sex. So far, they don't *do* sex. Although they do say, "Let's do it." But if the sex is overly aggressive, we say the person was "taken." I guess if one's not giving, the other's gonna take.

We take a lot of things. We take a lot of *good* things. We take time, we take heart, we take solace, medicine, advice; we take a job, take a break, take a vacation, a leave, a nap, a rest, a seat, we take a meal.

We take, take, take until we can't take anymore. Maybe it's because our inner nature is not primarily one of giving, but of taking. Even these things we take that should balance our lives and give us rest do not. We make work out of them. We do them aggressively; always in control. Take.

But when we give, we give a lot of bad things. We give trouble, heartache, sorrow, we give someone a hard time, a migraine, give 'em a heart attack, and give 'em a big pain in the ass.

So I say, "Give up, get fucked, take a hike, and have fun."

YOU'RE A NATURAL

This is for health food fiends, the natural-fabrics gang, and all those green-head environmental hustlers who stomp around in the "natural": Your key word is meaningless. Everything is natural. Everything in the universe is a part of nature. Polyester, pesticides, oil slicks, and whoopee cushions. Nature is not just trees and flowers. It's everything. Human beings are part of nature. And if a human being invents something, that's part of nature, too. Like the whoopee cushion.

Also: The experience called "natural childbirth" is not natural at all. It is freaky and bizarre. It is distinctly unnatural for a person to invite and welcome pain. Whose influence am I sensing here? Men's? It's nothing more than childbirth machisma. The woman wants it said of her that she can "take it like a man."

GOOD FOR HEADACHES

Sometimes on television they tell you a product is "good for headaches." I don't want something that's good for headaches. I want something that's bad for headaches. And good for me.

THROW YOUR BACK OUT

Several months ago, a friend told me that when he was cleaning his garage he threw his back out. I told him it was probably overenthusiasm. Sometimes when you're cleaning, you get carried away and throw out something you intended to keep. The next time I ran into him he seemed to have learned his lesson. He had recently cleaned out his attic, but this time he didn't throw his back out. He gave it to Goodwill.

FIRST THINGS FIRST

Many things we take for granted must have sounded unusual the first time they were proposed. For instance, imagine trying to explain to someone, for the first time, that you thought giving him an enema would be a real good idea. You'd have to proceed very subtly.

"Hey, Joey! I got a new idea. Turn around."

"New id–? Hey, what's that thing in your hand?"

"Nothing. Oh! I dropped my keys. Would you mind pickin' 'em up?"

Or imagine the very first guy who threw up. What did he think? What did he say to his friends? "Hey, Vinny, c'mere! Remember that yak we ate? Look!"

UNNECESSARY WORDS

There is a tendency these days to complicate speech by adding unnecessary words. The following phrases all contain at least one word too many.

emergency situation

shower activity

surgical procedure

boarding process

flotation device

hospital environment

fear factor

free of charge

knowledge base

forest setting

beverage items

prison setting

peace process

intensity level

belief system

seating area

sting operation

evacuation process

rehabilitation process

facial area

daily basis

blue in color

risk factor

crisis situation

leadership role

learning process

rain event

confidence level

healing process

standoff situation

shooting incident

planning process

The best known example of this problem is: "At that point in time." I've even heard people say, "At that particular point in time." Boy, that's pinning it down, isn't it?

This typing process is beginning to tire out my finger area. Not to mention what it's doing to my mind situation. I think it's time to consider the break factor here, before I have a fatigue incident.

SHORT TAKES (Part 1)

the wisest man I ever knew taught me something I never forgot. And although I never forgot it, I never quite memorized it either. So what I'm left with is the memory of having learned something very wise that I can't quite remember.

Just what exactly is the "old dipsy doodle"?

When I hear a person talking about political solutions, I know I am not listening to a serious person.

Sties are caused by watching your dog shit.

SOMETIMES A LITTLE BRAIN DAMAGE CAN HELP

A woman told me her child was autistic, and I thought she said artistic. So I said, "Oh, great. I'd like to see some of the things he's done."

Eventually there will come a time when everyone is in a band.

Weyerhauser, a company that makes its money by cutting down trees, calls itself "The tree-growing company."

If a man smiles all the time he's probably selling something that doesn't work.

Not only do I not know what's going on, I wouldn't know what to do about it if I did.

How likely is it that all the people who are described as missing are living together in a small town somewhere?

We're all fucked. It helps to remember that.

If lobsters looked like puppies, people could never drop them in boiling water while they're still alive. But instead, they look like science fiction monsters, so it's OK. Restaurants that allow patrons to select live lobsters from a tank should be made to paint names on their shells: "Happy," "Baby Doll," "Junior." I defy anyone to drop a living thing called "Happy" in rapidly boiling water.

The nicest thing about anything is not knowing what it is.

I feel sorry for homeless gay people; they have no closet to come out of. In fact, I imagine if you *were* gay and homeless, you'd probably be glad just to *have* a closet.

I've adopted a new lifestyle that doesn't require my presence. In fact, if I don't want to, I don't have to get out of bed at all, and I still get credit for a full day.

The sicker you get, the harder it is to remember if you took your medicine.

I can't bear to go to the children's zoo. I always wonder how their parents can allow them to be kept in those little cages.

If you take the corn off the cob, not only do you have corn-off-the-cob, you also have cobs-out-from-inside-the-corn.

Why do foreign soldiers march funny? Do they think we march funny? If we do, how would we know?

If you mail a letter to the post office, who delivers it?

On the fritz" is a useful expression only if you're talking about a home appliance. You wouldn't say, "The Space Shuttle is on the fritz." You'd never hear it in a hospital. "Doctor, the heart-lung machine is on the fritz."

Rarely does a loose woman have a tight pussy.

Some see the glass as half-empty, some see the glass as half-full. I see the glass as too big.

My uncle thought he would clean up in dirt farming, but prices fell, and he took a real bath. Eventually, he washed his hands of the whole thing.

Kilometers are shorter than miles. Save gas, take your next trip in kilometers.

Test of metal: Will of iron, nerves of steel, heart of gold, balls of brass.

WHITE PEOPLE FUCKED UP
THE BLUES

If you love someone, set them free; if they come home, set them on fire.

I've never owned a telescope, but it's something I'm thinking of looking into.

Whenever I see a large crowd, I always wonder what was the most disgusting thing any one of them ever did.

I think they ought to let guys like Jeffrey Dahmer off with a warning. They do it with speeding tickets. Sometimes all a guy needs is a good talking to. Why don't they say, "Listen, Jeff. Knock it off! Nobody thinks you're funny. Eat one more guy and we're comin' after ya."

hey kids! It's mostly bullshit and garbage, and none of the stuff they tell you is true. And when your dumb-ass father says he wants you to amount to something, he means make a lot of money. How do you think the word *amount* got in there?

Those nicotine patches seem to work pretty well, but I understand it's kind of hard to keep 'em lit.

In El Salvador, they declared a cease fire after ten years. Why didn't they think of that at the beginning? Anyway, the best thing about El Salvador is that they killed a lot of religious people. How often do you get 10 percent of the body count in clergy?

At one point in my haste to improve myself, I mixed up the telephone numbers of the Shick Center for the Control of Smoking and the Evelyn Woods Speed Reading School. As a result, I can now smoke up to 300 cigarettes a minute, but I gave up reading.

Preschool teacher": If it's not a school, why do they need a teacher? Don't they need a "preteacher"?

Most people are not particularly good at anything.

ow can someone be "armed with a handgun"? Shouldn't he be armed with an "armgun"? Can a handgun really be a sidearm? And shouldn't a hand grenade be an arm grenade? You don't throw it with your hand, you throw it with your arm.

Try explaining Hitler to a kid.

FUCK AL JOLSON

Why do we turn lights "out" when we turn most other things "off"?

The straightest line between a short distance is two points.

Working-class people "look for work." Middle-class people "try to get a job." Upper-middle-class people "seek employment."

Can you have just one antic? How about a lone shenanigan? A monkeyshine?

There are two pips in a beaut, four beauts in a lulu, eight lulus in a doozy, and sixteen doozies in a humdinger. No one knows how many humdingers there are in a lollapalooza.

It is a sad thing to see an Indian wearing a cowboy hat.

Those who dance are considered insane by those who can't hear the music.

THERE WILL BE NO MORE
PAPER TOWELS AFTER JULY

It is impossible to know accurately how you look in your sunglasses.

As he ages, Mickey Rooney gets even shorter.

Elevators and escalators do more than elevate and escalate. They also lower. The names tell only half the story.

No one ever refers to "half a month."

Don't you get discouraged each morning when you wake up and realize you have to wash again?

You show me the people who control the money, the land, and the weapons, and I'll show you the people in charge.

I'm not going to apologize for this, but I have my own personal psychic. He doesn't predict the future, and he can't tell you much about your past. But he does a really fantastic job of describing the present. For instance, he can tell you exactly what you're wearing, but he can't do it over the phone.

We're all amateurs; it's just that some of us are more professional about it than others.

When the going gets tough, the tough get fucked.

I was expelled from cooking school, and it left a bad taste in my mouth.

ast year, in Los Angeles, a robber threatened a store owner with a syringe that he claimed had HIV on it, saying "Give me the money or I'll give you AIDS." You know what I would've told him? "If you give me AIDS I'm gonna find your wife and daughter and fuck them."

I think we should attack Russia now. They'd never expect it.

I have as much authority as the Pope, I just don't have as many people who believe it.

What is the plural of "a hell of a guy"? "Hells of guys"?

The phrase *surgical strike* might be more acceptable if it were common practice to perform surgery with high explosives.

I never eat sushi. I have trouble eating things that are merely unconscious.

When you find existing time on a parking meter, you should be able to add it to the end of your life. Minus the time you spent on hold.

I recently went to a new doctor and noticed he was located in something called the Professional Building. I felt better right away.

You can't fight City Hall, but you can goddamn sure blow it up.

Just think, right now as you read this, some guy somewhere is gettin' ready to hang himself.

JESUS WAS A CROSS-DRESSER

I have no ax to grind, but I do have an ivory letter opener that could use sharpening.

feminists want to ban pornography on the grounds that it encourages violence against women. The Japanese consume far more violent and depraved pornography than we do, and yet there is almost no rape reported there. A woman is twenty times more in danger of being raped in the U.S. than she is in Japan. Why? Because Japanese people are decent, civilized, and intelligent.

The only good thing ever to come out of religion was the music.

I don't have to tell you it goes without saying there are some things better left unsaid. I think that speaks for itself. The less said about it the better.

Do kings have sweat bands in their crowns?

When someone is impatient and says, "I haven't got all day," I always wonder, How can that be? How can you not have all day?

There ought to be at least one round state.

for a long time it was all right for a woman to keep a diary, but it sounded too fruity for men. So they changed it to *journal*. Now sensitive men can set down their thoughts without appearing *too* sensitive.

In comic strips the person on the left always speaks first.

A courtesy bus driver once told me to go fuck myself.

Sometimes the label on the can says "fancy peas." Then, you get 'em home and they're really rather ordinary. Nothing fancy about 'em, at all. Maybe if they had little bullfight paintings on them, they would be fancy. But as it is . . .

SLAP A DEAD PERSON

If the shoe fits, get another one just like it.

Eventually, nature will produce a species that can play the piano better than we can.

I don't think we really gave barbarism a fair try.

Piano lessons sound like something a piano should take. Humans should take piano-playing lessons.

Did you hear about the man who left in a huff and returned in a jiffy? Another day, he arrived in a tizzy and left in a snit. His wife swept in in a fury and left in a daze, then left in a dither and returned in a whirl.

If you go to a bone bank, why can't you make a calcium deposit?

get down!" is a slang expression that would have been really useful in World War II. If soldiers had known this expression at the time, a lot of lives could have been saved.

WHY CAN'T THERE BE MORE SUFFERING?

There are no times that don't have moments like these.

Since 1983, more than thirty people have been killed in post office shootings. You know why? Because the price of stamps keeps changing. There's a lot of pressure. "How much are they now, Rob? Twenty-nine? Thirty-two? I can't keep track! Fuck it!" BANG BANG BANG BANG BANG BANG BANG BANG BANG BANG!!!

On Opening Day, the President doesn't throw *out* the first ball. He throws it *in*. If he threw it out, it would land in the parking lot and someone would have to go get it.

Where does the dentist go when he leaves you alone?

Why are there never any really good-looking women on long distance buses?

I almost don't feel the way I do.

We're not satisfied with forcing Russia to destroy its nuclear weapons and recant its ideology. Now we're really going to get even: we're sending experts to show them how to run their economy. Am I missing something? A country with a five-trillion-dollar debt is giving advice on handling money?

She "took him to the cleaners." Whenever I hear that I wonder if that was the only errand he had to run. Maybe she also took him to the adult bookstore.

I go to bed early. My favorite dream comes on at nine.

Best seller" really only means "good seller." There can only be one best seller. All the rest are good sellers. Each succeeding book on the list is a "better seller."

There should be some things we don't name, just so we can sit around all day and wonder what they are.

Everything is still the same. It's just a little different now.

The symphony orchestra had played poorly, so the conductor was in a bad mood. That night he beat his wife—because the music hadn't been beautiful enough.

You know why I stopped eating processed foods? I began to picture the people who might be processing them.

Whenever I see a large crowd I always think of all the dry cleaning they have out.

I didn't wash today. I wasn't dirty. If I'm not dirty, I don't wash. Some weeks I don't have to shower at all. I just groom my three basic areas: teeth, hair, and asshole. And to save time, I use the same brush.

I AM NOT IN COMPLIANCE

When you buy a six-foot dildo, and call it a marital aid, you are stretching not just the anatomy, but the limits of credibility.

At a formal dinner party, the person nearest death should always be seated closest to the bathroom.

The child molester skipped breakfast, but said he'd grab a little something on the way to work.

t HINGS YOU DON'T WANT TO HEAR: "Jeff? We're going to have to break your skull again and reset it. Okay? It's way out of line. It looks really strange. But we won't do it until we've opened up that incision and put some more fire ants inside of you. OK?"

In Panama, during the election that defeated Noriega, there were "dignity battalions" that wandered the streets beating and robbing and killing people.

S omeone said to me, "Make yourself a sandwich." Well, if I could make myself a sandwich, I wouldn't make myself a sandwich. I'd make myself a horny, 18-year-old billionaire.

Why would anyone want to use a flood light? I should think lights would be kind of dangerous during a flood. Better just to sit in the dark and wait for help.

There are nights when the wolves are silent, and only the moon howls.

The nicest thing about a plane crashing at an air show is that they always have good video of the actual crash.

How come none of these boxers seem to have a losing record?

Where ideas are concerned, America can be counted on to do one of two things: take a good idea and run it completely into the ground, or take a bad idea and run it completely into the ground.

If I only had one tooth, I think I would brush it a real long time.

If we could just find out who's in charge, we could kill him.

Whenever I hear that someone works in his shirtsleeves, I always wonder what he did with the rest of the shirt.

It is impossible to dry one hand.

The word *bipartisan* usually means some larger-than-usual deception is being carried out.

I saw an old woman who I thought was looking on the ground for a contact lens. As I drew closer, I realized she was actually all hunched over from osteoporosis.

GERMS LIVE IN MY HAT

You can lead a gift horse to water in the middle of the stream, but you can't look him in the mouth and make him drink.

deep Throat: Think about it. There is actually an important figure in American history who is named for a blow-job movie. How do grade-school teachers handle this?

Regarding the fitness craze: America has lost its soul; now it's trying to save its body.

Nothing is so boring as listening to someone else describe a dream.

What is all this stuff about a kick being "partially blocked"? It's either blocked, not blocked, or deflected. Partially blocked is like "somewhat dead."

I notice I don't see as many buck-toothed women as I used to.

The thing I like the most about this country is that, in a pinch, when things really get tough, you can always go into a store and buy some mints.

I've watched so many documentaries about World War II, I'm sure I've seen the same people die hundreds of times.

I'll bet there aren't too many people hooked on crack who can play the bagpipes.

I read that some guy was giving up the governor's chair to run for a Senate seat. Why would he give up a chair to run for a seat? Why not be a judge and sit on the bench?

How do primitive people know if they're doing the dances correctly?

THINGS YOU NEVER HEAR: "Please stop sucking my dick or I'll call the police."

Regarding smoking in public: Suppose you were eating in a restaurant, and every two minutes the guy at the next table threw some anthrax germs in the air. Wouldn't you want to sit in a different section?

The savings-and-loan associations that will cost $500 billion to bail out are called "the thrifts."

The idea of a walk-in closet sounds frightening. If I'm ever sittin' at home and a closet walks in, I'm gettin' outta there.

The reason they call it the American Dream is because you have to be asleep to believe it.

I'D RATHER
BE COMING

How can there possibly be a self-addressed envelope? They say now they even have envelopes that are self-sealing. This I gotta see!

I saw a sign: Park and ride. It's confusing. They really oughta make up their minds.

Park and lock. Here we go again. If you park and lock, you're stuck in the car. It should be park, get out, and lock.

"No comment" is a comment.

Why is it like this? Why isn't everything different?

If you have chicken at lunch and chicken at dinner, do you ever wonder if the two chickens knew each other?

She was only a prostitute, but she had the nicest face I ever came across.

It's odd that the word *breath* becomes *breathe* by adding a letter at the end, and yet the pronunciation changes in the middle. And *woman* becomes *women* by changing the vowel at the end, while the pronunciation changes near the beginning. Was somebody drunk when these decisions were made?

Russia actually has something called *vodka riots*.

I think it would be fun to go on "Jeopardy" and never buzz in. Just stand there for half an hour, never talk, and then go home.

Diplomatic immunity is necessary, because of the many diseases diplomats are exposed to in foreign countries.

Why is San Francisco in the "bay area," but Saudi Arabia is in the "gulf region"? Is a region really bigger than an area?

henever I hear about a spy ring, I always wonder if that's the only jewelry they wear. You'd think a spy wouldn't want to call attention to himself with a lot of flashy jewelry. For instance, you never hear about a spy necklace.

THIS IS JUST SOME PRINTING

It's better if an entire family gets Alzheimer's disease. That way they can all sit around and wonder who they are.

Time sharing got a bad name, so now they call it "interval ownership."

Harness racing may be all right for some people, but I prefer watching the horses.

If you get cheated by the Better Business Bureau, who do you complain to?

As soon as a person tells you they have a surprise for you, they have lost the element of surprise.

i saw a picture of the inventor of the hydrogen bomb, Edwin Teller, wearing a tie clip. Why would the man who invented a bomb that destroys everything for fifty miles be concerned about whether or not his tie was straight?

No one calls you "Bub" anymore.

Why is there such controversy about drug testing? I know plenty of guys who'd be willing to test any drug they can come up with.

If the Cincinnati Reds were really the first major league baseball team, who did they play?

I AM REPELLED BY WHOLESOMENESS

When they say someone is making a "personal tour," are they suggesting that, on the other hand, it is somehow possible to make a tour without actually being there?

After how much time does a persistent cough become a chronic cough?

Intelligence tests are biased toward the literate.

The carousel and Ferris wheel owners traveled in different circles so they rarely made the rounds together.

Which is more immoral? Killing two 100-pound people or killing one 300-pound person?

guest host is a bad enough oxymoron, but NBC raised the stakes when, a few years back, they installed Jay Leno as the "permanent guest host." Not to be outdone, Joan Rivers pointed out that she had been the "first permanent guest host." Check, please!

I don't own a camera, so I travel with a police sketch artist.

If JFK Jr. got into a taxi in New York to go to the airport, do you think he would say, "Take me to JFK?" How would he feel about that? And how does Lee Harvey Oswald's mother feel when she walks through JFK, knowing that if she had stayed single it would probably be Martin Luther King Jr. Airport?

Which is taller, a short-order cook or a small-engine mechanic?

Hobbies are for people who lack direction.

FUCK SOCCER MOMS

A graveyard always has to start with a single body. Unless the local people get lucky and there's a nice big bus accident in town.

A lot of times when they catch a guy who killed twenty-seven people, they say, "He was a loner." Well, of course he was a loner; he killed everyone he came in contact with.

Is it illegal to charge admission to a free-for-all?

read about some mob guy who was being charged with gambling, loan sharking, extortion, narcotics, prostitution, murder, pornography, labor racketeering, stolen cars, business fraud, mail fraud, wire fraud, bribery, corruption, perjury, and jury tampering. Here's a guy who didn't waste a minute. Busy, busy, busy!

My definition of bad luck: catching AIDS from a Quaker.

Dogs and cats get put to sleep, hogs and cows get slaughtered.

If a speed freak went to Rapid City to make a quick buck in fast food he might sell instant coffee in an express lane.

I worry about my judgment when anything I believe in or do regularly begins to be accepted by the American public.

Imagine how thick Japanese people's photo albums must be.

Some national parks have long waiting lists for camping reservations. I think when you have to wait a year to sleep next to a tree, something is wrong.

When football fans tear down the goalpost, where do they take it?

Just because your penis surgery was not successful is no reason to go off half-cocked.

n England in 1830, William Hukkison became the first person ever run over by a railroad train. Wouldn't that make you feel stupid? For millions and millions of years there were no trains, and then suddenly they have trains and you get run over?

NOTHING RHYMES WITH NOSTRIL

Shouldn't a complimentary beverage tell you what a fine person you are?

Only Americans could find as a prime means of self-expression the wave and the high five.

It is important to remember that although the Automobile Club has a health plan, the health club does not have an automobile plan.

Auto racing: slow minds and fast cars.

If you fuck a baseball player's wife while he's on the road, his team will lose the next day.

If Helen Keller had psychic ability, would you say she had a fourth sense?

Why do the Dutch people have two names for their country, Holland and the Netherlands, and neither one includes the word *Dutch*?

Late one night it struck me that for several years I had been masturbating to a Wilma Flintstone fantasy.

Why do we say *redheaded* but *brownhaired*?

does the water that signifies the passage of time flow under the bridge, or over the dam? I've heard both versions, and I'm concerned about the people who live near the dam.

In the movies, when someone buys something they never wait for their change.

I buy stamps by mail. It works OK until I run out of stamps.

Whenever someone tells me they're going to fix a chicken, I always think, Maybe it isn't really broken. Maybe it just needs a little oil.

My only superstition: if you drop a spoon, a wild pig will offer to finance your next car.

As a matter of principle I never attend the first annual anything.

Why is it with any piece of home electronics equipment there are always a few buttons and switches you never use?

There is actually a show on the lifetime channel called "Dentistry Update."

When you eat two different types of candy bars in succession, the second one is not as easy to enjoy because you get so used to how good the first one tastes.

BLOOD IS THICKER
THAN URINE

They said some guy arrested for murder in Las Vegas had "a history of questionable actions." Can you imagine if we were all held to that standard?

There is no will, and there is no wisdom.

Some people like to watch "monster trucks" drive on top of cars and crush them. Then there are the other people who can't get to the arena, because they don't have cars.

A lot of these people who keep a gun at home for safety are the same ones who refuse to wear a seat belt.

It's legal for men to be floorwalkers and illegal for women to be streetwalkers.

Look at the self-help titles in the bookstore, and you'll get a fews clues about our culture. They're all about aggression and acquisition. It wouldn't be at all surprising to see a book called *How to Force Your Will on Other People by Giving Them the Shaft and Fucking Them out of Their Money*.

When you sneeze, all the numbers in your head go up by one.

How can *crash course* and *collision course* have two different meanings?

I wanted to get a job as a gynecologist, but I couldn't find an opening.

Why don't they have dessert at breakfast?

Sometimes I look out the airplane window at a large city at night and wonder how many people are fucking.

Why don't they have rye pancakes? Grapefruit cookies? Fig ice cream? Canteloupe pie?

The *mai tai* got its name when two Polynesian alcoholics got in a fight over some neckwear.

I hope they do clone the dinosaurs, and they come back just in time for the ozone layer to disappear and wipe those ugly motherfuckers out again.

In most polls there are always about 5 percent of the people who "don't know." What isn't generally understood is that it's the same people in every poll.

I read that a patient got AIDS from his dentist. It wasn't from the blood; apparently, the dentist fucked him in the ass. "Open wide!"

Regarding Red Riding Hood: Wolves can't be all bad if they'll eat your grandmother. Even Grandpa won't do that.

I think we've outgrown the word *gripe*. When everyone has automatic weapons, a word like *gripe* is sort of irrelevant.

PIG
SNERV

"The friendly skies." "The skies are not cloudy." How is this possible? I look up, I see one sky.

Kids are now being born with syphilis *and* cocaine habits. There's nothing like waking up your second day on Earth and realizing that once you kick cocaine you're still gonna have the syph. And hey, kids! If you didn't get VD in the womb, don't worry, you still have a shot. Some toddlers recently picked up gonorrhea at a day care center.

I always thought a semi-truck driver was someone who dropped out of truck-driving school halfway through the course.

When Sammy Davis Jr. kissed a woman, do you think he closed his bad eye?

Environmentalists changed the word *jungle* to *rain forest*, because no one would give them money to save a jungle. Same with *swamps* and *wetlands*.

When a lion escapes from a circus in Africa, how do they know when they've caught the right one?

The safest place to be during an earthquake would be in a stationary store.

Wouldn't it be funny if you went to group therapy and the Mills Brothers were there?

I'm not an organ donor, but I once gave an old piano to the Salvation Army.

Cancer research is a growth industry.

Sometimes I sit for hours weighing the fine distinctions among *spunk*, *pluck*, *balls*, *nerve*, *chutzpah*, *gall*, and *moxie*.

It is impossible for an abortion clinic to have a waiting list of more than nine months.

YOU NEVER SEE A SMILING RUNNER

Carjackings, smash-and-grabs, snipers, home invasions, follow-home robberies, hostage incidents, barricade/standoff situations, drive-by shootings, walk-up shootings, traffic shootings, pipe bombs, mail bombs. Shit! We never had cool crimes like that when I was a kid. All we had was robbery and murder. I feel deprived.

In a hotel, why can't you use the house phone to phone your house?

I'm bringing out my own line of colognes. You've heard of Eternity, Obsession, and Passion? Mine is Stench! I'm offering a choice of five fragrances: Bait Shop, Animal Waste, Landfill, Human Remains, and Chemical Toilet.

When I was a kid I used to think it was all the same clouds that kept coming by.

SOMETHING IS DREADFULLY WRONG IN THIS COUNTRY: There is now an "empathy breast." It is a wrap-around vest that has a pocket for placing the baby's bottle in. The new father wears it while "nursing" the baby. Jesus!

Sometimes on a rainy day I sit around and weed the losers out of my address book.

They said on the news that tests on monkeys showed HIV can be transmitted through oral sex. What I want to know is, who had to blow the monkeys?

The other night I ate at a real nice family restaurant. Every table had an argument going.

I don't live in the fast lane, but have you ever seen one of those cars parked on the median with its hood up?

just think, right now, all over the world there are people exercising bad judgment. Somebody, right this minute, is probably making the mistake of his life.

Poor confetti. Its useful life lasts about two seconds. And it can never be used again.

human beings are kind of interesting from birth until they reach the age of a year and a half. Then they are boring until they reach fifty. By that time they're either completely defeated and fucked up, which makes them interesting again, or they've learned how to beat the game, and that makes them interesting, too.

THINK OFF-CENTER

The older I get, the more certain I am that I will not have to spend the rest of my life in prison.

Assisted suicide is controversial. There are moral, medical, legal, and ethical arguments. But the truth of it is, a lot of people just want to get the fuck outta here.

What exactly do you do when the Dalai Lama appears on "Nightline," and you're not satisfied with his answers?

whenever I see a picture of a group of people in the newspaper, I always wonder how many of them have had really depraved sex since the picture was taken.

A small town is any place too poor to have its own insane asylum.

exas canceled plans to put its motto, Friendship, on its license plates. People complained that it was too wimpy. Why don't they just change their motto? Let's Kill All the Niggers comes to mind as appropriate.

In Vienna, they recently had an opera riot.

Never get on an airplane if the pilot is wearing a hat that has more than three pastel colors.

hy is it when you buy five shirts, there's always one you never wear? To minimize this problem, when I shop for shirts I always put one back just before I pay.

My family and I are doing our bit for the environment. We've volunteered to have sixty metric tons of human waste stored in our home.

CANCER CAUSES HEART DISEASE

hopping and buying and getting and having comprise the Great American Addiction. No one is immune: When the underclass riots in this country, they don't kill policemen and politicians, they steal merchandise. How embarrassing.

I made a bargain with the devil: I would get to be famous, and he would get to fuck my sister.

ranola bars didn't sell very well when they were good for you. Now they have caramel, chocolate, marshmallow, saturated fat, and sweeteners; and a small amount of oats and wheat. Sales picked up.

ou know you're in trouble when you look behind the clerk and see one of your personal checks displayed on the wall as an example of why the store does not accept personal checks.

As grown-ups, we never get to "wave bye-bye." I think it would be fun. "Steve, the boss is sailing for Europe; we're all going down to the dock to wave bye-bye."

Some things a king never has to say:
"Can I play, too?"
"Hey, guys, wait for me."
"I never seem to get laid."

id you ever go somewhere and realize it used to be a different place? And it dawns on you that some things are not here anymore. Of course, some other things are not here *yet*. And nothing seems to be where it used to be; everything's been moved. Sometimes I think if we could just put everything back where it originally was, we might be all right.

I was surprised when I started getting old. I always thought it was one of those things that would happen to someone else.

ALUMINUM IS A
JIVE METAL

You know you're in a poor neighborhood when you give the store clerk a dollar and he asks you if you have anything smaller.

Since childhood is a time when kids prepare to be grown-ups, I think it makes a lot of sense to completely traumatize your children. Gets 'em ready for the real world.

With all that humping going on, JFK's administration shouldn't have been called Camelot, they should have called it Come-a-lot.

there is a new British rock band called So Long, Mate! During each performance one member of the band is ritually slaughtered. The music has a certain urgency, but the tours are nice and short. About five days.

When the convention of testicle transplant surgeons had its annual softball game, they asked me to throw out the first ball.

You know what would be fun? Drop acid, smoke PCP, and then take the White House tour with Jim Carrey.

i don't believe there's any problem in this country, no matter how tough it is, that Americans, when they roll up their sleeves, can't completely ignore.

Sometimes a fireman will go to great, strenuous lengths to save a raccoon that's stuck in a drainpipe and then go out on the weekend and kill several of them for amusement.

They debated the NAFTA trade bill for a long time; should we sign it or not? Either way, the people get fucked. Trade always exists for the traders. Anytime you hear businessmen debating "which policy is better for America," don't bend over.

Property is theft. Nobody owns anything. When you die, it stays here. I read about these billionaires: Sam Walton 20 billion, Daniel Ludwig 15 billion. They're both dead. They're gone, and the money is still here. It wasn't their money to begin with. Property is theft.

If you want to keep your dog in line, walk him past the fur shop a couple of times a week.

There are only two places in the world: over here and over there.

MILK CHOCOLATE IS FOR SCHMUCKS

I have a photograph of Judge Bork, but it doesn't do him justice.

Have you ever wondered why Republicans are so interested in encouraging people to volunteer in their communities? It's because volunteers work for no pay. Republicans have been trying to get people to work for no pay for a long time.

I finally accepted Jesus. Not as my personal savior, but as a man I intend to borrow money from.

It used to be, cars had cool names: Dart, Hawk, Fury, Cougar, Firebird, Hornet, Mustang, Barracuda. Rocket 88! Now we have Elantra, Altima, Acura, Lumina, Sentra, Corolla, Maxima. Tercel! What the fuck kind of lifeless, pussy names are these? Further proof America has lost its edge.

I'm starting a campaign to have Finland removed as a country. We don't need it.

What a spot! You're in surgery, the anesthetic wears off, and as you wake up you realize that someone in surgical clothing is carrying one of your legs over to a garbage can. The surgeon, holding a large power saw, says, "We're all out of anesthetic, but if you'll hold on real tight to the sides of that gurney, I'll have that other leg off in a jiffy."

You rarely meet a wino with perfect pitch.

Although the photographer and the art thief were close friends, neither had ever taken the other's picture.

Traditional American values: Genocide, aggression, conformity, emotional repression, hypocrisy, and the worship of comfort and consumer goods.

I read that Domino's Pizza trucks have killed more than twenty people. And that's not counting the ones who eat the pizza.

I like it when a flower or a little tuft of grass grows through a crack in the concrete. It's so fuckin' heroic.

A group of cult people has emerged who not only believe Elvis Presley is alive, but have decided that if they find him they will kill and skin him.

there are ten thousand people in the United States in a persistent vegetative state. Just enough to start a small town. Think of them as veggie-burghers.

Apparently, the Hells Angels are suing a movie producer because they said his film shows disrespect for the Hells Angels. OK.

SIMON SAYS, GO FUCK YOURSELF

SOMETHING IS DREADFULLY WRONG IN THIS COUNTRY: There is actually an organization called Wrestlers Against Drugs, and on TV there is now a Christian weight-lifting tour.

I once read that in Lebanon a peacekeeping force was attacked by a religious militia. They deserve each other.

Ross Perot. Just what a nation of idiots needs: a short, loud idiot.

When you visualize the recent past, do you see it as being somewhere over on the left?

Now the brainless New Age spiritual zombies are using bulldozers to vandalize the Ouachita National Forest in Arkansas in search of crystals. Nothing like that being-in-harmony-with-nature shit.

In some places, a seventeen-year-old girl needs a note for being absent from school, but she does not need one to get an abortion.

There's a moment coming. It's not here yet. It's still on the way. It's in the future. It hasn't arrived. Here it comes. Here it is . . . shit! It's gone.

A sure way to cure hiccups is to jam your fist down the affected person's throat and quickly open and close your hand several times. It relaxes the vega nerve.

SOMETHING IS DREADFULLY WRONG IN THIS COUNTRY: In a November 1990 Gallup Poll of 1,108 Americans, 78 percent said they believed there was a place where people who had led good lives were eternally rewarded, and 60 percent believed there was a place where those who led bad lives and died without repentance were eternally damned. I find this profoundly disturbing.

I always order the International Breakfast: French toast, English muffin, Belgian waffle, Spanish omelet, Danish pastry, Swedish pancakes, Canadian bacon, and Irish Coffee.

THERE ARE GHOSTS IN MY SINUSES

regarding local residents attempting to ban sex shops from their neighborhoods: You show me a parent who says he's worried about his child's innocence, and I'll show you a homeowner trying to maintain equity.

I thought it would be nice to get a job at a duty-free shop, but it doesn't sound like there's a whole lot to do in a place like that.

there's an odd feeling you get when someone on the sidewalk moves slightly to avoid walking into you. It proves you exist. Your mere existence caused them to alter their path. It's a nice feeling. After you die, no one has to get out of your way anymore.

Instead of school busing and prayer in schools, which are both controversial, why not a joint solution? Prayer in buses. Just drive these kids around all day and let them pray their fuckin' empty little heads off.

Lorena Bobbit only did what men do to each other all the time: She showed an asshole she meant business.

Americans are fucked. They've been bought off. And they came real cheap: a few million dirt bikes, camcorders, microwaves, cordless phones, digital watches, answering machines, jet skis, and sneakers with lights in them. You say you want a few items back from the Bill of Rights? Just promise the doofuses new gizmos.

I love it in a movie when they throw a guy off a cliff. I love it even when it's not a movie. No, especially when it's not a movie.

Owing to a basic programming flaw, many computer calculations, including mortgages and pensions, will be throw off by the arrival of the year 2000. It's because many computer programs use only the last two digits for calculating years. It will cost between 50 and 100 billion dollars to correct this mistake. I'm glad. I like anything that causes trouble.

Men don't show emotion, except rage, because it takes strength to show soft emotions. Most men don't have that kind of strength. They keep things inside. Then they kill someone.

Regarding Mount Rushmore: The Black Hills are sacred Indian ground. Imagine the creepy feeling of four leering European faces staring at your ancestors for eternity.

Who are all these people whose eyeglasses are attached to straps and bands around their necks? Please! Folks. Too precious. Hold your glasses, or set them down like the rest of us. Or perhaps, strange as it sounds, put them on. You need a dual correction? Get some bifocals.

HOUSES AND HOMES

housework/homework

houseboy/homeboy

housebreaker/homewrecker

housekeeper/homemaker

That thing you live in? Is it a house, or is it a home? Developers sell homes, but people buy houses.

Most people don't mind if you put 'em in a house. But under no circumstances do they want you to put 'em in a home. Unless it's a happy home. A happy home is not the same as a happy house. A happy house is one that's just been cleaned and painted. You'd be happy, too.

The madam Polly Adler once said, "A house is not a home." Of course, she meant a whorehouse is not a home. And it's not; no one would ever go to a whore home. Except a really old whore. That's where they go: The Old Whore's Home.

OPPOSITE-SAME-OPPOSITE

Sometimes the same words mean opposite things. Sometimes the opposite is true. Shock absorbers are called shocks. Slow down and slow up are interchangeable. Bad taste is tasteless. Sports fans say "turf" when they mean artificial turf. Something invaluable is very valuable. I'll bet you could care less. Or maybe you couldn't care less. Same difference. By the way, is it "from here on in" or "from here on out"?

INSIDE-OUT TALK

Here's something pretty stupid. You inflect these phrases the same way as the originals. It's inside-out talk! Tell your pals.

{ } Palsable celery

{ } The Arionese Syberation Limby

{ } Footday Night Monball

{ } Daise Don't Please the Eatsies

{ } A knocknical techout

{ } The New Bork Yockerknickers

{ } Beach the Combdanner

{ } Sylstoner Vallest

{ } Cronker Waltite

{ } The Unington of Washiversity

✖ Third Enkinders of the Close Count

{ } Kind Enclosures of the Third Count

{ } The Inhuldable Crelk

{ } Circy Flython's Pything Montus

{ } The Delaseverty Sixty Philyers

WHAT'S MY MOTIVATION?

What's all this stuff about motivation? I say, if you need motivation, you probably need more than motivation. You probably need chemical intervention or brain surgery. Actually, if you ask me, this country could do with a little *less* motivation. The people who are causing all the trouble seem highly motivated to me. Serial killers, stock swindlers, drug dealers, Christian Republicans. I'm not sure motivation is always a good thing. You show me a lazy prick who's lying in bed all day, watching TV, only occasionally getting up to piss, and I'll show you a guy who's not causing any trouble.

THE GEORGE CARLIN BOOK CLUB— "We've Got Books Out the Ass"
Offer #2: Advice and Self-Help Titles

☐ *Where to Go for a Free Fuck*

☐ *Eat, Run, Stay Fit, and Die Anyway*

☐ *You Give Me Six Weeks and I'll Give You Some Bad Disease*

☐ *Why You Should Never Mambo with a Policeman*

☐ *The Stains in Your Shorts Can Indicate Your Future*

☐ *Earn Big Money by Sitting in Your Car Trunk*

✖ *Where to Take a Short Woman*

❲❳ *I Gave Up Hope and It Worked Just Fine*

❲❳ *Why You Should Never Yodel During an Electrical Storm*

❲❳ *Fill Your Life with Croutons*

❲❳ *Six Ways to Screw Up Before Breakfast*

❲❳ *I Suck, You Suck*

✖ *Reorganizing Your Pockets*

❲❳ *Where to Hide a Really Big Snot*

❲❳ *Why You Must Never Give Yourself a Neck Operation*

❲❳ *The Wrong Underwear Can Kill*

✖ *Now You Can Cure Cancer by Simply Washing Up*

❲❳ *Lightweight Summer Ensembles to Wear on the Toilet*

❲❳ *Why No One Should Be Allowed Out Anymore*

❲❳ *A Complete List of People Who Are Not Making Progress*

❲❳ *Where to Throw Up Secretly*

❲❳ *Ten Things No One Can Handle at All*

❲❳ *Why You Should Not Sit for More Than Six Weeks in Your Own Filth*

THE NEW ZODIAC

We need new zodiac signs. The old ones depict an obsolete world: the archer, the water bearer, and—talk about obsolete—the virgin. What we need are modern zodiac signs that represent today's reality:

The Serial Rapist, the Lone Gunman, the Suicide Bomber, the

Paranoid Schizophrenic, the Transsexual Crackhead, the Money Launderer, the Disgruntled Postal Worker, the Diseased Homeless Veteran, the South American Drug Lord, the Third-Generation Welfare Recipient, the Human Immunodeficiency Virus, and . . . the Personal Trainer!

In case you're one of those people who doesn't relate well to the real world, here's a nice, safe zodiac for you: the Soccer Mom, the Sensitive Male, the Special Needs Child, the Role Model, the Overachiever, the Jogger, the Little Leaguer, the Recycler, the Anchorperson, the Codependent, the Domino's Delivery Boy, and . . . the Recovering Shopaholic.

GIVE A HOOT

I don't give a hoot. Not since 1959. That was the last one I gave. Wait! I think I gave a hoot in 1967. Just one. As a favor to a friend. But that was it. I'm not even sure I have any left. Frankly, I'd be afraid to look. I think I'm all out of hoots. If you want one, you're gonna have to find it on your own. Maybe you could rent a hoot. Or steal one. I'll bet by now there's a black market in hoots. Hot hoots. By the way, in addition to those who don't *give* a hoot, there are many others who will not *take* a hoot. Too proud. These are the same people who will not take any guff. But they might give you some lip.

BRING THE BODY CLOSER

I often hear otherwise intelligent people complaining about drivers who slow down when driving past a traffic accident. They curse them and call them "rubberneckers." I don't understand this at all. I am never in too big a hurry that I can't stop and watch someone else's suffering. The bigger the accident the better, as far as I'm concerned. I wanna see some guy whose neck is part of his gas tank. And if I can't see enough from my particular vantage point? I'll ask the policeman to bring the bodies over a little closer to my car. "Say, officer! Could you bring that twisted chap over here a little closer? I've never seen a man shaped quite like that." That's why the police are here: to protect, to serve, and to bring the bodies over a little closer to your car.

PAST-TENSE TV

I have a cable channel that shows old TV shows, but it shows them in different tenses from the originals. I don't know how they do it. Here's a sample:

Got Smart

Father Knew Best

It Was Left to Beaver

Daddy Had Had Room Made for Him

I Shall Have Been Loving Lucy

Car 54, Where Were You?

Had Gun, Would Have Traveled

What Had My Line Been?

I Have Had a Secret

That Had Been the Week That Had Been

ANYTHING BUT THE PRESENT

America has no now. We're reluctant to acknowledge the present. It's too embarrassing.

Instead, we reach into the past. Our culture is composed of sequels, reruns, remakes, revivals, reissues, re-releases, re-creations, re-enactments, adaptations, anniversaries, memorabilia, oldies radio, and nostalgia record collections. World War II has been refought on television so many times, the Germans and Japanese are now drawing residuals.

Of course, being essentially full of shit, we sometimes feel the need to dress up this past-preoccupation, as with pathetic references to reruns as "encore presentations."

Even instant replay is a form of token nostalgia: a brief visit to the immediate past for reexaminination, before slapping it onto a highlight video for further review and re-review on into the indefinite future.

Our "yestermania" includes fantasy baseball camps, where aging sad sacks pay money to catch baseballs thrown by men who were once their heroes. It is part of the fascination with sports memorabilia, a "memory industry" so lucrative it has attracted counterfeiters.

In this, the Age of Hyphens, we are truly retro-Americans.

And our television newscasts not only reflect this condition, they feed it. Everything they report is twisted into some reference to the past. If there's to be a summit meeting, you'll be told all about the last six summits; if there's a big earthquake, they'll do a story about big earthquakes of the past; if there's a mine disaster, you will hear about every mine disaster since the inception of mining. They're obsessed with looking back. I swear I actually heard this during a newscast, as the anchorman went to a commercial break: he said, "Still ahead, a look back." Honest.

"A look back: Hurricane Hugo, one year later." Why? The anniversary of the Exxon *Valdez* oil spill. For what reason? The anniversary of the Bay of Pigs, Pan Am Flight 103, the hostages in Iran, the fall of the Berlin Wall, V-J Day, V-E Day, Vietnam. Who gives a fuck?

Bugs Bunny's 50th birthday, Lassie's 55th, the Golden Jubilee of *Gone With the Wind*, the start of the Korean War, Barbie celebrates her 35th, the 25th anniversary of the New York blackout, Bambi turns 50. Shit, I didn't even like Bambi when I was supposed to, how much do I care now?

There's really no harm reviewing the past from time to time; knowing where you've been is part of knowing where you are, and all that happy horseshit. But the American media have an absolute fixation on this. They rob us of the present by insisting on the past. If they were able, I'm sure they would pay equal attention to the future. Trouble is, they don't have any film on it.

And so, on television news there is, oddly, very little emphasis on the present; on today's actual news. The present exists only in thirty-second stories built around eight-second sound bites. Remember, "sound bite" is their phrase. That's what they give you. Just a bite. No chewing, no digestion, no nourishment. Malnutrition.

Another way they avoid the present moment is to look ahead on their own schedules. The television news industry seems to revolve around what's coming next. "Still to come," "Just ahead," "Up next," "Coming up this half-hour," "More to come," "Stay with us," "Still ahead," "Also, later . . ."

They even preview what's going to happen as little as one hour later: During the "Five O'Clock News", the empty-headed prick who does the "Five O'Clock News" will suddenly say, "Here's a look at what's coming up on the 'Six O'Clock News.'" Then the empty-headed prick who does the "Six O'Clock News" will appear in shirtsleeves in the newsroom (to create the illusion of actual work) and tell you about several stories that the empty-headed prick who does the "Five O'Clock News" should already have told you about if he were really a newsman.

And so it goes, around the clock: On the "Five O'Clock News," they tell you about the "Six O'Clock News"; at six O'Clock, they tell you about eleven; at eleven, they plug the morning news; the morning man promos the noontime lady, and, sure enough, a little after noon, here comes that empty-headed prick from the "Five O'Clock News" to tell you what he's going to do . . . on the "Five O'Clock News."

You know, if a guy were paranoid, he might not be blamed for thinking that the people who run things don't want you dwelling too much on the present.

Because, keep in mind, the news media are not independent; they are a sort of bulletin board and public relations firm for the ruling class—the people who run things. Those who decide what news you will or will not hear are paid by, and tol-erated purely at the whim of, those who hold economic power. If the parent corporation doesn't want you to know something, it won't be on the news. Period. Or, at the very least, it will be slanted to suit them, and then barely followed up.

Enjoy your snooze.

SOME FAVORITE OXYMORONS

assistant supervisor

new tradition

original copy

plastic glass

uninvited guest

highly depressed

live recording

authentic reproduction

partial cease-fire

limited lifetime guarantee

elevated subway

dry lake

true replica

forward lateral

standard options

iF i WERE iN CHARGE OF THE NETWORKS

◊ I'm tired of television announcers, hosts, newscasters, and commentators, nibbling away at the English language, making obvious and ignorant mistakes.

◊ If I were in charge of America's broadcast stations and networks, I would gather together all the people whose jobs include speaking to the public, and I would not let them out of the room until they had absorbed the following suggestions.

◊ And I'm aware that media personalities are not selected on the basis of intelligence. I know that, and I try to make allowances for it. Believe me, I really try. But still . . .

There are some liberties taken with speech that I think require intervention, if only for my own sake. I won't feel right if this chance goes by, and I keep my silence.

◊ The English word *forte*, meaning "specialty" or "strong point," is not pronounced "*for*-tay." Got that? It's pronounced "fort." The Italian word *forte*, used in music notation, is pronounced "*for*-tay," and it instructs the musician to play loud: "She plays the skin flute, and her forte [fort] is playing forte [*for*-tay]." Look it up. And don't give me that whiny shit, "*For*-tay is listed as the second preference." There's a reason it's second: because it's not *first*!

◊ Irony deals with opposites; it has nothing to do with coincidence. If two baseball players from the same hometown, on different teams, receive the same uniform number, it is not ironic. It is a coincidence. If Barry Bonds attains lifetime statistics identical to his father's, it will not be ironic. It will be a coincidence. Irony is "a state of affairs that is the reverse of what was to be expected; a result opposite to and in mockery of the appropriate result." For instance:

If a diabetic, on his way to buy insulin, is killed by a runaway truck, he is the victim of an accident. If the truck was delivering sugar, he is the victim of an oddly poetic coincidence. But if the truck was delivering insulin, ah! Then he is the victim of an irony.

If a Kurd, after surviving a bloody battle with Saddam Hussein's army and a long, difficult escape through the mountains, is crushed and killed by a parachute drop of humanitarian aid, that, my friend, is irony writ large.

Darryl Stingley, the pro football player, was paralyzed after a brutal hit by Jack Tatum. Now Darryl Stingley's son plays football, and if the son should become paralyzed while playing, it will not be ironic. It will be coincidental. If Darryl Stingley's son paralyzes someone else, that will be closer to ironic. If he paralyzes Jack Tatum's son that will be precisely ironic.

I'm tired of hearing *prodigal* being used to mean "wandering, given to running away or leaving and returning." The parable in the Book of Luke tells of a son who squanders his father's money. *Prodigal* means "recklessly wasteful or extravagant." And if you say popular usage has changed that, I say, fuck popular usage!

The phrase *sour grapes* does not refer to jealousy or envy. Nor is it related to being a sore loser. It deals with the rationalization of failure to attain a desired end. In the original

fable by Aesop, "The Fox and the Grapes," when the fox real-
izes he cannot leap high enough to reach the grapes, he ratio-
nalizes that even if he had gotten them, they would probably
have been sour anyway. Rationalization. That's all sour grapes
means. It doesn't deal with jealousy or sore losing. Yeah, I
know, you say, "Well, many people are using it that way, so the
meaning is changing." And I say, "Well many people are really fuckin' stupid, too, shall we just adopt all their standards?"

Strictly speaking, *celibate* does not mean not having sex,
it means not being married. No wedding. The practice of
refraining from sex is called *chastity* or *sexual abstinence*. No
fucking. Priests don't take a vow of celibacy, they take a vow
of chastity. Sometimes referred to as the "no-nookie clause."

And speaking of sex, the *Immaculate Conception* does
not mean Jesus was conceived in the absence of sex. It
means Mary was conceived without Original Sin. That's all
it has ever meant. And according to the tabloids, Mary is
apparently the only one who can make such a claim. The
Jesus thing is called *virgin birth*.

Proverbial is now being used to describe things that
don't appear in proverbs. For instance, "the proverbial drop
in the bucket" is incorrect because "a drop in the bucket" is
not a proverb, it's a metaphor. You wouldn't say, "as welcome as a turd in the proverbial punchbowl," or "as cold as
the proverbial nun's box," because neither refers to a
proverb. The former is a metaphor, the latter is a simile.

Momentarily means *for* a moment, not *in* a moment. The word for "in a moment" is *presently*. "I will be there presently, Dad, and then, after pausing momentarily, I will kick you in the nuts."

No other option and *no other alternative* are redundant. The words *option* and *alternative* already imply otherness. "I had no option, Mom, I got this huge erection because there was no alternative." This rule is not optional; the alternative is to be wrong.

You should not use *criteria* when you mean *criterion* for the same reason that you should not use *criterion* when you mean *criteria*. These is my only criterions.

A *light-year* is a measurement of distance, not time. "It will take light years for young basketball players to catch up with the number of women Wilt Chamberlain has fucked," is a scientific impossibility. Probably in more ways than one.

An *acronym* is not just any set of initials. It applies only to those that are pronounced as words. MADD, DARE, NATO, and UNICEF are acronyms. FBI, CIA, and KGB are not. They're just pricks.

I know I'm fighting a losing battle with this one, but I refuse to surrender: Collapsing a building with explosives is not an *implosion*. An *implosion* is a very specific scientific phenomenon. The collapsing of a building with explosives is the collapsing of a building with explosives. The explosives explode, and the building collapses inwardly. That is not an implosion. It is an inward collapsing of a building, following a series of smaller explosions designed to make it collapse inwardly. Period. Fuck you!

Here's another pointless, thankless objection I'd like to register. I say it that way, because I know you people and your goddamn "popular usage" slammed the door on this one a long time ago. But here goes anyway:

A *cop out* is not an excuse, not even a weak one; it is an admission of guilt. When someone "cops a plea," he admits guilt to some charge, in exchange for better treatment. He has "copped out." When a guy says, "I didn't get to fuck her because I reminded her of her little brother," he is making an excuse. But if he says, "I didn't get to fuck her because I'm an unattractive schmuck," he is copping out. The trouble arises when an excuse contains a small amount of self-incriminating truth.

This one is directed to the sports people: You are destroying a perfectly good figure of speech: "Getting the monkey off one's back" does not mean breaking a losing streak. It refers only to ending a dependency. That's all. The monkey represents a strong yen. A losing streak does not compare even remotely. Not in a literary sense and not in real life.

Here's one you hear from the truly dense: "The proof is in the pudding." Well, the proof is not in the pudding; the rice and the raisins are in the pudding. The proof of the pudding is in the eating. In this case, proof means "test." The same is true of "the exception that proves (tests) the rule."

An *eye for an eye* is not a call for revenge, it is an argument for fairness. In the time of the Bible, it was standard to take a life in exchange for an eye. But the Bible said, No, the punishment should fit the crime. Only an eye for an eye, nothing more. It is not vindictive, it is mitigatory.

Don't make the same mistake twice seems to indicate three mistakes, doesn't it? First you make the mistake. Then you make the same mistake. Then you make the same mistake twice. If you simply say, "Don't make the same mistake," you'll avoid the first mistake.

Unique needs no modifier. *Very unique, quite unique, more unique, real unique, fairly unique,* and *extremely unique* are wrong, and they mark you as dumb. Although certainly not unique.

Healthy does not mean "healthful." Healthy is a condition, healthful is a property. Vegetables aren't healthy, they're dead. No food is healthy. Unless you have an eggplant that's doing push-ups. Push-ups are healthful.

There is no such thing or word as *kudo. Kudos* is a singular noun meaning praise, and it is pronounced *kyoo*-dose. There is also a plural form, spelled the same, but pronounced *kyoo*-doze. Please stop telling me, "So-and-so picked up another kudo today."

Race, creed, or color is wrong. Race and color, as used in this phrase, describe the same property. And "creed" is a stilted, outmoded way of saying "religion." Leave this tired phrase alone; it has lost its usefulness. Besides, it reeks of insincerity no matter who uses it.

As of yet is simply stupid. As yet, I've seen no progress on this one, but of course I'm speaking as of now.

Here's one you can win money on in a bar if you're within reach of the right reference book: *Chomping at the bit* and *old stomping ground* are incorrect. Some Saturday afternoon when you're gettin' bombed on your old stamping ground, you'll be champing at the bit to use this one.

Sorry to sound so picky, folks, but I listen to a lot of radio and TV, and these things have bothered me for a long time.

VIEWERS, BEWARE!

Television newscasters often warn viewers that something they're going to show might upset people: "Be warned that this next film clip is very graphic, and contains explicit language, so you might want to consider if you want to see it, or if it is suitable for your children." Imagine! Explicit and graphic! Here are the definitions of those words according to *Webster's Third New International Dictionary*:

Explicit: Characterized by full, clear expression; being without vagueness or ambiguity.

Graphic: Marked by clear and lively description or striking imaginative power. Sharply outlined or delineated.

So what is the problem here? Why do they feel it necessary to warn people against the possibility of seeing something clear, sharply outlined, unambiguous, and with striking imaginative power?

THE "PRE-" EPIDEMIC

Preboard, prescreen, prerecord, pretaped, preexisting, preorder, preheat, preplan, pretest, precondition, preregister. In nearly all of these cases you can drop the "pre" and not change the meaning of the word.

"The suicide film was not prescreened by the school." No, of course not. It was screened.

"You can call and prequalify for a loan over the phone. Your loan is preapproved." Well, if my loan is approved before I call then no approval is necessary. The loan is simply available.

NAME IT LIKE IT IS

The words *Fire Department* make it sound like they're the ones who are starting the fires, doesn't it? It should be called the "Extinguishing Department." We don't call the police the "Crime Department." Also, the "Bomb Squad" sounds like a terrorist gang. The same is true of *wrinkle cream*. Doesn't it sound like it causes wrinkles? And why would a doctor prescribe pain pills? I already *have* pain! I need relief pills!

MORE FAVORITE OXYMORONS

mandatory options

mutual differences

nondairy creamer

open secret

resident alien

silent alarm

sports sedan

wireless cable

mercy killing

lethal assistance (Contra aid)

business ethics

friendly fire

genuine veneer

full-time day care

death benefits

holy war

SUPER-CELEB KICKS BUCKET

I dread the deaths of certain super-celebrities. Not because I care about them, but because of all the shit I have to endure on television when one of them dies. All those tributes and retrospectives. And the bigger the personality, the worse it is.

For instance, imagine the crap we'll have to endure on TV when Bob Hope dies. First of all, they'll show clips from all his old road movies with Bing Crosby, and you can bet that some news anchor asshole will turn to the pile of clothing next to him and say, "Well, Tami, I imagine Bob's on the Road to Heaven now."

Then there'll be clips of all those funny costumes he wore on his TV specials, including the hippie sketch, where they'll show him saying,

"Far out, man, far out!" They'll show him golfing with dead presidents, kissing blonde bombshells, and entertaining troops in every war since we beat the shit out of the Peloponnesians. And at some point, a seventy-year-old veteran will choke up, and say, "I just missed seein' him at Iwo, 'cause I got my legs blowed off. He's quite a guy."

Ex-presidents (including the dead ones) will line up four abreast to tell us what a great American he was; show-business perennials will desert golf courses from Palm Springs to O.J.'s lawn to lament sadly as how this time, "Bob hooked one into the woods"; and, regarding his talent, a short comedian in a checkered hat will speak reverently about "Hope's incredible timing."

And this stuff will be on every single newscast day and night for a week. There'll be special one-hour salutes on "Good Morning America," the "Today" show, and "CBS This Morning." Ted Koppel will ask Henry Kissinger if it's true Bob Hope actually shortened some of our wars by telling jokes close to the frontlines. CNN will do a series of expanded "Show Biz Todays." One of the cable channels will do a one-week marathon of his movies. And it goes without saying that NBC will put together a three-hour, prime-time special called "Thanks for the Memories," but at the last minute they'll realize Bob Hope's audience skews older, and sell it to CBS.

Then there'll be the funeral, carried live on the Dead Celebrity Channel, with thousands of grotesque acne-ridden fans seeking autographs from all the show-business clowns who dug out their best black golfing outfits to attend "one of the hottest burials to hit this town in decades"—*Variety.*

And all this shit will go on for weeks and weeks and weeks. Until Milton Berle dies. And then it will start all over again. I dare not even contemplate Frank Sinatra and Ronald Reagan.

KEEP IT—WE DON'T WANT IT

Don't you get tired of celebrities who explain their charity work by saying they feel they have to"give something back." I don't feel that way. I didn't take nothin'. You can search my house; I didn't take a thing. Everything I got, I worked for, and it was given to me freely. I also paid taxes on it. Late! I paid late. But I paid. You celebrity people wanna give something back? How about giving back half the money? Or a couple of those houses? And you dickwads who collect cars? How about giving back 50 or 60 of them? Or maybe, if you people really want to give something back, you could let go of a little of that arrogance.

DESERVING CHARITIES

For my part, I like to work quietly in the background, helping my preferred charities raise money. If you'd like to help too, here are just a few you might consider.

✖ St. Anthony's Shelter for the Recently All Right

✖ The Christian Haven for the Chronically Feisty

✖ The Committee to Keep Something-or-Other from Taking Place

✖ The Center for Research into the Heebie Jeebies

✖ Free Hats for Fat People

✖ The Task Force for Better Pancakes

✖ The Home for the Visually Unpleasant

✖ The State Hospital for Those Who Felt All Right About a Year Ago

- The Committee to Challenge the Height Requirements of Mailmen
- The Beverly Hills Chamber of Poor Taste
- The Alliance of People Who Don't Know What's Next
- The Downtown Mission for the Permanently Disheveled
- The Malibu Home for the Unimportant
- The Nook for Needy Nuns
- Children of Parents with Bad Teeth
- The Rochester Home for Soreheads
- The League of People Who Should Know Better
- Hors d'Oeuvres for Bangladesh
- The Brotherhood of Real Creeps
- The Committee to Remove the "Bah" from "Sis Boom Bah"

PEOPLE I CAN DO WITHOUT

- A stranger on the train who wants to tell me about his bowel movements.
- People who whistle cowboy songs during a funeral.
- Anyone who refers to Charles Manson as "Chuck."
- A tall man with a Slavic accent wearing a bow tie of human flesh.

❪ ❫ Any couple who owns "his and hers" rectal thermometers.

❪ ❫ A girl whose wallet contains nude photos of Sam Donaldson or Yassir Arafat.

✖ A man with a tattoo that shows Joey Buttafuco dancing the Lambada with Leona Helmsley.

❪ ❫ Any man who can ingest a quart of vegetable soup through his nose in one long suck.

✖ A priest with an eye patch and a limp who's selling pieces of the cross.

❪ ❫ Any guy named Dogmeat whose body has over six square feet of scar tissue.

❪ ❫ Anyone who takes off work on Ted Bundy's birthday.

✖ A man with gold front teeth who wants to play stud poker on the floor of the bus station men's room.

❪ ❫ A crying woman with a harpoon gun entering a sports bar.

❪ ❫ Anyone who gets plastic surgery in an attempt to look more intelligent.

✖ A man with one cloven hoof who wants to give my daughter a hysterectomy.

❪ ❫ A seventy-year-old man wearing gag underpants that say "We visited the Grassy Knoll."

✖ Any man with a birthmark shaped like a hypodermic needle.

❪ ❫ Any woman who repeatedly gives me a high five during sex.

❪ ❫ A cross-eyed man in a New Year's hat reciting "Casey at the Bat" in Latin.

{ } Anyone who receives e-mail from Willard Scott.

{ } A man who plunges a bone-handled carving fork through his neck in order to get my attention.

{ } Anyone with three nostrils.

{ } A bag lady wearing over 200 garments, including nine separate hats.

{ } Any man who tries to pierce his ear with an electric can opener.

{ } A retarded twelve-year-old who carries more than six books of matches.

{ } Any man who gives himself a Harvey Wallbanger enema. On the rocks.

{ } Any person bleeding from three orifices who wants me to cosign on a loan.

{ } A homely, flat-chested woman wearing a Foxy Lady T-shirt.

SPACED OUT

You know something I could really do without? The Space Shuttle. Why don't these people go out and get real jobs? It's the same shit over and over. They get delayed, they blast off, they get in orbit, something breaks, they fix it, the President says hello, Mission Control wakes them up with a song no one has listened to in twenty years, the science experiment placed on board by the third-graders of Frog Balls, Tennessee, is a big success, and bla bla bla. It's time to end this shit. Besides, it's irresponsible. The last thing we should be doing is sending our grotesquely distorted DNA out into space.

EXPRESSIONS I QUESTION

IN THE PRIVACY OF YOUR OWN HOME. As opposed to what? The privacy of someone else's home? You have no privacy in someone else's home; that's why you got your own home.

DOWN THE PIKE. "He was the meanest guy ever to come down the pike." Fine. What about guys who come *up* the pike? Not everyone lives "north of the pike." Some guys have to come *up* the pike, and they're really mean, because nobody mentions them at all. And what about a guy who doesn't even *use* the pike? He arrives on Amtrak! "Boy, he was the meanest guy ever to arrive on Amtrak." Doesn't sound right.

LIKE A BAT OUT OF HELL. We say some guy was "goin' like a bat outta Hell." How do we know how fast a bat would leave Hell? Maybe he would leave real slow. In fact, why should we assume that a bat would even want to leave Hell? Maybe he likes it there. Maybe Hell is just right for a bat. Maybe it's bat heaven. And now that we're on this subject, how do we know Hell has bats in the first place? What would a bat be doin' in Hell? Usually a bat is in the belfry. Why would he want to split his time between two places? Then again, maybe that's why he's in such a hurry to leave Hell. He's due back at the belfry.

Why do we say **OUT LIKE A LIGHT**? The primary function of a light is to be lit, not to be out. Why choose a light to represent the concept of being out? Why not, "*On* like a light?" The same is true of **DROPPING LIKE FLIES**; the wrong quality is being emphasized. Flies are known for flying, not dropping. And let's forget **METEORIC RISE**. Meteors don't rise, they fall.

YOU CAN TALK UNTIL YOU'RE BLUE IN THE FACE, ETC. ETC. Well, you can't talk until you're blue in the face. In order to talk, you need oxygen. Blueness of the face is caused by a lack of oxygen. So, if you're blue in the face, you probably stopped talking a long time ago. You might be making some gestures. In fact, if you're running out of oxygen, I would imagine you're making quite a number of gestures. And rather flamboyant ones at that.

When we point out someone's lack of popularity, especially a politician's, we sometimes say, HE COULDN'T GET ELECTED DOG CATCHER. First of all, since when do they elect dog catchers? I've never seen one on the ballot, have you? The last time you were in the voting booth, did it say, "President, Vice President, Dog Catcher?" No. And why do they imply that getting elected dog catcher would be easy? I think it would be hard. A lot of people have dogs; they wouldn't vote for you. And many of the people who don't have dogs still like them. I should think it would be quite difficult to get elected dog catcher.

ONE THING LEADS TO ANOTHER. Not always. Sometimes one thing leads to the same thing. Ask an addict.

THE PEN IS MIGHTIER THAN THE SWORD needs to be updated. It's overdue. It should have been changed much earlier in the twentieth century to, "The typewriter is mightier than the machine gun." But at this point is should probably read, "The word processor is mightier than the particle-beam weapon."

UNIDENTIFIED PERSON. What exactly is an "unidentified person"? Doesn't everyone have an identity? Maybe they mean he's a person they can't identify. But that would make him an "unidentifiable person." I guess if nothing else, he could always be referred to as "that guy we can't identify."

OPEN A CAN OF WORMS. Why would you have to open it? Are there really sealed cans of worms? Who sealed them? Worms are usually put in a can *after* it has been opened, and emptied of something else, like corn or pumpkin meat. Uncover a can of worms, maybe. But not open.

WILD AND WOOLLY. Whenever I hear something described as wild and woolly, I always wonder where the woolly part comes in. Wild I understand. But woolly? I have some sweaters that are woolly, but they're kind of conservative. Not wild at all.

IN THE WRONG PLACE AT THE WRONG TIME. How can this be? Shouldn't it be, "In the *right* place at the wrong time?" If a guy gets hit by a stray bullet, he is in the right place (where his day's activities have taken him) at the wrong time (when a bullet is passing by). If it were the wrong place, the bullet wouldn't have been there.

IN THE RIGHT PLACE AT THE RIGHT TIME is also questionable. Let's say a guy wins a prize for being a bank's millionth customer. All you really have to say is, "He was in the right place." After all, it *had* to be the right time. That's the only time they were giving away the prize. If it hadn't been the right time, it wouldn't have been the right place. Twenty minutes later the bank wouldn't be "the right place" anymore.

YOU NEVER KNOW. Not true. Sometimes you know.

YOU DON'T HAVE TO BE A ROCKET SCIENTIST implies that rocket scientists are somehow smart. How smart can they be? They build machines that travel thousands of miles to drop fire and radiation on people. That doesn't sound smart to me.

THE OLDEST TRICK IN THE BOOK. Sometimes in the movies, when the bad guy is holding a gun on the good guy, the good guy says, "It won't work, Scarfelli. My men are right behind you with their guns drawn." And the bad guy says, "You can't fool me, Murdoch, that's the oldest trick in the book." Well, exactly what book are these guys talking about? Have you ever seen a book with a bunch of tricks in it? Magic tricks maybe, but I don't think the thing with the guns would be in there, do you? A prostitute might have a book of tricks, but once again, probably no mention of the two guys with the guns. And anyway, even if there really were a book with a lot of tricks in it, how would you know which trick was the oldest? They were all printed at the same time. You'd have to say, "You can't fool me, Murdoch, that's the trick that appears earliest in the book." But that's not good movie dialogue, is it?

When they say someone is **NOT GOING TO WIN ANY POPULARITY CONTESTS,** what popularity contests are they talking about? I've never heard of these contests. Where do they have them? And who wins? Whoever is winning these popularity contests can't be that popular. You never hear about them.

YOU COULD HEAR A PIN DROP. Well, you can't hear a pin drop. Not even a bowling pin. When a pin is dropping, it's just floating through the air. There's very little noise. You might be able to hear a pin land but certainly not drop.

WORDS AND PHRASES WE SHOULD HAVE

re-go = to return somewhere

un-park = to drive away

de-have = to lose something

re-get = to find it again

firmth = firmness

pocketry = a garment's pockets

way much: "Ice cream tastes way much better than sewage."

a lotta buncha: "I only slept with her once, and now I got a lotta buncha crabs.

a very lot: "The gold-plated dildos cost a very lot more than the rubber ones."

a whole much: "I love you a whole much."

real pretty good: "I'm real pretty good at math."

very pretty good: "But I'm very pretty good at history."

extremely not bad: "This prune cake is extremely not bad."

very thank you: "Oh, thank you. Very, very thank you!"

yesternight: "I couldn't get to sleep yesternight."

last morning: "So I was real tired last morning."

SOME FAVORITE REDUNDANCIES

added bonus

exactly right

closed fist

future potential

inner core

money-back refund

seeing the sights

true fact

revert back

safe haven

prior history

young children

time period

sum total

end result

temper tantrum

ferryboat

free gift

bare naked

combined total

unique individual

potential hazard

joint cooperation

POPULAR BELIEFS

There are many popular beliefs rooted in familiar expressions and sayings that simply aren't true.

EVERYTHING COMES IN THREES. Not true. In reality, everything comes in ones. Sometimes, when three "ones" come in a row, it *seems* like everything comes in threes. By the way, in medieval times it was widely believed that everything came in twenty-sixes. They were wrong, too. It just took them longer to recognize a pattern.

People say when you die, YOU CAN'T TAKE IT WITH YOU. Well, that depends on what it is. If it's your dark blue suit, you can certainly take it with you. In fact, not only can you take it with you, you can probably put some things in the pockets.

YOU LEARN SOMETHING NEW EVERY DAY. Actually, you learn something old every day. Just because you just learned it, doesn't mean it's new. Other people already knew it. Columbus is a good example of this.

THE SKY'S THE LIMIT. Well, how can the sky be the limit? The sky never ends. What kind of a limit is that? The Earth is the limit. You dig a hole and what do you keep getting? More earth. The Earth's the limit.

YOU GET WHAT YOU PAY FOR. Clearly this is not true. Have you been shopping lately? Only a naive person would believe that you get what you pay for. In point of fact, if you check your purchases carefully, you'll find that you get whatever they feel like giving you. And if corporations get any more powerful, you soon might not even get that.

TOMORROW IS ANOTHER DAY. Not true. Today is another day. We have no idea what tomorrow is going to be. It might turn out to *be* another day, but we can't be sure. If it happens, I'll be the first to say so. But, you know what? By that time, it'll be today again.

NICE GUYS FINISH LAST. Not true. Studies have shown that, on the average, nice guys finish third in a field of six. Actually, short guys finish last. By the way, in medieval times it was widely believed that nice guys finished twenty-sixth. You can see how limited those people were.

IF YOU'VE SEEN ONE, YOU'VE SEEN 'EM ALL. Do we even have to talk about this one? This should be obvious. If you've seen one, you've seen one. If you've seen them all, *then* you've seen them all. I don't understand how this one even got started.

THOSE WERE THE DAYS. No. Those were the nights! Think back. Weren't the nights better? Days you had to work. Nights you went to parties, danced, drank, got laid. "Those were the nights!"

THERE'S NO SUCH THING AS A FREE LUNCH. What about when you eat at home? I don't pay when I eat lunch at home—it's free! Sometimes I'll leave a tip, but basically, it's a free lunch. Yes, I know we had to buy the food at the store. But as the Zen Buddhists say, The Food Is Not the Lunch.

YOU PAYS YOUR MONEY, AND YOU TAKES YOUR CHOICE. I think what I said earlier still applies: You pays your money and you takes whatever they jolly well give you. Actually, when you get right down to it, you pays your money and you *loses* your money.

EVERYBODY HAS HIS PRICE. Not so. Would you believe there are millions of people who do not have their price? Thanks to a government mixup, many people have their neighbor's price.

THEY DON'T MAKE 'EM LIKE THEY USED TO. Actually they do make 'em like they used to, they just don't sell 'em anymore. They make 'em, and they keep 'em!

TWO WRONGS DON'T MAKE A RIGHT. Well, it just so happens that two wrongs do make a right. Not only that, but as the number of wrongs increases, the whole thing goes up exponentially. So that while two wrongs make one right, and four wrongs make two rights, it actually takes sixteen wrongs to make three rights, and 256 wrongs to make four rights. It seems to me that anyone who is stringing together more that 256 wrongs needs counseling, not mathematics.

IF IT'S NOT ONE THING, IT'S ANOTHER. Not always. Sometimes if it's not one thing, not only is it not another, but it turns out to be something else altogether.

YOU CAN'T WIN THEM ALL. Not true. Believe it or not, there is a man in Illinois who, so far, has won them all. But don't get too excited; it has also been discovered that under certain circumstances it is possible to lose them all. By the way, there is no record of anyone having tied them all.

YOU CAN'T HAVE IT BOTH WAYS. That depends on how intimately you know the other person. Maybe you can't have it both ways at once, but if you've got a little time, you can probably have it six or seven ways.

THINGS HAVE TO GET BETTER, THEY CAN'T GET ANY WORSE. This is an example of truly faulty logic. Just because things can't get any worse, is no reason to believe they have to get better. They might just stay the same. And, by the way, who says things can't get any worse? For many people, things get worse and worse and worse.

NOBODY EVER SAID LIFE WAS FAIR. Not so. I specifically remember as I was growing up, at least twelve different people, telling me life was fair. One person put it this way: "Life, you will find, is fair, George." Oddly enough, all twelve of those people died before the age of twenty-seven.

IT TAKES TWO TO TANGO. Sounds good, but simple reasoning will reveal that actually it takes only one to tango. It takes two to tango together, maybe, but one person is certainly capable of tangoing on his own. By the way, in medieval times it was widely believed that it took twenty-six to tango.

THERE'S A SUCKER BORN EVERY MINUTE, AND TWO TO TAKE HIM. This may have been true in the past, but now, if you adjust for the increased population base, birth control, and the so-called moral decline, not only are there five suckers born every minute, there are now fifty-three to take him.

LIFE IS SHORT. Sorry. Life is not short, it's just that since everything else lasts so long—mountains, rivers, stars, planets—life seems short. Actually life lasts just the right amount of time. Until you die. Death on the other hand, is short.

WHAT YOU DON'T KNOW WON'T HURT YOU. Why don't we just ask Abe Lincoln and John Kennedy about this one.

FROZEN MEXICAN DINNER

Sometimes on television they tell you to buy a frozen Mexican dinner. Well, it sounds like a good idea, but actually, before you take him out to dinner, I should think it would be a good idea to bring him in the house and let him warm up a little. A frozen Mexican probably wouldn't be thinking mainly about food. By the way, isn't Mexico a warm-weather country?

MORE FAVORITE REDUNDANCIES

total abstinence

subject matter

honest truth

join together

general public

harbinger of things to come

new initiative

audible gasp

advance warning

execution-style killing

future plans

gather together

Jewish synagogue

lag behind

manual dexterity

occasional irregularity

outer rim

plan ahead

basic fundamentals

first time ever

personal friend

shrug one's shoulders

WATCH YOUR MOUTH

BEWARE OF AGGRAVATING SPEAKERS

I am easily annoyed by people's speech habits, and I regard certain words and phrases as warnings to break off contact. In the interest of maintaining good mental health, I avoid the following people:

Those who can't resist saying, "God forbid" each time they mention the possibility of an accident or death, even though they don't believe in God.

People who say "God rest his soul" following the mention of a dead person, even if they hated the person and don't believe in God. These are the same ones who say "knock wood" and really mean it. Sometimes they'll even glance around halfheartedly for something to knock on, before giving up and just standing there like the morons they are.

And speaking of morons, can't we somehow prevent adults from using words like *tushie, boo-boo* and *no-no,* when speaking to grown-ups? Why don't we just send these people to their rooms without supper? Tell them there's not gonna be any yummy in their tummy. And while we're at it, let's include all those colorful risk-takers who actually use *heck* and *darn* for emphasis. What the fuck is this, 1850?

I also think we'd be better off if we could eliminate anyone who has a "can-do" attitude, or is referred to as "take-charge," "all-business," or "no-nonsense." Have these people sedated.

And let's include the ones who describe themselves as "goal-oriented." Please. Leave me alone.

And the ones who tell you, "I'm a people person." Yeah? Me too. Fuck people!

And what about these guys who have no job and say to you, "Are they keepin' ya busy?" I happen to resent even the assumption that there are people who have the authority to keep me busy. Least of all do I appreciate it from some guy who doesn't seem to have a whole lot to do, himself.

And let's punish every homely man who ever thought it was clever to say, "I'm not just another pretty face."

And I think it's time to start slapping around these people who can't tell a simple story without repeatedly saying, "Ya know what I'm sayin'?" Here I am, trying to listen to the guy, and he's a person who is constantly checking on how he's doing.

"Bla, bla, bla. Ya know what I'm sayin'?"

No, the question is not, do I know what you're saying, the

question is, do you know what you're saying? You follow me on that?

I'm also getting tired of *arguably*. It's weak. It tries to have things both ways. Take a stand!

And here are some jock/sports-fan adjectives that should be outlawed: Listening to a sports call-in radio station for about an hour, you will be amazed at the number of times you hear the following words: incredible, unbelievable, tremendous, outstanding, big, huge, large, major, and key. Do these guys sound like maybe someone's penis size is on their minds?

I can also do without people who tell me that something—anything—is either "the name of the game" or "what it's all about." Oh it is, huh? Well, fuck you!

And let's lose these guys who think it's cute to say, "Ouch!" when someone delivers a small put-down.

BEWARE ALSO OF THE PRETENTIOUS AND ARROGANT SPEAKER

People who refer to themselves as "yours truly." What kind of grandiose crap is this? Some even speak of themselves in the third person. Athletes and entertainers are big on this demented shit: "I'm gonna do what's right for Leon Spinks!" I think people like this are mentally ill. And you can include those very special people who use the royal "we."

I also instantly dismiss anyone who tells me that some other person "has class," "is classy," or "is a class act," the last of these being the most arrogant. What these speakers are telling you is that since they are among the few people who recognize class, it is their obligation to point it out to sorry-ass folks like you. If you manage to listen to them just a little longer, you'll find that they're completely full of shit.

This is the same type of person who uses the word "tasty" when referring to music.

The above sort of reference to class is of the same order of arrogance as the phrases "not too shabby," "he's no dummy," "I give him high marks," "he's got his head on straight," and "he really showed me something." All of these phrases reek of presumed superiority.

And just when I thought all those precious twerps were about to stop saying, "Not to worry," and "By the by," along came "What say you?" and "At the end of the day" to deepen my suffering. "At the end of the day" is probably the most pretentious expression to come along since the "moi-ciao" crowd descended on us.

"Just a tad" has a phony ring to it. So does "just a skosh."

And be on the alert for anyone who tells you that something they did was "life-affirming." Some celebrity said he quit doing his TV show because "it stopped being life-affirming." Hey, Skeezix, when you finish affirming your life, get over here and give my dick a coupla yanks.

And can't we figure out something evil to do to these people who call themselves "survivors"? Such self-regard!

"I'm a survivor."

"Good. We'll be sure to tell everyone at your funeral that you're a fuckin' survivor."

This one is almost too easy: guys who can't leave a room without saying, "I'm outta here." You know what I say to them? "Good! Stay the fuck outta here!"

There are also certain reckless people in this country who are abusing "ongoing" and "early on." Leave these terms alone, please. They mark you as a counterfeit. "Early on" has faux poetic aspirations, and "ongoing" has only a very narrow area where it is distinctly appropriate.

And some of these "ongoing" felons are the same ones who have vandalized the phrase "even as we speak." First they shortened it to "as we speak." Then they started using it every four minutes or so. Even as I write this, my pissed-off-edness is ongoing.

And fuck all the asshole people who say, "God bless," and then don't bother to complete the sentence. Who they are, I haven't the slightest. But, if I were God, I would not honor such a request. Anyway, enjoy.

More general lame overused expressions for which the users ought to be slain:

{ } From the git-go

{ } It works for me.

{ } You gotta love it.

{ } Go get 'em, tiger!

{ } Sounds like a plan.

{ } You know the drill.

{ } Get with the program.

{ } Take no prisoners.

{ } None of the above

{ } Up close and personal

{ } The whole nine yards

{ } May be hazardous to your health

✖ The Rodney Dangerfield of . . .

{ } Cut to the chase.

{ } Deal with it.

{ } Clean up your act.

{ } Bottom line

{ } Wannabe

{ } Been there, done that.

{ } Fifteen minutes of fame

{ } Joined at the hip

{ } Flavor of the month

{ } It's not over till it's over.

{ } Don't try this at home.

{ } Easy for you to say.

{ } Separated at birth.

✖ I'm mad as hell and, etc.

{ } Just when you thought it was safe . . .

{ } Humungous

✖ In your face

{ } Lean and mean

❪ ❫ Check it out.

❪ ❫ Doesn't take a rocket scientist

❪ ❫ Do a number

❪ ❫ Couch potato

❪ ❫ What's wrong with this picture?

❪ ❫ Or what?

❪ ❫ Born again

❪ ❫ Trash talk

❪ ❫ I love it!

❪ ❫ Go ballistic

✖ In your dreams

❪ ❫ I hate when that happens.

✖ Don't give up your day job.

❪ ❫ Tough act to follow

❪ ❫ No brainer

❪ ❫ Street smart

❪ ❫ I mean that in the nicest way.

❪ ❫ No biggie

❪ ❫ Tell us how you *really* feel.

❪ ❫ That's why he gets the big bucks.

PROBLEM!

I have a problem with guys who say "No problem." The phrase has outlasted its usefulness, and, more alarming, it has almost completely replaced "You're welcome."

"Thank you for carrying those ten bodies downstairs and putting them in the lime pit with all the dead puppies."

"No problem."

And, of course, there are the really cool guys who abbreviate it: "No prob!"

These are the same dipshits who say "bod" for body and "bud" for buddy.

And let's not forget the very special, very precious ones who can't resist saying "No problemo!"

Don't you love these guys? "No problemo!" Same ones who say "Correcta-mundo," and "Exacta-mundo." Mock foreign.

And "moi"! Of course, *moi* being a real word makes the person seem even more pretentious; same category as the "ciao" crowd.

I could really do without non-Italians who lay a worldly, continental "Ciao," on me and then wander off to hitchhike home. They're right up there with the freckle-faced, redheaded lads who belch up huge, moist beer clouds in my face and then insist on calling me "amigo."

YOU'RE GODDAMN RIGHT!

There are many replies you can make when you hear a statement you agree with. A real old-timer says, "You're darn tootin'!"

"I've noticed your granddaughter's nipples stiffen up when I moisten my lips."

"You're darn tootin'!"

In my father's day it was, "You can say that again."

"Hey, Dad, Mom's ass is starting to sag real bad."

"You can say that again."

When I was a kid we said, "I'm wise" or "I'm hip."

"Man, your sister gives a good blow job!"

"I'm hip."

Eventually, we grew tired of these expressions. Now there are new ones, and I'm getting tired of them, too. Examples:

"I hear ya."

"Wonderful. And are you picking me up visually as well?"

"Tell me about it."

"I just did."

"I heard that!"

"Oh, really? Well, isn't that exciting! What is this, a hearing test? Did I wander into a Beltone commercial? Of course you heard it, ya fuckin' nimrod, I'm standin' right next to ya! I'm gonna wander over here a little farther away. BLOW ME!!! By any chance, did ya hear that?"

"You got that right."

"What are you, Alex Trebek? Oh. Well, in that case, I'll take 'Bodies of Water' for $300."

EVEN MORE FAVORITE REDUNDANCIES

bond together

close proximity

ATM machine

PIN number

coequal

common bond

small minority

serious crisis

personal belongings

security guard

time clock

foreign imports

exact same

continue on

focus in

convicted felon

past experience

consensus of opinion

finished product

schoolteacher

linger on

THE PRIMITIVE SERGEANT

There was a first time for everything. At some point, every custom, every practice, every ritual had to be explained to people for the first time. It must have been tricky, especially in primitive societies.

For instance, the first human sacrifice. Not of the enemy, but the first ritual killing of a member of your own tribe. Someone had to announce it to the people. Someone with authority, but probably not the top guy. A sergeant. A primitive sergeant, addressing a band of early cave people—hunters, gatherers, whatever—explaining the human sacrifice. Of course, first he would have to get his other announcements out of the way.

"OK, listen up! You people in the trees, you wanna pay attention? The guys in the bushes, would ya put the woman down? All right. Now, is everybody here? Andy, check the caves. Make sure everybody's out here. And Andy, . . . don't wake up the bears! OK? Remember what happened last time. We can't spare any more people.

"OK, a few things I wanna go over, then I'm gonna tell ya about somethin' new. Somethin' we haven't tried before, so I don't want ya to be nervous. I know ya don't like new things. I remember last year a lotta people freaked out when someone came up with the wheel. People went nuts! They said, Well, this is it, it's all over, it's the end of the world, bla, bla, bla. Then somebody pointed out that we didn't have any axles. I think it was Richie. He said if we really wanted to invent something special, we oughta come up with the axle. I guess you're always gonna have a coupla wise guys.

"But anyway, we went ahead and made a coupla hundred of these big stone wheels, which is kinda stupid when you think about it. The only thing you can do with 'em is roll 'em down the hill. Which isn't such a top notch idea. I think the people who live at the bottom of the hill will bear me out on that.

"OK, movin' along here. It has come to my attention that some people have been drawin' pictures on the walls of the caves. Pictures of bulls, antelopes, a coupla horses. I think I even seen a goat on one wall. Listen, lemme tell you somethin'. It might seem like fun to you, but it looks awful. If ya can't keep the place clean, maybe ya don't deserve a nice cave. Ya don't see the bats drawin' pictures on the walls, do ya? No. They hang upside down, they take a crap, they don't bother anybody.

"You people don't know when you're well off. Maybe ya'd like to go back to livin' in the trees, huh? Remember that? Remember the trees? Competin' with the baboons and gibbons for hazelnuts and loganberries? Degrading! So there'll be no more drawin' on the walls! Coupla thousand years from now, people are gonna come here, and they're gonna study these caves. The last thing they wanna see is a lotta horse pictures on the walls.

"OK, continuin' on. As some of you mighta noticed, last night the fire went out. Coupla the guys on guard duty were jackin' around, playin' grabass, and one of 'em, Octavio, the short guy with the bushy hair. Well, one of the short guys with the bushy hair. Anyways, Octavio fell on the fire, and the fire went out. Unfortunately for Octavio, he died in the incident. Unfortunately for us, he was the only one who knew how to light the fire. So we're gonna have a contest. The first guy to get a fire goin', and keep it goin', wins a prize. It's a hat. Nothin' fancy. Just a regular hat. The kind with the earlaps.

"OK, next item. We're startin' to get some complaints from the women about dating procedures. This mainly concerns the practice of clubbin' the women on the head and draggin' 'em back to the cave by the hair. They would like to discontinue this practice, especially the hair part. It seems some of them go to a lot of trouble and expense to fix up their hair for a date, and they feel the draggin' has a negative effect on their appearance. As far as the clubbin' is concerned, they'd like to elminate that too, because what happens is a lot of 'em have an enjoyable date, and then they can't remember it in the mornin'.

"Movin' right along. As you all know, it's been our practice when we find a new plant that looks good to eat, we test it on the dogs to see if it's poison. Does everyone remember the berries we tested last week on the big brown dog? How many ate the berries simply because the dog didn't die that day? Quite a few. Well, I got bad news. The dog died last night. Apparently it was a slow-actin' poison. Yes, Laszlo? You didn't eat the berries? But this mornin' you ate the dog. Well, Laszlo, ya got about a week. Food chain! How many times do I gotta tell you people? Food chain! By the way, anyone who's gettin' into that new cannibalism crap—I won't mention any names—I'd strongly suggest not eatin' Laszlo—or anyone else for that matter.

"All right, now we gotta talk about the Hated Band of Enemy People Who Live in the Dark Valley. As some of ya might know, they snuck into camp last night and stole a bunch of our stuff. They got those sticks we were savin'. They got the rocks we piled up near the big tree. And they also took sixteen trinkets; the ones we got in a trade with the Friendly Bent-over People from the Tall Mountain Near the Sun. I think it was them. It was either them or the Guys with the Really Big Foreheads Down by the River. Anyways, as I recall, we came off a cool two hundred animal skins for those trinkets, and frankly, the Chief and I think we got screwed. By the way, speakin' of screwin', they also stole several of our women last night. Along with a couple of those sensitive men we've been usin' as women.

"OK, a new problem has come up that we're gonna have to deal with. It concerns the growin' menace of people chewin' the leaves of the dream plant. It's gotten completely outta hand. At first it wasn't so bad. After a long day of huntin', or gatherin'—whatever—people would chew a coupla leaves to relax. Recreational chewin'. No harm, no foul. But then some guys couldn't leave it alone. They would chew way too much and lose control. Some of them became verbally abusive. Of course, they couldn't help what they were sayin'. It wasn't them talkin', it was the leaves. But, hey, nevertheless!

"Then we found out some people were chewin' on the job. Not only endangerin' the lives of their co-hunters or co-gatherers—whatever—but also lowerin' the amount of food we acquire, while somehow, at the same time, greatly increasin' the rate of consumption of their own food. One of the gatherers, a short guy with bushy hair, I think it was Norris, got whacked outta his skull on leaves last week, and he came in from gatherin', with a grand total . . . get this . . . a grand total of six berries and one nut. And this guy had been out in the bushes for eight days!

"But now we're runnin' into an even more serious problem that affects the safety of everyone. It seems that some people are chewin' the leaves and then runnin' around in circles at high speed. As a result we're startin' to get a huge increase in the number of accidents. People are crashin' into each other. Please! Try to remember. Chewin' and runnin' around in circles at high speed don't mix. If you're gonna run around in circles, don't chew; and if you're gonna chew, for God's sake, don't be runnin' around in circles. Designate someone.

"So try to be aware of the signs of leaf abuse. If you're chewin' in the mornin', you got a problem. If you're chewin' alone, you got a problem. It's no disgrace. Get some help. Say no to leaves.

"OK, now, like I said earlier, we got a new thing we're gonna be doin', and I wanna announce it today. It's gonna be a custom. Remember customs? Who can name a custom? Nat? Goin' to sleep at night? Well, that's close, Nat. That's almost like a custom. Who else can name a custom? Killing the animals before we eat them? OK, actually, Jules, that's more like a necessity, isn't it? More like a necessity. Lookin' for a custom. Another custom. Dwayne? Washin' the rocks and dryin' them off before you throw them at the enemy durin' a rock fight? Is that what you been doin', Dwayne? Really! Well, I guess that would explain the disproportionately high number of rock injuries in your squad, wouldn't it?

"Anyway, this new custom is quite different, and it might come as somethin' of a surprise to ya, so make sure you're sittin' down. Or at least leanin' on somethin' firm. You people standin' over near the cliff, you might wanna drift over this way a little.

"Now. I want ya to remember that no matter what I say, this is gonna please the Corn God. OK? [Slowly, as if to children] The new custom . . . is gonna help . . . with the corn. Remember a coupla years ago we had no corn, and we hadda eat the trees? And a lotta people died? How many wanna go back to eatin' the trees? OK, I rest my case. Yeah? Dwayne? You thought the trees were pretty good? Ya never disappoint me, Dwayne, ya know that? Folks, ya don't have to look very far for a tragic example of abusin' the dream plant, do ya?

"All right, here's the new thing we're gonna do, it's called a human sacrifice. Each week, to appease the Corn God, we're gonna kill one member of the tribe. All right, calm down! C'mon, sit down! Hey! Hold on! Hear me out on this, would ya? Just relax and hear me out on this. We're gonna start havin' a human sacrifice every week, probably on Saturday night. That's when everybody seems to loosen up pretty good. So startin' next Saturday night, about the time we run outta berry juice, we're gonna pick one person, probably a young virgin, and we'll throw her in the volcano. All right, girls! Please! Siddown! Please! Stop with the rocks!! Calm down, ladies. We're not gonna do it today. I promise. Relax.

"OK, so we throw the virgin in the volcano. By the way, how many remember the volcano? Remember the fire? Remember the lava? What word comes to mind when we think about the volcano? Hot! Right. The volcano is hot. What's that, Dwayne? No. No way. If this idea's gonna work at all, it's gotta be done while the volcano is actually erupting. I don't think the Corn God is gonna be impressed if we throw some chick in a dormant volcano. It's meaningless. I think he's lookin' for somethin' with a little more screamin' involved.

"OK, so we throw the virgin in the volcano. What's that? How does this help with the corn? Good question. Look, Morley, I just make the announcements, OK? I'm not involved with policy. It came down from the high priests, that's all you gotta know. This is one of those things you just gotta accept on faith. It's like that custom we started last year of cuttin' off a guy's head to keep him from stealin'. At first it seemed severe, am I right? But ya gotta admit, it seems to work.

"OK, one last point: You say, Why does it have to be a young virgin; why can't we throw a wrinkled old man in the volcano? Lemme put it this way. Did y'ever get a real good, close look at the high priests? OK. Once again, I rest my case.

"Now, the only problem we anticipate with this new custom is the distinct possibility of runnin' out of virgins. Ya gotta figure best case scenario we're not gonna see any corn till late next year, so it looks like we're gonna be waxin' virgins at quite a clip. And hey! . . . girls, don't take this the wrong way . . . but we don't have that many virgins to begin with, do we? Ha-ha-ha-ha!! No offense, girls! Really! No, hey, you're very lovely.

"Well, that's it, folks. Thanks for listenin'. Good night. Walk home slowly. And walk safely. In case you didn't notice, the sun went down, and it's completely fuckin' dark."

SOME FAVORITE EUPHEMISMS
(all euphemisms actually observed)

blow job = holistic massage therapy

cheap hotel = limited service lodging

loan-sharking = interim financing

kidnapping = custodial interference

mattress and box spring = sleep system

shack job = live-in companion

truck stop = travel plaza

used videocassette = previously viewed cassette

wife beating = intermittent explosive disorder

theater = performing arts center

manicurist = nail technician

nude beach = clothing optional beach

peephole = observation port

baldness = acquired uncombable hair

body bags = remains pouches

drought = deficit water situation

recession = a meaningful downturn in aggregate output

in love = emotionally involved

room clerk = guest service agent

MORE FAVORITE EUPHEMISMS

uniforms = career apparel

seat belt/air bag = impact management system

prostitute = commercial sex worker

dildo = marital aid

nonbelievers = the unchurched

lying on a job application = résumé enhancement

miscarriage = pregnancy loss

police clubs = batons

smuggling = commodity relocation

porn star = adult entertainer

room service = private dining

nightclub = party space

monkey bars = pipe-frame exercise unit

cardboard box = makeshift home

fingerprinting = digital imaging

fat lady = big woman

junkies = the user population

apartment = dwelling unit

committee = task force

maid = room attendant

salesman = product specialist

EVEN MORE FAVORITE EUPHEMISMS

bad loans = nonperforming assets

seasickness = motion discomfort

gangs = nontraditional organized crime

civilian deaths = collateral damage

gambling joint = gaming resort

mole = beauty mark

garbage collection = environmental services

breast = white meat

thigh = dark meat

sludge = bio-solids

genocide = ethnic cleansing

Jeep = sports utility vehicle

library = learning resources center

junk mail = direct marketing

soda jerk = fountain attendant

soldiers and weapons = military assets

third floor = level three

illegal immigrant = guest worker

Jet ski = personal watercraft

loafers = slip-ons

poLiticaLLy corrEct LAnguAge

I know I'm a little late with his, but I'd like to get a few licks in on this bogus topic before it completely disappears from everyone's consciousness.

First, I want to be really clear about one thing: as far as other people's feelings are concerned—especially these "victim groups"—when I deal with them as individuals, I will call them whatever they want. When it's one on one, if some guy wants me to call him a morbidly obese, African-ancestored male with a same-gendered sexual orientation I'll be glad to do that. On the other hand, if he wants me to call him a fat nigger cocksucker, then that's what it will be. I'm here to please.

If I meet a woman who wishes to be referred to as a motion-impaired, same-gender-oriented Italian-American who is difficult to deal with, fine. On the other hand, I am perfectly willing to call her a crippled, Guinea dyke cunt if she prefers. I'm not trying to change anyone's self-image. But! But! When I am speaking generally, and impersonally, about a large group of people, especially these victim groups, I will call them what I think is honest and fair. And I will try not to bullshit myself.

OK, so, who exactly are these victims? Well, first of all, I don't think everyone who says he's a victim automatically qualifies. I don't think a homely, disfigured, bald minority person with a room-temperature IQ who limps and stutters is necessarily always a victim. Although I will say she probably shouldn't be out trying to get work as a receptionist. But maybe that's just the way it oughta be.

I'm more interested in real victims. People who have been chronically and systematically fucked over by the system. Because the United States is a Christian racist nation with a rigged economic system run for three hundred years by the least morally qualified of the two sexes, there were bound to be some real victims. People who've been elaborately fucked over.

The way I see it, this country has only four real victim-groups: Indians, blacks, women, and gays. I purposely left out the Spanish and Asians, because when you look at what happened to the Indians and blacks, the Spanish and Asian people have had a walk in the park. It's not even close. Not to downplay the shit they've had to eat, but in about one hundred years the Spanish and Asians are going to be running this country, so they'll have plenty of chances to get even with the gray people.

Let's get to some of these other non-victims. You probably noticed, elsewhere I used the word fat. I used that word because that's what fat people are. They're fat. They're not large; they're not stout, chunky, hefty, or plump. And they're not big-boned. Dinosaurs are big-boned. These people are not necessarily obese, either. Obese is a medical term. And they're not overweight. Overweight implies there is some correct weight. There is no correct weight. Heavy is also a misleading term. An aircraft carrier is heavy; it's not fat. Only people are fat, and that's what fat people are. They're fat. I offer no apology for this. It is not intended as criticism or insult. It is simply descriptive language. I don't like euphemisms. Euphemisms are a form of lying. Fat people are not gravitationally disadvantaged. They're fat. I prefer seeing things the way they are, not the way some people wish they were.

I don't believe certain groups deserve extra-special names.

For instance, midgets and dwarfs are midgets and dwarfs. They're not little people. Infants are little people; leprechauns are little people. Midgets and dwarfs are midgets and dwarfs. They don't get any taller by calling them little people. I wish their lives were different. I wish they didn't have to walk around staring at other people's crotches, but I can't fix that. And I'm not going to lie about what they are. The politically sensitive language commandos would probably like me to call them "vertically challenged." They're not vertically challenged. A skydiver is vertically challenged. The person who designed the Empire State Building was vertically challenged. Midgets and dwarfs are midgets and dwarfs.

Also, crippled people are crippled, they're not differently-abled. If you insist on using tortured language like differently-abled, then you must include all of us. We're all differently-abled. You can do things I can't do; I can do things you can't do. I can pick my nose with my thumb, and I can switch hands while masturbating and gain a stroke. We're all differently-abled. Crippled people are simply crippled. It's a perfectly honorable word. There is no shame in it. It's in the Bible: "Jesus healed the cripples." He didn't engage in rehabilitative strategies for the physically disadvantaged.

So, leaving aside women and gays for the moment, I've narrowed it down to blacks and Indians. Let's talk about what we ought to call them, and let's talk about what the language commandos would like us to call them. And remember, this has nothing to do with the people themselves. It has to do with the words.

And, by the way, when it comes to these liberal language vandals, I must say I agree with their underlying premise: White Europeans and their descendants are morally unattractive people who are responsible for most of the world's suffering. That part is easy. You would have to be, uh, visually impaired not to see it. The impulse behind political correctness is a good one. But like every good impulse in America it has been grotesquely distorted beyond usefulness.

Clearly, there are victims, but I don't agree that these failed campus revolutionaries know what to do about them. When they're not busy curtailing freedom of speech, they're running around inventing absurd hyphenated names designed to make people feel better. Remember, these are the white elitists in their customary paternalistic role: protecting helpless, inept minority victims. Big Daddy White Boss always knows best.

So, let me tell you how I handle some of these speech issues. First of all, I say "black." I say "black" because most black people prefer "black." I don't say "people of color." People of color sounds like something you see when you're on mushrooms. Besides, the use of people of color is dishonest. It means precisely the same as colored people. If you're not willing to say "colored people," you shouldn't be saying "people of color."

Besides, the whole idea of color is bullshit anyway. What should we call white people? "People of no color"? Isn't pink a color? In fact, white people are not really white at all, they're different shades of pink, olive, and beige. In other words, they're colored. And black people are rarely black. I see mostly different shades of brown and tan. In fact, some light-skinned black people are lighter than the darkest white people. Look how dark the people in India are. They're dark brown, but they're considered white people. What's going on here? May I see the color chart? "People of color" is an awkward, bullshit, liberal-guilt phrase that obscures meaning rather than enhancing it. Shall we call fat people, "people of size"?

By the way, I think the whole reason we're encouraged in this country to think of ourselves as "black and white" (instead of "pink and brown," which is what we are) is that black and white are complete opposites that cannot be reconciled. Black and white can never come together. Pink and brown, on the other hand, might just stand a chance of being blended, might just come together. Can't have that! Doesn't fit the plan.

I also don't say "African-American." I find it completely illogical, and furthermore it's confusing. Which part of Africa are we talking about? What about Egypt? Egypt is in Africa. Egyptians aren't black. They're like the people in India, they're dark brown white people. But they're Africans. So why wouldn't an Egyptian who becomes a U.S. citizen be an African-American?

The same thing goes for the Republic of South Africa. Suppose a white racist from South Africa becomes an American citizen? Well, first of all he'd find plenty of company, but couldn't he also be called an African-American? It seems to me that a racist white South-African guy could come here and call himself African-American just to piss off black people. And, by the way, what about a black person born in South Africa who moves here and becomes a citizen? What is he? An African-South-African-American? Or a South-African-African-American?

All right, back to this hemisphere. How about a black woman who is a citizen of Jamaica? According to P.C. doctrine, she's an African-Jamaican, right? But if she becomes a U.S. citizen, she's a Jamaican-American. And yet if one of these language crusaders saw her on the street, he'd think she was an African-American. Unless he knew her personally in which case he would have to decide between African-Jamaican-American and Jamaican-African-American. Ya know? It's just so much liberal bullshit. Labels divide people. We need fewer labels, not more.

Now, the Indians. I call them Indians because that's what they are. They're Indians. There's nothing wrong with the word Indian. First of all, it's important to know that the word Indian does not derive from Columbus mistakenly believing he had reached "India." India was not even called by that name in 1492; it was known as Hindustan. More likely, the word *Indian* comes from Columbus's description of the people he found here. He was an Italian, and did not speak or write very good Spanish, so in his written accounts he called the Indians, "Una gente in Dios." A people in God. In God. In Dios. Indians. It's a perfectly noble and respectable word.

So let's look at this pussified, trendy bullshit phrase, Native Americans. First of all, they're not natives. They came over the

Bering land bridge from Asia, so they're not natives. There are no natives anywhere in the world. Everyone is from somewhere else. All people are refugees, immigrants, or aliens. If there were natives anywhere, they would be people who still live in the Great Rift valley in Africa where the human species arose. Everyone else is just visiting. So much for the "native" part of Native American.

As far as calling them "Americans" is concerned, do I even have to point out what an insult this is? Jesus Holy Shit Christ! We steal their hemisphere, kill twenty or so million* of them, destroy five hundred separate cultures, herd the survivors onto the worst land we can find, and now we want to name them after ourselves? It's appalling. Haven't we done enough damage? Do we have to further degrade them by tagging them with the repulsive name of their conquerers?

And as far as these classroom liberals who insist on saying "Native American" are concerned, here's something they should be told: It's not up to you to name people and tell them what they ought to be called. If you'd leave the classroom once in a while, you'd find that most Indians are insulted by the term Native American. The American Indian Movement will tell you that if you ask them.

The phrase "Native American" was invented by the U.S. government Department of the Interior in 1970. It is an inventory term used to keep track of people. It includes Hawaiians, Eskimos, Samoans, Micronesians, Polynesians, and Aleuts. Anyone who uses the phrase *Native American*

---

* Before 1492 there were 25 million people in Central America. By 1579 there were 2 million.

is assisting the U.S. government in its effort to obliterate people's true identities.

Do you want to know what the Indians would like to be called? Their real names: Adirondack, Delaware, Massachuset, Narraganset, Potomac, Illinois, Miami, Alabama, Ottawa, Waco, Wichita, Mohave, Shasta, Yuma, Erie, Huron, Susquehanna, Natchez, Mobile, Yakima, Wallawalla, Muskogee, Spokan, Iowa, Missouri, Omaha, Kansa, Biloxi, Dakota, Hatteras, Klamath, Caddo, Tillamook, Washoe, Cayuga, Oneida, Onondaga, Seneca, Laguna, Santa Ana, Winnebago, Pecos, Cheyenne, Menominee, Yankton, Apalachee, Chinook, Catawba, Santa Clara, Taos, Arapaho, Blackfoot, Blackfeet, Chippewa, Cree, Cheyenne, Mohawk, Tuscarora, Cherokee, Seminole, Choctaw, Chickasaw, Comanche, Shoshone, Two Kettle, Sans Arc, Chiricahua, Kiowa, Mescalero, Navajo, Nez Perce, Potawatomi, Shawnee, Pawnee, Chickahominy, Flathead, Santee, Assiniboin, Oglala, Miniconjou, Osage, Crow, Brulé, Hunkpapa, Pima, Zuni, Hopi, Paiute, Creek, Kickapoo, Ojibwa, Shinnicock.

You know, you'd think it would be a fairly simple thing to come over to this continent, commit genocide, eliminate the forests, dam up the rivers, build our malls and massage parlors, sell our blenders and whoopee cushions, poison ourselves with chemicals, and let it go at that. But no. We have to compound the insult. Native Americans! I'm glad the Indians have gambling casinos now. It makes me happy that dimwitted white people are losing their rent money to the Indians. Maybe the Indians will get lucky and win their country back. Probably they wouldn't want it. Look what we did to it.

MISFORTUNE

People like to say that no matter how bad off your life is, there is always someone worse off than you. I guess it's a source of comfort. It's nice to know that while they're removing a bone from your throat, the man in the next room has a four hundred-pound tumor in his groin.

But the idea that there is always someone worse off leads to the logical conclusion that somewhere in the world there is a person who is in worse shape than everybody else. Some guy who has almost six billion people doing better than he is.

But, in reality, as you get down to the bottom of the bad-shape pile, it becomes harder and harder to know who's doing worse. Is a blind, paralyzed, maniac really better off than a three-foot, paraplegic imbecile? Tough call.

Then there's always my "Plus-a-Headache" formula. No matter how horrible and painful a person's condition may be, it can always be made worse by simply adding a headache: "He was poor, ignorant, diseased, lonely, depressed, and abandoned—plus he had a headache."

Look on the bright side: The headache will very likely go away.

THE GRIEF/TRAGEDY/SYMPATHY INDUSTRY

Everyone complains about this being a "victim society." Well, I don't know about the victim society, but I would like to talk about the "Grief, Tragedy, and Sympathy Industry."

The news media are playing a game with you. You're being fed a large ration of other people's troubles designed to keep your mind off the things that should really be bothering you. I guess the media figure if you're sitting around feeling sorry for every sick, injured, or dead person they can scrounge up, you'll have less time to dwell on how fucked up your own life is, and what bad shape this culture is really in.

I'm not so much opposed to grief per se, as I am to public media grief. My attitude is fuck sick people and fuck a dead person. Unless I knew them. And, if so, I'll handle it on my own, thank you. I don't need media guidance to experience sorrow.

Above all, I object to the abuse of the word *tragedy*. Every time some asshole stops breathing these days it's called a tragedy. The word has been devalued. You can't call every death a tragedy and expect the word to mean anything. For instance, multiple deaths do not automatically qualify as tragedies. Just because a man kills his wife and three kids, her lover, his lover, the baby-sitter, the mailman, the Amway lady, and the guy from Publishers' Clearing House and then blows his own brains out doesn't mean a tragedy has occurred. It's interesting. It's entertaining to read about. But it's not a tragedy.

The death of a child is also not automatically a tragedy. Some guy backing over his kid in the driveway is not a tragedy, it's a bad, bad mistake. A tragedy is a literary work in which the main character comes to ruin as a consequence of a moral weakness or a fatal flaw. Shakespeare wrote tragedies. A family of nine being wiped out when a train hits their camper is not a tragedy. It's called a traffic accident.

You wanna know what a tragedy is? A tragedy is when you see some fat bastard in the airport with pockmarks on his face and his belly hanging out, and he's with a woman who has bad teeth and multiple bruises, and that night he's gonna make her suck his dick. That's a tragedy. They don't mention that a lot on TV.

The media often refer to the killing of a white policeman as a *tragedy*. Why is that more tragic than the same white policeman killing an unarmed black kid? Why is it never a tragedy on TV when a white cop kills a black kid? It's never presented in that way. The whites save *tragedy* for themselves. Why is that?

The media have elevated the marketing of bathos and sympathy to a fine art. But I gotta tell ya, I really don't care about a paraplegic who climbs a mountain and then skis cross-country for 50 miles; I'm not interested in a one-legged veteran who ice skates across Canada to raise money for children's prosthetics. I have no room for some guy without a nervous system who becomes the state wrestling champion; or a man who loses his torso in Vietnam and later holds his breath for six months to promote spina bifida research; or someone born with no heart who lives to be ninety-five and helps everyone in his neighborhood neaten up their lawns.

Is this all we can find in America that passes for personal drama? People overcoming long odds? God, it's so boring and predictable.

And does this mean we are supposed to admire people simply because of the order of their luck? Because their bad luck came first? What about the reverse? What about people who start well and then fail spectacularly in life? People who were born with every privilege and given every possible gift and talent, who had all the money they needed, were surrounded by

good people, and then went out and fucked their lives up anyway? Isn't that drama too? Isn't that equally ineresting? In
fact, I find it more interesting. More like true tragedy.

I'd prefer to hear something like that once in a while,
rather than this pseudo-inspirational bullshit that the media
feel they have to feed us in order to keep our minds off
America's decline. If they're going to insist that we really need
to know about sick babies and cripples who tap dance and
quadraplegic softball players, why don't they simply have a
special television program called "Inspirational Stories"? That
way I can turn the fuckin' thing off. I'm tired of people battling
the odds. Fuck the odds. And fuck the people who battle them.

After a while don't you just get weary of being told that
some kid in Minnesota needs a new liver? Kids didn't need
new livers when I was growing up. We had good livers. What
are they feeding these kids that suddenly they all need new
livers? I think it's the gene pool. Nature used to eliminate the
weak, imperfect kids before they were old enough to repro-
duce their flaws. Now we have a medical industry dedicated
to keeping people alive just long enough to pass along their
bad genes to another generation. It's medical arrogance, and
it works against nature's plan. I'm sick of hearing about a
baby being kept alive on a resuscitator while doctors wait for
a kidney to be flown in on a private jet contributed by some
corporation seeking good publicity because they just killed
six thousand people in Pakistan with a chemical spill. I'm
tired of this shit being presented in the context of real news.
Prurient gossip about sick people is not real news. It's emotional pandering.

The real news is that there are millions upon millions of sick babies and cripples and addicts and criminals and misfits and diseased and mentally ill and hungry people who need help. Not to mention all the middle-class normals who swear things are just fine but spend three hours a day commuting, and whose dull, meaningless lives are being stolen from them by soulless corporations. But the media don't bother with all that. They like to simply cover their designated Victims of the Week, so they can see themselves as somehow noble. They highlight certain cases, making them appear exceptional. And when they do, they admit they are simply unable and unwilling to report the totality of the Great American Social Nightmare.

DEATH IS ALMOST FUN THESE DAYS

Seems to me it wasn't long ago that when an OLD PERSON DIED the UNDERTAKER put him in a COFFIN, and you sent FLOWERS to the FUNERAL HOME where the MORTICIAN held the WAKE. Then, after the FUNERAL, they put him in a HEARSE and DROVE him to the CEMETERY, where they BURIED his BODY in a GRAVE.

Now when a SENIOR CITIZEN PASSES AWAY, he is placed in a BURIAL CONTAINER, and you send FLORAL TRIBUTES to the SLUMBER ROOM where the GRIEF THERAPIST supervises the VIEWING. After the MEMORIAL SERVICE, the FUNERAL COACH TRANSPORTS THE DEPARTED to the GARDEN OF REMEMBRANCE, where his EARTHLY REMAINS are INTERRED in their FINAL RESTING PLACE.

R.I.P. ON THE VCR

You know where you never see a camcorder? At a funeral. Wouldn't that be fun? Especially if you didn't know any of the people there. Why not go to a stranger's funeral, and bring your camcorder? Have a little fun! Zoom in on the corpse's nose hairs. Then pull back, and pan over to the widow's tears. Get a tight shot of that. Do a montage of people wracked with grief. Then go home and put a laugh track on it! Smoke a joint and show it to your friends. That would be a lot of fun.

LEGAL MURDER ONCE A MONTH

You can talk about capital punishment all you want, but I don't think you can leave everything up to the government. Citizens should be willing to take personal responsibility. Every now and then you've got to do the right thing, and go out and kill someone on your own. I believe the killing of human beings is just one more function of government that needs to be privatized.

I say this because I believe most people know at least one other person they wish were dead. One other person whose death would make their life a little easier. A sexual rival; an abuser; a tormentor at school; a parent who's been draining the family nest egg by lingering too long on life support. It's a natural, human instinct. In fact, in the psychological literature it's technically referred to as, "Jesus, I wish that son of a bitch was dead!" Don't run from it. Society must find a way to accommodate this very understandable human instinct.

And so, I offer a plan: Legal Murder Once a Month. Under this plan, every thirty days each person in America will be allowed to kill one other person without incurring punishment. One murder per person, per month. But you can't kill just anybody. It's not random. Each month there will be a different type of person it's OK to kill. For instance, one month it would be all right to kill a business associate. (For you blue-collar guys, that means someone at work.) That month, kill anybody at work—no punishment. But you must have a good reason; none of this weak shit, "I caught him fucking my wife." It has to be a good reason. Like, "The guy is just a real asshole."

Another month we would have a day when it's OK to kill a relative. Actually, you might want two days for this, one for in-laws, and one for blood relatives. In fact, you might even need a week. Seven days, seven dead relatives. A festival! The Seven Dead Relatives Festival. Christmas week! There's a good time for family resentment. Lots of old, festering pathological flotsam bobbing to the surface like buoyant turds. Christmas! Peace on Earth and a nice stack of dead relatives under the tree. And forgive what may seem a tacky note, but this plan might also help simplify your Xmas shopping.

All right, what about spouses? You gotta have a day for killing spouses, although I don't think you'd want to do this one too often. You know how some guys are, they'd be goin' through ten or twelve old ladies a year. No, this one should be an annual event with a one-spouse limit. In fact, why not just have an annual spouse-hunting season? You must get a license, you must wear bright orange, and you must be accompanied by three drunken friends. And please take note, those of you who aren't married and are merely living together will not be allowed to kill each other until you have taken your sacred vows.

All right, we've covered relatives and spouses. Now, how about that certain someone else? Someone who really deserves to die? The ex-spouse! The exes of both sexes. The ex-husband, usually referred to in court documents as "the asshole." And, of course, that other towering archetypal figure in divorce law, "the cunt"!

In fact, I think we ought to just combine spouses and ex-spouses and stretch this one into a full week as well. Do I smell another holiday festival here? Is this possibly Easter week we're talkin' about? I think so! And I'm gonna give you a special deal. Not only will you be allowed to kill your ex-spouse, but you'll also get to kill their lawyer. It's a two-for-one, Easter Bunny, Resurrection special. One man rises from the dead, two people take his place. By the way, are you beginning to sense that perhaps there's a place for the Disney corporation in all of this? Just a thought.

And while we're at it, why don't we honor Freud by having a day for killing parents? This is something that doesn't happen nearly often enough as far as I'm concerned. Why should the Menendez Brothers have all the fun? Get into that living room, whip out the shotgun, and launch your parents into the great beyond so they can be with their loving God. Do the folks a favor. What kind of an ungrateful child are you? By the way, if you're wondering why parents aren't already covered in the Seven Dead Relatives

Festival, it's because parents are special people, and they deserve special treatment.

Here would be another handy event: Kill-a-Neighbor-Day. A perfect way to settle old scores and perhaps, at the same time, upgrade the neighborhood. And just to provide you a little flexibility, for our purposes a neighbor will be considered anyone who lives in your zip code.

You know, now that I think of it, it would probably make sense to simply have Wild-Card Day. One day a year when everyone can just go out and kill whomever the fuck they want. Many of us have long lists of specific, worthy targets who don't fall into any of the established categories. Retail clerks, landlords, teachers, salesmen, telephone solicitors; the asshole Connecticut people in the blue Volvo station wagon; the arrogant yuppie prick at the laundromat who acted so superior about his natural fibers; and how about that snotty blonde bitch on the "Six O'Clock News"? The one who keeps braying, "Thank God, no one was hurt," every time someone so much as backs into a lamppost.

Now, let me quickly point out that my Legal Murder Once a Month plan has three strict rules: First, it isn't cumulative. You can't save up all your murders for a year and then go waltzing into McDonald's and spoil everyone's Egg McMuffin. You get one murder a month, that's it. Use it or lose it.

Rule number two: You can't hire someone to do the killing for you. You have to do it yourself. And if you're squeamish, take my word for it, you'll get over that. There's nothing to it. I, myself, have killed six people. All random, all undetected, no way to trace them to me. And, let me tell you, there's nothin' like it. It's a great feeling. Yeah, I know, you're thinking. "Aw, he's a comedian. He's just sayin' that stuff." Good. That's exactly what I want you to think.

Rule number three: You can never kill your own off-spring. It's just off-limits. OK? No killing your own children. Of course, if they really deserve it; if they're really bad news, they'll probably piss someone else off, and that person will take care of the job for you.

And all you civic-minded dipshits, I want you to know there's nothing in the constitution to prevent any of this. The state doesn't actually oppose murder, it simply objects to those who go into business for themselves. When it comes to the taking of human life, the federal government doesn't want free-lance competition.

Life is cheap, never forget it. Corporations make marketing decisions by weighing the cost of being sued for your death against the cost of making the product safer. Your life is a factor in cost-effectiveness. So when you talk about murder, don't confine your discussion to individuals.

Besides, there's nothing wrong with murder in the first place. Murder is a part of life. My society taught me that. And my species is really good at it. I belong to the only species in the history of the world that systematically tortures and murders its own members for pleasure, profit, and convenience.

See how easily we figured all that out? How easy that was? People think life is real complicated. Actually, there's nothing to it. Once you leave out all the bullshit they teach you in school, life gets really simple.

FUN FOES

Since I hold no real national allegiances, when it comes to armed conflict around the world I tend to root for the side that will provide me with the most entertainment. Saddam Hussein is a case in point. Any head of state who says, "We will walk on your corpses and crush your skulls, and you will swim in your own blood," is my kinda guy. You just don't hear that kind of shit anymore. This man obviously has great potential to provide me with amusing diversion.

In fact, all these Middle-East religious fanatics are brimming with entertainment potential. On CNN I recently saw video of 200 Islamic student-suicide bombers who were graduating from suicide-bomber school. They were singing what was apparently the school fight song: "Our blessings to you who fight at the gates of the enemy and knock on heaven's door with his skulls in your hands." How can Christians and Jews ever hope to compete with these folks who obviously enjoy their work so much?

LET'S ALL KILL EACH OTHER ACCORDING TO THE RULES

I don't understand the Geneva Convention and the whole idea of having rules for fighting a war. Why? Is it really more than just a way of reassuring ourselves we're all quite civilized, as we pour our hearts and minds and fortunes into mass killing? It seems to me like hypocritical bullshit. If the object is to win, wars should be fought with no holds barred; otherwise, why bother suiting up? As it is now, a winner is declared, and yet the issue has not been settled by all possible means.

Additionally, if the object is to kill the enemy, why treat their wounded? Treating their wounded requires resources taken from your own effort to achieve victory. Does this make sense if you're trying to win? Oh, yeah. Civilized.

My doubts about having rules for combat likewise extend to street fighting. I've heard guys whine about someone throwing a "sucker punch." Are they kidding? A guy wants to reduce your ass to a small bloody pile, and you're going to warn him before hitting him? Get fucking lucid! And lose all that dopey shit about fair play. It's out of place if the object is to win. (Is it?)

Also, as far as kicking someone when he's down is concerned, what is the problem here? Again, the object is to win, yes? Well, if he gets up, you might lose; therefore he must not get up. He needs to be kicked. You said you wanted to win. Or are you people just fucking around? I suspect that might be the case. Well, stop fucking around and make up your mind. You're telling me a man will fuck another man's wife, drive him out of business, cut him off and nearly kill him in traffic, but he shouldn't sneak punch, or kick him when he's down? I don't get it.

Another thing I don't understand is the objection to so-called dirty play in sports such as football. These are big, tough guys who are desperate to prove how manly they are; that they're not soft. That's why they play these games in the first place. Well, why not let them play "dirty" and let's find out how tough they really are?

It's been shown that small, dedicated groups of men can easily find ways of policing and disciplining those among them who cross the line. It's called vigilantism, and it's very efficient. Please don't tell a bunch of six-foot-six, three hundred-pounders in helmets and pads they can't spear and punch and put their thumbs in each other's eyes.

You'll miss all the fun. And you'll be keeping them from pursuing their calling at its highest level.

I also don't understand terrorists who call the police to warn them about a bomb. Do I need even explain my dismay at this one?

You know, folks, if this old world had any imagination, wars would be fought without codes and conventions, alley fighting would be standard, and the only rules in sports would govern the uniforms. Then we'd have some real fun.

But I fear that doesn't suit you, and so I return to the notion that produced these thoughts in the first place: You people shouldn't be fighting at all.

UNKNOWN SOLDIER

I recently visited an interesting site in Washington, D.C. You've heard of the Tomb of the Unknown Soldier? This is the Tomb of the *Well*-Known Soldier. No one knows about it. Isn't that odd? Everyone knows about the Unknown Soldier, but no one knows about the Well-Known Soldier. Makes you think, doesn't it? Maybe not.

They're also planning the Tomb of the Well-Known-but-Widely-Disliked Soldier. And then they're gonna build the Tomb of the Well-Liked-but-Poorly-Understood Soldier.

One other interesting fact before we leave this subject. I assume you know that Britain, France, and Canada all have Unknown Soldiers of their own. Well, oddly enough, all three of those soldiers knew each other. Kinda makes the hair on the back of your neck stand up, doesn't it? Maybe not.

IF ONLY WE WERE HUMAN

This species is a dear, hateful, sweet, barbaric, tender, vile, intelligent, confused, virtuous, evil, thoughtful, perverted, generous, greedy species. In short, great entertainment.

As I said before, humans are the only species that systematically tortures and murders its own for pleasure and personal gain. In fact, we are the only species that systematically tortures and murders its own, period.

We are serial killers. All our poems and symphonies and oils on canvas will never change that. Man's noble aspect is the aberration.

Those who argue that art and philosophy are proof of human worth neglect to mention that, in the scheme we have devised, artists and philosophers are completely powerless and largely without prestige. Art, music, and philosophy are merely poignant examples of what we might have been had not the priests and traders gotten hold of us.

Most animals, when fighting one of their own, will show aggressive behavior, but very little hostility or intention to harm. And when the outcome of the struggle is inevitable, the losing animal will signal its defeat by exposing its most vulnerable part to the victor, affording it the opportunity to finish the kill. The victor then walks away without inflicting further harm. These are the creatures we feel superior to.

LOCK AND LOAD

The rate of U.S. Marine suicides has been rising in recent years. The biggest jump came at a time when the Marine Corps was being reduced in size, and so, many of these men were barred from reenlisting. I guess they realized that the odds against death had suddenly improved, and they might actually have to face life. So they killed themselves. Strange, huh? I like that sort of thing. It's entertaining.

PEACE ON YOU

I'm not disturbed by war. More like entertained. War may be a lot of things, but it's never a bad show. It's the original Greatest Show on Earth. Otherwise, why would they call it a "theater of war"? I love it. And as far as I'm concerned, the show must go on.

But I realize there are some people who really worry about this kind of thing, and so, as a good citizen, I offer two ideas for peace. It's the least I can do.

Many people work on war plans; not too many work on peace plans. They even have a war college at Ft. McNair, Washington. They call it the National Defense University, but it's a war college. They don't have a peace college.

And they have war plans for every contingency, no matter how remote. If Easter Island gives us some crap tomorrow, we have a plan in a computer that tells us exactly how to thoroughly bomb the shit out of Easter Island. You name the country, we've got the plan. Chad, Myanmar, Upper Volta, Burkina Faso, Liechtenstein. Just give us some crap, and we'll come there, and bomb the shit out of you! 'Cause we've got a plan.

Well, so do I. Two of them. George's plans for peace:

My first plan is worldwide, year-round, nonstop folk dancing. In short, everyone in the world would be required to dance all the time. It leaves very little time for fighting, and what combat does occur is inefficient, because the combatants are constantly in motion.

When it was suggested that this plan might be impractical, I offered an alternative wherein only half the people would be dancing at any given time. The problem with this was the distinct possibility that while half the people were dancing, the other half would be robbing their homes.

So now I've stripped it down to a symbolic plan: twenty-four-hour, nonstop, worldwide folk dancing, once a year. Each year, on a designated day, everyone in the world would stop what they were doing and dance for twenty-four-hours.

Any kind of dancing you want. Square dance, minuet, grind, peabody, cakewalk, mazurka, samba, mashed potato. Doesn't matter. Just get out there and dance. Even hospital patients, shut-ins, cripples, and people on life support; if you're too sick to dance, you just die. While the doctors and nurses keep dancing. This would be a good way to weed out the weaker people. Dance or die! Natural selection with a beat.

One good result, of course, would be that during the actual dancing, no fighting could take place. But the plan would also tend to reduce violence during the remainder of the year, because for six months following the dance, everyone would be talking about how much fun they had had, and for the six months after that, they would all be busy planning what to wear to next year's dance.

Another plan I have is World Peace Through Formal Introductions. The idea is that everyone in the world would be required to meet everyone else in the world, formally, at least once. You'd have to look the person in the eye, shake hands, repeat their name, and try to remember one outstanding physical characteristic. My theory is, if you knew everyone in the world personally, you'd be less inclined to fight them in a war: "Who? The Malaysians? Are you kidding? I know those people!"

The biggest problem with compulsory, world-wide formal introductions would be logistics. How would it work? Would you line up everyone in the world single file and have one person at a time move down the line meeting all the others? And then when they finish they get on the end of the line, and the next person starts?

Or would you divide everyone into two long lines and have them move past each other laterally? That seems inefficient, because, for at least part of the time, each line would have a large number of people with nothing to do. And also, once you finished the first pass, everyone would still have to meet the people in their own line.

Either way, it would take a very long time. In fact, children would be born during the introductions, and then you'd have to meet them, too.

And it's probably important to remember that because of their longer names, some nationalities would move through the line more slowly than others. Russians, for example. Russian names tend to be long. If you ever bought an ID bracelet for a Russian person, you know what I mean. The engraving alone can run over two hundred dollars.

I'm afraid the Russians would move through the line very slowly: "Vladimir Denisovitch Zhirinovski, this is Yevgeny Vasily Arbatov. Yevgeny Vasily Arbatov, meet Vladimir Denisovitch Zhirinovski." Major delay.

On the other hand, the Chinese tend to have short names. "Chin Lu, Wu Han. Wu Han, Chin Lu." Bing! See ya later! Movin' right along. Which is why there are so many Chinese: less time saying hello, more time to fuck.

Peace on you. But only if you really deserve it.

COME BACK AND SEE US, HEAR?

I suppose it would be nice if reincarnation were a reality, but I have problems with the math. At some point, originally, there must have been a time when there were only two human beings. They both died, and presumably their souls were reincarnated into two other bodies. But that still leaves us with only two souls. We now have nearly six billion people on the planet. Where are all the extra souls coming from? Is someone printing up souls? Wouldn't that tend to lower their value?

SHORT TAKES (Part 2)

I only respect horoscopes that are specific: "Today, Neil Perleman, wearing tight-fitting wool knickers, will kill you on the crosstown bus."

Sometimes we dismiss something by substituting the letters "s-h-m" for the initial consonant sound in the word and then repeating the word itself: "Taxes, shmaxes!" But suppose the thing you're dismissing already starts with the "s-h-m" sound? For instance, how do you dismiss a person named Schmidt?

When a ghostwriter dies, how many people come back?

I'm in favor of personal growth as long as it doesn't include malignant tumors.

Whenever I hear about a "peace-keeping force," I wonder, If they're so interested in peace, why do they use force?

The bigger they are, the worse they smell.

SATAN IS COOL

Once, at a school function, I received a dressing down for not dressing up.

The keys to America: the cross, the brew, the dollar, and the gun.

My watch stopped. I think I'm down a quartz.

A meltdown sounds like fun. Like some kind of cheese sandwich.

Sex always has consequences. When Hitler's mother spread her legs that night, she effectively canceled out the spreading of fifteen to twenty million other pairs of legs.

A parawhore is a woman who keeps you aroused until they can get you to a real whore.

No one can ever know for sure what a deserted area looks like.

Why don't they put child molesters in a fondling home?

The difference between show business and a gang bang is that in show business everybody wants to go on last.

Don Ho can sign autographs 3.4 times faster than Efrem Zimbalist Jr.

The truth is, Pavlov's dog trained Pavlov to ring his bell just before the dog salivated.

A scary dream makes your heart beat faster. Why doesn't the part of your brain that controls your heartbeat realize that another part of your brain is making the whole thing up? Don't these people communicate?

I never watch "Sesame Street"; I know most of that stuff.

I read that somewhere out west recently a National Wilderness Area was closed for two days because it was too windy.

e are conditioned to notice and emphasize the differences among ourselves, instead of the similarities. The corporate-style partitioning begins early in life: fetus, newborn, infant, toddler, preschool, lower school, middle school, junior high, senior high, pre-teen, teen. Get in your box and stay there!

THE STATUS QUO ALWAYS SUCKS

Is the kidney a bean-shaped organ, or is the bean a kidney-shaped legume?

I like Florida; everything is in the eighties. The temperatures, the ages, and the IQs.

When you cut the legs off jeans to make cutoffs, don't you feel foolish for just a moment as you stand there holding two useless denim legs?

Why does *Filipino* start with an *F* and *Philippines* start with *Ph*?

I think in retaliation the Jews should be allowed to kill six million Germans. It's only fair. With fifty years of compound interest. That would come to about 110 million Germans. That oughta put a nice dent in bratwurst consumption.

I heard about some guy called the Marrying Rapist. He operates with a minister-partner who performs a wedding ceremony just before the rape. Police are looking for two men in tuxedos and sneakers. Possibly carrying rice.

think tobacco and alcohol warnings are too general. They should be more to the point: "People who smoke will eventually cough up small brown pieces of lung." And "Warning! Alcohol will turn you into the same asshole your father was."

A fast car that passes you at night is going somewhere.

I recently had a ringing in my ear. The doctors looked inside and found a small bell.

IF IT AIN'T BROKE, BREAK IT

If Frank Sinatra owed you a favor, it would be fun to ask him to have one of his buddies kill Andy Williams.

I get a nice safe feeling when I see a police car, and I realize I'm not driving around with a trunkful of cocaine.

I'm offering a special prize for first Buick on the moon.

Why do shoelaces only come in certain sizes?

the public will never become concerned about global warming or the greenhouse effect. These words just aren't scary enough. Global means all-encompassing, warming connotes comfort, green equals growth, and house equals shelter. Growth, shelter, and all-encompassing comfort. Doesn't sound like much of a threat. Relax.

How can a color be artificial? I look at red Jell-O, and it's just as red as it can be.

Why is it the other side of the street always crosses the street when I do?

In Rome, the emperor sat in a special part of the Coliseum known as the Caesarian section.

Sometimes, when I'm told to use my own discretion, if no one is looking I'll use someone else's. But I always put it back.

BOTHER THE WEAK

I don't see the problem with devil worship.

You know what type of cosmetic surgery you never hear about? Nose enlargement.

My phone number is seventeen. We got one of the early ones.

What goes through a bird's mind when he finds himself flying through a fireworks display?

If you nail a tool shed closed, how do you put the hammer away?

Why are there no recreational drugs taken in suppository form?

When I'm working, and the television is on, I always tune in a program I like. If I'm going to ignore something, I want it to be something I enjoy.

No one is ever completely alone; when all is said and done, you always have yourself.

I admire an intelligent man with really unattractive, badly stained and crooked teeth who makes a lot of money and still doesn't get his teeth fixed. It's an interesting choice.

Imagine meeting your maker and finding out it's Frito-Lay.

have you ever groped blindly through the middle of a packed suitcase trying to find something and then suddenly realized with horror that the razor blades had come unwrapped?

I was taken to the hospital for observation. I stayed several days, didn't observe anything, and left.

A tree: First you chop it down, then you chop it up.

I'd hate to be an alcoholic with Alzheimer's. Imagine needing a drink and forgetting where you put it.

Whenever I see a huge crowd, I always wonder how many of the people have hazelnuts in their intestines.

Sometimes I can't recall my mental blocks, so I try not to think about it.

did you ever notice how important the last bite of a candy bar is? All the while you're eating it, you're aware that you have less and less remaining. Then, as you get to the end, if something happens to that last piece, you feel really cheated.

WOOD KILLS

If a cigarette smoker wakes up from a seven-year coma, does he want a cigarette?

There is a small town out west where the entire population is made up of the full-grown imaginary childhood friends of present-day adults.

If a painting can be forged well enough to fool experts, why is the original so valuable?

Valentine's Day is devoted to love. Why don't we have a day devoted to hatred? The raw, visceral hatred that is felt every hour of the day by ordinary people, but is repressed for reasons of social order. I think it would be very cathartic, and it would certainly make for an exciting six o'clock news.

I'm very lucky. The only time I was ever up shit creek, I just happened to have a paddle with me.

The Japanese culture is very big on martial arts and spiritual disciplines. So when a guy tells me he is studying something that has a Japanese name, I know he has either embarked on a mystical journey or is learning how to break someone's neck with two fingers.

Baseball is the only major sport that appears backwards in a mirror.

WHO STOLE THE BANANA GUACAMOLE?

Virginia has passed a law limiting people to the purchase of one gun per person per month. But if you can show the need for more than one gun a month, you can apply to the police for an exemption. "Listen, officer, we've got a really dysfunctional family here, and . . ."

Why does it always take longer to go somewhere than it does to come back?

People tell you to have a safe trip, as if you have some control over it.

Conservatives say if you don't give the rich more money, they will lose their incentive to invest. As for the poor, they tell us they've lost all incentive because we've given them too much money.

Why is the hot water on the left? I think it's so you can use your right hand to test how hot it is.

People love to admit they have bad handwriting or that they can't do math. And they will readily admit to being awkward: "I'm such a klutz!" But they will never admit to having a poor sense of humor or being a bad driver.

Have you ever noticed that the lawyer smiles more than the client?

E-I-E-I-O is actually a gross misspelling of the word *farm*.

If you can't beat them, arrange to have them beaten.

A recent story in the media said that some firemen in Chicago had refused to enter a burning building because it was too hot.

KILL YOUR PET

No one ever mentions when the swallows leave Capistrano. Do they die there?

The lazy composer still had several scores to settle.

At what point in his journey does an emigrant become an immigrant?

In a factory that makes bathroom disinfectant, the whole factory smells like the bathroom.

We have mileage, yardage, and footage, why don't we have inchage?

Travel tip: Economy-section farts on an inbound flight from the Third World are the deadliest a traveler will ever encounter.

Every time you use the phrase *all my life* it has a different meaning.

Great scientific discoveries: jiggling the toilet handle.

When will the rhetorical questions all end?

Why do they call it a garbage disposal? The stuff isn't garbage until after you dispose of it.

A cemetery is a place where dead people live.

do the people who hate blacks but think they're really good dancers ever stop to think how much better blacks would dance if fewer people hated them?

I do something about the weather. I stay home.

"Let's stop underage drinking before it starts." Please explain this to me. It sounds tricky.

When I'm really bored, I sit home and translate the writing on foreign biscuits.

Political discourse has been reduced to "Where's the beef?" "Read my lips," and "Make my day." Where are the assassins when we really need them?

GANDHI ATE MILK DUDS

Hard work is for people short on talent.

Alter and *change* are supposed to be synonyms, but altering your trousers and changing your trousers are quite different things.

My back hurts; I think I over-schlepped.

The news story said someone had overcome a fatal disease. Wow!

A Bible makes a delicious meal. Simply rub with olive oil and minced garlic, and bake one hour in a 375-degree oven. Serve with oven-roasted potatoes and a small tossed salad. Serves two. Dee-leesh!

Recently, in a public bathroom, I used the handicapped stall. As I emerged, a man in a wheelchair asked me indignantly, "Are you handicapped?" Gathering all my aplomb, I looked him in the eye and said, "Not now. But I was before I went in there."

Threatening postcard: "Wish you were here, but if you come here I will kill you!"

I wanted to be a Boy Scout, but I had all the wrong traits. They were looking for kids who were trustworthy, loyal, helpful, friendly, courteous, kind, obedient, cheerful, thrifty, brave, clean, and reverent. Whereas I tended to be devious, fickle, obstructive, hostile, impolite, mean, defiant, glum, extravagant, cowardly, dirty, and sacrilegious.

How is it possible to be seated on a standing committee?

I have come up with a single sentence that includes all of the seven deadly sins: greed, anger, pride, lust, gluttony, sloth, and envy. Here it is. "It enrages me that I, a clearly superior person, should have less money than my neighbor, whose wife I would love to fuck if I weren't so busy eating pork chops and sleeping all day."

Recent polls reveal that some people have never been polled. Until recently.

did you ever run over somebody with your car? And then you panic? So you back up and run over them again? Did you notice the second crunch was not quite as loud?

If I had just one wish it would be to write the letter z better in longhand.

have you noticed, whenever there's a problem in this country they get a bunch of celebrities or children together to sing a song about it? Drought, famine, drugs; they sing a song about it. This is an idea that grew out of the '60s peace movement. The idea then was that if enough "good" people sang, chanted, and held hands, all the "evil" people would give up their money, weapons, and power. Worked great, didn't it?

WE ARE ALL PRECANCEROUS

I read about a woman who had sixty-three distinct personalities. Jesus! It would take long enough just finding out how everyone was feeling in the morning, can you imagine trying to plan a vacation?

I put a dollar in one of those change machines. Nothing changed.

After the year 2000, I hope the crime of the century happens real soon, so I get to read about it.

They say if you outlaw guns, only outlaws and criminals will have guns. Well, shit, those are precisely the people who need them.

I once found a throw rug in a catch basin.

One time, a few years ago, Oprah had a show about women who fake orgasms. Not to be outdone, Geraldo came right back with a show about men who fake bowel movements.

It is now possible for a child to have five parents: sperm donor, egg donor, the surrogate mother who carries the fetus, and two adoptive parents. It renders the statement "He has his mother's eyes" rather meaningless.

The new, modern Swiss Army knife has an ear-piercing tool and a roach clip.

One of the best expressions in the English language is, "Who says so?" I guarantee, if you keep saying, "Who says so?" long enough, sooner or later someone will take you into custody.

It's hard for me to believe that the small amount of water I take from the water cooler can produce such a large bubble.

Infant crib death Is caused by grandparents' breath.

I've always wanted to place a personal ad no one would answer: "Elderly, depressed, accident-prone junkie, likes Canadian food and Welsh music, seeking rich, well-built, oversexed, female deaf mute in her late teens. Must be nonsmoker."

I went to the Missing Persons' Bureau. No one was there.

Beethoven was so hard of hearing he thought he was a painter.

I choose toilet paper through a process of elimination.

Meow means "woof" in cat.

On Thanksgiving, you realize you're living in a modern world. Millions of turkeys baste themselves in millions of ovens that clean themselves.

A day off is always more welcome when it is unexpected.

Some people see things that are and ask, Why? Some people dream of things that never were and ask, Why not? Some people have to go to work and don't have time for all that shit.

RIDE THE WILD PARAMECIUM

How can everyone's money be "hard-earned," and everyone's vacation be "well-deserved"? Sounds like bullshit to me.

What exactly is "diddley squat"?

We now buy watches primarily for their looks, price, or additional functions. The fact that they tell time seems lost.

I think you ought to be able to lease a dog.

I don't understand the particular importance of remembering where you were when JFK was assassinated. I remember where I was a lot of times.

What year did Jesus think it was?

There's a new lottery game called Blotto. You get drunk and pick the numbers.

With all this natural selection going on, why doesn't the human race get any smarter? Is this it? Why are there still so many stupid people? Apparently, being a real dumb jackoff has some survival value.

Why is there always a small hole near the tip of a pen?

I enjoy going to a party at one of the Kennedys' homes, dropping to the floor, and yelling, "Hit the deck, he's got a gun!"

You know what disease you never hear about? Cancer of the heart.

LIFE IS A NEAR-DEATH EXPERIENCE

Amy Vanderbilt, the foremost authority on etiquette, commited suicide and apparently didn't have the courtesy to leave a note.

If the bouncer gets drunk, who throws *him* out?

The world began going downhill when ticket-takers in movie theaters stopped wearing uniforms.

When primitive people practice the rain dance, does it rain at the end of practice? And if it doesn't, how do they know they did the dance correctly?

The original Shick Smoking Centers were very primitive. They gave you one lecture and then you came back a week later. If they smelled tobacco on your breath, they beat the shit out of you.

If you live to be a hundred, your lucky number goes up by one.

FUCK THE MIDDLE CLASS

Medical Progress: The medical profession is only now beginning to concede that maybe, just maybe, nutrition has something to do with good health. And that maybe, just maybe, the mind is somehow mysteriously linked to the body. Of course, there's not much money in such thinking.

If you mail a letter to your mailman, will he get it before he's supposed to?

I enjoy watching a woman with really bad teeth and a good sense of humor struggling to use her lips and tongue to hide her teeth when she's laughing. I just stand there and tell her joke after joke after joke.

Never tell a Spanish maid you want everything to be spic-and-span.

President Bush declared a National Day of Prayer for Peace. This was some time after he had carefully arranged and started the war.

They keep saying you can't compare apples and oranges. I can. An apple is red and distinctly non-spherical; an orange is orange and nearly spherical. So, what's the big problem?

After a big flood, where do all those rowboats go?

The Chinese have a saying: On a journey of a thousand miles, 512 is a little more than half.

McDonald's "breakfast for under a dollar" actually costs much more than that. You have to factor in the cost of coronary bypass surgery.

I don't like to lose my bearings, so I keep them in the cabinet near my bed.

When Popeye blows through his pipe, why doesn't he get sprayed with burning ash?

George Washington's brother was the Uncle of Our Country.

If you fall asleep on the couch in a house where a woman is present, there will be a blanket or a coat covering you when you awaken.

Politics is so corrupt even the dishonest people get fucked.

When blowing out your birthday candles, suppose you wish for one candle to stay lit? Is it possible for your wish to come true?

MY FIRST NINE DOGS ARE DEAD

I got a chest X-ray last month, and they found a spot on my lung. Fortunately it was barbecue sauce.

hen a masochist brings someone home from the bar, does he say, "Excuse me a moment, I'm going to slip into something uncomfortable?"

This year is the two-millionth anniversary of sperm.

hen you pick something up with your toes and transfer it to your hand, don't you feel, just briefly, like a superior creature? Like you could probably survive alone in a forest for a long time? Just briefly.

If all our national holidays were observed on Wednesdays, we might conceivably wind up with nine-day weekends.

The day after tomorrow is the third day of the rest of your life.

Why must hailstones always be the size of something else? And if it must be that way, why don't they have hailstones the size of testicles?

Cloud nine gets all the publicity, but cloud eight actually is cheaper, less crowded, and has a better view.

It is bad luck to kill a dog with a cooking spoon.

don't you love these people who end their sentences with a rising inflection? And they do it all the time? As though it were an intelligent way to talk? And everything they say sounds like a question? Even the answers? "How are you today?" "I'm fine?"

The swallows know that on the nineteenth of March the tourists come back to Capistrano.

hat's all this stuff about retirement I keep hearing on TV commercials? People planning, saving; they can't wait to retire. One woman on TV says to her husband, "At this rate, Jeff, we'll never be able to retire!" What is this all about? Why would someone spend his whole life doing something he can't wait to get away from?

One of my favorite things in the movies is seeing a person hanged.

DON'T GET YOUR CORTEX CAUGHT IN A VORTEX

I often think how different the world would be if Hitler had not been turned down when he applied to art school.

Don't you get tired of these cereal commercials where they show the milk being poured in slow motion, and it splashes off a raspberry?

I enjoy watching people in rush-hour traffic. Thousands of them, stressed, frustrated, hurrying to and from their chosen places of enslavement. It's especially enjoyable from an airplane, because you can see their houses as well. The houses, like the people, all the same. Towns and subdivisions all the same. Cul de sacs. Like their lives, going nowhere. "Not a through street."

I think they should lower the drinking age. I just want to see a sign in a bar that says, You Must Be 11 and Prove It.

Positive thinking doesn't sound like a very good idea to me. I'm sure it doesn't work. And if it does, it's probably real hard to do.

Sometimes when I watch a parade, I wonder how many of the marchers are in desperate need of a good long piss.

So far, the Ku Klux Klan has not produced any really great composers.

THINK CLOWN
VOMIT

Tomorrow is very much like today, except it's not here yet.

I admire a man who drives clear across town to a distant shopping center where no one knows him, and rides all afternoon on the children's coin-operated "horsie."

My fondest wish is that I learn to write a capital "X" in longhand without lifting the pen from the paper.

Always be careful what you say. Nathan Hale said,"I only regret that I have but one life to give for my country." They killed him.

The difference between the blues and the blahs is that you can't sing the blahs.

I find the high five repulsive. It's typical lame, suburban white-boy bullshit. Any "five" that takes place above the waist is lame white-boy bullshit. I sincerely hope these high fives are causing long-term arm and shoulder injuries.

DOES GOD REALLY HAVE TO
WATCH ALL THIS SHIT?

Bus lag: a low-level disorientation caused by riding on a bus. Almost impossible to detect.

Long before man discovered fire, he had sand and water to put it out with.

When you look at some of Picasso's paintings, it makes you wonder what kind of women he visualized when he masturbated.

Cancer is caused by a fear of malignant tumors.

honesty may be the best policy, but it's important to remember that, apparently, by elimination, dishonesty is the second best policy. Second is not all that bad.

You don't meet many Japanese guys named Biff.

We use the sun to make electricity, and then we use the electricity to operate sun lamps and tanning machines.

I'm unusual in one respect. My lucky number is 541,633.

A laugh is a smile with a hole in it.

People in the central and mountain time zones are getting too much sleep. Their late news comes on at 10 P.M., an hour earlier than in coastal time zones, and yet the morning talk shows come on at 7 A.M., the same as the rest of the country. So, central and mountain people are getting an extra hour's sleep. I think it makes them sluggish.

I NEVER LIKED A MAN I DIDN'T MEET

Preparation H is also good for a fat lip.

It's annoying to have a song running through your mind all day that you can't stop humming. Especially if it's something difficult like "Flight of the Bumblebee."

'll bet you and I are a lot alike. Did you ever get together with a bunch of people and hang someone? Isn't it awful? You just want the guy's body to stop spasming. Every time I do it, I say, "This is absolutely the last time I'm doin' this." And still I go back.

Most people work just hard enough not to get fired and get paid just enough money not to quit.

recently read that some guy had killed his girlfriend. You know, it's always been my contention that at the moment you decide to kill your girlfriend, that decision is tantamount to breaking off the relationship. Therefore, at the time you kill the person in question she is actually no longer your girlfriend.

In reverse order, our last eight presidents: A hillbilly wilh a permanent hard-on; an upper-class bureaucrat-twit; an actor-imbecile; a born-again Christian peanut farmer; an unelected college football lineman; a paranoid moral dwarf; a vulgar cowboy criminal; and a mediocre playboy sex fiend.

heard that crime has increased so much it is now a growth industry. My worry is that if it continues to grow at the current rate it will attract the criminal element.

I read that a Detroit man and his friend were arrested because they had forced the man's five-year-old son to smoke cigarettes, drink alcohol, and perform oral sex on them. Can you imagine? Cigarettes!

In New York State a fourteen-year-old can get married but he can't drive, so he is forced to go on his honeymoon on a bicycle or a skateboard.

SURF'S DOWN
FOREVER

there is something refreshingly ironic about people lying on the beach contracting skin cancer, in an attempt to acquire a purely illusory appearance of good health while germ-laden medical waste washes up on the sand all around them.

The New Testament is not new anymore; it's thousands of years old. It's time to start calling it The Less Old Testament.

I saw a fast-food commercial where they were selling a sandwich made of pork fat dipped in butter and egg yolk, deep-fried in lard, wrapped in bacon, and topped with cheddar cheese. They call it "Plaque on a Bun."

Crooked judges live on fixed incomes.

In the drugstore, how do you know if you're buying a sundry, a notion, or an incidental?

Prefix has no suffix, but *suffix* has a prefix.

I have no sympathy for single dads. They got into their marriages because they wanted steady pussy. Steady pussy leads to babies. After the novelty wears off, the marriage goes away. Single dads. Big fuckin' deal.

"It's neither here nor there." Well, folks, it's gotta be somewhere. I certainly don't have it.

If a really stupid person becomes senile, how can you tell?

germany lost World War II because Hitler was completely distracted by ill-fitting clothing that he was constantly adjusting during the last two years of the war.

The best example of a housekeeper is a divorced woman.

I read somewhere that in the last census 1.6 percent of the people were not counted. How can they know that?

MRS. GOODWRENCH IS A LESBIAN

blow your nose" is an interesting phrase. Because you don't really *blow* your nose, you blow out *through* your nose. If you blew your nose, I think they'd put you away. You might get someone *else* to blow your nose, but he would have to be a really close friend. Or completely drunk.

Just when I began to find myself, depersonalization came in.

I enjoy making people feel uncomfortable. Walking down the jetway to board my plane I'll often turn to a stranger and say, "Boy, I sure hope we don't crash into a cornfield today. If we *do* go down in flames, I hope we hit some houses. Or a school."

When are they gonna come up with some new Christmas carols?

You know you're getting old when you begin to leave the same smell in the bathroom your parents did.

Isn't it interesting that only sex and excretion can be found legally obscene in this country? Not violence, not neglect, not abuse of humans. Only shitting and fucking; two of nature's most necessary functions and irresistible forces. We're always trying to control and thwart nature, even in our language. Fuck that shit!

You show me something that doesn't cause cancer, and I'll show you something that isn't on the market yet.

Grown-ups have great power. They can order candy on credit over the telephone and have it delivered. Wow.

Heart disease changed my eating habits, but I still cook bacon just for the smell.

It has become very easy to buy a gun. It used to be, "I have a gun, give me some money." Now it's, "I have some money, give me a gun."

YOU ARE ALL DISEASED

If you ever meet twins, talk to just one of them. It drives the other one crazy.

to promote their hog-raising industry, each year the state of Iowa selects a young woman and names her Pork Queen. How would you like to tell the guys down at the gas station that your daughter is the Pork Queen?

What exactly is "viewer discretion"? If viewers had discretion, most television shows would not be on the air.

Someday I wanna see the Pope come out on that balcony and give the football scores.

A seven-day waiting period for purchasing a handgun is stupid. It just gives the buyer that much more time to think of people he'd like to kill. Now, instead of a single murder, you've got a multiple homicide on your hands.

Have you ever become suddenly, intensely aware of your legs?

OUR ONLY HOPE IS INSANE LEADERSHIP

Remember, inside every silver lining there's a dark cloud.

For the last twenty-five years I've done over one hundred shows a year, each one attended by about two thousand people. More than five million people in all. I often wonder if anyone was ever killed while driving to or from one of my shows. If so, I blame myself.

Where is this guy Christo when I need something wrapped at Christmas?

I'm not worried about guns in school. You know what I'm waitin' for? Guns in church! That's gonna be a lotta fun.

If you look around carefully the next time you go out, you'll notice that there are some really fucked-up-looking people walking around.

Dogs lead a nice life. You never see a dog with a wristwatch.

When you close your eyes and rub real hard, do you see that checker-board pattern?

If cockpit voice recorders are so indestructible, why don't they just build an airplane that's one big cockpit voice recorder?

GOOD NEWS: Ten golfers a year are hit by lightning.

n a trial, if they break for lunch during someone's testimony, they always remind him afterward that he's still under oath. That means that all during lunch he was sworn to tell the truth. So, if someone asks him, "How's the soup?" he better be goddamn sure he gives an honest answer. "How's the soup?" "Objection! Calls for a conclusion!"

I've been working on accepting my inner scumbag.

How do they get all those Down's syndrome kids to look the same?

Santa is satan spelled inside out.

Don't you lose faith in your dog's intelligence when he takes a piss and then steps in it?

There was no Big Bang. There was just a Big Hand Job.

At my supermarket, I get on a checkout line marked "no items," and pay for things other people forgot to buy.

My favorite country song is, "I Shoulda Fucked Old What's-Her-Name."

One consolation about memory loss in old age is that you also forget a lot of things you didn't intend to remember in the first place.

There's actually something called the Table Tennis Hall of Fame.

ometimes, during a big funeral that's being shown on TV, you'll see some really good-looking female mourners. But they never keep the cameras on them long enough to get a good careful look. And you can't see their eyes because a lot of times they're wearing sunglasses. It's frustrating. I happen to be particularly attracted to grief-stricken women.

THE DODGERS
EAT SHIT

What year in world history do you suppose the first person with really clean fingernails appeared?

What exactly is "midair"? Is there some other part of air besides the "mid" part?

Singing is basically a form of pleasant, controlled screaming.

The sound of one hand clapping is the same as the sound of a tree falling in the forest when no one is there to hear it.

What clinic did Betty Ford go to?

Wouldn't it be weird if the only way people could die was that their heads suddenly exploded without warning? If there was simply no other cause of death? One day you'd be sitting there having a hot chocolate, and suddenly your head would explode. You know something? I'll bet people would get used to it.

You know what they don't have? Cake-flavored pie.

I'd like to live in a country where the official motto was, "You never know." It would help me relax.

I can't wait until we get a really evil president. Not devious and cunning like Nixon and Johnson. But really, really evil. God, it would be so refreshing!

You know you're getting old when, after taking a leak, you shake your dick and dust comes out.

I avoid any restaurant that features Kaopectate on draft.

banks tell you to maintain a "minimum balance." I first learned about minimum balance from my uncle. He would come over to our house, drink a quart of wine, and try to stand up. That was minimum balance.

ANOTHER CRETIN FOR PEACE

Every now and then, on a certain days, in the late afternoon the air takes on a weird kind of purply, rose-colored light. What is that?

The neutron bomb is very Republican; it leaves property alone and concentrates on destroying large numbers of people indiscriminately.

being a comedian, I would love to see a production of *Hamlet* that included a drummer, so they could use rim shots to highlight the really good lines. "To be or not to be. That is the question." Ba-dum-bum!

I have no problem with the cigar smoking trend. If some guy wants to put a big, steaming turd in his mouth and suck on it, who am I to complain?

Why are we so surprised when terrorists manage to get a bomb on an airplane? Drug traffickers get things on airplanes all the time.

When you reach a certain age there comes a time when everyone you know is sick.

how can people take the Olympics seriously? Judges vote politically, athletes cheat on drugs, xenophobes run wild, and the whole thing is one big greed-driven logo competition.

Somehow, it's hard to picture butterflies fucking.

Do you know the nicest thing about looking at a picture of a 1950's baseball park? The only people wearing baseball caps are the players.

A deaf-mute carrying two large suitcases has rendered himself speechless.

It's way beyond ironic that a place called the Holy Land is the location of the fiercest, most deeply felt hatred in the world. And it makes for wonderful theater.

Whenever I see a picture of the General Assembly of the United Nations, I wonder how many of the delegates are whacked on drugs.

With all the cars, buses, trucks, airplanes, electric motors, gasoline engines, diesel engines, compressors, turbines, drills, fans, pumps, and generators running all the time, shouldn't the Earth now be making a loud humming sound as it moves around the sun?

The pores in a latex condom are one micron in size. The human immunodeficiency virus is one half micron. So, what's all this stuff about safe sex?

Mall walking. How perfect! Staying fit without having to take your eyes off the merchandise that got you out of shape in the first place.

I'm sixty, and I don't need child-resistant caps on my medicine bottles. They say, "Well, someone with children might come and visit you." Fuck 'em! They're on their own. Let 'em take their chances. Anyone who visits me is accepting a certain level of risk in the first place.

Can you imagine the increase in violence there would be if no one could lie? If we could all read each other's minds? Also, think of all the additional crying there would be.

A pager is an electronic leash, the better for your controllers to control you. One more sign that your life belongs to someone else.

Forty-five million people go to national parks each year. To get away from the other two hundred million.

Always do whatever's next.

That invisible hand of Adam Smith's seems to offer an extended middle finger to an awful lot of people.

If you want to know how fucked up the people in this country are, just look at television. Not the programs, not the news. The commercials. Just watch only the commercials for about a week, and you'll see how fucked up the people in this country really are.

theater and sports are similar, with minor differences: In theater, after rehearsing, the actors leave dressing rooms in costume to perform shows on stages in front of audiences. In sports, after practicing, the athletes leave locker rooms in uniform to play games on fields in front of spectators. And although it's true that both fields have agents, only the theater has makeup.

Sooner or later, your parents die.

Why do they put a suicide watch on certain death row prisoners? Why would you care if a man you're planning to kill kills himself? Does it spoil the fun? I also think about the death row prisoner in Texas who, on the day before his execution, managed to take a drug overdose. They rushed him to a hospital, saved his life, then brought him back to prison and killed him. Apparently, just to piss him off.

For many years, the Grand Ole Opry did not allow drums onstage.

ife has changed. The stores around the corner from my house used to be a grocer, butcher, laundry, tailor, barber shop, shoe repair, dry cleaner, and a beauty salon. Now it's a wig parlor, karate school, off-track betting, a software store, sushi, yogurt, video rentals, an adult bookstore, a T-shirt shop, a copying and printing center, a storefront law office, and a clothing store for fat women.

Sometimes, a city describes itself as a "Metroplex." This is one of those bull-shit word formations whereby a community tries to sound forward and pro-gressive, in spite of all the evidence to the contrary.

After every horror, we're told, "Now the healing can begin." No. There is no healing. Just a short pause before the next horror.

I think once people reach the age of forty they should be barred from using the words *girlfriend* or *boyfriend* in reference to someone they're fucking. It's creepy.

Attention, all camouflaged males: In the American Revolution, the militias broke and ran from battle. They ran home. Only the regular army stood fast.

RULES TO LIVE BY

Life is not as difficult as people think; all one needs is a good set of rules. Since it is probably too late for you, here are some guidelines to pass along to your children.

1. Relax and take it easy. Don't get caught up in hollow conceits such as "doing something with your life." Such twaddle is outmoded and a sure formula for disappointment.

2. Whatever it is you pursue, try to do it just well enough to remain in the middle third of the field. Keep your thoughts and ideas to yourself and don't ask questions. Remember, the squeaky wheel is the first one to be replaced.

3. Size people up quickly, and develop rigid attitudes based on your first impression. If you try to delve deeper and get to "know" people, you're asking for trouble.

4. Don't fall for that superstitious nonsense about treating people the way you would like to be treated. It is a transparently narcissistic approach, and may be the sign of a weak mind.

5. Spend as much time as you can pleasing and impressing others, even if it makes you unhappy. Pay special attention to shallow manipulators who can do you the most harm. Remember, in the overall scheme, you count for very little.

6. Surround yourself with inferiors and losers. Not only will you look good by comparison, but they will look up to you, and that will make you feel better.

7. Don't buy into the sentimental notion that everyone has short-comings; it's the surest way of undermining yourself. Remember, the really best people have no defects. If you're not perfect, something is wrong.

8. If by some off chance you do detect a few faults, first, accept the fact that you are probably deeply flawed. Then make a list of your faults and dwell on them. Carry the list around and try to think of things to add. Blame yourself for everything.

9. Beware of intuition and gut instincts, they are completely unreliable. Instead, develop preconceived notions and don't waver unless someone tells you to. Then change your mind and adopt their point of view. But only if they seem to know what they're talking about.

10. Never give up on an idea simply because it is bad and doesn't work. Cling to it even when it is hopeless. Anyone can cut and run, but it takes a very special person to stay with something that is stupid and harmful.

11. Always remember, today doesn't count. Trying to make something out of today only robs you of precious time that could be spent daydreaming or resting up.

12. Try to dwell on the past. Think of all the mistakes you've made, and how much better it would be if you hadn't made them. Think of what you should have done, and blame yourself for not doing so. And don't go easy. Be really hard on yourself.

13. If by chance you make a fresh mistake, especially a costly one, try to repeat it a few times so you become familiar with it and can do it easily in the future. Write it down. Put it with your list of faults.

14. Beware also of the dangerous trap of looking ahead; it will only get you in trouble. Instead, try to drift along from day to day in a meandering fashion. Don't get sidetracked with some foolish "plan."

15. Finally, enjoy yourself all the time, and do whatever you want. Don't be seduced by that mindless chatter going around about "responsibility." That's exactly the sort of thing that can ruin your life.

YOU KNOW?

When you're young, you don't know, but you don't know you don't know, so you take some chances. In your twenties and thirties you don't know, and you *know* you don't know, and that tends to freeze you; less risk taking. In your forties you *know*, but you don't know you know, so you may still be a little tentative. But then, as you pass fifty, if you've been paying attention, you know, and you know you know. Time for some fun.

HAVE A LITTLE FUN

Most people take life much too seriously and worry about all the wrong things: security, advancement, prosperity, all those things that give you heartburn. I think people would be better off if they relaxed and had a little more fun.

Think about it: We're all here on a big rock, zippin' around a bad star for no good reason. We don't know where we came from, we don't know where we're going, we don't know how long it's gonna last, and we keep having to go to the bathroom. And on top of that, the whole thing is completely meaningless.

Do you ever stop to think about that? It's all meaningless. All this detail. What's it for? This table. What's it doing here? What's the purpose? Who cares? I think the whole thing is someone's idea of a great big practical joke. So, relax that extra-tight American anal sphincter, folks, and have a little fun. Here are some suggestions:

In a public restroom, stand on the toilet and stare over the top of the partition at the man in the next stall. Tell him your therapist told you it's a good way of relaxing. Then lean out of the stall with your pants down, and ask someone if you can borrow a set of chopsticks and a nine-volt battery.

When you're out on the country-club dance floor with your wife, guide her over toward the orchestra and say to the conductor, "Tonight is our anniversary. Do you guys know 'Wong Has the Largest Tong in China'?"

Did you ever see these people who drive with their headlights on in the daytime, because they think it's safer? You know what would be fun? To smash head-on into a guy like that, just to show him that his idea doesn't work.

On the hotel "How-did-we-do?" form, write, "The maid offered to blow me for some candy," and "The room service waiter thrust his hand down my pants and manipulated my schwanz."

Here's some fun: At a taxi stand, give the first driver fifty dollars and tell him, "Go to the airport, and wait there for me." Then go to the second driver, give him fifty dollars and tell him, "Follow that cab, and under no circumstances allow it to get to the airport!" Then get in the third cab and tell the guy to follow the other two. When you're about halfway to the airport, take out a gun and start shooting at the first two cabs. Yell, "Hi-yo, Silver!" a lot.

Go into a store and tell the clerk you don't want to purchase anything. Then ask him if he'd be interested in buying sixty gallons of children's urine.

Next time you're on a plane, sit in the back row and place a boom box under your seat. Then, during takeoff, play high-pitched, metal-grinding noises on it, just loud enough to be heard over the engines. If possible, blend in the sound of a few small, muffled explosions. Keep saying, "Uh-oh!"

While seated at a nice dinner party, take a long look at the china service and say, "Hey, we had these same dishes in the army!"

Rush up to a hotel desk and mumble to the clerk, "Did the purple man with the dwarf in the cardboard box leave the Archbishop's phone number?" He will say, "What?" Repeat the sentence a little more loudly, but keep it hard to understand. Once again, a little annoyed, he will say, "What?" Keep this up until he reaches the breaking point and a small gathering of foam has appeared at the corner of his mouth. Then, when his supervisor comes over to inquire, tell her innocently, "I don't know what the problem is, ma'am. I simply asked this gentleman how late the restaurant is open, and he flew off the handle."

At a retail store, make a lot of large purchases hurriedly, and then, when signing the credit card slip, appear nervous and openly try to copy the signature that appears on your credit card. Then when the approval comes through, express visible relief. "Really? All right!!" Snicker a little, and mutter a barely audible, "Idiots."

HITCHHIKING FUN

There are some people who still hitchhike, although not as many as before. A lot of folks gave the practice up after being buried in shallow graves near the side of the road. But here's some fun you can have in case you still like to get out and hoist a thumb. Of course, you have to get a ride first. Someone has to stop.

When the guy says, "Where you going?" lean way into the car and bellow, "Turn this thing around, Zeke, I'm headin' back the other way!" Then make sure to step back quickly. No sense being dragged five hundred yards for the sake of a joke.

Or, when the guy stops, don't say anything; just jump in and sit down. When he says, "Where you going?" say, "I don't give a shit. Let's just ride around. I'm off till Thursday." Then make a lot of motor noises with your mouth.

Here's another good one: "Thanks for stopping. I don't actually need a ride today, but if you'd give me your phone number, I'd be glad to let you know when I *do*. It'll save you the trouble of driving all around looking for me." Once again, stepping back quickly might prevent a base case of gravel burn.

This one is my favorite. Guy stops, lowers the window and says, "Where you going?" You say, "Well . . . first we gotta go pick up my mother. Then we gotta go to the abortionist, the meth dealer, and the ammo shop. Then we gotta take her home. She lives in Indiana. By the way, do you know how to change a colostomy bag?"

So, have a little fun. Soon enough you'll be dead and burning in Hell with the rest of your family.

L'CHAIM!

If somehow you manage not to be canceled out by birth control pills, IUDs or condoms, and you are actually conceived; and then by some additional stroke of luck you are not aborted, miscarried, or given a birth defect by your mother's use of tobacco, alcohol, speed, heroin, or crack; and you are lucky enough to be born as a relatively normal child, then all you have to worry about is being beaten or sexually abused for your first 16 years. After that, you have a chance, at least a chance, of being chronically unemployed or killed in a war.

FIRST I WAS A KID

I'm sixty years of age. That's 16 Celsius. And I've never told you much about my childhood.

It seems I was unusual even before I was born. During pregnancy, my mother carried me very low. Indeed, for the last six weeks, my feet were sticking out. She was the only woman in the neighborhood who had maternity shoes. But she told me I was a big help when it came to climbing stairs.

I was a healthy baby, except for one ear that's folded and a little bent. The doctor said it happened because, apparently, at the precise moment I was being conceived, my mother and father fell off the hood of the car.

My parents chose what, at that time, was the very latest method of childbirth. You've heard of Lamaze? This was La Paz. The mother receives powerful narcotics, the father is sent to Bolivia, and the nurse does all the screaming.

As soon as I was born, I noticed that babies have it pretty easy: Wake up, cry, piss, roll over, drool, suck, eat, gag, belch, puke, giggle, crap, crawl, stand, fall, cry, scream, bleed, coo, sleep . . . and dream.

I went through the usual stages: imp, rascal, scalawag, whippersnapper. And, of course, after that it's just a small step to full-blown sociopath. I'm probably the only child who went directly from shenanigans to crimes against nature.

I was always a little different. Most kids had a dog named Spot. You know what I called my dog? Stain. Different. Instead of my thumb, I sucked my ring finger. And I had a strange ambition: I just wanted to live longer than Jesus. My mother said it was because I was sensitive, so she washed me in Woolite.

I was a hip kid. When I saw Bambi it was the midnight show. My cap gun had a silencer. My lemonade stand had dance hostesses. And one night at dinner, when I was about ten, I leaned over to my father and said, "Hey, man, when are we gonna load up on some of that breast milk again?" Still, I was practical. When one of my playmates died in an accident, I asked his mother if I could have his toys.

As a boy I was negatively affected by two things. First of all, I grew up on the side of a very steep hill. I think that can throw you off. Here's another thing: When you look at a map lying on a table, north is usually the direction pointing away from you. But my front door faced south, so you can see, as soon as I left my house, everything was backward. Things like that have an effect.

There's one other thing I should mention: You know how when you're real little your dad will throw you up in the air and catch you? Well, one day my dad threw me up in the air, and I went so high I could see the curvature of the earth. I believe I even caught a glimpse of Sri Lanka. At the time, of course, it was still called Ceylon. Dad and I had no idea its name would change someday. Anyway, after he threw me up in the air, he didn't wait around. He walked away. They said after that I was never really the same. They would whisper, "The boy is no longer playin' with a full bag of jacks!"

What happened was I became a loner; I just wanted to be by myself. I had an imaginary friend, but I didn't bother with him. Fuck 'im! Let him get his own friends. I got no time for people like that.

When you're a loner, of course, you have to make up your own games. Tag was difficult.

I used to play Cop. And instead of Hide and Seek, I would play a pathetic little game called Hide. One time I remained hidden for over a month before I realized that no one was looking for me. It was sad, really. But there are compensations. To this day, I remain unchallenged at Musical Chair.

My mother would say, "Why are you always playing alone?" And I would say, "I'm not playin', Ma. I'm fuckin' serious!" They first noticed I was strange when I insisted on listening to the circus on the radio. I guess I was a bad boy. Besides shitting in my pants, I would also shit in other people's pants.

Eventually, she sent me to a child psychologist. It was all the vogue at the time. So I went, and I honestly believe he was crazier than I was. I should've stabbed him many times in the eyes with a railroad spike when I still had the chance. I consider it a lost opportunity.

One problem was that my mother was very strict, and on top of that she was a physically imposing woman. Thinking back, the person she most reminds me of is Charles Kurault. I didn't really like her. I can remember staring at the orphanage and feeling envy.

Of course, it wasn't all bad; there are pleasant memories, too. Every Sunday after church, my mother and I would buy the Sunday papers and walk home together. Then she'd get drunk and try to make pancakes.

In a way, I take all the blame. I was hard to handle, and it wasn't easy on her. As I said, I'm sixty now, and she still isn't over her postpartum depression. And yet, she's a typical mom; she still tells me I'm going to be tall. And, you know something? Her wish is coming true. She's getting smaller. Soon I will be, too.

I guess the thing I miss most about childhood is riding piggyback, and here's something I don't tell too many people: I still like to ride piggyback occasionally. I really do. And I don't mean across the room. I'm talking about long trips. I went to Florida last winter. Piggyback. Fortunately, I have very indulgent friends. And I pay top dollar.

SCHOOL DAYS

As far as school was concerned, I did pretty well, if you don't count learning. My problem was, during the summer I would forget everything they had taught the year before. So, basically, when September rolled around, I was back to square one. The teachers told me, "You have an excellent mind. It just isn't readily apparent to an outside observer."

One of my problems was lying. I always got caught, because I told big lies. One morning, late for school, I told the teacher I'd had to iron my own shirt, because my parents had been strangled by a telephone lineman.

Actually, I was much too logical for school. For instance, after about a month in first grade, the teacher asked me something, and I said, "Why are you asking *me* these questions? I came here to learn from you."

They would try to keep me after school, but I knew my rights. Once again, logic: I told them, "When school is out, and the students have all gone home, this building is technically no longer a school. It becomes just another building, and you have no right to keep me in it." Staying after school wasn't actually all that bad. At least there wasn't any learning going on.

But it wasn't easy to learn in my school even during normal hours. Because we were a poor area, the school had a small budget and was unable to teach the second half of the alphabet. And so, to me, anything past the letter *m* is still pretty much a mystery. The Renaissance, the Reformation, Reconstruction. When these topics come up, I have no idea what people are talking about.

And so, I volunteered for being silly. I did so as soon as I discovered it was an option. One day, the teacher interrupted something I was doing and said, "Mister Carlin, you can either take responsibility and learn this material, or you can continue to act silly." Well, that was all I needed to hear.

It turned out I was pretty good in science. But again, because of the small budget, in science class we couldn't afford to do experiments in order to prove theories. We just believed everything. Actually, I think that class was called Religion. Religion was always an easy class. All you had to do was suspend the logic and reasoning you were being taught in all the other classes.

SPORTS, FIGHTING, AND GIRLS

I did better in sports, and was successful even before I entered school: As an infant, a particularly brutal uncle taught me full-contact pat-a-cake. I found it painful, but quite exhilarating. Later, in grammar school, I played intramural Simon Says and took several bronze medals in high-speed competition skipping.

I played basketball for three years, and when I left school, they retired my jersey. Primarily for reasons of hygiene. I wasn't a real stand-out at basketball, but I'm convinced that if I had been a lot taller, a lot faster, and had really good aim, I would have been a better player.

I wasn't much of a fighter, either. If a tough kid challenged me to a fight, I would make an excuse: "I'm not allowed to fight in this suit." Most of the time they would simply steal the suit. Which was fine with me, as I found I could run much faster in my underwear. I didn't have much of a "rep." They would say of me, "He can't dish it out, and he can't take it either."

The one time I did box, at camp, I fought as a walterweight: It turned out I was the exact same weight as my friend Walter. I lost my only bout. But I realize now it's probably just as well God didn't make me a good fighter, or else there'd have been a long trail of dead men across America.

Don't forget, I came from a pretty tough neighborhood. Not the toughest, maybe, but still fairly tough. You've heard of Hell's Kitchen? This was Hell's Dining Room. And we didn't live far from something really unusual, a tough rich neighborhood: Hell's Servants' Quarters.

We had some pretty tough characters. In fact, if Charles Bronson had lived in my neighborhood, he would've been a Playboy bunny. On Halloween, we would dress up funny and kill a person. And we always did things differently: Once a week, a bunch of us liked to get drunk and beat up heterosexuals. And although I broke a lot of laws as a teenager, I straightened out immediately upon turning eighteen, when I realized the state had a legal right to execute me.

It may surprise you that I wasn't very good with girls. Too smart. When I would play doctor, and "examine" a girl, I would often find an aneurysm. One time, in the midst of a particularly erotic physical exam, I discovered advanced hypertrophic cardiomyopathy. I continued to feel the girl up, of course, and only later, after reaching a private climax in my pants, did I inform her of my diagnosis. First things first. I can't tell you how many women over the years have written to thank me for finding a lump in their breasts.

My first girlfriend, however, was afraid of sex. Apparently, one night before falling asleep, she had been fondled by the sandman. As a result, she suffered recurring wet nightmares. I could sympathize with her, of course, as for years I had been the victim of wet daydreams. I realize now it was probably just as well God didn't make me a great lover, or else there'd have been a long trail of pregnant women all across America.

It was my uncle who taught me about the birds and the bees. He sat me down one day and said, "Remember this, George, the birds fuck the bees." Then he told me he once banged a girl so hard her freckles came off.

DR. BEN DOVER

Sooner or later, the young medical student has to tell his blue-collar father that he wants to be a proctologist:

"Wait a minute, Vinny, lemme get this straight. I busted my nuts for twenty years tryin' to save enough money to put you through college and now you tell me you want to stick your finger up a guy's ass?"

"Not finger, Dad. Hand!"

"Jesus!"

FUZZ BUSTER

Microwave radiation leaking from radar guns has caused at least eighty cases of testicular cancer in policemen. I'm glad. That's what they get for being sneaky. Cancer and radar both victimize silently; they sneak up on you. You think everything's OK, but unknown to you, something bad is happening. Then suddenly you're a victim. Also, it's quite appropriate that it's testicular cancer. These cops all think they have big balls. Now they do. Good.

LIGHTEN UP A LITTLE

Riot police sometimes use rubber bullets. Imagine! Someone, somewhere, had a lucid thought. And I think they might have provided a small opening here. This idea could be extended to larger weapons. Rubber bullets, naugahyde hand grenades, crushed velvet land mines, silk torpedoes, Nerf tanks, whiffle missiles. How about a neutron bomb made of fake fur?

They also have water cannons. Why not go further? How about cannons that shoot ginger ale? Skim milk? Orange juice from concentrate? And what unruly mob could possibly defy a police force armed with a vegetable soup cannon? Chunky style, of course.

And it's always struck me that our two most-used gasses produce only tears and laughter. How about a gas that creates crippling self-doubt? Or a gas that conjures up terrifying childhood memories? Okay, last one: How about a gas that fills you with an unquenchable desire for vanilla pudding?

BAG A BOOMER

I only hope that when the Generation Xers are finally running things, they'll have the courage to kill all these baby boomers, one by one, in their hospital beds and their nursing homes. Kill them and loot their pensions and estates, and throw them out into the streets with nothing. If they don't, the boomers will take everything they can and keep it for themselves. They're trying now to arrange for the next two generations to pay their debts, having already put young people deeply in hock. Boomers are living off their grandchildren's money and will try to steal everything else before they're gone.

If you young people want to know who to kill, I'll tell you. There are two schools of thought on this: Some say the baby boomers were born between 1946 and 1964. Others will tell you 1942 through 1960. Just to be on the safe side, I'd say kill everyone between the ages of thirty and fifty-five. The boomers used to say, "Don't trust anyone over thirty." Well, the stakes are a little higher now. So ask to see a driver's license and then strangle a boomer. That's my advice. I always like to have something uplifting to offer along with all the gloomy shit.

YOU GET NO CREDIT HERE

People should not get credit for having qualities they're supposed to have. Like honesty. What's the big deal anyway? You're *supposed* to be honest. It's not a skill.

Besides, people shouldn't get credit for skills in the first place. Do you think you should be praised for something you had no control over? I mean, if you were born with certain abilities and characteristics—things that are an essential part of your makeup—I don't see that you should be taking bows, do you? You couldn't help it; it was genetically encoded. No one deserves credit for being tall.

People say, "Well, talent can only get you so far. It still takes a lot of hard work." Yeah? Well, hard work is genetically encoded, too. Some people can't help working hard; it's enjoyable to them. They can no more remain idle than change the color of their eyes. People who work hard and display great talent do not deserve special praise. Quite often the credit should go to their grandparents. Or perhaps their grandparents' milkman.

Also, I don't understand why people who recover from illness or injury are considered courageous. Getting well should not be cause for praise. Just because someone is no longer sick doesn't mean they did something special. Getting well is a combination of seeking help, following advice, having a good attitude, and being the possessor of an effective immune system. All of these qualities stem from inborn genetic traits and characteristics. No one makes a conscious choice to be courageous. It's genetically encoded.

Believe me, when the only alternative is lying in a puddle of your own shit, it doesn't take much courage to get up and go to physical therapy. Courage comes into play when people have options, not when they're backed against a wall. It didn't take courage for Magic Johnson to announce he was HIV positive. He had no choice. Sooner or later people were going to find out. It was a matter of public relations, not courage.

And another type of courage, "bravery in battle," is to me even more suspect. Not only are there inherited genetic traits at work, there are also heavy doses of adrenaline and testosterone contributing to the situation, and those two hormones are affected and controlled by genes too. There are not really any heroes—there are only genetic freaks.

So relax, folks. The pressure's off. Everything's encoded. You heard it here.

BUNGEE THIS!

Remember the guy who paid one hundred dollars at a Michigan fair to try the bungee jump? And the cord broke, and he fell? The guy wanted his hundred dollars back. Is he kidding? I'd say, "Fuck you! You owe an extra hundred!" A hundred for goin' down, and a hundred for goin' down the rest of the way. Shit, he got twice the excitement, he oughta pay twice the price.

And they said he glanced off the side of the "air mattress." Air mattress? What kinda fuckin' bungee jump is that? Jagged rocks! That's what they oughta have at the bottom. If there's no risk, why bother? Fuckin' air mattress. My pulse wouldn't even change. If these guys are thrill seekers, let 'em seek a real thrill: I think every third bungee cord should be defective.

CHOW TIME ON DEATH ROW

Suppose you're on death row, and they tell you you can have one last meal. And it's an honorable thing, they take pride in it and they really try to live up to it. But you can't make up your mind. You have most of the meal figured out except you can't decide between steak and lobster. You honestly can't decide. Can they kill you? If you really can't decide? Truth serum, lie detector, psychologists; it becomes a big media thing: "MAN TELLING THE TRUTH. CAN'T REALLY DECIDE." Can they kill you? Can they honestly drag you down the last mile screaming, "Turf, surf, who knows?" But then, finally. Finally, after eighteen months of indecision, you say, "OK! I got it! Gimme the steak!" And everybody goes, "Ohh, cool, wow, he wants the steak." Then the warden says to you. "How would you like that steak done?" And you say, "Oh, Jeez . . . I have no idea. Can I get back to you on that?"

NUMBER FUN

If a picture is worth ten thousand words,* then one twenty-five-hundredth of a picture should be worth four words.

And if Helen of Troy had the face that launched a thousand ships, and a picture is worth ten thousand words, doesn't that mean one picture of Helen's face should be worth ten million ships?

And, if the night has a thousand eyes, and getting there is half the fun, that means to have fun getting there at night would require five hundred eyes.

And, if getting there is half the fun, and half a loaf is better than none, would getting halfway there with a whole loaf be more or less fun?

And if half a loaf is better than none, the night has a thousand eyes, a picture is worth ten thousand words, getting there is half the fun, and Helen of Troy had the face that launched a thousand ships,

*The actual proverb is "One picture is worth ten thousand words." —Confucius

then in a picture taken at night from a ship that is halfway there, how much fun would Helen be having if she were holding a full loaf? And could you see it in her eyes?

OK, now suppose Helen of Troy lived in a halfway house. . . .

SOMETHING'S MISSING

Why are there no B batteries? There aren't even any A batteries. In fact, it's almost as if they went out of their way to avoid A. They went straight to AA and AAA. Also, I never see any grade B milk, or type III audio cassettes. And there are no vitamins F, G, H, I, and J. Why? Why are certain airline seat numbers missing, and what ever became of the Boeing 717? And Chanel #4? Also, all I ever hear about are the Sixth and Seventh Fleets. Where are the other five? And why are there hardly any brown running shoes? Or green flowers? I dare not even mention blue food.

SCIENCE FRICTION

I'm gettin' sick of "scientific progress." Scientists are easily the least responsible class in society. If you're one of those "green" ass-holes who run around worrying about the condition of the planet all the time, you might as well just go ahead and blame it all on the scientists. They're the ones who fouled the nest. Without them, none of the bad shit gets done. Self-important, asshole scientists, most of them working for the Pentagon or big business, creating harmful products we don't need. They don't care what they produce as long as they get to publish their fuckin' papers.

And the idealistic ones? The ones who won't have anything to do with the weapons makers and greed-heads? The ones involved in "pure research"? They lay the groundwork for the truly dangerous scientists who move in later and apply the knowledge commercially. Scientists have consistently assaulted and violated your planet. That's why you have AIDS, that's why you have a hole in your ozone layer, that's why your atmosphere is overheating, that's why you have toxic and nuclear waste, and that's why everything has a thin coating of oil on it. And next, they're going to turn these irresponsible motherfuckers loose on human genetic engineering. That ought to be a real treat. Scientists. The only ones worth a fuck are theoretical physicists. At least they're nuts.

ANIMAL INSTINCTS

At the start, let me say I am not an animal rights activist. I'm not comfortable with absolutes.

And I know that every time something eats, something else dies. I recognize the Earth is little more than a revolving buffet with weather. So, the idea of eating animals is fine with me, but is it really necessary to make things out of the parts we don't eat? We're the only species that does this. You never see a mongoose with snakeskin shoes. Or a lion walkin' around in a wildebeest hat. And how often do you run into plankton that have phytoplankton luggage?

And I think people have a lot of nerve locking up a tiger and charging four dollars to let a few thousand worthless humans shuffle past him every day. What a shitty thing to do. Humans must easily be the meanest species on Earth. Probably the only reason there are any tigers left is because they don't taste good.

I respect animals. I have more sympathy for an injured or dead animal than I have for an injured or dead human being, because human beings participate and cooperate in their own undoing. Animals are completely innocent. There are no innocent human beings.

Here is an anecdote from the writer Patricia Highsmith: "Not so long ago I said to a friend of mine: 'If I saw a kitten and a little human baby sitting on the curb starving, I would feed the kitten first if nobody was looking.' My friend said: 'I would feed the kitten first if somebody *was* looking.'" I would too, Patricia.

Some people seem shocked and say, "You care more about animals than you do about humans!" Fuckin'-A well told!

I do not torture animals, and I do not support the torture of animals, such as that which goes on at rodeos: cowardly men in big hats abusing simple beasts in a fruitless search for manhood. In fact, I regularly pray for serious, life-threatening rodeo injuries. I wish for a cowboy to walk crooked, and with great pain, for the rest of his life.

I cheer when a bull at Pamplona sinks one of his horns deep into the lower intestines of some drunken European macho swine. And my cheers grow louder when the victim is a young American macho-jock tourist asshole. Especially if the bull is able to swing that second horn around and catch the guy right in the nuts.

But although I don't go out of my way to bother living things, I am not without personal standards. A mosquito on my arm, an ant or a cockroach in my kitchen, a moth approaching my lapel; these animals will die. Other insects in my home, however, the ones who merely wish to rest awhile, will be left alone. Or, if noisy and rowdy, lifted gently and returned to the great outdoors.

I am also perfectly willing to share the room with a fly, as long as he is patrolling that portion of the room that I don't occupy. But if he starts that smart-ass fly shit, buzzing my head and repeatedly landing on my arm, he is engaging in high-risk behavior. That's when I roll up the sports section and become Bwana, the great white fly hunter!

Sometimes there's an older fly in the room, one who flies slowly and can't travel too far in one hop–or it might be a female, heavy with eggs. In this case, even if the fly is bothering me, I don't kill it; instead, I adopt it as a short-term pet. I might even give it a name. Probably something based on mythology.

Generally, I like flies, but they'd be far more welcome if they would make a choice—and stick to it—between my bean burrito and that nice, hot, steaming dog turd out in the front yard.

Also, in keeping with my insect death policy based on the intentions of the insect, any bacterium or virus entering my body that does not wish me well will be slain. Normally, my immune system would accomplish this without notifying me, but if the old T-cells aren't up to the task, I am prepared to ingest huge amounts of antibiotics, even if they are bad for me.

And yet, in spite of all these examples of creature mayhem, I will not strike a dog, I will not chase and taunt a bull around a ring, and I will not squeeze an animal's testicles just to give the yokels a better show.

I'm also uneasy about the sheer number of scientific experiments performed on animals. First of all, animals are not always good models for medical experimentation: penicillin kills guinea pigs; an owl is not bothered by cyanide; monkeys can survive strychnine, etc., etc. Couldn't these scientific tests just as easily be performed on humans? Condemned prisoners, old people, the feeble, the terminally ill? I'm sure there are plenty of ignorant, desperate Americans who would be willing to volunteer in exchange for some small electrical appliance.

What makes me happy in the midst of all this is that ultimately animals get even. The major killers of humanity throughout recent history—smallpox, influenza, tuberculosis, malaria, bubonic plague, measles, cholera, and AIDS—are all infectious diseases that arose from diseases of animals. I pray that mad cow disease will come to this country and completely wipe out the hamburger criminals. Eating meat is one thing, but this whole beef-rancher-manure-cattle-hamburger side show is a different skillet of shit altogether.

Each year, Americans eat 38 billion hamburgers. It takes 2,500 gallons of water to produce one pound of red meat. Cattle consume one half of all the fresh water consumed on earth. The sixty million people who will starve this year could be adequately fed if Americans reduced their meat intake by just 10 percent. But if I were one of those sixty million people, I wouldn't be reachin' for the salt and pepper too quickly. It ain't gonna happen.

Ranchers raise pathetic, worthless cattle and sheep, animals who cannot live off the land without human supervision, and the same ranchers kill wolves, magnificent, individualistic animals fully capable of caring for themselves without assistance. Individualism gives way to sheep behavior. Sound familiar?

I root for a wolf to someday grab a rancher's kid. Yes I do. And you know something? The wolf would probably take the kid home and raise him, in the manner of Romulus and Remus; and probably do a better job than the rancher. Remember, wolves mate for life, and they care for their sick and infirm; they don't run them off, or kill them, or abandon them. Give me a wolf over some fuckin' jerkoff rancher any day of the week.

One last item to demonstrate the depth of human perversity: Some zoos now sell surplus animals to private hunting ranches where rich white men hunt them down and kill them for amusement.

No wonder they call it the *descent* of man.

GOOD DOGGIE

When your dogs lick a visitor and they say, "Oh, he's very affectionate," ask them, "Did you notice what he was doing prior to coming over and licking your face?" "No. Well, yes! I think he was cleaning himself. He's a very clean dog." "Well, his balls and asshole are very clean. In fact, he has a perfectly clean five-inch circle around his balls and asshole. His tongue, lips, and nose, however, are filthy with old dog shit and fermented ball sweat. Why do you think we taught him to shake hands?"

MOTHS AND LIGHTS

I don't like moths, because I can't predict their flight patterns. They don't seem to know where they're going. I don't like that.

And they're always hanging around light bulbs. Somehow they're even able to get inside the sealed light fixture between the bulb and the outer glass. How do they do that? One day you can clean out a hundred old, dead moths and then put the clean globe back on, and a month later there'll be another twenty or thirty full-grown dead moths inside the globe. How do they get in there?

And what is that attraction to light all about, anyway? You know what I think they're doing? Trying to read the writing on the light bulb. It's hard to read, isn't it? The writing on a light bulb is placed right where you can't read it when the light is on, because the light is too bright. And then, when the light is off, you can't read it, because there's not enough light. No wonder moths are so fucked up.

THE GEORGE CARLIN BOOK CLUB—
"We've Got Books Out the Ass"
Offer #3: General Interest Titles

〔 〕 *Twelve Things Nobody Cares About*

〔 〕 *The Picture Book of Permanent Stains*

〔 〕 *Firecracker in a Cat's Asshole: A Novel*

〔 〕 *The Complete List of Everyone Who Enjoys Coffee*

〔 〕 *The Official British Empire Registry of Blokes*

〔 〕 *Ten Places No One Can Find*

〔 〕 *Tits on the Moon* (science fiction)

〔 〕 *Why Norway and Hawaii Are Not Near Each Other*

✖ *The History of Envy*

✖ *The Pus Almanac*

〔 〕 *One Hundred People Who Are Only Fooling Themselves*

〔 〕 *Diary of a Real Evil Prick*

〔 〕 *Carousel Maintenance*

〔 〕 *Why It Doesn't Snow Anymore*

〔 〕 *The Dingleberry Papers*

✖ *A Treasury of Poorly Understood Ideas*

✖ *Why Jews Point*

✖ *The Golden Age of Tongue Kissing*

✖ *Famous Bullshit Stories of the Aztecs*

✖ *The Meaning of Corn*

✖ *Feel This: A Braille Sex Manual*

✖ *A Complete List of Everything That Is Still Pending*

✖ *Really Loud Singalongs for the Hard of Hearing*

GET A LIFE

One morning I get up, get out of bed, get showered, get some breakfast, and get to thinkin', "I'm not gettin' any." I get the urge to get some nookie, and get an idea. So I get dressed, get in my car, and get on the freeway.

When I get downtown, I get a few beers, get a buzz, and get lucky. I get a glimpse of a fine-looking woman. I get her a drink, get her talking, and we get acquainted. So I get up my courage and get her to agree to go get a room.

We get outta there, get some booze, get in a taxi, and get a hotel.

We get in the room, and get comfortable, and I'm gettin' excited 'cause I'm gonna get in her pants. So we get undressed, get in bed, and get started. And I'm gettin' hot 'cause she's gettin' horny. She wants to get down, and I wanna get my rocks off. I wanna get it up, get in, get it on, get off, and get out.

And it starts gettin' real good. But then I get thinking, "Suppose I get the clap? If I get the clap, I'll have to get shots. Might get worse. Could get AIDS. Shoulda got rubbers."

Now I get paranoid. Get a bit crazy. Get a bit scared.

Gotta get a grip.

Then it gets worse. Suppose she gets pregnant? Will she get an abortion? She might wanna get married. I can't get involved. If I gotta get married, I gotta get her a ring. How do I get it? I'd have to get credit. Or get hold of some money!

That means gettin' a job. Or gettin' a gun. And a getaway car. But suppose I get caught? Get busted by cops. Get thrown in the jail! Gotta get help. Get a good lawyer. Get out on bail.

No. I gotta get serious. Get it together. Get with the program. Get me a break, get me a job. Get a promotion, get a nice raise, get a new house, and get some respect. But if I get all of that, I can't get real cocky. Might get someone mad who'd get on my case, get me in trouble, and then I'd get fired.

Then I'd get mad, maybe get violent, get kicked outta work. Then get discouraged, start to get desperate, get hold of some drugs, get loaded, get hooked, and get sick. Get behind in my rent, get evicted, get thrown on the street.

Maybe get mugged, get beaten, get injured, get hospitalized, get operated on, get a blood clot, get a heart attack, get the last rites, get a stroke, get a flat line, get a trip to the graveyard, and get buried in a field.

So get this. You gotta get smart, and you gotta get real. Get serious. Get home, get undressed, get in bed, get some sleep. Or you might just get fucked. Get me?

A FEW RANDOM SEXUAL EJACULATIONS

In spite of all the wonderfully entertaining sex crimes we enjoy in this country, Americans are still a prudish lot. So now we've decided to use the word *gender* when referring to a person's sex. Gender has been borrowed from linguistics, and will soon include other meanings: "I think he's perverted, Stan. He told me he had gender with a woodchuck." "He's as ugly as shit, Gloria, but the gender is strangely dark and quite intense." "Pull up your pants, Russell. I told you, anal gender is high-risk fun!" And, of course, that once-exciting 1960s tripod of sex, drugs, and rock 'n' roll has been completely euphemized. Now it's, "gender, controlled substances, and alternative rock."

If a movie is "R-rated," it means that if you're under seventeen, you have to see it with an adult:

"What's he doing, Dad?"

"He's fucking her, son."

SEX QUIZ FOR MEN:

1. Have you ever been walking on the street toward three great-looking women who all have fabulous tits, and you don't know which set of tits to stare at? And you only have a few seconds to decide? Thank God you can at least study their asses while they're walking away.

2. Did you ever see a really attractive mannequin in a department store, and you think maybe you'd like to fuck her? But you know you can't, so you try to sneak a quick look at her crotch? And you don't worry about anyone seeing you, because they would never believe what you're thinking? Remember, ladies, the thought most often coursing through a man's mind is, "Boy, I'd sure like to fuck that."

3. Have you ever been talking to a married couple you just met, and the woman has really great tits? And you're dying to get a really long look at them, but you can't even take a quick glance, because her husband is staring right at you? Then, when he finally looks away for an instant, do you immediately look straight at her tits, regardless of whether or not it makes her uncomfortable?

News note: On TV recently, a guy was complaining that he was sexually "abused" by a female teacher when he was a boy. He said she touched him and made him touch her in their private parts. Yeah? So? Where's the abuse? Maybe I'm twisted or something, but as a child, I would've been willing to kill for this kind of special attention. I'd have had my hand in the air all day long, "Teacher! I need some more of that special help!" It would have really lent a stimulating new perspective to the idea of staying after school.

I'm glad I don't have any weird sexual fetishes. It's hard enough just getting laid, can you imagine cruising the bars searching for a submissive, albino rubber freak who wants you to throw canteloupes at his ass and shit on his chest?

I will, however, admit to being fascinated by a strange new perversion I've heard of. It's called S & W. Apparently just as you're about to come, your partner vomits root beer on you.

Actually, truth be known, my sexual fantasies are fairly prosaic: a woman takes off her dress, I fuck her, I drive home. Simple, neat, very little down side.

MARRY AN ORPHAN

Men, take my advice, marry an orphan. It's great. First of all, there are never any in-law problems. Second, there are no annoying Thanksgiving and Christmas visits sitting around pretending to enjoy the company of a couple of fifth-generation nitwits. In fact, when it comes to visiting her folks, the worst thing that might happen to you would be an occasional trip to the cemetery to leave some cheap flowers. And you might even get out of that by claiming a morbid fear of headstones.

But most important, as the relationship is just beginning, you won't have to worry about making a good impression on the girl's parents, nor will you have to get her father's approval. Believe me when I tell you, when you say, "I hope your father will approve of me," there is no greater thrill than having your beloved turn to you brightly and say, "My father's dead."

HAPPY NEW YEAR

How late in the new year can you say "Happy New Year" and not be considered weird? Actually, the whole thing starts on December 26. If on that day you think you're not going to see someone again until after New Year's, you wish them, "Happy New Year." And it's generally all right to say "Happy New Year" right on up through New Year's day. But after that, it begins to change a little. On January third or fourth, for instance, it still may be acceptable, but only if you haven't seen the person since the First. And then even as late as the sixth or seventh of January, you can still get away with it if you haven't seen the person for a really long time, say since Christmas. But once it starts gettin' into early April, if you're still running around telling people, "Happy New Year," you are simply begging to be fitted for one of those garments where the sleeves tie in the back. You are gonna wind up saying "Happy New Year" through that little food slot in the door. And no one, including you, will care what day it is. Or year, for that matter.

RHYMES YOU JUST DON'T HEAR IN SONGS ANYMORE

Easter/kiester

humor/tumor

Tonto/Toronto

surgery/perjury

manhandle/panhandle

nudist/Buddhist

postcard/Coast Guard

creditor/predator

pickup/hiccup

mobster/lobster

doormat/floormat

Eugene's/blue jeans

decaffeinated/decapitated

LOVE ME, LOVE MY SONG

There are entirely too many love songs. I know. Society probably demands a certain number of them, but, goddamn, is this the only thing people can sing about? As far as I'm concerned, the love song category is filled. Let's move on. There must be some other topics. Everything's a broken heart. "Broken heart. Broken heart." What about a broken rib cage? Hah? How would you like that? Or a ruptured spleen? You never hear a song about that. Wouldn't you like to see some nice tall woman with long hair and big tits up there beltin' out a song about a ruptured spleen? Or how about a nice song about a fire in a hotel? Or a guy who gets his legs caught in a threshing machine? How about someone who goes up into a hayloft and finds sixty dead Shriners? It seems to me we're passing up a lot of subjects that would make really good songs.

WHO'S TEACHING WHOM

What exactly is a "student teacher"? As I understand it, a student teacher is a person of student age who is far enough along in his education to be doing some teaching. But a "student teacher" could also be someone who simply teaches students, a *student* teacher. Which is what all teachers are.

Or a student teacher might be a student studying to become a teacher. Not yet a teacher, still a "student teacher." Such a student, studying to be a teacher, could also be called a "teaching student," which is, after all, what our original "student teacher" was: a teaching student.

Sometimes teachers, later in their careers, go back to school for further education, and once again they become students, while still remaining teachers. Well, if a younger student who is doing some teaching is a "student teacher," then wouldn't an older teacher who goes back to school logically be a "teacher student"? Or I guess you could call her a "student teacher," couldn't you? So far, that's three different kinds of student teachers.

Now, these teachers who go back to school obviously have to be taught by "teacher teachers." And if one of these teacher teachers were also taking a few courses on the side, that would make her a "student teacher teacher." And if she were just beginning that process, just learning to be a "student teacher teacher" wouldn't that make her a "student teacher teacher student"? I think it would.

CHANGING THE SUBJECTS

Talk about wrong priorities. We live in a country that has a National Spelling Bee. We actually give prizes for spelling! But when's the last time you heard about a thinking bee? Or a reasoning bee? Maybe an ethics bee? Never. Did you know the only people in our culture who are taught ethics are a handful of college students? Then they graduate and go to work for large corporations. So much for ethics training. Ethics and values should be taught early in grade school, not in college when the child has already been spiritually warped and perverted by his parents, friends, religion, and television set.

And while we're at it, why don't we teach courses in how to be responsible, or how to be married, or how to be a good parent, or, at the very least, how to be a reasonably honorable human being? Unfortunately, such courses will never be taught, because the information gleaned would have no application in real life.

"KIDS TODAY!"

I know this sounds like old-fart talk, but I think today's kids are too soft. They have to wear plastic helmets for every outdoor activity but jacking off. Toy safety, car seats, fire-resistant pajamas. Shit! Soft, baby boomer parents, with their cult of the child, are raising a crop of soft, fruity kids.

Here's another example of how adults are training children to be weak. Did you ever notice that every time some guy with an AK-47 shows up in a schoolyard and kills three or four students and a couple of teachers, the next day the school is overrun with psychologists, psychiatrists, grief counselors, and trauma therapists trying to help the children cope? Shit! When I was a kid, if somebody came to our school and killed three or four of us, we went right on with our work. We finished the arithmetic. "Thirty-five classmates, minus four equals thirty-one!" We were tough! I say if a kid can handle the violence in his home, he oughta be able to handle the violence in school.

What bothers me is all this mindless, middlebrow bullshit about children being "our future." So, what's new? Children have always, technically, represented our future. But what does that mean? What is so important about knowing that children are our future? Life as it is right now—today's reality in this country—the people lying on the streets and park benches, living in the dysfunctional homes, the prisons, and the mental institutions, the addicts and drunks and neurotic shoppers, these people were all once children described as "our future." So, this is it, folks. This is what the system produces. The adults you see today are what kids become. Is anything really going to make it any different? To me, they're just another crop of kids waiting to become wage slaves and good little consumers. You know what I see when I look at today's kids? Tomorrow's fucked-up adults.

PARENTAL GUIDANCE

What is all this nonsense about parental guidance, parental control, and parental advisories? The whole reason people in this country are as fucked up as they are and make such ignorant decisions on public policy; is that they listened too closely to their parents in the first place. This is an authoritarian country with too many laws, rules, controls, and restrictions. "Do this! Don't do that! Shut up! Sit still! No talking! Stand up straight!" No wonder kids are so fucked up; traditional authoritarian values. It starts in kindergarten: They give you a coloring book and some crayons, and tell you, "Be creative . . . but don't go outside the lines." Fuck parents!

VOLVO WISDOM

One of the more embarrassing strains of American thought is the liberal-humanist, touchy-feely, warm and fuzzy, New Age, environmental-friendly pseudo-wisdom that appears on bumper stickers: "Have you hugged your kid today?" "Think Globally, Act Locally," and most embarrassing, "Practice Random Kindness and Senseless Acts of Beauty." Isn't that precious? You know, if kindness and beauty require public reminders, maybe it's time we just throw in the jock. Here's another middlebrow abomination: "Our son is an honor student at Franklin School." I'm waiting for a bumper sticker that says, "We have a son in public school who hasn't been shot yet. And he sells drugs to your fuckin' honor student." Or, let's get real: "Our son was a teen suicide because of unrealistic expectations by his father." I think it's time we abandon sentimental, emotional kitsch as a prime means of public expression.

THINGS GO BETTER

I can identify my periods of heavy cocaine use by the years in which I have no idea who was in the World Series or the Superbowl. Bliss.

I remember one Saturday morning when I know I must have been high, because I found myself profoundly moved by Elmer Fudd and Petunia Pig who were appearing in something I took to be a drama.

There was another time when my right nostril was all plugged up, so I spent a whole night snorting in just my left nostril. The weird part is that only my left eye was dilated.

Late one evening, after scraping all the white powder and dust off my dresser top and making two lines out of it, I realized I was actually snorting some Desenex and my own dandruff.

Sometimes I'd get so wired I would do anything to come down a little. You ever chugalug a magnum of children's Tylenol?

Eventually, alas, I realized the main purpose of buying cocaine is to run out of it.

But long after I gave it up I was still self-conscious when I blew my nose in front of other people. And if I had to leave a group of people to go to the bathroom more than once, I was sure everyone thought I was going to do some blow. I used to say, "No, really! I have diarrhea! C'mon! I'll show you."

WE DON'T FEEL GOOD

I've always believed people get the diseases they ask for and deserve. The same is true of countries.

America. Chronic fatigue and anorexia. This is what we've become. "I'm tired!" and, "I don't wanna eat!" How plain. How pathetic. Years ago, a nice, horrifying, fatal consumptive disease would come along and completely eat your fuckin' organs away. Now it's, "I'm tired" and "I don't wanna eat." Christ!

Here's another one: "I'm depressed." Well, shit, look around! Of course you're depressed; you live in a neon sewer. You've earned it. There are supposed to be eleven million clinically depressed Americans. And those are just the ones they know about. I'm sure there are millions more nodding off in closets and attics all across the country. You wanna know why? Because it's one big fuckin' garbage can. At least those people with agoraphobia have found a good solution: "I'm not going out. I don't like it outside."

You say there's rampant cancer? How appropriate. We worship growth; everyone wants growth. Well, we got it. Exuberant cell growth. Lots of big cancers, lots of different kinds and plenty of 'em to go around. All part of who we are. Breast cancer? Who has a more distorted titty hang-up? Epidemic prostate cancer in a nation brimming with assholes? How unusual. Skin cancer? Vanity, thy name is tan. And how 'bout them lungs? The ones that suck up all that fine stuff we belch into the air. We got a cancer for everything. So don't worry, folks, if it's growin' on you, it's a part of the American dream.

Then we have the eating disorders. Is it really a surprise that with all our pathological feeding habits Americans have eating disorders? Who makes worse dietary decisions? Who wastes more food? And not just the ordinary waste of uncaring gluttons; that's easy. I'm talking about those grotesque, all-American food stunts the television news shows find so amusing: hands-behind-the-back pie-eating contests, the largest pizza in the world, the block-long omelet, the biggest banana split ever, the who-can-eat-the-most-hot-peppers-in-fifteen-minutes competition, and the swimming pool full of cherry Jell-O all schlocked up with bad fruit cocktail. And don't forget the wiener-eating contests, where the wieners are actually dipped in water so they'll slide down whole, eliminating all that bothersome chewing. Such healthy attitudes toward food!

And all of this conspicuous, deliberate waste takes place in the midst of global malnutrition and starvation. No wonder fucked-up teenage girls don't want to eat.

Here's another wonderful irony: with all our supposed superiority in food production, we provide our people with far higher rates of stroke, heart attack, colon cancer, and other diet diseases than most "inferior" Third-World food economies do. But don't you worry, those folks are catching up; social pathologies are our biggest export. And so, in a curious way, cancer turns out to be catching, after all.

Please note my restraint in ignoring "shopping disorders."

CONFESSIONS OF A MAGAZINE-OBSESSIVE

I'm always relieved when I see a magazine article I don't have to read, like "How to Turn Prison Rape into a Spiritual Quest." Or "Quesadillas for Quadraplegics." I'm practically giddy when I see an article about a disease I know I'll never get. I laugh heartily as I race past page after page of "Five Hundred Early Warning Signs of Cancer of the Labia." It's such a time-saver.

And I notice as I get older, the magazine articles that catch my eye have begun to change. For instance, in my early twenties, "Ten Career Choices that Lead to Suicide" was a must read. And "Achieving a Six-Hour Orgasm Without a Date" was duly clipped and laminated. But these days I find my interest caught by such titles as "Test Yourself for Alzheimer's," "Ten Tips on Surviving a Nursing Home Fire," and "How to Rid Yourself of Old-Person Smell." I guess the article I really need is "How to Extend Your Magazine Subscriptions Posthumously."

LIMERICKS

There was a young man from St. Maarten

Who saved all his odors from faartin.

If it passed through his crack

It went straight in a sack

And mistakes were all kept in a caarton.

A Jewess who lived in St. Croix

Fell in love with a handsome young goix.

Her parents forbade

She should marry the lad

So instead she eloped with the boix.

A flatulent actor named Barton

Had a lifestyle exceedingly spartan.

Till a playwright one day

Wrote a well-received play

With a part in which Barton could fart in.

KILLER COMIC

It goes without saying I'm not the only person who has noticed this, but I never got to spell it out my way before.

Comedy's nature has two sides. Everybody wants a good time and a couple of laughs, and of course, the comic wants to be known as a real funny guy. But the language of comedy is fairly grim and violent. It's filled with punchlines, gags, and slapstick. After all, what does a comic worry most about? Dying! He doesn't want to die.

"Jeez, I was dyin'. It was like death out there. Like a morgue. I really bombed."

Comics don't want to die, and they don't want to bomb. They want to go over with a bang. And be a real smash. And if everything works out, if they're successful and they make you laugh, they can say, "I killed 'em. I slaughtered those people, I knocked them dead."

And what phrases do we use when we talk about the comic? "He's a riot." "A real scream." "A rib-splitting knee-slapper." "My sides hurt." "My cheeks ache." "He broke me up, cracked me up, slayed me, fractured me, and had me in stitches." "I busted a gut." "I get a real kick out of that guy."

"Laugh? I thought I'd die."

Napalm & Silly Putty

George Carlin

HYPERION

New York

To sweet Sarah Jane,
the keeper of my magic.

Acknowledgments

To begin, I would like to acknowledge those of you who read *Brain Droppings*. It did better than I expected, and I want to say thanks. By the way, if you haven't read it yet, fear not. You can read this first and then rush out to the store to get *Brain Droppings*. The two are not sequential.

For those who did read the first book, you'll find this is the same sort of drivel. Good, funny, occasionally smart, but essentially drivel.

Thanks also to my boyhood friends from 123rd Street and Amsterdam Avenue who listened to my street-corner and hallway monologues when I was thirteen and gladdened my young heart by saying, "Georgie, you're fuckin' crazy!"

Most of all, thanks to my editor, Jennifer Lang, for her patience and support, and for putting these thoughts of mine in order.

Many native traditions held clowns and tricksters as essential to any contact with the sacred. People could not pray until they had laughed, because laughter opens and frees from rigid preconception. Humans had to have tricksters within the most sacred ceremonies lest they forget the sacred comes through upset, reversal, surprise. The trickster in most native traditions is essential to creation, to birth.

—Professor Byrd Gibbens,
Professor of English,
University of Arkansas at Little Rock.
From a letter to the author.

Those who dance are considered insane by those who can't hear the music.

—Anon.

If you can't dance you fuck a lot of waitresses.

—Voltaire

Sometimes gum looks like a penny.

—Sally Wade

Introduction

Hi, reader. I hope you're feeling well, and I hope your family is prospering in the new global economy. At least to the extent they deserve. For the next few hundred pages I will be your content provider.

Regarding the title of this book, *Napalm & Silly Putty*: Sometime ago I was struck by the fact that, among many other wondrous things, Man has had the imagination to invent two such distinctly different products. One, a flaming, jellied gasoline used to create fire, death, and destruction; the other, a claylike mass good for throwing, bouncing, smashing, or pressing against a comic strip so you can look at a backwards picture of Popeye. I think the title serves as a fairly good metaphor for Man's dual nature, while also providing an apt description of the kinds of thoughts that occupy me, both in this book and in my daily life: on the one hand, I kind of like it when a lot of people die, and on the other I always wonder how many unused frequent-flier miles they had.

The only difference between lilies and turds is whatever difference humans have agreed upon; and I don't always agree.

CARS AND DRIVING: PART ONE

Ridin' or Drivin'?

You wanna go for a ride? Okay, let's go for a ride. Well, actually, *you'll* go for a ride, I'll go for a drive. The one who drives the car goes for a drive. The other person goes for a ride. Most folks aren't aware of that. Tell 'em when they're gettin' into your car. Say, "You assholes are goin' for a ride, *I'm* goin' for a drive. 'Cause I'm the one who's makin' the payments on this shit-box."

Gettin' in the Car

Now, for purposes of description, you'll have to picture my car: an old, poorly maintained, dangerous collection of faulty parts from that wonderful time before safety became such a big goddamn deal in this country. And my car is like any other small car—real hard to get into. That's important, because, after all, you gotta get into the car first. Otherwise, the way I look at it, you ain't goin' nowhere.

And let's not forget, with *any* kind of car, just opening the driver's door and getting in involves a certain amount of risk. Have you noticed that? The terrific way they designed cars so the driver's door opens right out into the middle of goddamn traffic? Jesus! About the only intelligent thing the British ever did was putting that driver's seat right over there near the curb where it belongs. Of course then they went and moved the curb to the wrong side of the street.

Park like a Man

Anyway, like I said, no small car is easy to get into, but especially if you park the way I do: illegally, two feet out from the curb, on a busy, high-speed thoroughfare right in the middle of rush hour. And that sort of car entry is even riskier if you've got a two-door, and you're tryin' to stuff a coupla shopping bags full of groceries into the backseat while everyone else is zippin' past you, close enough to smell your breath.

Holy shit! Look out!! Here comes a drunken bus driver! Quick! Abandon groceries! Stand up straight! Squeeze against the car and pull that door as close to your body as you can, taking care of course not to cut off circulation to your feet. Holy shit, that was close! Good thing you went into emergency mode. And be honest, you didn't really need them groceries, did ya? Goddamn! Look at how flat that bus made everything; imagine a flank steak with tread marks. And might that just possibly be potato juice on the ground?

Handle with Care

Now, one more thing about car entry: my car has got one of them tricky kinda door handles that're recessed a little bit into the door itself. You know the ones I mean? Where your fingers actually go in a little bit, past the surface of the car, till you grab ahold of the handle? Don't ya like them? I do. That's why they don't make 'em anymore. They found out I like 'em. That's the way it is with everything. They find out I like it, they stop makin' it.

Open and Shut Case

Anyway, back to my car. I also got me one of them doors that when you open it, it swings a-a-a-all the way open. You know the kind I mean? *A-A-A-All* the way open; perpendicular to the car. I ain't got one of them fancy doors that hangs out there halfway and stays where you want it to. With my door, we got two things, open and shut. Pick one.

And if I should be tryin' to do somethin' really tricky, like get into the car? Well, in a case like that I gotta prop the door open with a broom handle. 'Cause otherwise, sure as hell, soon as I'm halfway in, that door's gonna swing back hard as it can and sever my leg just below the knee.

"Eeeeeyyyyaaaaaaaiiiiiaaaahhhhooooooooo!"

God! That shit hurts for about a year and a half, don't it? And them huge, purple blotches? Seems like they never go away.

An Up Front Guy

Now, I wanna mention one additional problem I have when I'm gettin' into my car. Like I told ya, it's kinda old, and upkeep has been minimal, so there's another thing I gotta deal with. A long time ago, my driver's seat got pushed way up forward on the runners about as far as it goes, and apparently it ain't never comin' back.

You see, what happened was, years ago, about thirty or forty of them little pop-top beer-can rings got wedged into the seat tracks, and now they're all fused into one solid piece of metal, and that fuckin' seat ain't never gonna move again. Unless, of course, there's an atomic attack, in which case it probably ain't gonna budge more than an inch or two.

So, because of all this unintentional seat redesign, when I get into full drivin' mode, I'm pretty much hangin' out right behind the radiator. In fact, if I wanna check my speedo, I gotta look straight down into my crotch. But, hey! At least I'm in the car.

Tight Squeeze

But maybe you're not! Maybe I oughta mention one more common car reentry problem: I know that some of you fainthearted folks like to play it safe by parkin' right in the mall parking lot. And, of course when you park the car, you do so in such a manner that leaves you full access to the door. But while you're in the mall chargin' all that worthless merchandise, some asshole parks right next to you, leaves about six inches between cars, and now you can't get your door open more than three or four degrees at best.

So, in order to gain access, you gotta try to wedge yourself through a tiny little crack, while balancing six gift-wrapped packages, all the time maintaining the integrity of a lit cigarette hangin' off your lip. Besides which, your own particular lumbar spine is not the best one God ever put together, and everybody knows that even a *proper* back is not made for gettin' into a car under circumstances such as these.

And, by the way, as most men know, tryin' to squeeze into a car in that manner also creates a potential for serious ball-injury from the steering wheel. Many's the family-planning program that's gone out the window due to poor parking. Solution: Always park way down at the far end of the lot, where the homeless people live. Your back and your balls will thank you. And the walk'll do ya good.

Door #4

Anyway, at this point I think we're all in the car, so now I'll just reach over here and . . . I'll just reach over here and . . . awww, shit! Goddamn door is still wide open. Well, maybe if I lean wa-a-ay out, and stretch my arm as far as it'll go; maybe without actually getting up, I can just reach out and . . . uuuuuhhhnnggh! Fuck it! It appears, folks, that today we're gonna be driving with the door wide open. What the heck, it's a lovely day, and they say an open driver's door actually helps you a little bit on left-hand turns. Acts like a rudder, increasing the drag factor on the port side.

Idiots and Maniacs

Okay, now we're gonna be takin' our little drive in just a minute or two, but first a philosophical question: Have you ever noticed that when you're drivin', anyone goin' slower than you is an idiot? And anyone goin' faster than you is a maniac?

"Will you look at this idiot!" [points right] "Look at him! Just creepin' along!" [swings head left] "Holy shit!! Look at that maniac go!"

Why, I tell ya, folks, it's a wonder we ever get anywhere at all these days, what with all the idiots and maniacs out there. Because no one ever drives at my speed.

Actually, I don't let people drive at my speed. If I see some guy in the next lane keepin' pace with me, I slow down. I let that asshole get a little bit ahead, so I can keep an eye on him. I like to know who I'm drivin' near. In fact, quite often at a red light I'll ask for personal references. You can never be too careful.

Getting Started

Okay. Now, a few basic points about driving. One of the first things they teach you in Driver's Ed is where to put your hands on the steering wheel. They tell you put 'em at ten o'clock and two o'clock. Never mind that. I put mine at 9:45 and 2:17. Gives me an extra half hour to get where I'm goin'.

Some Things Break Easy

Now, most drivers know that some things that happen in the car can cause great embarrassment. I've never done any of these things myself, of course, but I'm sure you'll recognize a few of them. Here's a good example: you ever been driving someone else's car, and for some reason they're in the car, too? You know what I mean? Let's say they got pushed off the balcony of a crack house and broke both their ankles, and they can't drive, so you're takin' them out to buy some crack? You're drivin' their car? But *you're* used to driving *your* car. And their gear shift handle is mounted on the opposite side from where yours is, and suddenly you go to shift gears and [CRACK!] break their fuckin' turn signal off! Just break it clean off the steering column!

"Holy shit, came right off, didn't it? God damn! You'll have to get a *new* one of them! Here, throw this old one out the window! It ain't no good to ya now. Shit, that broke easy, didn't it?"

Some things break easy. Just break right off. Like radio dials. The old kind, the knob kind. Damn, those things were fragile. You'd be drivin' along just tryin' to tune in somethin' on the radio. Tryin' to find some kinda music you could actually tolerate. And you'd just keep turnin' and turnin' and turnin' that dial, until finally you got way over onto the right-hand side of the dashboard and ran clean outta radio stations, and then . . . CRACK!!!

"Holy shit, came right off, didn't it? God damn! Gotta throw that mother away! Gimme a fresh one outta that little bag, would ya? I got about fifty of those motherfuckers. Damn, they break easy!"

So you stick a new knob onto the radio and keep turnin' and turnin' and turnin', until finally you wind up past the glove compartment listenin' to some radio station located over near the right-hand mirror. Damn. Some things break easy.

It's Your Car, Have a Little Fun!

I'm a great believer in using every piece of equipment on the car. Every feature, every option, even if you don't need it. Fuck it, you paid for the car, use everything!

Use the sun visor. Even on a cloudy day. Flip it up, flip it down; flip it over to the side like the French people do. Lower the passenger's visor, even if no one is sitting there. Open the ashtray, push in the lighter; who cares if you don't smoke? Turn all the knobs, press all the buttons. Have a lot of fun. Change the mirrors all around. Press the trunk release. Pop the hood open. Put your seat in a ridiculous position. Lower all the windows. Stick out your hand. Tell the other drivers to slow down. You have power. Use hand signals. Tell them to slow down. And then tell them to stop.

"Stop! Stop!"

Then let one guy go. Only one.

"Okay, you can go. Go! Go! Go! No, not you! Just him! Okay, *now* you! Go! Go!"

You have power. Use it. Fuck it. You're makin' the car payments, have a little fun.

EAT A BOX OF COOKIES

Did you ever eat a whole box of cookies right in a row? Did you ever do that? I don't mean take them into your bedroom or something. I mean open them right up in the kitchen as soon as you get home from the store and eat 'em while you're standing there? Just stare at the toaster while you're eatin' a whole goddamn box of cookies? Did you ever do that? Isn't it great?

And did you ever notice that printed right on the cookie box it says, "Open here"? Well, what did they think I was gonna do? Move to Hong Kong to open up their fuckin' cookies? Of *course* I'm gonna open 'em here. I'm gonna eat 'em here, I'd almost *have* to open 'em here. Thank God it doesn't say, "Open somewhere else." I'd be up all night tryin' to figure out an appropriate location.

SHORT TAKES

Ah, to be a bird. To fly the skies, sing my song, and best of all occasionally peck someone's eyes out.

When he got loaded, the human cannonball knew there were not many men of his caliber.

I don't like porno movies. They piss me off. First they show a great-looking naked woman who starts playing with herself. And while I'm watching, she sort of becomes my girlfriend. And then, suddenly, in walks a guy with a big dick, and he starts fucking my girlfriend. It pisses me off.

Most people with low self-esteem have earned it.

Haven't we gone far enough with colored ribbons for different causes? Every cause has its own color. Red for AIDS, blue for child abuse, pink for breast cancer, green for the rain forest. I've got a brown one. You know what it means? "Eat shit, motherfucker!"

I enjoy young people because they're really fucked up and don't know what they're doing. I like that. I support all fucked-up people regardless of age.

In that book *Tuesdays with Morrie,* Morrie Schwartz had Lou Gehrig's disease. But what isn't generally known is that because of a mix-up at the hospital, Lou Gehrig had Hodgkin's disease, Hodgkin had Parkinson's disease, and Parkinson had Alzheimer's disease. Unfortunately, Alzheimer couldn't remember whose disease he had. He thinks it might have been Wally Pipp.

Whenever you see more than two men sitting in a parked car after dark you can be sure drugs are involved.

You know what we haven't had in quite a while? A really big fire in a crowded nightclub. What's going on?

When I die I don't want to be buried, but I don't want to be cremated either. I want to be blown up. Put me on a pile of explosives and blow me up. Or throw my body from a helicopter. That would be fun. One stipulation: wherever I land, you have to leave me there. Even if it's the mayor's lawn. Just let me lie there. But keep the dogs away.

Isn't it nice that once your parents are dead they can't come back and start fucking with you again?

The trouble with a sitcom is that every week it's the same irritating group of assholes.

People who say they don't care what people think are usually desperate to have people think they don't care what people think.

I never see any black twins. What's the deal here?

You know what would be great? To be in a coma. You're still alive, but you have no responsibilities.

"He owes me six thousand dollars."

"He's in a coma."

"Oh, okay. Never mind."

If I had my choice of how to die I would like to be sitting on the crosstown bus and suddenly burst into flames.

Have you noticed fluorescent lights seem afraid to come on? When you turn on a fluorescent light it flickers and hesitates and is sort of unsure of itself. Then after several seconds it seems to gain confidence and light up at full strength. What's that all about? Cain't these lamps receive some sort of counseling?

You know what would be fun? To fuck a grief-stricken woman.

THE CHRISTIANS ARE COMING TO GET YOU, AND THEY ARE NOT PLEASANT PEOPLE.

I recently bought a book of free verse. For twelve dollars.

One of my favorite things to do at a party is smoke a bunch of PCP and start taking people's rectal temperatures without permission.

If the police never find it, is it still a clue?

You know an odd feeling? Sitting on the toilet eating a chocolate candy bar.

Have you ever started a path? No one seems willing to do this. We don't mind using existing paths, but we rarely start new ones. Do it today. Start a path. Even if it doesn't lead anywhere.

You can't argue with a good blow job.

True Fact: There is now an "interactive food" called SNOT—Super Nauseating Obnoxious Treat. It squirts out of a plastic dispenser that looks like a man's nose. God bless America.

I've thought it over, and I've decided pus is okay.

Every sixty seconds, thirty acres of rain forest are destroyed in order to raise beef for fast-food restaurants that sell it to people, giving them strokes and heart attacks, which raise medical costs and insurance rates, providing insurance companies with more money to invest in large corporations that branch out further into the Third World so they can destroy more rain forests.

When I was a kid, if a guy got killed in a western movie I always wondered who got his horse.

I have no sympathy for "single dads." Most of these guys got married because they wanted steady pussy. Well, steady pussy leads to steady babies, and steady babies tend to cut down the pussy. So, once the novelty wears off, the marriage disappears. Single dads. Big fuckin' deal.

AIRLINE ANNOUNCEMENTS: PART ONE

Here's something we all have in common: flying on big airplanes and listening to the announcements. And trying to pretend the language they're using is English. Doesn't always sound like it to me.

Preflight

It starts at the gate: "We'd like to begin the **boarding process**." Extra word. "Process." Not necessary. Boarding is sufficient. "We'd like to begin the boarding." Simple. Tells the story. People add extra words when they want things to sound more important than they really are. "Boarding process" sounds important. It isn't. It's just a group of people getting on an airplane.

To begin their boarding process, the airline announces they will **preboard** certain passengers. And I wonder, How can that be? How can people board before they board? This I gotta see. But before anything interesting can happen I'm told to get on the plane. "Sir, you can get on the plane now." And I think for a moment. "*On* the plane? No, my friends, not me. I'm not getting *on* the plane; I'm getting *in* the plane! Let Evel Knievel get *on* the plane, I'll be sitting inside in one of those little chairs. It seems less windy in there."

Then they mention that it's a **nonstop flight**. Well, I must say I don't care for that sort of thing. Call me old-fashioned, but I insist that my flight stop. Preferably at an airport. Somehow those sudden cornfield stops interfere with the flow of my day. And just about at this point, they tell me the flight has been delayed because of a **change of equipment**. And deep down I'm thinking, "broken plane!"

Speaking of potential mishaps, here's a phrase that apparently the airlines simply made up: **near miss.** They say that if two planes almost collide it's a near miss. Bullshit, my friend. It's a near hit! A **collision** is a near miss.

[WHAM! CRUNCH!]

"Look, they nearly missed!"

"Yes, but not quite."

Back to the flight: As part of all the continuing folderol, I'm asked to put my **seat-back forward.** Well, unfortunately for the others in the cabin, I don't bend that way. If I could put my seat-back forward I'd be in porno movies.

There's also a mention of **carry-on luggage.** The first time I heard this term I thought they said "carrion," and that they were bringing a dead deer on board. And I wondered, "What the hell would they want with that? Don't they have those little TV dinners anymore?" And then I thought, Carry on? "Carry on!" Of course! People are going to be carrying on! It's a party! Well, I don't much care for that. Personally, I prefer a serious attitude on the plane.

Especially on the **flight deck,** which is the latest euphemism for cockpit. I can't imagine why they'd want to avoid a colorful word like "cockpit," can you? Especially with all those lovely stewardesses going in and out of it all the time.

By the way, there's a word that's changed: **stewardess.** First it was hostess, then stewardess, now it's "flight attendant." You know what I call her? "The lady on the plane." These days, sometimes it's a man on the plane. That's good. Equality. I'm all in favor of that.

The flight attendants are also sometimes referred to as **uniformed crew members.** Oh, good. Uniformed. As opposed to this guy next to me in the Grateful Dead T-shirt and the FUCK YOU hat, who's currently working on his ninth little bottle of Kahlúa.

Safety First. Mine!

As soon as they close the door to the aircraft they begin **the safety lecture**. I love the safety lecture. It's my favorite part of the flight. I listen very carefully. Especially to the part where they teach us how to use the seat belt. Imagine that: a plane full of grown humans—many of them partially educated—and someone is actually taking the time to describe the intricate workings of a belt buckle. "Place the small metal flap into the buckle." Well, at that point I raise my hand and ask for clarification.

"Over here, please, over here. Yes. Thank you very much. Did I hear you correctly? Did you say 'place the small metal flap into the buckle,' or did you say 'place the buckle over and around the small metal flap'? I'm a simple man, I do not possess an engineering degree, nor am I mechanically inclined. Sorry to have taken up so much of your time. Please continue with your wonderful safety lecture." Seat belt. High-tech shit!

The lecture continues. The next thing they advise me to do is **locate my nearest emergency exit**. Well, I do so immediately. I locate my nearest emergency exit, and I plan my escape route. You have to plan your escape route. It's not always a straight line, is it? No. Sometimes there's a really big, fat fuck sitting right in front of you.

Well, I know I'll never be able to climb over him, so I look around for women and children, midgets and dwarfs, cripples, elderly widows, paralyzed veterans, and people with broken legs. Anyone who looks like they don't move too well. The emotionally disturbed come in very handy at a time like this. It's true I may have to go out of my way to find some of these people, but I'll get out of the plane a whole lot quicker, believe you me.

My strategy is clear: I'll go around the fat fuck, step on the widow's head, push those children aside, knock down the paralyzed midget, and escape from the plane. In order, of course, to assist the other passengers who are still trapped inside the burning wreckage. After all, I can be of no help to anyone if I'm lying in the aisle, unconscious, with some big cocksucker standing on my neck. I must get out of the plane, make my way to a nearby farmhouse, have a Dr Pepper, and call the police.

The safety lecture continues: "**In the unlikely event . . .**" This is a very suspect phrase, especially coming as it does from an industry that is willing to lie about arrival and departure times. "In the unlikely event of a **sudden change in cabin pressure . . .**" roof flies off!! ". . . an oxygen mask will drop down in front of you. Place the mask over your face and **breathe normally.**" Well, no problem there. I always breathe normally when I'm in an uncontrolled, 600-mile-an-hour vertical dive. I also shit normally. Directly into my pants.

Then they tell me to **adjust my oxygen mask before helping my child with his.** Well, that's one thing I didn't need to be told. In fact, I'm probably going to be too busy screaming to help my child at all. This will be a good time for him to learn self-reliance. If he can surf the fucking Internet, he can goddamn, jolly well learn to adjust an oxygen mask. It's a fairly simple thing: just a little elastic band in the back. Not nearly as complicated as, say, a seat belt.

The safety lecture continues: "In the unlikely event of **a water landing . . .**" A water landing! Am I mistaken, or does this sound somewhat similar to "crashing into the ocean"? ". . . your seat cushion can be used as a **flotation device.**" Well, imagine that. My seat cushion! Just what I need: to float around the North Atlantic for several days, clinging to a pillow full of beer farts.

The announcements suddenly cease. We're about to take off. Time for me to drift off to sleep, so the captain can later awaken me repeatedly with the many valuable sight-seeing announcements he will be making along the way. I'm always amazed at the broad knowledge these men have of the United States. And some of them apparently have really good eyesight:

"For you folks seated on the left side of the plane, that's old Ben Hubbard's place down there. And whaddeya know, there's Ben comin' out onto his porch right now. What's he doin? By God, he's pickin' his nose. Wow! Look at that one! That is one prize booger. And look, he's throwin' it into a bush. Ain't that just like old Ben? Over on the right . . ."

Zzzzzzzz.

AIRLINE ANNOUNCEMENTS: PART TWO

Suddenly I'm awake. The flight is almost over, and somehow, along the way, the captain has become politicized. His latest offering:

"Ladies and gentlemen, we have just begun our gradual descent into the Los Angeles area, similar in many ways to the gradual descent of this once great nation from a proud paragon of God-fearing virtue to a third-rate power awash in violence, sexual excess, and personal greed . . ."

I drift off again and awaken just as the end-of-flight announcements are being made: "**The captain has turned on the Fasten Seat Belt sign.**" Here we go again. Who gives a shit who turned on the sign? What does that have to do with anything? It's on, isn't it? And by the way, isn't it about time we found out who made this man a captain? Did I sleep through some sort of armed-forces swearing-in ceremony? Captain, my ass, the man is a fucking pilot, and he should be happy with that. If those sight-seeing announcements are any mark of his intelligence, the man's lucky to be working at all.

Having endured enough nonsense from this so-called captain, I finally raise my voice: "Tell the captain, Air Marshal Carlin says he should go fuck himself!"

The next sentence I hear is filled with language that pisses me off: "Before leaving the aircraft, please check around your **immediate seating area** for any **personal belongings** you **might have brought** on board." Well, let's start with "immediate seating area." Seat! It's a goddamn seat! "For any personal belongings . . ." Well, what other kinds of belongings do they think I have? Public? Do they honestly think I brought along a fountain I stole from the park? ". . . you might have brought on board." Well, I *might* have brought my Shoshone arrowhead collection. I didn't. So I'm not going to look for it.

Then they say we'll be "**landing shortly**." Doesn't that sound like we're going to miss the runway? "**Final approach**" is not too promising either. "Final" is not a good word to be using on an airplane. Sometimes the pilot will speak up and say, "**We'll be on the ground in fifteen minutes.**" Well, that seems a little vague. "On the ground" could mean any number of things. Most of them not very good.

By this time we're taxiing in, and the flight attendant is saying, "**Welcome to Los Angeles International Airport . . .**" Well, how can someone who is just arriving herself possibly welcome me to a place she hasn't gotten to yet? Doesn't this violate some law of physics? We've been on the ground barely four seconds, and she's comin' on like the mayor's wife. ". . . where **the local time** . . ." Well, of course it's the local time. What did they think I was expecting? The time in Norway?

"Enjoy your stay in Los Angeles or wherever your **final destination** might be." Someone should really tell these airline people that *all* destinations are final. That's what destination means. Destiny. It's final. Think of it this way: if you haven't gotten where you're going, you probably aren't there yet.

"**The captain has asked** . . ." More shit from the bogus captain. You know, for someone who's supposed to be flying an airplane, he's taking a mighty big interest in what I'm doing back here. ". . . that you remain seated until he has brought the aircraft to **a complete stop.**" A complete stop. Not a partial stop. No. Because during a partial stop, I partially get up, partially get my bags, and partially leave the plane.

"Please continue **to observe the No Smoking sign until well inside the terminal.**" Folks, I've tried this. Let me tell you it is physically impossible to observe the No Smoking sign, even from just outside the airplane, much less from well inside the terminal. In fact, you can't even see the *airplanes* from well inside the terminal.

Which brings us to "**terminal.**" Another unfortunate word to be using in association with air travel. And they use it all over the airport, don't they? Somehow, I can't get hungry at a place called the Terminal Restaurant. Then again, if you've ever eaten there, you know the name is quite appropriate.

A BEDROCK-SOLID ALIBI

Most vitamin pills don't have names or trademarks on them; they're just plain-looking unmarked pills. And if you're traveling with a lot of vitamins, and in order to save space you've put them all in one big jar, you have no way of proving what they are. If, for instance, the police should search your suitcase, all they're going to know is that you have a big jar of unmarked pills. And should they be in the mood to break your balls, they can hold you for twenty-four hours while they "send these little things down to the lab and see what we've got here." And you wind up in jail overnight for no reason at all.

That's why I always travel with Flintstone vitamins. Not only do Flintstone vitamins contain all the vital nutrients kids need each day, they also keep grown-ups out of jail.

"Honest, Officer, they're Flintstone vitamins. Look, there's Wilma and Barney."

"By God, Ben, he's right. Look at this. It's Dino! It's a little purple Dino!"

Suddenly, you're a free man. And a healthy one, too!

RICE KRISPIES

I had an interesting morning; I got into an argument with my Rice Krispies. I distinctly heard, "Snap, crackle, fuck you!" I'm not sure which one of them said it; I was reaching for the artificial sweetener at the time and not looking directly into the bowl. But I heard it and I said, "Well, you can all just sit right there in the milk as far as I'm concerned until I find out which one of you said it." Mass punishment. The idea is to turn them against one another.

Silly me. Big punishment! That's what Rice Krispies do. Sit in the milk. That's their job. You've seen them. Delicate, beige blisters of air, floating proudly in the milk. And you can't sink them. They refuse to sink. The navy ought to use Rice Krispies in life preservers. That's where they're really needed.

And do you know how Rice Krispies manage to float for such a long time? By clinging to one another; they buddy up. They gather in little groups of eight, ten, or sometimes twelve, but if you've noticed, it's always an even number. That's because the electromagnetic polarity of the Krispies attracts them to one another. It binds them into pairs, like subatomic particles. They form little colonies, and you can't sink them, not even with a spoon. They just come bobbing up over the sides of the spoon, laughing at you and reveling in their buoyancy. Hard to sink.

That's what the fruit is for. Not for added taste; not for nutrition; it's for sinking the Rice Krispies. Believe me, a good-sized peach, hurled at the bowl full force from a stepladder, can take down eighty or ninety of the little buggers in one glorious splash.

And I have absolutely no mercy. If I'm really pissed, I'll climb up to the upstairs balcony and drop a watermelon on them. That'll teach them to sass me at breakfast.

THE MORNING NEWS

* London police fired warning shots over the heads of rioters today. Unfortunately, they killed six members of the royal family watching from a balcony.

* A Wisconsin woman claims that last month she was taken aboard a space ship where aliens cleaned her teeth, fitted her with a diaphragm, and gave her a Valium prescription good for three refills. She also claims that while aboard the ship she was introduced to Richard Simmons.

* A spokesman for the Vatican announced today that in Rome a statue of St. Peter has come to life and is passing along fishing tips and veal recipes.

* The California Humane Society has filed a criminal complaint against a man they say is keeping tropical fish in a moving blender. The man admits it is true but says he has never turned the blender above Mix. The Humane Society claims he's had it up to Whip and Puree several times.

* John Barrow, a Vermont man, is suing his minister for religious malpractice. He claims the minister wrongfully included him in a prayer being said to shrink the size of another man's brain tumor. Although the cancer patient has completely recovered, Barrow says his own head is now the size of a walnut.

* A Florida man who wrestles alligators for a living was eaten alive today when the alligator apparently did not understand the universal signal for "time-out."

* Amtrak officials have announced that as of the first of July, all passenger service will be discontinued except for a single train that will operate only in an eastbound direction.

* Chief Justice William Rehnquist had an embarrassing moment in court last week. During an oral argument, the chief justice farted quite loudly. Recovering quickly, and displaying his vaunted wit, Rehnquist said, "One more outburst like that, and I'll clear the court."

* The Loch Ness monster surfaced today, and in a clear Scottish accent asked if she had any messages.

* A Kentucky man has been arrested for making an unauthorized deposit in a sperm bank.

* The U.S. Army has announced that although it is true they performed mind-destroying drug tests on hundreds of soldiers in the 1960s, none of the victims has been promoted beyond the rank of lieutenant colonel.

* An Ohio man whose library book was fourteen years overdue has taken his own life rather than pay the huge fine. Asked how such a thing could happen, his wife said, "I don't know. We looked and looked, and simply couldn't find it."

* And finally, here's one for *The Guinness Book of World Records*. A Baltimore man recently broke a longtime mental record when a forty-four-year-long thought he was having came to an end. When asked what he had been thinking of he said he couldn't remember, but that it would probably come back to him. He added that quite possibly it had something to do with his hat.

FIVE UNEASY MOMENTS

Moment #1

Have you ever been in one of those serious social situations when you suddenly realize you have to pull the underwear out of the crack in your ass?

"Do you, Enrique, take this woman, Blanca, to be your lawful, wedded wife?"

"Huh? Hold on, Rev." [Tugging violently at his pants] "Aah! Got it! Jesus, that was in deep. Yes. Yes, I do. Excuse me, Rev, sometimes my shorts get sucked up way inside my asshole." Ain't love grand?

Moment #2

Have you ever been at a really loud party where the music is deafening, and in order to be heard you have to scream at the top of your lungs? Even if you're talking to the person right next to you? But then often, the music stops suddenly and everyone quiets down at the same time. And only your voice can be heard, ringing across the room:

"CHARLIE, I'M GONNA GET MY TESTICLES LAMINATED!!"

And everyone turns to look at Charlie's interesting friend.

Moment #3

Have you ever been talking to a bunch of guys, and you laugh through your nose and blow a snot on your shirt? And then you have to just keep talking and hope they'll think it's part of the design? It works all right if you're wearing a Hawaiian shirt. But otherwise, they're gonna notice.

"Hey, Ed, check it out! Dave's got a big snot on his shirt! Howie, look! Phil, c'mere! Dave just blew a big snot all over himself."

Guys are such fun.

Moment #4

Did you ever meet a guy, and as you're shaking his hand you realize he doesn't have a complete hand? It feels like something is missing? And you're standing there holding a handful of deformed, knoblike flesh?

It's unnerving, isn't it? But you can't react; you can't even look down at his hand. You have to make believe it feels great.

You can't go, "Eeeaauuu! How creepy! Where's your other fingers?"

You can't say that. It's not even an option. You have to hang in, smile big, and say, "Hey, swell hand! Gimme three! Okay! A high-three! Yo! Okay!"

Moment #5

Have you ever been talking to yourself when someone suddenly comes in the room? And you have to make believe you were singing? And you hope to God the other person really believes there's a song called "Fuck Her"?

The American Bu$ine$$man's Ten Steps to Product Development

1. *Can I cut corners in the design?*

2. *Can it be shoddily built?*

3. *Can I use cheap materials?*

4. *Will it create hazards for my workers?*

5. *Will it harm the environment?*

6. *Can I evade the safety laws?*

7. *Will children die from it?*

8. *Can I overprice it?*

9. *Can it be falsely advertised?*

10. *Will it force smaller competitors out of business?*

   Excellent. Let's get busy.

THE BOVINE FECES TRILOGY

E Pluribus Bullshit

Every time you're exposed to advertising in America you're reminded that this country's most profitable business is still the manufacture, packaging, distribution, and marketing of bullshit. High-quality, grade-A, prime-cut, pure American bullshit.

And the sad part is that most people seem to believe bullshit only comes from certain predictable sources: advertising, politics, salesmen, and lawyers. Not true. Bullshit is everywhere. Bullshit is rampant. Parents are full of shit, teachers are full of shit, clergymen are full of shit, and law enforcement is full of shit. This entire country is completely full of shit—and always has been. From the Declaration of Independence to the Constitution to the "Star Spangled Banner," it's nothing more than one big, steaming pile of red-white-and-blue, all-American bullshit.

Think of how it all started: America was founded by slave owners who informed us, "All men are created equal." All "men," except Indians, niggers, and women. Remember, the founders were a small group of unelected, white, male, land-holding slave owners who also, by the way, suggested their class be the only one allowed to vote. To my mind, that is what's known as being stunningly—and embarrassingly—full of shit. And everybody bought it. All Americans bought it.

And those same Americans continue to show their ignorance with all this nonsense about wanting their politicians to be honest. What are these cretins thinking? Do they realize what they're wishing for? If honesty were suddenly introduced into American life, everything would collapse. It would destroy this country, because our system is based on an intricate and delicately balanced system of lies.

And I think that somehow, deep down, Americans understand this. That's why they elected—and reelected—Bill Clinton. Because given a choice, Americans prefer their bullshit right out front, where they can get a good, strong whiff of it. Clinton may have been full of shit, but at least he let you know it. And people like that.

In '96, Dole tried to hide his bullshit, and he lost. He kept saying, "I'm a plain and honest man." People don't believe that. What did Clinton say? He said, "Hi folks! I'm completely full of shit, and how do you like that?" And the people said, "You know what? At least he's honest. At least he's honest about being completely full of shit."

Will They Buy this Bullshit?

It's the same in the business world. Everyone knows by now all businessmen are completely full of shit; the worst kind of lowlife, criminal cocksuckers you can expect to meet. And the proof is, they don't even trust each other!

When a businessman sits down to negotiate with another businessman, the first thing he does is assume the other guy is a complete lying prick who's trying to fuck him out of his money. So he does everything *he* can to fuck the other guy a little bit faster and a little bit harder. And he does it with a big smile on his face. That big, bullshit businessman's smile.

And if you're a customer, that's when they give you the *really* big smile! The customer always gets that really big smile as the businessman carefully positions himself directly *behind* the customer, unzips his pants, and proceeds to "service" the account.

"I'm servicing this account . . .

[pelvic thrust!]

"This customer . . .

[thrust]

"needs

[thrust!]

"service!"

[thrust, thrust, thrust!]

Now you know what they mean when they say, "We specialize in customer service." Whoever first said, "Let the buyer beware" was probably bleeding from the asshole. But that's business. That's business, and business is okay.

Bullshit from the Sky

But folks, I have to tell you, in the bullshit department a businessman can't hold a candle to a clergyman. Because when it comes to bullshit. Big-time, major-league bullshit. You have to stand in awe—in awe!—of the all-time champion of false promises and exaggerated claims: religion. No contest.

Religion—easily—has the Greatest Bullshit Story Ever Told! Think about it: religion has actually convinced people—many of them adults—that there's an invisible man who lives in the sky and watches everything you do, every minute of every day. And who has a special list of ten things he does not want you to do.

And if you do *any* of these ten things, he has a special place, full of fire and smoke and burning and torture and anguish, where he will send you to remain and suffer and burn and choke and scream and cry, forever and ever, till the end of time. But he loves you!

He loves you, and he needs money! He always needs money. He's all-powerful, all-perfect, all-knowing, and all-wise, but somehow . . . he just can't handle money. Religion takes in billions of dollars, pays no taxes, and somehow always needs a little more. Now, you talk about a good bullshit story. Holy shit!

SHORT TAKES

Do you ever get that strange feeling of vuja de? Not déjà vu; vuja de. It's the distinct sense that, somehow, something that just happened has never happened before. Nothing seems familiar. And then suddenly the feeling is gone. Vuja de.

Spirituality: the last refuge of a failed human. Just another way of distracting yourself from who you really are.

I have a problem with married people who carry their babies in backpacks or frontpacks or slings, or whatever those devices are called. Those baby-carrying devices that seem designed to leave the parent's hands free to sort through merchandise. Hey, Mr. and Mrs. Natural Fibers, is it too much trouble to ask you to hold the fuckin' kid? Are you so busy picking out consumer goods and reaching for your credit card that you can't hold the baby? It's not an accessory or a small appliance. It's a baby.

Most of the time people feel okay. Probably it's because at that moment they're not actually dying.

You know what I like about the American form of government? They've worked things out so that you're never far from a 7-Eleven.

You know what you never hear about? A bunch of Jews being hit by a tornado.

Don't you hate it when people send you unsolicited pictures of their kids? What's that all about? It bothers me. I hate to keep throwing away perfectly good pictures.

When I see a guy with hair on his back I immediately relegate him to the animal kingdom.

Every six minutes there's a rape in this country, and boy, is my dick sore. I'm tellin' ya, every day, house to house, there's no letup. It's a fuckin' hassle.

I haven't eaten an ice cream sandwich in forty-seven years.

Next time you see Bing Crosby playing a priest in a movie, picture him beating his children in real life.

I've never been quarantined. But the more I look around the more I think it might not be a bad idea.

Here's some fun: Run into a bakery and ask if they can bake a cake in the shape of a penis. They're never quite sure; they always have to have a meeting.
"Well, I don't know. Wait just a moment."
While they're talking, pull out your schwanz and wave it all around.
"Good Lord, Helen! Quick! Order extra flour!"

I don't think we should be governing ourselves. What we need is a king, and every now and then if the king's not doing a good job, we kill him.

So far, this is the oldest I've been.

I think someone could make a lot of money if they set up a little stand at the Grand Canyon and sold Yo-Yos with 500-foot strings.

Road rage, air rage. Why should I be forced to divide my rage into separate categories? To me, it's just one big, all-around, everyday rage. I don't have time for fine distinctions. I'm busy screaming at people.

There's something I like about the clitoris, but I can't quite put my finger on it.

Driving is fun. Did you ever run over a guy? And then you panic? So you back up and run over him again? You ever notice the second crunch is not as loud as the first? I think it's because the guy already has tread marks on him. But there he is, lyin' right in front of your car. Might as well run over him again. What're you gonna do this time, drive around him?

When Ronald Reagan got Alzheimer's disease, how could they tell?

Sometimes they say the winds are calm. Well, if they're calm, they're not really winds, are they?

I think a good title for a travel book would be *Doorway to Norway*.

Next time they give you all that civic bullshit about voting, keep in mind that Hitler was elected in a full, free democratic election.

Would somebody please tell me what is so sacred about the Lincoln Bedroom? If it were the Ulysses S. Grant Bedroom, do you think people would've been as annoyed that Clinton rented it out to campaign donors? No. It's just the bullshit Lincoln myth that caused the uproar.

Why do they keep trotting out this Billy Graham character? He has nothing to say, and basically no one gives a fuck.

Murder investigators say that in most cases husbands kill wives, wives kill husbands, children kill parents, and parents kill children. Thank God for a little sanity in the world.

Regarding the Boy Scouts, I'm very suspicious of any organization that has a handbook.

If there really are multiple universes, what do they call the thing they're all a part of?

Where did this idea come from that if you're a celebrity, and something bad happens to you, you have to devote your life to eliminating the same problem for everyone else? Michael J. Fox, Christopher Reeve, Mary Tyler Moore; they all work on curing their own afflictions. Why doesn't a celebrity with milk leg ever do something about dandy fever? How about an actor with woolsorter's disease raising money for the victims of swimming pool granuloma? That's the trouble with Hollywood, no imagination.

Instead of warning pregnant women not to drink, I think female alcoholics ought to be told not to fuck.

YOUR CHILDREN ARE OVERRATED

Something else I'm getting tired of in this country is all this stupid bullshit I have to listen to about children. That's all you hear anymore, children: "Help the children, save the children, protect the children." You know what I say? Fuck the children! Fuck 'em! Fuck kids; they're getting entirely too much attention.

And I know what some of you are thinking: "Jesus, he's not going to attack children, is he?" Yes he is! He's going to attack children. And remember, this is Mr. Conductor talking; I know what I'm talking about.

And I also know that all you boring single dads and working moms, who think you're such fuckin' heroes, aren't gonna like this, but somebody's gotta tell you for your own good: your children are over-rated and overvalued, and you've turned them into little cult objects. You have a child fetish, and it's not healthy. And don't give me all that weak shit, "Well, I love my children." Fuck you! Everybody loves their children; it doesn't make you special.

John Wayne Gacy loved his children. Yes, he did. He kept 'em all right out in the yard, near the garage. That's not what I'm talking about. What I'm talking about is this constant, mindless yammering in the media, this neurotic fixation that suggests somehow everything—everything—has to revolve around the lives of children. It's completely out of balance.

Let's Get Real

Listen, there are a couple of things about kids you have to re-member. First of all, they're not all cute. In fact, if you look at 'em real close, most of them are rather unpleasant looking. And a lot of them don't smell too good either. The little ones in particular seem to have a kind of urine and sour-milk combination that I don't care for at all. Stay with me on this folks, the sooner you face it the better off you're gonna be.

Second premise: not all children are smart and clever. Got that? Kids are like any other group of people: a few winners, a whole lot of losers! This country is *filled* with loser kids who simply . . . aren't . . . going anywhere! And there's nothing you can do about it, folks. Nothing! You can't save 'em all. You can't do it. You gotta let 'em go; you gotta cut 'em loose; you gotta stop overprotecting them, because you're making 'em too soft. Today's kids are way too soft.

Safe *and* Sorry

For one thing, there's too much emphasis on safety and safety equipment: childproof medicine bottles, fireproof pajamas, child restraints, car seats. And helmets! Bicycle, baseball, skateboard, scooter helmets. Kids have to wear helmets now for everything but jerking off. Grown-ups have taken all the fun out of being a kid, just to save a few thousand lives. It's pathetic.

What's happened is, these baby boomers, these soft, fruity baby boomers, have raised an entire generation of soft, fruity kids who aren't even allowed to have hazardous toys, for Chrissakes! Hazardous toys, shit! Whatever happened to natural selection? Survival of the fittest? The kid who swallows too many marbles doesn't grow up to have kids of his own. Simple stuff. Nature knows best!

We're saving entirely too many lives in this country—of *all* ages! Nature should be permitted to do its job weeding out and killing off the weak and sickly and ignorant people, without interference from airbags and batting helmets. We're lowering the human gene pool! If these ideas bother you, just think of them as passive eugenics.

New Math

Here's another example of overprotection for these kids, and you've seen this one on the news. Did you ever notice that every time some guy with an AK-47 strolls into the school yard and kills three or four of these fuckin' kids and a couple of teachers, the next day the school is overrun with psychologists and psychiatrists and grief counselors and trauma therapists, trying to help the children cope?

Shit! When I was a kid, and some guy came to our school and killed three or four of us, we went right on with our arithmetic: "Thirty-five classmates minus four equals thirty-one." We were tough! I say if a kid can handle the violence at home, he oughta be able to handle the violence at school.

Out of Uniform

Another bunch of ignorant bullshit about your children: school uniforms. Bad theory! The idea that if kids wear uniforms to school, it helps keep order. Hey! Don't these schools do enough damage makin' all these children *think* alike? Now they're gonna get 'em to *look* alike, too?

And it's not even a new idea; I first saw it in old newsreels from the 1930s, but it was hard to understand, because the narration was in German! But the uniforms looked beautiful. And the children did everything they were told and never questioned authority. Gee, I wonder why someone would want to put our children in uniforms. Can't imagine.

And one more item about children: this superstitious nonsense of blaming tobacco companies for kids who smoke. Listen! Kids don't smoke because a camel in sunglasses tells them to. They smoke for the same reasons adults do, because it's an enjoyable activity that relieves anxiety and depression.

And you'd be anxious and depressed too if you had to put up with pathetic, insecure, yuppie parents who enroll you in college before you've even figured out which side of the playpen smells the worst and then fill you full of Ritalin to get you in a mood *they* approve of, and drag you all over town in search of empty, meaningless structure: Little League, Cub Scouts, swimming, soccer, karate, piano, bagpipes, watercolors, witchcraft, glass blowing, and dildo practice. It's absurd.

They even have "play dates," for Christ's sake! Playing is now done by appointment! Whatever happened to "You show me your wee-wee, and I'll show you mine"? You never hear that anymore.

But it's true. A lot of these striving, anal parents are burning their kids out on structure. I think what every child needs and ought to have every day is two hours of daydreaming. Plain old daydreaming. Turn off the Internet, the CD-ROMs, and the computer games and let them stare at a tree for a couple of hours. It's good for them. And you know something? Every now and then they actually come up with one of their own ideas. You want to know how you can help your kids? Leave them the fuck alone!

CARS AND DRIVING: PART TWO

Reverse Logic

Here's an embarrassing driving situation, the kind of thing that can haunt you for several hundred miles. One of those incidents you can't just shake off. Like the time you almost got killed by the big tractor-trailer, and had to pull off the road for about twenty minutes and listen to your heart slamming up against your rib cage? BAM! BAM! BAM! BAM! BAM! BAM! Well, this next thing is just like that, but this is one you do all by yourself.

Did you ever pull up to a red light, and go a little bit too far into the intersection? Just a few extra feet? So, you put the car in reverse and back up ju-u-u-u-st a little bit. And then you forget the car is in reverse? And so you sit there, innocently, waiting for the light to change. Looking around. Eager to get movin' again. Don't wanna keep the proctologist waiting. Da-dum, da-dum, dee-dee, da-dum.

At this point, folks, you are truly an accident waiting to happen. An insurance claim in progress. So, you sit some more, and you sit some more, and you wait, and you wait, and you wait. And you stare at the red light, and you look over at the woman on the right adjustin' her tits, and you look at the guy on the left pickin' his nose, and then finally—finally—the light changes and off you go! CRASH! CRUNCH! CRUMPLE! TINKLE! Directly backward into the grille of what was formerly a cute little red Yugo.

"Holy shit! How'd I get back here? This is where I was a coupla minutes ago!"

Apparently, you have to pay attention even at the red lights. I thought surely they were for resting. You know, drive a little, rest a little, drive a little, rest a little. Seemed that way to me. Guess not.

Oh, Brother!

Here's a little red-light story somebody told me a long time ago. This guy's drivin' along, he's got someone sittin' right next to him in the passenger seat, and he goes straight through a red light. ZOOOOM!

Passenger says, "Whaddaya doin'?"

Driver says, "Never mind! My brother drives like this."

They go a little farther, and come to another red light. ZOOM! Guy goes right through it!

"Whaddaya doin'?"

"Will you stop? I told ya, my brother drives like this."

He keeps on goin', and now he comes to a green light. He slams on the brakes.

"Whaddaya doin'?"

"Well, you never know. My brother might be comin' the other way!"

Turn, Turn, Turn

Now, a couple of things to remember when you're out in traffic. First of all, never get behind anybody weird. Y'ever get stuck behind a guy whose turn signal has been on for about eighty miles? And you're thinkin' to yourself, "Well, maybe he's just a really cautious man. I'm not gonna pass him now, he may turn at any moment."

And later you discover he was driving around the world—to the left!

Slow Dancin' in the Fast Lane

Another pain in the ass you don't want to get behind is anyone who drives real sss-l-l-l-o-o-o-ww. Boy, that's good for your arteries, isn't it? Someone really . . . really . . . sss-l-l-l-o-o-o-ww!

There are two classes of drivers in this category. The first is any four-foot woman in a Cadillac whose head you cannot see. This is certain death. At first you think, "Well, maybe it's a remote-controlled, experimental robot car. No, I can see tiny knuckles on the wheel and a small patch of blue hair." At this point I take no chances; I pull over immediately and take public transportation. I'm not about to fuck with a ghost car; let someone else flag down the Flying Dutchman, it's not my job.

Another driver you don't want to get behind is any man over seventy wearing a flannel cap with earflaps. In August. Keep your distance! Because, folks, you know how pissed you can get. Even though you think you're a mighty cool customer, you do get mighty pissed out there.

Gettin' Even

Don't you occasionally wish that instead of having headlights you had a couple of 50-caliber machine guns on the front of your car? So you could send several hundred rounds of burning lead into that slow-movin' gas guzzler up ahead? Just incinerate the motherfucker and get his ass off the road permanently?

Or don't you wish you were driving a rented car, so you could bash the asshole in the rear end, pay the deductible, and be done with the whole goddamn thing? BAM! BAM! BAM!

"Don't mind me, folks. I'm just tryin' to ease him into second gear." BAM! BAM! BAM!

God, it would do my heart good.

Or if the offender is directly behind you, wouldn't it be nice to have an electronic message board that would rise up out of the trunk of your car and let you type in any message you like? ATTENTION, ASSHOLE! YOU DRIVE LIKE OLD PEOPLE FUCK. SLOW AND SLOPPY!

You Light Up My Life

Speakin' of behind you, don't you just love it when there's one of those guys on your tail whose *brights are on*? Isn't that a treat? Some shit-stain who just had his headlights aimed and wants you to see what a wonderful job his mechanic did? You know how you handle a guy like that? Slam on your brakes and let him plow right into you. It might cost you a little money, but it sure puts them fuckin' lights out in a hurry. Let him find his way home in the dark.

Volume Control

Does this ever happen to you? You're driving through heavy downtown traffic, block to block, street to street. Busy area. People hurryin' home at five o'clock. Maybe it's winter, and it's already dark, raining a little bit. You got the window open, and you can hear the rain and the traffic noise. People honkin' at each other. Got the radio on. Got the windshield wipers going. Everything's happening at once: radio, rain, wipers, horns, traffic—lots of noise. And you're just trying to get across town to run an errand. And then, after all kinds of hassles, you get over there and park the car, turn off the key, go inside, and take care of business. And then when you come back out to the car and turn on the key, **THE GODDAMN RADIO IS THIS LOUD!!!**

And you sit there, stunned, thinking to yourself, "Could I . . . possibly . . . have been . . . listening to that?"

What's My Lane?

Here's one of those things you have to do every time you drive, especially if you're in a hurry. It happens as you approach a red light, and find several lanes of cars ahead of you. As you roll up to the pack, you have to decide which lane to get into. You have to guess which car looks like a good bet to take off quickly, so you can move out fast when the light turns green. With half a block to go you have to decide who's the really fast asshole in this group up ahead.

Forget the Volvo, she's listening to public radio, and drives the way she lives—with fear and caution. You'll also want to avoid that Toyota with the fish symbol; Christians drive as though Jesus himself was a traffic cop. And, by all means, ignore the Lexus with the heavily made-up, bejeweled pig-woman. She has the reflexes of an aging panda.

Ahhhhh! Here's the correct machine to get behind: a Camaro with four different shades of primer paint and a bumper sticker that says I DATE MY SISTER. This guy's a real risk-taker; full of crank, and on his way to an AC/DC concert. You'll be home before you know it.

Goin' Home

Now, one last reminder before I tow this trusty little shit-box of mine into the shop for its bimonthly overhaul. And this should go without saying. That's why I'm going to say it: Drinking and driving don't mix. Do your drinking early in the morning and get it out of the way. Then go driving while the visibility is still good.

HEIGH-HO, HEIGH-HO, IT'S OFF TO WORK WE GO

What wine goes with Cap'n Crunch? I have trouble selecting a wine in the morning. Sometimes I give up, smoke a bong full of Froot Loops, and just go back to bed. Try that sometime. Smoke a bong full of Froot Loops, go back to bed, and watch the midmorning movie. Call your boss and tell him you smoked some Froot Loops, you're watching a movie, and you'll be in around 2:30. That is, if you feel like it.

That's the way you handle a boss. You can't take shit from someone just because you work for him. Let him know who the real boss is. Tell him it's *your* job, and you'll do it *your* way. That's what bosses like—people with spunk. Act the same way when you go in for a job interview. Let 'em know what kind of person you are. Have a beer opener and some swizzle sticks sticking out of your breast pocket. Put a little confetti in your hair. Tell them your primary career is partying and work is kind of a sideline.

Tell the interviewer you'll need an office near the front door so you can leave in a hurry at five o'clock.

"I ain't stickin' around this fuckin' place after hours, I'll tell you that right now."

Let him know what's happening. Tell him you hope it's not one of those chicken-shit places where they dock your pay just for taking off Mondays and Fridays.

Then, if you still don't have the job, point to the picture on his desk and say, "Who's the cunt?" That'll clinch it. You'll probably have a nice long career with that firm. Once all your medical procedures have been completed.

SHORT TAKES

In the expression *topsy-turvy*, what exactly is meant by turvy?

I'd like to pass along a piece of wisdom my first-grade teacher shared with us kids. She said, "You show me a tropical fruit, and I'll show you a cocksucker from Guatemala." I'll always remember that.

I'm curious, what precisely is Zsa Zsa Gabor's job title?

If free trade can really turn all these Third World countries into thriving economies full of entrepreneurs and investors, who's gonna clean the fuckin' toilets around here?

You know what's fun? Go to a German restaurant and insist on using chopsticks.

I'm happy to say that during the 2000 Olympics I missed every single event without exception, managing even to avoid all the clips shown on newscasts. And although I sometimes watch NBC and MSNBC for other reasons, this time, whenever I ventured into those two locations it was with the remote control firmly in hand, ready to change channels instantly, in the event that depressing Olympic theme music or those repulsive five rings suddenly showed up.

If it requires a uniform it's a worthless endeavor.

True Stuff There is actually a TV commercial in Las Vegas that advertises a service called "Discount Bankruptcy."

There is now a Starbucks in my pants.

As long as you've decided to drink all day there's nothing wrong with starting early in the morning.

Odd Fact When two women with different colored hair walk together on a sidewalk, the one with the darker hair will always be positioned closest to the curb.

I hope we're not just human garbage drifting toward a big sewer. But I think so.

I like the fact that rap musicians are murdering each other. I don't have a problem with rap music, it's just that I like the idea of celebrities killing each other. Wouldn't it be great if Dan Rather snuck up on Tom Brokaw during the news and stabbed him in the head? Or imagine Julie Andrews putting rat poison in Liza Minnelli's triple vodka when she gets up to take a shit at Sardi's. Here's a great one: Richard Simmons and Louie Anderson grab Rosie O'Donnell and choke her to death. It's just fun to think about, isn't it?

Tennis tip You get a better return of serve if you let the ball bounce twice before hitting it.

People on a diet should have a salad dressing called "250 Islands."

Can anyone explain to me the need for one-hour photo finishing? You just saw the fuckin' thing! How can you possibly be nostalgic about a concept like "a little while ago"?

I tried to give up heroin, but my efforts were all in vein.

When I was a boy, on Good Friday in my parish, in order to dramatize the extent of Jesus' suffering, a group of the priests used to get together and crucify one of the children.

If the reason for climbing Mt. Everest is that it's hard to do, why does everyone go up the easy side?

By and large, language is a tool for concealing the truth.

What is all this shit about Dick Clark not looking his age? Take a closer look.

You know my favorite play in baseball? The bean ball. It's great, isn't it? It's dramatic. Especially if the guy is really hurt. Sometimes the ball hits the helmet, and you feel kind of disappointed. Even though it makes a good loud noise.

Do you ever open the dictionary right to the page you want? Doesn't that feel good?

Here's my idea for another one of those "reality-based" TV shows: "No Survivors!" One by one, a psychopathic serial killer tracks down and kills all of the "Survivor" survivors. Think of it as a public service.

As far as I'm concerned, humans have not yet come up with a belief that's worth believing.

People get all upset about torture, but when you get right down to it, it's really a pretty good way of finding out something a person doesn't want you to know.

How soon can we begin to execute these yuppie half-wits who name their golden retrievers Jake and put red bandannas around their necks? Apparently, this is viewed as amusing or ironic or some other quality yuppies value highly. It isn't amusing; it's precious, half-wit bullshit.

They say only 10 percent of the brain's function is known. Apparently, the function of the remaining 90 percent is to keep us from discovering its function.

Ethnic-wise, I'll tell you this: if I hadn't turned out to be Irish, I would've really liked to be a guinea.

You know the good part about all those executions in Texas? Fewer Texans.

I'm tired of hearing about innocent victims. It's fiction. If you live on this planet you're guilty, period, fuck you, next case, end of report. Your birth certificate is proof of guilt.

I enjoy watching reruns of *Saturday Night Live* and counting all the dead people.

AIRPORT SECURITY

I'm getting tired of all this security at the airport. There's too much of it. I'm tired of some fat chick with a double-digit IQ and a triple-digit income rootin' around inside my bag for no reason and never finding anything. Haven't found anything yet. Haven't found one bomb in one bag. And don't tell me, "Well, the terrorists know their bags are going to be searched, so now they're leaving their bombs at home." There are no bombs! The whole thing is fuckin' pointless.

And it's completely without logic. There's no logic at all. They'll take away a gun, but let you keep a knife! Well, what the fuck is that? In fact, there's a whole list of lethal objects they will allow you to take on board. Theoretically, you could take a knife, an ice pick, a hatchet, a straight razor, a pair of scissors, a chain saw, six knitting needles, and a broken whiskey bottle, and the only thing they'd say to you is, "That bag has to fit all the way under the seat in front of you."

And if you *didn't* take a weapon on board, relax. After you've been flying for about an hour, they're gonna bring you a knife and fork! They actually give you a fucking knife! It's only a table knife—but you could kill a pilot with a table knife. It might take you a couple of minutes. Especially if he's hefty. But you could get the job done. If you really wanted to kill the prick.

Shit, there are a lot of things you could use to kill a guy with. You could probably beat a guy to death with the Sunday *New York Times*. Or suppose you just had really big hands, couldn't you strangle a flight attendant? Shit, you could probably strangle two of them, one with each hand. That is, if you were lucky enough to catch 'em in that little kitchen area. Just before they break out the fuckin' peanuts. But you could get the job done. If you really cared enough.

So, why is it they allow a man with big, powerful hands to get on board an airplane? I'll tell you why. They know he's not a security risk, because he's already answered the three big questions. Question number one:

"Did you pack your bags yourself?"

"No, Carrot Top packed my bags. He and Martha Stewart and Florence Henderson came over to the house last night, fixed me a lovely lobster Newburg, gave me a full body massage with sacred oils from India, performed a four-way 'around-the-world,' and then they packed my bags. Next question."

"Have your bags been in your possession the whole time?"

"No. Usually the night before I travel—just as the moon is rising—I place my suitcases out on the street corner and leave them there, unattended, for several hours. Just for good luck. Next question."

"Has any unknown person asked you to take anything on board?"

"Well, what exactly is an 'unknown person'? Surely everyone is known to someone. In fact, just this morning, Kareem and Youssef Ali ben Gabba seemed to know each other quite well. They kept joking about which one of my suitcases was the heaviest."

And that's another thing they don't like at the airport. Jokes. You can't joke about a bomb. Well, why is it just jokes? What about a riddle? How about a limerick? How about a bomb anecdote? You know, no punch line, just a really cute story. Or, suppose you intended the remark not as a joke but as an ironic musing? Are they prepared to make that distinction? I think not! And besides, who's to say what's funny?

Airport security is a stupid idea, it's a waste of money, and it's there for only one reason: to make white people feel safe! That's all it's for. To provide a feeling, an illusion, of safety in order to placate the middle class. Because the authorities know they can't make airplanes safe; too many people have access. You'll notice the drug smugglers don't seem to have a lot of trouble getting their little packages on board, do they? No. And God bless them, too.

And by the way, an airplane flight shouldn't be completely safe. You need a little danger in your life. Take a fuckin' chance, will ya? What are you gonna do, play with your prick for another thirty years? What, are you gonna read *People* magazine and eat at Wendy's till the end of time? Take a fuckin' chance!

Besides, even if they made all of the airplanes completely safe, the terrorists would simply start bombing other places that are crowded: pornshops, crack houses, titty bars, and gang bangs. You know, entertainment venues. The odds of you being killed by a terrorist are practically zero. So I say, relax and enjoy the show.

You have to be realistic about terrorism. Certain groups of people—Muslim fundamentalists, Christian fundamentalists, Jewish fundamentalists, and just plain guys from Montana—are going to continue to make life in this country very interesting for a long, long time. That's the reality. Angry men in combat fatigues talkin' to God on a two-way radio and muttering incoherent slogans about freedom are eventually gonna provide us with a great deal of entertainment.

Especially after your stupid fuckin' economy collapses all around you, and the terrorists come out of the woodwork. And you'll have anthrax in the water supply and sarin gas in the air conditioners; there'll be chemical and biological suitcase-bombs in every city, and I say, "Relax. Enjoy the show! Take a fuckin' chance. Put a little fun in your life."

To me, terrorism is exciting. I think the very idea that you can set off a bomb in Macy's and kill several hundred people is exciting and stimulating, and I see it as a form of entertainment.

But I also know most Americans are soft, frightened, unimaginative people, who have no idea there's such a thing as dangerous fun. And they certainly don't recognize good entertainment when they see it. I have always been willing to put myself at great personal risk for the sake of entertainment. And I've always been willing to put you at great personal risk for the same reason.

As far as I'm concerned, all of this airport security—the cameras, the questions, the screenings, the searches—is just one more way of reducing your liberty and reminding you that they can fuck with you anytime they want—as long as you're willing to put up with it. Which means, of course, anytime they want. Because that's the way Americans are now. They're always willing to trade away a little of their freedom in exchange for the feeling—the illusion—of security.

What we now have is a completely neurotic population obsessed with security, safety, crime, drugs, cleanliness, hygiene, and germs! There's another thing. Fear of germs.

FEAR OF GERMS

Where did this sudden fear of germs come from in this country? Have you noticed this? The media constantly doing stories about the latest infections? Salmonella, *E. coli,* hantavirus, West Nile fever? And Americans panic easily, so now everybody's running around, scrubbing this, spraying that, overcooking their food, and repeatedly washing their hands; trying to avoid all contact with germs.

It's ridiculous, and it goes to ridiculous lengths. In prisons—and this is true—in prisons, before they give you a lethal injection, they swab your arm with alcohol. It's true! Well, they don't want you to get an infection. And you can see their point: wouldn't want some guy to go to hell *and* be sick! It would take a lot of the sport out of the whole execution.

Fear of germs. Buncha fuckin' pussies. You can't even get a decent hamburger anymore; they cook the shit out of everything, because everyone's afraid of food poisoning. Hey, where's your sense of adventure? Take a fuckin' chance! You know how many people die from food poisoning in this country every year? Nine thousand! That's all! It's a minor risk. Take a fuckin' chance. Buncha goddamn pussies!

Besides, what do you think you have an immune system for? It's for killing germs. But it needs practice. It needs germs to practice on. So if you kill all the germs around you and live a completely sterile life, then when germs do come along, you're not going to be prepared.

And never mind ordinary germs, what are you gonna do when some super-virus comes along that turns your vital organs into liquid shit? I'll tell you what you're gonna do. You're gonna get sick, you're gonna die, and you're gonna deserve it, because you're fuckin' weak, and you've got a fuckin' weak immune system.

Let me tell you a true story about immunization. When I was a little boy in New York City in the 1940s, we swam in the Hudson River. And it was filled with raw sewage. Okay? We swam in raw sewage! You know, to cool off.

At that time the big fear was polio; thousands of kids died from polio every year. But you know somethin'? In my neighborhood no one ever got polio. No one. Ever! You know why? Because we swam in raw sewage! It strengthened our immune systems. The polio never had a prayer; we were tempered in raw shit!

So, personally, I never take any special precautions against germs. I don't shy away from people who sneeze and cough, I don't wipe off the telephone, I don't cover the toilet seat, and if I drop food on the floor, I pick it up and eat it. Even if I'm at a sidewalk café. In Calcutta. The poor section. On New Year's morning during a soccer riot.

And you know something? In spite of all of that so-called risky behavior, I never get infections. I just don't get 'em, folks. I don't get colds, I don't get flu, and I don't get food poisoning. And you know why? Because I have a good, strong immune system, and it gets a lot of practice.

My immune system is equipped with the biological equivalent of fully automatic, military assault rifles with night vision and laser scopes. And we have recently acquired phosphorous grenades, cluster bombs, and anti-personnel fragmentation mines.

So, when my white blood cells are on patrol, reconnoitering my blood stream, seeking out strangers and other undesirables, if they see any—*any*—suspicious-looking germs of any kind, they don't fuck around. They whip out the weapons, wax the motherfucker, and deposit the unlucky fellow directly into my colon! Directly into my colon! There's no nonsense. There's no Miranda warning, there's none of that three-strikes-and-you're-out shit. First offense, BAM! Into the colon you go.

And speaking of my colon, I want you to know I don't automatically wash my hands every time I go to the bathroom. Can you deal with that? Sometimes I do, sometimes I don't. You know when I wash my hands? When I shit on them! That's the only time. And you know how often that happens? Tops—tops—two, three times a week. Tops! Maybe a little more frequently over the holidays. You know what I mean?

And I'll tell you something else, my well-scrubbed friends. You don't always need a shower every day. Did you know that? It's overkill! Unless you work out, or work outdoors, or for some reason come in intimate contact with huge amounts of filth and garbage every day, you don't always need a shower.

All you really need is to wash the four key areas: armpits, asshole, crotch, and teeth! Got that? The hooker's bath. Armpits, asshole, crotch, and teeth. In fact, you can save yourself a whole lot of time if you simply use the same brush on all four areas!

BUT FIRST, THIS FUCKIN' MESSAGE

Commercials use sex to sell things; why can't they use violence and bad language too? Not all families are as "functional" as the ones they show you on TV.

MOM: Eat your fuckin' corn flakes, ya cocksucker!

SON: Fuck you, Ma.

MOM: Why you little creep!
SLAM! SMACK! POW!

DAD: Here, Son, try this. It's new from Kellogg's.

SON: Holy shit, raisins!

MOM: Hey, asshole! What're ya tryin' to do, spoil the kid?

DAD: Listen, cunt, I'm tired of your meddlin'!
BLAM! POW! CRACK!

SON: Hey, Dad, when you get finished punchin' Mom, gimme some more of that shit with the raisins in it, will ya?

Advertising Lullabye

Quality, value, style,
service, selection, convenience,
economy, savings, performance,
experience, hospitality,
low rates, friendly service,
name brands, easy terms,
affordable prices, money-back guarantee,
free installation.

Free admission, free appraisal, free alterations,
free delivery, free estimates,
free home trial—and free parking.

No cash? No problem. No kidding!
No fuss, no muss, no risk, no obligation,
no red tape, no down payment,
no entry fee, no hidden charges,
no purchase necessary,
no one will call on you,
no payments or interest till September.

Limited time only, though,
so act now,
order today,
send no money,
offer good while supplies last,
two to a customer,
each item sold separately,
batteries not included,

mileage may vary,
all sales are final,
allow six weeks for delivery,
some items not available,
some assembly required,
some restrictions may apply.

So come on in for a free demonstration and a free consultation with our friendly, professional staff. Our experienced and knowledgeable sales representatives will help you make a selection that's just right for you and just right for your budget.

And don't forget to pick up your free gift: A classic, deluxe, custom, designer, luxury, prestige, high-quality, premium, select, gourmet pocket pencil sharpener. Yours for the asking, no purchase necessary. It's our way of saying thank you.

And if you act now, we'll include an extra, added, free, complimentary bonus gift, at no cost to you. A classic, deluxe, custom, designer, luxury, prestige, high-quality, premium, select, gourmet combination key ring, magnifying glass, and garden hose. In a genuine, imitation leather-style carrying case with authentic vinyl trim. Yours for the asking, no purchase necessary. It's our way of saying thank you.

Actually, it's our way of saying, "Bend over just a little farther, so we can stick this big advertising dick up your ass a little bit deeper [pelvic thrust!]. A little bit deeper [thrust!], a little bit deeper [thrust!], you miserable, no-good, dumb-ass, fucking consumer!"

SHORT TAKES

Here's some fun: Stand on line at the bank for a really long time. Then, when you finally get up to the window, just ask for change of a nickel. It's fun. They actually call other tellers over to look at you.

Regarding Pokémon, Beanie Babies, and such: something is really wrong when a major news story concerns how hard it is to buy a toy.

I don't know how you feel, but I'm pretty sick of church people. You know what they ought to do with churches? Tax them. If holy people are so interested in politics, government, and public policy, let them pay the price of admission like everybody else. The Catholic Church alone could wipe out the national debt if all you did was tax their real estate.

Whenever I see a large crowd of people, I wonder how many of them will eventually require autopsies.

Laptop. How can this be? A lap has no top; it has only two dimensions, length and width. It's not like a desk. A desk has a bottom, a top, and sides; you place your "desktop" on the top of your desk. A lap has only one plane; when you stand up your lap disappears. And your computer becomes a floortop.

Everything beeps now.

First there was rock 'n' roll, now there's just rock. What happened to "roll"? And what did Sears do with Roebuck? And exactly when did Montgomery leave Montgomery Ward? I have a theory. I believe that somewhere on a stage tonight a show will be performed by the Montgomery-Roebuck Roll Band.

I think there ought to be a feminine hygiene spray called "Sprunt."

Think of how strange we'd look if all the cuts, burns, scrapes, bruises, scratches, bumps, gashes, and scabs we've ever had suddenly reappeared on our bodies at the same time.

Regarding jam sessions: jazz musicians are the only workers I can think of who are willing to put in a full shift for pay and then go somewhere else and continue working for free.

When someone asks you what time it is, glance at your watch and say, "It's either six-fifteen, or Mickey has a hard-on." Guaranteed they'll ask somebody else.

What's with these super-cautious drivers who pull way over to the far end of a speed bump so their cars won't have to go over the highest point? Are they really worried that speed bumps hurt their cars?

Griddle cakes, pancakes, hotcakes, flapjacks: why are there four names for grilled batter and only one word for love?

I would like to open a restaurant, call it the Marilyn Monroe Café, and put hundreds of pictures of Jeff Goldblum on the wall.

I notice that unlike on other holidays, the police don't seem to make a big deal about drunk driving on Good Friday.

You know what I never liked? The high-five. I consider it lame white-boy shit. When a guy raises his arm to give me a high-five, you know what I do? Stab him in the arm. I'm tired of that shit. Sometimes I watch an old sports film on ESPN Classic, and I see a whole game without a single high-five. It's great.

When you think about it, 12:15 P.M. is actually 11:75 A.M.

At one time there existed a race of people whose knowledge consisted entirely of gossip.

A crazy person doesn't really lose his mind. It just becomes something more entertaining.

Instead of having truck scales on the highway, I think they ought to get one of those guys from the carnival and let him guess the weights.

An art thief is a man who takes pictures.

You know a phrase I never understood? King size. It's used to denote something larger, but most of the kings you see are short. You ever notice that? Usually a king is a short little fat guy. You never see a tall king. When's the last gangly king you can remember?

I hope the world ends during the daytime. I want to watch
"film at eleven."

Everywhere you look there are families with too many vehicles. You see them on the highways
in their RVs. But apparently the RVs aren't enough, because behind them they're towing
motorboats, go-carts, dune buggies, dirt bikes, jet-skis, snowmobiles, parasails, hang gliders,
hot-air balloons, and small, two-man, deep-sea diving bells. The only thing these people lack
is lunar excursion modules. Doesn't anybody take a fuckin' walk anymore?

The older a person gets, the less they care what they wear. Old people
come up with some of the strangest clothing combinations you'll ever
see. I think of it as "cancer of the clothing."

We're not supposed to mention fucking in mixed company,
but that's exactly where it takes place.

The other day I was thinking of how many peanuts elephants owe us.
Personally, I'm down about twenty-three or twenty-four bags.

Did you ever start hittin' a guy with a big club for no
reason? Just walk up to him and start beatin' him over
the head with a big, heavy club? It's great, isn't it?

If it's true that our species is alone in the universe, then I'd have to say
the universe aimed rather low and settled for very little.

INTERVIEW WITH JESUS

Interviewer: Ladies and Gentlemen, we're privileged to have with us a man known around the world as the Prince of Peace, Jesus Christ.
Jesus: That's me.

I: *How are you, Jesus?*

J: Fine, thanks, and let me say it's great to be back.

I: *Why, after all this time, have you come back?*

J: Mostly nostalgia.

I: *Can you tell us a little bit about the first time you were here?*

J: Well, there's not much to tell. I think everybody knows the story by now. I was born on Christmas. And actually, that always bothered me, because I only got one present. You know, if I was born a couple of months earlier I would've got two presents. But look, I'm not complaining. After all, it's only material goods.

I: *There's a story that there were three wise men.*

J: Well, there were three kings who showed up. I don't know how wise they were. They didn't *look* very wise. They said they followed a star. That don't sound wise to me.

I: *Didn't they bring gifts?*

J: Yes. Gold, frankincense, and I believe, myrrh, which I never did find out what that was. You don't happen to know what myrrh is, do you?

I: *Well, I believe it's a reddish-brown, bitter gum resin.*

J: Oh, great. Just what I need. What am I gonna do with a gum resin? I'd rather have the money, that way I could buy something I need. You know, something I wouldn't normally buy for myself.

I: *What would that be?*

J: Oh, I don't know. A bathing suit. I never had a bathing suit. Maybe a Devo hat. Possibly a bicycle. I really coulda used a bicycle. Do you realize all the walking I did? I must've crossed Canaan six, eight times. Up and down, north and south, walking and talking, doin' miracles, tellin' stories.

I: *Tell us about the miracles. How many miracles did you perform?*

J: Well, leaving out the loaves and the fishes, a total of 107 miracles.

I: *Why not the loaves and the fishes?*

J: Well, technically that one wasn't a miracle.

I: *It wasn't?*

J: No, it turns out a lot of people were putting them back. They were several days old. And besides, not all those miracles were pure miracles anyway.

I: *What do you mean? If they weren't miracles, what were they?*

J: Well, some of them were parlor tricks, optical illusions, mass hypnosis. Sometimes people were hallucinatin'. I even used acupressure. That's how I cured most of the blind people, acupressure.

I: *So not all of the New Testament is true.*

J: Naaah. Some of the gospel stuff never happened at all. It was just made up. Luke and Mark used a lot of drugs. Luke was a physician, and he had access to drugs. Matthew and John were okay, but Luke and Mark would write anything.

I: *What about raising Lazarus from the dead?*

J: First of all, he wasn't dead, he was hungover. I've told people that.

I: *But in the Bible you said he was dead.*

J: No! I said he *looked* dead. I said, "Jeez, Peter, this guy looks dead!" You see, Lazarus was a very heavy sleeper, plus the day before we had been to a wedding feast, and he had put away a lot of wine.

I: *Ahhh! Was that the wedding feast at Cana, where you changed the water into wine?*

J: I don't know. We went to an awful lot of wedding feasts in those days.

I: *But did you ever really turn water into wine?*

J: Not that I know of. One time I turned apple juice into milk, but I don't recall the water and wine.

I: *All right, speaking of water, let me ask you about another miracle. What about walking on water? Did that really happen?*

J: Oh yeah, that was one that really happened. You see, the problem was, I could do it, and the other guys couldn't. They were jealous. Peter got so mad at me he had these special shoes made, special big shoes, that if you started out walkin' real fast you could stay on top of the water for a while. Then, of course, after a few yards, badda-boom, down he goes right into the water. He sinks like a rock. That's why I called him Peter. Thou art Peter, and upon this rock I shall build my church.

I: *Well, that brings up the Apostles. What can you tell us about the Apostles?*

J: They smelled like bait, but they were a good bunch of guys. Thirteen of them we had.

I: *Thirteen? The Bible says there were only twelve.*

J: Well, that was according to Luke. I told you about Luke. Actually, we had thirteen. We had Peter, James, John, Andrew, Phillip, Bartholomew, Matthew, Thomas, James, that's a different James, Thaddeus. How many is that?

I: *That's ten.*

J: Simon, Judas, and Red.

I: *Red?*

J: Yeah, Red the Apostle.

I: *Red the Apostle doesn't appear in the Bible.*

J: Nah, Red kept pretty much to himself. He never came to any of the weddings. He was a little strange; he thought the Red Sea was named after him.

I: *And what about Judas?*

J: Don't get me started on Judas. A completely unpleasant person, okay?

I: *Well, what about the other Apostles, say for instance, Thomas, was he really a doubter?*

J: Believe me, this guy Thomas, you couldn't tell him nothin'. He was always asking me for ID. Soon as I would see him, he would go, "You got any ID?" To this day he doesn't believe I'm God.

I: *And are you God?*

J: Well, partly. I'm a member of the Trinity.

I: *Yes. In fact, you're writing a book about the Trinity.*

J: That's right, it's called *Three's a Crowd.*

I: *As I understand it, it's nothing more than a thinly veiled attack on the Holy Ghost.*

J: Listen, it's not an attack, okay? It happens I don't get along with the Holy Ghost. So I leave him alone. That's it. What he does is his business.

I: *What's the reason?*

J: Well, first of all, he's a wise guy. Every time he shows up, he appears as somethin' different. One day he's a dove, another day he's a tongue of fire. Always foolin' around. I don't bother with the guy. I don't wanna know about him, I don't wanna see him, I don't wanna talk to him.

I: *Well, let me change the subject. Is there really a place called hell?*

J: Oh yeah, there's a hell, all right. There's also a heck. It's not as severe as hell, but we've got a heck and a hell.

I: *What about purgatory?*

J: No, I don't know about no purgatory. We got heaven, hell, heck, and limbo.

I: *What is limbo like?*

J: I don't know. No one is allowed in. If anyone was in there it wouldn't be limbo, it would just be another place.

I: *Getting back to your previous visit, what can you tell us about the Last Supper?*

J: Well, first of all, if I'da known I was gonna be crucified, I woulda had a bigger meal. You never want to be crucified on an empty stomach. As it was, I had a little salad and some veal.

I: *The crucifixion must have been terrible.*

J: Oh yeah, it was awful. Unless you went through it yourself, you could never know how painful it was. And tiring. It was very, very tiring. But I think more than anything else, it was embarrassing. You know, in front of all those people, to be crucified like that. But, I guess it redeemed a lot of people. I hope so. It would be a shame to do it for no reason.

I: *Were you scared?*

J: Oh yeah. I was afraid it was gonna rain; I thought for sure I would get hit by lightning. One good thing, though, while I was up there I had a really good view; I could actually see my house. There's always a bright side.

I: *And then three days later you rose from the dead.*

J: How's that?

I: *On Easter Sunday. You rose from the dead, didn't you?*

J: Not that I know of. I think I would remember something like that. I do remember sleeping a long time after the crucifixion. Like I said, it was very tiring. I think what mighta happened was I passed out, and they *thought* I was dead. We didn't have such good medical people in those days. It was mostly volunteers.

I: *And, according to the Bible, forty days later you ascended into heaven.*

J: Pulleys! Ropes, pulleys, and a harness. I think it was Simon came up with a great harness thing that went under my toga. You couldn't see it at all. Since that day, I been in Heaven, and, all in all, I would have to say that while I was down here I had a really good time. Except for the suffering.

I: *And what do you think about Christianity today?*

J: Well, I'm a little embarrassed by it. I wish they would take my name off it. If I had the whole thing to do over, I would probably start one of those Eastern religions like Buddha. Buddha was smart. That's how come he's laughing.

I: *You wouldn't want to be a Christian?*

J: No, I wouldn't want to be a member of any group whose symbol is a man nailed onto some wood. Especially if it's me. Buddha's laughing, meanwhile I'm on the cross.

I: *I have a few more questions, do you mind?*

J: Hey, be my guest, how often do I get here?

I: *Are there really angels?*

J: Well, not as many as we used to have. Years ago we had millions of them. Today you can't get the young people to join. It got too dangerous with all the radar and heat-seeking missiles.

I: *What about guardian angels? Are there such things?*

J: Yes, we still have guardian angels, but now, with the population explosion, it's one angel for every six people. Years ago everybody had his own angel.

I: *Do you really answer prayers?*

J: No. First of all, what with sun spots and radio interference, a lot of them don't even get through. And between you and me, we just don't have the staff to handle the workload anymore. In the old days we took pride in answering every single prayer, but like I said, there were less people. And in those days people prayed for something simple, to light a fire, to catch a yak, something like that. But today you got people

praying for hockey teams, for longer fingernails, to lose
weight. We just can't keep up.

I: *Well, I think we're about out of time. I certainly want to thank
     you for visiting with us.*

J: Hey, no sweat.

I: *Do you have any words of advice?*

J: You mean like how to remove chewing gum from a suede
     garment? Something like that?

I: *No, I mean spiritual advice.*

J: Well, I don't know how spiritual it is, but I'd say one thing
     is don't give your money to the church. They should be giving
     their money to you.

I: *Well, thank you, Jesus, and good night.*

J: Well, good night, thanks for having me on here today. And
     by the way, in case anyone is interested, bell-bottoms will be
     coming back in the year 2015. Ciao.

I WISH I HAD MY MONEY BACK

Do you ever wonder who empties the wishing wells? That's our
money. I've never received an accounting. It's just gone. Someone,
apparently, is emptying the wishing wells and keeping the money.
And I'm wondering whether or not that cancels out the wishes. Sup-

pose it's a wish that takes time to come true. Like if you wish some friend of yours would develop cancer. That takes time. How can it come true if your nickel has already been rolled in a wrapper and deposited in a bank?

And when does this coin retrieval take place? I'm sure they don't do it on Sunday afternoon as some little girl is tossing in a penny, wishing for her daddy to come back from heaven. No, they probably do it at three in the morning, wearing black T-shirts and ski masks. I think this has gone far enough. I want to know what's going on. My friend is still perfectly healthy, and I'm concerned.

Punk Bands I Have Known

Tower of Swine
Room in My Shorts
Mary Krenwinkle's Revenge
Sphincter Hoedown
Basket of Fire
Trees for Lunch
Glandular Imbalance
A Fine Way to Die
Let's Pull Our Eyes Out
Sewer Transaction
Cosmic Groin Pull
Pudding Disease
A Rare Twinkie
Rubber Thoughts
Vaginal Spotting

The Note Fuckers
Puke All Night
Anal Lace
Gorilla Tits
Harmony Sucks
Warts, Waffles and Walter
Mess-Kit Germ Colony
Hideous Infant
Clots on the Move
Systematic Rejection
The Stillborn
Household Pest
Breach of the Peace
Thankless Child
Persistent Rain
Days of Doubt
Sack of Shit
Hole in My Scrotum
Ed, Formerly Don
Cocaine Snot Groove
Hilda Fucks
Waitress Sweat
Infected Mole
This Band Needs Practice

A CAT IS NOT A DOG

Most people understand that cats are completely different from dogs, and generally they like them for different reasons. One quality people like in cats is their independence; they appreciate a pet who can take care of himself. "I never have to do a thing. He cleans his room, makes his own clothing, and drives himself to work."

Unlike dogs, who are needy and dependent, and who like you merely because you know where the food is located, cats don't get all hung up on fake affection. They don't go nuts and slobber all over you when you come home, the way a dog does. They parcel out a certain limited amount of physical affection from time to time, but it probably has more to do with static electricity than anything else.

"Not Me!"

Cats have another quality I find admirable: blamelessness. When a cat makes a mistake, he doesn't accept responsibility or show embarrassment. If he does something really stupid, like jumping onto a table and landing in four separate coffee cups, somehow he passes the whole thing off as routine. Dogs aren't like that. If a dog knocks over a lamp, you can tell who did it by looking at the dog; he acts guilty and ashamed. Not the cat. When a cat breaks something, he simply moves along to the next activity.

"What's that? The lamp? Not me! Fuck that, I'm a cat! Something broken? Ask the dog."

"I Meant That!"

A cat can make any mistake appear intentional. Have you ever seen a cat race across a room and crash into a glass door? It doesn't faze him at all.

WHIZZZ! SPLAT!!

"I meant that! I actually meant that. That's exactly what I was trying to do."

Then he limps behind the couch, holding his head:

"Oh, Jesus! Fuckin' me-ooow! Goddamn fuckin' me-oooooooow!"

Your cat is much too proud to let you see him suffer. But if you look behind the couch, you'll see him recuperating from a domestic mishap.

"Hi. Tried to jump from the sofa to the window. Didn't make it. Tore a ligament. Got milk?"

Rub Me Tender

Cats are very tactile; they love to rub against your leg. If you own a cat, and you have a leg, you've got a happy cat.

"Oh boy, oh boy! I'm rubbing against his leg! How I love his leg!"

If you have two legs, you've got yourself a party.

"Oh boy, oh boy, *two* legs! Now I can do the figure eight."

They love to do the figure eight: around one leg, in between, and then around the other.

"Oh boy, oh boy. I'm doing the figure eight."

He'll rub against your legs even if you're not there yet. You might be twenty feet down the hall. As soon as he sees you coming he starts walking sideways. He doesn't want to miss a shot at your legs.

"Oh boy, oh boy! Here he comes! *Soon* I'll be doing the figure eight."

His Ass Is Yours

Cats are so tactile you don't even have to do the petting. All you need is to put your hand somewhere near him, and he'll lean into you and do all the work. They love to push back.

Then there's the ass trick. Did you ever stroke a cat who's lying absolutely flat, and before you've run your hand halfway down his back, his ass is sticking way up in the air? As if you pressed an "ass button" or something?

"Isn't he a cute little . . . holy shit! How did he do that?"

Or sometimes if he's on the bed with you he'll climb onto your chest and stick his ass right in your face:

"Hey, here's my ass! Check my ass, Daddy! Get a nice, clean look at my ass!"

And then while he's showing you his ass, he starts that kneading thing with his paws; like he's playin' the piano. God, I hate that.

"Get him offa me! Jesus, I hate that! I don't even know what it is, and I hate that. It's as if he got hold of some bad drugs. What is that?"

"It's an instinctive nursing behavior, honey. He misses his mommy."

"You always say that. You said that about the mailman."

DOG MOMENTS #1

Fido Doesn't Care

Dogs have no priorities or schedules. You rarely see a dog with a wristwatch. Most things they do they will do anywhere, at any time. Except for the things you teach them *not* to do:

"Laszlo! Don't ever do that again. If you do I'll beat the shit out of you!"

They do catch on to suggestions like that.

But basically, a dog doesn't care *what* he does. He'll simply do whatever's next. He doesn't really *know* what's next, but he'll think of something.

He might even do two things in a row that don't go together. Did y'ever see a dog trotting through a room, apparently headed somewhere, and suddenly he stops and chews his back for about eight minutes? As if the whole thing were scheduled for that exact moment? And then finally, when he's finished chewing, he forgets where he was going in the first place and just sort of looks around, confused.

"Let's see, where was I goin'? Shit, I forget. Seemed important at the time. Well, I guess I'll just lie down here under this chair. Hey, it's nice under here. I must do this more often."

He doesn't know, and he doesn't care.

A Little Light Buffet

Like I say, he'll do anything at any time. He might even embarrass you when you have company.

You might have some folks over to the house; folks you don't know that well; people you're tryin' to impress. Hell, you might even be tryin' to borrow money from one of these assholes.

And all these people are sittin' around the living room, and you've put out some chips and a little dip, carrot sticks, maybe a little light buffet, and everybody is eating nicely and chatting politely, and the dog is lying there on the floor, in full view.

And suddenly, you glance over, and realize that the dog . . . is licking . . . his balls! Vigorously! Big, long, loving licks, in full view of everyone. And no one is saying a word.

Remember now, a spectacular thing is taking place: a naked, living creature is administering a modified form of autofellatio in the presence of strangers. Not only is it a spectacular act, it's difficult to do. If I could do that I'd never leave the house.

And yet it goes unremarked. And if someone does say something, it's usually innocuous.

"Look. Isn't he cute? He's taking a bath."

"No, Carla, that's not a bath. That's called licking your balls. If that's a bath, I'd have to say it's a mighty selective one. He's been on that one spot for over an hour now."

Then the dog trots over and starts to lick your face.

"No, no! No, Bruno! Down! Down, Bruno! Nice doggie!"

"Oh, don't worry about it. Don't you know they have the cleanest mouth of any animal?"

"Well, I'm not a chemist, Velma. I'm just basing my judgment on his most recent activity, which you'll recall was licking his balls."

SHORT TAKES

Here's a word you don't see anymore: foodstuffs. I wish it would make a comeback.

Suppose you took an oath by placing your *right* hand on the Bible and raising your left? Would the oath still count? Does God really give a shit? Does anyone?

Let's give credit where it's due and admit that Scotch tape was a really great idea.

Here's a fun thing to do on a Saturday afternoon. As you watch the football scores on TV, try to visualize each college's campus. Then picture yourself fucking someone on the lawn in front of the Administration Building.

You live eighty years, and at best you get about six minutes of pure magic.

America would be better off if we took all these male Citadel and VMI students and simply castrated them. What kind of pig jackoffs go to these places in the first place? I say cut off their nuts.

I think the blacks in South Africa should just go ahead and kill all the whites and be done with it. Problem solved.

Remembering exactly where you were when some famous person died is a meaningless exercise. It's an attempt by ordinary people to connect their dull lives to important events. Can't we discourage this practice?

There are eleven teams in the Big Ten.

The gray-haired douche bag, Barbara Bush, has a slogan: "Encourage your child to read every day." What she should be doing is encouraging children to *question* what they read every day.

"Rivera Live" is such a good show. If only Rivera weren't on it.

Sometimes when you're burying a guy alive, for a moment or two you start feeling sorry for him. And then it passes, and you keep on shovelling.

I have a friend who loves to run through Der Weinerschnitzel yelling, "Bon appetito!"

I think everyone should treat one another in a Christian manner. I will not however be responsible for the consequences.

I wonder if an Elvis impersonator could ever get famous enough so that someone who looked like him could become a celebrity lookalike. Is there room in this culture for an Elvis-impersonator lookalike? Probably.

One objection to cloning human beings is that there's a chance for abnormal offspring. Yeah? So? You ever take a look at some of those families in the South?

Why do they bother saying "raw sewage"? Do some people actually cook that stuff?

I think pimps should have an Employee of the Month the way other businesses do. It would be good for morale. And I'll bet blow jobs would improve, too.

You rarely run into a damsel anymore.

Whenever I hear someone referred to as a spiritual leader, I wonder why the spirit world needs leaders.

Here's more bullshit middlebrow philosophy: "That which doesn't kill me makes me stronger." I've got something a little more realistic: "That which doesn't kill me still may sever my spinal cord, crush my rib cage, cave in my skull, and leave me helpless and paralyzed, soaking in a puddle of my own waste." Put that on your T-shirt, touchy-feely, New Age asshole!

These days many politicians are demanding change. Just like homeless people.

I think highways should have a beer lane.

Live and let live, that's what I say. Anyone who can't understand that should be killed. It's a simple philosophy, but it's always worked well in our family.

Isn't it time we stopped wasting valuable land on cemeteries? Talk about an idea whose time has passed: "Let's put all the dead people in boxes and keep them in one part of town." What kind of medieval bullshit is that? I say, plow these motherfuckers up and throw them away. Or melt them down. We need that phosphorous for farming. If we're going to recycle, let's get serious.

True Stuff: Because of all the lawsuits against "good Samaritans" whose efforts end badly, fewer people are willing to stop and lend assistance at the scene of an accident. As a result, experts are wondering whether or not we need laws compelling us to help each other.

Joan Rivers turned into one of the people she used to make fun of.

I'm thinking of buying a church and changing it around; maybe selling crack and having a few whores in the pews.

Here's a little car fun. If someone is driving alongside you in the right-hand lane, act concerned and wave them tnward the side of the road, yelling, "Pull over! Pull over! Pull over!" When they finally pull over, just keep going. Let 'em sit there and think it over for a while. It's certainly none of your concern. In fact, you don't want to have anything to do with a person like that.

Something I really don't like is claymation; that stop-action animation junk. Why don't they can that shit? It's fake-looking, and it detracts from the story.

DOG MOMENTS #2

Canine Standard Time

A dog doesn't understand time. Like a young child, he doesn't know the difference between eight o'clock and a week ago Tuesday. The only period of time a dog understands is forever. And that's how long he thinks everything is gonna last.

Y'ever scratch your dog behind the ears? They really love that, don't they?

"Oh boy, oh boy! Oh boy, oh boy, oh boy!! Daddy's scratchin' me behind the ears! My favorite thing. Oh boy, oh boy! This is great!"

And you're scratchin' and scratchin', and he's lovin' it, and lookin' up at you adoringly, his eyes rollin' back in his head, and then suddenly you stop. And he looks at you like you're some kind of diseased criminal pervert. He's disappointed. He thought the scratchin' was gonna last forever.

He can't help it—he just doesn't know what time it is.

Home Alone

It's especially bad when you go out and leave him alone. He thinks you're never coming back. Never. That must be what he thinks, or else why would he act the way he does when you finally get home? All hyper and excited and revved up like he just ate a pound and a half of methamphetamine:

"Oh-boy-oh-boy-oh-boy-oh-boy-oh-boy!! I thought you were never-gonnacomehome I thought you were nevergonnacomehome I thought you-werenevergonnacomehome! I was so scared. I was so lonely. Scared and lonely. I didn't know what to do. I was all alone. I thought I would never eat again. I don't know how to prepare food. I'm a dog. I can't cook. I can't do anything. I don't even know how to operate a can opener. How do ya do that? What do you do, push down the little handle? Couldn't figure it out. Gimme some food. Gimme a kiss. Shake hands. Here's my paw. You want me to roll over? I'll do it. Just don't leave me! Don't go! Don't go! I swear, I'll never pee in the house again! I'll never pee *anywhere* again! Just don't leave me alone!"

And it doesn't matter how long you've been gone. They go into this speed-freak mode even if all you did was forget your hat and come back a few seconds later.

"Oh-boy-oh-boy-oh-boy! Ithoughtyouwerenevergonnacomehome! Et cetera, et cetera. Is that how ya say that? Et cetera? Anyway, I got hungry. Again. The minute you left. I was gonna eat the cat. I couldn't find him. Where the fuck's the cat? What did ya do, hide the cat?"

"Lester, will you stop it? Calm down! I was just here a few seconds ago!"

They really miss you. And they have no idea what time it is.

SOME LIKE IT HOT

Think for a moment about flamethrowers. The fact that we have them at all. Well, actually we don't have them, the army has them. You know, I hadn't thought of that; the army has all the flamethrowers. I'd say we're jolly well fucked if we have to go up against the army, wouldn't you?

My point is that there are even such things as flamethrowers in the first place. What it indicates to me is that at some point, some person, Phil perhaps, said to himself, "Look at all those people across the road. What I wouldn't give to set them on fire. But I'm much too far away. If only I had some device that would shoot flames on them."

Well, the whole thing might've ended right there, but Phil happened to mention it to his friend, Dwyane, one of those people who's good with tools. About a month later, Dwayne was back.

"Phil, that idea of yours? Quite a concept. Watch!"

WHOOOOOOSH! WHOOOOOOMPH! CRACKLE! BURN!

Before long, the army came around. "Hi boys. We want to buy 500,000 of those flamethrowers. We have a long list of people we'd like to set on fire. Give us 500,000 and have them camouflaged. We don't want anyone seeing them until they're fully consumed by flames."

Phil and Dwayne made lots of money and died in a fireworks accident on the 4th of July.

MAYBE THEY'LL ADOPT

Concerning news coverage at the National Zoo: Do you care if the pandas fuck? I don't. Why don't they stop telling us the pandas didn't fuck again this year? I'm not concerned. I have no emotional stake in panda-fucking. If they want to they will, if not, they'll watch *The Price Is Right*.

Probably the only reason the pandas aren't fucking on schedule is because some environmental jackoff has moved into the cage with them. Could you get a hard-on if some loser in a green T-shirt was taking your girlfriend's rectal temperature? Leave these creatures alone. And please God, save the planet from environmentalists.

THE MISCELLANEOUS AILMENTS FOUNDATION

Not every human ailment has a telethon to help raise money. This space is donated to the Miscellaneous Ailments Foundation. If you or a loved one suffer from any of the following conditions, open your heart, dig deep, and give what you can. And please, no small donations. Try to give more than you can afford.

ITCH · TWITCH · WELTS · WARTS · PIMPLES · NITS · SCABS · SCARS · SORES · BOILS · RASH · GASH · HIVES · CYSTS · CRAMPS · POLYPS · BLISTERS · BLOTCHES · BUNIONS · BEDSORES · ROPE BURNS · PAPER CUTS · COCKEYE · BLACKHEADS · WHITEHEADS · GAG EASILY · SWOLLEN GLANDS · EYESTRAIN · NAUSEA · PILES · GAS · CRABS · PEG LEG · ABSCESSED TOOTH · PENICILLIN REACTION · PALENESS · NICKS & CUTS · BRITTLE NAILS · WOOZINESS · HOMESICKNESS · FALL DOWN A LOT · SICK & TIRED · JUST DON'T FEEL GOOD · CHILLS & FEVER · FEVER & CHILLS · CHILLS WITHOUT FEVER · FEVER WITHOUT CHILLS · SMALL POX · MEDIUM POX · LARGE POX · X-LARGE POX · CHICKEN POX · TUNA POX · ROAST BEEF POX · WHOOPING COUGH · WHOOPING SNEEZE · WHOOPING GIGGLE · WHEEZING · SNEEZING · FREEZING · MUMPS · BUMPS · LUMPS · BAD EYES · BAD FEET · BAD BLOOD · BAD BREATH · BAD BACK · BAD ATTITUDE · POOR POSTURE · COWARDICE · TRENCH MOUTH · PUFFY SKIN · COMPLETE PARALYSIS · ENLARGED PORES · OUT OF BREATH · ARM HURTS · BAD JUDGMENT · DUMB LOOK · OUT OF SORTS · BRUISE EASILY · WIND KNOCKED OUT OF YOU · SEEIN' THINGS · THE BLAHS · THE HOTS · THE RUNS · THE CREEPS · THE WILLIES · THE SHITS · THE VAPORS · THE BENDS · THE HEEBIE-JEEBIES · SHOCK · TREMOR · RELAPSE

▪ BOTULISM ▪ LEPROSY ▪ GANGOSA ▪ CANCER OF THE FIST ▪ JUNGLE ROT ▪ THE CREEPIN' CRUD ▪ THE 48-YEAR CREEPIN' JESUS ▪ MANGE ▪ GRUNGE ▪ SORE TITS ▪ JET LAG ▪ ROOT CANAL ▪ FACIAL TICS ▪ POOR BALANCE ▪ LOCKJAW ▪ CHARLEY HORSE ▪ EUPHORIA ▪ PRICKLY HEAT ▪ PEELING ▪ MISCARRIAGE ▪ CROW'S FEET ▪ CROW'S LEGS ▪ SLOPPY DICTION ▪ OVERBITE ▪ UNDERBITE ▪ SIDE EFFECTS ▪ DOUBLE LIMP ▪ SCABBY KNEE ▪ TONE DEAFNESS ▪ LOUD HEART ▪ POSTNASAL DRIP ▪ PRENASAL DRIP ▪ JAMMED THUMB ▪ COMA ▪ KNOCK KNEES ▪ STRETCH MARKS ▪ FAT LIP ▪ BLACK EYE ▪ BUM LEG ▪ OVERSIZE BIRTHMARK ▪ STRAWBERRY ▪ SPRING FEVER ▪ FORGETFULNESS ▪ SQUINTING ▪ SURGICAL BLUNDER ▪ FACIAL HAIR ▪ PLAGUE ▪ ADHESIONS ▪ SUNSTROKE ▪ BAD GENES ▪ SCRAWNINESS ▪ CROSSED NOSTRILS ▪ CALLUSES ▪ PREMATURE EJACULATION ▪ STARVATION ▪ SEEING STARS ▪ NERVOUS BREAKDOWN ▪ CORNS ▪ ORGAN REJECTION ▪ SWELLING ▪ BLOODY NOSE ▪ CATATONIA ▪ BAGS UNDER THE EYES ▪ FRECKLE LOSS ▪ NO URINE ▪ BIG EARS ▪ BAD COLD ▪ FREDDIE'S DISEASE ▪ NO TORSO ▪ SUICIDE ▪ HEN TOOTH ▪ NATURAL CAUSES ▪ CHRONIC PUSSY FARTS ▪ ONDINE'S CURSE ▪ PULLED GROIN MUSCLE ▪ CHAFING ▪ COLD SORES ▪ SPLIT LIP ▪ ACHES & PAINS ▪ TRICK KNEE ▪ TRICK NOSE ▪ TRICK DICK ▪ SLEEPING SICKNESS ▪ LOBOTOMY ▪ NIGHTMARES ▪ PIGEON TOES ▪ DOUBLE CHIN ▪ SHYNESS ▪ WINDBURN ▪ CHRONIC LETHARGY ▪ HOT FLASHES ▪ DOUBLE VISION ▪ CANCER OF THE JOWLS ▪ CLUBFOOT ▪ EXCESS EAR WAX ▪ SUFFOCATION ▪ REALLY GROSS SKIN ▪ FALLING NOSE HAIRS ▪ INFECTED TATTOOS ▪ GUNSHOT WOUNDS ▪ ELASTIC POISONING ▪ UNPROVOKED WEEPING ▪ DISLOCATED CROTCH ▪ COMPLETE HAIRLESSNESS ▪ NINE MILE FEVER ▪ MIGRATING BEAUTY MARK ▪ UNDESCENDED TESTICLE ▪ CHICKEN BREASTEDNESS ▪ BOTCHED CIRCUMCISION ▪ GHOST LIMBS ▪ INDUSTRIAL DEAFNESS ▪ HAMMERTOE ▪ DOUBLE RECTUM ▪ FALLEN WOMB ▪ INVERTED NIPPLES ▪ OUT-OF-CONTROL MOLES ▪ TRANSIENT SLURRED SPEECH ▪ WATER ON THE PROFILE ▪ SALINE DEPLETION ▪ GENDER AGONY ▪ NEGATIVE

BUOYANCY · CURVATURE OF THE MIND · INFECTED DIMPLE · BURNED AT THE STAKE · BUBONIC PLAGUE · BLACK DEATH · MORNING SICKNESS · SUBDURAL HEMATOMA · GRAND MAL SEIZURE · SPASTIC BLADDER · BRAIN TUMOR · NIPPLE SEEP · DRY TEETH · SIX-FOOT NOSE HAIRS · PASSED BALLS · MIDNASAL DRIP · CHAPPED ASS · SPEAR WOUNDS · TONSILLITIS · CLAP · CRUCIFIXION · TOTAL BODY DIMPLING · FEAR OF CLOTHING · SINGLE NOSTRIL · HORSE SERUM SENSITIVITY · COKE BOTTLE IN THE ASS · HEN WORKERS LUNG · SEXTUPLE AMPUTEEISM · HEREDITY FRUCTOSE INTOLERANCE · MORTON'S FOOT · HUTCHINSON'S FRECKLE · ORIENTAL NIGHTMARE DEATH SYNDROME · RUM FITS · LIDOCAINE POISONING · IRREGULAR GAIT · GEN-ITAL MEASLES · SPRAINED MIND · ICHTHYOSIS · LACK OF HUSTLE · HYPERDYDROSIS · FROTH-ING AT THE CROTCH · ALZHEIMER'S DISEASE · WET BRAIN · PRESENILITY DEMENTIA · LAETRILE OVERDOSE · MUNCHAUSEN'S SYNDROME · PAVEMENT BURN · NASAL HERPES · CLUSTER HEAD-ACHES · HUNCHBACK · VAGINAL CLOSURE · CANCER OF THE BRIDGE OF THE NOSE · CIR-CUMCISION BLUNDER · SEVERE UNREMITTING PAIN · COMPLETE NERVOUS COLLAPSE · SIXTY-YEAR COMA · RIGOR MORTIS · DECAPITATION · SWIMMER'S ITCH · BEEF TAPEWORM · SHORT-LIMBED DWARFISM · TICK-BORNE RICKETS · KOPLIK'S SPOTS · IMPETIGO · GAS GAN-GRENE · TRANSVERSE MYELITIS · MALNUTRITION · IRRITABILITY · NONPRODUCTIVE COUGH · SIMPLE MALAISE · EPIDEMIC KERATOCONJUNCTIVITIS · FURIOUS RABIES · BLACK VOMIT · DANDY FEVER · EUROPEAN TYPHUS · BRILL-ZINSSER DISEASE · CAT SCRATCH DISEASE · STITCH ABSCESSES · STRAWBERRY TONGUE · PASTIA'S LINES · AFRICAN SLEEPING SICKNESS · WOOL-SORTER'S DISEASE · CAULIFLOWER EAR · ZUCCHINI NOSE · PARACOCCIDIO IDOMYCOSIS · DES-ERT RHEUMATISM · LUMPY JAW · MADURA FOOT · HOOKWORM · ORIENTAL SORE · ALEPPO BOIL · FOREST YAWS · SWIMMING POOL GRANULOMA · CARDIAC DEATH · WHIPWORM INFEC-TION · GEOPHAGIA · RIVER BLINDNESS · TOTAL COLLAPSE · JEWELRY RASH · TERMINAL

BROWSING · MAIDENLY HYSTERICS · MARROW FAILURE · PICA · RIBOFLAVIN DEFICIENCY · MEDITERRANEAN ANEMIA · AIR EMBOLISM · VASCULAR FRAGILITY · DRUG-INDUCED PLATELET DEFECTS · FELTY'S SYNDROME · BOWEL INFARCTION · TETRALOGY OF FALLOT · BUNDLE BRANCH BLOCK · SUDDEN MEGACOLON · RAYNAUD'S PHENOMENON · YOUNG ORIENTAL FEMALE DISEASE · INTESTINAL APOPLEXY · OCCLUSION AT THE BIFURCATION · MILK LEG · HOMAN'S SIGN · CONSTANT SCREAMING · TOTAL BODY HEMORRHAGING · MISSING LUNGS · EXTRA STOMACH · LARVAE IN THE STOOL · BEBOP LEGS · FOREHEAD TRANSPLANT · TUMOR ON THE BUNS · HUGE SPLEEN · CHRONIC FALLING · CYSTS ON THE WRISTS · SUDDEN TOTAL WEIGHT LOSS ·

Give now. Somewhere, someone feels crappy. You can help.

GOT ANY MORE LEAVES IN THAT STALL?

Recently I came across a statistic published by the Population Reference Bureau in Washington. It stated that as of 1995 the number of people who had lived on earth was 105,472,380,169. The figure was based on the assumption that "the first two people" had emerged in 50,000 B.C. So I did a little arithmetic of my own, and I've concluded that as of 1995 there had been over 987 trillion bowel movements. I was very conservative: I assumed a mere thirty-year life span and only six bowel movements per week. Still, it means that at this point there have been almost 1 quadrillion human bowel movements and most of them occurred before people had anything to read. These are the kinds of thoughts that kept me from moving quickly up the corporate ladder.

DEATH ROW

The story is that if you're condemned to death they have to give you one last meal of your choice. What is that all about? A group of people plans to kill you, so they want you to eat something you like? Is it a joke? Do they think the food part will take your mind off the dying part? Or do they just prefer to kill you when you're coming off a peak experience and full of positive energy?

I'm not sure what kind of sick game is going on, but what the hell, you might as well play along. Have a little fun; order a Happy Meal. Tell 'em you want to go to Hooter's and eat on the patio.

Inform them you've converted to a religion that embraces cannibalism, and you'd like to eat a baby. With a small salad. I just think there's great potential here for fun and mischief. In fact, I'm thinking that if you worked it just right you might even squeeze a little extra time out of them. Time to file a couple of hundred more frivolous appeals.

Because, as I understand it, they have to give you any meal you ask for. Not including elephant, of course. You can't expect them to start on a whole new elephant for just one meal. But short of that, they have to give you pretty much what you want. It's part of the humanity involved: "Let's kill this fuck, but let's be civil."

So I say have a little fun; buy some time. When they ask what you want, tell them you can't decide. That's all there is to it. You can't decide.

"Gee, I don't know. I'm not sure if I want steak or lobster. I mean, I really love them both. I haven't had lobster in quite a while, but on the other hand, I really love chicken. It's my good luck food. And they're both rich in protein. I just can't figure it out."

What can they do? Can they kill you under those circumstances? Can they go ahead and kill you if you honestly don't know what you want for dinner? Tell them you're willing to take a lie detector test and truth serum, but you honestly can't decide. Can they kill you? Can they drag you down the last mile screaming, "Surf? Turf? I'm on the horns of a dilemma!" I think they'd have to give you a little more time.

Imagine if you kept it up for six months. Think of the headlines.

CONDEMNED MAN STILL ALIVE, CAN'T DECIDE. LEANS TOWARD LOBSTER.

Three years go by. Five. Seven. And then, finally, one morning you wake up, and it's clear as a bell:

"All right, I've decided. And I don't know why I didn't think of this long ago. I'm going to have the lamb chops."

"All right, lamb chops it is. And how did you want them cooked?"

"Geez, I hadn't thought of that. Lemme see. How do I want them cooked? Listen, guys, can I get back to you?"

HUNGRY MAN EXECUTED. DRAGGED DOWN LAST MILE SCREAMING "MEDIUM!"

CURRENT EVENTS

Here's a great idea. I think Texas should save up 500 condemned people and execute them all at once, in electric chairs. Five hundred electric chairs in a big gymnasium. Wouldn't that be fun? I realize Texas prefers lethal injection, but maybe they could make an exception just this once. Or how about executing people five at a time on electric couches. That would be interesting. Put a coffee table in front of them with magazines and some chips and dip. It would be fun. Here's another good idea. If a married couple kills their kid, they should be executed in an electric love seat. Force them to hug as you pull the switch.

THE UNKINDEST CUT

I don't know about you, but I think O. J. got screwed. Double jeopardy is just plain wrong. Civil trial, my ass! It's not fair. O. J. beat the system and he should be allowed to enjoy it. Geraldo and Charles Grodin don't like O. J. Simpson. Geraldo and Charles Grodin deal in certitude. Guys like that almost always impress me.

I'm really glad O. J. beat the rap. Personally, I'd like to see him on TV again, doin' commercials. There must be something he could do. Roach Motel. "They checks in, but they don't checks out." It would be fun. We need more fun. People get upset with all the wrong things.

Like these guys Jeffrey Dahmer and Timothy McVeigh. Right away everybody wants to kill them. Let me tell you, you don't kill guys like that. That's exactly what they want. You know what you do? You let them off with a warning. Just like a speeding ticket. Sometimes all a guy like that needs is a good talking-to. You sit him down, and you say, "Listen. Jeff. Nobody thinks you're funny. Okay? No one is amused. So calm down and knock off the shit. Stop trying to draw attention to yourself. You eat one more person, and you're in big trouble."

A lot of these guys never hear that sort of thing. I think it would make them think twice before they cooked another person's head and ate it. Don't you?

Now, as to Timothy McVeigh, you've got a slightly different situation. After all, the guy's a veteran, so you have to show him a little consideration. And don't forget, it's his first offense. So I say let him off with a warning. Throw a good scare into him: "Tim, one more trick like that, and it's gonna mean a hefty fine."

SMILE!

Camcorders are a good example of technology gone berserk. Everywhere you go now, you see some goofy fuck with a camcorder. Everyone's taping everything. Doesn't anybody stop and look at things anymore? Take them in? Maybe even . . . remember them? Is that such a strange idea? Does experience really have to be documented, brought home and saved on a shelf? And do people really watch this shit? Are their lives so bankrupt they sit at home watching things they already did?

These guys are so intense. And by the way, it's always guys. They won't let women touch the cameras; it's a highly technical skill. Look through a hole, push on a button. Big fuckin' skill. And they all think they're Federico Fellini. Did you ever see them at the soccer games? With the low angles and all the zooms and pans? And it's the same three ugly children in every shot. Same kids. Believe me, all the George Lucas magic in Hollywood is not going to change the unfortunate genetic configurations on the faces of these children. Do the world a favor, keep these unfortunate youngsters indoors, out of public view.

THE NOONTIME NEWS

* In Rome today, Pope John Paul removed his little hat and revealed he has a small map of Tombstone, Arizona, tattooed on his head.

* Out at the lake in City Park, police have arrested a one-armed man who was bothering the other boaters by continuously rowing in a circle.

* Authorities say a severely disturbed geography teacher has shot and killed six people who did not know the capital of Scotland. He is still at large and they remind everyone the capital of Scotland is Edinburgh.

* A man at a tool and die company died today when he was hit with a tool.

* A Detroit couple is suing Campbell's soups, claiming a bowl of alphabet soup spelled out an obscene message to their children. They state that at first the little letters floated around in a circle, and then they formed the words *suck my noodle.*

* Millionaire clothing executive Dacron Polyester died in his sleep yesterday. It was not a peaceful death, however, as he dozed off while hang-gliding.

* A large dog exploded on a downtown street corner this morning. No one was killed; however, several people were overcome by fur. Police estimate that more than 600 fleas also lost their lives in the blast.

* A woman in Montana was severely injured yesterday when she attempted to force-breast-feed a wolverine.

✳ A man wearing a Have a Nice Day button was killed yesterday by a man who works at night.

✳ The Centers for Disease Control has determined that the common cold is caused by a tall man who carries around a bag of germs.

✳ Twenty-six people were killed this morning when two funeral processions collided. Police say the list of fatalities does not include the two people who were already dead.

✳ The Mafia has killed an information clerk because he knew too much. His replacement, appointed today, says he has no further information.

✳ In San Francisco, a baby has been born wearing sunglasses and holding a small can of peas.

✳ A Milwaukee man has been arrested for the illegal use of food stamps. He was taken into custody while attempting to mail a bowl of chili to his sister.

✳ The Bureau of Indian Affairs has announced they have located another Mohican. Accordingly, all the books are being recalled and will be changed to read: *The Next to the Last of the Mohicans.*

✳ And finally, here's a Halloween prank that backfired. It seems that little thirteen-year-old Danny Obolagotz thought it would be great fun to soap the windows of all the cars on his street. He had soaped seven of them and was starting to soap the eighth, not knowing that the owner of the car, Earl Fletcher, was seated inside. Fletcher shot Danny in the head four times.

THE PLANET IS FINE,
THE PEOPLE ARE FUCKED

At some point, during every stage show I do, I take a sip of water and ask the audience, "How's the water here?" I haven't gotten a positive response yet. Not one. Last year I was in 100 different cities. Not one audience was able to give me a positive answer. Nobody trusts their water supply. Nobody.

And that amuses me. Because it means the system is beginning to collapse, beginning to break down. I enjoy chaos and disorder. Not just because they help me professionally; they're also my hobby. I'm an entropy buff.

In high school, when I first heard of entropy, I was attracted to it immediately. They said that in nature all systems are breaking down, and I thought, What a wonderful thing; perhaps I can make some small contribution to this process, myself. And, of course, it's not just true of nature, it's true of society as well. If you look carefully, you can see that the social structure is just beginning to break down, just beginning to come apart at the seams.

The News Turns *Me* On

What I like about that is that it makes the news on television more exciting. I watch the news for only one thing: entertainment. That's all I want. You know my favorite thing on television? Bad news. Accidents, disasters, catastrophes, explosions, fires. I wanna see shit being destroyed and bodies flyin' around.

I'm not interested in the budget, I don't care about tax negotiations, I don't wanna know what country the pope is in. But show me a burning hospital with people on crutches jumpin' off the roof, and I'm a happy guy. I wanna see a paint factory blowin' up, an oil refinery explode, and a tornado hit a church on Sunday. I wanna be told there's a guy runnin' through the Kmart shooting at customers with an automatic weapon. I wanna see thousands of people in the street killing policemen; hear about a nuclear meltdown in a big city; find out the stock market dropped 4,000 points in one day. I wanna see people under pressure!

Sirens, flames, smoke, bodies, graves being filled, parents weeping. My kinda TV! Exciting shit. I just want some entertainment! That's the kind of guy I am. You know what I like most? Big chunks of steel, concrete and fiery wood falling out of the sky, and people running around trying to get out of the way. Exciting shit!

Fuck Pakistan!

At least I admit it. Most people won't admit those feelings. Most people see somethin' like that, they say, "Ohhhh, isn't that awful?" Bullshit! Lyin' asshole! You love it and you know it. Explosions are fun. And the closer the explosion is to your house, the more fun it is. Have you ever noticed that?

Sometimes an announcer comes on television and says, "Six thousand people were killed in an explosion today." You say, "Where, where?" He says, "In Pakistan." You say, "Aww, fuck Pakistan. Too far away to be fun." But if he says it happened in your hometown, you say, "Whooa, hot shit, Dave! C'mon! Let's go down and look at the bodies!"

I love bad news. Doesn't bother me. The more bad news there is, the faster this system collapses. I'm glad the water sucks. You know what I do about it? I drink it! I fuckin' drink it!

This Is One Bad Species

You see, I'm not one of those people who worries about everything. Do you have people around you like that? The country's full of 'em now. People walkin' around all day, worried about everything. Worried about the air, the water, the soil, pesticides, food additives, carcinogens, radon, asbestos. Worried about saving endangered species.

Lemme tell you about endangered species. Saving endangered species is just one more arrogant human attempt to control nature. That's what got us in trouble in the first place. Interfering with nature. Meddling. Doesn't anybody understand that?

And as far as endangered species are concerned, it's a phony issue. Over 90 percent of all the species that ever lived on this planet are gone. They're extinct. We didn't kill them; they just disappeared. That's what species do: they appear, and they disappear. It's nature's way. Irrespective of our behavior, species vanish at the rate of twenty-five a day. Let them go gracefully. Stop interfering. Leave nature alone. Haven't we done enough damage?

We're so self-important. So arrogant. Everybody's going to save something now. Save the trees, save the bees, save the whales, save the snails. And the supreme arrogance? Save the planet! Are these people kidding? Save the planet? We don't even know how to take care of ourselves; we haven't learned how to care for one another. We're gonna save the fuckin' planet?

Greens Eat Shit

I'm gettin' tired of that shit. I'm tired of fuckin' Earth Day. I'm tired of these self-righteous environmentalist, white, bourgeois liberals who think the only thing wrong with this country is that there aren't enough bike paths. Tryin' to make the world safe for their repulsive Volvos.

Besides, environmentalists don't give a shit about the planet anyway. Not really. Not in the abstract. You know what they're interested in? A clean place to live. Their own habitat. That's all. They're worried that sometime in the future they might personally be inconvenienced. Narrow, unenlightened self-interest doesn't impress me.

And, by the way, there's nothing wrong with the planet in the first place. The planet is fine. The people are fucked! Compared with the people, the planet is doin' great. It's been here over four billion years. Did you ever think about that? The planet has been here four and a half billion years. And we've been here for what? A hundred thousand? And we've only been engaged in heavy industry for a little over two hundred years. Two hundred versus 4.5 billion! And we have the nerve, the conceit to think that somehow we're a threat? That somehow we're going to put this beautiful little blue-green ball in jeopardy?

Believe me, this planet has put up with much worse than us. It's been through earthquakes, volcanoes, plate tectonics, solar flares, sunspots, magnetic storms, pole reversals, planetary floods, worldwide fires, tidal waves, wind and water erosion, cosmic rays, ice ages, and hundreds of thousands of years of bombardment by comets, asteroids, and meteors. And people think a few plastic bags and aluminum cans are going to make a difference?

See Ya!

The planet isn't goin' anywhere, folks. We are! We're goin' away. Pack your shit, we're goin' away. And we won't leave much of a trace. Thank God for that. Nothing left. Maybe a little Styrofoam. The planet will be here, and we'll be gone. Another failed mutation; another closed-end biological mistake.

The planet will shake us off like a bad case of fleas. And it will heal itself, because that's what the planet does; it's a self-correcting system. The air and water and earth will recover and be renewed. And if plastic is really not degradable, well, most likely the planet will incorporate it into a new paradigm: The Earth Plus Plastic. Earth doesn't share our prejudice against plastic. Plastic came out of the earth. She probably sees it as one of her many children.

In fact, it could be the reason the earth allowed us to be spawned in the first place; it wanted plastic and didn't know how to make it. It needed us. That could be the answer to our age-old question: "Why are we here?" "Plastic, assholes!"

"I Just Can't Shake This Cold"

And so, our job is done. The plastic is here, we can now be phased out. And I think that's already begun, don't you? I mean, to be fair, the planet probably sees us as a mild threat, something to be dealt with. And I'm sure it can defend itself in the manner of a large organism; the way a beehive or an ant colony would muster a defense. I'm sure the planet will think of something. What would you be thinking if you were the planet, trying to defend yourself against this pesky, troublesome species?

"Let's see, what might I try? Hmmm! Viruses might be good; these humans seem vulnerable. And viruses are tricky, always mutating and developing new strains when new medicines or vaccines are introduced. And perhaps the first virus I try could be one that compromises their immune systems. A human immunodeficiency virus that makes them vulnerable to other infections that come along. And perhaps this virus could be spread sexually, making them reluctant to engage in the act of reproduction, further reducing their numbers."

Well, I guess it's a poetic notion, but it's a start. And I can dream, can't I?

No, folks, I don't worry about the little things. Bees, trees, whales, snails. I don't worry about them. I think we're part of a much greater wisdom. Greater than we will ever understand. A higher order. Call it what you like. I call it The Big Electron. The Big Electron. It doesn't punish, it doesn't reward, and it doesn't judge. It just is. And so are we. For a little while. See ya.

SHORT TAKES

You know what we need? Black Jell-O.

I don't understand why prostitution is illegal. Selling is legal, fucking is legal. So, why isn't it legal to sell fucking? Why should it be illegal to sell something that's legal to give away? I can't follow the logic. Of all the things you can do to a person, giving them an orgasm is hardly the worst. In the army they give you a medal for killing people; in civilian life you go to jail for giving them orgasms. Am I missing something?

Wouldn't it be great if you could make a guy's head explode just by looking at him?

Guys don't seem to be called Lefty anymore.

JOIN THE RANKS OF THE UNCLEAN.

In someone else's house, when I sit on a warm toilet seat after seeing another person leave the bathroom, if that person was a man I'm not quite comfortable. But if it was a woman I feel just fine. Unless it was a really fat or old woman. Then it feels kind of creepy.

The reason I talk to myself is that I'm the only one whose answers I accept.

To my great disgust, the trend of naming children with what, until recently, had been considered surnames continues unabated. The latest abominations: Walker, Parker, Kendall, Flynn and McKenna. God help us.

Why aren't there any really disturbing pop songs, like "Tomorrow I'm Gonna Fuck Your Wife"?

If you were trying to clean up the world with a gun, you could sure do a lot worse than starting with a whole bunch of dead prosecutors.

I was thinking the other day that they ought to make those handicapped ramps a little steeper. And put a few curves in them, too. I could use some laughs.

Think of how entertaining it would be if all the people on TV still had their original teeth.

I think we ought to just go ahead and make "zillion" a real number. "Gazillion," too. A zillion could be ten million trillions, and a gazillion could be a trillion zillions. It seems to me it's time to do this.

A long time ago in England a guy named Thomas Culpepper was hanged, beheaded, quartered, and disemboweled. Why do I have the impression women were not involved in these activities?

I read somewhere that in Mexico City 300 tons of fecal matter are deposited in the air every day. So I guess you could say that not only does shit happen, it also falls on your head.

In Maine, in order to save energy, there are several lighthouses that are closed at night.

What's all the fuss about same-sex marriages? I've been the same sex all my life, and I was married for years. No problem. What's the big deal?

I think the best home security system of all would be one that locks the burglar inside his own house.

Sometime when you're watching a street musician, walk over in the middle of a song and whisper to him that you don't like his music. Then take a dollar out of his cup and walk away.

Sometime after John Denver's airplane crashed, a sheriff on TV was speculating that a pelican had flown into the plane. He actually said, "Birds are a hazard to aircraft." Funny, I always thought it was the other way around.

You know what's a fun thing to do? Go through your address book every few years and cross out the dead people.

If a group of people stand around in a circle long enough, eventually they will begin to dance.

Jesus doesn't really love you but he thinks you have a great personality.

Baseball entered its death throes when it began referring to fielding as "defense."

Have Some Fun: Walk into a gift shop and tell them you came in to get your gift.

Sony would be real smart to come up with a combination CD player and colostomy bag called the Shitman.

May I ask what all these grown men are doing walking around with fruity-looking backpacks? You see some goofy, twenty-eight-year-old yuppie wearin' a backpack. Like he's out prospecting for borax. What's in these packs that's so important? The nuclear launch codes? It's embarrassing. I don't know why I've allowed it to go on as long as I have.

I don't understand people who protest things in the street by walking around holding signs. I say, if you're gonna be on the street, use the time productively. Destroy some property.

How can it be a spy satellite if they announce on television that it's a spy satellite?

Why is it every time some celebrity gets cancer the *National Enquirer* says he's "vowed to lick this thing." Just once I'd like to hear a guy say, "I've got cancer, and this is it. I'll be dead in a few months."

Why don't they have a light bulb that only shines on things worth looking at?

Even though men are complete assholes, you know what makes me sad about feminism? Somewhere along the way we lost "Hey, toots!"

BRAVE NEW WORLD OF SCIENCE

✳ Scientists in Switzerland announced today they have been able to make mice fart by holding them upside-down and tapping them on the stomach with a ballpoint pen.

✳ A pair of Siamese twins in Australia, surgically separated six months ago, has been sewn back together. Apparently, each of them could remember only half the combination to their locker.

✳ Medical researchers have discovered a new disease that has no symptoms. It is impossible to detect, and there is no known cure. Fortunately, no cases have been reported thus far.

✳ The Nobel Prize in mathematics was awarded yesterday to a California professor who has discovered a new number. The number is "bleen," which he says belongs between six and seven.

✳ The surgeon general warned today that saliva causes stomach cancer. But apparently only when swallowed in small amounts over a long period of time.

✳ A Swedish entomologist claims that common houseflies are highly intelligent and can be trained to fix umbrellas and dance in a circle.

✳ Botanists in England have developed a plant that may help solve the world's hunger problems. Although it has no food value of its own, when the plant reaches maturity it sneaks across the yard and steals food from the neighbors.

✳ An x-ray technician at New York Hospital has died from a rare disease known as cancer-of-the-part-in-the-hair. In a desperate attempt to treat himself, twenty-eight-year-old Norris Flengkt shaved his head completely bald. Unfortunately, the cancer thought it was simply a wider part and proceeded to devour his entire skull.

* Engineers at General Motors have developed a revolutionary new engine whose only function is to lubricate itself.

* Astronomers announced that next month the sun, the moon, and all nine planets will be aligned perfectly with the earth. They say, however, the only noticeable effect will be that the Nome to Rio bus will run four days late.

* Thanks to the sharp eyes of a Minnesota man, it is possible that two identical snowflakes may finally have been observed. While out snowmobiling, Oley Skotchgaard noticed a snowflake that looked familiar to him. Searching his memory, he realized it was identical to a snowflake he had seen as a child in Vermont. Weather experts, while excited, caution that the match-up will be difficult to verify.

* Geologists claim that although the world is running out of oil, there is still a two-hundred-year supply of brake fluid.

* According to astronomers, next week Wednesday will occur twice. They say such a thing happens only once every 60,000 years and although they don't know why it occurs, they're glad they have an extra day to figure it out.

* A team of microbiologists announced today they have discovered something they cannot identify. According to them it is long and thin and smells like a tractor seat.

IT'S NOT A SPORT

To my way of thinking, there are really only three sports: baseball, basketball, and football. Everything else is either a game or an activity.

Hockey comes to mind. People think hockey is a sport. It's not. Hockey is three activities taking place at the same time: ice skating, fooling around with a puck, and beating the shit out of somebody.

If these guys had more brains than teeth, they'd do these things one at a time. First you go ice skating, then you fool around with a puck, then you go to the bar and beat the shit out of somebody. The day would last longer, and these guys would have a whole lot more fun.

Another reason hockey is not a sport is that it's not played with a ball. Anything not played with a ball can't be a sport. These are my rules, I make 'em up.

Soccer. Soccer is not a sport because you can't use your arms. Anything where you can't use your arms can't be a sport. Tap dancing isn't a sport. I rest my case.

Running. People think running is a sport. Running isn't a sport because anybody can do it. Anything we can all do can't be a sport. I can run, you can run. For Chrissakes, my mother can run! You don't see her on the cover of *Sports Illustrated,* do you?

Swimming. Swimming isn't a sport. Swimming is a way to keep from drowning. That's just common sense.

Sailing isn't a sport. Sailing is a way to *get* somewhere. Riding the bus isn't a sport, why the fuck should sailing be a sport?

Boxing is not a sport either. Boxing is a way to beat the shit out of somebody. In that respect, boxing is actually a more sophisticated form of hockey. In spite of what the police tell you, beating the shit out of somebody is not a sport. When police brutality becomes an Olympic event, fine, then boxing can be a sport.

Bowling. Bowling isn't a sport because you have to rent the shoes. Don't forget, these are my rules. I make 'em up.

Billiards. Some people think billiards is a sport, but it can't be, because there's no chance for serious injury. Unless, of course, you welch on a bet in a tough neighborhood. Then, if you wind up with a pool cue stickin' out of your ass, you know you *might* just be the victim of a sports-related injury. But that ain't billiards, that's pool, and that starts with a *P,* and that rhymes with *D,* and that brings me to darts.

Darts could have been a sport, because at least there's a chance to put someone's eye out. But, alas, darts will never be a sport, because the whole object of the game is to reach zero, which goes against all sports logic.

Lacrosse is not a sport; lacrosse is a faggoty college activity. I don't care how rough it is, anytime you're running around a field, waving a stick with a little net on the end of it, you're engaged in a faggoty college activity. Period.

Field hockey and fencing. Same thing. Faggoty college shit. Also, these activities aren't sports, because you can't gamble on them. Anything you can't gamble on can't be a sport. When was the last time you made a fuckin' fencing bet?

Gymnastics is not a sport because Romanians are good at it. It took me a long time to come up with that rule, but goddammit, I did it.

Polo isn't a sport. Polo is golf on horseback. Without the holes. It's a great concept, but it's not a sport. And as far as water polo is concerned, I hesitate to even mention it, because it's extremely cruel to the horses.

Which brings me to **hunting.** You think hunting is a sport? Ask the deer. The only good thing about hunting is the many fatal accidents on the weekends. And, of course, the permanently disfigured hunters who survive such accidents.

Then you have **tennis.** Tennis is very trendy and very fruity, but it's not a sport. It's just a way to meet other trendy fruits. Technically, tennis is an advanced form of Ping-Pong. In fact, tennis is Ping-Pong played while standing on the table. Great concept, not a sport.

In fact, all racket games are nothing more than derivatives of Ping-Pong. Even **volleyball** is, technically, racketless, team Ping-Pong played with an inflated ball and a raised net while standing on the table.

And finally we come to **golf.** For my full take on golf, I refer you elsewhere in the book, but let it just be said golf is a game that might possibly be fun, if it could be played alone. But it's the vacuous, striving, superficial, male-bonding joiners one has to associate with that makes it such a repulsive pastime. And it is decidedly not a sport. Period.

GOLF COURSES FOR THE HOMELESS

War Is Heaven

When the United States is not invading some sovereign nation— or setting it on fire from the air, which is more fun for our simple-minded pilots—we're usually busy "declaring war" on something here at home.

Anything we don't like about ourselves, we declare war on it. We don't do anything about it, we just declare war. "Declaring war" is our only public metaphor for problem solving. We have a war on crime, a war on poverty, a war on hate, a war on litter, a war on cancer, a war on violence, and Ronald Reagan's ultimate joke, the war on drugs. More accurately, the war on the Constitution.

Be It Ever So Humble...

But there's no war on homelessness. You notice that? It's because there's no money in it. If someone could end homelessness and in the process let the corporate swine steal a couple of billion dollars, you'd see the streets of America clear up pretty goddamn quickly. But if you think it's going to be solved through human decency, relax. It's not gonna happen.

You know what I think they ought to do about homelessness?

Change its name. It's not *home*lessness, it's *house*lessness. It's houses these people need. Home is an abstract idea; it's a setting, a state of mind. These people need houses. Physical, tangible structures. They need low-cost housing.

Get It Outta Here!

But there's no place to put it. People don't want low-cost housing built anywhere near them. We have a thing in this country called NIMBY: "Not in my backyard!" People don't want social assistance of any kind located anywhere near them. Just try to open a halfway house, a rehab center, a shelter for the homeless, or a home for retarded people who want to work their way into the community. Forget it. People won't allow it. "Not in my backyard!"

People don't want anything near them, especially if there's a chance it might help somebody. It's part of that great, generous American spirit we hear so much about. You can ask the Indians about that. If you manage to find one. We've made Indians just a little hard to find. Should you need more current data, select any black family at random. Ask them how generous America has been to them.

Lock the Bastards Up ... Somewhere Else

People don't want anything near them. Even if it's something they think society needs, like prisons. Everybody says, "Build more prisons! But don't build them here."

Well, why not? What's wrong with having a prison in your neighborhood? It seems to me it would make for a fairly crime-free area. You think a lot of crackheads and thieves and hookers are gonna be hangin' around in front of a fuckin' prison? Bullshit! They ain't goin' anywhere near it.

What could be safer than a prison? All of the criminals are locked inside. And if a couple of them do manage to escape, what do you think they're gonna do? Hang around? Check real estate prices? Bullshit! They're fuckin' gone! That's the whole *idea* of breakin' out of prison: to get as far away as you possibly can.

"Not in my backyard." People don't want anything near them. Except military bases. They like that, don't they? Give 'em an army or a navy base; that makes 'em happy. Why? Jobs. Self-interest. Even if the base is loaded with nuclear weapons, they don't give a shit. They'll say, "Well, I don't mind a few mutations in the family if I can get a decent job." Working people have been fucked over so long, those are the kind of decisions they make now.

Putts for Putzes

But getting back to low-cost housing, I think I might have solved this problem. I know just the place to build housing for the homeless: golf courses. It's perfect. Plenty of good land in nice neighborhoods; land that is currently being squandered on a mindless activity engaged in by white, well-to-do business criminals who use the game to get together so they can make deals to carve this country up a little finer among themselves.

I'm sick of these golfing cocksuckers in their green and yellow pants, precious little hats, and pussified golf carts. It's time for real people to reclaim the golf courses from the wealthy and turn them over to the homeless. Golf is an arrogant, elitist game that takes up entirely too much space in this country.

Size Matters

The arrogant nature of golf is evident in the design and scale of the game. Think of how big a golf course is. It's huge; you can't see one end of it from the other. But the ball is only an inch and a half in diameter. So will someone please explain to me what these pinheaded pricks need with all that land?

America has over 17,000 golf courses. They average over 150 acres apiece. That's three million-plus acres. Four thousand, eight hundred and twenty square miles. We could build two Rhode Islands and a Delaware's worth of housing for the homeless on the land currently wasted on this meaningless, mindless, arrogant, racist game.

That's another thing: race. The only blacks you'll find in country clubs are carrying trays. And don't give me that Tiger Woods bullshit. Fuck Tiger Woods. He ain't black. He acts, talks, and lives like a white boy. Skin alone doesn't make you black.

Wake Me Up on the 19th Hole

And let's not forget how boring golf is. Have you ever watched it on television? It's like watching flies fuck. A completely mindless game. I should think it takes a fairly low intellect to draw pleasure from the following activity: hitting a ball with a crooked stick . . . and then walking after it! And then . . . hitting it again! I say, "Pick it up, asshole, you're lucky you *found* the fuckin' thing in the first place. Put it in your pocket and go the fuck home!" But, no. Dorko, in the plaid knickers, is gonna hit the ball again. And then he's gonna walk some more.

I say let these rich cocksuckers play miniature golf. Let 'em fuck with a windmill for an hour and a half. I wanna see if there's any real skill among these people. And yeah, yeah, I know there are plenty of golfers who don't consider themselves rich; people who play on badly maintained public courses. Fuck 'em! Fuck them and shame on them! Shame! For engaging in an arrogant, elitist, racist activity.

THE GOOD BREAD

When you make a sandwich at home, do you reach down past the first few slices to get the really good bread? It's a survival thing: "Let my family eat the rotten bread. I'll take care of Numero Uno."

And sometimes the issue isn't freshness but the size of the slice you're after. Everyone knows the wider ones are somewhere near the middle. So down you go past about six inferior slices to reach the ones you want. And, as you pull them up, you have to be careful they don't tear. Then, just before you get them out, the top six slices shift position and fall perpendicular to the rest of the loaf.

"Shit!"

I leave them that way. Let the family think a burglar made a sandwich.

SHORT TAKES

Did you notice that several years ago everything got different?

I never read memoirs; the last thing I need is someone else's memories. I have all I can do to deal with my own.

It takes two scales to find out how much a scale weighs.

In this era of "maxi," "mega" and "meta," you know what we don't have anymore? "Super-duper." I miss that.

Fuck whole-grain cereal. When I want fiber, I eat some wicker furniture.

Suggestions I ignore: "George, you go out and draw their fire, I'll sneak up on them from behind."

You men, next time a prostitute solicits your business, ask for the clergymen's rate.

I think doctors, who must always remain emotionally detached, should be accompanied on their hospital rounds by peasant women from the Middle East. The ones who cry and wail and throw themselves on coffins at those terrorist funerals you see on television. Just for balance.

The only thing high-definition television will do is provide sharper pictures of the garbage.

Have you noticed that some companies now call their menial employees "associates"? They're trying to make them feel better in spite of subsistence salaries. "Associates" is a very slippery job title. Don't be fooled by it.

God bless the homicidal maniacs. They make life worthwhile.

There are patriotic vegetarians in the American Legion who will only eat animals that were killed in combat.

Peg Leg Bates Jr.'s sole ambition was to follow in his father's footstep.

When I was a kid I can remember saying, "Cross my heart and hope to die." I'd like to confess now that I never really meant the second part.

Very few Germans know that in honor of her husband, Mrs. Hitler combed her pussy hair to one side.

You don't hear a lot from imps anymore.

FECES TAKE PLACE

I think TV remotes should have a button that allows you to kill the person on the screen.

The phrase "digging up dirt" seems wrong. If you use a shovel correctly, the very first time you stick it in the ground the thing you come up with is dirt. The dirt is right there on top. It doesn't have to be "dug up."

When you're at someone else's house, and they leave you alone in a room, do you look in the drawers? I do. I'm not trying to steal anything; I just like to know where everything is.

I don't understand this notion of ethnic pride. "Proud to be Irish," "Puerto Rican pride," "Black pride." It seems to me that pride should be reserved for accomplishments; things you attain or achieve, not things that happen to you by chance. Being Irish isn't a skill; it's genetic. You wouldn't say, "I'm proud to have brown hair," or "I'm proud to be short and stocky." So why the fuck should you say you're proud to be Irish? I'm Irish, but I'm not particularly proud of it. Just glad! Goddamn glad to be Irish!

Don't you think it's funny that all these tough-guy boxers are fighting over a purse?

I wonder: On rainy nights, does the sandman send the mudman?

I think they ought to have an annual ceremony at the White House called the Bad Example Award. They should give it to the one person in America who has made the most complete disaster of his own personal life. Someone who through drugs or alcohol or simply a bad attitude has been fired, arrested, killed a marriage, completely alienated friends and family, and perhaps even attempted suicide several times. But it must have happened because of personal behavior and conscious choices, not bad luck. It seems to me people like that never receive any recognition.

Christian deodorant: "Thou Shalt Not Smell"

Lou Gehrig was a pretty tough guy, but I wonder how he handled it when they told him he had Lou Gehrig's disease.

Most people don't know what they're doing, and a lot of them are really good at it.

Sea World should have a special aquarium that features fish sticks. In fact, I wouldn't mind seeing Mrs. Paul herself swimming around in there: "Hi, kids!"

Do you think Sammy Davis ate Junior Mints?

Have you noticed when you wear a hat for a long time it feels like it's not there anymore? And then when you take it off it feels like it's still there? What is that?

I can never decide if "what's-his-name" should be capitalized.

Do you know why they call it a blow *job*? So it'll sound like there's a work ethic involved. Makes a person feel like they did something useful for the economy.

As soon as someone is identified as an unsung hero, he no longer is.

It isn't generally known, but you can save money on phone calls by simply not letting the other person talk. Studies have shown that on many phone calls as much as 50 percent of the talking is done by the other person. If you can manage to dominate the conversation, you can save money.

DYING TO STAY ALIVE

You're all going to die. I hate to remind you, but it is on your schedule. It probably won't happen when you'd like; generally, it's an inconvenience. For instance, you might have your stamp collection spread out on the dining room table.

[Ominous music]

"Now?"

"Now."

"May I at least put away my commemoratives?"

"No."

Inconvenient.

Nobody wants to die. Nobody. Well, maybe Evel Knievel, but most other people don't like the idea. It doesn't seem like an enjoyable thing. People figure if being sick is no fun, dying must really be a bother. After all, part of the pleasure of being alive is the knowledge that you're not dead yet.

And when you get right down to it, people don't mind *being* dead, it's getting dead that bothers them. No one wants to *get* dead. But we're all gonna do it. Death is one of the few things that are truly democratic—everybody gets it once. But *only* once. That's what makes us nervous. No rehearsals.

TICKET TO NOWHERE

And actually, I think people should look forward to death. After all, it's our next big adventure. At last we're going to find out where we go. Isn't that what we've all been wondering? Where we go?

"Where do we go?"

"I don't know."

"We must go somewhere."

"True."

"Phil says he knows."

"I know he does. But take my word, Phil doesn't know."

Where do we go? Maybe it's nowhere; that would be interesting. On the one hand, you'd be nowhere, but on the other hand, you wouldn't know it. So at least you'd have something to think about. Or not.

Personally, I think we go wherever we *think* we're going to go. What you think is what you get. Have you ever heard one of those guys who says, "Don't even bother prayin' for me, I'm goin' straight to hell; I'm goin' to hell to be with all my friends"? Well, he is. He's going to hell, and he'll probably be with all his friends. What you think is what you get. If you keep saying you're going to heaven, chances are you'll get there. But don't look for any of your friends.

In my own case, I expect I'll be going to a public toilet in Honduras. And by the way, should you be interested, I can tell you on good authority that when Monty Hall dies he will be spending a lot of time behind door number three.

DEATH: THE SHOW

Die Big

My feeling is that as long as you're going to die, you should go out with a bang. Make a statement. Don't just "pass away." Die!

"Arnie passed away."

"He did?"

"Yes. Quietly, in a chair."

"I didn't know."

"Well, that's the idea; no one knows."

"True. On the other hand, they say Jim *died.*"

"Oh, yes, Jim died! He died, and now he's dead! He had a thirty-minute seizure in a hotel, danced across the lobby, and wound up in a fountain, twitching uncontrollably. Bellhops were actually applauding."

"God bless him, he went out big."

I say go out big, folks; it's your last chance to make a statement. Before you go, give 'em a show; entertain those you leave behind.

Two-Minute Warning

Now, you might be wondering why I would even suggest that someone can affect the manner and style of his death. Well, it's because of a mysterious and little-known stage of dying, the two-minute warning. Most people are not aware of it, but it does exist. Just as in football, two minutes before you die you receive an audible warning: "Two minutes! Get your shit together!" And the reason most people don't know about it is because the only ones who hear it are dead two minutes later. They never get a chance to tell us.

But such a warning does exist, and I suggest that when it comes, you use your two minutes to entertain and go out big. If nothing else, deliver a two-minute speech. Pick a subject you feel passionate about, and just start talking. Begin low-key, but, with mounting passion, build to a rousing climax. Finally, in the last few seconds, scream at those around you, "If these words are not the truth, may God strike me dead!" He will. Then simply slump forward and fall to the floor. Believe me, from that moment on, people will pay more attention to you.

Of course, such a speech is not your only option; circumstances may permit a more spectacular exit. Perhaps you'll get your two-minute warning during an aerobics class. If so, volunteer for something strenuous. Grab three sets of dumbells, strap on a lot of leg weights, and start running on the treadmill at a really steep grade. When they tell you to stop, turn the treadmill up to 20 miles an hour and start leaping in the air. Tell them it's a new exercise called the Hindu Death Leap. Then collapse on the treadmill, allowing it to fling you backward into the mirrored wall, breaking the mirror and showering everyone with small pieces of glass. I guarantee the police will search your locker carefully.

"Heal This!"

Or maybe you'll be lucky enough to receive your two-minute warning while attending Christian faith-healing services. This is a wonderful opportunity to give religion a bad name. After the sermon, when they ask for those to come forward who "need a miracle," stand up and get on line with the cripples. Try to time things just right. Cut into line if you have to. Then, with barely ten seconds left, kneel in front of the preacher. He will place his hands on you, shout, "Heal!" and you will croak at his feet. Not quite a miracle, but certainly an attention-getter. And the nice thing is they'll blame it on the preacher:

THOUSANDS LOOK ON AS
EVANGELIST SLAYS WORSHIPER.
POLICE STUDY VIDEOTAPE.

Posthumous Fun

But you needn't be satisfied with merely an impressive death scene. You can actually take it a bit further, past the moment of death, by preprogramming some posthumous reflexes into your brain. Remember, the central nervous system runs on electricity, and dying takes place in stages. So, not all of your electrical energy is fully discharged at the time you are pronounced dead; some of it remains stored. Morgue and funeral workers report that corpses often spasm and twitch as much as two days after death.

So I say, as long as you have that potential, be creative. Before you die, try using autosuggestion and visual imaging to preprogram into your brain a few posthumous reflexes. Things that will entertain the folks you leave behind and capture their imaginations. You might want to consider humming during your autopsy, or snapping your fingers during the embalming, or—always a big winner at a wake—bolting upright in your coffin and screaming, "I'm not really dead!" That one is especially fun if someone has brought along impressionable children.

But perhaps you're of a more conservative stripe. If so, at your wake, something as simple as squeezing off several dozen loud but artistically redeeming farts might bring a smile to the faces of those who knew you best: "Isn't that just like Uncle Bob," they'll chuckle, as they rush to open a window.

So, folks, I think my message is clear: even in death, obligations to your loved ones do not end. You still have the responsibility to entertain and ease their grief. And should you persist, and be truly creative with these postdeath efforts, you may accomplish the rare feat of leaving behind a group of incensed relatives who beat you with heavy clubs until they are satisfied that you're fully and completely dead.

FUNERALS

I don't like to attend funerals. When I die, I don't want a funeral, because I'm sure of one thing: if I don't like other people's funerals, I'm going to hate my own.

And I don't want a wake. I don't like the idea of lying on display, dead, in a mahogany convertible with the top down. Everybody looking, and you're dead. They have no idea you're wearing short pants, and have no back in your jacket. It's embarrassing. Especially if they use too much makeup, and you look like a deceased drag queen.

And as you're lying there half-naked, one by one they kneel down and stare silently into your coffin. It's supposed to look reverent. What they're really doing is subtracting their age from yours to find out how much time they have left. That is, if they're younger. If they're older, they just gloat because you died first.

"He looks good."

"Dave, he's dead."

"I know. But when he was alive he didn't look this good."

It's a perverse fact that in death you grow more popular. As soon as you're out of everyone's way, your approval curve moves sharply upward. You get more flowers when you die than you got your whole life. All your flowers arrive at once. Too late.

And people say the nicest things about you. They'll even make things up: "You know, Jeff was a scumbag. A complete degenerate scumbag. But he meant well! You have to give him that. He was a complete degenerate well-meaning scumbag. Poor Jeff."

"Poor" is a big word when discussing the dead.

"Poor Bill is dead."

"Yeah, poor Bill."

"And poor Tom is gone."

"Jeez, yeah, poor Tom."

"Poor John died."

"Poor John. Hey, what about Ed?"

"Ed? That motherfucker is still alive! I wish he would die."

"Yeah. The dirty prick. Let's kill him."

JUST FOR FUN

When writing a letter of reference for a friend, give him a glowing recommendation, but just for fun, conclude by saying, "Don't let Dave's legal history trouble you. There's reason to believe the little girl was lying."

Just for fun, knock on the door of any stall in a public rest room and say, "Sir! Please try to control the smell in there. Don't force us to bring in the hoses."

Call one of those How-Am-I-Driving 800 numbers and, just for fun, complain about a particular driver. Tell them he was driving on the sidewalk, vomiting, giving the finger to old women, and dangling a baby out the window.

Next time you're at a baseball game, sing the national anthem in a loud voice, but just for fun, alternate each line between English and complete gibberish:

O-oh say can you see,
Floggie bloom skeldo pronk,
What so proudly we hailed,
Clogga dronk slern klam dong blench.

See if that doesn't get the fans talking among themselves.

While strolling past a sidewalk café, just for fun, squeeze off several truly repulsive farts, silent or noisy. If silent, stand to one side and watch the results; if noisy, tip your hat and say, "Bon appetito."

Walk through a crowded amusement park carrying a small tape recorder that plays the sound of a little girl's voice screaming, "Help, Mommy, the man is touching me like Daddy does at home!" Just for fun.

SHORT TAKES

When you step on the brakes your life is in your foot's hands.

Attending college at a place called Bob Jones University is like putting your money in Nick & Tony's Bank.

I think what the authorities need is a SQUAT team. Here's how it would work: A squad of heavily armed police break into the house and take a shit in the living room.

Burma is now called Myanmar, Ceylon is Sri Lanka, and Upper Volta is Burkina Faso. How can they do that? How can they just change the name of a country? It doesn't seem right to me.

The Jews are smart; they don't have a hell.

No one ever says "half a week," although obviously there is such a thing. As in, "I'll be back in a week and a half."

FUCK RATIONAL THOUGHT

You know who would make an interesting murder—suicide?
Madeleine Albright and Yanni.

When they print the years of someone's birth and death, can you resist figuring out how old they were?

I hope reincarnation is a fact so I can come back and fuck teenagers again.

Let me tell you something, if we ever have a good, useful, real-life revolution in this country, I'm gonna kill a whole lot of motherfuckers on my list. For purposes of surprise, I'm not revealing the names at this time.

If a centipede wants to kick another centipede in the shins, does he do it one leg at a time? Or does he stand on fifty of his legs and kick with the other fifty?

McDonald's says "100 Billion Served." Bullshit, they hand them to you. There's a difference.

SPOTS ARE DOTS UP CLOSE.
DOTS ARE SPOTS FAR AWAY.

Why is it a pile of dirty clothes is called "the laundry"? "I'm about to do the laundry." And then, when it comes out of the machine, it's still called "the laundry"? "I just did the laundry." What's the deal here? Is laundry clean or dirty?

The reason county fairs don't have kissing booths anymore is because someone noticed that a lot of the men in line had hard-ons.

Wouldn't you like to read some of the things they found in the suggestion box after a meeting of the Aryan Brotherhood?

This year for the Oscars and Emmys I wore my usual outfit: filthy underwear. I enjoy television a lot more when I'm comfortably dressed.

Regarding "safe and sound": I've often been safe, but seldom have I been thought of as sound.

True Stuff: There is actually an auto race called the Goody's Headache Powder 500.

I think Kleenex ought to put a little bull's eye right in the middle of the tissue. Wouldn't that be great? Especially when you're hangin' out with your buddies: (KNNERRFFF! SNGOTT!) "Look, Joey, an 85!"

Dusting is a good example of the futility of trying to put things right. As soon as you dust, the fact of your next dusting has already been established.

What exactly is a wingding?

When Thomas Edison worked late into the night on the electric light, he had to do it by gas lamp or candle. I'm sure it made the work seem that much more urgent.

Have you noticed that in the movies lately a popular thing to do is stick someone's head in the toilet and flush the toilet repeatedly? Where did that come from? They never used to do that. You never saw Spencer Tracy stick Henry Fonda's head in the toilet. Maybe Katharine Hepburn's, but not Henry Fonda's.

A stone's throw is much farther than a hop, skip, and a jump, but it's not nearly as far as a whoop, a holler, and a stomp.

Amusement parks should have a ride where people are pursued by the police at high speed, and when they're caught they're beaten and tortured.

When you think about it, attention deficit disorder makes a lot of sense. In this country there isn't a lot worth paying attention to.

Why do they call one sport "women's tennis," and then turn around and call the other one "ladies' golf"?

Once a year they should have No Hairpiece Day. So everyone could see what all these baldy-headed, fake-hair jerkoffs really look like.

Who decides when the applause should die down? It seems like it's a group decision; everyone begins to say to themselves at the same time, "Well, okay, that's enough of that."

I'm tired of these one-sided heavyweight fights. I think Mike Tyson should just go ahead and fight a leopard. At least it would be an even match. And I wish he would bite more people. God, that was great. I think it would be fun if he just started biting people on the street for no reason.

As a child, I used to wonder if Charlie McCarthy had little wooden balls.

ADVENTURES IN THE SUPERMARKET

Have you ever selected an item in the supermarket and put it in someone else's cart? Then you realize what you're doing and you get sort of an alien feeling?

"Wait! This is not my cart. Look at this! Brown flour and sheep entrails. God, I almost put my capers in this cart. Where's mine? Oh, there it is! The one with the tapioca cupcakes and the mango popsicles. Thank God."

Or have you ever started to walk off with someone else's cart?

"Hey! That's my stuff!"

You have to think fast. "Not yet it isn't! It's not paid for. Technically, these things still belong to all of us. And if I feel like shopping out of your cart, that's what I'll do. Let's see, any organic scallions in there? What's this? Elk milk? That'll be just fine. You may leave now."

I've found the best way to shop for food is to work up a really big appetite. Fast for several days, smoke a couple of joints, take $700 . . . and go to the supermarket! It's great. You buy everything!

"Wow, canned bread! Just what I need!"

And all the good things, the things you really love and can't do without? Well, you buy two of them, because you know you're going to eat one of them on the way home at a red light.

Shopping hungry is great; you just keep loading things into your cart. But then, after several aisles, you realize you may have overdone it: You find yourself pushing a motorcade of three carts, all tied together with long loops of string cheese. Once again, you've lost control.

And so, as you realize you don't have enough money to pay for everything, you begin to put back some of the more expensive items. Like meat.

"Meat? Twenty-seven dollars? Bullshit! I'll put back these steaks and grab a few more pound cakes. The kids shouldn't be eating meat, anyway."

The nicest thing about putting things back in the supermarket is that you can put them anywhere you want. No one cares. You can leave the Robitussin next to the ham hocks and stick the marshmallows in with the Bacon Bits. They don't care. They have people who come around at midnight to straighten that stuff out, and in the morning everything is back where it belongs.

By the way, next time you shop at a supermarket in a neighborhood that has higher than average marijuana use, take a look at the cookie section. Combat zone. Half the packages have been opened, and all the really good cookies are gone.

"Where the hell are the Mallomars?"

"Oh, we can't get Mallomars into the store. Folks line up at the loading dock for Mallomars."

There are always plenty of crappy cookies. You ever notice that? Shitty, low-priced local cookies? Like "Jim's Home-Style Cookies. Twenty-six varieties." I say, "Damn, Jim, if you can't make cookies in twenty-five tries leave me out."

Time to head home, folks. Let's get on the checkout line here and read *People* magazine. By the way, I must admit I'm a real sucker on the checkout line. I'm an impulse buyer. Anything that's on display, I want it. I even buy things other people leave behind.

"Wow! Extra spicy diet fudge raisin tartar sauce. Must be a sale. Great. I got the last one!"

One last thought: have you ever been on the express line and tried to convince the tough-looking Hispanic girl with the tattoos that twenty-seven packages of hot dogs are really just one item? I'm always grateful when she finally gives in. "Go ahead, mister, it's quicker than beating the shit out of you."

WELL, AT LEAST THE PLATE WAS BLUE

I often wonder why there's no blue food. Every other color is well represented in the food kingdom: corn is yellow, spinach is green, raspberries are red, carrots are orange, grapes are purple, and mushrooms are brown. So where's the blue food?

And don't bother me with blueberries; they're purple. The same is true of blue corn and blue potatoes. They're purple. Blue cheese? Nice try. It's actually white cheese with blue mold. Occasionally, you might run across some blue Jell-O in a cafeteria. Don't eat it. It wasn't supposed to be blue. Something went wrong.

FUSSY EATER

When I was a kid, I was a fussy eater. That's what they called it at our house.

"He's a fussy eater."

"Fussy eater" is a euphemism for "big pain in the ass." They'd trot out some food, and I'd say, "I don't like that."

"Why?"

"I don't know. I know I don't *like* it. And I know that if I ate it, I would like it even less."

"Well, I like it. Mmmmm! Yum yum!"

"Hey, Ma. You like it? You eat it!"

Sometimes they would try to corner me with logic: "Well, how do you *know* you don't like it, if you've never even tried it?"

"It came to me in a dream." Big pain in the ass.

Some things I didn't like because of the way they sounded.

"Don't sound right to me, Ma. Say that again?"

"Asparagus."

"No, I don't like that." Imagine. I got away with that for eight or nine years.

To this day, there are still some things I won't eat because of how they sound. Yogurt sounds disgusting. I can't eat anything that has both a "y" and a "g" in it. Squash is also badly named.

"You want some squash?" Sounds like someone sat on dinner.

"How would you like a nice tongue sandwich? It's made from slices of a cow's tongue."

"Hey, Ma, are you fuckin' tryin' to make me sick?"

There are also foods that sound too funny to eat. Like guacamole. It sounds like something you yell when you're on fire. "Holy guacamole! My ass is burnin'!"

Or when you can't remember the name of something. "Ed, where's that little guacamole that plugs into the lamp?"

Another food too funny to eat: garbanzo beans. Sounds like acrobats. "Ladies and gentlemen, from Corsica, the fabulous Garbanzos!"

On the other hand, there were some foods I didn't like because of how they *looked*. That seems a bit more rational.

"I don't like that! It don't look right to me. Did you make that, Ma? Yeah? Is there a picture of it in the cookbook? I'll bet it don't look like *that*."

Of course, some people will eat anything, no matter how it looks. I saw guys like that on the chow line in the army.

"Hi, boys! Whaddaya got? I'll eat anything. What's that called? Never mind, gimme a whole bunch of it."

"It's rat's asshole, Don."

"Well, it sure makes a hell of a fondue."

Not me. I don't eat anything I don't recognize immediately. If I have to ask questions, I pass. I'm not at dinner to make inquiries. Gimme somethin' I recognize. Like a carrot. I know I can trust a carrot.

Now, there are some foods that even though I know what they are, I still don't like their looks. Tomatoes, for instance. My main problem with tomatoes is that they don't look as though they're fully developed. They look like they're still in the larval stage; thousands of tiny seeds and a whole lot of jelly-lookin' slime. "Get it off my plate! It's slimy!" It's like that stuff at the end of an egg.

Of course, I know it's not the end of an egg . . . it's the beginning of a chicken!! "It's hen come! Eeeeaaaaghhh! Get it off my plate!"

Oh, I'm fun in the coffee shop.

Lobsters and crabs don't look like food to me, either. Anything with big pinchers crawling toward me sideways doesn't make me hungry. In fact, my instinct is "Step on that fuck! Step on him before he gets to the children!"

And I definitely cannot eat oysters. Not for the usual reason—their similarity to snot—but because when I look at the whole oyster I think, "Hey, that's a little house. Somebody lives in there. I'm not gonna break in on a guy just to have a meal. He might be making a pearl. Maybe he just brought home a do-it-yourself pearl kit and cleared off the dining room table. Who am I to interfere with the plans of an oyster?"

RUNNING HOT AND COLD

The refrigerator butter warmer is a strange invention. Originally, humans were cold so they built a warm enclosure. A house. Cold outside, warm inside the house. Everything was fine until they realized that inside the warm enclosure the meat tended to spoil. So they built a cold enclosure—a refrigerator—inside the warm enclosure. Warm in the house, cold in the refrigerator. Everything was fine until they realized that inside the cold enclosure the butter got too hard to spread. So they built an even smaller warm enclosure—a butter warmer—inside the cold enclosure, which was already inside the larger warm enclosure. Strange.

ICEBOX MAN

Around our house I'm known as Icebox Man. One of my duties is keeping people from standing too long with the icebox door open while they decide what to eat. You know, someone smokes three joints and decides to inventory the refrigerator. Drives me crazy.

"Close the fuckin' door, will ya? You're letting out all the cold. Here's twenty dollars, go down to the Burger King! I'll save that much on electricity. Close the goddamn door! If you can't decide what you want, take a Polaroid picture, go figure it out, and come back later. You kids are lucky. We didn't have Polaroids, we had to make an oil painting."

I try not to let them get me down, though, because Icebox Man has an even bigger job: picking through the refrigerator periodically, deciding which items to throw away. Most people won't take that responsibility; they grab what they want and leave the rest. They figure, "Someone is saving that; sooner or later it'll be eaten." Meanwhile the thing, whatever it is, is growing smaller and denser and has become permanently fused to the refrigerator shelf.

Well, folks, Icebox Man is willing to make the tough decisions. And I never act alone; I always include the family.

"I notice some egg salad that's been here for awhile. Are we engaged in medical research I haven't been told about?"

"May I assume from the color of this meat loaf that it's being saved for St. Patrick's Day?"

"Someone please call the museum and have this onion dip carbon-dated."

"How about this multihued Jell-O from Christmas? It's July now. If no one wants this, I'm going to throw it away."

Did your mother ever pull that stuff on you? Offer you some food that if you didn't eat it she was "Just going to throw it away"? Well, doesn't that make you feel dandy?

"Here's something to eat, Petey. Hurry up, it's spoiling! Bobby, eat this quickly; the green part is spreading. If you don't eat it, I'm going to give it to the dog." It's so nice to be ahead of the dog in the food chain.

Icebox Man has had some interesting experiences. Have you ever been looking through the refrigerator and come across a completely empty plate? Nothing on it but a couple of food stains? It's unnerving. I think to myself: "Could something have eaten something else? Maybe the Spam ate the olives. Maybe that half-eaten chicken isn't really dead. He's living on *our* food." Sometimes I picture a little mouse in a parka, hiding behind the mustard, waiting for the refrigerator light to go off so he can resume his cold-weather foraging.

Probably the worst experience is reaching into the refrigerator and finding something you simply cannot identify at all. You literally do not know what it is. It could be meat; it could be cake. At those times, I try to bluff.

"Honey? Is this good?"

"What is it?"

"I don't know! I've never seen anything like it. It looks like, well, it looks like . . . meat cake!"

"Smell it!"

"It has no smell whatsoever."

"That means it's good! Put it back. Someone is saving it for something." That's what frightens me; that someone will consider it a challenge and use it in soup. Simply because it's there.

It's a leftover. What a sad word: leftover.

But think about this. Leftovers make you feel good twice. First, when you put them away, you feel thrifty and intelligent: "I'm saving food!" Then, a month later, when blue hair is growing out of the ham, and you throw it away, you feel *really* intelligent: "I'm saving my life!"

DOG MOMENTS #3

Big Dog, Little Dog

Dogs come in all sizes. There are lots of little dogs, and lots of big dogs. And when I say big dogs, I don't mean just big dogs. I mean BIG, FUCKIN', HUGE GODDAMN DOGS! Some people got huge dogs that look more like livestock. Dogs that oughta be wearin' commercial license plates.

"What the hell is that?"

"That's my dog."

"Jesus, man, he blocked out the sun!"

"That's Tiny. He's a Great Alaskan Horse Moose Dog. Say 'hello,' Tiny. No, no! Tiny! Put the man down! Bad dog!"

Little dogs are different. Little dogs jump all around, and their legs move real quick. They got those teeny little legs. They got legs that if you feel around under the fur it's like a pepperoni stick under there.

Sometimes they jump up high. Some of 'em can jump clear up onto a real high bed.

[Boing!]

"Holy shit, what a jump! Lemme see ya do that again."

Put him back on the floor.

[Boing!]

"God, I can't believe it. C'mon, one more time."

Back onto the floor.

[Boing!]

And I make him keep doin' it and doin' it, over and over, until he gets all tired out and can't quite reach the bed anymore. I let him fall short a few times and crash back onto the floor. Then and only then, if I decide I *want* him on the bed, I put him up there myself. It's my decision; I buy the dog food.

Fleeky Disappoints

Besides, if you *do* allow him on the bed, sooner or later he'll create an incident. Before the evening is over, he will force one of the humans to turn to the other and say,

"Honey, did you fart?"

"Not me. I thought *you* farted."

"Not me! Phewww! That's not even one of my farts! I told you, I've got four farts. My Heineken's fart, my broccoli fart, my rice pudding fart, and my nondairy creamer fart. And the fart I'm smellin' right now is definitely not one of mine."

[Sniffing]

"Wait a minute. I know! The dog farted!! Fleeky farted! Fleeky, why did you fart? Look at him! Look how guilty he looks. He knows he farted. I seen his asshole open up. I seen it. What? Well, I just happened to be lookin' at his asshole by chance, that's all. What kind of a question is that? I was simply glancin' at his asshole, and I saw it open up. I thought he was doin' some kinda deep-breathing exercise. I had no idea he was into chemical warfare."

SHORT TAKES

I don't mind leaving my house as long as I don't have to look at a lot of unattractive Americans in the process. Visors, logo hats, fat thighs, beer bellies, bad haircuts, halter tops, cheap sneakers, camcorders, and unattractive children wearing blank expressions. God, these people are ugly. I stay home a lot.

I always refer to any individual member of the Red Sox as a Red Sock.
Is this correct?

America: where the Irish, English, Germans, Scandinavians, Poles, and Italians all came together to kill Indians, lynch niggers, and beat the shit out of spics and Jews.

Next guy who says to me, "Badda-boom, badda-bing," is
gettin' kicked right in the fuckin' nuts.

I was one of the people at Woodstock who took the brown acid. Lemme tell ya, there was nothing wrong with it.

NEVER FORGET, HITLER WAS A CATHOLIC.

Here would be a good epitaph for some guy: "I want everyone to know it was great being alive, and I really enjoyed myself. I especially enjoyed fucking and going to the movies."

If you listen to his voice carefully without looking at the
screen, Ted Koppel sounds like he's taking a shit.

There's a thing called shaken-baby syndrome that people get upset about. Personally, I think you have to give 'em a good shake, or they don't bake uniformly.

The Golden Gate Bridge should have a long bungee cord for people who aren't quite ready to commit suicide but want to get in a little practice.

If a movie is described as a romantic comedy you can usually find me next door playing pinball.

Somehow I enjoy watching people suffer.

My most frequent sex fantasy: to work in a delicatessen and have a woman come in and ask me to give her a pound of tongue.
    And I'd say, "Well, I don't get off till four o'clock."
    And she'd say, "Well, I don't get off at all, that's why I want some tongue."

If they decide to cover Viagra under Medicare, we'll all be paying for other people's hard-ons.

You know what they ought to have? Mntherfucker's Day. The day aftcr Mother's Day uuyht to be Motherfucker's Day. Actually, when you think about it, Father's Day is Motherfucker's Day.

Attention men: The dumb-looking shaved-head thing has finally played out. Try finding some other way of pretending to be cool and different.

In applying the stereotype that all old people are slow-thinking and dull-witted, what's often overlooked is that many of these people were slow-thinking and dull-witted throughout their lives. At this point they're simply older versions of the same unimpressive people.

My main operating principle: Don't take any shit from the zeitgeist.

History is not happenstance; it is conspiratorial. Carefully planned and executed by people in power.

The mayfly lives only one day. And sometimes it rains.

You know what you never hear about anymore? Quicksand. When I was a kid, movies and comic books had quicksand all the time. What happened? Same thing with whirlpools. You never hear about some guy being sucked down into a whirlpool anymore. I miss that.

I think they ought to have black confetti. It would be great for funerals. Especially if the dead person wasn't too popular.

If you really want to put a faith healer to the test, tell him you want a smaller shoe size.

You never seem to get laid on Thanksgiving. I think it's because all the coats are on the bed.

In the United States, anybody can be president. That's the problem.

You know how you can tell when a moth farts? When he suddenly flies in a straight line.

Do you realize that somewhere in the world there exists a person who qualifies as the worst doctor? If you took the time, by process of elimination you could actually determine the worst doctor in the world. And the funny part is knowing that someone has an appointment to see him tomorrow.

I often think of something my grandfather used to say. He'd tell me, "I'm goin' upstairs and fuck your grandma." He was a really honest man. He wasn't going to bullshit a five-year-old.

Just beyond the edge of the solar system, in the Oort Cloud, there's a swarm of about a trillion comets orbiting the sun. Let's hope that right now one of them is turning slightly and pointing itself directly at Mississippi.

The police in Los Angeles said recently that some man had been stabbed in the San Pedro area. Believe me, I know how painful that can be; I was once bitten there by a dog. It's especially painful when you go to the bathroom.

Doesn't Jonesboro sound to you like a place where everyone has a drug habit?

DOG MOMENTS #4

Gimme a New One

I love my dog. I love *all* my dogs. Every dog I ever had, I still love 'em. And in my life, believe me, I have had me a bunch of goddamn dogs. Because you keep on gettin' a new one, don't ya? It's true. As life goes on, you keep gettin' one new dog after another. That's the whole secret of life. Life is a series of dogs.

Sometimes you can get a dog that looks exactly like the one you had before. It's true. If you shop around a little, you can find you a dog identical to your former dog. You just bring the dead one into the pet shop, throw him up on the counter, and say, "Gimme another one of these." And, by God, they'll give you a carbon copy of your ex-goddamn dog. And that's real handy, because then you don't have to go around your house changin' all the pictures.

That's the nice thing about dogs. They don't live too long, and you can go and get a new one.

Doggie Nose Best

Most people know the best size dog to have is a knee-high, midsize dog. It's the ideal pet. Because whenever some nice lady comes to visit you, the first thing that dog does is put his nose right in her crotch.

"Hi, Mrs. Effington."

"Hi, Stuart, how's the . . . oooooh! Ooooooh! What a friendly dog. Oooohhhh! You know, I'll bet he smells *my* dog."

"I'm not sure, Mrs. Effington. Judgin' by where he's placed his nose, I'd say he's got a completely different animal in mind. You don't by any chance own a pussy, do ya?"

"No. I mean . . . well, no!"

Some people get embarrassed by that nose-crotch behavior. The dog owner will often fall all over himself trying to save face.

"Stop that, Bongo! Stop it! I'm awfully sorry, Marzell. He's usually so polite. You musta not bathed."

Not me, folks; I never apologize. I'm a fun-lovin' guy. I say, "Get in there, Bongo! Get yourself some of that. Sniff it out. Listen, Marzell, would you mind spreadin' your legs a little bit, so he can get some sniffin' room? Plant your feet about three feet apart, would ya? That's it. Good. Air that thing out. Okay! So, how's everything goin' down at the church? Good. All right, Bongo, now go around back and sniff that other thing. Sorry, Marzell, there's two smells he likes, and one of 'em's in the back. What's that? You gotta go? Well, I'm awfully sorry. Listen, before you go, you wouldn't be willin' to let Bongo have about thirty seconds on your leg, would ya? No, I didn't think so. Okay, no problem. You take care, and tell the reverend Bongo says hello."

Those dogs are really great. They help to break the ice when a new neighbor comes to call.

"Hi, we're the Belchingtons. Ooooooh! What's his name?"

"Ballsniffer. He's a crotch hound. Lemme know if you wanna get circumcised; he's on duty 'round the clock."

Give the Little Dog a Big Hand

When they show a dog on TV, do you try to get your dog to look at him? Don't you want your dog to see the dog on TV? I do.

"Look at the doggie! Look at the dog! Over there! On TV! Look!"

He won't look. Even if you try to twist his head around and point it toward the TV, he won't look.

"Over there! Turn your head! Look! On TV! Look at the dog! Goddamn it, you asshole! Look at the fuckin' dog!!"

They never look where you want. If you point at something, they just stare at your hand. You try to show them something interesting, and they think you're showing them your hand.

"There he goes again, showing me his hand. Why does he do that? I guess he's really proud of it. Uh-oh! Now he's twisting my head around. Owww! Jeez, what did I do now?"

"Well, for one thing you completely missed the dog on TV."

A Cracker Jack Meal

A long time ago I had a little dog named Tippy. And one time when I was doin' drugs, I fed Tippy a whole bunch of Cracker Jack, because that's what I was havin'. Cracker Jack and tap water. Seemed like a reasonable meal to me. And even though Tippy was a little dog, she ate about two boxes of Cracker Jack. And the next day, when I took her out for a walk, she squatted and strained and grunted and shook, and you know what? By God, instead of taking a shit, she took a Cracker Jack! Right in front of my eyes I saw fully formed, undigested Cracker Jack coming out of my dog!

Well, you know me, I'm a practical guy. I kept waitin' for the little surprise to come out, hopin' it wouldn't be a whistle or a bird call. I figure there's a certain amount of basic hygiene you can't ignore.

NOT EXACTLY MARTHA STEWART

Did your dog ever eat a whole bunch of brightly colored balloons, and when he took a shit it turned out to be real festive looking? Or maybe at Christmas he'd eat some tinsel off the tree and take a dump near the manger, and it would glisten with light from the yule log, filling your heart with Christmas spirit? Isn't it great?

Dogs are a constant source of entertainment. Did you ever have a dog who ate cat turds? Some of them do. Some dogs will eat cat turds. Of course, you gotta have a cat; you can't be goin' down to the supermarket and buyin' cat turds.

But it's true. Sometimes a dog will eat cat turds. Don't let him lick your face that day. Get him a bottle of Listerine, and make him gargle. Pour it down his throat and tell him to howl. Then you can let him lick you.

One more thing about dog chow, and this includes a little household hint that'll help you keep your lawn neat and clean. Feed your dog rubber bands. Just mix ten or eleven rubber bands in with his food. He won't care. He'll eat anything as long as it's mixed in with something he likes.

Feed him a bunch of rubber bands, and then when he takes a shit, you'll notice there's a handy little rubber loop stickin' out of one end of the turd. Then, all you gotta do is pick up the loop, swing that turd around, and throw it in the next yard. Tell your neighbor it's a new thing: flying lawn food.

HAVE A NICE DAY

I don't have nice days anymore. I don't bother with that. I'm beyond the nice day; I feel I've outgrown the whole idea. Besides, I've already had my share of nice days. Why should I be hogging them all? Let someone else have a few.

Naturally, everyone still *wants* me to have one. Every person I meet wants me to have a nice day. Especially clerks.

"Have a nice day."

"Yeah, yeah, yeah. You wanna gimme my fuckin' change, please? I'm triple-parked!"

Some of them are really insistent.

"I said have a nice day! Do it!"

"All right, all right! I'll give it a shot."

That's the trouble with "Have a nice day." It puts all the pressure on you. Now you have to go out and somehow arrange to have a positive experience. All because of some loose-lipped clerk.

Have a nice day, indeed! Maybe I don't *feel* like having a nice day. Maybe—just maybe—I've had twenty-seven nice days in a row, and I'm ready for a crappy day. You never hear that, do you?

"Have a crappy day!"

"Why, thank you. Right back at ya! And to your wonderful family as well!"

A crappy day; that would be easy. No trouble at all. No planning involved. Just get out of bed and start moving around.

I think what bothers me most about the whole "nice day" thing is that word "nice." It's a weak word. It doesn't have a lot of character. Nice.

"Isn't he nice? He is so nice. And she's nice too! Isn't that nice? How nice they are!"

I don't care for it. It's like "fine." Another weak word.

"How are you?"

"Fine."

Bullshit! Nobody's fine. Hair is fine.

"How's your hair?"

"Fine."

That makes more sense to me.

Some guys are "great"! You ever meet those guys?

"This is great! Isn't this great? Goddamn, this is great! Look, they're gonna kill that guy! Isn't that great?"

Not me. I'm not nice, I'm not fine, I'm not great. People ask me how I am, I don't give them any superlatives; nothing to gossip about. I tell them I'm "fairly decent." Or "relatively okay." I might say, "I'm moderately neato." And if I'm in a particularly jaunty mood, I'll tell them, "I'm not unwell, thank you."

That one always pisses them off. Because they have to figure it out for themselves.

HELLO-GOODBYE

We have so many ways of saying hello. Howdy, hi there, how are ya, how ya doin', how's it goin', how do ya do, what's new, what's goin' on, whaddaya think, whaddaya hear, whaddaya say, whaddaya feel, what's happenin', what's shakin', que pasa, what's goin' down, and what it is?

You know my favorite? "How's your hammer hangin'?" That's a good one, isn't it? Doesn't work too well with women, though. Unless you're talking to a lady carpenter. Then it's perfectly acceptable.

I've always wanted to use that one on a high church official.

"Good evening, Your Holiness. How hangs thy hammer?"

So far, I haven't had the opportunity.

There's one form of saying hello that bothers me. It's when a guy says, "Are they keepin' you busy?" It's like he thinks someone has the right to come around and give me odd jobs.

Whenever a guy says, "Are they keeping you busy?" I always tell him, "Well, your wife is keeping me pretty busy!" And that seems to hold him for about a half an hour.

Of course, we also have many ways to say good-bye. Bye-bye, so long, see you later, ta-ta, be cool, take it easy, stay loose, hang in, take care, and keep on truckin'. You know my favorite? "Don't get run over." Well, I find some people need practical advice.

Occasionally, someone will say to me, "Have a good one!" I just laugh and say, "I already have a good one. Now I'm looking for a *longer* one!" And that seems to hold them for about a half an hour.

Then there are all the foreign ways we say good-bye. Some people when they leave you, they think they have to get fancy. They whip an "arrivederci" on you. Or an "au revoir." Some guys say, "adios." Or the American version, "Adios, motherfucker!"

In Hawaii they say, "aloha." That's a nice one. It means both "hello" and "good-bye." Which just goes to show, if you spend enough time in the sun you don't know whether you're coming or going.

Do you ever get in a rut with your manner of saying good-bye and find yourself using the same phrase, over and over? And you begin to feel a little stupid?

For instance, if you're leaving a party, and you have to say good-bye to five or six people standing in a group, you say, "Okay, hey, take it easy. Okay, hey, take it easy. Okay, hey, take it easy. Okay, hey, take it easy. Okay, hey, take it easy. Okay, hey, take it easy." And you feel like a goddamn moron.

You know what I do? Every month, whether I need to or not, I change the way I say good-bye; I start using a different phrase. People like that. They notice that little extra effort. They'll say to me, "Pardon me, but didn't you used to say 'Okay, hey, take it easy'?"

And I say, "Yes I did. But not anymore. Now I say, 'Farewell! Farewell, till we meet again. May the forces of evil become confused on the way to your house!' " That's a strong one, isn't it? People will remember you if you talk like that.

Sometimes, for a joke, you can combine several ways of saying good-bye that don't seem to go together. Like "Toodle-oo, go with

God, and don't take any wooden nickels." Then people don't know *what* the fuck you're talking about.

Or you can choose to say good-bye in a realistic manner. "So long, Steve. Don't let self-doubt interfere with your plans to improve your life."

Well, some people need practical advice.

LOVE AND REGARDS

Have you noticed that quite often when you leave someone they ask you to relay an affectionate message to someone else? They'll say, "Give my love to Klaus. Tell Klaus Rebecca sends her love."

Do you mind that? Do you mind being used that way? The awesome responsibility of carrying Rebecca's love to Klaus? Suppose you don't see Klaus? What do you do with Rebecca's love? Carry it around? Give it to someone else?

"Wilhelm! I can't find Klaus, here's some of Rebecca's love."

Suppose Wilhelm doesn't know Rebecca? Can he legally accept her love? Especially when it was originally intended for Klaus?

Or suppose you give Wilhelm Rebecca's love for Klaus, and then you run into Klaus, what do you give him? All you had was Rebecca's love, and you've already gone and given that to Wilhelm. Can you reasonably ask Wilhelm to give back Rebecca's love? Maybe he's gotten used to it by now. Can Klaus sue Wilhelm? Can Wilhelm be arrested? Can *you* be arrested for transporting love across a state line?

All right, back to reality. Just for the sake of argument, let's leave Wilhelm out of this altogether. Suppose Rebecca gives you her love to give to Klaus, and you *do* see Klaus, what form should the love take? Can you risk giving Klaus a tongue kiss? Which brings up another possibility: maybe Klaus is gay. Klaus doesn't *want* Rebecca's love, Klaus wants *Wilhelm's* love! If Klaus tells you to give his love to Wilhelm, just tell him, "Bullshit, Klaus. You give your *own* love to Wilhelm. I'm going to find Rebecca!"

Now, sometimes people don't quite want you to give their love to someone else; they only want you to give their "regards." That's all they're sending that day. Regards. That's not as important as love, is it? No. By the way, do you always relay the type of affection the sender intends? I don't. Generally, I wait till the last minute and then decide what the other person deserves.

For instance, Susan might say to me, "Give my love to Dave." Well, I might not feel Dave is deserving of Susan's love. Dave might be one of those people who piss me off. I'll probably just give him a few regards; keep him in his place. I feel it's my decision. After all, I'm the one who's doing all the work.

And if I *really* don't like the recipient, I might reduce the level of affection by an even greater degree. Susan might say, "Give all my love to Dave and tell him I can't wait to see him again so I can hold him in my arms, kiss his sweet, soft lips, and make love to him all night." And I'll say, "Dave! Susan says hello." Screw Dave! That's what he gets for pissing me off.

Then there are the recipients who try to anticipate what degree of affection they're going to receive.

"Did Susan send her love?"

"No, Dave. She only sent her regards."

"That's funny, usually she sends her love."

"Well, not this time. In fact, she specifically told me, 'Don't give Dave any of my love.' It seems she's running short of love and has to be careful whom she gives it to. However, she did say she's overstocked with regards and wants you to have a whole bunch of them. So, be satisfied, Dave. Take your regards, and get the fuck out of my life!"

Well, he should damn well be satisfied with regards; it's a lot better than simply being sent someone's "best." There are some people who just send you their best.

"Give my best to Dave."

"Your best what, Susan? If this is your best, perhaps you'd better keep it to yourself."

And yet, receiving someone's "best" is better than simply being "remembered to," isn't it? That's the lowest of all. Hardly worth even telling the poor person.

"Remember me to Dave."

"Okay."

"Dave? You remember Susan?"

"Yes."

"Well, she remembers you, too."

That's it, my job is done. I'm off now to find Tex, so I can tell him Billy Bob said "Howdy."

One final thing. There are times when someone wants you to convey more than simply love. They want you to give someone "a big hug and kiss." Now they've got you trafficking in sex.

"Give Joachim a big hug and a kiss for me."

Usually it's women. I find that women are a bit more expressive at times like these. And sometimes they're really explicit.

"Bye-bye, Elena. Drive carefully. Give Flaco a nice blow job for me. And don't forget to lick his asshole!"

"Okay, Belinda. But next time let's get Klaus to take care of that!"

EXPRESSIONS I QUESTION

There are many expressions we take for granted. We use them all the time, yet never examine them carefully. We just say them as if they really made sense.

Legally drunk. Well, if it's legal, what's the problem? "Leave me alone, officer, I'm legally drunk!"

You know where you can stick it. Why do we assume everyone knows where they can stick it? Suppose you don't know? Suppose you're a new guy, and you have absolutely no idea where you can stick it? I think there ought to be a government booklet entitled *Where to Stick It*. Now that I think of it, I believe there *is* a government booklet like that. They send it to you on April 15.

Undisputed heavyweight champion. Well, if it's undisputed, what's all the fighting about? To me, "undisputed" means we all agree. Here you have two men beating the shit out of one another over something they apparently agree on. Makes no sense.

It's the quiet ones you gotta watch. Every time I see a television news story about a mass murderer, the guy's neighbor always says, "Well, he was very quiet." And someone I'm with says, "It's the quiet ones you gotta watch."

This sounds like a very dangerous assumption. I'll bet anything that while you're busy watching a quiet one, a noisy one will kill you.

Suppose you're in a bar, and one guy is sitting over on the side, reading a book, not bothering anybody. And another guy is standing up at the front, bangin' a machete on the bar, screamin', "I'm gonna kill the next motherfucker who pisses me off!"

Who you gonna watch?

Lock him up and throw away the key. This is one you hear a lot from men. Men like to talk that way; it makes 'em feel tough. A guy sees a rapist on the TV news, he says, "You see that guy? They oughta lock him up, and throw away the key."

This is really stupid. First of all, every time the guy's gotta take a shit, you're gonna have to call the locksmith. If he's in prison thirty years, even if he's eatin' government cheese, it's gonna cost you a fortune.

Second, where do you throw the key? Right out in front of the jail? His friends'll find it! How far can you throw a key? Fifty, sixty feet the most. Even if you hold it flat on its side and scale it, whaddaya get? An extra ten feet, tops! This is a stupid idea that needs to be completely rethought.

Down the tubes. That's one you hear a lot. People say, "This country is goin' down the tubes." What tubes? Have you seen any tubes? Where are these tubes? And where do they go? And how come there's more than one tube? It would seem to me for one country all you need is one tube. Does every state have to have its own tube? One tube is all you need.

But a tube that big? Somebody would have seen it by now. Somebody would've said, "Hey Joey! Lookit the fuckin' tube! Big-ass fuckin' tube, over here!" You never hear that. You know why? No tubes! We don't have tube one. We are, sorry to say, tubeless.

Takes the cake. "Boy, he really takes the cake." Where? Where do you take a cake? To the movies? You know where I would take a cake? Down to the bakery, to see the other cakes. And how come he takes the cake? How come he doesn't take the pie? A pie is easier to carry than a cake. "Easy as pie." A cake is not too hard to carry, either. "Piece of cake."

The greatest thing since sliced bread. So this is it? A couple of hundred thousand years . . . sliced bread? What about the Pyramids? The Panama Canal? The Great Wall of China? Even a lava lamp, to me, is greater than sliced bread. What's so great about sliced bread? You got a knife, you got a loaf of bread. Slice the fuckin' thing!! And get on with your life.

Out walking the streets. This is another one you hear from men. Some guy sees a rapist on the news. Same rapist as before; only this time he's being released. The guy says, "You see that? You see that guy? They're lettin' him go! Now, instead of bein' in prison, he's out walkin' the streets!"

How do we know? How do we know he's out walkin' the streets? Maybe he's home bangin' the baby-sitter. Not everybody who gets a parole is out walkin' the streets. A lot of times they steal a car. We oughta be glad. "Thank God he stole a car. At least he's not out walkin' the streets."

Fine and dandy. That's an old-fashioned one, isn't it? You say to a guy, "How are ya?" He says, "Fine and dandy." Not me. I never say that. You know why? Because I'm never both those things at the same time. Sometimes I'm fine. But I'm not dandy. I might be close to dandy. I might be approaching dandy. I might even be in the general vicinity of dandyhood. But not quite fully dandy. Other times, I might indeed be highly dandy. However, not fine. One time, 1978. August. For about an hour. I was both fine and dandy at the same time. But nobody asked me how I was. I coulda told 'em, "Fine and dandy!" I consider it a lost opportunity.

Walking papers. Some guy gets fired, they say, "Well, they gave him his walkin' papers today." Lemme ask you something. Did you ever get any walking papers? Seriously? Believe me, in my life I got fired a lot of times. I never got any walkin' papers. I never got a pink slip, either. You know what I would get? A guy would come around to my desk and say, "Get the fuck outta here!!" You don't need paper for that.

The riot act. They keep saying they're going to read that to you. Tell the truth, have you heard this thing at all? Ever?

It's especially a problem when you're a kid. They like to threaten you.

"You wait'll your father comes home. He's gonna read you the riot act!"

"Oh yeah? Well, tell him I already read it myself! And I didn't like it! I consider it wordy and poorly thought out. If he wants to read me somethin', how about *The Gentleman's Guide to the Golden Age of Tongue-Kissing?*

More than happy. I'll bet you say that sometimes. I'll bet you say, "Oh, I'd be more than happy to do that." How can you be more than happy? To me, this sounds like a dangerous mental condition. "We had to put Laszlo under physical restraint; he was . . . well, he was more than happy."

One more of these expressions: **In your own words.** You hear it in classrooms. And courtrooms. They'll say, "Tell us . . . in your own words . . ." Do you have your own words? Personally, I'm using the ones everybody else has been using. Next time they tell you to say something in your own words, say, "Nigflot blorny quando floon."

SHORT TAKES

I don't hear much of that elevator music anymore. What's going on?

IT'S TIME TO START SLAPPING PEOPLE

Don't you think there were probably a lot of singers with great voices who never got famous because they were too ugly to stand up and be seen in public?

I can't wait to see one of those actor-assholes who drive race cars get killed on TV.

Why do women wear evening gowns to nightclubs? Why don't they wear nightgowns?

I think many years ago an advanced civilization intervened with us genetically and gave us just enough intelligence to develop dangerous technology but not enough to use it wisely. Then they sat back to watch the fun. Kind of like a human zoo. And you know what? They're getting their money's worth.

After you die, your "stuff" becomes your "personal effects."

GOD BLESS US ALL. RIGHT IN THE MOUTH

I think people should be allowed to do anything they want. We haven't tried that for a while. Maybe this time it'll work.

People ask me if I have an e-mail address, and I say, "www.fuckyou.com@blowme/upyourass." And they seem to understand.

Message to the Denver Nuggets regarding Columbine High School: There's no reason to cancel a sporting event just because some kids kill each other. Try to concentrate on basketball and leave the life-and-death shit to someone else.

Capitalism tries for a delicate balance: It attempts to work things out so that everyone gets just enough stuff to keep them from getting violent and trying to take other people's stuff.

Baseball bats are now the preferred weapon for many drug gangs and others who have a business need to administer behavioral reminders. They're cheap, lethal, legal, untraceable, and hey! It's the national pastime.

Dying must have survival value. Or it wouldn't be part of the biological process.

Why is it that, when making reference to something in the past, people often think they have to say, "I hope I'm not dating myself"? Listen, if you're so embarrassed by your age there's a simple solution: open a vein.

I don't have hobbies, I have interests. Hobbies cost money. Interests are free.

With all the presidential administrations we've had, I'm sure that by now there must have been at least one person who, besides being in the cabinet, was also in the closet.

I don't like it when I'm in an audience and the emcee tells us to give someone a welcome specific to that city: "Let's all get together and give this little lady a nice Toledo welcome." I've often thought if I were from Toledo it would be fun now and then to give someone a Baltimore welcome, just to break the emcee's balls. Or maybe slip in an exotic Budapest welcome when no one is expecting it. One thing I would never do is give someone a Dallas welcome. That's what JFK got. Dallas welcomes don't last too long.

You rarely see an elderly midget. Apparently their life spans are shorter too.

A PEAR IS A FAILED APPLE

You keep hearing that society's greatest tasks are educating people and getting them jobs. That's great. Two things people hate to do: go to school and go to work.

We busy ourselves with meaningless gestures such as Take Our Daughters to Work Day, which applies primarily to white, middle-class daughters. More help for the wrong people.

People seem to think that if there's some problem that makes them unhappy in this country, all they have to do is stage a big march and everything will change. When will they learn?

Complaint: Where did this dumb-ass Sammy Sosa thumping-your-chest, kissing-your-fingers, flashing-the-peace-sign nonsense come from? What's that stupid shit all about? Geraldo does a variation on it. It strikes me as pretentious, meaningless, pseudoreligious bullshit.

I don't know about you, but I really have no problem with atrocities. What's the big deal? Lighten up.

Can placebos cause side effects? If so, are the side effects real?

When hundreds of people are killed in an airplane crash I always wonder if maybe there wasn't one guy, a little behind schedule that day, who ran down the last few hundred yards of the airport concourse to make the plane on time. And when he finally sat down in his seat, out of breath, he was really glad he made it. And then an hour later the plane goes down. What goes through his mind? Do you think maybe in those last few moments, as he plunges to the Earth he wishes he'd had a heart attack while running through the airport?

Why do they bother with a suicide watch when someone is on death row? "Keep an eye on this guy. We're gonna kill him, and we don't want him to hurt himself."

I notice at Jewish weddings they break a glass. You ever been to an Irish wedding? Glasses, bottles, mirrors, tables, chairs, arms, legs, the band instruments, and the groom's neck. We don't fuck around. Mazel tov!

HOW SOON IS INTERMISSION?

I recently attended an avant-garde play. Here's what it said in the program:

An Anteater, a Tire Iron and a Blue Hat
by Zal Fenchley

Act One

SCENE 1 Laura's living room, several weeks later.

SCENE 2 Easter, aboard a Turkish woman's thigh.

SCENE 3 Deep within the colon of a woolly mammoth. 16,376 B.C.

SCENE 4 Inside a sailor's shorts during the attack on Pearl Harbor.

Act Two

SCENE 1 On a French sidewalk, six feet from escargot vomit.

SCENE 2 Inside a condom in Haifa. Jewish New Year.

SCENE 3 At your aunt's house. Soon.

Act Three

SCENE 1 In a Shriner's hatband following oral sex.

SCENE 2 Down where Arturo used to live. Not that long ago.

Act Four

John Lennon two songs. (not tonight)

HAVE A GOOD TIME

You know what bothers me? People who want to know the time. The ones who come up and ask me, "What time is it?" as if I, personally, were responsible for keeping track of such things.

Sometimes they phrase it a little differently. They'll say, "Do you have the time?" And I say, "No. I don't believe I do. I certainly didn't have it this morning when I left the house. Could you possibly have left it somewhere? You know, now that you mention it, I believe the navy has the time. In Washington. They keep it in an observatory or something, and they let a little of it out each day. Not too much, of course. Just enough. They wouldn't want to give us too much time; we might not use it wisely." Sometimes, in a playful mood, when asked if I have the time, I'll say, "Yes," and simply walk away.

When Is It, Anyway?

I do that because I hate to disappoint people. You see, there is no time. There's just no time. I don't mean, "We're late, there's no time." I mean, there is no time.

After all, when is it? Do you know? No one really knows when it is. We made the whole thing up. It's a human invention. There are no numbers in the sky. Believe me, I've looked; they're not there. We made the whole thing up.

So, when are we? Sometimes we think we know *where we are,* but we really don't know *when* we are. For all we know, it could be the middle of last week.

And the time zones are no help; they're all different. In fact, in parts of India the time zones actually operate on the half hour instead of the hour. What is that all about? Does anybody really know what time it is?

What Year Do You Have?

And never mind a piddly little half-hour difference in India, how about thousands of years? The major calendars disagree by thousands of years. To the Chinese, this is 4699; the Hebrews think it's 5762; the Muslims swear it's 1422. No telling what the Mayans and Aztecs would say if they were still around. I guess their time ran out.

Remember, folks, these are *calendars* we're talking about, instruments specifically designed to keep track of time. And they're all different. And they're not just off by a couple of weeks, this is thousands of goddamn years we're talking about. How did that happen?

Our current (Gregorian) calendar is such an amateur show that every four years we have to cram in an extra day just to make the whole thing work. We call it February 29. Personally, I don't believe it. Deep down, I know it's really March 1. I mean, it just *feels* like March 1, doesn't it?

But even that simple quadrennial adjustment doesn't fix things, so every 100 years we suspend that rule and dispense with the extra day. Unless, of course, the year is divisible by 400, in which case we suspend the suspension and *add* the extra day. But that's still not quite enough, so every 4,000 years we suspend that rule too, and back comes February 29!

Here's how we got to this sorry state: The Julian calendar was introduced in 46 B.C., the Roman year 709, but it was off by eleven minutes a year, so by 1582 there was an accumulated error of ten days. Accordingly, that year Pope Gregory XIII decreed that the day following October 4 would be called October 15. They just skipped ten days. Threw them out. Officially, in 1582, no one was born in France, Italy, Spain or Portugal during the period October 5 through October 14. Weird, huh?

But even weirder, Britain didn't adopt the Gregorian calendar till

1752, when they dropped eleven days out of September. Since this also applied to the American colonies, officially, no one was born here from September 3 through September 13, 1752. Except Indians. By the way, during that same year New Year's Day was moved from March 25 to January 1. The way it had been handled before, for example, was that March 24, 1750, would be followed by March 25, 1751. Pretty fucked up, huh? And you thought that big millennium party you went to was being held right on time.

Staying in the "Now"

We try hard to keep track of time, but it's futile. You can't pin it down. For example, there's a moment coming . . . it's not here yet . . . it's still in the future . . . it's on the way . . . it hasn't arrived . . . it's getting closer . . . here it is . . . Oh shit, it's gone!

We use words like "now." But it's a useless word, because every time you say it, it means something different.

"Can you tell me the time?"

"Which time did you want? Now? Or the time you asked me? Or how about now? Is this the time you want? Speak up, this stuff isn't standing still."

And think of the phrase "just now."

"Did you hear that?"

"What?"

"Just now."

"You mean, 'Just then.' "

"Yes, just then. Wait, there it is again!"

"When?"

"Just now."

Everything we think of as "now" is either the very recent past or

the very near future. There's no present. "Welcome to the present."
ZOOM! Gone again!

Keep It Vague

It's all so imprecise that people sometimes don't bother with
minutes and hours at all; they keep things purposely vague.

"What time you got?"

"Just after."

"Just after? Jeez, my watch is slow. I got 'goin' on.' "

It's amazing how something as precisely calibrated as time can be
described so loosely. Especially where short periods of time are concerned. We say "at once," "immediately," "right away," "just like that,"
"no time at all," "nothing flat," "at a moment's notice."

And one that I never understood: "Before you can say Jack Rob-
inson." You don't hear that much anymore, do you? Maybe Jack ran
out of time. Maybe he was an Aztec.

And let's not forget a "jiffy." Or a "flash." Do you know which
is quicker? Well, I looked it up; in fact, there are two jiffies in a flash.
And there are six flashes in the twinkling of an eye. No one seems to
know how many twinklings of an eye there are in two shakes of a lamb's
tail. And, by the way, why is it *two* shakes of a lamb's tail? Wouldn't
the basic unit of measurement be one shake of a lamb's tail?

All of a Sudden

Another vague word is "soon." For me, soon has an emotional
quality; it has great potential for sadness.

"Is Daddy ever coming to visit us again?"

"Yes."

"When?"

"Soon."

Here's a spooky one: "Sooner than you think." Wow! Sooner than I think. That's like "before you know it."

"I'll be back before you know it."

ZOOM!

"Holy shit! He did it!!"

"Sooner or later," "one of these days," "any day now," "from time to time," "every now and then," "a little while."

"A little while" is nice. So gentle. "I'll be home in a little while." That wouldn't bother you, would it? I think anyone could wait a little while. It doesn't sound too threatening.

"Your father is sick, but he still has 'a little while.'" That's different from "a short time." A short time sounds terminal.

"Your father has only a 'short time.'"

If I were about to be executed, I'd much rather have a little while than a short time.

A Good Time

By the way, do you have a favorite period of time? It isn't easy to select a favorite period of time, there are so many appealing ones. I have a few.

To me, the most useful period of time is five minutes. That seems to be the one most people choose when they're pressed. "I'll be there in five minutes." "Give me five minutes, will ya?" "Whattaya, kiddin'? I could fix that thing in five minutes!"

That's all most people want. Five minutes. A good, solid, respectable period of time. And it goes by fast. I think I could do just about anything for five minutes. Even the most distasteful task.

"Let's go talk to George Bush."

"Are you kiddin'? He's an asshole."

"Look, just five minutes, okay?"

"Okay, five minutes. But no more! After that I'm gonna puke."

Fifteen minutes is a popular period of time. But it has an institutional ring to it. A regulatory quality. It sounds like it's associated with something either compulsory or forbidden.

"The exchange window will only be open for fifteen minutes."

"You have fifteen minutes to fill out the forms . . ."

"In fifteen minutes we will be coming around and . . ."

I like twenty minutes better. Twenty minutes sounds kind of free and sporty.

"I'll be back to pick up those test papers in fifteen minutes. Then you'll have a twenty-minute break."

"Hey guys, cover me with the boss, will ya? I'll be back in twenty minutes."

Twenty minutes. Just enough time to get laid.

Have a good time.

SHORT TAKES

Why was brown excluded from the rainbow? And where did indigo come from? I was taught there were three primary colors and three secondary colors. What's with this indigo shit?

After the hurricane is gone, where do people put all that plywood?

Standing ovations have become far too commonplace. What we need are ovations where the audience members all punch and kick one another.

Watching television these days, I often wonder what happened to the "vertical hold" knob. I miss that.

Don't you hate when a rock band comes onstage and apparently the drummer has decided that somehow it's cool to wear a funny hat?

There's a store near my house with a sign that says, Unfinished Furniture. I must go in there. I'm looking for a nice three-legged table.

If you live long enough, everyone you know has cancer.

I once was dancing with a woman who told me she had a yeast infection. So I asked her to bake me a loaf of bread.

Why don't these people who live in hurricane-prone areas just keep some batteries on hand at home? Seems like a simple thing to me. There's too much last-minute shopping.

I'm always relieved when someone is delivering a eulogy and I realize I'm listening to it.

Why don't network TV shows have a warning that says "Caution: You are about to watch a real piece of shit." Actually, they could just leave it on the screen all the time.

All music is the blues. All of it.

I think it would be interesting if old people got anti-Alzheimer's disease where they slowly began to recover other people's lost memories.

Electricity is really just organized lightning.

You know what they ought to have on planes? A passenger voice recorder. So we could hear all the screaming when a plane goes down. I'm not really interested in the cockpit recorder; the pilots are always talkin' a bunch of technical shit anyway. But the passengers! That would be fun.

When you rub your eyes real hard do you see that checkerboard pattern? What is that?

"Coming soon to a theater near you." Actually, there is no theater near you. Look around your street. Is there a theater near you?

Attention certain women: Transporting children is not a license to drive slowly.

I saw a sign that said, Coming Soon—a 24-Hour Restaurant. And I thought, Well, that's unusual. Why would they open and close it so quickly? At least try it for a week or two, and see if you can build a clientele.

Why is it when the two main characters in an action movie have their big climactic fight it always turns out that both of them are really good fighters? Just once, wouldn't you like to see a fight between two leading male characters where one of them gets the shit completely beat out of him in about eight seconds? Especially the hero.

I've noticed my flax bill is not too high.

Would someone please explain to me the supposed appeal of having grandchildren? People ask me, "Are you a grandfather yet?" as if it's some great thing. I'm sure it has its charms, and I imagine some dull-witted people want to see their genes passed along just for the sheer novelty of the idea. But overall, I don't get it.

It's been on my mind for some time, but I've never said it publicly. So here goes: "Vo-do-de-o-do and a scoddie-woddie doo-dah day." Thank you.

Boy, am I glad to finally be rid of that fuckin' Mother Teresa.

Masturbation is not illegal, but if it were, people would probably take the law into their own hands.

It used to be you got a tattoo because you wanted to be one of the few people who had a tattoo. Now you get a tattoo because you don't want to be one of the few people who don't have a tattoo.

Just when I discovered the meaning of life, it changed.

People in Washington say it's not the initial offense that gets you in trouble, it's the cover-up. They say you should admit what you did, get the story out, and move on. What this overlooks is the fact that most of the time the cover-up works just fine, and nobody finds out a thing. I would imagine that's the rule rather than the exception. My advice: Take a chance. Lie.

The IQ and the life expectancy of the average American recently passed each other going in opposite directions.

Hotel fun: Smoke a big fat joint and then watch a complex spy movie with a lot of characters and plot twists. Then a few weeks later at a different hotel, smoke another joint and watch the same movie. It's like seeing a whole new film. But the real fun is that about every fifteen minutes something happens in the plot that you seem to know already. It's an odd feeling. By the way, this exercise can probably be repeated indefinitely with the same movie. As long as the grass holds out.

This is just one more way of starting a sentence with the word "this" and ending it with the word "that."

Odd Slang: A woman who fucks a priest is said to have "taken a ride on the holy pole."

PEOPLE I CAN DO WITHOUT

* Guys in their fifties named Skip.

* Anyone who pays for vaginal jelly with a platinum credit card.

* An airline pilot wearing two different shoes.

* A proctologist with poor depth perception.

* A pimp who drives a Ford Escort.

* A gynecologist who wants my wife to have three Quaaludes before the examination.

* Guys with a lot of small pins on their hats.

* Anyone who mentions Jesus more than 300 times in a two-minute conversation.

* A dentist with blood in his hair.

* Any woman whose hobby is breast-feeding zoo animals.

* A funeral director who says, "Hope to see you folks again real soon."

* A man with only one lip.

* A Boy Scoutmaster who works at a dildo shop.

* People who know the third verse to the "Star Spangled Banner."

* Any lawyer who refers to the police as "the federales."

* A cross-eyed nun with a bullwhip and a bottle of gin.

* Guys who have their names printed on their belts.

✳ A brain surgeon with BORN TO LOSE tattooed on his hand.

✳ Couples whose children's names all start with the same initial.

✳ A man in a hospital gown, directing traffic.

✳ A waitress with a visible infection on her serving hand.

✳ People who have large gums and small teeth.

✳ Guys who wear the same underwear until it begins to cut off the circulation to their crotch.

✳ Any woman whose arm hair completely covers her wristwatch.

CANCER IS GOOD FOR YOU

A lot of people worry that their drinking water isn't safe, because it contains things that cause cancer. Not me. I don't care if the water is safe or not, I drink it anyway. You know why? Because I'm an American, and I expect a little cancer in my water. I'm a loyal citizen and I'm not happy unless government and industry have poisoned me a little every day.

Besides, cancer never hurt anybody. People need a little cancer. It's good for you; it keeps you on your toes. I ain't afraid of cancer, I had broccoli for lunch. Broccoli kills cancer. A lot of people don't know that. It's not out yet.

It's true. You find out you got some cancer, get yourself a fuckin' bowl of broccoli. That'll wipe it right out. Cauliflower, too. Cauliflower kills the really big cancers, the ones you can see from across the street through heavy clothing. Broccoli kills the little ones, the ones that are slowly eating you away from inside. While your goofy, half-educated doctor keeps telling you, "You're doin' fine, Jim."

In fact, bring your doctor a bowl of broccoli, he's probably got cancer, too. Probably picked it up from you. They don't know what they're doing. It's all guesswork in a white coat. What you gotta try to do is develop more than one kind of cancer, so you can turn 'em against one another. That's what you gotta hope for: that the cancers eat each other up instead of you. Fact is, the way I look at it, the more cancer you got, the healthier you are.

THE HUMOROUS SIDE OF RAPE

Many people in this country want to tell you what you can and can't talk about. Or sometimes they'll tell you you can talk about something, but you can't joke about it. Like rape. People say you can't joke about rape. They say rape's not funny. And I say, Fuck you, I think it's hilarious. How do you like that? I can prove rape is funny: Picture Porky Pig raping Daisy Duck. See? Hey, why do you think they call him Porky?

And I know what men are gonna say. Daisy was askin' for it; she was comin' on to Porky, she had on tight feathers. Porky got horny, and he lost control. A lot of men talk like that. They blame it on the woman. They say, "She had it comin'. She was wearing a short skirt."

Doesn't seem fair to me; doesn't seem right. But I believe you can joke about it. I believe you can joke about anything. It just depends on how you construct the joke, what the exaggeration is. Every joke needs one exaggeration. Every joke needs one thing to be way out of proportion.

I'll give you an example. Have you ever seen a news story like this? Some burglar breaks into a house, steals some things, and while he's in there, he rapes an eighty-one-year-old woman. And you think to yourself, "Why? What the fuck kind of social life does this guy have?" I want to ask him, "Why did you do that?" But I know what I'd hear: "Hey, she was comin' on to me. She had on a tight bathrobe." And I'm thinkin', "Next time, be a little more selective, will you?"

Now, speaking of rape, but changing the subject slightly, you know what I wonder? Is there more rape at the Equator or the North Pole? I mean, per capita; I know the populations are different. I think it's the North Pole.

Most people think it's the Equator. Because it's hot down there, people don't wear a lot of clothing, guys can see women's tits, they get horny, and there's a lot of rape and a lot of fucking in general. But that's exactly why there's *less* rape at the Equator; because there's a lot of fucking, in general. You can tell the Equator has a lot of fucking; look at the population figures. Billions of people live near the Equator. How many Eskimos we got? Thirty? Thirty-five?

No one's gettin' laid at the North Pole; it's too cold. An Eskimo says to his wife, "Hey, honey, how about some pussy?" She says, "Wally, are you crazy? The windchill is 150 below!" Eskimo guys are deprived, they're horny, they get pent up, and every now and then they gotta rape somebody.

Now, the biggest problem an Eskimo rapist has is trying to get wet leather leggings off a woman who doesn't want to take them off. Have you ever tried to pull leather pants off someone who's trying to kick you in the nuts? It takes a lot of effort. And, in the process, you would lose your hard-on. In fact, at the North Pole your dick would shrivel up like a stack of dimes.

That's another thing I wonder. Does a rapist have a hard-on when he leaves the house in the morning? Or does it develop during the day while he's walking around checkin' out the gals? Just wondering.

THE EVENING NEWS

* Police in Maine announced today they have broken up a ring of amphetamine users. Six of the speed freaks were arrested on the spot. Another four got away by sprinting completely across Canada.

* It has been disclosed that several years ago when Mother Teresa won the Nobel Peace Prize, she returned the money, claiming it had germs on it.

* A man who was attempting to walk around the world drowned today on the first leg of his journey, which would have taken him from San Francisco to Honolulu.

* The owner of a Florida massage parlor has been arrested by police. "There weren't any serious violations," said the officers, "she just rubbed us the wrong way."

* Doctors treating a ninty-year-old pregnant woman claim that because of her advanced age she will have a grown-up.

* A Boston man who last year shot and killed all twelve members of a jury that convicted him of murder goes on trial again today. Courtroom insiders say jury selection is expected to take quite some time.

* Silent film star Mark Dunbar died today in Hollywood. He had no last words; however, he did wiggle his eyebrows and make several exaggerated gestures with his arms.

* A Cincinnati man has revealed that last month a local hospital, instead of giving him a vasectomy, castrated him. A hospital spokesman explained, "It all started as a joke. The doctors pre-

tended they were going to castrate him, but he got real snotty so they went ahead and did it to teach him a lesson." The patient, though upset, seemed philosophical. "The way I look at it, it's that much less to wash."

* A New Hampshire inventor has developed a machine he claims will grant him any wish. Reporters were greeted at his home by hundreds of naked women who said they had been blowing him for the past six months.

* A sixty-five-year-old fitness expert trotting backward from Winnipeg to Chile in an effort to promote backward trotting was killed today when she was hit by a truck head-on from the rear.

* And finally, on the lighter side, here's a human-interest story about man's best friend. It seems sixty-five-year-old James Driscoll was asleep in his downtown hotel room last week when he was awakened by the sound of a dog barking. When he awoke the room was filled with smoke, and he could not see to get out. The dog led him out of the room, down the hall, and into an elevator shaft, where he plunged eight stories to his death. It seems it wasn't his dog.

DANCE CALLED BECAUSE OF RAIN

When I think of the rain dance the American Indians used to do, I often wonder if they had to practice first. Wouldn't you want to have rain-dance practice just to go over things again? To make sure everyone was doing the correct steps in the correct order? Maybe there were some new guys; maybe the dance master had some new things he wanted to try out. There are all sorts of reasons why the Indians might want to play it safe and practice first.

My question is, if they did hold practice, and the rain didn't come immediately, how would they know they had done it right? If the dance is done correctly, shouldn't it rain? Or did the Indians figure the rain god knew it was only practice and was waiting for the real thing?

Then again, if it did rain right after practice, why not just cancel the dance and figure the next time you need rain all you have to do is practice?

These are the kinds of thoughts that made it necessary to separate me from the other kids in school.

THINGS THAT ARE PISSING ME OFF

Cigars

Haven't we had about enough of this cigar smoking shit? When are these fat, arrogant, overfed, white-collar business criminals going to extinguish their cigars and move along to their next abomination?

Soft, white, business pussies suckin' on a big brown dick. That's all it is, folks, a big, brown dick. You know, Freud used to say, "Sometimes a cigar is just a cigar." Yeah? Well, sometimes it's a big brown dick! With a fat, criminal-business asshole sucking on the wet end of it!

But, hey. The news is not all bad for me. Not all bad. Want to hear the good part? Cancer of the mouth. Good! Fuck 'em! Makes me happy; it's an attractive disease. So light up, suspender-man, and suck that smoke deep down into your empty suit. And blow it out your ass, you miserable cocksucker!

Angels

What is all this nonsense about angels? Do you realize three out of four Americans now believe in angels? What are they, fuckin' stupid? Has everybody lost their goddamn minds?

Angels, my ass! You know what I think it is? I think it's a massive, collective, chemical flashback from all the drugs—all the drugs!—smoked, swallowed, snorted, and shot up by all Americans from 1960 to 2000. Forty years of adulterated street drugs will get you some fuckin' angels, my friend!

Angels, shit. What about goblins? Doesn't anybody believe in goblins? And zombies. Where the fuck are all the zombies? That's the trouble with zombies, they're unreliable. I say if you're gonna buy that angel bullshit, you may as well go for the goblin-zombie package as well.

Bike Frauds

Here's another horrifying example of a declining American culture. The continued pussification of the male population, this time in the form of Harley Davidson theme restaurants. What is going on here?

Harley Davidson used to mean something; it stood for biker attitude; grimy outlaws and their sweaty mamas full of beer and crank, rollin' around on Harleys, lookin' for a good time. Destroying property, raping teenagers, and killing policemen. All very necessary activities.

But now . . . theme restaurants! And this soft shit obviously didn't come from hard-core bikers, it came from weekend motorcyclists. These fraudulent, two-day-a-week lames who have their bikes trucked into Sturgis, South Dakota, for the big rally and then ride around town like they just came off the road. Lawyers and dentists and pussy-boy software designers gettin' up on Harleys because they think it makes 'em cool. Well hey, Skeezix, you ain't cool, you're fuckin' chilly. And chilly ain't never been cool.

The House of Blues

I have a proposition: I think if white people are going to burn down black churches, then black people ought to burn down the House of Blues. What a disgrace that place is. The House of Blues. You know what they ought to call it? The House of Lame White Motherfuckers! Inauthentic, low-frequency, lame white motherfuckers.

Especially these male movie stars who think they're blues artists. You ever see these guys? Don't you just want to puke in your soup when one of these fat, overweight, out-of-shape, middle-aged, pasty-faced, baldy-headed movie stars with sunglasses jumps onstage and starts blowin' into a harmonica? It's a fuckin' sacrilege.

In the first place, white people got no business playing the blues ever. At all! Under any circumstances! What the fuck do white people have to be blue about? Banana Republic ran out of khakis? The espresso machine is jammed? Hootie and the Blowfish are breaking up?

Shit, white people ought to understand . . . their job is to *give* people the blues, not to get them. And certainly not to sing or play them! I'll tell you a little secret about the blues: it's not enough to know which notes to play, you have to know why they need to be played.

And another thing, I don't think white people should be trying to dance like blacks. Stop that! Stick to your faggoty polkas and waltzes, and that repulsive country line-dancing shit that you do, and be yourself. Be proud! Be white! Be lame! And get the fuck off the dance floor!

A Day in the Life of Henry VIII

Wake up

Fuck the queen

Take a shit

Kill the queen

Eat six chickens

Get married

Kill the new queen

Eat a cow

Take a shit

Start dating

Belch for an hour

Eat a sheep

Kill my date

Defy the pope

Eat a goat

Take a shit

Fuck a bishop

Get engaged

Kill my fiancée

Eat a pig

Marry a pig

Kill the pig

Eat the pope

Vomit

Go to sleep

FAMILIES WORTH LOATHING

Are you sick of this "royal family" shit? Who gives a fuck about these people? Who cares about the English in general? The uncivilized, murderous, backward English. Inbred savages hiding behind Shakespeare, pretending to be cultured. Don't be misled by the manners; if you want to know what lurks beneath the surface, take a look at the soccer crowds. That's the true British character. I'm Irish and I'm American, and we've had to kick these degenerate English motherfuckers out of both of our countries.

But most Americans are stupid; they like anything they're told they like. So when the duke and duchess of Wales or Windsor, or whatever, visit America, and people are asked if they like them, the simpletons say, "Yes, I like them a lot. They're sort of fun." If they asked me I would say, "Well, I'm Irish, and they've killed a lot of my people, so I wish they'd die in a fire. Maybe someone will blow up their limousine."

The English have systematically exploited and degraded this planet and its people for a thousand years. You know what I say? Let's honor the royal ladies: Queen Elizabeth, the Queen Mum, Margaret, Fergie, and all the rest. Let's give them the hot-lead douche. Get out the funnel, turn them upside-down, and give them the hot-lead douche. Right in their royal boxes. That's my message from the IRA to the English.

And I'm really glad the black, tan, and brown people of the world, fucked over by the English for so long, are coming home to Mother England to claim their property. England is now being invaded by the very people she plundered. They're flying, sailing, swimming, and rowing home to the seat of Empire, looking to the Crown: "Hey, mon! What about de food stamps?"

WHERE WAS I STANDING LAST TIME WE DID THIS?

When Britain returned Hong Kong to China there was a long, formal ceremony. The whole thing looked well-rehearsed, and I wondered how everyone knew exactly where to stand and what to do. After all, the event had never taken place before; how could there be a set of procedures? Do the British have a manual on returning colonies? If so, they won't be needing it much longer.

I notice the same thing is true when a pope or king dies.

The elaborate funerals involve at least thirty or forty groups of participants, each with different roles and different garb, and each of whom seems to know exactly where to walk, when to stop, and where to stand. And everyone knows all the songs and prayers by heart.

Can someone tell me when these people practice all this pageantry?

LIFE'S LITTLE MOMENTS

* Do you ever look at your watch and immediately forget the time, so you look again? And still it doesn't register, so you have to look a third time. And then someone asks you what time it is, and you actually have to look at your watch for the fourth time in three minutes? Don't you feel stupid?

* Do you ever find yourself standing in a room, and you can't remember why you went in there? And you think to yourself, "Maybe

if I go back where I was I'll see something that reminds me. Or maybe it would be quicker if I just stand here and hope it comes back to me." Usually as you're weighing those options, two words float across your mind: "Alzheimer's disease."

✳ Do you ever have to sneeze while you're taking a piss? It's frightening. Deep down you're afraid you'll release all sorts of bodily fluids into your pants. What people don't realize is that it's physically impossible to sneeze while pissing; your brain won't allow it. Because your brain knows you might blow your asshole out. And wind up having to repaint the entire apartment.

✳ Have you ever noticed how sometimes all day Wednesday you keep thinking it's Thursday? Then the next day when you're back to normal, you wonder, why don't you think it's Friday?

✳ Have you ever been sitting on a railroad train in the station, and another train is parked right next to you? And one of them begins moving, but you can't tell which one? And then it becomes obvious, and all the magic is gone? Wouldn't it be nice if we could spend our whole lives not knowing which train was moving? Actually, we do.

✳ Do you ever fall asleep in the late afternoon and wake up after dark, and for a moment you can't figure out what day it is? You actually find yourself thinking, Could this be yesterday?

✳ Did you ever tell someone they have a little bit of dirt on their face? They never rub the right spot, do they? They always assume the mirror image and rub the wrong side. Don't you just want to slap the bastard?

* Have you noticed that when your head is on the pillow, if you close one eye the pillow is in one position? But when you switch eyes the pillow seems to move? Sometimes I lie awake for hours doing that.

* Do you ever reach the top of a staircase and think there's one more step? So you take one of those big, awkward steps that doesn't accomplish anything? And then you have to do it a few more times, so people will think it's something you do all the time. "I do this all the time, folks. It's the third stage of syphilis."

The 10 Most Embarrassing Songs of All Time

1. *I Gotta Be Me*

2. *My Way*

3. *I Write the Songs*

4. *That's Life*

5. *Let Me Entertain You*

6. *Hey, Look Me Over*

7. *You're Gonna Hear From Me*

8. *Impossible Dream*

9. *I Will Survive*

10. *If They Could See Me Now*

SHORT TAKES

People often say, "That's a fine how-do-you-do," when deep in their hearts they know it's really only a fairly good how-do-you-do.

I've noticed there's such a thing as disposable douche. And I wonder Why would someone want to keep that stuff in the first place?

When I was young I used to read about the decline of Western civilization, and I decided it was something I would like to make a contribution to.

Have you noticed when you look in the top drawer of someone's desk there are always a few pennies in the pencil tray? I take them.

In a package of bacon, underneath all the neat horizontal strips there's always one oddly-folded piece that seems to have been thrown in at the last moment.

You rarely see one oat all by itself.

The best thing about living at the seashore is that you only have assholes on three sides of you. And if they come at you from the water, you can usually hear them splash.

Although it's untrue that rubbing a toad causes warts, it does give the toad a hard-on.

We will never be an advanced civilization as long as rain showers can delay the launching of a space rocket.

THE POPE WEARS LOAFERS

I never worry that all hell will break loose. My concern is that only part of hell will break loose and be much harder to detect.

What is all this dinner-and-a-movie shit? Why can't people just go somewhere and fuck for three or four hours?

In restaurants where they serve frog's legs, what do they do with the rest of the frog? Do they just throw it away? You never see "frog torsos" on the menu. Is there actually a garbage can full of frog bodies in the alley? I wouldn't want to be a homeless guy looking for an unfinished cheeseburger and open the lid on that.

I hope no one asks me to show them the ropes; I have no idea where they are. Maybe I could pull some strings and find out.

If you practice throwing the discus alone, you have to go get it yourself.

It's fun to go into the hospital room of a terminal patient and whisper to him, "Hang on. We're working on a miracle drug. It'll be ready in about five years."

I really don't care if we have a nuclear war as long as I can get some French fries.

I'm one of those people who hope Elvis Presley is really dead. Buddy Holly too. "The day the music died," shit. As far as I'm concerned, it was the day the music got better. All those guys did was steal and water down black music to make it safe and easy to digest for fearful white kids. Here's a toast to all the great black artists who got ripped off by no-talent white thieves.

One thing nice about being dead is that you immediately become eligible to appear on stamps and money.

Cat's thought: "I sure could do with a nice rat."

Oxen can be trained to genuflect and whistle softly in the moonlight.

Have you ever noticed the escalator handrail and the thing you're standing on don't move at the same speed?

You know what you rarely see? A ninety-three-year-old guy workin' on his résumé.

I don't mind government regulation, but requiring people to wear helmets during intercourse is a bit much.

Whom does a male ladybug dance with?

Did you ever notice that apparently the Lone Ranger and Tonto never got their laundry done?

I pray each night that someday on a single afternoon, several major news stories will break within a few hours of each other. I would love to see two 747s colliding above Times Square, the president and vice president getting assassinated, Iran and Israel having a nuclear exchange, the Dow Jones dropping 8,500 points, and California having an earthquake measuring 13.7. It would be fun watching the news channels try to cope with it all. And you know what would really be fun? Reading the newspapers for the following few weeks.

I know a transsexual guy whose only ambition is to eat, drink, and be Mary.

Not Much to Do Dept.: Someone has actually gone to the trouble of determining that Columbus, Ohio, has the best-dressed police force.

Here's how you get rid of counterfeit money: Put it in the collection plate at church.

I don't understand the problem some people have with paroling Charles Manson. I say set him free and let him get on with his work. I have a long list of celebrities I'd be glad to share with him.

When people say "clean as a whistle," they forget that a whistle is full of spit.

ORGAN DONOR PROGRAMS

I'm not too enthusiastic about this organ donor idea. What bothers me most is that it's run by the Motor Vehicles Bureau. I figure if I have to wait in line that long for a kidney, fuck it. I'll do without.

They send you a little card you're supposed to carry in your wallet next to your driver's license. You're supposed to list the organs you're willing to donate in case you die. Are these people crazy? Do you honestly believe that if a paramedic finds that card on you after an accident he's gonna be trying to save your life? No way! He's lookin' for parts.

"Look, Sid! Here's that lower intestine we've been hoping for. Never mind the CPR, this man's a donor!"

Fuck that. If these people want something of mine, they can have my appendix. That's it. That's all I'm giving. Put it in the cooler and get the fuck outta here.

Plugging Along

And don't go pulling any plugs on me, either. That's another bunch of macho bullshit floating around. People talkin' about, "Aw, just pull the plug on me. If I'm comatose? Lyin' there like a vegetable? Just go ahead and pull the plug."

And I say, FUCK YOU! LEAVE MY PLUG ALONE!! Get an extension cord for my plug! I want everything you got: tubes, cords, plugs, probes, electrodes, IVs. You find I got an orifice that's not bein' used, stick a fuckin' tube in it. Vegetable, shit! I don't care if I look like an artichoke. Save my ass!

If you ever find out I'm comatose just remember there are three things I gotta have: ice cream, morphine, and TV. Give me that ice cream about every two hours; give me that morphine about, oh, every ten minutes; and turn on the fuckin' TV!! I wanna watch *Survivor!*

And don't be comin' to visit me, either. I got no time for live people. I'm brain-dead, here. Ain't you people got no respect for the brain-dead? Hey, you gotta be brain-dead to watch *Survivor!* in the first place; you might as well watch it when you're clinically brain-dead.

Now, one more thought concerning this comatose stuff. This might come in handy someday. If you know a homosexual who is comatose, remember, you can always comfort his family by saying, "Look at it this way, folks. He was a fruit, now he's a vegetable. At least he's still in the produce section."

ON THE BEACH: THE MOVIE

It is said that just before you die your life flashes before your eyes; especially if it's a sudden death. It's like a little personal movie of your own. But it doesn't make sense to me. Mathematically, how would it work?

Let's say you're swimming at the beach, you get caught in a riptide, and it pulls you out to sea. You panic and begin swallowing water. Since you're about to die, the flashback movie begins to roll.

It seems to me that if it's really a flashback of your entire life, you'd have to watch the whole thing, and that would include the ending. Which means seeing yourself arrive at the beach, walk into the surf, start to drown, and have the movie start all over again. Therefore you'd have to watch it a second time, which would include arriving at the beach, walking into the surf, and . . . you get what I mean? Thanks to the flashback, you can never die. The movie runs forever.

"I COULDN'T COMMIT SUICIDE IF MY LIFE DEPENDED ON IT"

So Little Time

Whenever I hear that someone has committed suicide I wonder one thing. Not Why did he do it? or What was he thinking? I wonder, How did he find the time? Who has time to be running around committing suicide these days? Aren't you busy? Don't you have things to do? I do. Suicide would be way down on my list. It would come much later, for example, than setting my neighbor's house on fire. Believe me, I would have to work suicide into an already very crowded schedule. I'd probably try a little self-mutilation at first, just to get started. See if I like the general concept.

When you think about it, the planning alone would create all sorts of tasks. First, you'd have to choose a method. That's big. And that might take a while; there are so many good ways to go.

"Let's see. How about firing a gun in my mouth? Naaah! Jesus, that would hurt. And suppose I lived? My head would have a big hole in the top. Fuck that. Maybe I should just hang myself. No, too weird. I don't want people to think I'm weird. Just sad. Really, really sad. I guess I could put my head in the oven and turn on the gas. Shit, it's an electric oven. What am I gonna do? I'm afraid of heights, I have trouble swallowing pills, and I can't stand the sight of blood. God, this is depressing. I know! I'll throw myself in front of a subway train. No, I live in Cheyenne. Damn! Maybe I'll just eat some infected dog shit."

Dear Survivor

You also have to decide whether or not to leave a note. You might just think, Fuck 'em. Let 'em figure it out for themselves. And I really think not leaving a note is a nice touch, especially if you're a perky, optimistic, happily married person and recently got a big promotion. Let 'em figure it out for themselves.

But, remember, if you do leave a note you'll have to come up with a version you're satisfied with. You have to get it right.

"Let's see, 'To whom it may concern.' No, too impersonal. 'Dear Myra.' No, that leaves out the kids. I've got it! 'Hi, everybody. Guess what?' "

Or you may want to go for maximum survivor-guilt: "To all of you who drove me to this, you know who you are. I hope you're satisfied, now that I've destroyed myself."

How about simply saying, "Hi. Hope this note finds you healthy and happy. Not me. Healthy, not happy. In fact, wait'll you read the rest of this note."

Suppose you're a writer? Seems to me, a writer would get so involved revising and polishing the note that he'd never get around to the suicide. He would cheer up just by writing a really good note. Then he'd turn it into a book proposal.

Another problem for suicide people is the timing. "Okay, Tuesday's out, gotta take Timmie to the circus; Wednesday's my colon cleansing; the play-offs start on Friday; my folks'll be here for the weekend. Hmmm! The weekend . . ."

I feel sorry for these suicide people. There are so many things to think about. Don't get me wrong, I'm still glad they do it; I find it highly entertaining. It certainly qualifies as drama: an irreversible act that puts a permanent end to your consciousness. Talk about a big decision; you'd better be thinking clearly. You gotta be at your best for suicide.

Must-Die TV

I just love the whole idea. I could really appreciate an all-suicide channel. Boy, you talk about reality programming: One person after another, destroying themselves permanently in front of the entire nation. And never mind that V-chip shit, let the kids watch. Teach 'em they have options in life. I would show every method imaginable. And when there's a lull in the action, I'd run films of World War II kamikaze raids and Arab suicide bombers.

I think you could get big ratings with suicide. Especially if you had unusual methods. I'll bet anything you could get 200 people in this country to hold hands and jump into the Grand Canyon. Sick people, old people, the chronically depressed. And to get young folks involved, instead of calling it suicide, you bill it as "extreme living." Put it on TV and give some of the profits to the surviving relatives.

CEO Is D.O.A.

But I digress. You know what I really like about suicide? The reasons some people give. Like those Japanese businessmen who bankrupt their companies through bad management and decide to end it all. Imagine a guy in a three-piece gray suit and red tie, opening his briefcase, taking out a fourteen-inch fish knife, and slashing his stomach open eighteen inches from side to side. Wow! If that tie wasn't red before it sure is now. By the way, this would be a really good idea for those Firestone and Ford executives.

No Coin Return

I love suicide. You know what they ought to have in amusement arcades? Coin-operated suicide machines. Simple idea. You sit down at a steel table and deposit 50 cents. There's a thirty-second delay as you lean forward, place your head on the table, and put your arms behind your back. Before long, you hear, "Five, four, three, two, one." Then a large cast-iron hammer comes slamming down with 2,000 pounds of force and smashes your head to bits. And it keeps on smashing for about twenty minutes, to give you your money's worth. Lets you rest in pieces.

EUPHEMISTIC BULLSHIT

I don't like euphemistic language, words that shade the truth. American English is packed with euphemism, because Americans have trouble dealing with reality, and in order to shield themselves from it they use soft language. And somehow it gets worse with every generation.

Here's an example. There's a condition in combat that occurs when a soldier is completely stressed out and is on the verge of nervous collapse. In World War I it was called "shell shock." Simple, honest, direct language. Two syllables. Shell shock. It almost sounds like the guns themselves. That was more than eighty years ago.

Then a generation passed, and in World War II the same combat condition was called "battle fatigue." Four syllables now; takes a little longer to say. Doesn't seem to hurt as much. "Fatigue" is a nicer word than "shock." Shell shock! Battle fatigue.

By the early 1950s, the Korean War had come along, and the very same condition was being called "operational exhaustion." The phrase was up to eight syllables now, and any last traces of humanity had been completely squeezed out of it. It was absolutely sterile: operational exhaustion. Like something that might happen to your car.

Then, barely fifteen years later, we got into Vietnam, and, thanks to the deceptions surrounding that war, it's no surprise that the very same condition was referred to as "post-traumatic stress disorder." Still eight syllables, but we've added a hyphen, and the pain is completely buried under jargon: post-traumatic stress disorder. I'll bet if they had still been calling it "shell shock," some of those Vietnam veterans might have received the attention they needed.

But it didn't happen, and one of the reasons is that soft language; the language that takes the life out of life. And somehow it keeps getting worse.

Here are some more examples. At some point in my life, the following changes occurred:

toilet paper = bathroom tissue

sneakers = running shoes

false teeth = dental appliances

medicine = medication

information = directory assistance

the dump = the landfill

motels = motor lodges

house trailers = mobile homes

used cars = previously owned vehicles

room service = guest room dining

riot = civil disorder

strike = job action

zoo = wildlife park

jungle = rain forest

swamp = wetlands

glasses = presciption eyewear

garage = parking structure

drug addiction = substance abuse

soap opera = daytime drama

gambling joint = gaming resort

prostitute = sex worker

theater = performing arts center

wife beating = domestic violence

constipation = occasional irregularity

Health

When I was a little boy, if I got sick I went to a doctor, who sent me to a hospital to be treated by other doctors. Now I go to a "family practitioner," who belongs to a "health maintenance organization," which sends me to a "wellness center" to be treated by "health-care delivery professionals."

Poverty

Poor people used to live in slums. Now "the economically disadvantaged" occupy "substandard housing" in the "inner cities." And a lot of them are broke. They don't have "negative cash flow." They're broke! Because many of them were fired. In other words, management wanted to "curtail redundancies in the human resources area," and so, many workers are no longer "viable members of the workforce." Smug, greedy, well-fed white people have invented a language to conceal their sins. It's as simple as that.

Government

The CIA doesn't kill anybody, they "neutralize" people. Or they "depopulate" an area. The government doesn't lie, it engages in "disinformation." The Pentagon actually measures nuclear radiation in something called "sunshine units." Israeli murderers are called "commandos," Arab commandos are called "terrorists." The contra killers were known as "freedom fighters." Well, if crime fighters fight crime and firefighters fight fire, what do freedom fighters fight?

Physical Disorders

And some of this softened language is just silly and embarrassing. On the airlines they say they're going to preboard "passengers in need of special assistance." Cripples. Simple, honest, direct language. There's no shame attached to the word "cripple." No shame. It's a word used in Bible translations: "Jesus healed the cripples." It doesn't take six words to describe that condition.

But we don't have cripples anymore; instead we have the "physically challenged." Is that a grotesque enough evasion for you? How about "differently abled?" I've actually heard cripples referred to as differently abled. You can't even call them handicapped anymore. They say, "We're not handicapped, we're handi-capable." These poor suckers have been bullshitted by the system into believing that if you change the name of the condition, somehow you'll change the condition. Well, it doesn't happen that way.

I'm sure you've noticed we have no deaf people in this country. "Hearing impaired." And no one's blind. "Partially sighted" or "visually impaired." And thank God we no longer have stupid children. Today's kids all have "learning disabilities." Or they're "minimally exceptional." How would you like to be told that about your child? Actually, it sounds faintly positive.

"He's minimally exceptional."

"Oh, thank God for that, I guess."

Best of all, psychologists now call ugly people "those with severe appearance deficits." Things are so bad that any day I expect to hear a rape victim referred to as an unwilling sperm recipient.

Gettin' Old

Of course, it's been obvious for some time that there are no old people in this country. They all died, and what we have are "senior citizens." How's that for a lifeless, typically American, twentieth-century phrase? There's no pulse in a "senior citizen."

But that's a term I've come to accept. That's what old people are going be called. But the phrase I will continue to resist is when they describe an old person as being "ninety years young." Imagine how sad the fear of aging that is revealed in that phrase. To be unable even to use the word "old"; to have to use its antonym.

And I understand the fear of aging is natural; it's universal, isn't it? No one wants to get old, no one wants to die. But we do. We die. And we don't like that, so we bullshit ourselves.

I started bullshitting myself when I reached my forties. I'd look in the mirror, and say, "Well, I guess I'm getting ... 'older!' " Older sounds better than old, doesn't it? Sounds like it might even last a little longer. Bullshit. I'm getting old. And it's okay. But the Baby Boomers can't handle that, and remember, the boomers invented most of this soft language. So now they've come up with a new life phase: "pre-elderly." How sad. How relentlessly sad.

Gettin' Dead

But it's all right, folks, because thanks to our fear of death, no one has to die; they can all just pass away. Or expire, like a magazine subscription. If it happens in the hospital, it will be called a terminal episode. The insurance company will refer to it as negative patient-care outcome. And if it's the result of malpractice, they'll say it was a therapeutic misadventure.

To be honest, some of this language makes me want to vomit. Well, perhaps "vomit" is too strong a word. It makes me want to engage in an involuntary, personal protein spill.

BEER AND POT

When I was young, most kids in my neighborhood drank beer before they discovered pot. Everybody drank first. Saturday night we drank beer and puked on our shoes. It was an Irish neighborhood. Drink and puke, that was it. A great American tradition. It still goes on today.

Then in 1950, when I was thirteen, we heard about pot. We discovered that on pot you didn't stagger, you didn't puke on your shoes, and your breath didn't smell. Which was important. Because, as a kid, when you came home from drinking there were two breath smells that could give you away: alcohol and puke.

So, we found that when you smoked pot, you could withstand your mother's closest scrutiny. Because, let's face it, you had come home drunk so often wearing someone else's clothing that your mother was now openly asking to smell your breath.

"Come here, mister! Let me smell the breath. Ahhh! No booze or puke. That's a good boy. What's that under your arm?"

"Two boxes of Oreos."
"That's a good boy."
"Good night, Ma."
Cool.

HIGH ON THE PLANE

Airlines disappoint me. Why don't they have a flight attendant whose job it is to hand out drugs? They're certainly aggressive enough when it comes to alcohol. Even before the meal begins they're in the aisles: "Champagne, red wine, white wine?" Can't they spare one person to wander around muttering, "Coke? Smoke? Chance to get high. Crank? Acid? Smack? You're high in the plane, now get high *on* the plane!"

For me, on a long flight it used to be that gettin' high was half the fun. Hell, even a short flight. Lockin' myself in the bathroom, firin' up a joint. That's what flyin' was all about. Now you can't smoke anything at all, not even a good old-fashioned ready-roll. They have smoke detectors. Jesus! The people in this country have really become a pack of fearful, ignorant sheep. Everybody's a God-fearing, law-abiding asshole now. Fair warning, my friend: if you're gonna smoke a joint on the airplane these days, you better be an old pro.

In the old days I always did my pot-smoking in the forward lavatory, because I fantasized that the mirror was two-way, and the crew could see me. I can't help it, I just like an audience. But I knew my manners; I always offered the crew a hit or two. I'd make little gestures with the joint toward the mirror. "C'mon, boys, lighten up. Life isn't all azimuth indicators." Never any takers; real straight folks up there.

Now, I'm sure all of you high-minded, non-chance-takers out there are thinkin', "What about the smell? Doesn't the bathroom fill up with pot smoke?" Well, folks, this is where a background in physics comes in handy. Follow me closely on this.

Before the airlines introduced those fancy new toilets, the ones that tear your genitals off when they flush, the old toilets, in order to control odors, had a slow, steady stream of air that flowed from the lavatory itself down into the bowl. And you could increase the speed of that airflow by simply sitting on the toilet, thereby reducing the size of the air passage down to that little wedge-shaped space between your thighs. Narrower channel, stronger flow. And your cheeks acted as a gasket, sealing off the rest of the opening.

Then, if you carefully pointed a lit cigarette down into the toilet between your thighs, all the smoke got sucked away into that mysterious, blue-chemical void. No smoke, no smell, no problem. By the way, I cannot overemphasize the importance of the word *carefully* in the above sentence.

Of course, not all planes had equally strong airflow, so a system test was always in order. A good physicist never proceeds without checking conditions. In this case, we use a common match. A lit match, quickly extinguished, produces a small, visible wisp of smoke. If the match is held deep in the bowl, one can observe whether that smoke is sucked straight downward or rises gently back into the lav. In the former case all systems are "go," in the latter case the No Smoking sign is wisely observed. Unless, of course, we decide to go to Plan B. One must always have a backup.

And so, we turn our attention to the sink. The sink is a magnificent device: it fills with water, holds it awhile, and then, when the drain is released, it empties. And on an airplane, when it empties it is helped along by what? Why, it's helped along by our old friend, Mr. Air Pressure! And, whaddaya know, just by pressing down on the drain-release plunger we can produce an even stronger flow of air than we can with the toilet, because the sink drain is so much smaller. A quick test with a lit match confirms this.

But remember, the drain-release lever is spring-loaded, and therefore if the airflow is to remain constant, the plunger must remain depressed and open during the entire period the joint is lit. And that means we have to prop the drain cap open by wedging some object underneath it. A matchbook cover, or perhaps one of those little bars of soap the airlines used to leave near the sink. Isn't science fun?

All right, gang, we're almost ready to light up and get wasted, but there is still one further consideration. If you're going to smoke a joint while seated on the toilet (as opposed to standing up, leaning down into the sink), at some point, you have to decide whether or not you should pretend to be taking a shit. In other words, whether or not to pull your pants down.

If you really have to take a shit at the time, that's great; you're all set. But if you don't, you have a decision to make. Because, although ethically there is nothing wrong with taking a fake shit, in a practical sense if the crew thinks you've been in there too long, and they decide to break down the door, you want to be sure that when they arrive you appear to be taking a genuine shit. Don't forget, they're going to check. And nobody wants to be arrested for shitting with his pants on, am I right? Although personally I can tell you I don't care what the charge is as long as I get rid of the joint. Besides, shitting with your pants on is only a misdemeanor. And in my case it would be a first offense.

Which brings us back to my own personal airline-bathroom experience. One problem I always had was that after I got high I would wind up staying in the bathroom way too long. Pot brought out the superorganizer in me, so once I'd had a few good, deep hits and was securely locked in, I tended to go to work.

First thing I did was open up all those little compartments under the sink and rearrange the supplies stored in there. I'd restack all
the sanitary napkins according to strength: regular, super, jumbo,
teeny-bopper. I'd remove the outer wrappers from the spare toilet paper, making it readily available in the event some nasty bacterium
found its way into the first-class entrees. Then I'd refill the paper
towel dispenser, being careful to pack it so tightly that the towels
would not come out without shredding. And—again, the old days—
I'd make sure there were plenty of those little bars of soap lying out
for people to steal. In the occasional instance when cologne, after-
shave, and other amenities were made available, I would be sure to
take them home for further quality-control testing. Ford is not the
only place where quality is job one.

Then, my chores done, I would relax somewhat and reflect on the
environment around me. I'd become fascinated by the little slot they
had for used razor blades, and I wondered whether or not the blades
actually dropped out of the airplane and fell on people's houses, or if
they just rusted and rotted somewhere behind the wall. I'd read the
various signs posted in three languages and try to translate precisely the
corresponding words in each language. Then, finally, a long, lingering
look in the mirror, usually resulting in the discovery of some hideous
facial flaw, previously undetected.

And then, suddenly, the little lighted sign would flash on telling
me to Return to Cabin! Return to Cabin! Return to Cabin!

I'd think, Oh shit, trouble in the cabin. They need me. I should
never have left them alone. I'd better see what's up. And then on my
way out, I'd spot one last sign: Please Leave Lavatory Clean for the
Next Passenger. Well, that's all I needed to see. And because I'm really
into detail now—and even though I didn't make a mess—I'm experi-
encing "felon's guilt." And I decide to clean up for the next person.

I rinse and dry and thoroughly polish the entire sink area, scouring all the burst-pimple residue off the mirror, and I even wash off the dried, gray dirt bubbles left on the soap by the previous person. Now I'm gettin' into it! Pretty soon I find myself washing the walls and ceiling, throwing open the door, and yelling, "You people got some Spic and Span and a hard-bristle brush out there? I think I can get these blue stains off the toilet!"

And suddenly I realize my fantasy world has collapsed; the real world is watching. Adjusting quickly, and relying on my identity as a comedian, I chuckle weakly and say, "You gotta clean up for the next person."

Then, as the fat woman waiting to take a shit passes me on her way into the john, I hiss, "Don't fuck it up, lady. I worked my ass off in there." And back to my seat I go, secure in the knowledge that, once again, thanks to my highly developed work ethic, along with some great Humboldt weed, I've managed to make the skies a little friendlier.

SHORT TAKES

You know one of the biggest rip-offs in the world? Flowers. They grow free all over the world, and yet we pay for them. And then they die. That seems strange. Flowers are one of the few things we buy, bring home, watch die, and we don't ask for our money back. Normally, we'd be screaming at a merchant over something like that: "Hey, what kind of shit is this? Gimme my money back! The fuckin' things keeled over right on the piano!"

The caterpillar does all the work, but the butterfly gets all the publicity.

Tits always look better in a pink sweater.

You know what you don't see enough of on television? A good parachute accident. It's kinda fun.

Ask your dry cleaner if he can remove the stains from one pair of pants and put them in another. He should be able to do that for the same amount of money. While you're in there, ask if he can remove semen from a wedding veil. That's the test of a really good dry cleaner.

To me, fast food is when a cheetah eats an antelope.

Two men whose names you see a lot on air-conditioner dials: Norm and Max.

Have you ever been kissing someone, and one of you has a snot that's whistling? It takes your mind off the sex, because it requires a three-step solution. First of all, you have to figure out whose nose it's in. Then you have to determine which nostril. Finally, someone has to dig in there and, if not remove it completely, at least push it to one side so it doesn't whistle anymore. By the way, during all this activity the man usually loses his hard-on.

A crumb is a great thing: If you break a crumb in half you don't get two half-crumbs, you get two crumbs. Doesn't that violate some law of physics?

I think I am, therefore, I am. I think.

Have you ever noticed that when you're torturing a person, after a while you get real tired and you don't know what to do to him next? Then you think of something, and you sort of get your energy back?

Any man with a small moustache wearing a bow tie and a loud vest is an asshole.

A cat will blink when struck with a hammer.

Reception lines would be a lot more interesting if instead of shaking hands, people greeted each other with a kick in the groin.

The reason the mainstream is thought of as a stream is because of its shallowness.

Actual bumper sticker: HORN BROKE—WATCH FOR FINGER.

Fun at the ballpark: Y'ever notice a lot of guys bring a glove to the game to catch a foul ball? Never mind that, bring a bat! When a foul ball comes flying toward you, BAM! Hit it back to the players. Everyone will sense you're a fun fan. They'll be glad they came to the ballpark on straitjacket night.

I read somewhere that for the average person fourteen farts a day are considered normal. Based on these figures, and judging from my own output, I have to assume there are millions of people who never fart at all.

I don't have a fear of heights. I do, however, have a fear of *falling* from heights.

Isn't it a good feeling when you read the tabloids and realize that a lot of famous people are just as fucked up as you are?

The justice system should have a penalty whereby they send you to prison, and for ten years the guards take turns doing that Three Stooges, jabbing-two-fingers-in-your-eyes thing. I think that would straighten a lot of guys out.

.backwards sentences say to used I !shit Oh !again go I
There

I noticed in the newspaper that track and field has an event called the women's pole vault. It makes me wonder: With all the options available to her in this age, how does a young woman get interested in pole-vaulting? It seems like a bizarre choice. By the way, I hope you noticed I completely ignored the obvious opportunity for a cheap phallic joke.

If I ever lose my mind I hope some honest person will find it and take it to Lost and Found.

In some hotels they give you a little sewing kit. You know what I do? I sew the towels together. One time I sewed a button on a lampshade. I like to leave a mark.

What's wrong with America: There are schools in Fairfax County, Virginia, where kids are not allowed to win soccer games. Whenever a team gets two goals ahead they have to give up one player. Pathetic.

The Asian country known as Mongolia used to be called Outer Mongolia. And just below the Outer Mongolian border with China there was an autonomous region called Inner Mongolia. And since each of them had its own inner and outer regions, that means that at one time there existed, fairly close to one another, an "outer Inner Mongolia" and an "inner Outer Mongolia." I like that sort of thing. I like picturing the road signs and all the people taking wrong turns.

When someone with an artificial heart dies, I think they should take out the heart, hook it up to an artificial body, and let it go at that.

I never bite my nails; I consider it a health risk. Instead, I twist my nails off with pliers and burn away any excess tissue with a cigarette lighter.

SPORTS SHOULD BE FIXED: FIRST HALF

Everyone knows by now, sports is big business. But the major sports have grown boring and predictable, and the public has become jaded. So I'm suggesting a few changes that would add excitement to the games and increase their entertainment value.

Take Me Out to the Hospital

Baseball has one major problem: not enough serious injuries. A lot of baseball's so-called injuries are just "a strained this" or "a sore whatchamacallit." In today's culture that's not good enough. Fans are crying out for someone to be hurt really badly.

So, to raise the injury level, what I would do is place thirty to forty land mines in the outfield; the kind of mines that spray thousands of tiny nails when they explode. Not only would this add excitement, it would also provide a refreshing element of surprise: "There's a high, lazy fly ball to right field. O'Neill drifts over, pats his glove . . ." BOOOOOOM! "Holy fuckin' shit! Oh, good Lord! Oh, precious, precious Lord!"

Baseball is also accused of being too slow. Here's something that would not only speed up the game but also provide a welcome opportunity for serious injuries. Like most good ideas, it's uncomplicated: if the pitcher hits the batter with the ball, the batter is out. That's it. A simple idea, but it could make quite a difference.

And maybe if the ball hits the batter in the head it could be a double play. I don't know, I'm not an expert on rules. But it's certainly worth a try. And just think: a good "control pitcher" could have a perfect game just by hitting twenty-seven guys in a row. In fact, if you had two quality pitchers out there, the fans could be out of that ballpark in half an hour, on their way home to watch football on TV. Where they could see some *serious* goddamn injuries.

Gettin' My Kicks

Now, football. For many of you fans, football is already a perfect game. Its particular combination of speed, strategy, and brute force seems just right for the American psyche. But even a well-thought-out game like football can use a little help from a fun-loving guy like me.

I would start by improving the coin toss, by making it a full-contact event. While the coin is in the air, the team captains should be allowed to kick the officials. It would get things going on a positive note. Remember, this is a sport that owes its origin to the practice of English soldiers playfully kicking around the head of a Dane during the lulls in combat.

Now, to the game itself. I think football should limit itself to only one rule: Each down begins in an orderly manner. That's it. After that, the players should be allowed to do whatever they want. If there's a fight, you move it off to one side of the field. Let it run its course; no restrictions. If several 300-pound linemen are crippling a placekicker, fine. Let them continue. We shouldn't be trying to suppress the natural exuberance of athletes. Keep in mind these men are physical freaks, full of drugs and anger, and they're here to entertain us. They enjoy being injured; let them go about their business.

So much for upgrading the violence. Here's my suggestion for adding excitement. Currently, each team is allowed forty-five players on the squad, but most of them stand around watching the game from the sidelines. If I were in charge, this would not be happening. Instead, I would have all ninety men out on the field at all times. Offense, defense, special teams. Everyone. What football really needs is ninety steroid monstrosities geeked on amphetamines racing around the field trying to hurt one another.

Here's another way to spice up the game: leave the injured players on the field. Let them lie there. These men are supposed to be tough, you can't coddle them just because they break something. Let the other guys play around them. If they get stepped on, tough titty. These macho pinheads are always talking about how it's "a big war goin' on out there." Fine. Let the Red Cross come around and pick them up.

And regarding this taunting behavior that so many people find offensive, I don't see the problem. In fact, I don't think taunting goes nearly far enough. In my opinion—and I'm certainly no professional athlete—after a good hard tackle the defensive player should be allowed to pull down his pants and masturbate on the man he tackled. It seems like a simple thing, but it would change the whole tempo of the game. And if he can't ejaculate because 60,000 people are watching, you hit him with a 15-yard penalty for delay of game.

I end my suggestions for improving football by taking a look at one of those game-end rituals: the pouring of Gatorade on the winning coach. To my mind, this is far too fruity for football. It's barely appropriate for a sixth-grade dodgeball team. What ought to happen is the winning team should be allowed to come across the field and spike the losing coach. Just spike him. Four linebackers turn him upside-down and pile-drive him headfirst into the ground. Give him an incentive to work a little harder on the next week's game plan.

CAPITAL PUNISHMENT

Many people in this country want to expand the death penalty to include drug dealers. This is really stupid. Drug dealers aren't afraid to die. They're already killin' each other by the hundreds every day. Drive-bys, turf wars, gang killings. They're not afraid to die. The death penalty means very little unless you use it on people who are afraid to die. Like the bankers who launder the drug money. Forget dealers. If you want to slow down the drug traffic, you have to start executing some of these white, middle-class Republican bankers. And I don't mean soft American executions like lethal injection. I'm talkin' about crucifixion, folks. I say bring back crucifixion! A form of capital punishment the Christians and Jews of America can really appreciate.

And I'd take it a step further: I'd crucify these people upside-down. Like St. Peter. Feet up, head down. And naked! I'd have naked, upside-down crucifixions once a week on TV, at halftime of the Monday Night Football games. The Monday Night Crucifixions! Shit, you'd have people tunin' in who don't even care about football. Wouldn't you like to hear Dennis Miller explain why the nails have to go in at a specific angle?

And I'll guarantee you one thing: you start nailin' one white banker per week to a big wooden cross on national television, and you're gonna see that drug traffic begin to slow down mighty fuckin' quick. Why you won't even be able to buy drugs in schools and prisons anymore.

Personally, I don't care about capital punishment one way or another, because I know it doesn't do anything. It doesn't really do anything, except satisfy the biblical need for revenge. You know, if you read the Bible, you see it's filled with violence, retribution, and revenge.

So capital punishment is really kind of a religious ritual. A purification rite. It's a modern sacrament.

And as long as that's true, I say let's liven it up. Let's add a little show business. I believe if you make capital punishment a little more entertaining, and market it correctly, you can raise enough money to save Social Security.

And remember, the polls show the American people want capital punishment, and they want Social Security. And I think even in a fake democracy people ought to get what they want once in a while. If for no other reason than to feed the illusion that they're really in charge. Let's use capital punishment the same way we use sports and shopping in this country: to take people's minds off how badly they're bein' fucked by the upper 1 percent.

Now, unfortunately the football season only lasts about six months. What we really need is capital punishment year-round. Put it on TV every night with sponsors. Ya gotta have sponsors. I'm sure as long as we're killing people, Dow Chemical and Marlboro cigarettes will be proud to participate. Save Social Security.

And not only do I recommend crucifixions, I'm also in favor of bringing back beheadings. Wouldn't that be great? Beheadings on TV, complete with slow-motion and instant replay. And maybe you could let the heads roll down a little hill and fall into one of five numbered holes. Let the folks at home gamble on which hole the head is gonna fall into. Interactive television snuff-gambling! Give the people what they want.

And you do it in a stadium, so the rabble can gamble on it too. Raise a little more money. And, if you want to extend the violence a little longer—to sell a few extra commercials—instead of using an ax, you do the beheadings with a handsaw. And don't bother getting queasy at this point, folks, the blood's already on your hands; all we're talking about now is a matter of degree. You want something a little more delicate? We could do the beheadings with an olive fork. That would be good. And the nice part is, it would take a real long time.

There are a lot of good things you could do with capital punishment. When's the last time we burned someone at the stake? It's been too long! Here's another form of state killing that comes from a rich religious tradition: burning people at the stake. Put it on TV on Sunday mornings; the Sunday-morning, evangelical, send-us-an-offering, praise Jesus, human bonfire. You don't think that would get big ratings? In this sick fuckin' country? Shit, you'd have people skippin' church to watch this stuff. And then you take the money from the prayer offerings and use it to save Social Security.

And whatever happened to boiling people in oil? Remember that? Let's bring it back. On TV. First you get the oil goin' good with a nice high rolling boil. And then slowly, at the end of a rope, you lower the prisoner, headfirst, into the boiling oil. Boy, you talk about fun shit! And to encourage citizen participation, you let the rabble in the stadium control the speed of the rope. Good, clean, wholesome family entertainment. The kids'll love it. No V-chip to spoil the fun. And all the while they're enjoying themselves, we're teachin' them a nice Christian moral lesson. Boiling people in oil.

And maybe, instead of boiling all these guys, every now and then you could French-fry a couple of 'em. French-fried felons! Or dip a guy in egg batter, just for a goof. Kind of a tempura thing. Jeffrey Dahmer never thought of that, did he? Jeffrey Dahmer, eat your heart out! Which is an interesting thought in and of itself.

All right, enough nostalgia. How about some modern forms of capital punishment? How about throwin' a guy off the roof of the World Trade Center, and whoever he lands on wins the Publishers Clearinghouse?

Or perhaps something more sophisticated. You dip a guy in brown gravy and lock him in a small room with a wolverine who's high on angel dust. That's one guy who's not gonna be fuckin' with the kids at the bus stop.

Here's a good one. Something really nice. You take a high-speed catapult, and you shoot a guy straight into a brick wall. Trouble is, it would be over too quickly. No good for TV. You'd have to do a whole bunch of guys right in a row. Rapid-fire capital punishment. Fifteen catapults! While you're shootin' off one, you're loadin' up the others. Of course, every now and then you'd have to stop everything to clean off the wall. Cleanliness! Right next to godliness.

Finally, high-tech! I sense you're waitin' for some high-tech. Here you go. You take a highly miniaturized tactical nuclear weapon, and you stick it straight up a guy's ass and set it off. A thermonuclear suppository. Preparation H-Bomb. Boy, you talk about fallout! Or, a variation: You put a bomb inside that little hole on the end of a guy's dick. A bomb in a dick! And when it goes off, the guy wouldn't know whether he was comin' or goin'! I got a lotta good ideas. Save Social Security.

FARM SYSTEM: THUGS, PERVS, NUTS, AND DRUNKS

Here's another one of my really good ideas. I'm going to save us a whole lot of money on prisons, but at the same time I'm going to remove from society many of our more annoying citizens. Four groups are goin' away—permanently!

First group: Violent criminals. Here's what you do: You take the entire state of Kansas and you move everybody out. You give the people a couple of hundred dollars apiece for their inconvenience, but you get them out. Next you put a 100-foot-high electric fence around the entire state, and Kansas becomes a permanent prison farm for violent criminals. No police, no parole, no supplies; the only thing you give them is lethal weapons and live ammunition. So they can communicate in a meaningful manner.

Then you put the whole thing on cable TV. The Violence Network. VNN. And for a corporate sponsor, you get one of those companies that loves to smear its logo-feces all over the landscape. Budweiser will jump at this in half a minute.

Second group: Sex criminals. Completely incurable; you have to lock them up. Oh, I suppose you could outlaw religion and these sex crimes would disappear in a generation or two, but we don't have time for rational solutions. It's much easier to fence off another rectangular state. This time, Wyoming.

But this is only for true sex offenders. We're not going to harass consenting adults who dress up in leather Boy Scout uniforms and smash each other in the head with ball-peen hammers as they take turns blowing their cats. There's nothing wrong with that; it's a victimless hobby. And think of how happy the cat must be. No, we're only going to lock up rapists and molesters; those hopeless romantics who are so full of love they can't help gettin' a little of it on you. Usually on your leg.

You take all these heavy-breathing fun-seekers, and you stick them in Wyoming. And you let them suck, fuck, and fondle. You let them blow, chew, sniff, lick, whip, gobble, and cornhole one other . . . until their testicles are whistlin' "O Come All Ye Faithful." Then you turn on the cameras, and you've got . . . the Semen Channel! And don't forget our corporate sponsor. We're going to let Budweiser put little logo patches on the rapists' pants: "This pud's for you!"

Next group: Drug addicts and alcoholics. Not all of them, don't get nervous. Just the ones who are making life difficult for at least one other person. And we're not gonna bother first offenders; people deserve a chance to clean up. So, everyone will get twelve chances to clean up. Okay okay, fifteen! Fine! That's fair, and that's all you get. If you can't make it in fifteen tries, off you go . . . to Colorado! The perfect place for staying loaded.

Each week, all of the illegal drugs confiscated in the United States—at least those drugs the police and DEA don't keep for their own personal use—will be air-dropped into Colorado. That way, everyone can stay stoned, bombed, wasted, smashed, hammered, and fucked up around the clock on another new cable channel: Shitface Central. This is the real Rocky Mountain high.

Now, I've saved my favorite group for last. **The Maniacs and Crazy People.** The ones who live out where the buses don't run. And I always take care to distinguish between maniacs and crazy people. A maniac will beat nine people to death with a steel dildo. A crazy person will beat nine people to death with a steel dildo, but he'll be wearing a Bugs Bunny suit at the time.

So you can't put them all away. You have to keep some of them around just for the entertainment. Like the guy who tells you the King of Sweden is using his gallbladder as a radio transmitter to send anti-Semitic, lesbian meat loaf recipes to Marvin Hamlisch. A guy like that, you want to give him his own radio show.

No, the Maniac Farm will be used strictly for hopeless cases. Like a guy who gets a big tattoo on his chest of Madonna taking a shit. You know? Then he tells you that if he flexes certain muscles it looks like she's wipin' her ass. A guy like that, you wanna get him into custody as quickly as possible.

Now, for the Maniac Farm I think there's no question we have to go with Utah. Easy to fence, and right next to Wyoming and Colorado. And Colorado is right next to? Right, Kansas! And that means that *all four groups* of our most amusing citizens are now in one place. Except for the big electric fences. And, folks, I think I have another one of my really good ideas for cable TV. Gates! Small sliding gates in the fences.

Think what you have here. Four groups: degenerates, predators, crackheads, and fruitcakes. All separated by 900 miles of fence. And here's how you have some fun: every ten miles, you put a small, sliding gate in the fence. But—the gates are only ten inches wide, and they're only opened once a month. For seven seconds.

And you know something? Fuck cable, this stuff belongs on pay-per-view. Because if those gates are only open seven seconds a month, you are gonna have some mighty interesting people trying to be first on line. Deeply disturbed, armed, cranky lunatics on drugs! You know the ones: a lot of tattoos; a lot of teeth broken off at the gum line. The true face of America. And every time you open the gates a few of the more aggressive ones are gonna slip through. The crème de la crème. The alphas! They're gonna slip through, they're gonna find each other, and they're gonna cross-breed.

And pretty soon you'll have the American melting pot: child-killers, corpse-tuckers, drug zombies, and full-blown twelve-cylinder wackaloons. All wandering the landscape in search of truth. And fun. Just like now. Everyone will have guns, everyone will have drugs, and no one will be in charge. Just like now. But Social Security will be fully funded.

I'LL BE RIGHT BACK

I've never been impressed with people who tell me what they plan to do when they go to the bathroom. Doesn't that bother you? People who announce their intentions?

"I'll be right back, Trevor, I'm gonna take a shit."

"Never mind, Pietro! Do what you have to and leave me out of it. And please don't describe it when you get back."

[Time, among other things, passes.]

"Boy, you shoulda seen . . ."

"Never mind!"

"It set off the smoke alarm."

"Never mind!"

"The rest room attendant passed out."

I've never understood people who describe their bowel achievements. Nor have I much cared for it. Especially at a fine restaurant.

NOT EVERY EJACULATION DESERVES A NAME

Have you noticed that most people who are against abortion are people you wouldn't want to fuck in the first place? Conservatives are physically unattractive and morally inconsistent. They're obsessed with fetuses from conception to nine months, but after that they have no interest in you. None. No day care, no Head Start, no school lunch, no food stamps, no welfare, no nothin'. If you're preborn, you're fine; if you're preschool, you're fucked.

Once you leave the womb, conservatives don't care about you until you reach military age. Then you're just what they're looking for. Conservatives want live babies so they can raise them to be dead soldiers.

Pro-life. How can they be pro-life when they're killing doctors? What sort of moral philosophy is that? "We'll do anything to save a fetus, but we might have to kill it later on if it grows up to be a doctor"? They're not pro-life; they're antiwoman. Simple. They're afraid of women, and they don't like them. They believe a woman's primary role is to function as a brood mare for the State. If they think a fetus is more important than a woman, they should try getting a fetus to wash the shit stains out of their underwear. For no pay.

Pro-life. You don't see many white, antiabortion women volunteering to have black fetuses transplanted into their uteruses, do you? No. You don't see them adopting any crack babies, do you? No, that's something Jesus would do.

And you won't see many pro-lifers dousing themselves with kerosene and lighting themselves on fire. Remember the Buddhist monks in Vietnam? Morally committed religious people in Southeast Asia knew how to stage a protest: light yourself on fire! C'mon, you Christian crusaders, let's see a little smoke. Let's see if you can match that fire in your bellies.

Separate thought: Why is it when it's a human being it's called an abortion, and when it's a chicken it's called an omelet. Are we so much better than chickens? When did that happen? Name six ways we're better than chickens. See? No one can do it. You know why? Because chickens are decent people.

You don't see chickens hanging around in drug gangs, do you? No. You don't see chickens strappin' someone to a chair and hookin' up their nuts to a car battery. And when's the last time you heard about a chicken who came home from work and beat the shit out of his hen? Huh? It doesn't happen. You know why? Because chickens are decent people.

Back to abortion: The central question seems to be "Are fetuses human beings?" Well, if fetuses are human beings, why aren't they counted by the census? If fetuses are human beings, why is it there's no funeral following a miscarriage? If fetuses are human beings, why do people say, "We have two children and one on the way," instead of saying, "We have three children"?

Some people say life begins at conception; I say life began a billion years ago, and it's a continuous process. And actually, it goes back farther than that. What about the carbon atoms? Human life could not exist without carbon. So is it possible that maybe we shouldn't be burning all this coal? I don't mean to be picky, I'm just lookin' for a little consistency.

The hard-core pro-lifers tell us that life begins at fertilization, when the sperm fertilizes the egg. Which usually occurs a few minutes after the man says, "Sorry, honey, I was gonna pull out, but the phone startled me."

But even after fertilization it's still six or seven days before the egg reaches the uterus and pregnancy begins. And not every egg makes it. Eighty percent of a woman's fertilized eggs are rinsed out of her body once a month during those delightful few days she has. They end up on sanitary napkins, and yet they are fertilized eggs. So, what these antiabortion people are actually telling us is that any woman who's had more than one period is a serial killer. I don't mean to be picky, I'm just looking for a little consistency.

And speaking of consistency, Catholics—which I was until I reached the age of reason—Catholics and other Christians are against abortions, and they're against homosexuals. Well, who has less abortions than homosexuals? Here's an entire class of citizens guaranteed never to have an abortion, and the Catholics and Christians are just tossin' them aside. You'd think they'd be natural allies.

And regarding the Catholics, when I hear that the Pope and some of his "holy" friends have experienced their first pregnancies and labor pains, and raised a couple of children on minimum wage, I'll be glad to hear what they have to say about abortion. In the meantime, what they ought to do is tell these priests who took a vow of chastity to keep their hands off the altar boys. When Jesus said, "Suffer the little children come unto me," pedophilia is not what he was talking about. He had something else in mind.

I'VE GOT YOUR SANCTITY OF LIFE

One phrase that comes up quite a bit in abortion discussions is "sanctity of life." What about that? Do you think there's such a thing as sanctity of life? Personally, I think it's a bunch of shit. Who says life is sacred? God? Great, but if you read your history you know that God is one of the leading causes of death and has been for thousands of years. Hindus, Moslems, Christians, Jews, all taking turns killing one another, because God told them it was a good idea. The sword of God, the blood of the lamb, vengeance is mine. Millions of dead people. All because they gave the wrong answer to the God Question:

"Do you believe in God?"

"No."

BAM! Dead.

"How about you? Do you believe in God?"

"Yes."

"Do you believe in *my* God?"

"No."

BAM! Dead!

"My god has a bigger dick than your god."

For thousands of years all the bloodiest and most brutal wars have been based on religious hatred. Which, of course, is fine with me; any time "holy" people are killing one another, I'm a happy guy. But please, don't kill each other and then give me that shit about "sanctity of life." Even if there were such an absurd thing, I don't think you could blame it on God.

You know where the sanctity of life comes from? We made it up. You know why? Because we're alive. Self-interest! Living people have a strong incentive to promote the idea that somehow life is sacred. You don't see Bing Crosby runnin' around talking about this shit, do you? You don't hear much from Mussolini on the subject. And what's the latest from JFK? Not a goddamn thing! You know why? Because JFK, Mussolini, and Bing Crosby are all fuckin' dead. They're fuckin' dead, and dead people give less than a shit about the sanctity of life.

The only people who care about it are the living. So the whole thing grows out of a biased point of view. It's a self-serving, man-made bullshit story; one of those things we tell ourselves in order to feel noble. "Life is sacred." Makes us feel good. But let me ask you this: If everything that ever lived is dead, and everything alive is going to die, where does the sacred part come in? Can you help me on that?

Because even with all we preach about the sanctity of life, we don't practice it. Look at what we kill: Mosquitoes and flies, because they're pests. Lions and tigers, because it's fun. Chickens and pigs, because we're hungry. And people. We kill people. Because they're pests. And because it's fun!

And here's something else I noticed. Apparently, the sanctity of life doesn't apply to cancer cells, does it? You rarely see a bumper sticker that says Save the Tumors. Or I Brake for Advanced Melanoma. No. Viruses, molds, mildew, maggots, fungus, weeds, intestinal worms, *E. coli* bacteria, the crabs. Nothin' sacred about those things. Just us.

So, at best, the sanctity of life is a selective thing. We choose which forms of life we feel are sacred, and we get to kill the rest. Pretty neat deal. You know how we got it? We made the whole thing up! Same way we made up the death penalty. The sanctity of life, and the death penalty. We're such a versatile species.

READY OR NOT, HERE WE COME!

The latest disaster for the solar system is that the United States has decided go to Mars. And, of course, later we intend to colonize deep space with our Salad Shooters and Snot Candy and microwave hot dogs. But let me ask you this: What are we going to tell the Intergalactic Council the first time one of our young women throws her newborn baby out of a seventh-story window? And how do we explain to the Near-Stellar Trade Confederation that our representative was late for the meeting because his breakfast was cold, and he had to spend thirty minutes beating the shit out of his wife?

Do you think the elders of the Universal Board of Wisdom will understand that it's simply because of quaint local customs that over 80 million of our women have had their clitorises and labia cut off and their vulvas sewn shut in order to make them more marriageable and unable to derive pleasure from sex and thus never be a threat to stray from their husbands' beds?

Can't you just sense how eager the rest of the universe is for us to show up?

NEVER HEARD OF HIM!

You ever notice that suddenly overnight someone you never heard of becomes a big celebrity; and you never heard their name before? Ever? And you think, Who the fuck is this? How can this happen without me noticing? Usually it's because the person is in some line of work you're not interested in, like popular music or network television. They're on some TV show you wouldn't watch unless you were strapped in bed in a nuthouse, but suddenly there are big magazine articles about them, and they're on Leno and Letterman. Don't you feel really good two years later when they've completely disappeared; gone back to the supermarket? It's very satisfying.

SHORT TAKES

Have you ever been on trial for murder? It's weird. You don't know what to do with yourself. Singing is out. Mostly I stare at the judge.

Is a vegetarian permitted to eat animal crackers?

I've figured out how to commit the perfect double murder. You pick one person up by the ankles and beat the other person to death with him. They both die, and there's no murder weapon.

Peg Leg Bates's wife is one person who never had to wait for the other shoe to drop.

Have you ever had a hatchet go right through your face? Not a glancing blow, but a full-on shot, deep into your forehead? Deep enough so you can shake your head and the hatchet doesn't fall out? It's the strangest feeling. Because just after the hatchet goes in, and before there's any pain, you can feel a gentle puff of cool air on your brain. It feels good. But since it's the only way to get that feeling, I try not to get too hung up on it.

Wouldn't it be great if just one of these times at Daytona or Indianapolis, because of accidents and various mechanical failures, there were simply no cars at all left to finish the race? What color flag would they wave then?

Suggested bumper sticker We Are the Proud Parents of a Child Whose Self-Esteem Is Sufficient that He Doesn't Need Us Advertising His Minor Scholastic Achievements on the Bumper of Our Car.

When did they pass a law that says the people who make my sandwich have to be wearing gloves? I'm not comfortable with this; I don't want glove residue all over my food. It's not sanitary. Who knows where these gloves have been? Let's get back to human hands making sandwiches for human beings.

As you swim the river of life, do the breast stroke. It helps to clear the turds from your path.

YOU PICK IT, I'LL LICK IT.

Have you ever tried to throw away an old wastebasket? You can't do it. People keep bringing it back: "Here, Howie, I found your wastebasket in the garbage." Apparently, you have to completely destroy a wastebasket in order to convince people you really don't want it anymore.

In Los Angeles, there's a hotline for people in denial. So far no one has called.

Just once I'd like to see a high-speed funeral procession. A hearse, some flower cars, and a bunch of limousines tearin' ass through town at 70 miles an hour, on their way to the cemetery. Maybe someday a race-car driver will put that in his will.

You know a business that doesn't lend itself too easily to the Internet? Pay toilets.

Here's something I consider a crime against society: women with hyphenated names. Hey, lady, pick a fuckin' name, will you?

"Hi. I'm Emily Jarrikov-Fortescu."

"Hi. I'm George Jerkmeoff-Fuckyoutoo!"

Attention women: You don't attain self-esteem or personal dignity by adding a name to your name. Modern feminists apparently think hyphenation is a radical act. It's not. Castrating a man in a parking lot with a Coke bottle is a radical act. Hyphenating your name is pretentious, middle-class bullshit.

No one ever knows what's next, but they always do it.

You know what they don't have? A really good French football player. You never hear about some guy named Pierre La Doux smashing through the line of scrimmage and picking up a first down. Why is that?

The only hip thing left to do in America is to blow up a building. Believe me.

Fun Stuff: Walk into a gun store, buy three guns and a bunch of ammunition. Then ask them if they have any ski masks.

I have a very inexpensive security system. If someone breaks into my house, I run next door and throw a brick through my neighbor's window. That sets off his alarm and when the police arrive I direct them to my house.

As Asian immigrants become more completely assimilated into American society over the next few generations, their standards of hard work and academic excellence will drop, and they will feel more at home here.

Some teenage girls delay getting abortions because they're afraid to comply with the parental notification laws. Especially if one of the parents also happens to be the father of the child.

Here's a plastic surgery option: have one nostril sewn shut. I feel like I might be ready for that.

Regarding the Pledge of Allegiance and other patriotic nonsense: what does placing your hand over your heart have to do with anything? Or removing your hat when the flag is passing by? Am I missing something?

True Stuff: There is actually a Tow-Truck Hall of Fame.

I just realized I haven't been scared in a really long time.

Didn't the first guy who wore a sombrero realize it was completely impractical when eating pussy?

I don't understand motivation books. What happened here? Suddenly everybody needs to be motivated? It's a fairly simple thing: either you want to do something or you don't; there's no mystery. Besides, if you're motivated enough to go to the store to buy a motivation book, aren't you motivated enough to do that? So, you don't need the book. Put it back. Tell the clerk, "Fuck you, I'm goin' home. I'm already motivated."

Safety Tip: Always wear a leather glove when giving a porcupine a hand job.

You know a word you don't hear enough anymore? Hosiery.

SPORTS SHOULD BE FIXED: SECOND HALF

Basketball: No Harm, No Fun

Continuing my attempt to improve professional sports with basketball, once again I propose to make the game more exciting by changing the rules. But in this case I concentrate less on violence and injuries and a bit more on spicing up the game.

To begin with, basketball would be faster and a whole lot more exciting if they had a three-second shot clock. Never mind that passing shit; as soon as the ball is in play, get that son of a bitch up in the air. I didn't pay to watch a game of catch, I'm lookin' for a 700-point ball game.

Here's another good suggestion: all free throws should be taken as jump shots. Players should have to drive from half-court, pull up at the foul line, and shoot the jumper. Much more exciting. And speaking of foul shots, I would retain the six-foul limit, but I would increase it to six fouls per quarter per man. This way you avoid that stupid foul-trouble shit and keep the stars on the court.

Next, I think before anyone touches a rebound, it should be allowed to bounce one time and then let the players fight over it. And if a rebound goes into the stands, the spectator who catches the ball should be allowed to shoot two free throws for his team. Get the fans involved.

And here's something interesting no one else has thought of: when one of those hyperactive players dives into the crowd trying to keep a ball from going out-of-bounds, he should have to stay and sit in the stands for three minutes. Like the penalty box in hockey. And by the way, when is one of those diving, Charlie Hustle guys gonna break his fuckin' neck on a chair? You just don't see enough of that sort of thing.

Here's another good idea: fifty points for any shot made from beyond the half-court line. It would be great for those lopsided games in the fourth quarter. And I'll guarantee you some guys would practice that shot and get good at it. Then they could just hang around half-court the whole game, and when the teams switch baskets at halftime, all they'd have to do is turn around and face the other way.

Something else I'll bet has never come up at a meeting of the rules committee: bonus points for any shot that goes in the basket after bouncing off another guy's head. Fifty points if it's a teammate, 100 if it's an opponent. Believe me, you'd see a lot of good fights. And, actually, the brain injuries alone would make this one well worth trying.

Two more suggestions. If a team falls behind by more than 15 points, they have to let their girlfriends come in and help them on defense. It's just the kind of motivation these macho duds need to keep the games close.

And last—and, honestly, I do not think this is excessive—during overtime periods I would allow the players to use small personal weapons, excluding firearms. I think knives and blackjacks, employed sparingly, would contribute to some rousing finishes in these evenly matched games.

DON'T BLAME THE LEADERS

You, the People

In the midst of all my bitching, you might've noticed that I never complain about politicians. I leave that to others. And there's no shortage of volunteers; everyone complains about politicians. Everyone says they suck.

But where do people think these politicians come from? They don't fall out of the sky; they don't pass through a membrane from a separate reality. They come from American homes, American families, American schools, American churches, and American businesses. And they're elected by American voters. This is what our system produces, folks. This is the best we can do. Let's face it, we have very little to work with. Garbage in, garbage out.

Ignorant citizens elect ignorant leaders, it's as simple as that. And term limits don't help. All you do is get a brand new bunch of ignorant leaders.

So maybe it's not the politicians who suck; maybe it's something else. Like the public. That would be a nice realistic campaign slogan for somebody: "The public sucks. Elect me." Put the blame where it belongs: on the people.

Because if everything is really the fault of politicians, where are all the bright, honest, intelligent Americans who are ready to step in and replace them? Where are these people hiding? The truth is, we don't have people like that. Everyone's at the mall, scratching his balls and buying sneakers with lights in them. And complaining about the politicians.

Vote? No!

For myself, I have solved this political dilemma in a very direct way. On Election Day, I stay home. Two reasons: first of all, voting is meaningless; this country was bought and paid for a long time ago. That empty shit they shuffle around and repackage every four years doesn't mean a thing.

Second, I don't vote, because I firmly believe that if you vote, you have no right to complain. I know some people like to twist that around and say, "If you *don't* vote, you have no right to complain."

But where's the logic in that? Think it through: if you vote, and you elect dishonest, incompetent politicians, and they screw things up, then you're responsible for what they've done. You voted them in. You caused the problem. You have no right to complain.

I, on the other hand, who did not vote—who, in fact, did not even leave the house on Election Day—am in no way responsible for what these politicians have done and have every right to complain about the mess you created. Which I had nothing to do with. Why can't people see that?

Now, I realize last year you folks had another one of those really swell presidential elections you treasure so much. That was nice. I'm sure you had a good time, and I'm sure that everyone's life has now improved. But I'm happy to tell you that on Election Day I stayed home. And I did essentially what you did. The only difference is when I got finished masturbating I had something to show for it.

The 20th Century World-Hostility Scoreboard

The following is a list of hostilities that took place in the 20th Century among the civilized peoples of the world. The uncivilized were unable to provide reliable statistics.

2	world wars	691	wars of honor
250	civil wars	296	declared wars
311	holy wars	856	undeclared wars
1	cold war	4	brushfire wars
516	wars of liberation	2	vest-pocket wars
331	wars of containment	413	limited wars

1,987	acts of war	946	carpet bombings
7,756	warlike acts	4,288	threats to security
88	police actions	286	popular uprisings
2	nuclear attacks	1,877	areas of unrest
6,578	government massacres	622	strife-torn regions
4	holocausts	165	internal upheavals
943	jihads	745	political repressions
693	pogroms	12,194	acts of sabotage
614	longterm persecutions	1,633	swift reprisals
12,111	acts of treachery	818	armed resistances
575	betrayals of the masses	639	repressive measures
958	grabs for power	1,126	violent outbursts
400	putsches	9,876	mass detentions
50	total enslavements	11,904	guerilla operations
837	partial enslavements	3,466	suicide missions
4	total genocides	823	slaughters
461	partial genocides	1,200	bloodbaths
13,658	cease-fire violations	43,096	atrocities
3,115	boundary disputes	161	reigns of terror
1,432	border clashes	715	rebellions
3,047	social conflicts	28	revolutions
798	sectarian rivalries	21	counterrevolutions
13,678	civil disturbances	746	coups

745	countercoups	515	regional tinderboxes
457	insurgencies	818	military flashpoints
458	counterinsurgencies	2,415	heated exchanges
4,622	covert operations	911	shows of force
3,422	direct interventions	668	heightenings of tension
617	enemy incursions	735	deliberate provocations
13	measured responses	921	military confrontations
295	commando strikes	639	dangerous escalations
694	retaliatory raids	3,721	terrorist bombings
844	surprise attacks	438	preemptive strikes
236	protective reactions	630	outside aggressions
2,155	frontal assaults	8,571	violent disturbances
213	responses in kind	646	surgical strikes
17,867	hostile incidents	4,392	diplomatic deadlocks
4,756	belligerent moves	82,879	ultimatums
938	naked aggressions	788,969,747	heated arguments
849	foreign adventures	823,285,571	shoving matches
601	overseas entanglements	917,704,296	fistfights
307	arms races	942,759,050	snotty phone calls
98	international powder kegs		

That's how we did, folks. Not a bad record, although we could have done better, considering the number of fools in our ranks.

ROCKETS AND PENISES IN THE PERSIAN GULF

History Lesson

I'd like to talk a little about that "war" we had in the Persian Gulf. Remember that? The big war in the Persian Gulf? Lemme tell you what was goin' on.

Naturally, you can forget all that entertaining fiction about having to defend the model democracy those lucky Kuwaitis get to live under. And for the moment you can also put aside the very real, periodic need Americans have for testing their new weapons on human flesh. And also, just for the fun of it, let's ignore George Bush's obligation to protect the oil interests of his family and friends. There was another, much more important, consideration at work. Here's what really happened.

Dropping a Load for Uncle Sam

The simple fact is that America was long overdue to drop high explosives on helpless civilians; people who have no argument with us whatsoever. After all, it had been awhile, and the hunger gnaws. Remember that's our specialty: picking on countries that have marginally effective air forces. Yugoslavia is another, more recent, example.

Surfing Unnecessary

But all that aside, let me tell you what I liked about that Gulf War: it was the first war that appeared on every television channel, including cable. And even though the TV show consisted largely of

Pentagon war criminals displaying maps and charts, it got very good ratings. And that makes sense, because we like war. We're a warlike people. We can't stand not to be fucking with someone. We couldn't wait for the Cold War to end so we could climb into the big Arab sandbox and play with our nice new toys. We enjoy war.

And one reason we enjoy it is that we're good at it. You know why we're good at it? Because we get a lot of practice. This country is only 200 years old, and already we've had ten major wars. We average a major war every twenty years. So we're good at it!

And it's just as well we are, because we're not very good at anything else. Can't build a decent car anymore. Can't make a TV set, a cell phone, or a VCR. Got no steel industry left. No textiles. Can't educate our young people. Can't get health care to our old people. But we can bomb the shit outta your country, all right. We can bomb the shit outta your country!

If You're Brown, You're Goin' Down

Especially if your country is full of brown people. Oh, we like that, don't we? That's our hobby now. But it's also our new job in the world: bombing brown people. Iraq, Panama, Grenada, Libya. You got some brown people in your country? Tell 'em to watch the fuck out, or we'll goddamn bomb them!

Well, who were the last white people you can remember that we bombed? In fact, can you remember *any* white people we ever bombed? The Germans! That's it! Those are the only ones. And that was only because they were tryin' to cut in on our action. They wanted to dominate the world. Bullshit! That's our job. That's our fuckin' job.

But the Germans are ancient history. These days, we only bomb brown people. And not because they're cutting in on our action; we do it because they're brown. Even those Serbs we bombed in Yugoslavia aren't *really* white, are they? Naaah! They're sort of down near the swarthy end of the white spectrum. Just brown enough to bomb. I'm still waiting for the day we bomb the English. People who really deserve it.

A Disobedient American

Now, you folks might've noticed, I don't feel about that Gulf War the way we were instructed to feel about it by the United States government. My mind doesn't work that way. You see, I've got this real moron thing I do, it's called "thinking." And I guess I'm not a very good American, because I like to form my own opinions; I don't just roll over when I'm told. Most Americans roll over on command. Not me. There are certain rules I observe.

Believe You Me

My first rule: Never believe anything anyone in authority says. None of them. Government, police, clergy, the corporate criminals. None of them. And neither do I believe anything I'm told by the media, who, in the case of the Gulf War, functioned as little more than unpaid employees of the Defense Department, and who, most of the time, operate as an unofficial public relations agency for government and industry.

I don't believe in any of them. And I have to tell you, folks, I don't really believe very much in my country either. I don't get all choked up about yellow ribbons and American flags. I see them as symbols, and I leave them to the symbol-minded.

Show Us Your Dick

I also look at war itself a little differently from most. I see it largely as an exercise in dick-waving. That's really all it is: a lot of men standing around in a field waving their dicks at one another. Men, insecure about the size of their penises, choose to kill one another.

That's also what all that moron athlete bullshit is about, and what that macho, male posturing and strutting around in bars and locker rooms represents. It's called "dick fear." Men are terrified that their dicks are inadequate, and so they have to "compete" in order to feel better about themselves. And since war is the ultimate competition, essentially men are killing one another in order to improve their genital self-esteem.

You needn't be a historian or a political scientist to see the Bigger Dick Foreign Policy Theory at work. It goes like this: "What? They have bigger dicks? Bomb them!" And of course, the bombs, the rockets, and the bullets are all shaped like penises. Phallic weapons. There's an unconscious need to project the national penis into the affairs of others. It's called "fucking with people."

Show Us Your Bush

So, as far as I'm concerned, that whole thing in the Persian Gulf was nothing more than one big dick-waving cockfight. In this particular case, Saddam Hussein questioned the size of George Bush's dick. And George Bush had been called a wimp for so long, he apparently felt the need to act out his manhood fantasies by sending America's white children to kill other people's brown children. Clearly the worst *kind* of wimp.

Even his name, "Bush," as slang, is *related* to the genitals without actually being the genitals. A bush is sort of a passive, secondary sex characteristic. It's even used as a slang term for women: "Hey, pal, how's the bush in this area?" I can't help thinking, if this president's name had been George Boner . . . well, he might have felt a little better about himself, and he wouldn't have had to kill all those children. Too bad he couldn't locate his manhood.

Premature Extraction

Actually, when you think about it, this country has had a manhood problem for some time. You can tell by the language we use; language always gives us away. What did we do wrong in Vietnam? We "pulled out"! Not a very manly thing to do. No. When you're fucking people, you're supposed to stay with it and fuck them good; fuck them to death; hang in there and keep fucking them until they're all fucking dead.

But in Vietnam what happened was by accident we left a few women and children alive, and we haven't felt good about ourselves since. That's why in the Persian Gulf, George Bush had to say, "This will not be another Vietnam." He actually said, "this time we're *going all the way*." Imagine. An American president using the sexual slang of a thirteen-year-old to describe his foreign policy.

And, of course, when it got right down to it, he *didn't* "go all the way." Faced with going into Baghdad he punked out. No balls. Just Bush. Instead, he applied sanctions, so he'd be sure that an extra half a million brown children would die. And so his oil buddies could continue to fill their pockets.

If you want to know what happened in the Persian Gulf, just remember the first names of the two men who ran that war: Dick Cheney and Colin Powell. Dick and colon. Someone got fucked in the ass. And those brown people better make sure they keep their pants on, because Dick and Colin have come back for an encore.

OLD AND STINGY

Here's something that pisses me off: retired people who don't want to pay local property taxes, because they say it's not their grandchildren who go to the schools. Mean-spirited retirees usually from out of state. Cheap, selfish, old Bush voters. The ones I read about were in Arizona. AARP members. They take a shit the size of a peanut and think it's an accomplishment.

And it's not like these retirement people can't afford the tax money. Not all old people are as dependent on Social Security checks as they'd like you to think. Some of them get all kinds of checks: Social Security, the VA, private pensions, government pensions. They also have stock dividends, bank interest, and whatever else they've managed to squeeze out of the system.

And still they begrudge their local property taxes simply because their own fucked-up, cross-eyed grandchildren aren't gonna use the schools. Fuck 'em! I say pay your taxes and die like everybody else. I hope they choke on an early-bird dinner.

SHORT TAKES

What exactly is wrong with inmates running the asylum? It seems to me they're in an ideal position to know just what's needed.

HOORAY FOR MOST THINGS!

When it comes to my organs, I've decided to donate only my prostate and testicles, with the stipulation that they go to one of those lovely feminists.

Here's something no one ever wrote before: "Big bats down to one five, five over cross, up the thingo. Nose, baseball, hieroglyphics, hopscotch, pouch. Inevitably, two four eight, four eight, four eight, four eighth. I. I with a two, two, two. Three. Four. Five. Down here, Mother, we're all home now. So long, Jill. Beep beep. Hungry, hungry. Are you? I couldn't stand it. Not in my house. Up yours, too, Don. He's packin' them in! We'll all try it. Fifty-fifty? Okay, but not me." No one ever wrote that before. Not even Shakespeare. I'm proud of that.

Civilization began its downhill path the day some guy first uttered the words, "A man's gotta do what a man's gotta do."

Have you ever been in the middle of a nice, pleasant dream, when you suddenly wake up and realize someone is trying to kill you? You know what I do? I go back to sleep.

They say if you live to be 100 your lucky number goes up by one.

Near as I can tell, "jack shit" and "diddly-squat" are roughly the same amount.

What do you think about some guy who hears a voice in his head that tells him to kill his entire family, and he does it? Is that the only thing these voices ever tell paranoid guys to do? Kill people? Doesn't a voice ever say, "Go take a shit on the salad bar at Wendy's!" Doesn't a voice tell a guy to take out his dick on the merry-go-round? Actually, some guys do take out their dicks on the merry-go-round. But usually it's their own idea.

In the old days white people used to put black greasepaint on their faces and perform menstrual shows. That must have been really interesting.

When I first heard the song "Don't Worry, Be Happy," I realized it was exactly the kind of mindless philosophy that Americans would respond to. It would make a great national motto. Right along with Me First.

Little-Known Fact: When the stock exchange closes, the guy who comes out on the balcony with that big hammer slams it on the head of the person who lost the most money that day.

America has too many fake Irish pubs. Giving your bar an Irish name doesn't make it a pub. The word pub is earned the hard way: tons and tons of puke and thousands of shattered cheekbones.

McDonald's breakfast for under a dollar is actually more expensive than that. You have to factor in the cost of bypass surgery.

May I make it clear that I don't care what country the pope is in? I'm really not interested. All the pope ever does is go around to places where people make six dollars a year and tell them to have more children. Isn't that bright? And responsible! And compassionate. Such a bright, responsible, compassionate man. If the pope wants to travel around, flaunting his wealth and encouraging poor people to have children, let him do it privately. And for God's sake, keep it off television. The pope is not news.

No one who has ever had "Taps" played for them has been able to hear it.

Although it's true blondes have more fun, it's important to remember that they also have more venereal disease.

If you watch a sitcom carefully, you can see that it's really nothing more than a series of doors opening and closing with a series of jackoffs entering and exiting.

Here's a great idea: A roach spray that doesn't kill the roach, but, instead, fills him with self-doubt as to whether or not he's in the right house.

I'm sure looters don't call it looting. They probably think of it as extreme shopping.

FUCK THE POLITICAL CENTER

America got what it deserved in Elvis Presley: a big fat, drug-addict squealer. And don't get me wrong, there's nothing wrong with being a drug addict. But he wasn't even addicted to a cool drug like heroin. It was medicine. Fuckin' doctor drugs.

One good reason for maintaining only a small circle of friends is that three out of four murders are committed by people who know the victim.

If you live on the wrong side of the tracks but get up on the right side of the bed, do those things cancel each other out? Probably not.

Professional soldiers are people who die for a living.

Here's Some Fun: Go into a photography shop and ask the man if you can buy the pictures of the other people in the window. Say, "How much for that heavy-set couple?" I guarantee they'll stare at you a long time. In fact, they might even back up several feet.

Whenever they say someone got hit by a "stray bullet" I wonder about the choice of words. It seems to me the bullet isn't stray at all. It's doing exactly what physics predicts: travelling in a straight line. What's so stray about that?

AT LEAST EAT A FUCKIN' LIMA BEAN, WILL YA?

Beverly Hills has a new restaurant for bulimia victims. It's called The Scarf and Barf. Originally, they were gonna call it The Fork and Bucket. Thank God, once again good taste prevailed in Beverly Hills.

They're also planning a restaurant for anorexics, but again, having trouble with the name. It's a toss-up between The Empty Plate and Lonesome Chef. I suggested Start Without Me, Guys.

Tell you the truth, I don't feel sorry for an anorexic. Do you? Some rich cunt doesn't wanna eat? Fuck her! Don't eat. I give a shit. Like I'm supposed to be concerned.

"I don't wanna eat!"

"Go fuck yourself! Why don't you lie down in front of a railroad train after you don't eat?"

What kind of a goddamn disease is anorexia, anyway? "I don't wanna eat!" How do we come up with this shit? Where do we get our values?

Bulimia. There's another all-American disease. This has gotta be the only country in the world where some people are digging in the dumpster for a peach pit while other people eat a nice meal and puke it up intentionally. Where do we get our values?

FACE-TO-FACE WITH THE CLOCK

I remember when they tried to teach me to tell time as a little boy. What they didn't know, of course, was that you don't tell time; time tells you. Still they tried.

"Now, George, the big hand is on . . ."

"I don't have a big hand. Both my hands are little."

"Never mind. Just look at the clock."

And I did. It was wonderful. I love the face of a clock. To me, there is great emotion attached to the face of a clock. A conventional analog clock.

Digital clocks are all right in their place, I suppose, but they lack the friendly spatial relationships that exist between the hands and the numerals on an analog clock.

There's a psychological component: to me, the first half of any hour, as the minute hand falls from 12 to 6, passes a lot more quickly than the second half, when it has to struggle upward, fighting gravity all the way.

I'll say this much: If I had only half an hour to live, I'd want it to be the second half. I just know it would last a little longer.

GOD HAS GOTTA GO

I make fun of people who are religious, because I think they're fundamentally weak. But I want you to know that on a personal level, when it comes to believing in God, I tried. I really, really tried. I tried to believe there is a God, who created us in his own image, loves us very much, and keeps a close eye on things.

I tried to believe it. But I have to tell you, the longer you live, the more you look around, the more you realize . . . something is fucked. Something is wrong. War, disease, death, destruction, hunger, filth, poverty, torture, crime, corruption, and the Ice Capades. Something is definitely wrong.

If this is the best God can do, I'm not impressed. Results like these do not belong on the résumé of a supreme being. This is the kind of stuff you'd expect from an office temp with a bad attitude. In any well-managed universe, this guy would've been out on his all-powerful ass a long time ago.

So, if there is a God—if there is—I think reasonable people might agree he's at least incompetent and maybe, just maybe, he doesn't give a shit. Which I admire in a person, and which would explain a lot of his results.

I Got the Sun in the Mornin'

So, rather than becoming just another mindless, religious robot, blindly believing that everything is in the hands of some spooky, incompetent father figure who doesn't give a shit, I decided to look around for something else to worship. Something I could really count on. And immediately, I thought of the sun. It happened in an instant. Overnight, I became a sun worshipper.

Well, not overnight; you can't see the sun in the dark. But first thing the next morning, I became a sun worshipper. For several reasons: First of all, I can see the sun. Unlike some other gods I could mention, I can actually see the sun. I'm big on that. If I can see something, it kind of helps the credibility.

Every day I can see the sun as it gives me everything I need: heat, light, food, flowers in the park, reflections on the lake. An occasional skin cancer, but, hey! At least there are no crucifixions. And we sun worshippers don't go around killing other people simply because they don't agree with us.

Sun worship is fairly simple. There's no mystery, no miracles, no pageantry, no one asks for money, there are no songs to learn, and we don't have a special building where we all gather once a week to compare clothing. And the best thing about the sun . . . it never tells me I'm unworthy. It doesn't tell me I'm a bad person who needs to be saved. Hasn't said an unkind word. Treats me fine.

Praying on My Mind

So I worship the sun. But I don't pray to the sun. You know why? Because I wouldn't presume on our friendship. It's not polite. I've often thought people treat God rather rudely. Trillions and trillions of prayers every day, asking and pleading and begging for favors. "Do this; give me that; I need this; I want that." And most of this praying takes place on Sunday, his day off! It's not nice, and it's no way to treat a friend.

But still people do pray and they pray for many different things. And that's all right with me. I say, pray for anything you want. Pray for anything. But . . . what about the Divine Plan? Remember that? The Divine Plan? A long time ago, God came up with a Divine Plan. He gave it a lot of thought, he decided it was a good plan, and he put it into practice. And for billions and billions of years the Divine Plan has been doing just fine.

But now you come along and pray for something. Well, suppose the thing you're praying for isn't in God's Divine Plan? What do you want him to do? Change his plan? Just for you? Isn't that sort of arrogant? It's a Divine Plan! What good is being God if every rundown schmuck with a two-dollar prayer book can come along and fuck with your plan?

And here's another problem you might encounter. Suppose your prayers aren't answered? What do you do then? What do you say? "Well, it's God's will. Thy will be done"? Fine. But if it's God's will, and he's going to do what he wants anyway, why bother praying in the first place? Doesn't it seem like a big waste of time? Couldn't you just skip the praying part and go straight to "his will"? It's all very confusing to me.

To Each His Own

So, to get around all this, I decided to worship the sun. But as I said, I don't pray to the sun. You know who I pray to? Joe Pesci. Two reasons. First of all, I think he's a pretty good actor. To me, that counts. Second, he looks like a guy who can get things done. Joe doesn't fuck around. In fact, he came through on a couple of things that God was having trouble with. For years I asked God to do something about my noisy neighbor's barking dog. Nothing happened. But Joe Pesci? He straightened that shit out with one visit. It's amazing what you can accomplish with a simple piece of athletic equipment.

So, I've been praying to Joe for a couple of years now, and I've noticed something. I've noticed that all the prayers I used to offer to God and all the prayers I now offer to Joe Pesci are being answered at about the same 50 percent rate. Half the time I get what I want, half the time I don't. Same as God. Fifty-fifty. Same as the four-leaf clover, the horseshoe, the wishing well, and the rabbit's foot. Same as the mojo man, or the voodoo lady who tells you your fortune by squeezing a goat's testicles. It's all the same, fifty-fifty. So just pick a superstition you like, sit back, make a wish, and enjoy yourself.

Tell Me a Story, Daddy

And for those of you who look to the Bible for its moral lessons and literary qualities, I have a couple of other stories I'd like to recommend. You might want to try "The Three Little Pigs." That's a good one, it has a nice happy ending. Then there's "Little Red Riding Hood," although it does have that one X-rated part where the Big Bad Wolf actually eats the grandmother. Which I didn't care for.

And finally, I've always drawn a great deal of moral comfort from

Humpty Dumpty. The part I like best: "All the king's horses and all the king's men couldn't put Humpty Dumpty back together again." That's because there is no Humpty Dumpty. And there is no God. None, not one, never was. No God. Sorry.

BULLETS FOR BELIEVERS

I don't worry about guns in school. You know what I'm happy about? Guns in church! This is a terrific development, isn't it? And finally it's here! I'm so happy. I prayed for this. Oddly enough, I actually prayed for this. And I predicted it, too.

A couple of years ago I said that pretty soon there'd be some fuckin' yo-yo Christian with a Bible and a rifle who'd go apeshit in a church and kill six people. And the media would refer to him as a "disgruntled worshiper." I had no idea it would be a non-Christian. That's a really nice touch.

And my hat is off to the people of Texas for once again leading the way when it comes to the taking of human life. Texans are always in the vanguard of this important activity, and here they are again, setting a good example, showing the way. And finally they're going after the right people: the churchgoers. Let's face it, folks. They're askin' for it. They just want to be with Jesus. Give them a helping hand.

"Wanna see the Lord?" BANG! "Off you go!" BANG! "Are you a Christian?" BANG! "Say hello to Jesus!"

Give 'em a Christian helping hand. Don't think they wouldn't do the same for you. They don't call themselves "Christian soldiers" for nothing.

THE LATE-NIGHT NEWS

* The Supreme Court has reversed a lower court ruling which had let stand a Circuit Court decision allowing an injunction that restrained a defendant from contesting a court order forcing him to show cause why he should not be enjoined from suing his lawyer.

* A government witness who has been demanding twenty-four-hour protection today was given a roll-on deodorant.

* A woman who left her two-year-old son at a day care center yesterday morning says that when she returned to pick him up in the afternoon he was completely grown. Day care officials are crediting the hot-lunch program.

* Here are the results of the Blind Person's Golf Tournament. The winner was Johnny Dowling, with 2,829 strokes, just enough to beat Larry Powell, who lost any chance he may have had when he took a 612 on the final hole, including 115 separate putts.

* A priest who has performed over 300 exorcisms was eaten today by a green boogeyman.

* Twenty-one patrons of a Miami bar suffered numerous gunshot wounds to their feet and ankles as two armed dwarfs ran amok in a downtown tavern. Police say the two tiny men entered the bar riding horsey-back, and things got out of hand when the one on the bottom began to get drunk. In addition to the many foot wounds, extensive damage to the baseboards and electrical outlets was also reported.

✳ Mary Pierce, a woman who claimed she was filled with great love for everyone in the world, was killed today by a man who says he didn't know that.

✳ An unregistered nurse in Phoenix has been arrested for sending obscene get-well cards.

✳ In a bizarre accident, a man who looks like Dean Martin ran over and killed a man who resembles Jerry Lewis. Police spokesman Dave Brewster, who looks like Sammy Davis Jr., said they can find no significance.

✳ The international sword-swallowing championships were held in Sweden yesterday. The judges say the level of competition was especially fierce this year, and they will announce the winners as soon as they are able to remove them from the platform.

✳ Hollywood film star Vicki Lick, and her husband, Mark Stain, have called it quits after a seventeen-minute honeymoon in a pew in the back of the church.

✳ And finally, on the lighter side: *The Guinness Book of World Records* announced today that Harold Twirlfine of Boston has amassed the world's largest collection of chocolate pudding. Twirlfine, a carnival organist, has over 6,000 separate servings on display in his living room. He says that on many of the older servings an almost impenetrable skin has now formed, and in some cases the pudding has pulled completely away from the side of the dish. This has caused the formation of huge crevices where Twirlfine now stores part of his award-winning collection of Raisinets.

But Twirlfine's feat is nothing compared to the largest single mass of Jell-O in the world. That title belongs to the good citizens of Lemon Lime, Minnesota, who last year poured 200,000 boxes of Jell-O powder into the lake. Most of the locals are happy with the results; however, some people diving at the lake's shallow end have injured their heads on large pieces of fruit cocktail.

I NEVER FUCKED A 10

I never fucked a "10," but one night I fucked five 2s. And I think that ought to count. It ought to go down in my record as a positive achievement. But here's something I'm *really* proud of: I never fucked a 1. Well, I never got drunk enough. You have to swallow a lot of chemicals to even *talk* to a 1, much less actually fuck one.

Of course, some guys will fuck anybody. We know that. There's always one guy in every crowd who'll go,

"Hey, guys! Look! Let's fuck her!"

"That's a coat rack, Bob."

"So?"

Some guys will fuck anybody. Not me. Not anymore. Not since herpes and AIDS have been floating around. I'm playin' it safe these days. In fact, I'm being so careful I've stopped jerking off. You never know where your hand has been.

But if you're one of these guys who's still happily bashing the candle, I strongly suggest that you practice safe-sex masturbation. Don't take chances. If you're going to lie in bed and pretend you're fucking some unsuspecting female, for God's sake use a condom. It doesn't take much time out of your fantasy to get up and go over to the dresser and get a condom. She's not goin' anywhere, that's for sure! In fact, if you handle your fantasy correctly, you can probably talk her into goin' over and gettin' the condom for you.

SHORT TAKES

To spice up the Miss America contest, I think they ought to make the losers keep coming back until they win. Wouldn't that get spooky-looking after about thirty years? How would you like to see some seventy-year-old woman in a bathing suit?
   "I'd like everyone in the world to live in peace and harmony."
   "Fine. Sit down before you fall down. And pick up all those fuckin' batons!"

The Muslims observe their sabbath on Friday, the Jews observe on Saturday, and the Christians on Sunday. By the time Monday rolls around God is completely fuckin' worn out.

A lot of times when a package says Open Other End, I purposely open the end where it says that.

Looking back, I realize that my life has been a series of incidents where one person has said to another, "Get this asshole outta here!"

In the doggie dictionary, under "bow wow" it says, "See 'arf arf.'"

You know what you never see? A black guy with buckteeth.

When you look at the average American you realize there's nothing nature enjoys more than a good joke.

The future will soon be a thing of the past.

Can't we silence these Christian athletes who thank Jesus whenever they win and never mention his name when they lose? You never hear them say, "Jesus made me drop the ball," or, "The good Lord tripped me up behind the line of scrimmage." According to Christian athletes, Jesus is undefeated. Meanwhile, a lot of these Holy assholes are in sixth place. Maybe it's one of those miracles we hear so much about.

How come the Midwest is in the United States, and the Mideast is way the fuck overseas somewhere?

On Thanksgiving, most people give thanks for the things they have. Not me, I use Thanksgiving to ask for more things.

I think if a person doesn't immediately answer a public page in an airport, the paging should get increasingly hostile each time it is repeated. Until finally they're saying, "Goddammit, would the miserable jackoff calling himself David Klosterman please pick up the fuckin' white courtesy phone?"

Regarding these famous boxers who make comebacks when they're in their forties, don't you wish one of them would get killed in the ring? Just for a goof?

Here's a good example of practical humor, but you have to be in the right place. When a local television reporter is doing one of those on-the-street reports at the scene of a news story, usually you'll see some onlookers in the background of the shot, waving and trying to be seen on television. Go over and stand with them but don't wave. Just stand perfectly still and, without attracting attention, move your lips, forming the words, "I hope all you stupid fuckin' lip-readers are watching. Why don't you just blow me, you goofy deaf bastards." The TV station will enjoy taking the many phone calls.

I feel sorry for bisexuals. Can you imagine wanting to fuck everybody you meet? Jesus, think of all the phone numbers you'd come home with. Might as well walk around with the white pages under your arm.

Hitler never bothered with restaurant reservations; he just dropped by. And somehow they always found him a table.

I'm glad the *Peanuts* comic strip is finished; I never understood its appeal. I'm looking forward now to the disappearance of *Garfield* and *Doonesbury*.

One of the more pretentious political self-descriptions is "Libertarian." People think it puts them above the fray. It sounds fashionable and, to the uninitiated, faintly dangerous. Actually, it's just one more bullshit political philosophy.

When a plane crashes, and a lot of people die, I always wonder what happens to their frequent flier miles.

Why don't they have waiters in waiting rooms?

I'm glad Americans have trashed their national parks. I especially like that they can't blame it on Jews, blacks or immigrants. It was all done by ignorant, white-slob American tourists.

When you read about all the presidents who had affairs, you feel sorry for Gerald Ford. Apparently no one wanted to fuck him. Except Betty. And she was drunk a lot.

THE FOLLOWING STATEMENT IS TRUE.
THE ABOVE STATEMENT IS FALSE.

Many people think they have to lie to get out of jury duty. You don't have to lie; tell the judge the truth. Tell him you'll make a really good juror because you can spot guilty people just by looking at them. Explain that it has to do with how far apart their eyes are. I guarantee you'll be out of that courtroom before you can say "justice sucks."

You know what I like? A big fire in an apartment house.

Ecology note: In an economy measure, the number of bees in a squadron has been reduced from 35 to 20.

I often wonder if movie directors have credits at the end of their dreams?

SPORTS SHOULD BE FIXED: OVERTIME

Auto Racing

I'd like to improve auto racing. This is a sport that's very big in the South; a perfect marriage of fast cars and slow minds. I think if they want to liven up these races, what they ought to do is have one guy driving in the wrong direction. Simple thing: one guy, moving against the traffic. Maybe with a deer strapped to the hood, and a muffler dragging, makin' sparks. You could also stick three children with rickets in the backseat. Racing fans would appreciate seein' something familiar. Make 'em feel right at home.

Here's another thing that would increase the danger and excitement in these races: You offer an irresistibly huge sum of money—$50 million—to any driver who completes ten laps while driving in reverse. Doesn't matter which direction he's going, with or against the traffic; it's his choice. Fifty million dollars! Some guy would try it. Count on it. In fact, for $50 million you might wind up with everybody in the race goin' backward. Perfect metaphor for the South.

It would also be highly entertaining if the pit crews had to change tires right out on the track, during the race. I'd like to see them try those ten-second pit stops under some *really* stressful conditions. And maybe if you gave 'em longer hoses they could refuel the cars out there, too. Adds a fire hazard, heightens the danger, increases the fun. Just a thought.

And speakin' of danger, isn't it about time they eliminated that boring pace-car shit? They oughta start these races by havin' a couple of Air Force F-18's zippin' around the track, real low. Keep them ten feet off the ground, so the locals can get a real good look. Just watchin' them make those turns would be worth the whole trip to the track. Most of those racing fans are soldier-sniffers and patriotic halfwits anyway, so I'm sure they'd be honored to have the occasional military jet slam into the crowd and send a couple of hundred of them off to be with Jesus.

And, speaking of such possibilities, it goes without saying that the most satisfying part of auto racing is the high number of fatal accidents. So maybe we could do a few things that would increase the frequency of these accidents or, if not, at least make them a little more dangerous.

One idea I had, although it's decidedly offbeat, would be to spray olive oil on the track about every twenty minutes. Not only would this add driving excitement, it would produce an interesting aroma as it mingled with the gasoline fumes, the stale beer, and the pervasive body odor.

Another good accident enhancer would be requiring the drivers to race single file, except for two short, 100-yard passing lanes at each end of the track. Let them jockey for position just as they're heading into the turns. And guess what? This might be the perfect spot for the olive-oil release.

Here's another thrill provider: line the interiors of the cars with plastic explosives rigged to go off when anything touches the exterior of the car. Anything: the wall, another car, debris from the track. Shit, you could probably make it sensitive enough so that one of those heavy clouds of corn-dog farts that come rolling out of the grandstand from time to time would set it off. And just think, the fart cloud itself would probably add several lovely colors to the pyrotechnic display of the explosion.

SEVEN DEATH WISHES

#1 You're in a leather bar with 200 heavily armed, wildly drunk, ex-convict, sadomasochistic butch lesbians. You climb on the bar and say, "Which one of you sweet little cupcakes wants the privilege of being the first in line to suck me off? If you're the lucky one, and you give me a real good blow job, I might do you a favor and throw you a quick fuck and let you cook me a nice meal. C'mon, line up, you repulsive cunts, and I'll change your sexual orientations. I dare you to cut off my balls!"

#2 Walking through the woods one day, you encounter a group of devil worshipers who are disemboweling a small boy. You tell them what they're doing is cowardly, unnatural, and morally wrong, and you're sure they would never try it on a grown-up. Especially one like yourself, who loves Jesus, and always wears his crucifix proudly. You also say that you just arrived from Australia, have no local friends or living relatives, and are planning to establish a Christian church called Fuck Lucifer. Then you order them to stay where they are, because you're leaving to get the police.

#3 You and your wife are the only nonbikers at a Hell's Angels' wedding, where all the others have been drinking, shooting methamphetamine, and smoking PCP for eleven straight days. At the height of the celebration, you whip out your dick, grab the bride's crotch, and shout to the crowd, "I understand you filthy, greasy asshole motorcycle cowards are supposed to be real good at gang rape, but I'll bet you can't fuck like me! Watch this!" You begin ripping the wedding gown off the bride, pointing out that your own wife is a virgin, and that you, yourself, have never been fucked in the ass.

#4 At a white supremacists' convention in remote Idaho, you take the stage wearing an ATF helmet and a Malcolm X T-shirt, and holding a United Nations flag. You perform a rap song that says morally and intellectually inferior white people should submit themselves to black rule and turn over their wives and daughters to black men as a way of apologizing for slavery. You mention that following your recent conversion to Judaism, you have become ashamed of your white skin and would gladly have it removed if you could just find a way to do it.

#5 Three sadistic sex maniacs have entered your house, and they find you naked in the shower. The most coherent among them asks if he can play with your genitals. You lose your temper and say, "Listen, you perverted, lunatic fuck, leave my sex organs alone. And tell your drooling, fruitcake buddies I would rather place my cock in that paper shredder located by the window, or stuff my testicles into the Cuisinart, which is in the kitchen on the right-hand shelf, than let you disgusting degenerates touch my private parts."

#6 While attending the First Communion of a Mafia boss's grandson, you suddenly begin to pistol-whip the boy's mother, screaming, "I'm gonna hit you some more, you ugly dago bitch, and if one of these greasy, dickless criminal morons who call themselves men makes a move on me, I'll break his guinea neck. I'm hungry! Make me some fuckin' spaghetti and go easy on the oil, ya hairy greaseball cunt!"

#7 You're standing in a crowded Harlem bar dressed in the robes of a Ku Klux Klan Grand Dragon, holding a Confederate flag, and singing "Dixie" in a real loud voice with a Mississippi accent. You jump on the bar, shit in the drink of a huge man with numerous razor scars on his face, wipe your ass with a picture of Martin Luther King, and yell at the man, "Hey, boy! Get your momma down here, I want some dark meat. And get that fuckin' jungle-bunny music off the juke box, or I'm gonna start killin' me some boogies!"

Have a nice afterlife.

MONOPOLY

I never did well at Monopoly. I guess I don't have a business mind. Oh, I'd usually manage to own a couple of railroads. And Water Works, of course. I'm not a complete asshole; I know a monopoly when I see one. Everybody needs water. But it always frustrated me that the other guys wouldn't let me build houses on Water Works. They said it was zoning or some shit like that. I think they were jealous that I had vision. The worst fight I ever got into was when I tried to put hotels on the Electric Company. Vision.

As far as other properties were concerned, naturally I'd snap up Baltic Avenue as soon as that became available.

"How much is that son of a bitch? Sixty bucks? Gimme that mother. I gotta have a place to live."

About the best thing I'd ever own would be one or two properties in the light blue series. Maybe Oriental Avenue. No houses, of course. Just an excavation or two. That's about all I ever had on my property—plans. Surveyor's marks. I just couldn't get financing. All my friends would have shopping centers, malls, condominiums, industrial parks. And they liked to rub it in.

"Oh boy, Carlin, you're comin' down my side of the board now! Get ready to pay up!"

"Ohh, no! Please God, gimme a big one."

Then I'd roll.

"Hot shit!! A twelve! Thank you, God! JUMP! JUMP! JUMP! JUMP! JUMP! JUMP! JUMP! JUMP! JUMP! JUMP! JUMP! JUMP! Fuck you, Tony. I ain't even stoppin' on your side. Fuck you and Boardwalk, too!"

"That's all right, Carlin, you'll be around again."

Of course, you can't move your token until you remember which one is yours.

"Which one is mine? Am I the hat? I could swear I was the hat. No, that was yesterday. Wait! I know. The racing car. I'm the racing car. Hey, who's the ship? Richie, are you the ship?"

"No, he's not the ship, I'm the ship. I get the ship every game. Don't even touch the ship." Tony was the biggest guy.

None of them wanted to be the iron. Too feminine.

The worst token to have was the cannon. The big gun. It was the only topheavy token. It kept falling over. Throw the dice anywhere near it, and it fell on its side. And then some anal retentive would say, "Who has the gun? Are you the gun? Would ya pick it up, please? And you, Paulie, are you *in* jail or just visiting? Well, if you're just visiting, put the car on the *side* of the jail, not on the actual jail part."

Some guys really cared. That's why they won.

I never won, but I was always in there at the end. Because I had all the one-dollar bills. Twenty-five hundred dollars in singles, and they needed me to make change.

I would try to borrow money.

"Please, Tony. Just five bucks. I wanna buy some gum."

"Fuck you, Carlin. I'll give you five bucks for Water Works."

"Ten."

"Seven-fifty."

"Tony, they don't have a fifty-cent bill."

"Tough shit. Tear a dollar in half."

No, I wasn't very good at the game, but I spent a lot of time landing on Chance. And I always tried to buy it. I got in more fights trying to buy Chance.

I'd move my token. "... three, four, five, six, seven, eight, nine ... Chance!" Turn over the card, a little man with a hat: "Two hundred dollars for being an asshole."

"Hey, Richie, shuffle those cards, will ya? That's the second time I got that one."

WHEN WILL JESUS BRING THE PORK CHOPS?

GEORGE CARLIN

HYPERION NEW YORK

This book is dedicated to my amazing daughter, Kelly: keeper of the sacred DNA, citizen of the universe, and one of America's few really good Buddhist poker players.

Major funding for this book was made possible by deliberately starving a family of four in Tennessee.

ACKNOWLEDGMENTS

Everlasting thanks to my editor, Gretchen Young, who withstood a last barrage of changes and pulled everything together. She also did an outstanding job protecting me from certain evil people in the publishing company who were jealous of my nice teeth and never stopped plotting against me.

All love to my troll-mate, the sweet Sara Jane.

"Of course the people don't want war. But after all, it's the leaders of the country who determine the policy, and it's always a simple matter to drag the people along whether it's a democracy, a fascist dictatorship, or a parliament, or a communist dictatorship. Voice or no voice, the people can always be brought to the bidding of the leaders. That is easy. All you have to do is tell them they are being attacked, and denounce the pacifists for lack of patriotism, and exposing the country to greater danger."

—HERMANN GÖRING AT THE NUREMBERG TRIALS

"All tears are the same."

—IRISH WOMAN

"So little time. So little to do."

—OSCAR LEVANT

"The main obligation is to amuse yourself."

—S. J. PERELMAN

"Today's another day. Time to play."

—SALLY WADE

PREFACE

I'm an outsider by choice, but not truly. It's the unpleasantness of the system that keeps me out. I'd rather be in, in a good system. That's where my discontent comes from: being forced to choose to stay outside.

My advice: Just keep movin' straight ahead. Every now and then you find yourself in a different place.

George's Holiday Message

Since this book comes out in the fall, I'd like to take advantage of this early opportunity to wish all of you an enjoyable Christmas season and a happy New Year filled with good fortune. Of course, I realize this can't happen for everyone. Some of you are going to die next year, and others will be crippled and maimed in accidents, perhaps even completely paralyzed. Still others will be stricken with diseases that can't be cured, or will be horribly scarred in fires. And let's not forget the robberies and rapes—there'll be lots of them. Therefore, many of you will not get to enjoy the happy and fortunate New Year I'm wishing for you. So just try to do the best you can.

A Note of Appreciation

FROM THE DESK OF:

SPOT WADE

On the occasion of the publication of his new book, *When Will Jesus Bring the Pork Chops?*, I want to wish the author good luck and let the readers know that as my rep and personal assistant—hired to deny rumors of my marriage and subsequent same-sex divorce to Sir Elton John's dog, Arthur, and how now I'm an expectant dad—George Carlin was easy to work with and followed instructions well—although he was often tardy, with lame excuses like "other things to do."

Similar to that of a cocker spaniel, who wants nothin' more than our complete and undivided attention, his personality is pleasant, well-tolerated, and meets with my approval—except for the time when, like Jesus, he forgot to bring the pork chops. But now's not the time to dwell on food. Well . . . maybe it is.

At any rate, I'm proud that one of my employees—especially you, Mr. Carlin—has demonstrated that you're more than just a flash in the pan, as is so often the case with seared tuna. And by the way—as long as we're still talkin' about food—regardin' Jesus bringin' the pork chops, lemme know when they finally arrive. We'll eat them religiously, and enjoy a fine glass of wine.

What are you lookin' at?

A MODERN MAN

I'm a modern man,
digital and smoke-free;
a man for the millennium.

A diversified, multi-cultural,
post-modern deconstructionist;
politically, anatomically and ecologically incorrect.

I've been uplinked and downloaded,
I've been inputted and outsourced.
I know the upside of downsizing,
I know the downside of upgrading.

I'm a high-tech low-life.
A cutting-edge, state-of-the-art,
bi-coastal multi-tasker,
and I can give you a gigabyte in a nanosecond.

I'm new-wave, but I'm old-school;
and my inner child is outward-bound.

I'm a hot-wired, heat-seeking,
warm-hearted cool customer;
voice-activated and bio-degradable.

I interface with my database;
my database is in cyberspace;
so I'm interactive, I'm hyperactive,
and from time to time I'm radioactive.

Behind the eight ball, ahead of the curve,
ridin' the wave, dodgin' the bullet,
pushin' the envelope.

I'm on point, on task, on message,
and off drugs.

I've got no need for coke and speed;
I've got no urge to binge and purge.

I'm in the moment, on the edge,
over the top, but under the radar.

A high-concept, low-profile,
medium-range ballistic missionary.

A street-wise smart bomb.
A top-gun bottom-feeder.

I wear power ties, I tell power lies,
I take power naps, I run victory laps.

I'm a totally ongoing, big-foot, slam-dunk
rainmaker with a pro-active outreach.

A raging workaholic, a working rageaholic;
out of rehab and in denial.

I've got a personal trainer,
a personal shopper,
a personal assistant,
and a personal agenda.

You can't shut me up;
you can't dumb me down.

'Cause I'm tireless, and I'm wireless.
I'm an alpha-male on beta-blockers.

I'm a non-believer,
I'm an over-achiever;
Laid-back and fashion-forward.
Up-front, down-home;
low-rent, high-maintenance.

I'm super-sized, long-lasting,
high-definition, fast-acting,
oven-ready and built to last.

A hands-on, footloose, knee-jerk head case;
prematurely post-traumatic,
and I have a love child who sends me hate-mail.

But I'm feeling, I'm caring,
I'm healing, I'm sharing.
A supportive, bonding, nurturing
primary-care giver.

My output is down, but my income is up.
I take a short position on the long bond,
and my revenue stream has its own cash flow.

I read junk mail, I eat junk food,
I buy junk bonds, I watch trash sports.

I'm gender-specific, capital-intensive,
user-friendly and lactose-intolerant.

I like rough sex; I like tough love.
I use the f-word in my e-mail.
And the software on my hard drive
is hard-core—no soft porn.

I bought a microwave at a mini-mall.
I bought a mini-van at a mega-store.
I eat fast food in the slow lane.

I'm toll-free, bite-size, ready-to-wear,
and I come in all sizes.

A fully equipped, factory-authorized,
hospital-tested, clinically proven,
scientifically formulated medical miracle.

I've been pre-washed, pre-cooked, pre-heated,
pre-screened, pre-approved, pre-packaged,
post-dated, freeze-dried, double-wrapped
and vacuum-packed.

And . . . I have unlimited broadband capacity.

I'm a rude dude, but I'm the real deal.
Lean and mean.
Cocked, locked and ready to rock;
rough, tough and hard to bluff.

I take it slow, I go with the flow;
I ride with the tide, I've got glide in my stride.

Drivin' and movin', sailin' and spinnin';
jivin' and groovin', wailin' and winnin'.

I don't snooze, so I don't lose.
I keep the pedal to the metal

and the rubber on the road.
I party hearty, and lunchtime is crunch time.

I'm hangin' in, there ain't no doubt;
and I'm hangin' tough.
Over and out.

EUPHEMISMS: It's a Whole New Language

Euphemistic language turns up in many areas of American life in a variety of situations. Not all euphemisms are alike, but they have one thing in common: They obscure meaning rather than enhance it; they shade the truth. But they exist for various reasons.

Sometimes they simply replace a word that makes people uncomfortable. For instance, the terms *white meat, dark meat* and *drumstick* came into use because in Victorian times people didn't like to mention certain body parts. No one at the dinner table really wanted to hear Uncle Herbert say, "Never mind the *thighs*, Margaret, let me have one of those nice, juicy *breasts.*" It would've made them uncomfortable.

And at the same time, for the same reason, *belly* became *stomach*. But even *stomach* sounded too intimate, so they began saying *tummy*. It's actually a bit sad.

I first became aware of euphemisms when I was nine years old. I was in the living room with my mother and my aunt Lil when I mentioned that Lil had a *mole* on her face. My mother was quick to point out that Lil didn't have a mole, she had a *beauty mark*.

That confused me because, looking at Lil, the beauty mark didn't seem to be working. And it confused me further, because my uncle John also had a brown thing on his face, and it was clearly not a beauty mark. And so on that day, I discovered that on some people what appeared to be moles were actually beauty marks. And as it turned out, they were the same people whose *laugh lines* looked a lot like *crow's-feet.*

By the way, that whole beauty-mark scam worked so well that some women routinely began using eyebrow pencils to apply fake beauty marks—a "fake mole" being something no self-respecting woman would ever think of giving herself. Somehow, I can't imagine Elizabeth Taylor turning to Joan Crawford and saying, "Lend me your eyebrow pencil, Joanie, I'm gonna put a fake mole on my face."

By the way, it was only a few years after the Aunt Lil incident that I took comfort in the fact that some people apparently thought my ugly *pimples* were nothing more than minor *skin blemishes.*

Another role euphemisms play is to simply put a better face on things, to dress up existing phrases that sound too negative. *Nonprofit* became *not-for-profit,* because nonprofit sounded too much as though someone didn't know what they were doing. Not-for-profit makes it clear that there was never any intention of making a profit in the first place.

But some words that are euphemized aren't even vaguely negative, they're merely considered too ordinary. For that reason, many things that used to be *free* are now *complimentary.* Asking the hotel clerk if the newspapers are free makes you sound like a mooch, but "Are the newspapers complimentary?" allows you to retain some small bit of dignity. This is the reason some hotels offer their guests *complimentary continental breakfasts,* while others give their customers *free doughnuts.*

If you're one who would enjoy a closer look at euphemisms, you'll find a number of sections in the book that will interest you. I broke the euphemisms into segments, because they play such a large and varied role in American speech. And I call it The New Language, because it's certainly new to me; I know I didn't grow up with it. And that's my larger point: that it's gotten worse over time. There were probably a few early signs I noticed, but I knew the problem was getting serious when I began to hear ordinary people refer to *ideas* as *concepts*.

More to come.

STIFF UPPER LIP, YOU KNOW

Imagine two different commercial airliners taking long, fatal plunges directly into the ground from high altitudes. One is a British Airways plane filled with staid English diplomats and upper-class landed gentry. The other plane is Alitalia, filled with uneducated Sicilian, Greek and Turkish peasants. As the two planes dive toward certain destruction, which one do you think will have the louder screaming and the more colorful praying, cursing and blasphemy? You get one guess. Hint: It isn't the British plane.

Eye Blaster: Get One Now

Are your eyes dry and itchy? It's possible you may have dry, itchy eyes. Don't take a chance. Call now for Eye Blaster, a special, self-powered unit that blasts hot, refreshing steam directly into the eyes to relieve symptoms fast. Just plug in the Eye Blaster and wait forty-five minutes for full heat and steam pressure to build up. Then blast the scalding hot steam directly into your eyes for thirty to forty minutes. Submerge your head immediately in ice water for fifteen minutes, then repeat the steam treatment. Repeat these steps seven times and then take a breather. Do not use more than fifteen times in one twenty-four-hour period. Children under five should not use Eye Blaster unsupervised. When using on pets, tie pet to a chair before blasting. Safe for old people. Doctor approved, but not eye doctors. Call now.

HAND ME MY PURSE

Boxing is an activity in which each of two men, by delivering a series of repeated, sharp blows to the head, attempts to render the other senseless, leaving him lying on the floor, unable to act rationally, defend himself or even stand up. If one of the two men is knocked down and beaten into an only partially blank and helpless mental state, the other is made to stand aside and the contest is halted momentarily, while the damaged man regains just enough strength to stand up and have the beating continue—to the point where he is again lying on the floor, this time completely immobile and functionless. Afterward, the two men embrace in a display of good sportsmanship.

REMEMBER YOUR UNCLE JOHN?

Hi Billy. I'm Uncle John. I came up to say goodnight. You remember your Uncle John, don't you? You remember the time I took you down to the beach and we set the hot dog stand on fire and three people died? Wasn't that fun? Remember runnin' away from the police? And how we hid in the sewer and Uncle John got poo-poo all over him? And he wiped it on your coat? You remember? And then I took you to the bar and got drunk and vomited on the jukebox? And sparks started flyin' out of the jukebox and a fire started? And all the people were screamin'? Remember that? Remember the screamin'? And the ambulances? Wasn't that fun?

And do you remember that other time? The time I took you to the circus? The lion got loose and ate a monkey? Wasn't that fun? And they had to kill the lion? And the monkeys got real sad, so they had to kill the monkeys, too? Wasn't that fun? And then the man fell off the trapeze and smashed into the ground, and they had to kill him? And all the other trapeze people got real sad and they had to kill them too? Hah? Wasn't that fun?

Why are you cryin', Billy? Please don't cry. If you stop cryin', I'll take you to the rodeo. Wouldn't that be fun? Maybe someone will get trampled, or gored. They've got horsies and cows, too, you know. Maybe they'll have to kill a horsie. Or a cow. And if they kill a cow, maybe we'll get to eat him in a hamburger. Wouldn't that be fun? Please don't cry.

Remember the time you fell outta my car? Remember, you were lookin' out the window, and we went around a corner real fast to keep from hittin' that lady? And you went flyin' out the window and hit the pole, head first? And the doctor had to sew your head up with a big needle? I've got a boat now, Billy. You wanna go out on my boat? I promise I'll be careful. Are you asleep yet? Billy? Please stop cryin'.

COUNT THE SUPERFLUOUS REDUNDANT PLEONASTIC TAUTOLOGIES

My fellow countrymen, I speak to you as coequals, knowing you are deserving of the honest truth. And let me warn you in advance, my subject matter concerns a serious crisis caused by an event in my past history: the execution-style killing of a security guard on a delivery truck. At that particular point in time,

I found myself in a deep depression, making mental errors which seemed as though they might threaten my future plans. I am not over-exaggerating.

I needed a new beginning, so I decided to pay a social visit to a personal friend with whom I share the same mutual objectives and who is one of the most unique individuals I have ever personally met. The end result was an unexpected surprise. When I reiterated again to her the fact that I needed a fresh start, she said I was exactly right; and, as an added plus, she came up with a final solution that was absolutely perfect.

Based on her past experience, she felt we needed to join together in a common bond for a combined total of twenty-four hours a day, in order to find some new initiatives. What a novel innovation! And, as an extra bonus, she presented me with the free gift of a tuna fish. Right away I noticed an immediate positive improvement. And although my recovery is not totally complete, the sum total is I feel much better now knowing I am not uniquely alone.

THE CONTROL FREAKS

Hello. We're the ones who control your lives. We make the decisions that affect all of you. Isn't it interesting to know that those who run your lives would have the nerve to tell you about it in this manner? Suffer, you fools. We know everything you do, and we know where you go. What do you think the cameras are for? And the global-positioning satellites? And the Social Security numbers? You belong to us. And it can't be changed. Sign your petitions, walk your picket lines, bring your lawsuits, cast your votes, and write those stupid letters to whomever you please; you won't change a thing. Because we control your lives. And we have plans for you. Go back to sleep.

THEY CAME FROM OUT OF THE SKY

I find it discouraging—and a bit depressing—when I notice the unequal treatment afforded by the media to UFO believers on the one hand, and on the other, to those who believe in an invisible supreme being who inhabits the sky. Especially as the latter belief applies to the whole Jesus-Messiah-Son-of-God fable.

You may have noticed that, in the media, UFO believers are usually referred to as *buffs*, a term used to diminish and marginalize them by relegating them to the ranks of hobbyists and mere enthusiasts. They are made to seem like kooks and quaint dingbats who have the nerve to believe that, in an observable universe of trillions upon trillions of stars, and most likely many hundreds of billions of potentially inhabitable planets, some of those planets may have produced life-forms capable of doing things that we can't do.

On the other hand those who believe in an eternal, all-powerful being, a being who demands to be loved and adored unconditionally and who punishes and rewards according to his whims are thought to be worthy, upright, credible people. This, in spite of the large numbers of believers who are clearly close-minded fanatics.

To my way of thinking, there is every bit as much evidence for the existence of UFOs as there is for the existence of God. Probably far more. At least in the case of UFOs there have been countless taped and filmed—and, by the way, unexplained—sightings from all over the world, along with documented radar evidence seen by experienced military and civilian radar operators.

This does not even begin to include the widespread testimony of not only highly trained, experienced military and civilian pilots who are selected for their jobs, in part, for their above-average eyesight and mental stability, but also of equally well-trained, experienced law-enforcement officers. Such pilots and law-enforcement people are known to be serious, sober individuals who would have quite a bit to lose were they to be associated with anything resembling kooky, outlandish beliefs. Nonetheless, they have taken the risk of revealing their experiences because they are convinced they have seen something objectively real that they consider important.

All of these accounts are ignored by the media.

Granted, the world of UFO-belief has its share of kooks, nuts and fringe people, but have you ever listened to some of these religious true-believers? Have you ever heard of any extreme, bizarre behavior and outlandish claims associated with religious zealots? Could any of them be considered kooks, nuts or dingbats? A fair person would have to say yes.

But the marginal people in these two groups don't matter in this argument. What matters is the prejudice and superstition built into the media coverage of the two sets of beliefs. One is treated reverently and accepted as received truth, the other is treated laughingly and dismissed out of hand.

As evidence of the above premise, I offer one version of a typical television news story heard each year on the final Friday of Lent:

"Today is Good Friday, observed by Christians worldwide as a day that commemorates the crucifixion of Jesus Christ, the Son of God, whose death redeemed the sins of mankind."

Here is the way it *should* be written:

"Today is Good Friday, observed worldwide by Jesus buffs as the day on which the popular, bearded cultural figure, sometimes referred to as *The Messiah*, was allegedly crucified and—according to legend—died for mankind's so-called sins. Today kicks off a 'holy' weekend that culminates on Easter Sunday, when, it is widely believed, this dead 'savior'—who also, by the way, claimed to be the son of a sky-dwelling, invisible being known as God—mysteriously 'rose from the dead.'

"According to the legend, by volunteering to be killed and actually going through with it, Jesus saved every person who has ever lived—and every person who ever *will* live—from an eternity of suffering in a fiery region popularly known as hell, providing—so the story goes—that the person to be 'saved' firmly believes this rather fanciful tale."

That would be an example of unbiased news reporting. Don't wait around for it to happen. The aliens will land first.

THE TWO COMMANDMENTS

I have a problem with the Ten Commandments. Here it is: Why are there ten? We don't need that many. I think the list of commandments was deliberately and artificially inflated to get it up to ten. It's clearly a padded list.

Here's how it happened: About five thousand years ago, a bunch of religious and political hustlers got together to figure out how they could control people and keep them in line. They knew people were basically stupid and would believe anything they were told, so these guys announced that God— God personally—had given one of them a list of ten commandments that he wanted everyone to follow. They claimed the whole thing took place on a mountaintop, when no one else was around.

But let me ask you something: When these guys were sittin' around the tent makin' all this up, why did they pick ten? Why ten? Why not nine, or eleven? I'll tell you why. Because ten sounds important. Ten sounds official. They knew if they tried eleven, people wouldn't take them seriously. People would say, "What're you kiddin' me? The Eleven Commandments? Get the fuck outta here!"

But ten! Ten sounds important. Ten is the basis for the decimal system; it's a decade. It's a psychologically satisfying number: the top ten; the ten most wanted; the ten best-dressed. So deciding on ten commandments was clearly a marketing decision. And it's obviously a bullshit list. In truth, it's a political document, artificially inflated to sell better.

I'm going to show you how you can reduce the number of commandments and come up with a list that's a bit more logical and realistic. We'll start with the first three, and I'll use the Roman Catholic version because those are the ones I was fed as a little boy.

- I AM THE LORD THY GOD, THOU SHALT NOT HAVE STRANGE GODS BEFORE ME.
- THOU SHALT NOT TAKE THE NAME OF THE LORD THY GOD IN VAIN.
- THOU SHALT KEEP HOLY THE SABBATH.

Okay, right off the bat, the first three commandments—pure bullshit. "Sabbath day," "Lord's name," "strange gods." Spooky language. Spooky language designed to scare and control primitive people. In no way does superstitious mumbo jumbo like this apply to the lives of intelligent, civilized humans in the twenty-first century. You throw out the first three commandments, and you're down to seven.

- HONOR THY FATHER AND MOTHER.

This commandment is about obedience and respect for authority; in other words it's simply a device for controlling people. The truth is, obedience and respect should not be granted automatically. They should be earned. They should be based on the parents' (or the authority figure's) performance. Some parents deserve respect. Most of them don't. Period. We're down to six.

Now, in the interest of logic—something religion has a really hard time with—I'm going to skip around the list a little bit:

- THOU SHALT NOT STEAL.
- THOU SHALT NOT BEAR FALSE WITNESS.

Stealing and lying. Actually, when you think about it, these two commandments cover the same sort of behavior: dishonesty. Stealing and lying. So we don't need two of them. Instead, we combine these two and call it "Thou shalt not be dishonest." Suddenly we're down to five.

And as long as we're combining commandments I have two others that belong together:

- THOU SHALT NOT COMMIT ADULTERY.
- THOU SHALT NOT COVET THY NEIGHBOR'S WIFE.

Once again, these two prohibit the same sort of behavior; in this case, marital infidelity. The difference between them is that coveting takes place in the mind. And I don't think you should outlaw fantasizing about someone else's wife, otherwise what's a guy gonna think about when he's flogging his dong?

But marital fidelity is a good idea, so I suggest we keep the idea and call this commandment "Thou shalt not be unfaithful." Suddenly we're down to four.

And when you think about it further, honesty and fidelity are actually parts of the same overall value. So, in truth, we could combine the two honesty commandments with the two fidelity commandments, and, using positive language instead of negative, call the whole thing "Thou shalt always be honest and faithful." And now we're down to three.

· THOU SHALT NOT COVET THY NEIGHBOR'S GOODS.

This one is just plain stupid. Coveting your neighbor's goods is what keeps the economy going: Your neighbor gets a vibrator that plays "O Come All Ye Faithful," you want to get one, too. Coveting creates jobs. Leave it alone.

You throw out coveting and you're down to two now: the big, combined honesty/fidelity commandment, and the one we haven't mentioned yet:

· THOU SHALT NOT KILL.

Murder. The Fifth Commandment. But, if you give it a little thought, you realize that religion has never really had a problem with murder. Not really. More people have been killed in the name of God than for any other reason.

To cite a few examples, just think about Irish history, the Middle East, the Crusades, the Inquisition, our own abortion-doctor killings and, yes, the World Trade Center to see how seriously religious people take Thou Shalt Not Kill. Apparently, to religious folks—especially the truly devout—murder is negotiable. It just depends on who's doing the killing and who's getting killed.

And so, with all of this in mind, folks, I offer you my revised list of the Two Commandments:

First:

· THOU SHALT ALWAYS BE HONEST AND FAITHFUL, ESPECIALLY TO THE PROVIDER OF THY NOOKIE.

And second:

· THOU SHALT TRY REAL HARD NOT TO KILL ANYONE, UNLESS, OF COURSE, THEY PRAY TO A DIFFERENT INVISIBLE AVENGER THAN THE ONE YOU PRAY TO.

Two is all you need, folks. Moses could have carried them down the hill in his pocket. And if we had a list like that, I wouldn't mind that brilliant judge in Alabama displaying it prominently in his courthouse lobby. As long he included one additional commandment:

· THOU SHALT KEEP THY RELIGION TO THYSELF!!!

THE FILTHY, DIRTY NEWS

ANNOUNCER: It's six o'clock, time for *Action-6 News* with Leslie Crotchmonger and Dick Hopshteckler. Here's Leslie with today's top stories.

L: Good evening. First the headlines:

· A giant man shits on Philadelphia.
· An old man shows his soiled anus to a waitress at an Olive Garden.
· A small dog eats a man's balls and dies.
· A crippled couple is arrested for fucking on a roller coaster.

Now the stories behind the headlines: In Philadelphia today, a giant man dropped his huge pants and squatted over Independence Hall. He then unleashed a . . .

(Dick reaches over and grabs Leslie's script.)

D: Fuck you, you cunt, you did the headlines.

L: Lick my asshole, you dimwitted prick. My name comes first on the opening announcement.

D: That's because you blew the news director.

L: At least I didn't blow a homeless guy who has the siff.

D: Oh yeah? Well, he wouldn't have the siff if you didn't fuck him in the Dumpster out back.

L: Eat my box.

D: Not without a gas mask, Dearie.

L: Keep fuckin' with me, Little Dick, and I'll tell your wife about the Cub Scouts you went down on.

D: Leslie, the way we're acting is crazy. Let's put all this petty, personal stuff behind us and act like professionals. What do you say?

L: Good idea. I agree.

D: So, what's coming up at six o'clock?

L: How the fuck should I know? What do you think I am, a fuckin' psychic?

D: No way! If you were psychic, you would've known you were gonna wind up with labia that hang down like satchel handles.

L: Thanks, Dick, that's real clever. By the way, doesn't that get to you? Being called Dick?

D: Being called Dick is a lot better than being called Dick Licker.

L: Eat shit, raisin balls! I hope you swallow a turd. Well, folks, that's it for *Action-6 News*. Don't miss *News at Eleven* tonight as Rod Holder interviews a nun who's been receiving obscene phone calls from a man who says he wants to chew her bush during a funeral mass.

ANNOUNCER: *Action-6 News* has been brought to you by First Bank, meeting community needs since 1849. First Bank: Experience Out the Ass.

THAT'S THE SPIRIT

I don't understand these people who call themselves spiritual advisors. Franklin Graham, the unfortunate son of Billy Graham, is George Bush's spiritual advisor. Bill Clinton had Jesse Jackson.

Here's the part I don't understand: How can someone else advise you on your spirit? Isn't spirit an intensely personal, internal thing? Doesn't it, by its very nature, elude definition, much less analysis? What kind of advice could some drone who has devoted his life to the self-deception of religion possibly give you about your spirit? It sounds like a hustle to me.

GUYS CALLED JUNIOR

I have no respect for any man who allows people to call him Junior; I immediately think he's a chump and a loser. To me, Junior means lower than, lesser than, beneath. Putting "Junior" on a kid's name is just a way for a father to control and demean his son and prevent him from having an identity of his own. I don't like that whole cult-of-the-father thing in the first place. But apparently some guys' self-esteem is just low enough that they accept it. I have no respect for them.

Pro sports is full of these hopelessly Daddy-addicted athletes who wouldn't think of taking a shit without their fathers' approval. I especially have no respect for the ones whose fathers coached them in high school or college, or whose fathers played the same position they did. When I hear the sons of coaches and former athletes talking on television, they sound to me like parent-pleasers and ass-kissers. Why don't they grow up?

GUYS & DOLLS:PART 1

Ladies First

I notice a lot of this "comedy" they have on television is about relationships. Do you ever see this stuff? Relationship comedy? Well, I don't know much about relationships, but over the years I've noticed a few things about the two sexes, and I'd like to discuss them. Men and women: the big, hairy, noisy male creatures, and the smaller, smoother, but nonetheless also quite noisy, female creatures.

Here's all you need to know about men and women: Women are crazy, men are stupid. And the main reason women are crazy is that men are stupid. It's not the only reason, but it's a big one. And by the way, if you don't think men are stupid, check the newspaper. Ninety-nine percent of all the truly horrifying shit going on in this world was initiated, established, perpetrated, enabled or continued by men. And that includes the wave and the high five, two of history's truly low points.

But as I say, besides knowing that men are stupid, it's also important to remember that women are crazy. And if you don't think women are crazy, ask a man. That's the one thing men aren't stupid about; they know for sure, way down deep in their hearts, that women are straight-out fuckin' nuts.

But it doesn't just happen; it isn't an accident. Women have good reason to be nuts, the main one being that in the course of life, compared with men, they have far more to put up with; they bear greater burdens. Think of it this way: In the Big Cosmic Cafeteria, as human beings move down the chow line of life and reach that section where the shit is being spooned out, women are given several extra portions.

And please understand, my motives here are not selfish or personal. I'm not saying all this stuff to get in good with women—although an occasional blow job would be nice. But it's not a requirement. It's optional. BJO: Blow Job Optional. No, I just think it should be evident to any person who's being honest—and thinking clearly—that women carry a lot more of life's baggage than men.

To begin with, they're smaller and weaker, so they get slapped, punched, raped, abused and, in general, get the shit beaten out of them on a rather regular basis. By men, of course, who are stronger. If women were stronger, this wouldn't be happening. Men would not raise a hand if they thought the balance was more equal; they would back down quickly. Then again, if women were stronger, they would probably be beating the shit out of men just for the fun of it. It's only fair.

APPEARANCE IS EVERYTHING

Another major problem for women: They have to look good all the time—or at least they think they do. So they'll be attractive to their male protectors. "Gotta look good tonight, Joey's gonna beat the shit out of me. Maybe I can get a nice kick in the fuckin' mouth. Gotta look my best."

And looking one's female best requires a lot of things. Start with cosmetics. Just think of all the products and procedures a woman is forced to deal with in the world of cosmetics: cleansers, toners, foundation, blush, face powder, lipstick, lip gloss, lip liner, eyeliner, eye shadow, eyebrow pencil, mascara, nail polish, nail polish remover, manicures, pedicures, fake fingernails, fake eyelashes . . .

GIMME SOME SKIN

. . . face cream, neck cream, eye cream, thigh cream, foot cream, day cream, night cream, cold cream, wrinkle remover, makeup remover, hand lotions, body lotions, bath oils, bath beads, shower gels, bubble baths, scented baths, perfumes, colognes, toilet water, astringents, moisturizers, emulsions, exfoliants, peels, scrubs, depilatories, body wraps, facial masks . . .

HAIR HAIR!

. . . shampoos, conditioners, bleaches, dyes, rinses, tints, perms, straighteners, wigs, falls, rats, extensions, combs, barrettes, bobby pins, hairpins, hairnets, hair curlers, scrunchies, ribbons, bows, tiebacks, headbands . . .

PROCEDURES

. . . streaking, frosting, teasing, spraying, moussing, blow drying, cutting, layering, curling, eyelash curling, eyebrow plucking, armpit shaving, leg shaving, crotch shaving, crotch waxing, leg waxing, eyebrow waxing . . .

And a purse! A big fuckin' purse so she can carry all this shit around with her. Especially the makeup, which must be close at hand at all times. "Gotta have my makeup. In case I run into Joey and he wants to beat the shit outta me. I gotta look my best. Maybe he'll punch me repeatedly in the kidneys and the stomach so it doesn't mark up my face. He's so thoughtful."

I HAVE NOTHING TO WEAR

And, my friend, I hope you're aware that when we talk about women looking good, we're also talking about clothing. Clothing is what generates all this shopping shit that occupies so much of a woman's time. Because the truth is, women have to buy, own and wear an unbelievably bewildering number of garments:

TAKE IT OFF!!!

Slips, half-slips, camisoles, thongs, panties, pantyhose, stockings, half hose, knee-highs, anklets, socks, leg warmers, garter belts, girdles, corsets, training bras, padded bras, sports bras, nursing bras, push-up bras, strapless bras, Wonderbras, bustiers, teddies, petticoats, peignoirs, negligees, nightgowns, shorties, muumuus, body stockings . . .

TOP TO BOTTOM

. . . blouses, sweaters, jerseys, pullovers, halter tops, miniskirts, maxiskirts, slacks, suits, sunsuits, business suits, pants suits, culottes, capris, shorts, short shorts, hot pants, formal gowns, bridal gowns, evening gowns, street dresses, sundresses, cocktail dresses, housedresses, housecoats, winter coats, fall coats, spring coats, hats and scarves . . .

BAUBLES & BANGLES

. . . brooches, pins, necklaces, pendants, medallions, lockets, bracelets, ankle bracelets, earrings, wedding rings, engagement rings, friendship rings, thumb rings, toe rings and (optional, of course) nipple, nose and labia rings.

And let's not even begin to talk about shoes. Oh, God! Sorry girls! I take it back. But at least let's keep it brief: tennis shoes, sandals, open-toes, slingbacks, mules, wedgies, flats, half-heels and . . . high heels. High heels that damage a woman's feet, ankles and knees, but make her ass and legs look great, so how can you blame a guy for the occasional rape? "Hey, the bitch was askin' for it, she was wearin' high heels."

DOWN THE AISLE

Now, generally, all this obsession with appearance has one purpose. It's supposed to lead to romance and—it is devoutly wished by some—a wedding. A wedding is another one of those good deals women get: The man "takes a wife," the woman is "given away," her family pays for the whole thing, and everyone stands around hoping she gets pregnant immediately.

KNOCK KNOCK!

Pregnant! Hey, another terrific treat for the gals! A chance to gain forty pounds, puke in the morning, walk like a duck, get sore tits and develop a nice case of hemorrhoids. What a deal! And such attractive clothing. Plus, she can't get up off the couch without help. Well, it's her own fault. This wouldn't have happened if she had taken her birth contol pill or used her diaphragm. Notice: her pill, her diaphragm.

AND BABY MAKES WORK

But think of how fulfilling it can be. After all, now she has a baby; a baby she gets to raise practically alone. And if she decides to be a stay-at-home mom, she gets to cook, clean, sew, scrub, scour, wax, wash, dry, iron, do the shopping, drive the van and entertain the guests. She's a housewife! An unpaid, in-family domestic servant. Admittedly, that description is a bit more in line with the old model. The new model is so much better: She "gets a fuckin' job so she can be bringin' somethin' in." But, somehow, she still winds up being an unpaid, in-family domestic servant—after she gets home from the job.

You know, the job? Where she gets paid less than men for the same work, does not rise beyond a certain level in the company and gets harassed all day long by some oversexed moron with a lump in his pants.

Probably better just to stay home where she doesn't have to be bothered with that pesky paycheck crap, and there's none of that nonsense about Social Security, pension plans and unemployment money in case of divorce. Just alimony and child support . . . if the ex-husband can be located. The ex who probably thought she was looking a little used up and dumped her for someone whose milk glands hadn't sagged yet.

Can't forget those milk glands, can we, girls? Tits! Two tits, sticking straight out of your chest; in some cases sticking *straight* out. Well, for a few years, anyway. Yes, girls, just by virtue of being female, you get to walk around all your life with two vulnerable milk glands hanging out in front of you like lanterns. And if, somehow, you should get the idea that men don't approve of the size and shape of those milk glands, you'll find plenty of social pressure to have them artificially "enhanced." Such enhancement usually will be performed and supervised by men.

Here's another physical treat for females: periods! Cramping, bloating and bleeding five days a month. Fifteen percent of the time. And you can add the time spent with premenstrual syndrome. PMS. Men gave it that name. If women had named it, it would be called "My several days of shrieking and crying and depression, just before my several days of bleeding, cramping and bloating." Men don't quite see it from that angle. Men experience PMS as a problem for them. "What's the matter, Joey? You don't look so good." "Ahhhh, my wife's got the PMS."

Here are some more special female advantages in case you haven't had enough: pap smears, mammograms, hysterectomies, mastectomies, miscarriages, abortions, labor pains, childbirth pain, episiotomies, stretch marks and breast-feeding. And postpartum depression. Can't imagine why she wouldn't feel good. And just to top it all off, menopause. Menopause! More strange behavior and exciting physical sensations.

And in exchange for all this, in exchange for all this abuse from nature, what is the woman's payoff? Why, she's allowed to get into the lifeboat first. At least theoretically. How often do you think that really happens? Oh, and let's not forget, many men are quite willing to hold the door open for her. In fact, some men are quite impressed with their willingness to do this; they brag about it: "Yeah, I beat the shit out of her a lot, but when she runs from one room to the other, I always hold the door open."

I'll tell you what a bad deal women got: They're in the majority on this planet, and they still wound up with the shitty end of the stick. That's how big a hosing they got.

Oh, and one other inequity I neglected to mention; very unequal. But this one works in women's favor: They live longer than men. And remember this happens in spite of all the shit they have to put up with. So who do you think is tougher? Men or women? Why don't you guess. And don't forget, women have the huge added burden of having to put up with men.

FREE BREAST EXAMINATIONS

As a public service, the Hell's Angels will be conducting free breast examinations this weekend at their clubhouse behind the Chrome Sprocket Bar. If you prefer privacy, the Bikers' Mobile Breast Patrol will be happy to perform their services in the privacy of your bedroom. Pelvic examinations and pap tests are also available but usually take a little longer.

IT'S A FEMALE PROBLEM

Beside a dusty road, in the open air, a physically repulsive man dressed in filthy doctor clothes stands at a rusted out examination table wearing a coal miner's hat and heavy work gloves. A woman lies in front of him on the examination table, her legs extending out from under a torn sheet, the ankles resting in stirrups. Nearby, an unattractive "nurse" sits at a desk picking her nose and wiping it on a lamp. Women squat nearby on tree stumps, reading magazines, waiting their turns. Just above this tableau is a large sign reading DISCOUNT ROADSIDE GYNECOLOGY.

SMOOTH FLIGHT

I really enjoyed my recent airplane trip to Africa; everything went just perfectly. I had no trouble at all making reservations a month in advance, and I had my tickets in hand, including seat selection, a week before the flight. I even ordered a special vegetarian meal. I left home early the day of the flight and arrived at the airport with several minutes to spare. My friend dropped me off at the curb and left immediately.

My one bag, which was a light one, was easy to carry and did not have to be checked. I was able to take it on board and save time at each end. I walked into the terminal. There was no line at the security area, my carry-on bag passed inspection, and I didn't ring any bells walking through the metal detector. Looking for my gate number on the departures board and spotting it without breaking stride, I headed for Gate 1, the nearest gate. With just a few minutes left until takeoff, I walked the few steps to the gate and boarded the plane.

The seat I had reserved was right next to the window, and the seat next to me was unoccupied; plenty of room to spread out. I was in first class with only three other passengers. The two female flight attendants were pleasant . . . and very attractive. They said my special meal was on board. I had plenty of legroom, and all my seat controls worked perfectly; seat-back tilt, contour button, leg rest, light switch, even the stereo controls.

Everything continued flawlessly. The plane's door was closed exactly on time, and we taxied immediately to the end of the runway. Pausing barely an instant, we began our takeoff roll, which sounded and felt extremely smooth. There was very little vibration; just a steady increase in power and speed as we became airborne and gently glided up. I felt no bumps or strain, and we quickly leveled off to a quiet cruise speed at our assigned altitude. Then the plane went into a steep dive and crashed into the ground, killing all but two of us.

Fortunately, my cosurvivor was a fantastic-looking woman; a registered nurse who had taken survival courses. After a quick check, we realized neither of us was hurt, and then I remembered I still had two joints tucked into my sock. We got high and made love several times. The sex was great for both of us and we promised to see each other often if we somehow managed to get out of there. The only condition on her part was that there be no commitment of any kind between us; she wanted to be independent. I agreed.

After a short time, we found some sandwiches and beer. We ate and drank and laughed for about an hour and then we noticed that a signal-flare gun had landed nearby. We fired off one flare, and, almost immediately, saw a small private plane flying overhead. They spotted us and began to circle. They made a low pass at us, waggling their wings, and then headed off, presumably to get help. Thank God, everything was still going smoothly.

That's when the gorilla showed up.

IF LOOKS COULD KILL

I don't think it's right that ugly women should be allowed to get plastic surgery and get fixed up to look real nice. I think if you're born ugly you ought to stay that way. That should be it. It's not right to let people get fixed up. It's creepy to think that you could possibly find yourself fucking some woman you picked up because you thought she was great-looking, but underneath she's really ugly. She got her nose fixed, her lips, her eyes; she got nipped and tucked and liposuctioned, and the surgeon did a good job—he didn't overdo it—and now she looks really great. But underneath it all, she's horrible-looking and you're actually fucking a pig; someone you wouldn't even ask for change of a dollar if you could see her real face. It's not right. Ugliness should be a permanent condition.

THE CONTINUING STORY OF
MARY & JOSEPH: "IT'S A BOY"

MARY: Joe, we're gonna have a baby.

JOE: What? That's impossible. All I ever do is put it between your thighs.

MARY: Well, I don't know. Something must've gone wrong.

JOE: Who says you're pregnant?

MARY: An angel appeared to me in the backyard and said so.

JOE: An angel?

MARY: An angel of God. His name was Gabriel. He had a trumpet and he appeared to me in the backyard.

JOE: He what?

MARY: He appeared to me.

JOE: Was he naked?

MARY: No. I think he had on a raincoat. I don't really know. He was glowing so brightly.

JOE: Mary, you're under a lot of stress. Why don't you take a few days off from the shop. The accounts can wait.

MARY: I'm telling you, Joe. This Angel Gabriel said that God wanted me to have his baby.

JOE: Did you ask for some sort of sign?

MARY: Of course I did. He said tomorrow morning I'd start getting sick.

JOE: But why should God want a kid?

MARY: Well, Gabriel said that according to Luke it's kind of an ego thing. Plus, he promised the Jews a long time ago, it's just that he never got around to it. But now that he feels *ready* for children he doesn't want to just make them out of clay or dust. He wants to get humans involved.

JOE: Well, is he going to help toward raising the kid? God knows we can't do it alone. I could use a bigger shop, and maybe he could throw a couple of those nice crucifix contracts my way. The Romans are nailin' up everything that walks.

MARY: Honey, Gabriel said not to worry. The kid would be a real winner. A public speaker and good with miracles.

JOE: Well, that's a relief. Anyway, I guess now that you're officially pregnant I can start puttin' it inside you.

MARY: I'm sorry, honey. God wants it to be strictly a virgin birth.

JOE: I don't get it.

MARY: That's right, Joe.

JOE: Don't I get to do anything?

MARY: He wants you to come up with a name for the kid.

JOE: Jesus Christ!

MARY: Joe, you're so heavy.

GUYS & DOLLS, PART 2

Man, Oh Man!

To my way of thinking, men have only one real problem: other men. That's where all the trouble starts. A long time ago, men gave away their power. To other men: princes, kings, wizards, generals and high priests. They gave it away, because they believed what these other men told them. They bought the okeydoke. The bullshit. Men always buy the okeydoke when it comes from other men.

Some stranger probably stood up at a campfire and said, "All right, boys, from now on, I'm the king. The sun is my father, the moon is my mother and they're the ones who tell me when to throw the virgins into the volcano. I'll be expecting all of you to bow deeply when you see me, and give me half your crops. Plus I'm allowed to fuck your wife. And don't forget, if I want to I can concentrate real hard and make your head explode."

And the other men around the campfire nodded their heads and said to one another, "This guy makes a lot of sense." A man will always buy the bullshit, because a man is not too bright.

But I'm not suggesting a man doesn't have a great deal to put up with. He does. First of all, a man has to make believe he knows what he's doing at all times. And while he's doing whatever it is he's doing, he has to make believe he doesn't need any help.

He has to make believe he can fix *anything*. And if he can't fix it now, he'll fix it later. And if he can't fix it later, he has a friend who can fix it, and if not, it was no good to start with, it's not worth fixing, and besides, he knows where he can get something better, much cheaper, but they're all outta them right now, and besides, they're closed. This is the male disease. It's called being full of shit.

The male disease includes the need to be in charge at all times. In charge, in control, in command. A "real man" sees himself as king of the hill, leader of the pack, captain of the ship. But all the while, in order to fit in and belong, he has to act like all the other men and do what they do, so he'll be accepted. And get a good job and a promotion and a raise and a Porsche, and a wife. A wife who will immediately trade in the Porsche on a nice, sensible Dodge van with folding seats so they can be like all the other boring families. The poor fuck. The poor stupid fuck.

His manliness also requires that he refuse to go to a doctor or a hospital unless it can be demonstrated to him that he has, in fact, been clinically dead for six months. "No sense goin' to the hospital, honey, I don't seem to be in a coma." Therefore, he must learn to ignore pain. "It doesn't really hurt. Bleeding from six holes in the head doesn't really hurt. Just gimme the remote and get me a beer. And get the fuck outta here."

Most men learn this stupid shit from their fathers. Fathers teach their sons not to cry. "Don't let me hear you cryin' or I'll come up there and give you something to cry about!" Great stuff, hah? All the problems in the world—repeat, *all* the problems in the world—can be traced to what fathers do to their sons.

So, little boys learn to hide their feelings, and society likes that because, that way, when they get to be eighteen, they'll able to go overseas and kill strangers without feeling anything. And of course, that bargain includes a certain reluctant willingness to have their balls shot off: "Honey, I have to go overseas and have my balls shot off, or else the rest of the guys will think I'm too afraid to go overseas and have my balls shot off." The poor fucks. The poor stupid fucks.

And so, as a result of all this repression of feelings, the extent of the average man's emotional expression is the high five. Or sometimes, when really deep feelings emerge, both hands. The high ten. This is raw emotion. And that's about all they're capable of. And they have Dad to thank. Thanks, Dad.

But wait! Don't think dads can't be fun at times, too. After all, dads introduce their sons to the Wonderful World of Men—the male subcultures. The really tough-guy, masculine, he-man stuff. No wimps, no pussies, no softies.

There are five deadly male subcultures and they all overlap: the car and machinery culture, the police and military culture, the outdoors and gun culture, the sports and competition culture and the drug and alcohol culture. And, as a bonus, I'm gonna throw in one more: the "Let's go get some pussy and beat the shit outta queers" culture. As I say, they all overlap. Many men belong to all six.

This male universe is, of course, detectable by analyzing its combustible chemical formula: gasoline, gunpowder, alcohol and adrenaline. A chemistry rendered even more lethal by that ever-present, ever-delightful accelerant: testosterone. Talk about substance abuse! If it's chemical dependency you're interested in, you might want to look into testosterone. TESS-TAHSS-TER-OWN!!—the most lethal substance on earth. And it does not come from a laboratory, it comes from the scrotum; a scrotum located, interestingly enough, not far from the asshole. How fitting.

And, as it happens, all these male subcultures share a particular set of features: homophobia, coupled with an oddly ironic, complete, childlike trust in male authority. Men are attracted to powerful men. They also share a strong fear and dislike of women. This in spite of a pathological obsession with pussy. TESS-TAHSS-TER-OWN!!

So why are men like this? I think the overriding problem for men is that in life's main event, reproduction, they're left out; women do all the work. What do men contribute? Generally, they're just looking for a quick parking space for some sperm. A couple of hits of hot jism, and the volume on the TV goes right back up. It's my belief that most of these flawed male chromosomes should not be allowed to go forward for even one more unfortunate generation. But such is biology.

And so, excluded as they are from reproduction, men must find other ways to feel useful and worthwhile. As a result, they measure themselves by the size of their guns, the size of their cars, the size of their dicks and the size of their wallets. All contests that no man can win consistently.

And let me tell you why all this happened. Because women are the source of all human life. The first human being came from the belly of a female. And all human fetuses begin as females. The brain itself is basically female until hormones act on it to make it structurally male.

So, in reality, all men are modified females. Where do you think those nipples came from, guys? You're an afterthought. Maybe that's what's bothering you. Is that what's on your mind, Bunkie? That would explain the hostility: Women got the good job, men got the shitty one. Females create life, males end it. War, crime and violence are primarily male franchises. Man-shit.

It's nature's supreme joke. Deep in the womb, men start out as the good thing and wind up as the crappy thing. Not all men, just enough. Just enough to fuck things up. And the dumbest part of it all is that not only do men accept all this shit . . . they do it to themselves.

By the way, I'm not letting women completely off the hook. After all, the one part of the lower anatomy that is the same in both sexes is the asshole. But women who are assholes aren't called that. They're named for a different part of their lower anatomy. They're called cunts. Isn't it nice that cunts and assholes are next-door neighbors?

NINETY-NINE THINGS YOU NEED TO KNOW

There are ninety-nine things you need to know:

Number one: There are more than ninety-nine things you need to know.

Number two: Nobody knows how many things there are to know.

Number three: It's more than three.

Number four: There is no way of knowing how many things you need to know.

Number five: Some of the things you need to know are things you already know.

Number six: Some of the things you need to know are things you only think you know.

Number seven: Some of the things you need to know are things you used to know and then forgot.

Number eight: Some of the things you need to know are things you only *thought* you forgot and actually still know.

Number nine: Some of the things you need to know are things you know but don't really know you know.

Number ten: Some of the things you need to know are things you don't yet know you need to know.

Number eleven: Some of the things you think you need to know are things you probably don't really need to know.

Number twelve: Some of the things you need to know are things known only by people you don't know.

Number thirteen: Some of the things you need to know are things nobody knows.

Number fourteen: Some of the things you need to know are things that are unknowable.

Number fifteen: Some of the things you need to know are things that can only be imagined.

Number sixteen: At any time the list of things you need to know can be abruptly suspended.

Now you know.

EUPHEMISMS: Shell Shock to PTSD

Earlier in the book, in the first section on this subject of euphemistic language, I mentioned several reasons we seem to employ so much of it: the need to avoid unpleasant realities; the need to make things sound more important than they really are; marketing demands; pretentiousness; boosting employee self-esteem; and, in some cases, just plain, old political correctness.

But no matter their purpose, the one thing euphemisms all have in common is that they soften the language. They portray reality as less vivid. And I've noticed Americans have a problem with reality; they prefer to avoid the truth and not look it in the eye. I think it's one of the consequences of being fat and prosperous and too comfortable. So, naturally, as time has passed, and we've grown fatter and more prosperous, the problem has gotten worse. Here's a good example:

There's a condition in combat—most people know it by now. It occurs when a soldier's nervous system has reached the breaking point. In World

War I, it was called *shell shock*. Simple, honest, direct language. Two syllables. Shell shock. Almost sounds like the guns themselves. Shell shock!!

That was 1917. A generation passed. Then, during the Second World War, the very same combat condition was called *battle fatigue*. Four syllables now. It takes a little longer to say, stretches it out. The words don't seem to hurt as much. And *fatigue* is a softer word than *shock*. Shell shock. Battle fatigue. The condition was being euphemized.

More time passed and we got to Korea, 1950. By that time, Madison Avenue had learned well how to manipulate the language, and the same condition became *operational exhaustion*. It had been stretched out to eight syllables. It took longer to say, so the impact was reduced, and the humanity was completely squeezed out of the term. It was now absolutely sterile: operational exhaustion. It sounded like something that might happen to your car.

And then, finally, we got to Vietnam. Given the dishonesty surrounding that war, I guess it's not surprising that, at the time, the very same condition was renamed *post-traumatic stress disorder*. It was still eight syllables, but a hyphen had been added, and, at last, the pain had been completely buried under psycho-jargon. Post-traumatic stress disorder.

I'd be willing to bet anything that if we'd still been calling it *shell shock,* some of those Vietnam veterans might have received the attention they needed, at the time they needed it. But it didn't happen, and I'm convinced one of the reasons was that softer language we now prefer: The New Language. The language that takes the life out of life. More to come.

ELEGY FOR "MILLENNIUM"

You don't hear the word *millennium* much anymore, do you? It's kind of sad. Here's a word that lies around for long periods of time looking for work, but never really doing very much. Then, every thousand years, things suddenly pick up and there's a flurry of activity. The word is on everyone's lips, and is heard in almost every conversation. It stays red-hot for several years, enjoying its popularity—seeing its name in newspapers and magazines, making appearances on radio and TV. But then a peak is reached, and, after a while, things begin to slow down. The activity tapers off, and before long, it's once again relegated to history books, academic journals and reference works. Goodbye, poor *millennium*. I'm going to miss you. When you return, I may not be here to welcome you back.

WHO, ME? HATE?

I saw two bumper stickers on a car: HATE IS NOT A FAMILY VALUE and VALUE ALL FAMILIES. What is the purpose of having things like this on your car? Certainly it's not to change someone else's opinion of family life at a red light. More likely, the purpose is to inform us that the driver doesn't hate anyone, and that he considers himself pure and virtuous and better than the rest of us. So it's actually self-righteousness. The driver apparently forgot that the seven deadly sins include both anger *and* pride.

JACKO BEATS THEM ALL

I don't care if Michael Jackson freaked off with little boys or not. It doesn't bother me. Fuck those kids. And fuck their greedy parents too. What's important to me is that Michael is the greatest entertainer who ever lived. Bar none. Watch him dance; pay attention to the showmanship. No one ever came close.

Elvis was a bogus white guy with sex appeal and good looks who ripped off a lot of great black music, watered it down, and made it safe for lame whites who couldn't handle the experience of raw, emotional black music. Never grew as an artist; remained an entertainer. Fuck Elvis.

Sammy Davis Jr.? Nice try. Ordinary dancer, ordinary singer, second-rate impressionist. I also didn't like the insincere sincerity. But he was a nice man, personally; I give him credit for that.

Frank Sinatra? Great singer of songs, among the best. Superb musician. Grew as an artist. No showmanship, though. Arrogant, too. And mean to ordinary people. Fuck him.

Michael Jackson buries them all. I say give him a bunch of kids and let him dance.

LET'S GET REAL, HERE

I've decided to cash in on TV's reality-show trend. I have several ideas, but they may need some work before I approach the networks. Here's what I'm working on:

ISLAND CUISINE

This idea grew out of *Survivor*, but I have a new twist: You put twelve people on a barren island, and you let them starve to death. You make sure they get no food, but you provide plenty of fresh drinking water—you don't want them to die of thirst, you want them to starve to death.

That would be entertaining enough, but here's the fun. You make sure half the contestants are large, aggressive, physically fit individuals, and the other half are small, mild-mannered and physically weak. Then you wait them out and see who survives—and, more fun, you watch how they do it. The show is called *Guess Who's for Dinner*. The only part I haven't decided yet is whether to provide utensils.

GETTIN' HIGH AND HAVIN' FUN

Here's another idea I think has a good shot: *Maniac on Drugs*. Each week you put a different homicidal maniac in a van filled with assault rifles and you provide him with large amounts of speed, crack, acid and PCP. Then you let him drive around New York City for several days, and you videotape everything he does. Naturally, you clear all this with the police, so they don't interfere with the smooth flow of the show. At the end of thirteen weeks, you take all the psychos, give them a fresh supply of drugs and turn them loose at Disney World with rocket-propelled grenades. Actually, now that I think about it, this idea is too good for the networks; I'm gonna put it on pay-per-view.

Here's a variation for the finale, in case the Disney people get squeamish. You give the maniacs the same drugs, but instead of grenade launchers, you go back to the assault rifles. Everything's the same, but this time you put them on an ordinary, nonstop passenger train from New York to Los Angeles. You strap video cameras to their heads and let them run loose on the train, allowing them to befriend the other passengers. Remember, it's nonstop, no one can get off. I guarantee you'd get some really great footage. By the way, to save a little money, this could also be done on a Greyhound bus. But you'd need a really good driver who isn't easily distracted.

GUYS' NIGHT OUT

Here's the one I'm proudest of because it took the most thought. I call it *Lucky Bachelor*.

Our chosen guy is selected from letters sent in to the show. In step one, the lucky bachelor is sent out on three separate occasions to pick up women in cheap bars and bring each of them to a hotel where he tries to fuck them. If they go along easily, he then convinces them to commit a perverted act involving a floor lamp, a woodpecker and a box of rubber bands—an act most people would consider completely depraved. All this activity is videotaped.

In step two, we stop three men at random on the street, show them the videos and ask them which of the women the lucky bachelor should marry. That woman is called the designated bride. We then ask the two losing women to vote on which one of the three random street guys looks like the best fuck. That guy is called the designated, best-fuck street guy.

In step three, we take the two losing street guys and the two losing bar girls and feed them near-fatal doses of aphrodisiacs, put them in thong bathing suits and turn them loose in an adult sex shop with unlimited credit. This footage, strictly an added feature, could possibly be some of the liveliest on the show.

Now, the alert reader is probably wondering what happened to our original lucky bachelor. Well, in step four we arrange for him and the designated best-fuck street guy to stage a bare-knuckle fistfight—to the death—in the center aisle of St. Peter's in Rome during a papal high mass. The two men must keep fighting until one of them dies; it's important to the show. As a side feature, we keep a camera trained on the pope, and every time he falls asleep during the fight, we give the guys an extra hundred dollars.

The reason it's important that one of the two men dies is because the next day, in the same church, we're going to hold step five: a combination wedding and funeral. The loser of the fight gets the funeral, the winner gets to marry the designated hotel-fuck bride, with the remaining, losing bar and hotel participants serving as bridesmaids and pallbearers. We then give the newlyweds all the leftover drugs from *Maniac on Drugs* and send them on a honeymoon to some nice, conservative golfing resort on Hilton Head Island, where they are required to take large amounts of drugs and two weeks of golf and tennis lessons.

LOOKS AREN'T EVERYTHING

This next one is a makeover show. My working title is *Try Looking Like That For a Change!* You start by picking three incredibly beautiful, successful supermodels and then, against their wills, you sedate them, strap them down and subject them to extensive plastic surgery. You give them big, misshapen noses; sagging eye-bags; and plenty of wrinkles and drooping skin on their faces. Then you pump enough fat into their asses, hips and thighs to make them really unhappy. When they come out of the anesthesia, the audience yells, "Try Looking Like That For a Change!" I'm so excited about this one that I'm working on a variation that involves involuntary sex-change surgery.

WRAP-UP

Well, that's about it. I suppose all that's left would be for me to tell you about a show called *Bowel Movement.* Basically, it's a show that involves a fixed-position camera, a toilet and a series of guys with diets organized primarily around beer and extra-spicy Mexican food. Perhaps it's better if I don't go into too much detail at this time. And you know something? This one might actually belong on cable.

That's it, folks. I've done all I can to develop a hit show. But the creative process can only go so far; the rest is up to you, the public, and I'm counting on your good taste.

WE JUST WANNA WATCH

First, let me say that most people take these so-called tragedies like Columbine and Oklahoma City far too seriously. You have to remember, it's all part of the American way of life. If you live in America you have to go along with these things. You can't be sitting around whining, "Ohh, a lot of people got killed." These things happen, folks. People get killed.

But concerning the guys (it's always men) who commit these mass killings—and other less dramatic murders for that matter: After the sentence of death is passed, you will usually see the whining families of the "victims" insist on watching the execution up close, through a little window. They want to see the guy die. Don't these people know there's nothing to see? It's uneventful. An attendant gives the guy an injection; it's like watching someone get a flu shot. There's nothing to see. But they often get their wish and are allowed to witness what's little more than a medical procedure.

Now, my feeling is, if you're going to let people watch some guy get executed, it would make much more sense to put on a little show for these ghouls. Entertain them. Place the guy in a small steel room and send in four or five of these sadistic prison guards with steel pipes and let them beat the guy to death. For about an hour. A constant, uninterrupted, sixty-minute clubbing would seem far more in keeping with our national values.

And, of course, this method would be much more satisfying to the families of these so-called victims; these fine, upstanding religious families who believe in a merciful God. They'd enjoy watching these psychotic, animalistic prison guards doing what comes naturally—administering a nice, brutal clubbing. Prison guards who, by the way, dare I say, are also all fine, upstanding religious people as well. Folks, if you're gonna do these things, don't settle for halfway measures. Do them right. Do them the Christian way.

KEEP AMERICA CLEAN

As a public service, next weekend Boy Scouts will be picking up litter and trash from America's highways and dumping it in America's rivers. If you'd like to pitch in and help the Boy Scouts, bring some of your own trash from home and throw it out the window of your car as you drive along your favorite road. You'll be doing your part to keep the highways clean. By the way, if you have any ideas about cleaning up the rivers, let us know.

GET THE FUCK OOT

I'm tired of these Canadians who have worked in the American news media for years and still haven't learned to pronounce the words *out* and *about*. Peter Jennings is one of them, and there are about three or four more. These people need to be taught that it's *OUT* and *uh-BOUT*, not *OOT* and *uh-BOOT*. I say if you can't learn the language, it's aboot time you got the fuck oot of here. Besides, Canadians are just disguised English people, and it's a well-known fact that all English people deserve to die.

UNCLE SAM WANTS YOU

Things I wonder about the FBI's list of the "Ten Most Wanted" criminals: When they catch a guy and he comes off the list, does number eleven automatically move up? And does he see it as a promotion? Does he call his criminal friends and say, "I made it, Bruno. I'm finally on the list"?

How about when a new, really dangerous guy comes along and they absolutely have to put him at the top of the list without delay? (Call it "Number one with a bullet," if you wish.) Doesn't everyone else have to move down a notch? And doesn't one guy get dropped off? How do they decide which guy to drop? Is it automatically number ten? And how does he feel about that? Does he feel slighted? Does he feel maybe it should've been someone else? Has anyone who was demoted ever killed the new guy to gain his spot back?

One last question: Does the FBI search harder for number three than they do for number seven? I would. Otherwise why have the numbers at all? These are the kinds of thoughts that keep me from making any real progress in life.

TOO MANY PEOPLE

There are too many people. Period. There have *always* been too many people. From the beginning. If these diaper-sniffing Christian babymongers would stop having so many of these cross-eyed little kids, maybe the rest of us would have a chance to spread out and have a little fun. Excess children waste our natural resources. If this society wants me to conserve energy, it had better get some of these child-worshipping religious fanatics to stop having five, six or seven babies. When they do that, I'll start turning off the lights. And yes, I know the fertility rate is down. Good. It should go down even further. Every family should be allowed half a child. If that.

AN L.A. STREET PROBLEM

Who are all these guys in their twenties, out on the streets skateboarding at two and three in the afternoon? Get off the streets and find work, mother-fucker! And by the way, I'm not talking about X Games guys who are really good at it; that's different, that's a way of life. I'm talking about these skate-board fucks who look like they're actually *going* somewhere. As if the skate-board were a means of transportation. What the fuck's the deal with these guys?

Same with these Rollerblading and scooter fucks. Why are these fully grown men out on the street, playing with children's toys during working hours? And wearing helmets, for chrissakes! Jesus, I would be so embarrassed to wear a helmet. Grow up, motherfucker. And, while you're at it, stay out of the range of my car; I might just decide to run some consumer tests on those helmets. I might also decide to clear the streets of all nonessential traffic. So get a job or play on the sidewalk with the rest of the kids.

BITS AND PIECES

· I'm starting to get more compassionate. I gotta watch that.

· Children's Hospital in New York is quite an amazing place. On a recent visit, I saw two seven-year-olds performing a kidney transplant.

· Be careful whom you befriend. They will eventually ask you for something.

· When she was getting fucked by Roy Rogers, do you think Dale Evans ever screamed, "Giddyup, Roy"?

· Here's a dead-end business: a shoeshine stand at the beach.

· Mexico has a new holiday known as the "Name-Calling Fiesta." People dress up in colorful costumes and do a series of folk dances while they call each other "cocksucker" and "motherfucker." Then they all get drunk and eat a big meal.

· Michael Jackson missed his calling. If he had become a Catholic priest, he could've spent thirty or forty years blowing all the little boys he wanted, and no one would have said a word.

· *Hard work* is a misleading term. Physical effort and long hours do not constitute hard work. Hard work is when someone pays you to do something you'd rather not be doing. Anytime you'd rather be doing something other than the thing you're doing, you're doing hard work.

· Cosmologists are just now beginning to accept the possibility that the big bang was actually caused by a huge explosion in a meth lab.

· "Hello. I'm Howard Finely, and I'm running for state's attorney general. This is my pledge to you: If I am elected, and someone breaks the law, I will personally go to his house and beat the shit out of him. Thank you."

· Why does it always take longer to get somewhere than it does to come back?

· What's with these recumbent bicycles? Listen, buddy, if you wanna take a nap, lie down. If you wanna ride a bike, buy a fuckin' bicycle.

· I prefer people with imagination: dictators, serial killers, schizophrenics, assassins, skinheads, drug lords, violent bikers, devil worshippers. To me, these are the interesting people. To get its edge back, I think what America really needs is more evil. Intense, unalloyed, concentrated evil.

· I was reading a fitness magazine that had an article about cross-training, and I realized this would have been a good idea for Jesus.

· People who see life as anything more than pure entertainment are missing the point.

· The future ain't what it used to be.

· Wouldn't it be fun if, all at once, everybody just forgot everything they knew?

· These professional child-worshippers say we should put the needs of children first. Why? What about the needs of adults? We come second? It's stupid. If you put the needs of children first, you're going to wind up with way too many diapers and lollipops and not nearly enough bongs and condoms.

· WHAT HAPPENED? Washington, Jefferson, Franklin, Madison, Adams, Hamilton. Things were going well. Then Ford, Quayle, Mondale, Agnew, Nixon, Clinton, Dole, Bush I, Bush II. What happened?

· This morning I had a great idea, but it was too late to put it into the book. I just wanted you to know this is where it would have gone.

TRUE FACT: A radio commercial says that a certain diet pill works three times faster than starvation. Question: Are they guessing, or did they really run these tests?

· Here's something you can't do by yourself: practice shaking hands.

· Stop in today at Anne Bennington's Quality Cyst Removal. Regular cysts, five dollars. Really big, difficult cysts, a dollar a pound. Anne Bennington's: Cyst removal for the discerning.

· THE OPTIMIST: "I have no friends, no family, no money, no food, no job, no credit, no luck, no hope and no future. However, I do have matches, toothpicks, chewing gum, paper clips, rubber bands, shoelaces and Scotch Tape. Maybe things aren't so bad."

· Am I the only one who thinks the Muppets weren't funny?

· If you have twins, a good idea is to sell one of them. What the hell, you've got two, why not pick up a few dollars?

· When child abuser Father John Geoghan was killed in prison, he was sixty-eight years old. If a psychic had attended his ordination forty years earlier and told his parents, "When John is sixty-eight, he will be strangled to death in prison while serving time for touching children's penises," at the very least there would have been a small commotion.

TRUE FACT: There is now a gay softball World Series.

· A children's museum sounds like a good idea, but I would imagine it's not easy to breathe inside those little glass cases.

· Why is it the only time you ever hear the word *figment* it's in relation to the imagination? Aren't there any other kinds of figments?

· If everyone in the world sat quietly at the same time, closed their eyes and concentrated as hard as they could on peace and goodwill, all the killing and cruelty in the world would continue. And probably increase.

· You know what you never see? A Korean guy with freckles and a big hook nose.

· I wonder when we pick up the telephone, does each of us get his own individual dial tone, or is there just one systemwide, master dial tone that each of us jumps on and off when we need it? These things eat at me.

· If a safe is unlocked, is it still a safe?

· Here's an optical illusion you can try at home. Take a pencil and make a small black dot in the middle of an ordinary piece of paper. Cover your left eye and stare at the dot from a distance of about two inches. You will see the Battle of Chancellorsville. If you don't, check the paper. Or maybe you made the dot wrong.

· Just because you don't have a lot of money to spend is no reason you shouldn't spend what little you have.

· A good promotional idea for a singles bar would be to have "Date-rape Friday." Drinks half-price, free GHB, free Plan-B pills, free RU-486 morning-after pills, free rape counseling and generous rebate coupons for an abortion clinic. That takes care of attracting the men; I'm still working on how to get some women to show up.

· I had no shoes, and I felt sorry for myself until I met a man with no feet. I took his shoes. Now I feel better.

· You know what would have been a smart thing to do in these developing countries that need electricity? To have tried large-scale experiments with alternative energy sources: solar, wind, geothermal, etc. We could have tested and tried to perfect these technologies on a large scale in places that need it. That would have been smart. That's why we didn't do it.

· You know what you never see? A really good-looking homeless couple.

· I've always wondered if the Library of Congress provides books in their public toilets to promote reading. I should think they wouldn't want to pass up a captive audience like that.

· A GENERIC JOKE: A person goes into a place and says something to another person. The second person says something back to the first person, who listens to that and then says something back to the second person. The thing he says back is really funny.

· Stick around. China's gonna win it all.

TRUE FACT: In Moscow there's a professional entertainer who is described as a Hitler impersonator. Show biz.

· Get one now! Everybody has one! They're almost gone! New, super-deluxe, jumbo, handy, portable, lightweight, convenient, collapsible, prewrapped, easy to use, guaranteed, available in all sizes in designer colors. Get one now! Won't rust tarnish, blister, crack or peel, but it will cause tumors.

KEEPIN' IT REAL IN THE AIR

OFF WE GO, INTO THE WILD BLUE YONDER

I think the safety instructions that airline flight attendants deliver before departure could be greatly improved if they were simply a bit more honest and complete. They should include graphic descriptions—accompanied by animated and live-action video—of the devastating physical damage done to the human body during a crash. They should cite examples of various anatomical mutilations. They should also include a detailed description of the damage done to the lungs and skin by fire and smoke inhalation, to demonstrate that surviving the impact of the crash alone is not always sufficient. People deserve the truth.

Then, how about a more relaxed, breezy pre-flight announcement made in the cadences of young people: "Hi. Listen, we'll be leaving soon? Then we're gonna fly a while and get there possibly this afternoon? Okay? Later on, we'll chow down, have some brews and maybe catch a movie? Okay? And hey, try not to ring your bell a lot and wake us up . . . unless something really scary is going on. Okay? Thanks. Oh, and by the way, the captain says do that thing with the belts."

LEVELING OFF

"Ladies and gentlemen, we're leveling off at our cruising altitude. That means the cockpit crew will soon be lighting up and enjoying a few hits of something really nice we picked up in Hawaii. After about six hits, they're gonna turn off the autopilot, take their hands off the controls and let the plane do what it wants for a couple of minutes. The captain suggests you keep your seat belts fastened unless you have a strong appetite for blunt trauma."

"The captain has just turned on the fasten-seat-belt sign. He didn't mean to, but the joint he was smoking fell in his lap, and when he jumped up, his head hit the switch."

"The captain has turned off the seat-belt sign. But he cautions you to stay alert, as sometimes these planes don't work as well as we'd like them to."

"The captain has just turned the seat-belt sign on again. Of course, he also just stuffed a pound of walnuts up his nose, one by one, so you can decide for yourselves what you want to do about the belts."

STILL CRUISIN' ALONG

A socially responsible pilot: "On your right, you will see Las Vegas, where millions of visitors are fleeced out of their hard-earned money each year by huge, impersonal hotels originally built by brutal, criminal syndicates and now owned by brutal, criminal corporations. These large, impersonal hotels have no concern for service or quality, but merely wish to generate more gambling activity, because the advantage is heavily weighted toward the house. Whores and drugs are available at all hours."

A poetic pilot: "Off to your right you'll see the Colorado River as it snakes its way carefully through the ancient, multicolored walls of the Grand Canyon, echoing mutely the dreams and disappointments of countless generations of red-skinned people who inhabited the Great Southwest."

An interesting pilot: "There's the house where John Gacy lived. If you look carefully, in his backyard you can see the top of the chute where he dropped the bodies of the twenty-six children he killed. Over on the right, we'll soon be coming up to the gas station where Ted Bundy picked up his twenty-third victim. Altogether, he is thought to have killed between thirty-six and fifty young women, almost all of whom parted their hair in the middle."

A political pilot: "Most of the farms you see used to belong to small farmers. But their land has been brutally repossessed by the greedy, grasping bankers, only to be bought up by huge agribusiness corporations who poison the land and produce tasteless food. These corporations receive billions of dollars a year from the taxpayers for no good reason except to enhance their wealth."

Pilot with the blues: "Ladies and gentlemen, I've been feeling kind of depressed lately, and I think you'll agree, we all share guilt for the world's suffering and deteriorating condition. Sometimes I ask myself, 'Is it all worthwhile?' Quite often, I give up hope completely and try to think of interesting ways of killing myself that would get my name on television." (Sounds of a struggle in the cockpit)

COMIN' DOWN

"Ladies and gentlemen, we have just begun our gradual descent into the Indianapolis area, a descent similar in many ways to the gradual slide of the United States from a first-class world leader to an aggressive, third-rate debtor nation of overweight slobs, undereducated slob children and aimless elderly people who can't afford to buy medicine. The current conditions in Indianapolis: Temperature sixty-one degrees, partly cloudy skies, winds from the southwest and intense Midwestern boredom."

TIRED OF THE HANDI-CRAP

Now, listen, I gotta tell you somethin' and I'm not gonna sugarcoat this because it is what it is. But boy, oh boy, am I gettin' tired of this handicapped business. Aren't you? Hah? Don't you think this handicapped shit has gone far enough?

And I'm like you, folks; normally I would feel sympathy for these people. But the first thing they tell you is that they don't want sympathy. You ever hear 'em say that? "I don't want your sympathy." And I say, fine, fuck you. No sympathy.

And by the way, if there are any handicapped people reading this, I'm not talking about you, all right? I'm talking about the other handicapped people, the ones who'll never see this book. So don't get all excited and start rolling around causing trouble in your electric go-cart or whatever the fuck it is. Calm down. I'm on your side.

I NEED MY SPACE

And just to show you my heart's in the right place, I'm gonna start out by mentioning a few of the positive things about the handicapped, okay? First of all, the big blue parking spaces. This was a great idea. I think most people would agree, those spaces come in mighty handy (which is where the word "handycapped" came from in the first place—a lot of people don't know that). They're always right near the entrance to the store or the building, and I find that I can get in and out of the place in a hurry and complete my business with a minimum of delay.

STALLING AROUND

Another handicapped feature I enjoy are the extra-large toilet stalls in public restrooms; once again, an excellent idea. There's so much room in there to spread out; it's like a gymnasium. I can do some pushups, work on my kickboxing, try out a few dance steps. Occasionally I bring a picnic lunch. Nothing fancy; just a small salad, a bit of cheese, perhaps a delicate Bordeaux.

I find that once you're locked in there, you can pretty much do what you want. About the only limitations might be common decency and a sensible regard for personal safety. One time, I had a few friends over and we played cards all night. The good thing was when one of the players had to take a shit, he didn't have to drop out of the game for several hands. He simply traded places with the person who was using the toilet as a chair and it worked out great.

I mention all this because I want you to know I recognize some of the positive things that have grown out of this unfortunate obsession America has with the handicapped.

THEY'RE EASILY BOARD

But on this subject I also have a few complaints to make, the main one being this business at the airport of letting the handicapped get on the plane early. I don't like the idea of people boarding ahead of me just because they've had a run of bad luck. It doesn't seem fair. I think if a person's had some bad luck, it should apply across the board to all segments of his life. We shouldn't be going around trying to selectively fix people's bad luck.

And what bothers me most about the process is, I'm not sure all these people are truly handicapped; some of them don't look that fucked up. I think there's a fairly hefty amount of bullshitting going on at the check-in counter.

ROLLIN', ROLLIN', ROLLIN'

The whole fiasco begins just before the flight, with the parade of wheelchairs. And apparently, just about anyone can get their hands on one of those airport wheelchairs. You know the ones I mean? The ones the airlines provide? Not a wheelchair some guy brings from home; I don't mind that. I figure if a guy's laid out money for his own wheelchair, he's probably legitimately fucked up. And I don't mind a guy gettin' ahead of me if he's legitimately fucked up. You know? Like if a huge chunk of his head is missing, or he's got a whole caved-in chest and two or three of his limbs don't work. Generally, in a case like that, I'm gonna give the guy the benefit of the doubt. I say roll his ass down the jetway and let's get the fuck outta town.

But, to me, some of these airline-wheelchair people don't look that fucked up; they just look old—and my guess is they're lazy.

A lot of old people are lazy, because somehow when they hit their 80s or 90s, they think it's time to take it easy. Old people aren't "spry" and "full of ginger" anymore. Now they're all just lazy. And frankly, I think they're just tryin' to get a free ride to the gate.

RAISING CANES

But let's get back to the actual process of boarding. As soon as the wheelchair derby is over the next thing you have to contend with is these people who show up with canes and crutches; what I call the quasi-handicapped. And even though I'm willing to cut the wheelchair people some slack, I'm not so easy on the cane folks. I'm convinced most of these jokers with canes don't really need them.

And once again it's the old people, tryin' to gain sympathy and get to the front of the line. It's obviously a scam; have you noticed, for instance, how suddenly these canes materialize? Out of nowhere? One minute everyone at the gate looks perfectly healthy, the next minute half of 'em have a limp. And before you know it there are twenty or thirty people leanin' on canes. I'm convinced that somewhere in the airport (which has now become a large mall with airplanes as a side attraction) there must be a little place where you can rent canes. "Canes for Planes."

But you know something? I'm not that upset. Not really. Because the best part about these "handicapped" people gettin' on the plane first is that they have to get off last. Fuck 'em, they always get off last. While they're still lookin' for their carry-on bags and rectal thermometers, I'm halfway into town. You see? Life has a way of evening things out.

EUPHEMISMS: The March of Time

As we resume our look at the advance of euphemisms, we have to keep a close eye on the image-makers: advertisers, marketers, public-relations people. And to repeat an earlier point, it's important to remember that, over time, this trend toward softer language has only gotten worse.

IT ALL GOT DIFFERENT

I don't know when the whole thing started, but I do know that at some point in my life, *toilet paper* became *bathroom tissue.* I wasn't consulted on this. I didn't get a postcard, I didn't get an e-mail, no one bothered to call. It just happened. One day, I simply found myself using bathroom tissue.

And then, just as my *loafers* were becoming *slip-ons,* my *sneakers* turned into *running shoes,* and in no time, my running shoes became *athletic footwear.* It was about then that a trip to the department store revealed that my lazy-slob uniform of *sweatpants* and *sweatshirt* were now located in a section called *Activewear.*

The world was changing. I saw *second-hand clothing* referred to as *vintage apparel;* I saw *toupees* advertised as *hair appliances,* in keeping, I would imagine, with the *dental appliances* that had long since replaced *false teeth.*

YA GOTTA HAVE A SYSTEM

Of course, if you didn't want to wear a *hairpiece* or a *rug* (nice old-fashioned term), you could always look around for a good, reliable *hair-replacement sys-*

tem. Keep an eye out for *systems,* folks, they're everywhere. The clerk who sold me my *answering machine* said I was purchasing a *voice-processing system; a mattress and box-spring set* is now called a *sleep system;* and the people who sell *mops* have not been resting. According to a commercial I saw recently, the Clorox ReadyMop is now America's favorite *mopping system.*

And if you think you can escape these systems by going for a drive, forget it; your car has been systematically (get it?) infiltrated, too. The *heater and air conditioner* became the *climate-control system,* your *brakes* have been replaced by a *braking system,* and your *seat belts and air bags* are now known as the *impact-mangement system.* You can't beat the system.

Marketers will always strive to make things sound more impressive than they really are; that's why *dashboards* became *instrument panels.* But how's this for laying it on thick? A magazine ad recently informed me that the cars depicted were equipped with leather *seating-surfaces.* When you get right down to it, you have to admit, marketing people have a ton of balls.

THAT'S ENTERTAINMENT

The upgrading continued: At home, I found myself watching *animation* instead of *cartoons.* And it turns out, all those TV shows I'd seen before were not really *reruns,* they were *encore presentations.* At about that time I noticed *soap operas* had begun billing themselves as *daytime dramas.*

Theaters felt overdue for an upgrade, too, so they became *performing arts centers,* or sometimes *performance spaces*—in keeping with the spirit of certain *nightclubs* who now speak of themselves as *party spaces.* (The really hip just call them *spaces.*) While all this was happening in smaller locations, the big arenas decided they wanted to be known as *events centers.*

Center is another word that's become important. Hospitals have long thought of themselves as *medical centers,* but now libraries have joined the chorus, calling themselves *learning resources centers*. And just to wrap this section up—and returning to show business for a moment—no matter what size the place where entertainment was being presented, at some point it was decided they would all just be called *venues*.

Systems, facilities, spaces, centers and *venues*: They're all words to keep an eye on in today's atmosphere of increasing self-importance.

YOU WANT MORE CHANGES?

Profits became *earnings*, *personnel* became *human resources*, the *complaint department* became *customer relations*. People started offering *feedback* instead of *criticism; car sickness* turned into *motion discomfort; messengers* became *couriers; junk mail* morphed into *direct marketing; special delivery* was suddenly *priority mail*; and after all these years, I picked up the phone and discovered *information* was identifying itself as *directory assistance*. I don't even want to mention my dismay at the fact that every old-fashioned, shady *used-car* dealer in a plaid jacket was suddenly selling *certified pre-owned vehicles*.

By this time, the *dump* had become the *landfill*. I guess it was inevitable; the *garbagemen* who fill it had long since become *sanitation engineers*, and in some cities, *garbage collection* was going by the fancy (and misleading) name *environmental services*.

The changes even got me where I lived. According to the Census Bureau, my *apartment* had become a *dwelling unit*, and when I asked my *janitor* to put a *peephole* in the door, I discovered later that actually the *custodial engineer* had installed an *observation port*.

Change of pace: One day, a *bucktoothed* girl told me she had *overbite*. That was the day I traded in my *glasses* for *prescription eyewear*.

Of course, some of these language upgrades are more widespread than others; admittedly, they're not all universal. For instance, we still have *motels,* but some of them wanted to charge a little more, so they became *motor lodges.* We also still have *house trailers,* but if they're for sale and profits are involved, they become *motor homes, mobile homes, modular homes* or *manufactured housing.*

So apparently, what we thought all this time was a *trailer park* is actually a *manufactured-home community.* I guess the lesson is we never quite know what we're dealing with. Could it be that all these years on the *Jerry Springer* show we've actually been watching manufactured-home-community trash?

I HAVE A DRUG (STORE) PROBLEM

I guess you've noticed a trip to the drugstore has changed a lot too; the products have all been transformed. To start with, the *medicine* I used to take is now called *medication.* (I have a hunch medication costs more than medicine.) *Mouthwashes* are *dental rinses, deodorants* have been joined on the shelf by *antiperspirants* (probably because *sweat* has become *nervous wetness*), a plain old bar of *soap* these days is being described variously as a *bath bar,* a *cleansing bar* and a *clarifying bar.* Can you imagine a mother saying, "Young man, if I hear that word out of you one more time, I'm going to wash your mouth out with a *clarifying bar*"? Doesn't sound right, does it?

The hair people have taken liberties, too: *hair spray*—too ordinary. Try *holding mist.* Of course, if you don't want holding mist, you can always turn to *shaping mousse* or *sculpting gel.* Anything to get you to pay a little more. *Cough drops* have grown up and turned into *throat lozenges,* some even calling themselves *pastilles* or *troches.* Guess what? Right! Two dollars more for lozenges, pastilles and troches.

I can remember, in television's early years, when *constipation* was called *occasional irregularity.* These days, in a kind of minor, reverse-euphemism trend, we're back to constipation, which parallels the recent TV comeback made by *diarrhea*. No more *lower gastric distress*. Diarrhea! "Gotta go, gotta go, gotta go, gotta go!" The new TV candor. (Even though you still can't say *shit*.) By the way, doctors used to claim that constipation could be relieved by eating more *roughage*; now they're pushing *fiber*. I still prefer roughage. If I want fiber, I eat a basket.

And hey, lady! Advancing age causing *vaginal friction?* Tell the pharmacist you have a *personal dryness problem*. I'm sure he has some sort of *intimate feminine-lubricating solution* to recommend. That's the way they describe crotch products now. Even a good old-fashioned *douche* has turned into a *feminine wash*. And remember *feminine hygiene sprays?* Personally, they didn't sound very tasty to me. If they had come in flavors they might have been more successful. Vagin-illa, crotch-ocolate, labia-lime. Just a thought. Anyway, the latest female product I've heard of is *protective underwear*, which, frankly, folks, I don't even want to think about. More later.

TIPS FOR SERIAL KILLERS

Because I enjoy following the exploits of serial killers, I'm always hoping they never get caught. So I've compiled a list of suggestions to help them stay on the loose longer; that way they can provide me with maximum entertainment.

TO THE KILLERS: If you're looking for some form of perverted attention and publicity I can't help you. But if you just want to kill a lot of people, one by one, I'm your guy: Here's how you can maximize the time it will take the police to apprehend you.

 • Make sure your victims are not all the same types. Kill a variety of people: tall, short, rich, poor, male, female, young, old. But don't kill them in any particular order. Do two old men in a row, then do a young woman, then a teenage boy. Mix blondes and brunettes and long hair and short. And don't bother with prostitutes.

· Vary the types of locations where you grab your victims and vary the times of day.

· Try to do the work in heavily populated areas where there are more murders to begin with.

· If at all possible, travel around the country and kill each victim in a different state. Never kill two people in the same city within a year. And don't travel in a straight line. Randomness is your greatest ally.

· Kill each of your victims in a completely different manner: Do some really weird ones, and then do some ordinary ones. Sexual, non-sexual; ritual, non-ritual. Don't specialize. Patterns are your enemy.

· Dispose of the bodies as far from the murder sites as possible, always at least a hundred miles. Bury some, burn some and dissolve others in lime and acid. If you encounter any chance witnesses to any part of the killings or the disposals, they should be killed and disposed of with a minimum of fuss. And be sure to dispose of them separately.

· When driving to the murder or especially the disposal sites, be careful not to break the law or have an accident. Use cash for everything. Don't stay in motels. Drive a late-model van-type vehicle you can sleep in, and don't park it where police might be expected to patrol. Have a large food supply and eat in the vehicle. If possible, change vehicles after every murder.

· Don't write notes to the police or taunt them in any way. It's dumb.

· Don't save newspaper clippings. In fact, don't even read the newspaper accounts.

· Don't keep souvenirs from any of the victims.

· Start watching the *CSI* shows on CBS and the *Law & Order* shows on NBC. Every now and then you will pick up some piece of information that will help you avoid mistakes.

Be smart and stay alive. Some of us are counting on you.

Wall Street Journal: Subscribe Now

The *Wall Street Journal* reminds you that your job as a businessman is to fuck the other guy before he fucks you. Sometimes you have to do such a complete job of fucking the other guy that he stays fucked for a long time, even to the point of going out of business and losing everything he owns. Quite often, the difference between getting fucked and being the one who does the fucking can be one small piece of business information, such as they're not making steam locomotives anymore, or the zeppelin travel market has begun to decline. Those two important business facts appeared recently in the *Wall Street Jour-*

nal. If you're a reptilian lowlife on your way up, stop getting fucked and start doing the fucking. Read the *Wall Street Journal.*

CRIPPLED, UGLY AND STUPID

In an earlier book, *Brain Droppings*, I wrote some things about politically correct language, but left out a few areas. I neglected three important groups of people who have had this awkward, dishonest language inflicted on them by liberals: I omitted those who are crippled, ugly or stupid. And so, to address these earlier omissions, I'd like to make a brief return visit to that playground of guilty white liberals: political correctness.

Political correctness is America's newest form of intolerance, and it is especially pernicious because it comes disguised as tolerance. It presents itself as fairness, yet attempts to restrict and control people's language with strict codes and rigid rules. I'm not sure that's the way to fight discrimination. I'm not sure silencing people or forcing them to alter their speech is the best method for solving problems that go much deeper than speech.

Therefore, those among you who are more politically sensitive than the rest of us may wish to take a moment here to tighten up those sphincter muscles, because I'm going to inject a little realism into the dream world of politically correct speech. Especially the words we use to describe one another.

CRIPPLED LIBERALS

Perhaps you've noticed that when the politically correct, liberal rule-makers decide to rename a group of humans they view as victims, they begin by imparting a sense of shame to the group's existing name. And so, somewhere over the years, the word *cripple* has been discarded. No one mentions cripples anymore.

That's because, in yet another stunning attempt to stand reality on its head, cripples have been assigned a new designation, the *physically challenged*. The use of *physically challenged* is an obvious attempt to make people feel better, the idea being, "As long as we can't cure these people, let's give their condition a more positive name, and maybe it will distract everyone." It's verbal sleight of hand.

The same is true of the ungainly phrase *differently abled*. I believe that if a person is going to insist on using tortured language such as differently abled, then he should be forced to use it to describe everyone. We're all differently abled. You can do things I can't do, I can do things you can't do. Barry Bonds can't play the cello, Yo-Yo Ma can't hit the curveball. They're differently abled.

It should be explained to liberals—patiently—that crippled people don't require some heroic designation; it's a perfectly honorable condition. It appears in the Bible: "Jesus healed the cripples." He didn't engage in rehabilitative strategies to improve the conditions of the physically disadvantaged. Can't these liberals hear how unattractive this language is? How poorly it sits on the ear? Personally, I prefer plain, descriptive language.

For instance—and this is a suggestion that will bother some, but I'm serious about it—why don't we just call handicapped people *defective*? We don't mind talking about birth defects; we don't flinch from that. We say, "Gunther has a birth defect." Isn't that a concession to the fact that people can be defective? Then what would be wrong with calling those people the *physically defective*? At what point in life does a person with a birth defect become a person who is differently abled? And why does it happen? I'm confused.

UGLY LANGUAGE

Then there are those who don't quite measure up to society's accepted standards of physical attractiveness. The worst of that group are called ugly. Or at least they used to be. The P.C. lingo cops have been working on this, too.

And to demonstrate how far all this politically correct, evasive language has gone, some psychologists are actually now referring to ugly people as "those with severe appearance deficits." Okay? Severe appearance deficits. So tell me, psychologist, how well does that sort of language qualify for "being in denial"? These allegedly well-intentioned people have strayed so far from reality that it will not be a surprise for me to someday hear a rape victim referred to as an *unwilling sperm recipient.*

Back to ugly. Regarding people's appearance, the political-language police already have in place one comically distorted term: *lookism.* They say that when you judge a person, or rather, size them up (wouldn't want to judge someone; that would be judgmental) if you take their looks into account, you're guilty of lookism. You're a *lookist.*

And those valiant people who fight lookism (many of them unattractive themselves) tell us that one problem is that in our society, those who get to be called beautiful and those who are called ugly are determined by standards arbitrarily set by us. Somehow, there is some fault attached to the idea that we, the people, are the ones who set the standards of beauty. Well, we're the ones who have to look at one another, so why shouldn't we be the ones who set the standards? I'm confused. I would say the whole thing was stupid, but that's my next topic, and it would sound like a cheap transition.

STUPID PEOPLE

So, stupid. It's important to face one thing about stupidity: We can't get away from it. It's all around us. It doesn't take a team of professional investigators to discover that there are stupid people in the world. Their presence (and its effects) speaks for itself.

But where do these stupid people come from? Well, they come from

American schools. But while they're attending these schools, they're never identified as stupid. That comes later, when they grow up. When they're kids, you can't call them stupid. Which may be contributing to the problem. Unfortunately, kids, stupid or otherwise, come under a sort of protective umbrella we've established that prevents them from being exposed to the real world until, at eighteen, their parents spring them on the rest of us, full grown.

There are stupid kids. And I do wish to be careful here how I negotiate the minefield of the *learning disabled* and the *developmentally disadvantaged*—in other words, "those with *special needs*." (All of these being more examples of this tiresome and ridiculous language.) I just want to talk about kids who are stupid; not the ones with dings.

One of the terms now used to describe these stupid kids is *minimally exceptional.* Can you handle that? Minimally exceptional? Whatever happened to the old, reliable explanation, "The boy is slow"? Was that so bad? Really? "The boy is slow. Some of the other children are quick; they think quickly. Not this boy. He's slow." It seems humane enough to me. But no. He's minimally exceptional.

How would you like to be told that about your child? "He's minimally exceptional." "Oh, thank God for that! We thought he was just kind of, I don't know, slow. But minimally exceptional! Wow! Wait'll I tell our friends."

Political correctness cripples discourse, creates ugly language and is generally stupid.

I haven't quite finished this section. (I'm sure I needn't remind you P.C. people that "The opera isn't concluded until the *full-figured woman* offers her vocal rendering.") I know. I really had to strain to get that in. I'm thoroughly ashamed.

But before I leave this section, I wanted to make the point that, on a practical level, this language renders completely useless at least one perfectly good expression: "In the kingdom of the blind, the one-eyed man is king" becomes "In the kingdom of the visually impaired, the partially-sighted person is fully empowered." Sad, isn't it?

LOCATION LOCATION LOCATION

I've noticed that when people speak these days, location seems important to them; and one location in particular: *there*. They say such things as *don't go there; been there, done that;* and *you were never there for me.*

They don't say much about *here*. If they do mention here, they usually say, *"I'm outta here."* Which is really an indirect way of mentioning there, because, if they're outta here, then they must be going there, even though they were specifically warned not to. It seems to me that here and there present an important problem because, when you get right down to it, those are the only two places we have. Which, of course, is really neither here nor there.

So, let's first talk about don't go there. As we all know—painfully, by now—when you mention something someone thinks you shouldn't go into any further, they say, "Don't go there." What they fail to realize, of course, is that, technically, by the time they've told you not to go there, it's too late. You're already there, because you've already mentioned whatever it is they're uncomfortable with. At a time like that, what they should be saying is, "Don't stay there." Or, at the very least, "Please hurry back." Sort of like "Wish you were here."

The only time I would tell someone "Don't go there" is if they told me they were planning a trip to Iraq. If someone said, "We're going on our honeymoon to Fallujah," I would immediately say, "Don't go there."

By the way, when one of those TV newsmen on MSNBC recently tried to get his co-anchor lady to react to some juicy celebrity rumor, she said to him, "I am *so* not going there." And I thought, "Why am I allowing a person like this to bring me the news?"

BEING AND DOING

Another phrase I don't care for is *been there, done that.* I, personally, am not so cocky. I prefer the modest approach. Instead of "Been there, done that," I will usually say, "Been nearby, done something similar." And by the way, most people don't seem to know the complete expression. I heard Drew Barrymore say it on *The Tonight Show:* "Been there, done that, got the T-shirt." It's a little smarter and it hasn't been overused yet.

WHERE WERE YOU?

Staying with this subject of location, when someone is ending a long-term relationship, quite often they'll tell the other party, "You were never there for me." Here, again, what they may be forgetting is that possibly at some time in the past they had told that very same person, "Don't go there." So how can they blame the person for not being there when they themselves had issued specific instructions not to go there in the first place? It seems unfair.

SO MOVE!

Additionally, many people who are ending relationships use another bothersome phrase: *moving on.* They'll say, "I found Steve in bed with a carnival worker and they were doing unpleasant things to a chipmunk. So I'm moving on." And I think to myself, "Actually, Steve sounds more like the one who's moving on."

Or they might say, "I'm leaving Armando. He beat me up yesterday in the frozen-food section of the supermarket. He struck me in the head repeatedly with a Stouffer's Lean Cuisine. I believe it was the Chicken Cordon Bleu. I'm moving on." Occasionally, I get impatient with these people. When they tell me they're moving on, I look at my watch and say, "Well, isn't it about time you got started? No sense standing around here, talking to me, when you could be out there . . . moving on."

I don't know, I guess it all works out, because when I run into the same person a few months later, they usually say, "I'm in a *whole different place* now." And I don't think they're referring to Pittsburgh.

KNOW YOUR PLACE

And by the way, speaking of geographic locations, why is San Francisco always said to be in the *Bay Area,* while Saudi Arabia is in the *Gulf Region*? Is a region really bigger than an area? And what about a *belt*? How big is a belt? The *Bible Belt* is bigger than the *Borscht Belt.* Maybe that's because there are more Christians than Jews. But that doesn't explain the *Rust Belt.* In the last several decades, a good deal of the U.S. population has moved from the Rust Belt to the *Sun Belt.* People changed belts. By the way, part of the Sun Belt runs right through the Bible Belt. That must be confusing.

ZONING OUT

And let's not forget zones, especially *war zones.* The media like that phrase. If there's any kind of explosion at all, even a small gas heater, they'll say, "The living room looked like a war zone." Most of the time it's an overstatement. Because when you get right down to it, the only thing that looks like a war zone is a *combat area.*

Then there's the opposite of a war zone: a *demilitarized zone.* Korea has one of those, separating the North and South. A demilitarized zone sounds like a good idea, but I've noticed that wherever they have a demilitarized zone, there are always a lot of soldiers nearby. I guess that's in case the demilitarized zone suddenly becomes a combat area.

Now, the Gulf Region has been both a war zone and a combat area. That's because there were some countries who wanted to expand their *spheres of influence*. And also because of the big oil companies, who, of course, are in the *private sector*. The private sector is quite different from the *public arena*. Dick Cheney was in the private sector, then he moved to the public arena. Although many of his acts in the public arena have benefited his interests in the private sector.

Getting back a little closer to my own experience, on a recent visit to my hometown, New York City, I was walking through the area that we used to call the *Garment District*. I noticed that the local trade association now wanted people to call it the *Fashion Center*. Not everyone wanted that, just the ones who would like to raise the rents. Fashion Center is another example of how desperately people feel the need to upgrade themselves; they just want to feel better. They want to expand their *comfort zones*.

Your comfort zone is not the same as your *zone of privacy*. A few years ago, when the press was hounding Congressman Gary Condit about Chandra Levy's disappearance, he asked them to please grant him a *zone of privacy*. But of course, they couldn't do that. Because Gary Condit was in the public arena.

As I wind up our little journey through Location Land, I regret not getting to one other place: *where*. And if you wonder *where I'm going with this,* it's because you don't know *where I'm coming from.* Or maybe you simply don't know *where it's at.* Either way, I'm leaving now. *I need my space.*

POLITICIAN TALK #1:
Term Limits

When people mention term limits to me, I usually tell them the only politicians' terms I would like to limit are the ones they use when speaking. They have an annoying language of their own.

And I understand it's necessary for them to speak this way, because I know how important it is that, as they speak, they not inadvertently say something. And according to the politicians themselves, they don't *say* things, they *indicate* them: "As I *indicated* yesterday, and as I *indicated* to the president . . ."

And when they're not *indicating,* they're *suggesting:* "The president has *suggested* to me that as I *indicated* yesterday . . ." Sometimes instead of *indicating* or *suggesting,* they're *outlining* or *pointing things out:* "The president *outlined* his plan to me, and, in doing so, he *pointed out* that he has not yet *determined* his position."

Politicians don't *decide* things, they *determine* them. Or they make *judgments.* That's more serious: "When the hearings conclude, I will make a *judgment.* Or I may simply give you my *assessment.* I don't know yet, I haven't *determined* that. But when I do, I will *advise* the president."

They don't *tell,* they *advise;* they don't *answer,* they *respond;* they don't read, they *review;* they don't *form opinions,* they *determine positions;* and they don't *give advice,* they *make recommendations.* "I *advised* the president that I will not make a *judgment* until he has given me his *assessment.* Thus far, he hasn't *responded.* Once he *responds* to my initiative, I will *review* his *response, determine my position,* and *make my recommendations.*"

And so it is, at long last, that after each has *responded* to the other's *initiatives,* and after they have *reviewed* their *responses,* made their *judgments, determined* their *positions* and *offered* their *recommendations,* they begin to approach the terrifying possibility that they now may actually be required to do something.

Of course, that would be far too simple, so rather than *doing something,* they *address the problem:* "We're *addressing the problem,* and we will soon *proceed to take action.*"

Those are big activities in Washington: *proceeding* and *taking action.* But you may have noticed that, as they *proceed,* they don't always *take action;* sometimes they simply *move forward. Moving forward* is another one of their big activities.

"We're *moving forward . . . with respect to* Social Security." *With respect to* is lawyer talk; it makes things sound more important and complicated. So they're not *moving forward* on Social Security, they're *moving forward with respect to* Social Security. But at least they're *moving forward.* To help visualize this forward motion, you may wish to picture the blistering pace of the land tortoise.

Now, sometimes when they themselves are not *moving forward,* they're moving something else forward. Namely, *the process:* "We're *moving the process forward* so we can *implement* the provisions of the *initiative.*" *Implement* means *put into effect,* and an *initiative* is similar to a *proposal.* It's not quite a *measure* yet, but there's a possibility it may become a *resolution.*

Now, one may ask, "Why do we need all these *initiatives, proposals, measures* and *resolutions?*" Well, folks, it should be obvious by now: We need them in order to *meet today's challenges.* As I'm sure you've noticed, our country no longer has problems; instead we face *challenges.* We're always facing *challenges.* That's why we need people who can *make the tough decisions.* Tough decisions like: "How much money can I raise in exchange for my integrity, so I can be reelected and continue to *work in government?*"

Of course, no self-respecting politician would ever admit to *working in government;* they prefer to think of themselves as *serving the nation.* This is one of the more grotesque distortions to come out of Washington. They say, *"I'm serving the nation,"* and they characterize their work as *public service.*

To help visualize this service they provide, you may wish to picture the activities that take place on a stud farm.

POLITICIAN TALK #2:
Trouble on the Hill

Continuing our review of the language of the elected, it seems that, linguistically, politicians hit their truest stride when they find themselves in trouble. At times like these, the explanations typically begin with a single word: *miscommunication.*

"How do you answer these felony charges, Senator?"

"The whole thing was a *miscommunication.*"

"But what about the tapes?"

"They took them out of context. They twisted my words." Nice touch. A person who routinely spends his time bending and torturing the English language telling us that someone has twisted his words.

But as the problem gets worse, and his troubles increase, he's forced to take his explanation in a new direction. He now tells us that *"The whole thing has been blown out of proportion."* And by the way, have you noticed with these blown-out-of-proportion people that it's always "the whole thing"? Apparently, no one has ever claimed that a only a small part of something has been blown out of proportion.

But as time passes and the evidence continues to accumulate, our hero suddenly changes direction and begins using public-relations jujitsu. He says, *"We're trying to get to the bottom of this."* We. Suddenly, he's on the side of the law. *"We're trying to get to the bottom of this, so we can get the facts out to the American people."* Nice. The American people. Always try to throw them in; it makes it sound as if you actually care.

As the stakes continue to rise, our hero now makes a subtle shift and says, *"I'm willing to trust in the fairness of the American people."* Clearly, he's trying to tell us something: that there may just be a little fire causing all the smoke. But notice he's still at the *I-have-nothing-to-hide* stage.

But then, slowly, "I'm willing to trust in the fairness of the American people" progresses to *"There is no credible evidence,"* and before long, we're hearing the very telling, *"No one has proven a thing."*

Now, if things are on track in this drama, and the standard linguistic path of the guilty is being followed faithfully, "No one has proven a thing" will precede the stage when our hero begins to employ that particularly annoying technique: Ask-yourself-questions-and-then-answer-them:

"Did I show poor judgment? Yes. Was there inappropriate behavior? Yes. Do I wish this never happened? Of course. But did I break the law? That's not the issue."

The calendar is marching, however, and it soon becomes clear that our friend is most likely quite guilty, indeed. We know this, because he now shifts into that sublime use of the passive voice: *mistakes were made.* The beauty of mistakes were made is that it doesn't really identify who made them. You're invited to think what you wish. Bad advice? Poor staff work? Voodoo curse?

But it's too late. Mistakes were made quickly becomes *eventually I will be exonerated,* which then morphs into *I have faith in the American judicial system,* and the progression ends with that plaintive cry, *whatever happened to innocent until proven guilty?* Whatever happened to innocent until proven guilty; well, he's about to find out.

Eventually, in full retreat (and federal custody), he shuffles off in his attractive orange jumpsuit, and can be heard muttering that most modern of mea culpas: *"I just want to put this thing behind me and get on with my life."* And to emphasize how sincere he is, he announces, *"I'm taking responsibility for my actions."* How novel! Imagine; taking responsibility. He says it as though it were a recently developed technique.

Whenever I hear that sort of thing on the news, I always want to ask one of these I'm-taking-responsibility-for-my-actions people whether or not they'd be willing to take responsibility for *my* actions. You know, gambling debts, paternity suits, outstanding warrants. Can you help me out here, pal?

Regarding this whole put-this-thing-behind-me idea in general, here's what I'd like to do. I'd like to put this I-want-to-put-this-thing-behind-me-and-get-on-with-my-life thing behind *me* and get on with *my* life. May I repeat that for you? I'd like to put this I-want-to-put-this-thing-behind-me-and-get-on-with-my-life thing behind *me* and get on with *my* life.

I think one of the problems in this country is that too many people are screwing things up, committing crimes and then getting on with their lives. What is really needed for public officials who shame themselves is ritual suicide. Hara-kiri. Like those Japanese business executives who mismanage corporations into bankruptcy. Never mind the lawyers and the public relations and the press conferences, get that big knife out of the kitchen drawer and do the right thing.

POLITICIAN TALK #3:
Senator Patriot Speaks

To take up a thread from an earlier section of this politico-lingo trilogy, we noted at the time the fact that most politicians operate under the delusion that what they're is doing is serving the nation. Of course, if they really feel this way, they're more than simply misinformed, they're obviously not playing with a full bag of jacks.

So, citizens; a question. Do you think it's at all possible that these politicians whose judgment is so faulty that they actually believe they're serving the nation might be expected to indulge occasionally in some, oh, I don't know, exaggerated patriotism? Hah? Whaddya think? Maybe? Hah?

Well, fans, it's not just possible, it's downright inevitable. And should they be so indulging themselves on the Fourth of July, you'll want to be sure to have hip boots and shovels handy, because brown stuff is going to be piling up at an alarming rate. And I suggest you shovel fast, because your elected heroes will be squeezing every last ounce of counterfeit patriotism out of their blood-starved brains.

And so, as you see them rushing madly across the landscape, pushing all the buttons marked red, white and blue, be on the alert for phrases such as *Old Glory; Main Street; the stars and stripes; the heartland; all across this great land of ours; from Maine to California;* and, of course, *on American soil.* And don't forget all those *freedom-loving people around the world who look to us as a beacon of hope.* Those, I assume, would be the ones we haven't bombed lately. And you'd also better be ready to be reminded, over and over, that you live in a country that somehow fancies itself *leader of the free world.* Got that? Leader of the free world. I don't know when we're going to retire that stupid shit, but personally, I've heard it quite long enough.

And what exactly is the free world, anyway? I guess it would depend on what you consider the non-free world. And I can't find a clear definition of that, can you? Where is that? Russia? China? For chrissakes, Russia has a better Mafia than we do now, and China is pirating *Lion King* DVDs and selling dildos on the Internet. They sound pretty free to me.

Here are some more jingoistic variations you need to be on the lookout for: *The greatest nation on Earth; the greatest nation in the history of the world;* and *the most powerful nation on the face of the Earth.* That last one is usually thrown in just before we bomb a bunch of brown people. Which is every couple of years. And bombing brings me to the language used by politicians when referring to our armed forces.

Now, normally, during peacetime, politicians will refer to members of the military as *our young men and women around the world.* But since we're so rarely at peace for more than six months at a time, during wars Senator Patriot and his colleagues are fully prepared to raise the stakes. (Don't you just love that word, *colleagues?* It makes them sound so . . . I don't know, legitimate.) And so it is, that in times of combat, our young men and women around the world quickly become *our brave young fighting men and women stationed halfway around the world in places whose names they can't pronounce.* And for added emotional impact, they may also mention that these military folks spend a lot of time *wondering if they'll ever see their loved ones again.* That one gets people right in the belly button. And should the speaker be going for maximum emotional effect, he will deliver the above passage, substituting *sons and daughters* for *men and women.*

And isn't that reference "places whose names they can't pronounce" a lovely little piece of subtle racism? That's an all-American, red-meat bonus they throw in for you.

Here's another way politicians express their racist geographic chauvinism: *young men and women stationed in places the average American can't find on a map.* I've always thought it was amusing—and a bit out of character—for a politician to go out of his way to point out the limited amount of intelligence possessed by the American people. Especially since his job security depends on that very same limitation. It would also appear to contradict that other well-traveled and inaccurate standby: *The American people are a lot smarter than they're given credit for.*

Amazingly, politicians have mastered the art of uttering those words with a perfectly straight face, even though the proposition is stated precisely backward. Judging from the results of focus groups, polls and election returns that I've seen, and watching the advertising directed at Americans, I'd say the American people are a lot *dumber* than they're given credit for. As one example, just look at the individuals they keep sending to their statehouses and to Washington to represent them. Look also at what they've done to their once-beautiful country and its landscape.

Wrapping up this modest review of patriotic political language, I think it's safe to conclude that the degree of a politician's insincerity can best be measured by how far around the world our soldiers are, and whether or not any of them is able to pronounce the name of the place. And whether or not their neighbors back home can find it on a map.

ZERO TOLERANCE

I get weary of this zero tolerance bullshit. It's annoying. To begin with, it's a fascist concept; it's what Hitler and Stalin practiced. It allows for no exceptions or compassion of any kind. All is black and white—no gradations. But even more important, it doesn't solve anything. The use of such a slogan simply allows whichever company, school or municipality is using it to claim they're doing something about a problem when, in fact, nothing is being done at all and the problem is being ignored. It's a cosmetic non-solution designed to impress simpletons. Whenever you hear the phrase zero tolerance, remember, someone is bullshitting you.

Dempsey's Department Store: Drop In Today

Shoppers! For a limited time only, Dempsey's Department Store is offering a complete line of cheap crap at extremely high prices. Come in today and be treated rudely by our poorly trained clerks. Remember, at Dempsey's we're not just talking about the high cost of living, we're doing something about it: We're raising our prices.

ENJOY A PLEASANT DIURNAL EXPERIENCE

I'm not sure you've noticed it, but I'm always trying to improve society. And in my relentless pursuit, I feel the time may finally have arrived for me to address "Have a nice day." I think we can agree it has gotten completely out of hand.

Just to give you some background on my long-standing interest in this subject, when I was a young man we didn't have "Have a nice day." It isn't that we didn't have nice days, of course—offhand I can remember several, most of them in 1949—but somehow, we had them without any prompting. No coaching was necessary. The nice days just sort of happened. Perhaps at that time the days were simply nicer, and we took them for granted. It could be that today's days leave much to be desired and actually need a little help. But if that's true, I'm not convinced that "Have a nice day" is the best solution.

And so, in my ongoing effort to elevate human experience, I think I have come up with an improved version of "Have a nice day." It's an alternative system of well-wishing, and frankly, something I hope will become the next big trend.

But before I tell you about it, it's important to remind you that there is a limiting factor at work here: Most people have very little control over what sort of day they're going to have. For instance, when one person says, "Have a nice day," the other may well be thinking, "I've just been diagnosed with hypertrophic cardiomyopathy, and I'm also coughing up thick black stuff." In this case the well-wisher's words will fall on deaf ears.

And so, I feel that perhaps, in the interest of realism, instead of being directed arbitrarily to have a nice day, people should simply be encouraged to do the best they can.

It is also probably unrealistic to expect someone to have a nice day all day long. How often does that happen? The day is simply too long and comprises too many parts. One's day may start off well enough, but quite often the niceness is difficult to sustain over an extended period of time.

And so, instead of the now standard, and far too general, "Have a nice day," I have devised a new, more specific system of selective, short-term well-wishing that puts much less pressure on the recipient. In my system, the time of day a person offers good wishes determines what should be said.

As an example, under my method, if I run into an acquaintance at 9 A.M., I'm likely to say, "Have a satisfying midmorning." I believe in getting someone off to a good start, and it's a modest enough goal to suggest at such an early hour. Had the encounter taken place a bit earlier, I may have been inclined to offer a simple, yet cheerful, "Here's wishing you a refreshing post-sleep phase."

And, turning the clock back even further, if the two of us had been out late and parted at three in the morning, I'm sure I would have told him to "Have yourself a stimulating pre-dawn." As you can see, I'm fully prepared for any time of day.

Twelve noon, you ask? "May your midday be crammed with unfettered joy and myriad delights." Two in the afternoon? "I hope you experience a rewarding post-lunch."

Likewise as the day draws to a close. Can you guess what I tell a person at five-thirty in the afternoon? "Enjoy your sundown." It's short, it's pleasant, it doesn't demand a lot. Here's one for the same time of day which I reserve for more serious-minded friends : "Have a profound dusk." I like it. I feel it shows a certain respect for the other fellow's depth of soul. Or—and this is a particular favorite of mine—"Have a challenging twilight." I enjoy giving the other person something to struggle with just as happy hour is getting under way.

By the way, I have a playful side as well. If my friend is a Scottish person I may say, "Have a bonnie gloaming." But not too often; I don't like to show off my command of foreign languages.

Well, folks, I hope you've enjoyed this little explanation of my new system, but more important, I hope you'll put it to work in your daily lives. And so now, dear reader, as we prepare to take our leave, you may be tempted to think I'll be hard-pressed to offer a parting wish that hasn't already been suggested. Don't underestimate me.

You see, I'm not limited to the short form. Occasionally, in an expansive mood, I get carried away and my rhetoric becomes ornate. And so, as we part, let me state that I hope you have a memorable tomorrow, including, but not limited to, the promising, golden hours of morning, the full, rich bloom of afternoon, and, of course, the quiet, gentle hours of evening, when time, pausing for an instant and breathing a small sigh, rushes forward to greet the newly forming day.

I hope you appreciate the extra effort.

LET'S KILL A TREE FOR THE KIDS

Regarding public Christmas displays: At some point, someone who worked at Rockefeller Center must have said, "Boys, I have a great idea for Christmas. Let's kill a beautiful tree that's been alive for seventy-five years and bring it to New York City. We'll stand it up in Rockefeller Plaza and conceal its natural beauty by hanging shiny, repulsive, man-made objects on it, and let it stand there slowly dying for several weeks while simpleminded children stare at it and people from Des Moines take pictures of it. That way, perhaps we can add our own special, obscene imprint to Christmas in Midtown."

A SORE POINT

Regarding the criticism of Al Gore's actions upon being elected president in 2000 and realizing that the Bush family would do everything in its power to reverse the results illegally: I recall at the time hearing some of the usual morons in this country refer to President-elect Gore as a sore loser because he sought legal redress in the courts.

Sore loser? You bet your fuckin' ass! What on earth is wrong with being a sore loser? It shows you cared about whatever the contest was in the first place. Fuck losing graciously—that's for chumps. And losers, by the way.

Americans have just flat-out lost their spirit; you see it everywhere. Have you ever watched these hockey assholes? When the game is over, they're forced to line up and shake hands with one another after spending three hours smashing each other in the mouth with sticks. Biggest load of shit I ever witnessed. Whatever happened to "In victory, magnanimity; in defeat, defiance." So said Frederick the Great.

EUPHEMISMS: Write If You Get Work

MARX MY WORDS

These days, people who have jobs are called *members of the workforce*. But I can't help thinking the Russian Revolution would have been a lot less fun if the Communists had been running through the streets yelling, "Members of the workforces of the world, unite!"

And I'm sure Marx and Lenin would not be pleased to know that, today, employees who refuse to work no longer go out on strikes. They *engage in job actions* that result in *work stoppages*. And if a work stoppage lasts long enough, the company doesn't hire *scabs*, it brings in *replacement workers*.

READY, AIM, NON-RETAIN!

When it comes to firing people, companies try desperately to depersonalize the process so that no human being is ever seen to fire another. The language is extremely neutral, and whatever blame there is goes to something called *global market forces*. Fuckin' foreigners!

And these companies go through some truly exotic verbal gymnastics to describe what's taking place—although I'm not sure it makes the individuals in question feel any better. After all, being *fired, released* or *terminated* would seem a lot easier to accept than being *non-retained, dehired* or *selected out.*

Nor would I be thrilled to be told that, because the company was *downsizing, rightsizing* or *scaling down*, I was part of an *involuntary force-reduction*. I really don't care that my company is *reshaping* and *streamlining*, and that, in order to *manage staff resources*, a *focused reduction* is taking place, and I'm one of the workers being *transitioned out*. Just fire me, please!

I read somewhere that apparently one company's senior management didn't understand the fuss about this issue. After all, they said, all they were doing was *eliminating the company's employment security policy* by *engaging in a deselection process* in order to *reduce duplication.*

P.S. By the way, when those deselected people begin to look for new jobs, they won't have to be bothered reading the *want ads.* Those listings are now called *employment opportunities.* Makes you feel a lot better, doesn't it?

EUPHEMISMS:
What Do You Do for a Living?

American companies now put a great deal of effort into boosting their employees' self-esteem by handing out inflated job titles. Most likely, they think it also helps compensate for the longer hours, unpaid overtime and stagnant wages that have become standard. It doesn't.

However, such titles do allow an ordinary *store clerk* to tell some girl he's picking up at a bar that he's a *product specialist.* Or a *retail consultant.* If it turns out she's a store clerk, too, but her store uses different euphemisms, then she may be able to inform him that she's a *sales counsellor.* Or a *customer service associate.* And, for a while there, they're under the impression that they actually have different jobs.

These are real job titles, currently in use to describe employees whose work essentially consists of telling customers, "We're all out of medium." Nothing wrong with that, but it's called store clerk, not retail consultant, and not customer service associate. Apparently, stores feel they can charge more for merchandise sold by a customer service associate than they can for the same junk sold by a clerk. By the way, if a clerk should be unhappy with his title, he can always move to a different store, where he may have a chance of being called a *product service representative*, a *sales representative* or a *sales associate.*

And I hope you took note of that word *associate*. That's a hot word with companies now. I saw a fast-food employee mopping the floor at an In-N-Out Burger and—I swear this is true—his name tag said "associate." Okay? It's the truth. Apparently, instead of money, they now give out these bogus titles.

At another fast-food place, Au Bon Pain, I noticed the *cashier's* name tag said *hospitality representative*. The cashier. The name tag was pinned to her *uniform*. The people who sell these uniforms now refer to them as *career apparel*. Or—even worse—*team wear*. I had to sit down when I heard that. Team wear.

Teams are also big in business; almost as big as associates. In Los Angeles's KooKooRoo restaurants the employee name tags say "team member." At a Whole Foods supermarket, I talked to the head of the meat department about ordering a special item; I figured he was the *head butcher*. But his name tag identified him as the *meat team leader*. Throw that on your résumé. I guess the people under him would have been *meat team associates*. I didn't stick around to ask.

So it's all about employee morale. And in a lot of companies, as part of morale-building, the *employees* are called *staff*. But it's all right, because most *customers* are now called *clients*. With those designations, I guess the companies can pay the staff less and charge the clients more.

I'm not sure when all this job-title inflation began, but it's been building for a while. At some point in the past thirty years *secretaries* became *personal assistants* or *executive assistants*. Many of them now consider those terms too common, so they call themselves *administrative aides*.

Everyone wants to sound more important these days:

Teachers became *educators*,
drummers became *percussionists*,

movie directors became *filmmakers,*
company presidents became *chief executive officers,*
family doctors became *primary-care providers,*
manicurists became *nail technicians,*
magazine photographers became *photojournalists,*
weightlifters became *bodybuilders*
and *bounty hunters* now prefer to be called *recovery agents*

And speaking of lifting, those *retail-store security people* who keep an eye on shoplifters are known as *loss-prevention managers.* Still more to come. Later.

Schmuck School: Call Now!

Why not be a schmuck? A licensed, practicing schmuck. Or, if you qualify, a CPS, a certified public schmuck. It may not seem like it when you look around, but there's actually a shortage of schmucks in America. As a result, there's big money in schmucking. The average schmuck earns $28,000 a year, plus benefits. And there are openings for schmucks in every field: The government is run by schmucks; big business is run by schmucks; and the retail field is crawling with schmucks. And, more and more, people are becoming independent, freelance schmucks on their own. Call the Schmuck Technical Institute today and get our free booklet, *Hey Putz, Be a Schmuck!* Most people only manage to be schmucks at parties, but here's your chance to become a full-time, year-round schmuck. Give us a call. Don't be a schmuck, be a schmuck.

IN THE FUTURE:

- The human life span will be extended to 200 years, but the last 150 will be spent in unremitting pain and sadness.

- No one will take drugs, but people will still buy them and conceal them from the police.

- Children will be required to attend school only when something comes up in conversation they do not understand.

- All people will speak the same language, but no one will speak it well.

- Science will develop exotic flowers capable of producing music. Most of these plants will be exploited by record companies.

- All farming will cease and the land will be used for loitering.

- Although people will not keep pets of any kind, someone will still occasionally step in dogshit.

- A race of people living in the center of the Earth will be discovered when one of them comes out to buy a sunlamp.

- Miners will exploit the ocean floor, and, when trapped in a mine, the wives who gather to wait at the entrance will be forced to tread water.

- A team of astronauts will attempt to harness a comet and never be seen again.

- The human body will develop fins and gills, and beach property will increase tenfold in value.

- Man will learn to control the weather with a large hammer.

- A time machine will be built, but no one will have time to use it.

- At birth, religions will charge people an initial fee of $50,000 and then pretty much leave them alone.

- All the knowledge in the world will be contained on a single, tiny silicon chip which someone will misplace.

- People will be born with just enough money to last until they get seriously ill.

- The speed of the Earth's rotation will increase and everyone less than five feet tall will be flung off into space, including Paul Anka.

- The sun's light will diminish until it is the equivalent of a forty-watt bulb, and people with highly developed squinting skills will have a survival advantage.

- Every part of the human body will become replaceable, but all parts will be back-ordered six months.

- A utopian society ruled by women will emerge, and there will be peace and plenty for all. However, many men will still act like macho assholes.

· People will change clothes every six minutes but still never be quite happy with their appearance.

· Cities will be built under huge glass domes which, in time, will be completely covered by graffiti.

· Chickens will operate on gasoline and, surprisingly, many of them will get good mileage.

· Genetic scientists will develop vegetables too big to be transported and they will have to be eaten right at the farm.

· The insane will no longer be housed in asylums; instead, they will be displayed in department store windows.

· The oceans will dry up, and people will find things they dropped in the toilet many years ago.

· There will be no doctors or medicines of any kind and everyone will be really sick.

· Eventually, it will no longer be necessary to forecast the future, because time will disappear and everything will happen at once.

DIG THIS!

Whenever we go into some country we've bombed, burned and occupied, we always find mass graves full of dead people who were killed by the deposed dictator before we got there. And everybody in the United States acts like they're real surprised and disgusted. But when you think about it, what's a guy supposed to do with all those bodies after he's killed a couple of thousand people? Dig a separate hole for each one? Put up little markers with their names on them? Get real, for chrissakes. The whole idea of killing a couple of thousand people all at once, in one place, is to save time. Besides, all the United States ever does is complain a little, take a picture and then leave. So what's the fuckin' difference?

FALL DOWN, GO BOOM!

You know what I find interesting? Land mines. Here are a few great statistics. Listen to this:

There are 340 different types of land mines made by a hundred different companies. Every day—that's every day—roughly six thousand fresh mines are placed in the ground. Right now, there are 110 million land mines in seventy-two countries; and every twenty-two minutes, one of them explodes. Seventy-five mines explode every day, and each month seven hundred people are maimed or killed. That's twenty-six thousand people a year. Don't you find that interesting?

Mines cost only three dollars to make and to put in the ground. But they cost a hundred dollars to disarm and remove. If you tried to remove them all, it would cost $33 billion and it would take eleven hundred years. They cost three dollars apiece, and they last indefinitely. Wouldn't it be nice if other products could make that claim?

Here's another funny statistic: In Cambodia, one out of every 236 civilians is missing a limb or an eye from an exploded land mine. Cambodia now has thirty thousand people with at least one missing limb. And they still have 4 million mines in the ground.

It makes you wonder whether or not some unlucky, one-legged Cambodian guy has ever stepped on a land mine with his good leg. I'll bet it's happened. I'll bet anything there's some guy in Cambodia who has hit the lottery twice.

I tried to think of what would be the most entertaining way of setting off a land mine, and I decided it would be to land on one while doing a cartwheel. Wouldn't that be weird to see? Makes you wonder if the high-school cheerleading squads in Cambodia keep mine detectors handy.

These are the kinds of thoughts I have when I'm sitting home alone and things are slow.

Be a Doctor: Act Now!

Be a doctor in just three weeks! Yes, thanks to our accelerated learning program, you can be a doctor in just three weeks—and you only have to study twenty minutes a day. Or become a dentist in just one afternoon. Don't like your present job? Don't fit into the current job market? Be a doctor. Or a dentist. It's easy. Call now and we'll include a nursing course for your wife. In fact, we can make your wife a nurse over the phone. Call Accelerated Medical School now! Don't be an asshole. Be a doctor.

WHO KNOWS?

A: "I don't know. Or at least I don't know if I know. And I don't even know if I care to know if I know."

B: "I don't know what you mean."

A: "You know, I mean I don't *know* what I mean. You know what I mean?"

B: "What do you mean you don't know what you mean? I don't know what you mean."

A: "I mean, you know, I don't know."

B: "You don't know? You mean that?"

A: "I don't know."

A CONTINUING NEWS STORY ALL IN ONE PLACE

Chicago, May 1: Police announced today they have found evidence of a murder-dismemberment. In a North Side Dumpster, they have found a right arm, a left leg and the eyebrows of an adult white male. Police say the eyebrows are bushy and had recently been plucked. According to spokesmen, the search for additional body parts will continue.

May 6: Here is further news on that North Side dismemberment. Police have now found a set of blond sideburns, a lower lip, two matching buttocks, a middle finger, a knee and two and a half grams of armpit hair. As yet they have no identification, but sources say they're glad that at least it's still only one person they appear to be finding.

May 12: More on the dismemberment story: The police theory that they were dealing with only one body was shattered today when they discovered forty-four male nipples in a vending machine. Twenty-six of the nipples have hair, eighteen do not. One of them has a nipple ring inscribed LONNIE AND MARIE. They have also come across a belly button, a calf and several hundred warts, all found in a Hooters parking lot. Lint from the belly button leads police to believe the navel's owner was wearing a plaid shirt. The investigation continues.

May 23: Here is the latest from the North Side: Police are now puzzled as to just how many bodies are involved. Today they found an Adam's apple, a hunchback, six heels, a pair of un-matching nostrils, a large bag of freckles, two dozen additional belly buttons, a blond goatee, half a neck, and a suitcase full of knuckles. They say all the knuckles have recently been cracked. Cannibalism may be involved, as police have found a rib cage that shows traces of barbecue sauce. More later.

LETTER TO A FRIEND

Dear Manny,

It was great to see you at the hospital last Sunday. You looked good and sounded very positive about yourself. Each time I visit, I can see how much you've improved. I will say, though, it was a lot more fun when you were really fucked up and couldn't remember anything.

Sincerely, Arlo

Krellingford's Restaurant: Cooking Tips

Here are today's cooking tips from Krellingford's Family Restaurant: Hamburger meat that has become slightly hardened by sitting at room temperature for more than nine days can be perked up by soaking it in a mixture of gasoline and varnish remover. Soak the meat overnight and leave it in the sun for several days. Be sure to add a lot of extra-hot spices to offset the gasoline taste. Then try to put the meat to use immediately. By the way, food prepared this way should never be cooked over an open flame.

Here's another valuable cooking tip: You can prepare a delicious stew with just a volleyball, an old fatigue hat and six gallons of bathwater. Put the ingredients in a big pot and cook for thirty-six hours, or until the volleyball is tender. Serves twelve. Excellent with broccoli or corn. Try it over the holidays when the people you serve it to are people you don't see too often.

That's it, folks. Remember, these cooking tips are brought to you by Krellingford's, the home of the Ham and Cheese Caramel Corn Flake Surprise. Why not drop by and take a chance? No one lives forever.

UNCLE D'ARTAGNAN

Uncle d'Artagnan was known as a fancy dan, because he circumcised himself with pinking shears. His wife, Velveeta, the only woman ever to go down on

Newt Gingrich, claimed that to the very end, d'Artagnan wore a golden tassel on his penis. He once told me that as a young man he caught the clap from one of the Doublemint twins and gave it to the other on the same night. He was a lot of fun. He could make his cat shit by pointing the TV remote at it and pressing the VOLUME button. His hobby was falling to the floor in hotel lobbies and pretending to have a stroke. Eventually, he was beaten to death with a cello by a classical musician he befriended at a juice bar.

UNCLE TONTO

Uncle Tonto had a tough life; intercourse with a pelican is not an easy thing to live down. He drank excessively. One time he was so hungover he had to consult a cottage cheese carton to determine the approximate date. At parties, he was the designated drinker, his preference being crème de menthe, Sterno and goat droppings. When stopped and tested by police, he usually set the Breathalyzer on fire. Refusing to drive when he was sober, in the mornings he rode to work on an electric floor buffer, claiming the one drawback was the time he wasted traveling from side to side. He was sentenced to ten years for defecating in a cathedral, but was released immediately when the warden felt Tonto was lowering the prison's standards. After his release, he hitchhiked through Pennsylvania where he was beaten to death by a buggyload of Quakers.

UNCLE JUDAS

Uncle Judas, a man smaller than life, never had a heyday. He peaked in third grade. Not only did opportunity fail to knock, it had deliberately thrown away his address. His existence was so boring he once proudly showed me his neighbor's parking space. In an effort to improve his life, he decided to sell his soul; unfortunately, he sold it on eBay and was never paid. He didn't accomplish much; his autobiography was entitled *Whaddya Want from Me?* One thing he did take pride in: He was one of the few men who, at the age of eighty-five, could still remember the names of all his dentists. He died on the feast of St. Dismas, after mistakenly eating a bag of after-dinner mints before lunch.

UNCLE MONTEZUMA

Uncle Montezuma wasn't too bright; he thought Irving Berlin was the Jewish section of Germany. As a young man he wanted to be a gynecologist, but claimed he couldn't find an opening. He was proud of the fact that while serving a prison term for sodomizing a prairie dog, he learned to drink beer through his nose. For years, he managed a gay car wash but lost all his money investing in a roadside sausage museum. His last job was managing a Playboy club in Auschwitz. When he retired, he wasn't given a gold watch, but his former boss would call him once a week and tell him what time it was. Finally, after marrying a woman who had repeatedly blown Strom Thurmond during a military funeral, he died from eating a batch of carelessly made hollandaise sauce.

EUPHEMISMS: Hotel Lingo

There is no part of American life that hasn't been soiled by the new, softer, artificial language. It's everywhere. When you travel, you notice it in the hotel business, or as they prefer to think of themselves now, the *hospitality industry*. And by the way, hotels are one more place where you will run into job-title inflation.

There was a time in a hotel when you checked in with the *desk clerk*; now he's the *front-desk agent*. But when he answers the phone he becomes *guest services*. I guess it's only fair, everyone else in the hotel has been upgraded. The *bellhop* has somehow become a *luggage assistant*, and he claims to work in *luggage services*. The *maids* have been upgraded several times over the years: *cleaning woman, maid, housekeeper*; now they're *room attendants*.

And on the subject of rooms, depending on where you're staying, *room service* is likely to be called *in-room dining*. Or *private dining*. One brochure I read called it *your private dining experience*. Pretentiousness. Never underestimate the role pretension plays when it comes to creating euphemistic language. Here's another example of it:

At one hotel where I stayed, the restaurant was temporarily located on the lower level. I was told the reason was that they were undergoing *restaurant enhancement*. Okay? The concierge actually uttered that phrase. Not remodeling—restaurant enhancement. And he said it as if it were something people say all the time.

By the way, I shouldn't have to remind you that that *lower level* he referred to was once called the *basement*. I guess I don't really mind the phrase lower level; at least it's *descriptive*, although it is the comparative form and not an absolute. Lower than what? It also bothers me when they tell me the gym is located on *level three*. Level three is just plain old pretentiousness.

And I wish hotels would make up their minds on what to call the *gym*. It's been everything: *gym, fitness center, exercise room, health club. Spa.* God! Spa a-a-ah! Used to be you had to go to Europe to find a spa. Now any place that has a sink and more than three towels is a fucking spa!

One more thing about hotels. A lot of them have replaced the DO NOT DIS-

TURB signs with signs that say PRIVACY, PLEASE. It seems like a small thing, but there's a difference that's worth noting:

Do not disturb is assertive; it's strong. Do not disturb! It means GO AWAY! But *privacy, please* is weak; it sounds as if you're pleading with people: "Privacy . . . please?" Softness. To my mind, it's one more example of the feminization of language that has taken place in this country. And, more important, it represents a retreat from reality.

PUT IT OUT, FUCKO!

Here's another example of the same problem:

THANK YOU FOR NOT SMOKING. Now, speaking strictly for myself, I find nothing wrong with the phrase *no smoking.* It's simple, it's direct, it's firm. No smoking! Any questions? Fine.

But thank you for not smoking. First of all, it's weak. And second, for God's sake, why are you thanking them? It's as if you think they're doing you a favor by not giving you emphysema.

Personally, if I were trying to discourage people from smoking, my sign would be a little different. In fact, I might even go too far in the opposite direction. My sign would say something like, "Smoke if you wish. But if you do, be prepared for the following series of events: First, we will confiscate your cigarette and extinguish it somewhere on the surface of your skin. We will then run your nicotine-stained fingers through a paper shredder and throw them into the street, where wild dogs will swallow and then regurgitate them into the sewers, so that infected rats can further soil them before they're flushed out to sea with the rest of the city's filth. After such time, we will systematically seek out your friends and loved ones and destroy their lives."

Wouldn't you like to see a sign like that? I'll bet a lot of smokers would think twice about lighting up near a sign like that. You have to be direct. Thank you for not smoking is simply embarrassing.

Personally, I think all of this upgraded, feel-good language is a further sign of America's increasing uncertainty about itself.

GIMME A BURGER

Have you noticed that many restaurants can't simply say "cheeseburger" on the menu. They have to get cute and over-descriptive? Well, why not go along with them? Why not use the menu's own language when you place your order? But if you do, you must do it right; no fair reading directly from the menu. Instead, you must memorize the exact description given of the item you've chosen, and then look the waiter directly in the eye as you say:

"I'll have the succulent, fresh-ground, government-inspected, choice, all-beef, eight-ounce, charbroiled sirloin patty, served on your own award-winning, lightly toasted sesame-seed bun, and topped with a generous slice of Wisconsin's finest golden cheddar cheese, made from pure, grade A, premium milk recently extracted from a big, fat, smelly cow infected with flesh-eating bacteria." See if that doesn't get you good service.

But before the waiter leaves your table, ask for a glass of water. Say, "Would you mind bringing me a clear, cylindrical, machine-crafted, moderate-capacity, drinking vessel filled with nature's own colorless, odorless, extra-wet, liquid water?" Pisses them off.

ROLL 'EM

I'm never critical or judgmental about whether or not a movie is any good. The way I look at it, if several hundred people got together every day for a year or so—a number of them willing to put on heavy makeup, wear clothes that weren't their own and pretend to be people other than themselves—and their whole purpose for doing all this was to entertain me, then I'm not gonna start worrying about whether or not they did a good job. The effort alone was enough to make me happy.

NOTHING CHANGES

Dear Political Activists,

All your chanting, marching, voting, picketing, boycotting and letter-writing will not change a thing; you will never right the wrongs of this world. The only thing your activity will accomplish is to make some of you feel better. Such activity makes powerless people feel useful, and provides them the illusion that they're making a difference. But it doesn't work. Nothing changes. The powerful keep the power. That's why they're called the powerful.

This is similar to people's belief that love can overcome everything, that it has some special power. It doesn't. Except one on one. One on one, love is incredibly powerful. It is a beautiful thing. But if love had any power to change the world, it would have prevailed by now. Love can't change the world. It's nice. It's pleasant. It's better than hate. But it has no special power over things. It just feels good. Love yourself, find another person to love and feel good.

Love, George

BITS AND PIECES

· Remember, drinking and driving don't mix. Safety experts suggest you do your drinking first and get it out of the way. Then go driving.

· When your toilet won't stop running, and you put your hand in the tank to fix the chain, don't you wonder, briefly, whether or not the water in the tank has already been in the toilet bowl?

· If you can't say something nice about a person, go ahead.

· I'm not taking sides here, but in listening to a discussion about the Middle East on C-SPAN the other night, I realized I would rather tongue-kiss Yasir Arafat than ass-fuck Ariel Sharon. It's got nothing to do with politics, it's just a feeling I had.

· "Is Bruno a sadist?"
  "Beats me."

· They say that rather than cursing the darkness, one should light a candle. They don't mention anything about cursing a lack of candles.

· Beethoven was a pupil of Haydn, and Schubert lived near the two of them. Supposedly they all frequented the same little cafés. I wonder if they ever got together and gang-banged a lady piano player. Just a thought.

· If you're a criminal, the best way to be is "at large."

· We have classifications called "legally blind" and "legally dead." What about "legally tired"? I think a guy should be able to declare himself legally tired, so he could get out of doing things he didn't want to do.

· If I ever have a stroke, I hope it will be early in the morning, so I don't take my vitamins that day for no reason.

· The American Eye Association reminds you that sties are caused by watching young girls get undressed.

· You know what kind of guy you never see anymore? A fop.

· I typed the word *Google* into Google. Guess what came up? Everything.

TRUE FACT: The Professional Bowlers Association sanctions a tournament called the Odor Eaters Open. It's probably because of all those rented shoes.

· I wonder how many eventual homicides have resulted from wedding ceremonies performed at the Happy Wedding-Bell Chapel in Las Vegas.

· I'll never forget Spondo. Spondo wasn't able to sit around and talk about the good times, because in the sixty years he lived he'd had only one good time. And he would never tell anyone what it was, because he was afraid that if he talked about it, it wouldn't seem as good anymore.

· I notice Connie Chung has faded away again.

· Personal ad: "Hello, I am Henri. I am fifty-five years old, and I am looking for someone who will leave me alone. Please respond. And then leave me alone."

· Christians must be sick in the head. Only someone who hates himself could possibly think of the pleasures of masturbation as self-abuse.

· I believe the next trend in cosmetic surgery will be a procedure that leaves the person with a cryptic smile. Occasionally, of course, the surgeon's hand will slip, and the patient will wind up with a baffled look.

· Are you sick of crime? Well, some communities are doing something about it; they're putting people to death for no reason. Why not start a similar program in your town? Hang a few people in a public area and watch those crime statistics improve. You'll be amazed.

· Ignore these four words.

· There are some people who are so nondescript that if their identities were stolen it would be an improvement.

TRUE FACT: It's against the law to mutilate grave remains. So apparently, it's not illegal to be in *possession* of grave remains, the trouble starts when you mutilate them. Nice distinction.

· I have an *im*personal trainer. We meet at the gym, we don't talk, he works out alone and I go home.

· Here's how money can buy happiness: Money gives you options, options give you breathing room, breathing room gives you control and control can offer you a measure of happiness. Maybe.

TRUE FACT: You can now buy vibrating panties. They're a kind of thong with a built-in vibrator. Just what we needed.

· If no one knows when a person is going to die, how can we say he died prematurely?

· I can't help it, I just have this gut feeling that the Mafia is controlled by organized crime. I don't know what it is, but something fishy is going on.

· I wonder if a classical music composer ever intentionally composed a piano piece that was physically impossible to play and then stuck it away in a trunk to be found years after his death, knowing it would forever drive perfectionist musicians crazy.

· Why don't these guys named Allen, Allan, Allyn and Alan get together and decide how the fuck to spell their name? I'm tired of guessing. The same with Sean, Shaun and Shawn. Stop with all these cute attempts to be different. If you wanna be different, call yourself Margaret Mary.

· All patriarchal societies are either preparing for war, at war, or recovering from war.

· Somebody said to me, "I can't believe Jerry Garcia is dead." And I thought, Doesn't this guy know? Everybody's dead. It's all a matter of degree.

· I can't wait for the sun to explode; it's gonna be great. Just three billion years. I'm so fuckin' impatient.

· If you have a legal problem, guess how you determine whether or not you need a lawyer. You see a lawyer. Isn't that weird?

· Middlebrow bumper sticker in California: IF YOU CAN DREAM IT, YOU CAN DO IT. Yeah, sure. Unless the thing you're dreaming is impossible. Then, chances are, you can't do it. But try to enjoy life anyway.

· "I collect rocks."
 "How many you got?"
 "One. I just started."

· Advice to kids: Get high on sports, not drugs. But if there are no sports in your neighborhood, go ahead and get high on drugs.

· If you had yourself cloned, who, exactly, would be your parents? Can you raise yourself? I guess so. And it might be fun. Just think, by the age of six you'd be driving yourself to school.

· Regarding creationists: Aren't these the same people who gave us alchemy and astrology, and who told us the earth, besides being flat, was at the center of the universe? Why don't we just kill these fuckin' people?

· Idle thought: Do you suppose a perverted priest has ever tried to stick a crucifix up a kid's ass? Just wondering.

· The wrong two Beatles died first.

· I wonder if anyone who was working in or near the World Trade Center that day took advantage of all the confusion to simply disappear. What a great way to get away from your family.

· Indoor electric illumination is often referred to as "artificial light." How can it be artificial? The way I look at it is this: If I can read by it, see myself in the mirror and recognize my friends, it's probably as real as I'm ever going to need it to be.

· You know what you never see anymore? A guy with a pencil behind his ear.

TRUE FACT: One of those clubs that feature nude dancers recently got in trouble with the government because it didn't have wheelchair ramps.

I JUST DON'T SEE IT

Here's something I don't care about in a movie or a TV show: a blind girl. "This is the story of a blind girl who . . ." *CLICK!* You know what? As far as I'm concerned, there's nothing they can do with a blind girl . . . well, maybe a couple of things, but there's nothing they can tell me about a blind girl that's going to interest me. I don't care that she's blind; I don't care if she learns how to communicate with geese; I don't care if she can identify three hundred different flowers from their smell. I really don't care. Does she fuck? Now you're talkin'!

FART RETRIEVAL LEAGUE

"Hello. I'm Fred Ponsaloney III, president of the Fart Retrieval League. We all know that millions of farts are released by Americans each day, but did you know not all of them are free to rejoin the atmosphere? It's true. A small but significant number of farts each day are hopelessly trapped in seat cushions, suspended forever in cotton padding or foam rubber. We're asking you to help rescue these forgotten farts by sending your donations to the Fart Retrieval League. We'll send you a booklet entitled *The Facts on Farts*. And next time you're in a hotel lobby, do your part: Jump up and down on a seat cushion for several minutes and liberate a few trapped farts."

AS THE TURD WHIRLS

The Noodleman Twins Television Network proudly presents America's longest-running daytime drama, *As The Turd Whirls*, a day-to-day chronicle of ordinary people desperately in need of professional intervention and perhaps even cranial surgery. Take a break in your day as once again we flush the toilet of life, and as blue water fills the bowl, we watch, fascinated. . . . *As the Turd Whirls*.

(Romantic violin music is heard as a well-built man approaches a beautiful woman in an upscale bar)

VINNY: Hi. You wanna play a game?

NADIA: What kind of game?

VINNY: It's called Count the Man's Balls.

NADIA: Die in a fire, bourgeois scum!

VINNY: We really should get together, I'm an interesting guy. I can take a live cock-a-roach and put it up my nose and pretend it's not there. I also like to do unusual things to small woodland mammals, but not until I pull out all their claws. Otherwise, look out! Lots of screaming from Vinny. I'll bet you never dated a guy like me. Believe me, I'm worth a try.

NADIA: I wouldn't go home with you if you had six dicks.

VINNY: Come on. I purposely didn't jerk off today just so I could take someone home. You wanna compare hard-ons?

NADIA: I'm a woman, trouser-stain!

VINNY: So? Lemme see your hard-on.

NADIA: Listen! I can't take the time to explain anatomy to you. I've been waiting all day just to get out of this tight underwear. I'm getting real moist in my groin area. I'd love to take off my clothes and have someone massage me, firmly but gently, all around my crotch. My female organs are warm and pulsating, and I can smell the sexual fluids and secretions flowing out of me and mingling with my sweat.

VINNY: Now you're talkin'. Let's go to my house.

NADIA: Okay, but no sex. Understand?

VINNY: Fine by me. But can I at least jerk off? I waited all day.

Join us again tomorrow on *As the Turd Whirls*, as Trent has to decide whether to blow the mailman in exchange for free stamps.

THE FARMING RACKET

Farmers are on government welfare and you pay for it. Good year, bad year—doesn't matter. They still get money. In a bad year—drought or floods—the crop is poor, incomes drop, farmers can't make their payments and they need financial help; you pay for it. In a good year—favorable weather—there's a bumper crop, prices fall, income drops, farmers can't make their payments and they need financial help; you pay for it. Either way, farmers win, you lose. Oh well, I guess we should be grateful; at least there's plenty of tasteless food, all safely sprayed and filled with contaminants. You know, "Bless us, O Lord, and these, thy gifts . . ."

CELLULAR CHITCHAT

You know what I don't understand? People on the street having casual conversations on a cell phone. Casual stuff. Walking along, just visiting.

"So how's Ellen? Good. Tell her I said hello."

Too casual for me. You know what a cell-phone call oughta sound like?

"Hello, Tony? Listen, my pants are on fire. I'm goin' to the fire house. What? Take my pants off? Good idea. Thanks. Listen, say hello to Ellen, will ya? I gotta go, my bush is catching fire."

Now that's a fuckin' cell-phone call. Not this shit:

"So, what are you doin', Joey, watchin' TV? Really? I was only guessin'. What's on? Oh, I saw that. Try another channel. Yeah, go ahead, I'll wait."

Try to find a phone plan that provides more than just free minutes. See if any companies are offering free brains.

IS ANYONE THERE?

(Phone rings)

MAN: Hello. Philosophy Department.

CALLER: Is Jack there?

MAN: Well, what do we mean when we say, "Jack"? Is there really such an entity? Or is Jack simply a description? A label. There are countless people who call themselves Jack. Can they all be doing so accurately? And by the way, where is this "there" you speak of? As I listen to you, I experience your voice as a physical sensation within my head. Certainly Jack isn't in *there*. Wherever your entity called Jack is, it's probably safe to say that that is where he is. At least for the moment.

CALLER: I just would like to speak with Jack.

MAN: I'm sorry, Jack was killed this morning. Or was he? After all, here we are, talking about him. Is he truly gone? One way of looking at it would be—

(*Click!*)

IT'S NO BULLSHIT!

AN ASTOUNDING COLLECTION OF AMAZING STORIES FROM THE SECRET FILES OF *BELIEVE IT OR ELSE* MAGAZINE. READ THESE ASTONISHING FACTS AND FEEL YOUR FUCKIN' BRAIN MELT.

The sun does not really give off light. It merely appears to give off light because everything around it is so dark.

The Belzini tribe of South American Indians will eventually be extinct, because they initiate their young by putting them to death at the age of three.

During her entire sixty-four-year reign, Queen Victoria never once went to the bathroom. She said she was holding it in for a more appropriate time. Her words were, "We don't have to go just now."

Indianapolis, the capital of Indiana, is actually located in Brazil. It only seems to be in Indiana when viewed on a map.

When the Alexander Farkington family moved from Boston to San Diego, they had to leave their dog, Peckerhead, behind. Miraculously, two weeks later the dog showed up in Key West, Florida. Mistakenly, Peckerhead had taken Interstate 95 south instead of getting on the Massachusetts Turnpike.

Contrary to popular belief, Babe Ruth did not call his famous home-run shot. He was actually giving the finger to a hot-dog vendor who had cheated him out of twelve cents.

Incredibly, there was no Hitler. There is no record of any such person. It's true, there was a little German man with a small moustache who combed his hair to one side and started World War II. He also killed six million Jews. But he was not Hitler. He was, in fact, a shoemaker named Hank Fleck.

A cheetah is actually slower than an armadillo. It only appears to be faster, because the armadillo moves so slowly.

Unbelievably, a goldfish can kill a gorilla. However, it does require a substantial element of surprise.

It's now possible to travel completely around the world without money or credit cards. You must be prepared, however, to walk and swim extremely long distances.

A forty-two-year-old man from Ballbender, Wyoming, drove a riding lawn mower backward from Vermont to Argentina. The trip put him under such stress that he is now incapable of thought.

The pyramids are not really old. They were built in 1943 as a joke by drunken Italian soldiers on leave in Egypt at the time. All photographs of the area taken before that time have been retouched.

The sky is not blue. It merely looks that way because blue is the name we have given that color.

Two times two is not four. It is nine. Actually, everything is nine except seventeen. Seventeen is actually six.

Placing a two-hundred-pound pile of cooked garlic, dogshit and choco-late chips on the doorstep of your newly purchased home will keep your enemies away. However, it will not prevent your new neighbors from considering you a family that bears watching.

The record for the greatest amount of Jell-O in one location belongs to Lemon Lime, Minnesota, where residents poured twenty thousand boxes of Jell-O into a lake and heated it, just to claim the title. Most of them are happy with the results. However, some local residents, diving in the shallow areas, claim to have hit their heads on small pieces of fruit cock-tail.

BELIEVE IT OR ELSE, BUT IT'S NO BULLSHIT!

Buy This and Get One of These: Act Now

Here's one more thing you don't need that costs too much and won't last long. Even if you've never had credit before; even if you owe money; even if you're bankrupt; even if you don't intend to pay; we don't care. Thousands of customers come back to us year after year, and they all say the same thing: "Please, give us our money back!" Remember, it costs a little more, but it doesn't work as well. And, it's loaded with things you can't pro-nounce. Special prices for senior citizens—triple. Don't forget, we're big enough to give you a good screwing and small enough to smile while we're doing it.

SMART SHOPPER

Usually, when you go to someone's house they offer you coffee. They say, "You want some coffee?" I tell them, "No thanks, I have coffee at home. But I could use a little pancake mix." I try to get things I need. If I don't need coffee, I'm usually prepared with options:

"Do you have any of those Chef Boyardee SpaghettiOs? The ones with the little hunks of weenie in 'em? Good, I'll take a couple of cans of them. Large, if you have 'em. By any chance, you don't have any Hebrew alphabet soup, do you? No? Okay. I didn't think so. How do the wax beans look today? I see, the produce didn't come in yet. Well, I guess you better just give me a couple of rolls of toilet paper and some Glass Wax and I'll be on my way. I have to get over to Farley's house and do my drugstore shopping. He's havin' a special on gauze pads." Be a smart shopper. And don't forget to bring your coupons.

FRUIT-FLAVORED TEAS

I would like to talk to you about fruit-flavored teas. These would be teas that are flavored like fruit. Fruit-flavored teas. You need to understand that. These are not fruits. They're teas.

But they taste like fruit. All right? They have names like strawberry kiwi, lemon berry, orange mango, wild cherry, blackberry and cranberry. They taste like fruit. And they sound like fruits, too, don't they? They're not. They're teas. Fruit-flavored teas. And frankly, I don't understand this.

Personally, I've always been of a mind that if you're looking for fruit flavor, if you're genuinely interested in something that tastes like fruit, and you find yourself in the tea section, you're probably in the wrong aisle.

My advice is, if it's fruit flavor you're after, play it safe, go ahead and get some fruit. I have found in my experience that fruit almost always turns out to be a reliable source of fruit flavor.

Another good place you may wish to look for fruit flavor would be in fruit juice. Fruit juice is made by squeezing the juice out of the fruit. Apparently, the juice that runs out of the fruit has a fruit flavor. Perhaps that's why they call it fruit juice. It doesn't taste like tea. For tea taste, you would need to get some tea.

So let's sum this up: If it's fruit flavor you want, you can't go wrong with fruit. Or, as I've pointed out, fruit juice. Don't be ordering tea. Tea has a tea flavor. It's not like fruit. It's more like tea. If you want tea, I say order tea. That's a different experience. It's known as "having tea."

Have you noticed, by the way, there are no tea-flavored fruits? Take a clue from nature.

LEAVE MY CHOCOLATE ALONE

I don't understand why a chocolate dessert should include raspberries or strawberries. Intrusions of that type spoil the dessert. Leave the chocolate alone; it was doing fine by itself.

I mean, here I am, innocently sitting at my table, waiting for a nice chocolate thing with lots of whipped cream and chocolate sauce to arrive, and I find that some asshole in the kitchen has decided to show off by throwing a bunch of strawberries around. Chef's ego! Strawberries belong in strawberry shortcake, not in chocolate desserts.

I wouldn't want a bunch of chocolate in my strawberry shortcake, would you? No. Ergo, I don't want strawberries hangin' around my chocolate cake.

Chocolate cake is called chocolate cake for a reason—it's chocolate. Leave it alone. Put the strawberries in a nice sherbet if you must. Or put 'em in a bowl by themselves, over there near the raspberries. But please don't spoil my chocolate.

Hey, chef! You want to exercise your ego? Weave the berries into fabric and make a strawberry chef's hat. Be as creative as you want, but stop fucking with my chocolate.

P.S.—People who dip sweetly tart stawberries into liquified chocolate, wait for it to cool, and then eat the whole thing ought to be placed in mental institutions. What you should do is this: Drink the chocolate before it cools, then put the strawberries on your kids' cereal.

And while we're at it folks, nuts have no business in ice cream. Ice cream should be creamy. Nuts interrupt the creamy idea. Chunks of nuts don't belong in ice cream. Put 'em in a little bowl by themselves; put 'em in a candy bar; stick 'em up your nose for all I care, but leave my ice cream alone. And, in general, please folks, stop fucking with my desserts!

EUPHEMISMS: Food and Restaurants

Euphemisms and politically correct speech have also infiltrated the food and restaurant businesses. We may as well begin with the inflated job titles, since they seem to be showing up everywhere we visit.

In a truly absurd departure from reality, at some point *waiters* temporarily became *waitpersons*, as if *waiters* and *waitresses* were somehow sexist terms. For a while there, a few of them even became known as *waitrons*—until everyone involved simply refused to call them that. Now they seem to have settled on *servers*. These servers are said to be on the *waitstaff*. Waitstaff seems forced, doesn't it? And it goes without saying, no restaurant today would dare allow a *cook* to *cook* the *food*; instead, the *cuisine* must be *prepared* by a *chef*.

An important factor to keep in mind with all of this restaurant and food talk is yuppie pretentiousness. I was in a Yuppie joint last year where the cover of the noontime menu, instead of saying *menu*, actually had the words *lunch solutions*. There I sat, unaware that I even had problems, and those nice folks were ready to provide solutions. Once again, I feel the need to emphasize that I actually saw this. Every example I offer you on these euphemism topics has been personally observed.

And before we get to the food itself, I just want to remind you that you can usually determine a restaurant's price range by noticing how it advertises. If it uses the word *cuisine*, it will be expensive; if it mentions *food*, the prices will be moderate; however, if the word *eats* is employed, rest assured any savings you make on the food will be more than offset by high medical expenses.

Now, on the subject of food itself, I'm sure you know that certain foods have been altered. I don't mean genetically, I mean euphemistically. They tried to do it to prunes. The California Prune Board wanted to change the word *prunes* to *dried plums*, because research told them that women in their thirties reacted more favorably to the phrase dried plums. California women in their thirties—does that tell you enough?

And the poor prunes were not alone. A long time ago the same thing happened to *garbanzo beans*. Apparently, someone thought the word *garbanzos* sounded too much like a circus act, so they began using the older name, *chickpeas*. Also at about that time—again, for marketing purposes—*Chinese gooseberries* became *kiwifruit*. And since it was obvious feminists would never use an oil derived from *rapeseed*, we were all introduced to *canola oil*. And just to round out our meal, the reason *Chilean sea bass* became so trendy a few years ago was because it was no longer being called *Patagonian tooth fish*. That item needs no comment.

And let's not even mention *capellini*, which became *angel-hair pasta*. Jesus! Angel hair. And by the way, who was it that took the perfectly nice word *macaroni* and started calling it *pasta* in the first place? That sounds like more of that marketing bullshit. Never underestimate the relentlessness of the marketing people. Because long before we had yuppies, consumer goods had been getting image upgrades from the marketers.

For example, *seltzer water* has variously been known as *seltzer, carbonated water, soda water, club soda* and, finally—enter the yuppies—*sparkling water*. Sometimes these days, the label on the sparkling water says *lightly carbonated*. Of course, that means they had to find a name for water that wasn't carbonated, and since *noncarbonated* sounded far too ordinary, the trendier restaurants decided on *flat water*. There are even a few places that refer to it as *still water*. It's subtle, but it's clearly a decision that when it comes to beverages, flat may possibly be seen as negative.

Never overlook pretentiousness. Pretentiousness is the reason we don't *drink water* anymore; instead we *hydrate ourselves*. Hey, I'll hydrate myself to that.

EUPHEMISMS: Buy This and Eat It
FOOD LINGO

Food-advertising language. You're familiar with the words. You hear them all the time: *Fresh, natural, hearty, old-fashioned, homemade* goodness. In a can. Well, if those are the words they want to use, let's take a look at them.

Old-fashioned

When they say old-fashioned, they want us to think about the old days, don't they? The old days. You know, before we had sanitation laws; before hygiene became popular; back when E. coli was still considered a condiment.

Homemade

Right next to old-fashioned in the warmth and nostalgia department is home-made. You see it on packages in the supermarket: *homemade flavor*. Folks, take my word for this, a food company operating out of a ninety-acre processing plant is functionally incapable of producing anything homemade. I don't care if the CEO is living in the basement, wearing an apron and cooking on a hot plate. It's not gonna happen.

Same with restaurants. *Homemade soup*. Once again, it doesn't matter how much the four-foot, amphetamine-laced waitress with the bright orange hair smoking the three Marlboros reminds you of your dear old mother, the soup is not homemade. Unless the chef and his family are sleeping in the kitchen. And if that's the case, I'm not hungry.

Homemade is a myth. You want to know some things that are homemade? Crystal meth. Crack cocaine. A pipe bomb full of nails. Now we're talkin' homemade. If you need further information, check the notes of Timothy McVeigh. Old Tim knew how to cook up little homemade goodies.

Home-style

Sometimes the advertising people realize that homemade sounds too full of shit, so they switch to *home-style*. They'll say something has *home-style flavor*. Well, whose home are we talking about? Jeffrey Dahmer's? Believe me, folks, there's nothing home-style about the boiled head of a Cambodian teenager. Even if you sprinkle parsley on the hair and serve it with oven-roasted potatoes.

Style

Style is another bullshit word you have to keep an eye on. Any time you see the word *style* added to another word, someone is pulling your prick. *New York–style deli.* You know why they call it that? Because it's not in New York. That's the only reason. It's probably in Bumfuk, Egypt, the owner is from Rwanda and the food tastes like something the Hutus would feed to the Tutsis.

Another bogus use of the word *style* is in *family-style restaurant.* What that means is that there's an argument going on at every table. And the eldest male is punching the women. You know, "family-style."

Gourmet

Here's another word the advertising sluts have completely wiped their asses with. Everything is gourmet now: *gourmet* cuisine in a can, *gourmet dining in a cup.* Folks, try not to be too fuckin' stupid, will ya? There's no such thing as *gourmet coffee, gourmet rolls* or *gourmet pizza.* Gourmet means one thing: "We're going to charge you more."

The same is true of the word *cuisine.* The difference between food and cuisine is sixty dollars. That's it. They're stealing from you. You want to know some real gourmet food? Toasted snail penises; candied filet of panda asshole; deep-dish duck dick. Now you're talkin' cuisine.

Hearty

This is a word only a bullshitter could love: *hearty.* Soups are hearty, breakfast is hearty. Folks, next time you see the word *hearty*, take a good look at the rest of the label. "Hmmm! Six hundred grams of saturated fat." You know, hearty. As in heart attack.

The *y* words

It's a good idea to be wary of any words ending in *y*, in particular such words as *butter-y, lemon-y* and *chocolate-y*. Any time marketers add a *y* to the name of a food, you can be sure they're yanking your schwantz. *Real chocolatey goodness.* Translation? No fuckin' chocolate!

And while we're at it, *zesty* and *tangy* are not real words that normal people use in conversation. Has anyone ever turned to you in a restaurant and said, "This pork is really zesty. And it's tangy, too"? My comment? "Hey, Zesty, I got somethin' tangy for ya!"

Flavored

Folks, watch out for the word *flavored. Lemon-flavored drink.* Oh yeah? Lemme know if you spot any trace of a goddamn lemon in there.

There's even a pet food that calls itself a *chicken-flavored treat.* Well, a dog doesn't know what chicken tastes like. He might like it if you give him some, but he's not gonna say, "Oh good, I was hoping we'd have something chicken-flavored again. One grows tired of beef."

Natural

The last one of these bullshit food words is *natural.* And these comments are directed at all you environmental jackoffs out there. The word *natural* is completely meaningless. Everything is natural. Nature includes everything. It's not just trees and flowers and the northern spotted owl. It's everything in the universe. Untreated raw sewage, polyester, toxic chemical waste, used bandages, monkey shit. It's all perfectly natural. It's just not real good food. But you know something? It is zesty. And it's tangy, too. Bon appétit, consumers.

RETAIL BLUES

LET'S TAKE THE GLOVES OFF

When did they pass a law that says the people who make my sandwiches have to be wearing gloves? I'm not comfortable with this. I don't want glove residue all over my food; it's not sanitary. Who knows where these gloves have been? Let's get back to the practice of human hands making sandwiches for human beings.

And we have to stop this tipping-people-for-counter-service thing. No one should get a tip for standing erect, moving a few feet to one side and picking up a muffin. The sign on the pathetic little tip cup says TIPS WOULD BE APPRE-CIATED. Well, so would some fuckin' decent service. Let's be honest, folks, there's not a great deal of IQ floating around behind these counters. Maybe in their homelands some of these people might pass for intelligent, but to me, if they live in this country and can't speak English, their IQ plunges about three hundred points. I shouldn't have to leave a tip in order to pay for someone's English lessons.

DON'T BE A PHONEE

Store clerks! You should not be on the phone when you're waiting on me. When I, the customer, walk up to the counter, the phone should be put down. And if it rings while you're waiting on me, let it ring. After ten rings, pick it up, and, without even saying hello, say, "I'm currently waiting on an actual, paying customer who has money and has had the courtesy to come into the store to transact business. I will get to you when the store is empty. Stay on the line if you wish, but I may not get to you till sundown." Then smile at me and say, "Where were we?" The in-store customer should always come first.

MOVIN' ON UP

And where did this new rule come from that says the second person standing on line in a store has to hang back and leave about six feet of space between himself and the customer being waited on? You know, one person is already up at the counter and the next person is standing back five or six feet, leaving all this unused space. When did this shit start?

And I'm not talking about stores where there's an obvious central feeder-line—one line that feeds a number of counter positions. I'm talking about an individual line that feeds a single counter, and these dopey people hang back like they're afraid of offending someone. This has obviously grown out of some perverted, politically correct impulse. Move up, mother-fucker! Take up the slack! You know what I do when I'm behind one of these timid jackoffs? I step right in front of him and take his place in line. If he doesn't like it, I say, "You should have moved up, twat-face. Don't you know space is at a premium? I gave you a full minute and you didn't move. Now *I'm* next!"

THE UNDECIDEDS

I also get very unhappy with people in supermarkets who stop their carts in the middle of the aisle and just stand there looking at the soup. They don't know what they want, so they're looking. Parked. Middle of the aisle. They're trying to decide. Why would you go to the supermarket if you didn't know what you wanted? You know how I shop? I enter the store with a list in my hand, and I move quickly through the aisles from item to item, and I'm in the parking lot before Hamlet has figured out if the cream of mushroom is a better bargain than the chicken with stars. I say, know what you want, get what you need, and get the fuck out of there. That's how ya shop.

MESSAGE FROM A COCKROACH

"Hello there, I'm a cockroach. Listen, I'm gonna keep this to a minimum, because I gotta get back to the kitchen and eat a bunch of crumbs that I spotted on the table. Plus there's a little puddle of gravy on the left side of the sink near the drain that nobody noticed. Okay, here's my deal: Bug sprays. We don't like 'em, we don't need 'em, we don't want 'em. We say get rid of 'em. Okay? That's it. Otherwise, if you don't do what we want, we're gonna crawl all over your face while you're asleep. We'll even go up your nose. We don't care. Thanks. I'll see you later. And for chrissakes, turn out the lights, will ya?"

FLY THE FRIENDLY SKIES

When I'm on a commercial flight, and I see a fly flying down the center of the airplane from back to front, I like to take him off to one side and ask him if he understands how fast he's moving. They never really know. So the first thing I do is briefly explain Newton's laws of motion, complete with a small diagram to make it a bit easier. But the only thing their little fly egos are interested in is how fast they're moving. So I tell them that in order to calculate their velocity relative to the ground, all they have to do is add their own flying speed to the speed of the airplane. I show them how it works and they can't believe it when they discover that they're actually traveling over five hundred miles an hour. The first thing most of them mention is that a frog's tongue wouldn't stand a chance against that kind of speed.

PLEASE DON'T SAY THAT

Here is a small sampling of embarrassing societal clichés that I find tiresome and, in some cases, just plain ignorant.

IF IT SAVES JUST ONE LIFE

You often hear a new policy or procedure justified by the specious idea that "If it saves the life of just one (insert here 'child' or 'American soldier'), it will be worth it." Well, maybe not. Maybe a closer look would show that the cost in time, money or inconvenience would be much too high to justify merely saving one life. What's wrong with looking at it like that? Governments and corporations make those calculations all the time.

EVERY CHILD IS SPECIAL

An empty and meaningless sentiment. What about every adult? Isn't every adult special? And if not, then at what age does a person go from being special to being not-so-special? And if every adult *is* also special, then that means all people are special and the idea has no meaning. This embarrassing sentiment is usually advanced to further some position that is either political or fund-raising in nature. It's similar to "children are our future." It's completely meaningless and is probably being used in some self-serving way.

HE'S SMILING DOWN

After the death of some person (even many years after) you will often hear someone refer to the deceased by saying, "I get the feeling he's up there now, smiling down on us. And I think he's pleased." I actually heard this when some dead coach's son was being inducted into the Football Hall of Fame.

First of all, it's extremely doubtful that there's any "up there" to smile down from. It's poetic, and I guess it's comforting. But it probably doesn't exist. Besides, if a person *did* somehow survive death in a non-physical form, he would be far too busy with other things to be smiling down on people.

And why is it we never hear that someone is "smiling up at us." I suppose it doesn't occur to people that a loved one might be in hell. And in that case the person in question probably wouldn't be smiling. More likely, he'd be screaming. "I get the feeling he's down there now, screaming up at us. And I think he's in pain." People just refuse to be realistic.

THIS PUTS EVERYTHING IN PERSPECTIVE

This nonsense will often crop up after some unexpected sports death like that of Cardinals pitcher Darryl Kile. After one of these athletes' sudden death, one of his dopey teammates will say, "This really puts everything in perspective." And I say, listen, putz, if you need someone to die in order to put things in perspective, you've got problems. You ain't payin' enough attention.

AMERICA'S LOST INNOCENCE

I keep hearing that America lost its innocence on 9/11. I thought that happened when JFK was shot. Or was it Vietnam? Pearl Harbor? How many times can America lose its innocence? Maybe we keep finding it again. Doubtful. Because, actually, if you look at the record, you'll find that America has had very little innocence from the beginning.

LET THE HEALING BEGIN

This bothersome sentiment is usually heard following some large-scale killing or accident that's been overreported in the news. Like Columbine, Oklahoma City or the World Trade Center. It's often accompanied by another meaningless, overworked cliché, "closure." People can't seem to get it through their heads that there is never any healing or closure. Ever. There is only a short pause before the next "horrifying" event. People forget there is such a thing as memory, and that when a wound "heals" it leaves a permanent scar that never goes away, but merely fades a little. What really ought to be said after one of these so-called tragedies is, "Let the scarring begin." Just trying to be helpful here.

Consolidated International: We Need You

We're Consolidated International, and we might be looking for you. Are you one of those submissive people who show up, punch in, put out, pitch in, punch out, clean up, head home, throw up, turn in, sack out and shut up? That's what we need, people we can keep in line. We just might have a place for you. Consolidated International: People making things, so people have things to do things to other people with.

THE FANATICS WILL WIN

I hope you good, loyal Americans understand that in the long run the Islamist extremists are going to win. Because you can't beat numbers, and you can't beat fanaticism—the willingness to die for an idea.

A country like ours, preoccupied with Jet Skis, off-road vehicles, snow boards, Jacuzzis, microwave ovens, pornography, lap dances, massage parlors, escort services, panty liners, penis enhancement, tummy tucks, thongs and Odor Eaters doesn't have a prayer—not even a good, old-fashioned

Christian prayer—against a billion fanatics who hate that country, detest its materialism and have nothing really to lose. Maybe fifty years ago, but not today when germs and chemicals and nuclear materials are for sale everywhere.

People who don't give a shit and have nothing to lose will always prevail over people who are fighting for some vague sentiment scrawled on a piece of parchment. Folks, they're gonna getcha; and it ain't gonna be pleasant.

We can't drop a five-thousand-pound bomb on every one of them. They will either run all over us or, in trying, they will turn us into even bigger monsters than we already are.

And don't get all excited about this goofy idea, "the spread of democracy." No matter who the United States puts in charge to bring peace and order in Iraq or Palestine or anywhere else, those people will be killed. It's that simple. Anyone who supports the United States will be killed. Peace and order will not be tolerated. Start saving your cash for the black market, folks, you're gonna need it.

THE CHANNEL SEVEN EDITORIAL REPLY

ANNOUNCER: Channel seven recognizes its obligation to provide equal time to viewers who disagree with its editorial policy. Here, then, with an editorial reply, is Dr. Steven Wanker, a clinical psychologist. Dr. Wanker speaks as a private citizen.

DR. WANKER: Thank you. Are these channel seven people kidding? Hah? What kind of crap are they trying to pull? Did you hear that shit they said last week about the budget? Jesus Christ! I couldn't believe it! What kind of assholes do they think we are?

And they're always acting so self-righteous, like they know what's good for us and we're too stupid to think. I'm gettin' tired of this shit. How about you? Hah? Fuck these people! Who do they think they are, with their goddamn three-piece suits and fancy eyeglasses?

And, by the way, do you know how long it takes to get one of these goddamn editorial replies on the air? Three fuckin' years! Three years ago I started asking to do this shit! They kept sayin', "Well, we're not sure you're stable enough to be allowed on the air." And I said, "Stable? What're you fuckin' people, crazy? I'm as stable as the next cocksucker!" I said to 'em, "Bend over and I'll give you somethin' stable!"

Fortunately, they were able to recognize the logic of my argument and here I am. But you know what I found out these assholes can do? They can cut you off the air if they want to. For instance, if they don't like what you're saying, they can just fuckin' interru—

ANNOUNCER: That was Steven Wanker, a clinical psychologist. Tune in to channel seven tomorrow night for another editorial reply, as schoolteacher Howard Boudreaux delivers an opinion titled, "What's All This Phony Bullshit about Drunk Driving?" And, later in the week, don't miss Mayor Cosmo Drelling as he addresses another important issue: "What's So Bad about Slavery?" Thank you, ladies and gentlemen. We now join *Blowjobs of the Rich and Famous* in progress.

And later this evening, tune in *Doctor Jim* as he removes a wart from a lesbian.

KEEP TV FAMILY-FREE

I'm always glad when some group of American hostages is released overseas, and they finally get to come home to their families. I'm not glad because I particularly care about them, but because I get sick of hearing about them on TV, and I get sick of listening to their families. Jesus, did I get tired of all those whining hostage-families during that bullshit in Iran in the 1970s. "My husband's a hostage! The government's not doing enough!"

Hey, lady, if you don't want your husband to be a hostage, tell him to stay the fuck out of Iran or places like it in the first place. It's a simple thing; you don't have to be a theoretical physicist to figure it out. If you stay out of these places, you've got a good chance of not becoming a hostage.

And the media always refers to them as "innocent Americans." Bullshit. There are no innocent Americans. And whatever they are, they're certainly not news. First thing you know, once they're back they start writing books, one by one, and you have to endure the whole thing all over again, seeing them on every talk show, regurgitating the whole fuckin' boring story again.

Here are some more families I'm not interested in: astronauts' families. Who cares about these people? Astronauts' wives and children. They're not news—keep 'em off TV. I don't even care about the astronauts themselves. Anal-retentive robots wasting money in space. And—not incidentally—spreading our foul, grotesquely distorted DNA beyond this biosphere.

I say, keep the infection local. God! Haven't we done enough damage on *this* planet? Now we're going to go somewhere else and leave our filth and garbage all over the universe? Jesus, what a pack of fuckin' idiots we are. Thank you.

SEEMS LIKE OLD TIMES: A DIALOGUE

KEVIN: Boy, a lot has changed in twenty years.

RAY: Yeah.

KEVIN: Is Naughton still around?

RAY: Frankie?

KEVIN: No, Jimmy.

RAY: Jimmy's dead. And Frankie died at the funeral. They're both dead.

KEVIN: What about Bobby? How's he?

RAY: He's dead, too. A lot of 'em are dead.

KEVIN: What was the other Naughton kid's name? Tommy? Is he dead?

RAY: No. Tommy's not dead.

KEVIN: Thank God for that.

RAY: He's dying.

KEVIN: Jeez! The mother must be heartbroken.

RAY: The mother was killed in a boiler explosion. Blown to pieces.

KEVIN: Jeez. I'll never forget that house the Naughtons lived in. Kind of a cute little place with green shutters.

RAY: Hit by lightning fifteen years ago. Burned to the ground. All the pets were killed.

KEVIN: Jeez. That's too bad. I remember the Naughtons always liked that house because it was so close to the church.

RAY: Our Lady of Perpetual Suffering?

KEVIN: Yeah.

RAY: The church is gone. Condemned by the city last year and demolished on Good Friday.

KEVIN: So where do the neighborhood kids go to school?

RAY: Most of the neighborhood kids were killed a few years ago by a rapist who worked at the grocery store.

KEVIN: Dorian's?

RAY: No, Babington's.

KEVIN: I liked Dorian's. They always had good produce.

RAY: Dorian's collapsed ten years ago and killed nineteen customers. The entire Halloran family was decapitated at the butcher counter while they were pickin' out meat.

KEVIN: Jeez. Times really change.

RAY: Well, life goes on.

REAL REALISM FOR REALISTS
DRINK UP

I think the warning labels on alcoholic beverages are too bland. They should be more vivid. Here are a few I would suggest:

"Alcohol will turn you into the same asshole your father was."

"Drinking will significantly improve your chances of murdering a loved one."

"If you drink long enough, at some point you will vomit up the lining of your stomach."

"Use this product and you may wake up in Morocco wearing a cowboy suit and tongue-kissing a transmission salesman."

"Men: When emptying your pockets after a night of using this product, you may come across a human finger, a wad of Turkish money and a snapshot of a naked ex-convict named Dogmeat. The photo will be inscribed, 'To Dave, my new old lady.'"

"Women: Drink enough of this and you will spend the rest of your life raising malnourished children in a rusting trailer with a man who sleeps all day. Except for the rapes."

GOD REST HIS SOUL

Newspaper death notices could also be written more honestly. Have you seen the lies they print? "Cherished and beloved husband of Kathleen, devoted and esteemed father of Thomas; loving brother of Edward"? Bullshit. Let's be realistic:

"Ryan, James D.; jealous and abusive husband of Kate; lustful, wanton father of Maureen; controlling and manipulative father of Matthew; cruel, envious and conniving brother of Thomas, died yesterday to the great relief of the family. May he burn a long time in the worst parts of the deepest pits of the hottest precincts of hell. It is good to have him out of our lives.

"Funeral at the Church of the Holy Bleeding Wounds, burial in Crown of Thorns Cemetery. No flowers; donations should be made in cash directly to the family for purposes of celebration."

ON BENDED KNEE

This idea could spread. It might even inspire young men to make more realistic marriage proposals: "Honey, let's get married. I realize I'm asking you to take a chance on a proven loser—I don't have any money or stuff like that—but maybe—hear me out—maybe we could find a cheap, unclean apartment in a dangerous neighborhood and have more kids than we can afford. If we're lucky, maybe a few of them won't be born sickly and disfigured, in spite of our genetic histories. Meanwhile, I could find a dehumanizing, low-paying, dead-end job with no benefits, while you stay home watching TV and gaining weight.

"And if things get bad—like if I get paralyzed, and you get raped by Mexican sailors and lose your mind and start crying all the time—we can always move in with my parents. They love kids, and their incest counseling is almost complete. And I've noticed Dad's 'episodes' are starting to result in far less property damage than before. What do you say, honey? You want to give it a shot? Maybe our second set of HIV tests will turn up negative."

EARLY BOARDING: Children

If I may renew a theme found elsewhere in the book, I have a bit more to say about early boarding on the airlines. It's not just favoritism to the "disabled" that bothers me; that's unfair enough. But! Immediately after the various cripples, limpers and wheelchair jockeys have been unfairly allowed to board early, the airline then has the nerve to allow people with children to get on the plane. Once again, at the expense of the rest of us. I do not understand this policy at all.

Why should people board early simply because they have children? What's so special about having kids? After all, a lot of kids are accidents; many people wind up with children simply because they're unlucky. Is that something we should be rewarding? I don't think being careless in bed should qualify someone for special treatment on an airplane.

And by the way, as with the devious methods of the cane-and-crutch crowd mentioned earlier, I think there are some couples who bring their kids along on a trip for the sole purpose of early boarding. What other reason would you have for including kids on a trip? Enjoyment? Hardly.

In fact—and this may seem extreme to some—it's my conviction that there are some couples who have intentionally gotten married and had families specifically for the purpose of getting on the plane early. I know it sounds unlikely to you, but don't forget, these are cold, pragmatic, striving yuppie-boomers; unsentimental people who largely regard children as props and commodities, anyway: "Honey, let's have a kid, so we can board planes early." "Great idea, Scott! You start making a list of good preschools, and I'll get the lubricating jelly." Believe me, it happens more than you may think.

So, during this preflight, pre-boarding fiasco, after the crippled and the maimed have been safely strapped in, the airline people tell us they will now "preboard passengers traveling with small children." Well, that's fine as far as it goes, but what about passengers traveling with large children? Suppose you have a six-month-old son with a growth-hormone disorder? One of those seven-foot infants with oversized heads that you see in the *National Enquirer*. Actually, with a kid like that I think you're better off checking him in at the curb, don't you? He'd probably enjoy it in the luggage compartment. It's dark in there, and I would imagine he's used to that.

But I digress. Forgive me for indulging my weakness for flights of colorful narration. Back to the real problem: people with children on airplanes. Here's how you solve this. You make the following announcement:

"Ladies and gentlemen, this is a pre-boarding announcement only. We would like to address those of you who, both today and in your lives generally, find yourselves burdened with needy and annoying children. We sympathize with you, but as long as you've decided to drag them along with you to Pittsburgh, we wish to minimize the inconvenience of their presence to the rest of us. Here is what is going to happen:

"First of all, you're getting on last—if there's room. Before that, we're going to board the full-grown humans and allow them to settle in, get comfortable and have a drink or two. You may be standing out here for an hour or more. Then, you and your children will be swiftly escorted onto the aircraft and placed in a special, soundproof, walled-off area in the rear of the plane. There will be standing room only. For safety purposes, you will be tethered to one another and secured to the wall with leashes and straps.

"More than likely, there will not be any food left for you, but your children will be allowed to scavenge the trays of those passengers who did not finish their meals. Aside from that food service, you will be left alone and expected to keep the children quiet.

"And now, we ask that you please gather your precious creatures around you, and, when you hear the whistle, see to it that they move smartly and swiftly onto the plane, remaining quiet and avoiding any eye contact with grown-ups. Thank you for flying the friendly skies of Sensible Airlines."

TRAFFIC ACCIDENTS
NEVER HANG AROUND

I don't often write about my own experiences; it's not my style. But I had a recent incident in traffic that I'd like to tell you about. And before I begin, there are a couple of things you ought to know about me: I drive kind of recklessly, I take a lot of chances, I never maintain my vehicles and I don't believe in traffic laws. And so, because of these practices, I tend to have what a picky person would probably refer to as a lot of traffic accidents.

And wouldn't you know, last week I ran over a sheep.

Or, possibly, I ran over a small man wearing a sheepskin coat. I'm not sure, really, because I didn't stop. That's another rule of mine: I never stop when I have a traffic accident. Do you? No. You can't. Who has time? Not me.

If I hit something, or I run somebody over, I keep moving! Especially if

I've injured someone. I refuse to involve myself in other people's injuries. I'm not a doctor, I've had no medical training; I'm just another guy, out, driving around looking for a little fun. And I can't be stopping for everything.

Listen, folks. Let's be logical about it. If you stop at the scene of the accident, all you do is add to the confusion. These people you ran over have enough troubles of their own without you stopping and making things worse. Think about it—they've just been involved in a major traffic accident! The last thing they need is for you to stop, get out of your car, go over to the wreckage and start bothering them with stupid questions: "Are you hurt?"

Well, of course they're hurt. Look at all the blood! You just hit them with a ton and a half of steel—of course they're hurt. Leave these people alone. Haven't you done enough? For once in your life do the decent thing—don't get involved.

Look at it this way, it's none of your business in the first place; the whole thing took place *outside* of your car. Legally speaking, these people were not even on your property at the time you ran them over. They were standing in the street; that's city property. You are not responsible! If they don't like it, let 'em sue the mayor.

And besides, the whole thing is over now; it happened back *there, behind you!* For God's sake, stop living in the past. Do yourself a favor, count your blessings, be glad it wasn't you. As it is, there's probably a substantial dent in your fender. So be satisfied, my friend, you got off easy.

And I'll give you a truly practical reason not to stop. If you *do* stop, sooner or later the police are going to show up. Is that what you want? To waste even more of your time, standing around with a bunch of worthless civil servants, filling out forms, answering a lot of foolish questions . . . lying to the authorities?

And one more thing: Didn't anyone *else* see this accident? Are you the only one who can provide information? Surely the people you ran over caught a glimpse of it at the last moment. So, let *them* tell the police what happened. They certainly had a better view of it than you did.

There's just no sense in having two conflicting stories floating around about the same dumb-ass traffic accident. Things are bad enough: People are dead, families have been destroyed, it's time to *get moving!* Chances are you're late for dinner as it is.

EXCEPTION TO THE RULE

Now, folks. There are two sides to this. Helping people by leaving them alone when they're injured is one thing, that's my altruistic side; people need to be self-reliant, and I want to do what I can to foster that. But it's often hard for me to drive away from a nice fiery accident scene, because I have a self-indulgent side, and that needs to be honored too.

And so, on the other hand, if I'm out driving, enjoying a lovely day, and I *see* a traffic accident—one I'm not involved in—I stop immediately! I wanna get a good look at what's goin' on. I enjoy that sort of thing. If people are injured, I wanna take a look! I am Curious George.

Of course, the police don't like that. They say you're rubbernecking and blockin' traffic. I tell 'em, "Never mind that rubberneckin' shit, I wanna take a look!" My philosophy: I'm never too busy that I can't stop to enjoy someone else's suffering. I'm looking for a little entertainment. To me, traffic accidents are one more form of entertainment.

You want to hear my dream accident? Two buses and a chicken truck gettin' hit by a circus train in front of a flea market. Entertainment! I'm lookin' for an antique lamp stickin' out of a clown's ass. If I'm gonna take the time to stop, I expect a couple of fuckin' laughs.

And if the traffic situation is such that I can't quite see what's going on—can't get a good enough look—I'm not the least bit shy about asking the police to bring the bodies over a little closer to the car.

"Pardon me, Officer. Would you fellows mind dragging that twisted-looking chap over here a little closer to the car? My wife has never seen anyone shaped quite like that. Look at that, Sugarlips! Those are his testicles hanging from the rearview mirror. Thank you, Officer, that will be all now, you can throw him back on the pile. We'll be moving along."

And off we go, out onto the highway looking for a little fun. Perhaps a flatbed truck loaded with human cadavers will explode in front of a *Star Trek* reunion. One can only dream and hope.

A CRY FOR HELP

Dear Friend:

Your name has been provided to us, because we have discovered that, in spite of America's recent economic problems, you may still have a few dollars tucked away that you are saving for a future financial emergency. Well, that emergency is here. We're hoping you will be sympathetic to our effort and express it with your generosity.

Stated quite simply, we're raising money to help the rich and powerful. These hard-driving people continue to require large amounts of money, and most of them are far too busy to attend to this sort of direct appeal for themselves. We are here to help.

The rich and powerful need your financial support in order to increase their wealth and power, so they can exercise even greater influence over na-

tional events, and, of course, over your lives. Remember, these people are small in number and, therefore, inadequately represented in our system of proportional government. They consequently lack influence and suffer the fate of many minorities, i.e., being ignored by the very government they have helped elect. It is for these reasons they have decided to band together to better present their ideas and especially to expand their influence with elected officials. But first they need your help. They need money.

In the first stage, your money is needed for basics: stationery, office supplies, postage, phones and rent (first month, last month, security deposit). The rich and powerful need to set up a headquarters so they can start really raising money in order to live properly. But once they reach that level that doesn't mean your job is done. Not at all.

In fact, once things are running smoothly there'll be a continuing and even greater need for more and more of your money in order to provide all of the expensive clothing, imported cars, fine jewelry, gourmet foods and exotic pets that these people require. That's when your dollars will really count, helping provide the lifestyle to which the rich and powerful are not only accustomed but entitled.

In addition to these considerable personal expenses, there will, of course, be a need for large amounts of money to persuade and influence the many politicians and government officials who, after all, have financial obligations of their own. Most of these dedicated public servants are underpaid and must find ways of supplementing their income without taking time off from work. Your money, funneled through the rich and powerful, can go a long way toward solving their financial problems. And you will have the satisfaction of knowing you have helped advance the selfless agenda the rich and powerful have laid out in their effort to improve our country.

Can we count on you? Will you help? Will you give yourself the opportunity to say you helped the rich and powerful when they really needed it? Do it now. Do it for yourself and for your children. Sit down and write out a check for a substantial amount, maybe even more than you can afford. Make it payable to The Fund for the Rich and Powerful. You'll take satisfaction knowing you have done your part. And you'll be secure in the knowledge that whenever you have a problem, the rich and powerful will always be there to help.

Sincerely,
Esterbrook Winslow
Somewhere Offshore

P.S. Your canceled check is your receipt.

BOB CALLING

Bob dials a number.

DON: Hello?

BOB: Hi, is this Don?

DON: Yes.

BOB: Hi, Don, this is Bob.

DON: Oh. Hi, Bob.

BOB: Hi. Well, I guess I'll let you go now. Bye.

DON: Okay. Bye.

Bob dials again.

CARL: Hello?

BOB: Hi, is this Carl?

CARL: Yes.

BOB: This is Bob.

CARL: Oh. Hi, Bob.

BOB: Hi. Well, you're probably a busy guy. I'll let you go. Bye.

CARL: Bye.

Bob dials again.

TOM: Hello?

BOB: Hello, Tom?

TOM: Yes. Who's this?

BOB: Bob.

TOM: Hi, Bob. What's goin' on?

BOB: Not much, how about you?

TOM: Same old same old.

BOB: Great. Well, I gotta go. I've got a bunch of calls to make.

TOM: Okay. Bye.

Bob opens his phone book and makes a list of more people he wants to bond with. His phone rings.

BOB: Hello?

VOICE: Hi, is this Bob?

BOB: Yes.

VOICE: This is Steve.

BOB: Oh, hi, Steve. How are you?

STEVE: Well, that's the reason I'm calling.

BOB: Oh?

STEVE: Yes. I'm doing fine. So I thought I'd let you know that and maybe save you a call.

BOB: Well, that's mighty thoughtful of you. Thanks.

STEVE: That's okay. Well, that's it. I guess we'll talk tomorrow.

BOB: You got a deal. Bye.

STEVE: Bye.

Bob scratches Steve's name from his list of calls and reaches for the receiver. So much still to do.

BITS AND PIECES

- Remember, kids, Mr. Policeman is your friend. Always cooperate with him. Mr. Policeman wants to help you, so you must help Mr. Policeman. Don't forget, if you refuse to cooperate, Mr. Policeman will beat you to death. Especially if you're not white.

- I'm not a person who thinks he can have it all, but I certainly feel that with a bit of effort and guile I should be able to have more than my fair share.

- You know what would be fun? To have a set of twins, name them Dumbo and Goofy and then just sit back and see how their personalities develop. I'll bet they'd really enjoy going to school every day.

- I'd like to point out that during the twentieth century, white, God-fearing, predominately Christian Europe produced Lenin, Stalin, Franco, Hitler and Mussolini.

- Next time you're in an elevator, blow your nose real loud into your bare hands and then ask if anyone has a Kleenex. Or blow your nose into a Kleenex, open it up and stare at the stuff and say, "Wow! Look at this. It's all green and yellow." Then show it to the other people. I guarantee you won't pass many floors before you have the elevator all to yourself.

- I've never seen a homeless guy with a bottle of Gatorade.

· One great thing about getting old is that you can get out of all kinds of social obligations simply by saying you're too tired.

· You know who you have to admire? A Catholic hit man who blesses himself just before he strangles someone.

· I've noticed that a Jew will sometimes use a little paper clip to hold on his yarmulke. Shouldn't that be God's responsibility? I mean, you did your part, you put the thing on. Shouldn't it be God's job to keep it there? Or why don't Jews just wear larger yarmulkes that grip the head better? Maybe with an elastic strap that could go under the chin. By the way, I know a hip-hop Jew who wears his yarmulke backward. It's hard to detect, but I think it looks great.

· Suppose you tried to fuck a woman who had ten personalities, and nine of them said okay, but one of them resisted and tried to fight you off. Would that still be a rape?

· "Where do we go from here?"
"Who says we're here?"

· Because of mad cow disease, they're now going to leave certain cow parts out of hamburger meat, including the skull. Well, I don't know about you folks, but I can't imagine enjoying a hamburger that doesn't have at least a hint of cow skull in it.

· I was looking in the mirror the other day and I realized I haven't changed much since I was in my twenties. The only difference is I look a whole lot older now.

· Here's a safety tip from the Fire Department: Kitchen-grease fires can be quickly and safely extinguished by dousing them with a mixture of benzine and lighter fluid. Apply quickly and stand clear.

TRUE FACT: More children in the United States are molested each year than wear braces.

· I'd like to know the suicide rate among people who call in to radio psychologists and actually follow the advice they get.

· I have no regrets in life. Although I am kind of sorry I never got to beat a man to death while wearing a tuxedo.

· There's a message window that comes up on my computer screen whenever I type in a command the computer doesn't like. It says, "Fuck you, I don't do that."

· When people use the phrase *call it quits*, why do they use the plural? It would make more sense to say, "I'm going to call it quit."

· I recently witnessed something I'll never forget: an eclipse of the earth. But because it was an eclipse of the earth, there was no place to look. So I looked at the earth. And as I did, the earth got very dark. But the period of darkness was brief because of how close we are to the earth. Remember, kids, never look directly at an eclipse, always get someone else to tell you about it.

• The National Rifle Association reminds its members: Never fire a gun at your own body. Unless you're trying to seriously injure yourself.

• As a part of those displays that honor rock stars in the Rock and Roll Hall of Fame, I think they should show the amount of money each artist spent on drugs, year by year. Also, it wouldn't be a bad idea to list which drugs the artists were taking while recording particular songs and albums. Just so we'd all know.

TRUE FACT: In 1733, the Russian army had a treatment for soldiers who suffered severe homesickness. At the first sign of the condition, they buried the soldier alive. That's good. I like people who go right to the heart of a problem.

• Do you have any perfectly good possessions you don't need? Send them to Ill Will Industries, where our completely healthy and able-bodied employees earn money by breaking things and rendering them useless. Call Ill Will. Help those who are already doing fine.

• I'm in favor of anything that destabilizes the republic.

• Regarding the Menendez brothers, my opinion is that you can rarely get two kids to agree to kill their parents unless the parents really deserve it.

TRUE FACT: Purina now has a cat food made especially for cats who live indoors. "Indoor cat food for indoor cats." Meanwhile, I'm sure you're aware that some human beings have no food at all.

· The worst thing about e-mail is that you can't interrupt the other person. You have to read the whole thing and then e-mail them back, pointing out all their mistakes and faulty assumptions. It's frustrating and it's time-consuming. God bless phone calls.

· I can't understand a grown man whose nickname is Fuzzy and who actually allows people to call him that. Do these guys really introduce themselves that way? "Hi, I'm Fuzzy." If some guy said that to me, I would say to him, "Well, you don't look very fuzzy to me."

· If you vote once, you're considered a good citizen. If you vote twice, you face four years in jail.

· In this country, alcohol is hardly ever seen as a drug problem. Instead, we think of it as more of a driving problem.

· Life is simple: Your happiness will be based completely on luck and genetics. Everything comes down to luck and genetics. And when you think about it, even your genetics is luck.

· Seems as though I never get to do the fox-trot anymore.

· What's going on with these people who tell you to "have a safe trip"? I would never tell a person that. Because if they died it would feel really creepy.

· If I had been in charge of reorganizing the government's security agencies into a homeland defense organization, I would have divided the responsibilities into two agencies: The Bureau of What the Fuck Was That? and The Department of What the Fuck Are We Gonna Do Now?

READ ONLY

Don't you get tired of this simpleminded Laura Bush nonsense about children reading, or reading to children, or teaching children to read, or reading to children about teaching, or whatever the fuck it is? What is it with these Bush women? His mother—the big silver douche bag—was into the same sort of nonsense. These women should not be encouraging children to read, they should be encouraging children to *question* what they read. Content is far more important than the mere act of sitting with your mother and dragging your eyes across text. By the way, I noticed that, apparently, the idea of teaching children to read didn't work when Barbara tried it on George.

EUPHEMISMS: Political-Interest Groups

Not all the political manipulation of language is done by the big bad politicians. A lot of it comes from people who think of themselves as good and virtuous: the politically active. Activists. As opposed, I guess, to "passiv-ists." Who should not be confused with pacifists, who are, after all, quite often activists.

GOD HELP US

Let's start with *faith-based*, which was chosen by right-wing holy people to replace the word *religious* in political contexts. In other words, they've conceded that religion has a bad name. I guess they figured people worry about *religious fanatics*, but no one's ever heard of a *faith-based fanatic*.

And by the way, none of the Bush religious fanatics will admit this, but the destruction of the World Trade Center was a *faith-based initiative*. A fundamentalist-Moslem, faith-based initiative. Different faith, but hey, we're all about diversity here.

The use of faith-based is just one more way the Bush administration found to bypass the Constitution. They knew Americans would never approve of government-promoted religious initiatives, but faith-based? Hey, what's the problem?

The term faith-based is nothing more than an attempt to slip religion past you when you're not thinking; which is the way religion is always slipped past you. It deprives you of choice; *choice* being another word the political-speech manipulators find extremely useful.

CHOOSING SIDES

School choice, and the more sophisticated version, *parental choice*, are code phrases that disguise the right wing's plan to use government money to finance religious education. If you hear the word *voucher*, watch out for the religious right. Again, though, be alert for the more sophisticated term for vouchers: *opportunity scholarships*.

It's impossible to mention the word *choice* without thinking of the language that has come out of the abortion wars. Back when those battles were first being joined, the religious fanatics realized that *antiabortion* sounded negative and lacked emotional power. So they decided to call themselves *pro-life*. Pro-life not only made them appear virtuous, it had the additional advantage of suggesting their opponents were *anti-life*, and, therefore, *pro-death*. They also came up with a lovely variation designed to get you all warm inside: *pro-family*.

Well, the left wing didn't want to be seen as either anti-life or pro-death, and they knew *pro-abortion* wasn't what they needed, so they decided on *pro-*

choice. That completed the name game and gave the world the now classic struggle: pro-choice vs. pro-life. The interesting part is that the words *life* and *choice* are not even opposites. But there they are, hangin' out together, bigger than life.

And by the way, during this period of name-choosing, thanks to one more touch of left-wing magic, thousands of *abortionists' offices* were slowly and mysteriously turning into *family-planning clinics.*

And on the subject of those places, I think the left really ought to do something about this needlessly emotional phrase *back-alley abortions.* "We don't want to go back to the days of back-alley abortions." Please. It's over-descriptive; how many abortions ever took place in back alleys? Or, okay, in places where the entrance was through a back alley? Long before *Roe v. Wade,* when I was a young man, every abortion I ever paid for took place in an ordinary doctor's office, in a medical building. We came in through the front door and took the elevator. The three of us. Of course, as we were leaving, the elevator carried a lighter load.

A BUNNY IN THE OVEN?

Then there's the *fetus–unborn child* argument. Even leaving aside personal feelings, the semantics of this alone are fun to unravel. To my way of thinking, *whatever* it is, if it's unborn, it's not a child. A child has already been born; that's what makes it a child. A fetus is not a child, because it hasn't been born yet. That's why it's called a fetus. You can call it an unborn fetus if you want (it's redundant), but you can't call it an unborn child. Because—not to belabor this—to be a child, it has to be born. Remember? The word *unborn* may sound wonderful to certain people, but it doesn't tell you anything. You could say a Volkswagen is unborn. But what would it mean?

The fanatics have another name for fetuses. They call them the *pre-born*. Now we're getting creative. If you accept pre-born, I think you would have to say that, at the moment of birth, we go instantly from being pre-born to being pre-dead. Makes sense, doesn't it? Technically, we're all pre-dead. Although, if you think about it even harder, the word pre-dead probably would best be reserved for describing stillborn babies. The post-born pre-dead.

By the way, I think the reason conservatives want all these babies to be born is that they simply like the idea of birth. That's why so many of them have been *born again*. They can't get enough of it.

TARZAN WOULD BE MORTIFIED

Here's some more left-wing nonsense, this time from the environmentalists, the folks who gave us the *rain forest*. "Save the rain forest." They decided to call it that because they needed to raise money, and they knew no one would give them money to save a *jungle*. "Save the jungle" doesn't sound right. Same with *swamp*. "Save the swamp!" Not gonna work. Swamp became *wetland!* Nicer word. Sounds more fragile. "Save the wetlands." Send money.

But I think the environmentalists still have their work cut out for them when it comes to *global warming* and the *greenhouse effect*. As I see it, these terms are far too pleasant for people to get all worked up about. For one thing, global is too all-embracing for Americans; it's not selfish enough. "Isn't globalization that thing that's been stealing our jobs?" Global doesn't make it. And *warming* is such a nice word. Who wouldn't want a little warming?

Similarly, greenhouse effect will never do. A greenhouse is full of plants and flowers, full of life and growth. Green equals life, house equals shelter. The greenhouse effect sounds like something that gives you life and shelter and growth. You're never gonna turn something like that into a villain.

And the environmentalists have another language problem, this one concerning nuclear energy: *meltdowns*. They like to warn us about meltdowns. But a meltdown sounds like fun, doesn't it? It sounds like some kind of cheese sandwich. "Would you like some fries with that meltdown?"

EUPHEMISMS: POLITICAL-INTEREST GROUPS
A Few Afterthoughts

Here is more of the distorted language of political persuasion:

- Conservatives oppose *gun control*. Liberals know *control* is a negative word, so they call it *gun safety*. That's about what you'd expect, but it's hard to find words to describe the following distortion: some of the pro-gun people are referring to gun control as *victim disarmament*. Isn't that stunning? Victim disarmament! It takes your breath away. Like a gun.

- Liberals call it *affirmative action*; conservatives are less positive. They refer to *government-mandated quotas, racial preferences* and *unfair set-asides*.

- Rich Republicans want to keep their money in the family, and so the Republican party began to call the *inheritance tax* (a pro-tax term) the *estate tax* (a neutral term), which they later changed to the *death tax* (an anti-tax term).

· When liberals talk about *spending*, they call it *investing* or *funding*. Funding means *spending money*. "We need to do more to fund education." On the other side of the ledger, when Republicans need to *raise taxes*, they call it *revenue enhancement*.

· The energy criminals now refer to *oil drilling* as *oil exploration*. Instead of Mobil and Exxon, they'd rather you picture Lewis and Clark.

· When the original Enron story was developing, Bush's people referred to the crimes as *violations*. They said a *review* might be necessary, but not an *investigation*. So I guess if the other guys do it, it's a *crime* that should be *investigated*, but if your guys do it, it's a violation that should be reviewed.

· Liberals call it *global warming*, conservatives call it *climate change*.

· If you want the individual to sound shady and suspicious, you call him an Eye-racky. If you want to upgrade him a bit, he becomes an *Iraqi-American*. If you're trying to clean him up completely, you call him an *American citizen of Iraqi descent*.

· When people came to this country, primarily from Europe, they were called *immigrants* and *refugees*. As they began arriving from Latin America and the Caribbean, we started calling them *aliens*. Some of them are here illegally. Those in this country who sympathize with that group don't call them *illegal aliens*, they refer to them as *undocumented workers*. Or *guest workers*. Sometimes they're identified by the purely descriptive term the *newly arrived*.

- *Most-favored-nation* trade status was considered too positive a term for China, so it was decided instead to call it *normal trade relations*. Aside from the language, there is no difference between the two policies.

- The Nazis referred to the extermination of the Jews as *special action*. In their version, the Jews were not killed, they were *resettled, evacuated* or *transferred*. The dead were referred to as the *no longer relevant*.

- In Palestine, Arabs refer to the areas Jews have taken over as *occupied territories*. Jews call them *disputed areas*. The Israelis call their assassinations of Palestinian leaders *focused thwartings, pinpoint elimination* and *preventive measures*.

- At one time in Iraq Hussein called the hostages he was holding his *guests*.

- Countries we used to call *rogue nations* are now referred to as *nations of concern*, so we can talk with them without insulting them outright. But as a result of bad behavior, North Korea has been downgraded from a *state of concern* to a *rogue state*. Likewise, *failed nations* are now called *messy states*. *Underdeveloped countries* have also been upgraded. They're now *developing nations*.

And finally . . .

- During the election that defeated Manuel Noriega in Panama, there were groups of thugs that wandered around beating and killing people and looting stores. They called themselves *dignity battalions*.

HOW GOES IT?

If you enjoyed my earlier description of my new system for wishing people a nice day, perhaps you'll be interested in the following, equally innovative method I employ in similar situations. The difference is that this attempt to relieve the tedium of short exchanges involves the replies I give, as opposed to the good wishes I offer.

As an example, when someone asks me how I am, I try to make my answer as specific as possible. I'm not the type to toss off a casual, "I'm fine." I take care to express my exact condition. And thanks to my creative flair, I can choose from a number of options:

If I'm in a self-protective mood, a simple "guardedly well" often does the job. I find also "tentatively keen" doesn't give too much away. Of course, if there is the least bit of doubt, I simply rely on my old standby, the ever-cautious, "I'm fairly well, comparatively speaking." That works nicely, especially if I feel I genuinely have something to hide.

If I wish to be a little more open, "I'm semi-dandy, thank you for inquiring" is effective, and has the added advantage of acknowledging the other person's contribution to the exchange.

By the way, should it be one of today's trendy kids, I'm quick to drop a hip and with-it "moderately neato," in order to show that I'm really a cool guy and not just some old fuddy-duddy. Once again, with "moderately neato" I reveal only a limited bit of information.

TAKE THAT!

But sometimes I'm having one of my really great days, and I'm in a jaunty and expansive mood. In these situations I tend to throw caution to the wind and express my full feelings. Innocently enough, the person will inquire, "How are you?" And he has no idea what's coming. So I give him both barrels.

I lean forward, look him squarely in the eye, and hit him with a quick and cheery "I'm good, well, fine, keen, dandy, swell and excellent! And, might I add, fabuloso!" Believe me, I've bowled over more than one unsuspecting inquirer with this sudden volley of positive energy.

WEEKEND WISHES

Just so you know, I'm prepared for other situations as well. If someone says, "Have a nice weekend," I never say, "You too." Because I never know if, perhaps, by the time the weekend rolls around, I will have other plans for that person. Come Friday, I may wish to have them slain.

YULETIDE

Also, I never say, "A merry Christmas to you and yours." I don't like the possibilities suggested by that use of the possessive pronoun *yours*. One never knows when the other person may be a slave owner. I certainly wouldn't want to encourage that sort of behavior.

CLOSING THOUGHTS

One last thing: My stingingly clever remarks sometimes extend to retail encounters. When the supermarket checkout person asks, "Paper or plastic?" I often say, "Woven silk," just to keep him on his toes. "Rolled steel" is not a bad answer either.

I'm happy to pass along to you these methods of mine for making the world a better place. I hope you use them wisely, and, may I be so bold as to say, "Have an excellent immediate future."

TOO MANY THANK-YOUS

HOSTS & GUESTS

I find it bothersome that on radio and TV interview shows, once the host says, "Thank you for being here," the guest always thinks he has to say, "Thank you for having me." It's not necessary. All that's needed is a simple "You're welcome" or "Nice to be here." "Having people on" is what they do on interview shows; they're looking for guests all the time. There's no need to thank them.

The same is true of radio call-in shows. The people who call in say, "Thank you for taking my call." Why do they bother? Think about it. Taking calls is what these shows do. They're call-in shows; they take calls. That's their function. Why thank them for doing what they can't avoid? It bothers me that people even *think* they need to say these things. It's all very insincere.

TELEPHONE OPERATORS

And on the subject of insincerity, let's not forget the nonsense that telephone operators are ordered to say by their corporate-drone bosses. Keeping in mind, of course, that telephone operators are not operators anymore, they're *attendants. Telephone attendants.* Or *telephone representatives.* I've also heard them called *communications facilitators,* and *customer care professionals.*

Anyway, these operators used to say, "Who did you want to speak with?" Now it's, "How may I direct your call?" I don't like that. It sounds artificial. And it has a ring of self-importance. "How may I direct your call?" Jesus, everyone wants to direct; it's not just actors anymore. And when you tell them who you're trying to reach, they say, "Thank you, it's a pleasure to forward your call." Sounds polite, doesn't it? It's not. It's insincere.

TOO MANY TELEPHONE THANK-YOUS

And on the subject of telephone operators, another complaint I have about these people takes me back to my original point—the unnecessary overuse of thank you. These days, I think there are far too many thank-yous being thrown around on the telephone. "Thank you for this," "Thank you for that," "Thank you for something else." I find myself being thanked for everything I do, and then some.

I recently called a friend who was staying at the Marriott. He was staying at the Marriott. I called him there—at the Marriott. I intentionally dialed the number of the Marriott, because that's where I expected him to be. The connection went through. Guess what the operator said? Right. "Thank you for calling the Marriott." Well, what did she think I was going to do? Call the Hyatt? He was staying at the Marriott. It wouldn't do me much good to call the Hyatt. We all know what they would have said: "Thank you for calling the Hyatt."

They even thank you for doing things you can't avoid. Did you ever have an operator say, "Thank you for calling the operator?" I've had that happen. Well, who did she think I was gonna call, the night watchman? The chairman of the board? Jesus! Thank you, thank you, thank you. It's annoying.

One time, at a hotel, I wanted to get my car. Naturally, I needed to call valet parking. I noticed the little plastic card next to my telephone. It said "Press nine for valet parking." I was about to press nine, but then I noticed I didn't have to press nine, because right there on the phone one of the speed-dial buttons had a little picture of a car next to it, and it said "Valet parking." So I pushed that button. The one that said "Valet parking." The one with the picture of the car. Someone answered. You know what he said? Right. "Thank you for calling valet parking."

Well, fuck! Didn't he know that if a guest wants to retrieve his car, he more or less *has* to call valet parking? That's where the cars are! And doesn't he know the designers of hotel telephones have gone to a great deal of trouble to make it easy for people to get their cars? I had simply taken advantage of their skills; I had called valet parking by pressing a single button. A button marked with a little picture of a car.

And I can assure you, folks, if I had thought for even a split second that valet parking *didn't* have my car—for instance, if I'd thought the bartender had it—I would have called the cocktail lounge. I would have pressed the little button with the picture of the martini next to it. Which would, of course, have given the bartender a chance to say, "Thank you for calling the cocktail lounge."

One further complaint: These days, if I call a hotel from the outside, the telephone operators waste an awful lot of my time: "Hello. Thank you for calling the Lincoln Plaza Hotel-Resort and Conference Center, my name is Taneesha, have a nice day, and how may I direct your call?" And I say, "I'll have to get back to you. I forgot why I called." Sometimes, just to scare the operator, I'll sob, "It's too late. He just died."

Thank you, thank you, thank you. It's too much. Occasionally, a *recording* will thank me. "Thank you for using AT&T." How can this be? Isn't gratitude a personal feeling? Recording devices don't have personal feelings, do they? No. But I do. And I feel this showy, hyper-politeness must be stopped. Thank you for reading this far.

FURTHER THOUGHTS ON EXPLODING HEADS

Wouldn't it be interesting if the only way you could die was that suddenly your head blew up? If there were no other causes of death? Everyone died the same way? Sooner or later, without warning, your head simply exploded? You know what I think? I think people would get used to it. I believe people can learn to take anything in stride if they think it's unavoidable.

Picture a bunch of guys singin' "Happy Birthday":

"Happy birthday to you, Happy birthday to you, Happy birthday, dear Charlie . . ." BOOM!! And Charlie's head blows up. But all the candles go out, so it's actually a form of good luck. And everyone applauds.

Of course, there'd be an occasional downside. "God, another head? That's two this week. I just had this suit cleaned." But we'd learn to deal with it.

Let's say you were sitting in a restaurant with your girlfriend, and the waiter was reciting the specials:

"Tonight we have the marinated bat nipples on a bed of lightly sautéed panda assholes . . ." BOOM!! The waiter's head explodes. I'll bet you wouldn't miss a beat.

"Honey, did he say *bat* nipples or *cat* nipples? We'd better get another waiter. And some fresh salsa. I'm not eating this stuff; he was holding it when he blew. So anyway, I'm allergic to bat nipples. I think I might go with the free-range penguin dick or the deep-dish moose balls. How about you? Wait, hold still. There's a little piece of eyebrow on your cheek. There, I got it. By the way, honey, what wine goes with brain?"

JUST A STONE'S THROW

When I watch news tapes of the Intifada from Palestine, and see the Arab kids throwing stones at Israeli tanks, I always have fun watching for the kids who are lefthanded, because lefthanders have kind of a natural curveball. It's really interesting. I can't wait till major league baseball comes to the Middle East. Incidentally, I also noticed that Arab kids usually throw in a high arc, whereas the Catholic kids in Northern Ireland throw more of a line drive. Either way is all right with me as long as they're accurate. Kids are great.

Bud's Medical Center: C'mon In!

"Hi. I'm Bud, president and head doctor of Bud's Medical Center. Come on in to Bud's. This weekend we're havin' a special on head injuries: any sort of head injury you got, from a black eye to a completely caved-in skull, just a dollar fifty this weekend at Bud's. We'll also give a free estimate to anyone who's bleedin'. So if you're sick, injured, diseased, hurt, maimed, disfigured or just plain don't feel good, come on in to Bud's Medical Center. Bud's: Where all the sick people go."

BURIED ALIVE AT 65

Wouldn't it be weird if they just buried you alive when you got to be sixty-five? If that was the deal for everyone? Right after your sixty-fifth birthday party they came and got you and dumped you in a big pit with a bunch of other people your age, threw in all your birthday presents and buried you all alive?

Wouldn't that be weird? Jesus, I'm glad they don't do that. That would be weird.

But sooner or later we'll have to do something like that; we'll have to. We can't take care of old people as it is, and there are going to be millions more of them. Good, early medical care is a mixed blessing; it leads to too many old people. What are you going to do with them? No one wants to take care of them. Their children put them in homes. Even the people whose job it is to take care of them in the homes don't give a shit; they abuse them. No one cares. It's my belief that, sooner or later, we're going to have to start killing old people before they become a burden. One good thing, though: We'll save a lot of money on Social Security and maybe the country won't go broke.

There's always a bright side.

MOMENT OF SILENCE

The custom of observing a moment of silence before an athletic event to honor dead people strikes me as meaningless. And arbitrary. Because, if you'll notice, only certain people get this special treatment. It's highly selective. Therefore I've decided that someday, when the time comes that every single person in the world who dies receives a moment of silence, I will begin paying attention. Until then, count me out. It's ridiculous. Here's what I mean.

Let's say you live in Cleveland, and you decide to go to the Browns game. There you are in the football stadium, with a hot dog and a beer, ready to enjoy the action, and a somber-sounding public-address announcer interrupts the festivities, intoning darkly:

"And now, ladies and gentlemen, we ask that you remove your hats and join us in observing a moment of silence for the forty-three unattractive, mentally retarded, overweight Bolivian dance instructors who lost their lives this morning in a roller coaster accident at an amusement park near La Paz. Apparently, they all stood up on a sharp turn and went flying off, willy-nilly, into the cool, crisp, morning La Paz air. And, being heavier than air, crashed through the roof of the funhouse, landing on several clowns, killing them all and crushing their red noses beyond recognition."

Snickering is heard in the crowd. The American announcer continues:

"And, ladies and gentlemen, lest you think this amusing, lest you think this a time for laughter, I ask you please—please—to put yourself in the place of a bereaved Bolivian who may be seated near you this afternoon. Try reversing places. Imagine yourself visiting Bolivia and taking in a soccer game. Imagine yourself seated in the stadium with a burrito and a cerveza, ready to enjoy the action, and a somber-sounding, Spanish public-address announcer interrupts the festivities, intoning darkly:

" 'Señors y señoritas, we ask that you remove your sombreros and join us in observing un momento de silencio for the forty-three mentally retarded, overweight, unattractive American meat inspectors who lost their lives this morning in a Ferris wheel accident at a carnival near Ashtabula, Ohio.'

"The Spanish announcer continues:

" 'Apparently, the huge wheel flew out of control, spinning madly, flinging the poor meat inspectors off, willy-nilly, into the hot, humid, Midwestern air. And, being heavier than air, they crashed through the roof of the carnival freak show, crushing the dog-faced boy, and destroying many of his chew-toys.'

"And let's say, as you sit there in La Paz listening to this, you find yourself seated next to some Bolivian smart-ass who's giggling and poking his friend in the ribs. May I suggest you'd be highly pissed at this lack of respect for Americans? And, might I add, rightly so."

The American announcer continues his plea:

"And so, ladies and gentlemen, considering the many grieving Bolivians who may be seated among you today, and trying to keep in check that normal human impulse to laugh heartily when another person dies, let us try again—really hard this time—to observe a moment of silence for the forty-three unattractive, mentally retarded, overweight Bolivian dance instructors who went flying, willy-nilly, off the roller coaster in La Paz. Not to mention the poor, unsuspecting clowns who at the time were innocently filling their water pistols."

You can see the problem either announcer would face; the fans would simply not be able to get into it. But I understand that; I can empathize with the fans. Because, frankly, I don't know what to do during a moment of silence, either. Do you? What are you supposed to do? What do they expect? Do they want us to pray? They don't say that. If they want me to pray, they should ask. I'll pray, but at least have the courtesy to make a formal request.

But no. They offer no guidance, no instruction at all. I honestly don't know what to do. Sometimes I resort to evil thoughts: I wish my seatmates ill fortune in days to come; I fantasize about standing naked in front of the Lincoln Memorial and becoming sexually aroused; I picture thousands of penguins being hacked to death by boatloads of graduate students. More often, though, I wind up bored silly, searching for something to occupy my thoughts.

One time I inventoried the pimples on the neck of the man in front of me, hoping to find one with a hair growing through it, so I could quietly pluck it out during the confusion of halftime. On a happier occasion, I once found myself staring at the huge but perfectly formed breasts of the woman to my left, her fleshy mounds rising and falling softly in the late October sun. And my thoughts turned tenderly romantic:

"Holy shit! Look at the fuckin' knobs on her! Great fuckin' knobs! I think I'm gonna go to the refreshment stand, buy myself a weenie and hide it in my pants. Then, during halftime, I'm gonna whip out the weenie and force her to watch while I eat the bun and stuff the weenie up my . . . naaah! She's probably one of those uptight chicks who'd think I'm weird. She doesn't know the problem is I'm shy."

Those are my thoughts, and I can't help it. During a moment of silence my imagination runs away with me. I don't know what to do. And why is it silence they're looking for? What good is silence? The ones being remembered are already dead, they're not going to wake up now. Why not a moment of screaming? Wouldn't that be more appropriate for dead people? Wouldn't you like to hear 60,000 fans screaming, "Aaaaaiiiiiieeeeeaaagghh!!" It sure would put me in the mood for football.

And one more criticism. Why honor only the dead? Why this favoritism? Why not the injured, as well? There are always more injured than there are dead in any decent tragedy. What about them? And what about those who aren't dead or injured, but are simply "treated and released"? How about, if not silence, at least a moment of muffled conversation for those who were treated and released? It's an honorable condition. Personally, I've always wanted to be treated and released. Usually, I'm treated and detained. Perhaps it's for the best.

TERRORISM MISNOMERS:
DOMESTIC TERRORISM

When they talk about domestic terrorism, they often cite the Oklahoma City bombing. But that wasn't terrorism. Terrorism involves a series of acts intended to put a civilian population in a state of panic, fear and uncertainty, in order to achieve some political goal. Oklahoma City wasn't terrorism, it was payback. Revenge. Timothy McVeigh wanted to punish the federal government for what it did at Waco and Ruby Ridge. Revenge, not terrorism.

TERRORISM EXPERT

Television news channels will often present some guest they identify as a *terrorism expert*. But you can take one look at him and see that he's clearly not a terrorism expert. He's a guy in a suit who obviously works in an office. And I say he's not a terrorism expert.

You wanna know who's a terrorism expert? Osama bin Laden. Ayman al-Zawahiri. The people they hang around with. Those are the terrorism experts. Has this guy in the suit ever blown anyone up? No. So why is he a terrorism expert?

I'm sure the TV people would say, "Well, because he's made a study of terrorism." Oh, I see. So really, he's an expert in the study of terrorism, the subject of terrorism. But can he make a suicide vest? Fuck, no. And if he can, he should make one, put it on and press the button. Then he'll be a real terrorism expert. Like those people he now only reads about.

SUICIDE BOMBER

No. Sorry to disagree; it's anything *but* suicide. A person who commits suicide is someone who places no value on his life: "My life is worthless, I'm going to end it." These so-called suicide bombers don't feel that way. They feel their lives are worth something, and that by giving them up they make a statement to the world, furthering a cause they believe in deeply. In their eyes, their lives (when sacrificed) have value. And, by the way, the "suicide bombers" themselves don't call it that. In a stunning example of euphemism, they call it a *sacred explosion*. Holy smoke!

"HOMICIDE BOMBERS"

And in spite of what Bush has been ordered to say, they're not *homicide bombers*, either. All bombings are intended to kill people, to produce homicides. Anyone who packs a bomb with nails and bits of steel, and sets it off in a public place, is hoping to commit homicide. This is true of any bomb, whether you drop it out of an airplane or leave it on a doorstep; you're hoping to kill people. That's the purpose. Killing people. In the case of these so-called suicide bombs, what's different is that the people setting them off are intentionally ending their own lives in the process. That's why we confuse the act with suicide.

HUMAN SHIELDS

During bombing raids in Iraq, the media liked to say that Saddam Hussein used people as *human shields*. That's not accurate. Although it's true they were used as shields, the fact is they were humans already. So if these humans were used as shields, they *were* human shields. They weren't *being used as* human shields.

Got that?

COWARDS

Bush calls the al Qaeda people cowards, and says, "They like to hide." Well, isn't that what the American Continental Army did during the American Revolution? Our beloved patriots? They hid. They hid behind trees. Then they came out, killed some British soldiers, and ran away. Just like al Qaeda. That's what you do when you're outnumbered and have less firepower than the enemy. It's called "trying to win." It's not cowardly.

Bill Maher may have stretched the point a bit when he said that air force pilots who release their bombs from hundreds of miles away are cowards; flying combat jets doesn't attract many cowards. But it's not nearly as courageous an act as deliberately strapping a bomb to your chest and heading for the disco with no intention of dancing.

I will say this. Getting out of the Vietnam war through Daddy's connections and then not living up to your end of the bargain is probably a form of cowardice.

"HEROES" WHO "DIED FOR THEIR COUNTRY"

The Port Authority of New York and New Jersey said that changing the name of Newark Airport to Liberty International Airport would be a way of honoring "the more than 3,000 heroes who died for their country in the World Trade Center." Pardon me for pointing this out, folks, but stock traders, clerks, receptionists, cooks, waiters and building maintenance people in the World Trade Center didn't *die for their country*. They died because they went to work. Not one of them would have shown up for work that day if you had told them they would die as a result. Try to get your heroes straight.

Not everyone who died in 9/11 was a *hero*. Hero is a very special word, that's why we reserve it for certain special people. Not every fireman and policeman who was on duty that day was a hero. The ones who risked or lost their lives trying to rescue people were heroes. They acted heroically. The others probably did a good job and were very helpful, but heroes?

If everyone's a hero, then the word doesn't mean much anymore. And sooner or later we'll have to give the real heroes (the heroic ones) a new name, to distinguish them from the rest of the pack. Too bad "superheroes" is already taken; it would have been perfect. But relax, folks, if I know us, "megahero" can't be too far over the horizon. Although to be honest, I kind of like the alliteration in "hyperhero." Let's shoot for that.

WAR, GOD, STUFF LIKE THAT

These anti-war demonstrators are really unimpressive people. They're against war? How groundbreaking; what a courageous stand. Listen, angry asshole, pick something difficult. Like religion. Why don't you get out on the street and start marching around against religion—something that's really harmful to mankind. War is simply nature's way of doing things; of keeping down the count. Religion is the problem. Get rid of religion and you've done the planet a favor. So how about getting out there next weekend and marching around with a sign that says HO HO HO! RELIGION MUST GO!? Come on, protesters, show some balls.

. . . AND THE HORSE YOU RODE IN ON

I can't understand what it is people like about John Wayne movies; I think they suck. I find him inauthentic. Sometimes, when I'm clicking around the channels, looking for the least objectionable program, I come across a movie scene in progress. It's in black and white, it's clearly a Western, and it looks old enough that it could actually be fun to watch. I see guys like John Ireland, Barton MacLane, Ward Bond, Anthony Quinn, Charles Bronson, Dan Duryea, Thomas Mitchell, Lee Van Cleef and Brian Donlevy shooting each other, drinking and playing cards, and I get this great nostalgic feeling. Then John Wayne rides up. And I have to reach for the remote. It's a fuckin' shame. He spoils war movies in the same way. By the way, I feel the same about Jimmy Stewart. These people should not have been allowed to spoil so many perfectly good movies.

DON'T ASK THE DOCTOR

ANNOUNCER: Good afternoon, folks. This is Pedro Fleming. Welcome to *Don't Ask the Doctor*, America's only medical advice program based on questions that are not pertinent to the field of medicine. Here is our medical expert, Dr. Ned Gittles. How are you today, Doctor?

DOCTOR: Not bad, Pedro, considering all the sick people I see. How about you?

PEDRO: Well, I have a malignant tumor inside my nose.

DOCTOR: Don't ignore that. Take some pills. Do you have any pills at home?

PEDRO: Sure, lots of different kinds.

DOCTOR: Good, take some of them. That's my advice.

PEDRO: And good advice it is. Well, let's get started. Here's a question from Elaine Trickler in Frog Balls, Tennessee. She writes, "Doctor, my car seems to hesitate a little when I accelerate from a red light, and I'm afraid it will stall. What should I do?"

DOCTOR: Don't ask me.

PEDRO: That's right. Don't ask the doctor. How would he know? That's obviously a question for a mechanic.

DOCTOR: Righty-ho!

PEDRO: For having her question used on *Don't Ask the Doctor*, Elaine Trickler will receive a free rectal thermometer by Recto-Swell, the last word in rectal thermometers. See the new Recto-Swell line of monogrammed thermometers at leading rectal equipment dealers in your area. Try Orifice Max or Brown's Personal Items for Inside the Rectum.

DOCTOR: Recto-Swell is a good one, Pedro. Sometimes I use mine when I'm cooking a turkey.

PEDRO: Great idea, Doctor. Well, folks, that's it for today. Tune in again tomorrow when Dr. Ned Gittles will answer the question, "How can I increase my soybean yield?" on America's favorite medical advice program, *Don't Ask the Doctor*.

Stay tuned for *Video Magazine*, as beauty expert Mavis Davis shows a young albino girl how to keep her hair from turning prematurely brown. You're tuned to Elaine and Joe's Radio Network.

IT'S NO USE

USAGE-USE

I object to the use of *usage* when it's used in place of *use*. There's nothing wrong with using *use*; it's been in use a long time and I'm used to it. It isn't that *usage* isn't useful; I simply have no use for its current usage. The use of *usage* should be consistent with good usage: I'd prefer to say, "My use of the Internet" rather than "my usage." If I meant it collectively, I might say, "American usage of the Internet." But so far I haven't meant that.

And, as I'm using space on *usage*, I'll use some more on *utilize*. Using *utilize* instead of utilizing *use* is one of those attempts to make things sound more important than they really are. Sports announcers do that all the time; they misapply big words: "He's not utilizing all his skills." They don't understand that an athlete doesn't utilize his skills, he uses them. The coach utilizes his players, but the players use their skills. Don't use *utilize* when you should be utilizing *use*.

MAKING A DIFFERENCE

Another sports-announcer crime is the use of the word *differential* when they mean *difference*. "There was a twelve-point differential at halftime." No. Sorry. There was a twelve-point *difference*. Differential is a mechanical or mathematical term. And by mathematical I don't mean Knicks 55, Pacers 43. *Difference* and *differential* are different. Go Knicks!

ON THE LINKS

It also annoys me that people sometimes claim to see a *linkage* when they actually see a *link*. I think link is fine. *Linkage* reminds me of my car's transmission. In fact, I think my car's linkage is located somewhere near the differential.

STOPPAGE

Stoppage is another ungainly word. The most frequently heard euphemism for a labor strike is *work stoppage*. Apparently, *labor strike* sounded too Marxist for loyal Americans. But stoppage sounds like an obstructed bowel. And *stoppage* is much too close to *sewage* for my comfort.

OUTAGE

Usage, *linkage* and *stoppage* remind me of *outage*. This is a word I simply dislike. It's an awkward, ugly word. *Outage*. It sounds like something that's done when a gay person's identity is revealed. But actually its most frequent use is in describing a loss of electricity: *power outage*. We used to say *power failure*, but I guess Americans don't like to admit failure—even when it's manifest. Regardless, we ought to find a better way to answer the question, "What happened to the lights?"*

*I recently heard the following sentence on CNN: "Because of high winds, about 250,000 people in New England are without power." I thought, "Gee, when you think about it, about 275 million people in the United States are without power. They just aren't aware of it."

UNCALLED-FOR EDITORIAL COMMENTS:

WHO'S RESPONSIBLE FOR THIS?

When reporting a bombing by some radical group, the news media will often inform us that *"No one has claimed responsibility."* Why is this wording used instead of *"No one has taken credit"*? To save the feelings of the dead people's relatives? The people who did the bombing surely see it as credit. Let them have their moment in the sun. Look at all the trouble they went to.

UNFORTUNATELY, THEY ALL GOT OUT ALIVE

Here's another gratuitous editorial appendage often heard on the TV-news coverage of a fire or an accident: "Luckily, no one was hurt" or "The good news is no one was injured." I consider those to be editorial comments. After all, I may not think it's such good news that no one was hurt. I'm entitled to decide for myself whether or not injuries to strangers are good or bad news. I may prefer hearing, "It's a shame no one was hurt." It's entirely possible. Please save the commentary for the editorial page.

PUT ON A HAPPY FACE

And I could also do without these grim, mock-serious facial expressions and sad voices the television-news people affect when reporting these so-called tragedies. Diane Sawyer is one of the worst offenders. She lowers her voice dramatically and puts on this really sad face and tells you all about the baby who died in a washing machine. If you weren't listening carefully, you'd think the goddamn "tragedy" happened to her. Is that good? I don't think so. Just let me have the news, please; I'll get Meryl Streep to handle the sad faces.

THOUGHTS ON "THOUGHTS"

Another empty sentiment concerning the death of people; you hear it on the news, and you hear it in real life: *"Our thoughts are with the family."* What exactly does that mean? Sympathies I can understand; prayers, as ineffective as they are, I can understand. But thoughts? Why thoughts? What kind of thoughts? Just thoughts? Like, "Gee, he's dead"? How does that help?

When first reporting on Michael J. Fox's Parkinson's disease, one newslady announced that *"Everyone's thoughts are with Michael."* Well, I'm by no means happy that he's sick, and he happens to be one of the few celebrities I genuinely like. But to be perfectly honest with you, for most of the day my thoughts were definitely not with Michael. I wish him well, and I admire the way he copes. But at any given moment, my thoughts are probably on pussy.

THE EXPLICIT TV CHANNEL

The satellite service I get has this great channel, Explicit TV. It's not nearly as limited in content as the standard channels you see. Here are a few excerpts from their program guide:

DAYTIME DRAMA

Harper Darrow and Mary Jane Crotchjockey star in the continuing story of hardship, sorrow, fear, pain, disillusionment, guilt and suicide in a blue-collar family living in a run-down neighborhood. Don't miss the acclaimed daytime drama *Fuck This Shit*. In tomorrow's episode, Velma is given a cesarean section by Nick and Artie, two neighbors who are handy with tools, only to discover that she wasn't really pregnant. (Partial nudity, heavy drinking, spousal abuse, despair, home-improvement tips)

PUBLIC SERVICE PROGRAM

Every evening at seven-thirty, citizens and consumers get a chance to sound off and air their complaints. Don't miss *Blow It Out Your Ass!*, with consumer ombudsman Susan Dorkalot. If you have a complaint to register, be sure you call in, talk to Susan, explain your grievances and complaints and then listen carefully as she bellows, "Blow It Out Your Ass!" (Con games, larceny, gullibility, anger, hostility)

FINANCIAL NEWS

Every evening at six o'clock, catch the Wall Street buzz on *Money Talks, Shit Walks.* Tonight, Ron Insana interviews Windfall Profitz III, one more worthless cocksucker who makes his living on Wall Street. Don't be left behind in the fast-changing world of business and finance. Keep up-to-date by watching *Money Talks, Shit Walks,* brought to you by Pennington-Craymore: Wall Street scumbags since 1869. (Greed, envy, arrogance, predatory males)

OLD-TIME COMEDY FAVORITES

Comedy rules the house on Wednesday night with four of your all-time favorites in a row. First, on *Mork and Mindy,* Mork is caught performing cunnilingus on a gumball machine. The fun begins and the gumballs fly when Mindy tries to work Mork's tongue loose, gets sexually aroused and has her first quintuple orgasm. (Gum-chewing, moaning, Lord's name taken in vain)

Then, on *All in the Family,* Archie Bunker kills a nigger, blames it on a spic and two chinks and hires a yid lawyer to bribe the judge. Don't miss the laughs as two guineas beat the shit out of Archie just for the fun of it. Meanwhile, police arrest Michael for pimping out Gloria to Louise Jefferson for a mixed-race, dyke gangbang in the back of George's dry cleaners. (Racism, bigotry, vaginal bruising)

After that, on *I Love Lucy,* Ricky pays Ethel twenty dollars for a quick hand job in the broom closet, but things get really hilarious when Fred is caught placing a kosher knockwurst in Lucy's asshole. Things get worse when Ricky's nightclub show is canceled as twelve members of the band come down with anal warts and have to play standing up. (Nudity, sex, sphincter jokes, bogus Latin music)

Our quartet of madcap sitcoms concludes with *Leave It to Beaver*, as Beaver and Wally fall out of a maple tree while masturbating each other. Imagine everyone's surprise when they land smack on top of a flustered June Cleaver, who is giving Eddie Haskell a blow job under the tree. (Pee-pee jokes)

FRONTIER NOSTALGIA

Next week, back to back on *Nostalgia Theater*, you'll see two of America's favorite episodes of *Little House on the Prairie*. First, the 1975 Christmas show, "A Douche Bag for Clara." Little Clara comes of age and asks Santa for her own douche bag. At first it looks like a disaster when, out of inexperience, she sticks it in the wrong hole. But Luke, the disturbed neighbor boy, saves the day when he distracts everyone by removing his dog's vital organs with a stick. Clara later learns to douche properly after several long sessions with old Doc Flathammer.

Then, you'll see just about everyone's favorite *Little House on the Prairie*, the hilarious "Missy Takes a Dump in the Woods," as our young heroine answers nature's call while wearing high heels and a long dress. Watch her as she tries to maneuver through bramble bushes and poison sumac. Then, too late, she finds out there's no toilet paper and has to wipe herself with several pine cones. The fun (and the screaming) begins when she unknowingly pulls the cones in the wrong direction. (Partial nudity, douche lessons, unpleasant language)

DUELING TALK SHOWS

Since last month Oprah had a special show, "Women Who Fake Orgasms," this month, not to be outdone, Jerry Springer is presenting a nighttime special, "Men Who Fake Bowel Movements." (Graphic video, foul odors)

DR. PHIL

In a special program, Dr. Phil welcomes famed psychic medium John Edwards to the show and they try to contact dead whores. Then, in a special pre-taped segment, Dr. Phil cures a woman's fear of flying by throwing her out of an airplane. (Limited intellects)

EVEN MORE TALK

Two fascinating glimpses into the medical world as Montel Williams investigates "Doctors Who Intentionally Give Patients the Siff" and Maury Povich interviews "Twins Who Eat Each Other's Feces." (Indigestion)

DOCUMENTARY

Award-winning documentary maker Ken Burns continues his penetrating look at America's history as he takes on a three-part study, *The Great Cabbage-Fart Panic of 1860*. The disaster, which lasted an entire summer, took the lives of thirty-five hundred people, mostly from lung diseases. The special sound effects heard required the services of over three-hundred Milwaukee men who were fed only beer and cabbage for seven weeks. Fourteen stuntmen died during the re-creations.

MUSIC SPECIAL

Then, Friday at midnight, don't miss Willie Nelson's pay-per-view concert, *Wankin' with Willie*. Willie kicks off the festivities in great fashion as he gets right into one of his all-time best sellers, "Too Drunk to Jerk Off."

Then he introduces his guest star, Loretta Lynn, who sings her big hit "Your Love Ran Down My Leg and Now You're Gone." Willie then joins her onstage and they warble a pair of romantic love songs: "Kiss Me I'm Coming" and "You Blew My Mind, Now Blow Me." The pair's tandem segment concludes as Willie serenades Loretta with his special new arrangement of "We Kissed and My Balls Exploded."

Willie then takes the solo spotlight again with his familiar country lament, "I Shoulda Fucked Old What's-Her-Name."

And what would a Willie Nelson show be without a good ol' cowboy song? This time he honors the late Roy Rogers and does an authentic western ballad written by Roy called "It's Midnight in Montana and I Can't Get My Dick Outta This Cow." Home-movie footage of the original incident, taken by Roy's beloved wife, Dale Evans, adds to the song's authenticity. His faithful horse Trigger is seen off to the side brandishing a huge hard-on.

The whole shebang then ends with more vintage video, this time from Willie's first special. Two of Willie's great buddies, Johnny Cash and Waylon Jennings, both now gone to that big corral in the sky, are seen with Willie as they all deliver a rousing version of that definitive honky-tonk anthem, "Drinkin' Beer, Takin' a Shit, and Passin' Out."

As the closing credits roll and his band plays "God Bless America," Willie is seen smoking a big joint rolled in American flag paper.

CONCERNED PARENTS

DAD: How was Debbie's checkup?

MOM: The dentist was very pleased. Only six extractions this time.

DAD: Great.

MOM: Plus she needs a jawbone graft and twelve implants.

DAD: Must be that new gel toothpaste we've been using.

MOM: Yes! Patented new Choppersheen! Removes unwanted pulp, enamel and bone.

DAD: Choppersheen. Now in refreshing mint!

MEMO TO SELF

Here's a piece of graffiti I saw scrawled in black marking pen on one of those newspaper dispensers you see on New York sidewalks. It said, "Rosie O'Donnell sleeps with her head between a woman's legs." I couldn't help wondering who had written it, and under what circumstances.

I wondered, had someone simply awakened that morning and decided the time had come to share this little tidbit he'd been thinking about for a long time? And had he gone out that day determined to find a good place to write it? And this seemed like the best spot? Was it that simple?

Or was the person just out walking around and had this sudden burst of inspiration—something he didn't want to forget—but didn't have a piece of paper handy? And why didn't he take the newspaper dispenser home with him to refer to later?

And I also wondered, if that was it, what kind of person was walking around with one of those thick, felt-tip marking pens in his pocket in the first place? This wasn't no Sharpie, folks, this was one of those serious, thick, chisel-tip pens that gets you high if you leave it open too long.

It's thoughts of this sort that seriously limit the size of my circle of friends.

ANSWER THIS, YOU PRICK

(Drum roll)

ANNOUNCER: Good evening, ladies and gentlemen, this is your announcer, Dondelayo Prell. Join us now as we play America's favorite game, *Answer This, You Prick!* The show where folks just like you, although, perhaps, less attractive, have a chance to win fabulous prizes. And now here's America's favorite prick, Anthony Boff.

(Applause, cymbal crash)

BOFF: Hi, folks. I'm your genial host, Anthony Boff. Our jackpot today is one hundred and eleven dollars, plus a trip up north. Let's meet our first two contestants, Clark Fark and Dolly Drelman. What do you do, Clark?

FARK: I pretty much just sit around, Anthony.

BOFF: Swell. What about you, Dolly?

DOLLY: No sitting around for me, Mr. Boff. I stand near the window.

BOFF: All day?

DOLLY: Except for meals. Unless I'm fasting.

BOFF: Well, you sound like interesting people. Let's get right to our game. Just before airtime, a short backstage shoving match determined that Clark would get the first question. So here it is. Are you ready, Clark?

FARK: Ready as a bastard, Mr. Boff.

BOFF: Okay. Remember, the category is "People." Now then, Clark Fark, as America watches, please . . . answer this, you prick!

(Sound of a clock ticking)

Damon and Sylvia Prongster live in Thighmaster, Maine, on the corner of Watkins and Schermerhorn. Last Tuesday, at six in the evening, a brown Chevrolet drove past their house. What was the name of the last mechanic to change the oil on that car, and what was the name of his grandfather's first-grade teacher? You have three seconds.

(Music and ticking)

FARK: Jason Warburton and Mrs. Amelia Day Higgins.

BOFF: Oh, I'm awfully sorry, Clark. Your answer is incorrect. The correct answer is Dudley Manoosh and Clara Wheatley.

FARK: Well, I just took a wild guess.

DOLLY: I knew that answer.

BOFF: Not fuckin' likely, Dolly.

FARK: I agree, Mr. Boff. I think she's full of shit.

BOFF: Clark, I'm awfully sorry you did such a poor job. I see your family in our audience and they look ashamed. But you do win a roll of quarters and the home version of teacher-approved *Answer This, You Prick!* Play it with your kids. And we'll add a dollar to our jackpot, bringing our total to one hundred and twelve dollars. It's too late for us to get to Dolly Drelman, but that's just too bad for her.

Don't forget to join us again in June or May to play *Answer This, You Prick!* when one of our main questions will be "Who was the first person to strangle someone he had known for more than six years?" Goodnight, everybody.

ANNOUNCER: Guests on *Answer This, You Prick!* receive a framed picture of Henry Kissinger and stay at the luxurious Hotel for the Malformed in downtown Watsonville. Watsonville: the last place you wanna be.

(Music, applause up and out)

THREE SHORT CONVERSATIONS

BLESS ME, FATHER

PENITENT: Bless me, Father, for I have sinned. Yesterday, I killed my third priest in a month. The first time it scared me. The second time I had no feelings at all. The third time . . . I actually began to like it.

PRIEST: I'm not really a priest, son. I'm just cleaning the confessional.

THANKSGIVING, IN THE KITCHEN

BART: You look great in that dress, Marian. Really sexy. I was thinkin', if, God forbid, something ever happened to Joe and Estelle, I'd sure like to spend some time with you.

MARIAN: I feel the same way about you, Bart.

BART: Really? Look, maybe we wouldn't have to wait for something to happen to Joe and Estelle. Whaddya think?

WALK/DON'T WALK

JOEY: I heard Phil Hanley died. What happened?

SID: It's the strangest thing. He was walkin' down Fifth Avenue on his way to Times Square. He took a right at Forty-second Street and headed over to Broadway. He was just strollin' along, mindin' his own business, when suddenly a big chunk of concrete fell on him and crushed him to death.

JOEY: Jesus! What a way to go!

SID: I know. I woulda taken a right at Fiftieth Street, gone over to Broadway and then headed down to Times Square.

UNCLE LOCHINVAR

Uncle Lochinvar, although a moral vegetarian who only ate meat if the animal had died in its sleep, once punched out his twin daughters because they wouldn't lend him fifteen cents. He could speak seven languages, but unfortunately, he was disliked in all those countries. His hobby was visiting cemeteries in poor areas and guessing which people had the worst lives. He fell in love with a fish dentist named Chiquita, and a week later she died from using infected toilet paper while watching a TV show called *Progress in Medicine*. Inconsolable, Lochinvar, after composing his own epitaph, "Believe me, I wasn't a schmuck," died as part of a group-enema suicide pact.

UNCLE SHERLOCK

Uncle Sherlock was a proctologist's mate in the navy who fought in Korea and the Philippines. Unfortunately, it was just last year and he was jailed in both countries. He was the only man ever brought before the World Court for unpaid parking tickets. His personal checks did not depict nature scenes, they showed animal euthanasia and the Allied fire-bombing of Dresden. During a bungee jump, he fell in love with a Dutch courtroom artist and they were married in a windmill the next day, during a relative calm. They drifted apart when he realized that all she wanted to do was sit for hours and listen to skiing on the radio. Later he moved to Milan and was killed when a riot broke out at the La Scala candy counter during the second act of *Rigoletto*.

UNCLE DAGWOOD

Uncle Dagwood was a fun guy. He once claimed the most difficult thing he ever did was to take a shit in a phone booth without removing his overcoat. He met his wife, Spatula, at a UFO convention where she was conducting a basketball clinic for abductees. The instant they met, Dagwood knew she was his kind of woman: She had peach preserves in her hair and brown gravy caked on her neck. Spatula worked for years as an unregistered nurse and eventually ran off with an ironmonger. She and her new lover, Rolf, died in a blimp fire over Newfoundland, and Dagwood was killed in a Barcalounger, having rough sex with a Norwegian fisherman.

UNCLE LUCIFER

Uncle Lucifer was my most interesting uncle. He was an elk hunter, but he wouldn't kill the elk. Instead, he would chase it down, knock it to the ground and suck all the gristle out of its neck through a Donald Duck straw. He was fun to be with; he could eat a whole bowl of alphabet soup and then vomit up the vowels and consonants separately. His hobby was attending reunions of groups he never belonged to and pretending to be people who were long dead. Till the end of his days, Lucifer remained bitter that when he was a boy there had been no seedless red grapes. He died in an Indiana furniture outlet when he was torn to pieces by a pack of Cape hunting dogs.

CHILD CARE TIP

Never use a hammer to smooth out the lumps on a newborn baby's head. Instead, wrap a soft, clean cloth around a ten-inch length of wood and pound each lump repeatedly until the larger ones are gone and the area is smooth. Follow up by rubbing vigorously with a wire brush. Remember, never use a hammer on a child of any age, especially an infant.

NEWS REPORT: THE DEATH OF HUMPTY DUMPTY

ANCHORMAN: From the Nursery Newsroom, this is Keith Blanchgetter. A mystery on the West Side today with the apparent death of the beloved Humpty Dumpty. We begin our *Action Central News* team coverage tonight with Joanie Wong at the scene of the tragedy.

WONG: Thank you, Dan. Well, it's true, Humpty Dumpty is dead. The cause of death was apparently a great fall from this wall behind me.

ANCHORMAN: Joanie, what's the scene like out there right now?

WONG: Well, as you can see, police have taped off the area and are treating it as a crime scene, and no one seems to know why. According to one eyewitness, all the king's horses and all the king's men tried to put Humpty Dumpty back together again, but were unable to do so. We have with us now one of the king's men. What is your name, sir?

KING'S MAN: Dooley. Kevin Dooley.

WONG: And you're one of the king's men?

KING'S MAN: That's right. I've been one of the king's men for seventeen years.

WONG: And were you the first on the scene?

KING'S MAN: That is correct. My partner and I responded to a 10–43. That's an egg-on-a-wall.

WONG: Egg on a wall?

KING'S MAN: Right. It's a routine call, we get them all the time. Usually, by the time we arrive the egg is gone. Or else we arrive and the egg is intoxicated and we have to remove him.

WONG: And what was different this time?

KING'S MAN: Well, this time we've got a dead egg on our hands. He either fell or jumped. There's a chance he was pushed; we can't rule it out.

WONG: Is that why you're treating it as a crime scene?

KING'S MAN: That is correct. Crime-scene people are checking the area for trace evidence. Hair and fibers, stuff like that.

WONG: We've been told that all the king's horses and all the king's men tried to put Humpty Dumpty back together again.

KING'S MAN: That's not completely true. Some of the king's horses and a few of the king's men. But not all. The king has a lot of horses and men. They're needed for parades.

WONG: So they weren't able to put him back together again?

KING'S MAN: No. He never had a chance. His yolk was broken. Once the yolk is gone on these eggs, it's all over.

WONG: Do the police have any theories?

KING'S MAN: We're developing leads at this time, questioning some other eggs who were seen with him earlier today. Apparently, there was some drinking going on at a picnic. All in all, we're told there were about a dozen eggs out there, and I guess it got pretty rowdy. They were singing dirty songs and harassing females.

WONG: Can the public help?

KING'S MAN: We're asking people who may have information to call our tip-line, 800-429-EGGS. All calls will be held in strict confidence.

WONG: Thank you for talking with us, Officer Dooley. Well, that's it from the scene, Keith. Humpty Dumpty dead, at the bottom of a wall. Now let's send it over to Marcia Lopez at the Dumpty family residence. Marcia?

LOPEZ: Thank you, Joanie. I'm standing here with Humpty's best friend, Vinny Omeletta. Vinny, what kind of an egg was he?

OMELETTA: Easygoing. Nice guy. One time, when some kids were teasing him about bein' fat, he bought 'em all an ice cream.

LOPEZ: What do you think happened?

OMELETTA: I don't know. I saw him just yesterday, he was fine. I told him to stay off that wall. It's not safe, some of those bricks are loose. But he was headstrong; he never listened.

LOPEZ: Thank you, Vinny. We're going to talk now with his widow, Arlene Dumpty. Mrs. Dumpty, thanks for taking a moment with us. This must be a very difficult time for you.

MRS. DUMPTY: Yes. I'm still in shock. My thoughts are all scrambled.

LOPEZ: How did you feel when you found out he was dead?

MRS. DUMPTY: It was no fun, I can tell you that. He was a good egg.

LOPEZ: What do you suppose he was doing on the wall?

MRS. DUMPTY: He went up there all the time. He would just sit there and think. He was very deep. For an egg.

LOPEZ: What are your plans for services? Will there be services?

MRS. DUMPTY: Well, he was very conservative, so we'll probably stick with a traditional egg funeral.

LOPEZ: What is that?

MRS. DUMPTY: You know, skillet, a little butter, salt and pepper. Maybe some peppers and onions.

LOPEZ: Will you have an open casket?

MRS. DUMPTY: I'm not sure. A lot of him has already soaked into the ground. But we'll Krazy Glue the shell together as best we can, and go from there.

LOPEZ: How can people express their condolences?

MRS. DUMPTY: We're asking people just to send bacon. Or ham, if
they like. And maybe some home fries, but not too
greasy. Or they can just make a contribution to the
Humpty Dumpty Foundation for Research on Safer
Egg Salad.

LOPEZ: Thank you so much, Mrs. Dumpty.

MRS. DUMPTY: No sweat, my pleasure. I'm sure he's smiling down on
us from wherever it is eggs go. Although he *was* an egg-
nogstic. Ha ha, he would've liked that.

LOPEZ: Well, that's it. Humpty Dumpty is dead and no one knows why.
A story we'll undoubtedly hear more about. From the scene, this
is Marcia Lopez—now back to our studio.

GOODNIGHT, TIMMY

Here's a good way to provide some entertainment for your four-year-old when
you tuck him in at night, and at the same time, stimulate his imagination.

"I came up to say goodnight and tuck you in, Timmy. You had a big day,
so make sure you get a good night's sleep. And don't forget to watch out for the
Boogie Man. Remember what Daddy and I told you about the Boogie Man?
How he kills little boys? What do you think, Timmy? Is the Boogie Man here
in your room, hiding somewhere? Is he in the closet? Is he going to jump out
and kill you when I leave the room? He might; you never know.

"Maybe he's under the bed. He likes to hide there, too. He might claw his way through the mattress and kill you. Don't let him kill you, Timmy. You know what he does? He sticks a sharp metal tube up your nose and sucks the fluid out of your brain. It really hurts a lot.

"I'm going to turn out the light now and leave you alone in the dark. All by yourself. And I don't want to hear a peep out of you. If I hear any noise coming out of this room, I'm going to come up here and beat you. Try to get a good night's sleep. By the way, Daddy saw a monster walking up and down the hall last night. The monster had a piece of paper in his hand with your name on it. Night-night."

BITS AND PIECES

· Here's a surefire way to stimulate the economy and increase productivity at the same time: From now on, when someone asks what time it is, it costs a dollar; that would stimulate the economy. Then, if they don't want to pay, they have to go find out for themselves; that would increase productivity. Some of my ideas may not be perfect, but they're always worth considering.

· The best thing about visiting a hospital is that you see a lot of people who are much sicker than you, and it kind of makes you feel good.

TRUE FACT: I read that there's a rich couple in the Hamptons on Long Island who have palm trees on their property, and in the winter they fly the trees to Palm Beach to get them out of the cold weather. I can't help wondering how they treat their servants.

· You know how sometimes you have a song going through your head over and over all day long, maybe even two or three days? And it's driving you crazy because you can't get it out of your mind? Well, I know how to fix that. It's extreme, but it works every time. You kill yourself.

· They're always talking about what separates the men from the boys. Well, I'm gonna tell you what separates the men from the boys. The sodomy laws.

· · Regarding a wild-goose chase, why are these wild geese supposed to be so hard to find? They're right up there in the sky. I see them flying over in big flocks all the time in the spring and fall. They don't seem to be hiding. So why do we make such a big deal out of this?

· Live every day as if it's your last and eventually it will be. You'll be fully prepared.

· I hope I meet Senator Dole someday. I plan to grab his bad right arm and shake it like crazy. By the way, I'm glad he didn't get to be President. I prefer a guy who can push the nuclear button with either hand.

· The feminists have this thing, "Take Our Daughters to Work Day." Why don't the men have "Take Our Sons to the Cat-House Night"?

· At the beginning of the Iraq war I saw a red, white and blue bumper sticker that said UNITED WE STAND. What is that supposed to mean? During the Revolutionary War it referred to the American colonies. What does it mean now? That we should all think alike and there should be no dissenting opinions? As far as I'm concerned, United We're Fucked.

· O. J. Simpson has already received the ultimate punishment: For the rest of his life he has to associate with golfers.

· I don't believe in road rage; I prefer the gentle rebuke. If I don't like the way someone is driving, I pull up alongside the other car and say, "I hope your children turn out poorly." Only once have I lost my cool. That was the time I said to a woman, "I hope you get a blister on your cunt." But I said it with a smile.

TRUE FACT: A headline said "Peacekeeper killed in safe haven." Good. That'll show him.

· A lot of gay men stay in the closet because they're interested in fashion.

· I wonder if a person who comes out of a coma feels refreshed and well rested.

· One day it dawned on me that Hitler had a mom and dad. The phrase "Hitler's mom and dad" has an odd ring to it, doesn't it? It's kind of like when CNN used to talk about the city of Tikrit in Iraq being "Saddam Hussein's hometown." The two ideas don't seem to go together.

· You know what's good about being in your sixties? Your children are in their forties, so you don't have to worry about child molesters anymore. Unless, of course, one of your forty-year-old children is a child molester.

· I drove past a school with a sign that said WE'RE DRUG-FREE AND GUN-FREE. Later that day I drove past another school that didn't have a sign like that. What am I supposed to infer from this about the second school?

· REASONS FOR GIVING UP HOPE: Nothing works, nothing counts, nothing fits, no one cares, no one listens, standards have fallen, everyone's fatter, lines are longer, traffic's worse, kids are dumber and the air is dirty. I'll be back later with more reasons for giving up hope. In the meantime, try to come up with a few of your own.

· Here's a thought: If you have a perfectly DNA-matched identical twin, technically, it's possible to go fuck yourself.

· Sometimes you hear people say, "What kind of message does that send to our children?" And I think, What messages are these people talking about? When I was a kid, I never got any messages. Maybe an aunt would send me a birthday card or something; or once in a while my mother would get a Western Union telegram. But at our house, that was about it.

· Good news for senior citizens: Death is near!

· During one of those patriotic orgies of self-congratulation that followed the first Gulf War, as General Schwarzkopf was bragging about dropping fire on women and babies, a protester interrupted his speech. The man who had killed a few hundred thousand civilians continued to speak. The protester was charged with disturbing the peace.

· In New York State, there's a town called Eastchester. It's in a county called Westchester.

· I think we need some new Christmas carols with a more modern approach. Of course, I wouldn't abandon the religious theme completely. How about "Holy Christ, the Christmas Tree's on Fire"? Or "Jesus, Can You Believe It's Christmas Again?" This ought to get the ball rolling; I'm hoping you people will take it from here.

TRUE FACT: In 2002, in the U.S. Supreme Court, the surviving heirs of the famous film comedy trio were awarded "the intellectual rights to the Three Stooges."

· I don't know about you, but years ago, when Evel Knievel was jumping across the Snake River, I was rooting for the river.

· In the news from Israel, I keep hearing about the "cycle of violence." It reminded me that when I was a kid I had one of them, too. After school, I used to pedal it around the neighborhood, hitting other kids over the head with a big steel pipe.

· They always say the vice president is just a heartbeat away from the presidency. Don't they mean the *lack* of a heartbeat?

· I always feel good when I visit a sickroom supply store and see all the things I don't need.

· The last thing a young girl needs is a hands-on father.

· I feel really good. I wish I felt even more like this.

Dear Mom,

How are you? I am fine. I tried to donate my liver to science but they wouldn't take it. Next time I'm going to add some sautéed onions and a light sauce. I'll let you know how it goes.
Love, Neil

There's nothing wrong with a man who enjoys a good blow job.
—Anonymous

- I read an article that cautioned people against shaken-baby syndrome. Do people really need to be told this sort of thing? And if some people do need to be told, are these the kind of people who are very likely to heed the advice? Personally, I never shake a baby. Unless the recipe calls for it.

- Imagine how creepy it would be to be sexually abused by your great-great-grandparents.

- Do you know why it is that when a rancher fucks a sheep he does it at the edge of a cliff? It's so the sheep will push back.

TRUE FACT: A guy somewhere in the Midwest was sued for having too many Christmas lights on his house. Happy holidays.

- I think Western Union should have a service where women with big tits come to your house and sing "Happy Birthday." They could call it a mammogram.

- Whenever I hear about someone who "died for the flag," I always wonder about his real motives. And then I remember, Oh yeah, they shoot deserters.

- A lot of the people who worry about the safety of nuclear plants don't bother using their seat belts.

· HERE'S SOME FUN: Just keep calling telephone numbers at random and yelling, "Get off the line."

· This is National Disabled Month. Do your part. Cripple someone today.

· Two soldiers get into a fight. Two other soldiers pull them apart and tell them not to fight. Then they all pick up their guns and go kill people.

· "Which came first, the chicken or the egg?"
"The chicken."
"What about the egg?"
"Okay, the egg."

· Using technology to clean up the mess made by technology doesn't seem too intelligent.

· At one time, if you had had a telephone in a restaurant it would have been a novelty and attracted more attention than the food. Now if you have a telephone in a restaurant it's considered a nuisance.

· Why don't they just let these gay Boy Scouts join the Girl Scouts? What the fuck, you've got two groups. Use them both.

· There's a whole different now now.

· When you drive into California from Las Vegas they have an agricultural inspection station where they ask you if you have any fruits or vegetables with you. And then they just believe whatever you tell them. What's the point of that? You know what I do? On every trip I put a yam in the glove compartment, just to be sure I'm breaking the law.

· We ought to have a name for the day before yesterday. Dayforeday? Yesterforday? Why don't you people just come up with something and get back to me.

· I don't own any stocks or bonds. All my money is tied up in debt.

· A good motto to live by: "Always try not to get killed."

· If Marilyn Monroe were alive today she would be seventy-five, and I'll bet there would still be guys lining up for a chance to fuck her.

· Why not join the army? Join up and die. How do you expect to keep America free if you won't die? I'm dead; I died in Vietnam. I'm dead, and all my old army buddies are dead. Can you say that? No. What's wrong with you?

EUPHEMISMS: It's Gettin' Old

Perhaps you've noticed, we no longer have *old people* in this country; they're all gone, replaced by *senior citizens*. Somehow we wound up with millions of these unfortunate creatures known as *golden-agers* and *mature adults*. These are cold, lifeless, antiseptic terms. Typically American. All ways of sidestepping the fear of aging.

And it's not difficult to understand the fear of aging. It's natural. And it's universal; no one wants to get old. No one wants to die. But we do. We die. And we don't like that, so we shade the truth. I started doing it when I reached my forties. I'd look in the mirror at that time and think, "Well, I guess I'm getting . . . *older!*" That sounded a little better than *old*. It sounded like it might even last a bit longer.

But people forget that older is comparative, and they use it as an absolute: "She's an *older woman*."

"Oh, really? Older than what? Than she used to be? Well, yeah, so?"

People think *getting* old is bad, because they think *being* old is bad. But you know something? Being old is just fine; in fact, it can be terrific. And anyway, it's one of those things you don't get to choose. It's not optional.

But that insufferable group among us known as baby boomers (ages forty-two through fifty-nine, as of 2005) are beginning to get old, and they're having trouble dealing with that. Remember, these baby boomers are the ones who gave us this soft, politically correct language in the first place.

So rather than admit they're getting old, the baby boomers have come up with a new term to describe themselves as they approach the grave. They don't care for *middle-aged*, so instead—get this, folks—instead, they claim to be *pre-elderly*. Don't you love that? Pre-elderly. It's a real word. You don't hear it a lot, but it's out there. The boomers claim that if you're between fifty and sixty-five, you're pre-elderly.

But I'd be willing to bet that in 2011, when they begin turning sixty-five, they will not be calling themselves *elderly*. I have a hunch they'll come up with some new way of avoiding reality, and I have a suggestion for them. They should call themselves the *pre-dead*. It's a perfect term, because, for them, it's accurate and it's highly descriptive.

By the way, those ever-clever boomers have also come up with a word to describe the jobs they feel are most suitable for retired people who wish to keep working. They call these jobs *elder-friendly*. Isn't that sad? God, that's just really, really sad.

And so, to sum up, we have these senior citizens. And, whether I like that phrase or not, unfortunately, I got used to it, and I no longer react too violently when I hear it. But there is still one description for old people that I will never accept. That's when I hear someone describe an old guy as being, for instance, *eighty years young*. Even though I know it's tongue-in-cheek, it makes my skin crawl. It's overly cute and precious, and it's an evasion. It's junk language.

More: On CBS's *60 Minutes*, Leslie Stahl, God help her, actually referred to some old man as being a *ninety-something*. Please. Leslie. I need a small, personal break here.

One last, pathetic example in this category: On the radio, I heard Matt Drudge actually refer to *people of age*. And he wasn't being sarcastic. He said, "The West Nile virus is a particular threat to people of age." Poor Matt. Apparently, he's more fucked up than he seems.

Now, going to an adjacent subject: One unfortunate fact of life for many of these eighty- or ninety-somethings is that they're forced to live in places where they'd rather not be. Old-people's homes. So what name should we use for these places where we hide our old people? When I was a little boy, there was a building in my neighborhood called the *home for the aged*. It had a copper sign on the gate: HOME FOR THE AGED. It always looked deserted; I never saw anyone go in. Naturally, I never saw anyone come out, either.

Later, I noticed people started calling those places *nursing homes* and *rest homes*. Apparently, it was decided that some of these old people needed nurses, while others just needed a little rest. What you hear them called now is *retirement homes* or *long-term-care facilities*. There's another one of those truly bloodless terms: long-term-care facility.

But actually, it makes sense to give it a name like that, because if you do, you make it a lot easier for the person you're putting in there to acquiesce and cooperate with you. I remember old people used to tell their families, "Whatever you do, don't put me in a home. Please don't put me in a home." But it's hard to imagine one of them saying, "Whatever you do, don't put me in a long-term-care facility." So calling it that is really a trick. "C'mon, Grandpa, it's not a home. It's long-term care!"

By the way, while we're on the subject of the language of getting old, I want to tell you something that happened to me in New York on a recent evening. I was standing in line at the Carnegie Deli to pay my check, and there was a guy ahead of me who looked like he was in his sixties. He gave the cashier a ten-dollar bill, but apparently, it wasn't enough. When the cashier mentioned it to him in a nice way, he said, "Oh, I'm sorry. I guess I had a *senior moment*." And I thought how sad that was. To blame a simple mistake on the fact that you're in your sixties, even if you're just sort of joking. As if anyone would think a twenty-year-old couldn't make the same mistake. I only mention this because it's an example of how people can brainwash themselves by adopting popular language.

I wanted to pull him aside and say, "Listen, I just heard you refer to yourself as a senior. And I wanted to ask, were you by any chance a junior last year? Because if you weren't a junior last year, then you're not a senior *this* year." I wanted to say it, but I figured, why would he listen to me? After all, I'm only a freshman.

EYE SAFETY TIP

Here's a safety tip from the American Eye Association: Never jab a knitting needle directly into your eye and repeatedly thrust it in and out. You could be inviting vision problems. If you should suffer an eye injury, rinse the eye immediately with a caustic solution of Clorox and ammonia, and rub the surface of the eye vigorously for about ten minutes with #3 sandpaper. The American Eye Association reminds you: Don't fuck around with your eyes. They're the key to vision.

BODY OF WORK: PART 1

(Not for the queasy.)

DON'T GIMME NO LIP

Do you ever get lip crud? That sticky film that sometimes forms on your lips? Especially the lower lip? It's a kind of gooey crud that builds up, and when it dries it turns into a gummy, crusty coating? Thicker at the corners of the mouth, but thinning out as it works its way down toward the center of the lip?

And when it's really bad, the corners of your mouth look like parentheses? Do you ever get that? Lip crud?

Well, here's how you get rid of it. It's a simple, low-tech operation, and it requires just a single tool: the thumbnail. That's all you need. You scrape the crud off with your thumbnail. You just scrape, scrape, scrape it on down, scrape it on down, and you keep on scrapin'—don't worry about those people watchin' from the bus stop; if they knew anything they wouldn't be ridin' the bus. You scrape it on down, you scrape it on down, and finally, when it's all off, you take it and roll it up into a little ball, and then you *save that son of a bitch!* That's my practice, folks. I save it. Personally, I'm a lip-crud buff.

IT PAYS TO SAVE

In fact, I save everything I remove from my body. Don't you? At least for a little while? Don't you look at things when they first come off you? Study them? Aren't you curious? Don't you spend a few minutes lookin' at somethin', trying to figure out what it is and what it's doin' on you in the first place? Sure you do. You don't just pull some growth off your neck and throw it in the trash. You study it. You wanna know what it is.

Besides, you never know when you're gonna need parts. Isn't that true? Have you ever seen these guys on TV, they're in the hospital? One guy's waitin' for a kidney, another guy's waitin' for a lung. I say, "Fuck that shit, I've got parts at home! I have a freezer full of viable organs. Two of everything, ready to go. Whaddya need? A spleen? An esophagus? How about a nice used ballbag? Hah? Come on. Caucasian ballbag, one owner, good condition. He only scratched it on Sundays. Come on, folks, take a chance. I've got everything you need."

THE THRILL OF DISCOVERY

But regardless of your need for parts, the larger point is true: Most people study the things they pick off their bodies before they throw them away. Because you want to know what somethin' is. You don't want to spend fifteen minutes peeling a malignant tumor off your forehead, just to toss it out the window, sight unseen, into the neighbor's swimming pool. No! You want to take a good, long look at it. You may even want to share the experience:

"Holy shit, Honey! Looka this thing! Ho-ly jump-in' fuck-in' Jesus! Looka this! Hey! Honey? Come in here, will ya, goddammit! Fuck the Rice-A-Roni! Get your ass in here! (Displaying item proudly) Look at this thing. Ain't it somethin'? Guess where I got it? A minute or two ago it was a part of my head. Not anymore. I pried the bastard off with paint thinner and a Phillips-head screwdriver.

"But look at it, Honey! Look at the colors! It's green, blue, yellow, orange, brown, tan, khaki, beige, bronze, olive, neutral, black, off-black, champagne gold, Navajo white, turquoise . . . and Band-Aid color! Plus—get this—it's exactly the same shape as Iraq. That is, if you leave out that northern section where the Kurds live. I'm not throwin' this bastard away, it might become a collectible! Dial up those dickheads on eBay. We can make some fuckin' money on this thing."

STRAP IT ON AND PUMP ME UP

It annoys me when people complain about athletes taking steroids to improve athletic performance. It's a phony argument, because over the years every single piece of sports equipment used by athletes has been improved many times over. Golf balls and clubs; tennis balls, racquets; baseball gloves and bats; football pads and helmets and so on through every sport. Each time technology has found a way to improve equipment it has done so. So why shouldn't a person treat his body the same way? In the context of sports, the body is nothing more than one more piece of equipment, anyway. So why not improve it with new technology? Athletes use weights, why shouldn't they use chemicals?

Consider the Greek Phidippides, a professional runner who, in 490 B.C., ran from Athens to Sparta and back (280 miles) to ask the Spartans for help against the Persians in an impending battle that threatened Athens. Don't you think his generals would have been happy to give him amphetamines if they had been available? And a nice pair of New Balance high-performance running shoes while they were at it? Grow up, purists. The body is not a sacred vessel, it's a tool.

IT'S NOT POLITE TO POINT

I don't care for athletes who point to the sky after they've accomplished something on the field. Even worse are the ones who kneel down, bow their heads and make a big show of being "believers." You know something? God doesn't like that shit. He's not impressed with spiritual grandstanding; it embarrasses him. He says, "Get up, you phony, showoff bullshit artist and pay attention to the fuckin' game. I took the points!" Imagine the conceit of these people who think God is helping them and is looking for their acknowledgment. I say, play now, pray later.

ATTITUDE CHECK

Let's straighten out this whole "attitude" thing. Someone on TV said the sports anchor guys on ESPN have a lot of attitude. Let me tell you something, what these guys have is not attitude.

Here's attitude: One day, when I was about eighteen, I was standing at the bar in the Moylan Tavern with a couple of guys from my New York neighborhood. The Moylan had big windows, so if you were standing at the bar, you could easily see the people walking by on Broadway.

One of the guys in our group was a little older than the rest of us—an exconvict named John Cooney. All of a sudden, in the middle of the conversation, he looked out the window and saw someone walking past. He reached behind the bar for the baseball bat—the one the bartenders used for settling sports and political arguments—and he went outside, walked up to the guy on the sidewalk and just started smashing him with the baseball bat. The guy fell down, John walked back into the bar and put the bat away. He said, "The guy owes me money." That's attitude.

The guys on ESPN don't have that. What they have is a kind of smart-mouth, white-boy, college mentality. They're snotty, superficial white guys. Even the black anchors on ESPN are nothing more than snotty white guys. Snotty is not attitude. Snotty is just bad manners. And it's boring.

John Cooney knew attitude. He also knew more about how to swing a bat than any one of these blow-dried, never-were-athletes sitting safely behind their fruity little desks.

GOOD CHEER

Twenty-five years ago, two lovely girls in San Carlos, California, were kind enough to perform this football cheer for me, and in 1984 I used it on an HBO show. I'm passing it along now and would like to point out that it's actually quite useful at sporting events of any kind. In fact, I've found it to be a big crowd pleaser at weddings, baptisms and first communions, as well. Here it is. Chant it in good health:

> Rat shit! Bat shit!
> Dirty ol' twat!
> Sixty-nine assholes
> Tied in a knot!
> Hooray!
> Lizard shit!
> Fuck!

Let's go over that again, this time with a few comments:

Rat shit! Bat shit!
    (How nice to begin with a reference to nature.)
Dirty ol' twat!
    (A perfectly normal sports reference, as far as I'm concerned.)
Sixty-nine assholes
Tied in a knot!
    (No, I don't know what that means, either.)
Hooray!
    (There's the cheer part.)

Lizard shit!

   (Back to nature once again.)

Fuck!

   (And we end on an uplifting note.)

Now here's the happy postscript: About ten years later, I met a guy named Michael who gave me the second verse to the cheer. I hope those San Carlos girls will see this and accept it as my way of saying thanks:

Eat, bite, fuck, suck!

Nibble, gobble, chew!

Finger fuck! Hair pie!

Dick, cunt, screw!

Hooray!

Bat fuck!

Blow me!

Let's go over that again:

Eat, bite, fuck, suck!

   (Once again, off to an excellent start.)

Nibble, gobble, chew!

   (I notice verbs are more prominent this time.)

Finger fuck! Hair pie!

Dick, cunt, screw!

   (More good sports references.)

Hooray!

   (Can't have a cheer without it.)

Bat fuck!

(Truly an interesting thought.)

Blow me!

(Once again, ending on an uplifting note.)

Cheers!

ONE AT A TIME, PLEASE

Never buy two different garments of the same type at the same time, such as two sport shirts. Inevitably, you will like one better than the other and you will choose to wear it every time. The second one will always remain second choice and it will stay in the closet, coming out only occasionally, when you hold it in front of you at arm's length and decide not to wear it. Here's how you handle this problem: Exercise a little discipline at the store and buy just one shirt. Then, if you like it, wait a month and buy another. That's it. Next, I'm gonna work on nuclear proliferation.

KEEPIN' IT REAL IN THE RING

Another area of speech that could benefit from a bit more realism would be those announcements that are made just before a boxing match:

"Ladies and gentlemen, the main event of the evening: twelve rounds of heavyweight boxing. In this corner, from Cornhole, Mississippi, weighing two hundred pounds and wearing soiled white trunks, an utter and complete loser who is wanted in six states for crimes against the animal kingdom. Considered a complete scumbag by his family, he once fucked his sister at a church picnic and forced her to walk home alone. Also, on at least four occasions he has taken out his dick at the circus and waved it at the trapeze lady. Here is, He-e-e-n-r-y-y Gonz-a-a-a-lez!

"In the other corner, wearing a pair of lame, out-of-style zebra-skin shorts that he found on the street, from Sweatband, Arkansas, an unattractive and disturbed young man who, by court order, is not permitted to be alone for more than two minutes at a time. In and out of sixteen mental institutions over the years, he is a dangerous sociopath who once killed a nun for blocking his view. He has been legally barred from more than fifteen hundred bars in the New York City area, and recently, while visiting a supermarket, he forced a fat woman to blow him in the meat section. Here he is, Ma-a-a-tty Mu-u-u-urphy-y-y!"

The fighters move out to the center of the ring to have the boxing rules recited to them.

"All right, boys, you know the rules: No biting, scratching, clawing or tripping. No yanking dicks. No grabbing the other guy's testicles and snapping them up and down. No using a small screwdriver to punch holes in the other guy's neck during clinches. And if you're gonna call the other guy's mother a diseased, two-dollar whore, please, in the interest of accuracy, use her full name."

WELL-WISHING

When taking leave of one another, we often say, "Be well." Perhaps we should be more precise and a bit more practical. Reasonably, we can't expect everyone to be healthy all the time. Good wishes should be more realistic: "I hope you remain reasonably healthy during the next eighteen months or so, and if you have a stroke, I hope it only paralyzes you on one side, leaving you free to take phone calls." I think people would appreciate such thoughtfulness and precision.

PREPOSITIONAL PHRASES

We Americans love our prepositional phrases.

Out of sight, off the charts, in the groove, on the ball; up the creek, down the tubes, in the dumper, out the yin-yang; off the wall, 'round the bend, below the belt, under the weather.

And of course . . . *under the table.*

TABLE TALK

But rather than <u>under</u> the table, let us begin <u>on</u> the table. That's a phrase you hear a lot in the news, especially from Washington. In negotiations of any kind, certain things are said to be *on the table.* Implying that other things are *off the table.* And sometimes, regardless of what's on the table, a settlement is reached *under the table.*

The table seems important. If a person is highly qualified, we say he brings a lot *to the table.* Unfortunately, those who bring a lot *to the table* often have too much *on their plates.* Still, they're guaranteed a seat *at the table,* because they think *outside the box,* which puts them *ahead of the curve.*

Now, if the negotiators agree on what's on the table, then they're *on the same page.* Personally, I don't like people on my page. If someone says to me, "We're on the same page," I say, "Do me a favor, please, turn the page; I'd rather not be on that page. In fact, I'd rather be in a completely different book." But that's *beside the point;* I've wandered *off the track.*

Returning to negotiations, if the sides are getting close, we're told they're *in the ballpark*. This often comes from people *in the know*, speaking *off the record*. And in Washington, many in the know are also *in the loop* because, after all, they work *inside the beltway*.

Now, there are other government people, <u>outside</u> the beltway, who, nonetheless, remain in the know and in the loop. They function in foreign countries and we say they're *on the ground*. If they're CIA, they're *under the radar* and paid *off the books*. Much of what they learn is picked up *on the street*. But they don't always need to be on the street, because a lot of information comes in *over the transom*.

HOUSE PARTIES

Putting aside government for the moment, I wonder if you're aware that a completely different group of people has recently emerged in America. They're not on the ground and they're not on the street. You know where they are? They're *in the house!* Apparently, they never went out! And there must be a lot of them, because you hear it all the time: "He's in the house!"

And, if I may broach a delicate subject here, some of these people who are in the house are also *in the closet*. Fortunately for them, if they somehow manage to get out of the closet, they'll still be in the house. That is, they will be until they've . . . *left the building!* How often these days we hear that someone has left the building.

LEAVE ME TENDER

And I'm sure you've noticed it's mostly show business people who leave buildings—the accepted belief being that Elvis was the first to master this maneuver, although you can also find Beatles fans who will argue that the

Fab Four were known to have left several buildings, as well, thereby accomplishing what would have been the first multi-star building-departures. Unfortunately, at the time, no one realized the significance of what the Beatles were doing.

Now, there are no doubt those among you who are seething because *has left the building* is not a prepositional phrase. I grant that, but you'd have to agree that nonetheless, it fits here very nicely. Because, after all, only people who are in the house can leave the building. But, alas, it's impossible to leave the building if you're still in the closet. In fact, you can't even get to the front door.

COMING OUT

However, let's say everything breaks your way, and somehow you manage to leave the building; guess where you'll be? Right! Back on the street. With the CIA. So you'd better be *on your toes*. Because the CIA will get *on your case*, and they'll be *in your face*. Who knows? They might even go *upside your head*.

I'm sorry, folks, this is really getting *off the wall*, so let's return to where this whole thing began: under the table—where those shady deals are made. And isn't it interesting that under the table is similar to *under the counter*, where illegal products are sold? Under the counter, as opposed, of course, to *over the counter*, which describes a drug that does not require a prescription.

COUNTERPOINT

But when you think about it, even drugs that require a prescription are sold over the counter. I mean, the pharmacist doesn't somehow give them to you <u>underneath</u> the counter; you don't get them by going around <u>behind</u> the counter. What happens is, you stand <u>at</u> the counter, pay the man, and he hands them to you _across_ the counter. Or he sets them down _on_ the counter, and you pick them up _off_ the counter. Or, if you want, you can completely eliminate the counter by having the drugs delivered to your home. Provided, of course, that, at the time, you're _in the house._

Well, folks, it turns out that one of the phrases I used at the beginning of this piece was more appropriate than I suspected at the time. It's clear to me now that _in the dumper_ is exactly where this piece has wound up.

So that's it. I'm _out the door._

PASS ME A DAMP TOWEL

Here are some interesting sex facts from Thailand, accurate as of fifteen years ago. And I apologize for the dated quality of this information, but I find it fascinating, and since it's accurate, I wish to include it here. In 1990 alone, 5 million "sex tourists"—mostly affluent men from Japan—spent $4.5 billion on sex in Thailand. The country at that time had 800,000 child prostitutes under the age of sixteen, prostitution being the major occupation for children between ten and sixteen. The girls earn twenty to eighty cents a week, and their recruitment begins at six years of age.

Additionally, at that time there were 200,000 Thai prostitutes working in Europe. In 1993, there were 600,000 Thais infected with AIDS, with 1,200 new cases occuring every day. I have only one question: Doesn't anyone in Asia jerk off anymore?

P.S. I can't get newer statistics because, apparently, everyone in Thailand is too busy getting undressed.

PUTTING THE CAT OUT

It was nearly eleven-thirty, and I had just put the cat out. But it hadn't been easy. He had burned more fiercely than I anticipated.

The poor thing had caught fire earlier in the evening when, in an effort to test his reflexes, I had thrown his favorite toy mouse into the fireplace, and instinctively he raced in after it.

"WHOOOOOOOOM!!!" you might say.

At first, I let him burn awhile just to teach him a lesson, and to peel off a couple of layers of the mud, mange and matted hair which seemed lately, sadly, to have robbed him of a step or two. But I must admit I was also quite fascinated by the many spectacular colors he began to glow with. Colors, no doubt, owed in part to the countless hours he spent killing time in the toxic dump next door. It was quite a show. In fact, I saw several pyrotechnic effects I dare say have not been witnessed since the Grucci home exploded during the Bicentennial.

Then, as the feline conflagration began to burn itself out and I could see the clear, stark outline of his hairless body, he began to emit a dense cloud of smoke, along with some other gaseous substance which I can only describe as "cat steam." Acting quickly, I covered him with several cheap sweaters that no longer fit and pounded him gently, although not without anger, for just over an hour, or until the smoke died down and he stopped his by then bothersome screeching.

At that point, energized, apparently, by a sudden burst of pain and fear, he leapt several feet into the air, went stiff and spread-eagled and began to spin violently, giving off an ominous low-frequency hum and circling the ceiling fan in an elliptical orbit. He circled for the better part of an hour. Finally, exhausted, or, I thought, maybe dead, he went suddenly limp, his orbit decayed and he smashed into an eighteenth-century breakfront, landing heavily on the floor. For three days he lay motionless. When finally he awoke, I opened a can of Bits O' Kidney and fed him by hand.

I can tell you this: Although he looked quite unusual, and he smelled god-awful, I was glad I could be there for him when he needed me.

BODY OF WORK: PART 2
TOENAIL CLIPPINGS

Saving the little things we remove from our bodies comes from our natural curiosity. We all have it. We're curious about ourselves, we're curious about our bodies, so we're curious about the little parts that we clip, snip, pluck, pull or pick off of ourselves. Toenail clippings are a good example.

I'll set the scene for you: You're sittin' on the bed at home one night, and somethin' really shitty comes on TV. Like a regularly scheduled, prime-time network program. And you think, "Well, I'm not gonna watch *Raymond Blows the Milkman*. I'm gonna clip my fuckin' toenails."

So you start to clip your toenails. And every time you clip one of them, the little clipped part flies several feet away. You notice that? These things fly all over the bed. So when you're finished clipping, you have to gather them all back into a little pile. You can't leave them all over the bed, they make dents in your legs. You don't need that. You have to gather them back into a pile. And did you ever notice this? The bigger the pile gets, the more pride you have in the pile.

"Look at this, Honey. The biggest pile of toenail clippings we've had in this house since the day the Big Bopper died. Get the fuckin' camcorder! Call the Museum of Natural History! Tell them we have a good idea for one of those diorama things."

And then you search the bed for the largest clipping of all, the biggest one you can find, usually from the big toe, and you bend it for a while. Don't you? Yes! You do! You bend it, you squeeze it, you play with it. You have to. Why? Because you *can!* Because it's still lively and viable; it just came off your body, there's still moisture in it. *It's almost alive!!*

And sometimes I save my toenail clippings overnight. Do you ever do that. You put 'em in an ashtray and try to save them till the morning? It's no use. They're no good in the morning; they're too dry. You can't bend them. I say, fuck 'em, throw 'em away. Who needs unbendable toenails? Not me. I'm not that sick. I don't need parts that badly. No sir.

PICK OF THE LITTER

Little things, folks. Little things you pick off your body—and your curiosity about them. Especially if it's something you can't really see before you pick it off.

For instance, you know how sometimes you're picking your ass? You know what I mean, just standing out in the driveway, idly picking your ass? And as you're picking and probing, you come across something that seems to be . . . a small object! And let's be real, here, folks. After you manage to pull it free, don't you smell it? Just a little bit? Sure you do. You have to, it's only natural. And you get excited!

"Honey, c'mere! Look! (He sniffs) You want a couple of hits off this thing? While it's still fresh? Remind me, baby. Did we eat at Fatburger this week? We did? (Sniffs again) Well, I don't remember orderin' anything that smelled like this. I believe this is a Shitburger. You know, tastes like a burger, smells like shit. Actually, it smells more like Ethel Merman. Call that Andrew Lloyd Webber fella. Tell him we have a great idea for one of those fine shows he's always puttin' on Broadway. Then gimme the scrapbook, baby. This son of a bitch is goin' right next to that Lithuanian toe-jam we found at the Olympics."

It's an exciting moment the whole family can enjoy.

THE BIRTHDAY PARTY

(Two bachelors at a neighborhood bar.)

CHESTER: Tomorrow's my fortieth birthday. I gotta go get candles and pick up my cake.

LESTER: You're buyin' your own birthday cake?

CHESTER: No, I ain't buyin' my own birthday cake. My mother's buyin' it, I'm just pickin' it up. She's givin' me a surprise party but she don't feel good, so she can't pick up the cake.

LESTER: It's a surprise party, and you're pickin' up the cake?

CHESTER: I ain't gonna *look* at it, okay? It's already wrapped. I'm just gonna pick it up.

LESTER: But how can it be a surprise party if you're pickin' up the cake and you know the party is comin'?

CHESTER: I don't know *when* it's comin', do I? It could be eight in the morning, it could be midnight.

LESTER: Eight in the morning? How can you have a birthday party at eight in the morning? Who the fuck is gonna come, the milkman?

CHESTER: Don't laugh, my mother would do it. One year, on my birthday, I got drunk and didn't come home. She threw the party without me.

LESTER: What'd she sing? "Happy Birthday to Him"?

CHESTER: You're a fuckin' riot, ya know that?

LESTER: How many candles ya gonna get?

CHESTER: Well, we already got sixteen from my kid's birthday last year, and twenty-four is how many come in a box. I'm forty, so I only gotta get one box. I guess I could go ahead and get two boxes and leave my kid's candles alone, but two boxes would be forty-eight candles, and what am I gonna do with the eight extras?

LESTER: Save 'em?

CHESTER: Don't laugh. At my house we do save 'em. In fact, we don't even light 'em up.

LESTER: Why not?

CHESTER: Well, if you light 'em up, they look crappy the next time you wanna use 'em—believe me, we don't waste nothin' at my house. In fact, listen to this: A couple of years ago, my grandfather turned ninety-six. Ninety-six is four boxes, right? Four times twenty-four?

LESTER: Right.

CHESTER: Well, we only had sixty candles on hand, 'cause that's all we ever need for my mother—she's one of them people, when she turned sixty she decided to "stop havin' birthdays." So sixty is all we need. Two and a half boxes. So we bought three boxes. But that's seventy-two, givin' us twelve left over. Right?

LESTER: I'm takin' your word for it.

CHESTER: Trust me, okay? So, we got twelve extra candles, and we decided to give them to my niece. She was just turnin' thirty-six, and she already had a brand-new box of twenty-four of her own. She's a widow with no kids, so she don't need too many candles. I think maybe on her cat's birthday or somethin' she sticks one on a cupcake. So with her, a box lasts a long time.

LESTER: Keep goin'.

CHESTER: Anyway, like I say, it's my grandfather's ninety-sixth birthday and we only had sixty candles. That means we need thirty-six more, a box and a half. So we borrow thirty-six from my brother. He had two full boxes, because in about six months it's his forty-eighth birthday. But that's still a ways off, so we borrow thirty-six from him, which leaves him with twelve, and that works out nice, because his kid is gonna be twelve next week, so we're covered all the way around.

LESTER: You got an interesting family.

CHESTER: Anyways, we put the ninety-six candles on my grandfather's cake, and we start to light them up, okay? But there's so many of them, that by the time we get the last one lit, half of them are just little holes in the frosting with smoke comin' out. But if you looked down into the holes, you could still see the flames. So, my grandfather blew out all ninety-six candles, but he had to do 'em one at the time because he had to blow down each individual hole. Plus he's short-winded. You know the good part?

LESTER: I can't imagine.

CHESTER: He got ninety-six different wishes.

LESTER: Did any of 'em come true?

CHESTER: I think three.

LESTER: You believe in wishes? I mean, you believe they come true?

CHESTER: Nah. I believe in wishes, but I don't believe they come true. Not unless it's a real easy wish, like "I wish I was at a birthday party." But you gotta blow out all the candles, or else the wish don't come true. If one candle stays lit, you don't get your wish.

LESTER: Well, suppose you wished one candle would stay lit.

CHESTER: Whaddya mean?

LESTER: I mean suppose you wished that one candle would stay lit, and then you blew them all out. What would happen?

CHESTER: Well, it couldn't happen. Unless you blew them all out.

LESTER: But if you blew them all out, then one candle wouldn't have stayed lit, so your wish wouldn't have come true.

CHESTER: Don't give me that college shit, will ya? Jesus! Herbie, y'ever notice this guy? As soon as you start talkin' about somethin' intelligent, he has to throw in that college shit. He says, "If you wish for one candle to stay lit, it won't happen unless you blow all the candles out." That's the kind of shit they teach in college now.

LESTER: That's right. It just so happens my major was Comparative Birthday Cakes, with a minor in Frosting.

CHESTER: It wouldn't surprise me.

LESTER: Ya gonna have hats? It ain't a party without hats.

CHESTER: Naaah. No hats.

LESTER: How come?

CHESTER: They come fifty in a box. What am I gonna do with forty-eight extra hats?

LESTER: In your family it might work out.

CHESTER: I know. That's why I ain't gonna do it. See ya next week.

LESTER: Okay, so long. Have a happy birthday!

CHESTER: I'll do my best.

MERRY CHRISTMAS, LIL

One Christmas, when I was little, my aunt Lil gave me a book about railroads. It was just the kind of gift I hated. A book. I wanted a toy. Preferably a little car or truck, or maybe a few soldiers; I didn't ask much. Just some kind of toy a boy could play with every day and not get tired of. No. A boring fucking book about railroads with pictures of fucking trains.

My mother forced me to tell Aunt Lil that I really liked the book; she made me lie and say "thank you" and all that other drivel-shit parents are constantly trying to push into your head. She didn't want to hurt Lil's feelings. (Actually, she didn't want to look bad in Lil's eyes.)

Well, I made the mistake—common in childhood—of listening to my mother and following her advice. I thanked Lil. Guess the result. Right! Every Christmas and every birthday from then on, I got a fucking boring book from my fucking boring aunt fucking boring Lil. First buses, then airplanes, then trucks and then cars. And on and on through the years, until she ran out of conveyances and had to switch to buildings. I weep when I think of all the soldiers I could have had. Probably a battalion or two. Ah, well.

I realize the problem now: I was too young to have learned the following sentence: "Hey Lil! Take your fucking railroad book and stick it up your ass. And get me some goddamn soldiers!" That would have nipped the whole thing in the bud.

TURN DOWN THE RADIO!

Does anybody really listen to that shitty music they play on the radio? FM radio music? What's it called? Adult contemporary? Classic rock? Urban rhythm and blues? You know what the official business name for that shit is? "Corporate standardized programming." Just what an art form needs: corporate standardized programming. Derived from "scientific" surveys conducted by soulless businessmen.

Here's how bad it is: One nationwide chain that owns over a thousand radio stations conducts weekly telephone polls, asking listeners their opinions on twenty-five to thirty song "hooks" they play over the phone; hooks that the radio people have already selected. (Hooks are the short, repeated parts of pop songs that people remember easily.) Depending on these polls, the radio chain decides which songs to place on their stations' playlists.

Weeks later, they record the hooks of all the songs they're currently playing on their stations across the country, label them by title and artist and sell that information to record companies to help create more of the same bad music. They also sell the information to competing radio stations that want to play what the big chain is playing. All of this is done to prevent the possibility of original thinking somehow creeping into the system.

Lemme tell you something: In the first place, listening to music that someone else has picked out is not my idea of a good time. Second, and more important, the fact that a lot of people in America actually like the music automatically means it sucks. Especially since the people who like it have been told in advance by businessmen what it is they're supposed to like. Please. Save me from people who've been told what to like and then like it.

In my opinion, if you're over six years of age, and you're still getting your music from the radio, something is desperately wrong with you. I can only hope that somehow MP3 players and file sharing will destroy FM radio the way they're destroying record companies. Then, even though the air will probably never be safe to breathe again, maybe it will be safer to listen to.

OH SAY, CAN YOU HEAR?

What is the purpose of having a person "sign" "The Star-Spangled Banner"? Don't deaf people know the words by now? Besides, signing can't possibly convey the exact, personalized musical rendition the singer may be offering. How could a signer ever convey to a deaf person the elaborate, note-bending vocal gymnastics that black female singers put that anthem through? Especially those last few lines; the ones from "O'er the land . . ." all the way through ". . . of the brave," which sometimes can take more than six or seven minutes to complete. Why, I should think a signer would break an arm trying to get that stuff across.

Besides, what does the national anthem have to do with sports in the first place? I never understood that. Play Ball!

PRACTICE, PRACTICE, PRACTICE

During the Middle Ages, it seems as though every castle had a group of trumpet players who stood in a line and played loud, intricate fanfares whenever something important happened. And it occurred to me that occasionally those guys must have needed to practice. You know, "Fanfare practice, three o'clock, near the moat." There could be any number of reasons: new guys in the group, new fanfares, the brand-new trumpets came in.

So I'm wondering, when these guys did hold practice—and they kept playing the fanfares over and over—were the people working around the castle required to constantly keep snapping to attention? Did maybe some of them do it anyway, out of force of habit? Or did everyone pretty much ignore the fanfares since they knew it was really only practice?

And, if so, at a time like that, when everyone had been lulled into a false sense of security, what if the king decided to walk across the yard to visit his sister in the dungeon? And they blew a fanfare for him? Half the people would probably just keep on working. Would that piss him off, or would he understand?

And what about coming-to-attention practice? Seems like fanfare practice would be a perfect time to hold it. You know, kill two birds . . . Ah well, fuck it. These are the sort of thoughts that hold me back in life.

JUMP, DON'T SCREAM

Here's why I'm opposed to singing. Singing strikes me as an indicator of limited language skills. My feeling is that if someone has a valid thought, deserving of expression, but somehow that thought can't be communicated without the assistance of a banjo or a tambourine, then maybe it's a thought the rest of us don't need to hear.

People will argue, "Singing has more to do with expressing emotion than it does with expressing thought." Well, fine. But from my point of view, when it comes to expressing emotion, singing is not nearly as effective a tool as screaming. Let's face it, if you want to express emotion, screaming is where it's at.

And to be fair, the more I think about it, the more I realize that singing itself is nothing more than a modified form of screaming. It's actually just carefully organized, socially acceptable screaming. And, folks, I think we have enough screaming in the world as it is.

Now, dancing, on the other hand, I can understand. Dancing is a highly developed form of jumping around, and there's certainly nothing wrong with jumping around. Jumping around is fine in my book. In fact, I feel it's essential. So, please, feel free to jump around all you want. But if you fall and break a leg, don't come screaming to me. Write a song.

CAN YOU HEAR ME NOW?

Have you noticed that whenever someone at a large gathering tries to get the attention of the crowd on a public address system, they always yell into the microphone? "ATTENTION!! ATTENTION PLEASE!! LADIES AND GEN-TLEMEN!! YOUR ATTENTION PLEASE!!" Don't these people understand that the whole purpose of a voice-amplifying system is to amplify the voice? I think the idea is that when you speak into it, it makes your voice sound louder. Maybe I'm way off on this, but it seems to me that if there is a device that makes your voice sound louder, there's probably no reason to yell into it. I don't know, maybe I'm just wrong on this. I'm willing to listen. But hold it down, will ya?

CARS AS PERSONAL BILLBOARDS

NEVER MIND THE BIOGRAPHY

I'm tired of people using their cars as biographical information centers, informing the world of their sad-sack lives and boring interests. Keep that shit to yourself. I don't want to know what college you went to, who you intend to vote for or what your plan is for world peace. I don't care if you visited the Grand Canyon, Mount Rushmore or the birthplace of Wink Martindale. And I'm not interested in what radio station you listen to or what bands you like. In fact, I'm not interested in you in any way, except to see you in my rearview mirror.

Furthermore, I can do without your profession of faith in God, Allah, Jehova, Yahweh, Peter Cottontail or whoever the fuck it is you've turned your life over to; please keep your superstitions private. I can't tell you how happy it would make me to someday drive up to a flaming auto wreck and see smoke curling up around one of those little fish symbols with *Jesus* written inside it.

And as far as I'm concerned, you can include the Darwin/fish-with-feet evolution symbol too. Far too cute for my taste.

So keep the personal and autobiographical messages to yourself. Here's an idea: Maybe you could paste them up inside your car, where you can see them and I can't.

PROUD PARENTS OF ANOTHER DRONE

Here's another segment of the bumper-sticker population that ought to be locked into portable toilets and set on fire. The ones who want us to know how well their kids are doing in school. Doing well, that is, according to today's lowered standards:

"We are the proud parents of an honors student at the Franklin School." Or the Midvale Academy. Or whatever other innocent-sounding name has been assigned to the indoctrination center where their child has been sent to be stripped of his individuality and turned into an obedient, soul-dead, conformist member of the American consumer culture.

What kind of empty people need to validate themselves through the achievements of a child? How would you like to live with a couple of these blockheads? "Say, Justin. How's that science project coming along?" "Fuck you, Dad, you simpleminded prick! Mind your own business and pass the Froot Loops. Fucking cunt dork."

Here are a few parental bumper stickers I'd like to see:

"We are the proud parents of a child whose self-esteem is sufficient that he doesn't need us promoting his minor scholastic achievements on the back of our car." That would be refreshing.

"We are the proud parents of a child who has resisted his teacher's attempts to break his spirit and bend him to the will of his corporate masters." A little Marxist, but what's wrong with that?

Here's something realistic: "We have a daughter in public school who hasn't been knocked up yet." And, for the boy: "We have a son in public school who hasn't shot any of his classmates yet. But he does sell drugs to your honors student. Plus, he knocked up your daughter."

And what about those parents who aren't too proud of their children? "We are the embarrassed parents of a cross-eyed, drooling little nitwit, who, at the age of ten, not only continues to wet the bed, but also shits on the school bus." Something like that on the back of the car might give the child a little more incentive. Get him to try a little harder next semester.

PLATE TECTONICS

My car complaints include personalized license plates, which in California have reached really bothersome levels. Among my least favorites are the ones where the guy tells me what kind of car it is, in case I'm fucking blind: BEAMER, BENZ, PORSH. How helpful. Then there are those very special guys who not only tell me what kind of car it is, but also who owns it: GARY'S Z, DON'S JAG, BOB'S BMW. What's wrong with these cretins? Have they never owned a car before?

And what's with these pinheads who feel compelled to announce their occupations? LAWYUR, SKINDOC, PLMBR, SHRYNK, POOLMAN. Why this pressing need to reveal one's profession? Drumming up business? Job insecurity? Identity crisis? Or is it just the usual American disease: being a jackoff.

And since these things are called "vanity plates" (they should be called "ego tags"), it comes as no surprise that the show-business professions abound with this nonsense. Among the worst offenders are writers. If you drive the streets and freeways of Los Angeles long enough, sooner or later you will see every variation of license plate these allegedly creative people have managed to come up with.

Here are the best of the lot: WRITTIR, WRYTRE, WRYTR, WRYYTRR, WRYTAR, RITER RITEUR, WRYTER, RYTER, TV RTR. God help them. Isn't a scriptwriting credit recognition enough? Or carrying a Writers Guild card? What are they looking for? Do they expect to be nominated for an Emmy at a red light? If these hacks spent half the time working on their scripts they spend thinking up license plates, entertainment in America would be vastly improved.

But writers aren't alone. It seems that any job in television demands an acknowledgment: TVGUY, TVMAN, TVHOST1, TVNUZE, TVVDEO, TVSOWND, TVBIZ, TVBIZZ, TVBIZZZ, TV SHOW. I suppose the idea is, "Why be involved in television at all if I can't tell the world?" After all, everyone knows what an outstanding field it is to be proud of.

One last item. To me, the biggest mystery of all is why a good-looking woman would get a license plate that says HOT BABE, PARTYGAL, HOTLIPS or BABE4U? Isn't she just asking for some crazy fuck with a hard-on to follow her home so he can find out if she's as hot she says she is? Maybe that's the point; to pick up horny freaks at random. Sounds dumb. I wonder how many of these women have been raped and killed by guys whose license plates said BIGDICK, HOTROD, KILLGAL or RAPEDUDE?

BODY OF WORK: Part 3
SCAB LABOR

Here's another item you can't see while it's still on you: a scab on the top of your head. Did y'ever have that? Sure you have. A little scab on the top of your head? Not a big, red, juicy blood scab, like you get when someone at work hits you in the head with a Stilson wrench. Just a little scaly, scabby, dry spot. You find it one day by accident, when you're scratchin' your head. You come across it as if by good luck.

"Dum-dee-dee-da . . . Da-dum-da . . . Whoooaaa! What's this? A scab! Hot shit, a scab! I love fuckin' scabs. This is gonna be a lot of fun. I can't wait to pick off my scab and look at it. Oh boy, oh boy! I can't wait to pick off my scab and place it down on a contrasting material such as a black velvet tablecloth in order to see it in greater relief. Oh boy, oh boy, I can't wait to pick off my scab, this is gonna be a lot of fun.

"Wait! Wait! Wait! (Picking at scalp) Wait just a minute. It's not ready to come off yet! It's immature, it's still not ripe. It's not ready for plucking. I'll save this for Thursday! Thursday will be a good day. I only have half a day of work on Thursday. I'll come home early, masturbate in the kitchen, wash the floor and then I'll watch *The Montel Williams Show*. And while I do, I'll pick off my scab. Oh boy, oh boy! I can't wait to pick off my scab, this is gonna be a lot of fun."

THE WAITING GAME

So you wait. And you wait. And you wait, and you wait, and you wait. And you try not to knock it off by accident with the little plastic comb you bought in the vending machine at the Easy Livin' Motel when you hooked up with the two skanky-lookin' chicks who gave you the clap that night.

And now, finally, Thursday arrives. It's harvest time! Harvest time on the top of your head. So you come home early, and you masturbate, but you do it in your sister's bedroom just to give it a little extra thrill. Know what I mean? Then you shampoo the rug, and you watch *The Montel Williams Show*. Pretty interesting topic: "Women Who Take It up the Ass for Fifty Cents." Not the best show he's ever done, but you know somethin'? Not bad, either!

And now it's time. Time to go get this little scab. But you want to proceed carefully. You want to pry this thing off slowly and evenly, around the perimeter of the scab, so that it lifts off all in one piece. You don't want it to break into pieces. Who needs a fragmented scab? Not me. I don't need parts that badly, I'm not that disturbed.

What you really want; what you really need; what you really must have is a complete, whole scab you can set down, study, make notes on and perhaps write a series of penetrating articles on for *Scab Aficionado Magazine.* Who knows? You might rise to the top of the scab world in a big hurry. It's a small community and they need people at the top.

And so you proceed. With a single fingernail extended—always choosing your best peeling and scraping nail—you find your way through the thicket of hair and locate the target. You make a careful, initial probe, and surprisingly, the prey yields easily, coming off all in one piece. And you lift it off carefully, through the hair, and position it on the tip of your picking finger.

And you look at the little thing, so pathetic there on your finger. Isolated, alone, out of its environment. And your heart begins to melt. So you take your new friend carefully between thumb and forefinger, and gently place it back on your head, setting it loose in the wild. And you feel the better man. You're in harmony with your body.

Think of it as catch and release.

EUPHEMISMS: Broke, Nuts and On the Street

I GOT NO MONEY

While we in America have been busy creating politically correct euphemisms for old people—thereby making their lives infinitely easier—we've also been working on our poor-people language problem. And we now have language that takes all the pain out of being poor. Having no money these days is easier than ever.

I can remember, when I was young, that *poor people lived in slums*. Not anymore. These days, the *economically disadvantaged occupy substandard housing in the inner cities*. It's so much nicer for them. And yet they're still considered *socially marginal*.

But as it turns out, many of these socially marginal people receive *public assistance*—once known as *welfare*. Before that it was called *being on relief*, or *being on the dole*. And at that time, being on the dole was the worst thing you could say about a family: "They're on the dole." People were ashamed. It was tough to get a date if you were on the dole.

But public assistance! That sounds good. Who of us hasn't benefited from some form of public assistance? Even huge businesses and agricultural interests receive public assistance. Ditto all the wealthiest taxpayers. So apparently, there is no shame attached to being on the dole after all.

I GOT NO HOME

In this country, about the only thing worse than having no money is having no place to live. And over the years, those with no place to live have had many different names: *vagrants, tramps, hoboes, drifters* and *transients* come to mind. Which name applied to a person sometimes depended on his, his— God, this is difficult to say—*lifestyle*. There, it's out.

But can having no place to live actually be a lifestyle? Well, it seems to me that if you're going to use a questionable word like *lifestyle* at all, you should be forced to use it across the board. After all, if there's a *gay lifestyle*—which I doubt—and a *suburban lifestyle*—which seems more arguable—it stands to reason there must be a *homeless lifestyle*. And even, one would assume, a *prison lifestyle*.

Indeed, is it possible that those doomed souls in places like Buchen-wald were actually enjoying a *concentration-camp lifestyle?* If they were, don't tell their families; you'll be misunderstood. And, taking this unfortu-nate word to its ultimate, logical extreme, I will not be surprised to some-day see one of those spiritual mediums doing a TV show called *Lifestyles of the Dead*. (Incidentally, shouldn't a group of mediums be called *media?* Just asking.)

Back to the subject: vagrants, tramps, hoboes, drifters and transients. Without using a dictionary (which in many cases is no help at all), here are the distinctions I picked up in years past by listening to how people used these words. The sense I got was: Vagrants simply had no money; tramps and hoboes had no money, but they moved around; drifters moved around, but occasion-ally worked for a while and then drifted on, whereas tramps and hoboes didn't work at all. We'll get to transients in a moment.

There's one other distinction between tramps and hoboes that's worth mentioning. The word *tramp* might also have been used to describe the young woman your son brought home. Rarely did anyone's son bring home a hobo. Unless, of course, he was into the *gay hobo lifestyle*. Actually, there weren't too many gay hoboes. That's because if a hobo didn't have a home, he certainly didn't have a closet either to be in or to come out of. (Sudden thought: hobo rhymes with homo. Sorry.)

Another way to categorize this class of people was to call them transients. Sometimes, on skid row, where they had a lot of *bums* and *winos* (we'll get to them in a minute), you'd see a cheap hotel with a sign that said TRANSIENTS WELCOME.

Transients were like drifters, except transients seemed to stay in cities, whereas drifters moved through small towns and rural areas. You *had* to move through those places, because they weren't as tolerant as cities; they didn't have signs that said DRIFTERS WELCOME. It was usually just the opposite. Ask Clint Eastwood. By the way, isn't a hotel that says it welcomes transients a little like a restaurant that says it prefers people with stomachs? Just asking.

First cousin to a *transient hotel* was a *flophouse*, a magnificently descriptive piece of language that has all but disappeared. (Just for the record, these days transient hotels are called *limited service lodgings*.) Several cuts above all these places were *furnished rooms*, these days known by the phrase *SROs*, short for *single room occupancy*.

So, staying on track here, we began this section with people who have no place to live, which brings us to today's hot designation, *the homeless*, also known as *street people*. When I was a boy, we never heard those words; a dirty, drunk man on the street who wanted money was normally called a bum. Simple word, three letters, one syllable: *bum*. And a bum was usually also a wino. You know, a *substance abuser*. He had a *chemical dependency*. Little did we know.

By the way, it should be pointed out that bum might also have been used to describe the young man your daughter brought home. Many's the bum who didn't pass muster with Dad. I wonder how many of those bums the daughters brought home wound up marrying the tramps the sons brought home? That might explain all those *homeless children*.

But the word *homeless* is useless. It's messy, it's inaccurate, it's not descriptive. It attempts to cover too many things: poverty, alcoholism, drug addiction, schizophrenia, no place to live and begging on the street.

Homeless should mean only one thing: no home. No place to live. Many of these people who beg on the street actually have places to live. I had one guy tell me he needed money to buy tires for his van. I gave him a dollar; I considered him both honest and enterprising.

The first word I remember for these people was *bag ladies*. I don't know why men were left out of this; I never heard anyone say *bag men*. I guess that's because a bag man is a different thing. A bag man is someone who delivers bribes or illegal gambling money. Probably, in today's evasive, dishonest, politically correct language, they'd be called *bag persons*. In my opinion, the closest we're ever going to get to a good descriptive name for these lovable grimy folks is street people.

And by the way, isn't it ironic that shopping bags (and shopping carts)—symbols of plenty—should be the objects most preferred by people who have nothing at all? I guess if you have nothing, you need something to carry it around in. Especially if you're crazy.

WILD AND CRAZY GUYS

That's what a lot of these street people are, you know. They're crazy. I avoid terms like *mentally disturbed* and *emotionally impaired*. You can't let the politically correct language police dictate the way you express yourself. I prefer plain language: crazy, insane, nuts. "The whole world is crazy, and many of its inhabitants are insane. Or am I just nuts?" And for the most part, we humans do enjoy being colorful and creative when describing the condition of someone who's crazy. Here are a few descriptions of craziness that I enjoy:

- *One wheel in the sand.*
- *Seat back not in the full, upright position.*
- *Not playing with a full bag of jacks.*
- *Doesn't have both feet in the end zone.*
- *Lives out where the buses don't run.*
- *The cheese fell off his cracker a long time ago.*
- *His factory's still open, but it's makin' something else.*

Here's an odd one: *His squeegee doesn't go all the way to the bottom of the pail.* I think you have to have some serious time-management problems to be sitting around thinking up stuff like that. But there you are. This next one sounds really good, but I confess I don't quite understand it: *He belongs in a cotton box.* For some reason it sounds exactly right, though, doesn't it?

And if you're going to be irreverent about describing crazy people, you can't get soft when it comes to describing the places we keep them. Or used to keep them. In the 1980s, Ronald Reagan decided the best place to keep them was on the streets, which actually makes a lot of sense, because the streets are nothing more than a slightly larger, open-air asylum, anyway.

But around the turn of the nineteenth century, many states had places called *institutions for the feebleminded.* That name seemed too long for some people, so instead they referred to them as *madhouses.* "They took him to the madhouse. Boy, was he mad." Then these places became *insane asylums, mental homes, mental institutions* and, finally, *psychiatric facilities.*

I have three personal favorites. I always liked the *hoo-hoo hotel.* To me, that says it all. Here's another one that's not bad: *the puzzle factory.* It has a certain class to it, doesn't it? But if you prefer a gentler approach, you really can't beat *the enchanted kingdom.* "They took him away to the enchanted kingdom." And guess how they took him there? The *twinkymobile.* Now that's descriptive language.

A TOAST TO THE CLASSICS

When I see a symphony orchestra, a hundred or so people playing some incredibly difficult piece of music in complete and perfect unison as if they were a single organism, I remind myself that each one of them started the day in a different kitchen. A hundred different musicians in a hundred different kitchens, scattered across the city. And sometimes I find myself wondering how many of them had eggs that morning and how many chose cereal. I try to guess whether the percentage of muffin eaters is greater among the strings or the brass section. I ponder whether or not the percussionists drink a lot of coffee, whereas, perhaps, the piccolo players lean more toward flavored teas. I don't know why these thoughts come to me. But they sure fill the time between scherzos.

FUCK YOU, FATHER, FOR YOU HAVE SINNED

Catholic kids are stupid; they don't know how to handle a pedophile priest. Here's what you do: First of all, you don't get all scared and do whatever he tells you. Who wants to get sucked off by a forty-three-year-old clergyman with beard stubble? Not me. Instead, what you do is kick him in the nuts. You kick him squarely in the nuts, and you get the fuck out of there as fast as you can, and you go tell somebody right away; you tell as many grown-up people as you can—one of them is bound to believe you.

That's what you do. You don't wait thirty years. You kick the priest in the nuts and say, "Fuck you, Father, I don't do that shit. Try Jimmy Fogarty, I heard he blew the choirmaster." And you're out the door. And don't forget to take your rosary. On second thought, leave the rosary. A lot of good it did you in the first place.

THREE SHORT STORIES
THE VELVET HAT

She wore a velvet hat. She walked down the steps slowly, as if each one were a significant achievement. Her arm, bent severely at the elbow, pinned her purse close to her side. The surface of the last few steps was cracked and uneven, and so she extended her tiny arm to grip the railing. At that moment a man ran up and jammed an entire box of peppermints into her mouth.

NOT MARTHA STEWART

Vinny had just squeezed off three really vicious, warm, partially liquid farts and was now trying with all his might to suck down from the back of his nose a huge gob of hardened snot that felt as big as a human embryo. Ignoring the dog shit encrusted under his fingernails from several weeks earlier, he reached deep into his throat, pulled loose some partially digested food, swallowed it again and continued to make hamburger patties for the kids.

GARNISH

The man in the tweed hat stood by a tree, rolling a half-dried snot between his thumb and forefinger. Moments later, the snot now completely dry, he strolled casually past a sidewalk café and gently flicked it into a young lady's lemonade.

. . . FINISH YOUR SENTENCES?

STAN: Why do you always . . .

DAN: . . . finish your sentences?

STAN: Yes, it's something that's . . .

DAN: . . . been bothering you for a long time?

STAN: Yes.

DAN: Well, it's a habit that started in grade school. When the teacher called on another kid, sometimes the kid would start to answer and then get stuck. So I would supply the rest of the answer.

STAN: And this habit has stayed with you . . .

DAN: . . . ever since that time.

STAN: But there must be something you can . . .

DAN: . . . do about it? The only thing I could do about it would be to find some person who might be willing to . . .

STAN: . . . finish *your* sentences?

DAN: Yes, if I could just find someone to finish *my* sentences . . .

STAN: . . . it would put a little balance in your life?

DAN: Right.

STAN: But why does it have to be someone *else*? Why couldn't it be . . .

DAN: . . . the same person? Why couldn't the same person whose sentences I finish . . .

STAN: . . . be the same person who finishes your sentences?

DAN: I don't know. Let's ask this . . .

MAN: . . . man over here. What can I do for you fellows?

A Person I Know Day

The American Retail Association reminds you that next Sunday is A Person I Know Day. It's a lot like Mother's Day or Father's Day, but instead of honoring your parents, you take the time to honor some other person you know. It can be anyone at all: mailman, delivery boy, gas station attendant, drugstore clerk, even that interesting fellow who stands on the corner all day displaying his penis. Any person you know is eligible; in fact, *every* person you know is eligible. So why not honor them all? Go out today and buy gifts for all the people you know. It's the perfect way of showing your love and saying, "Hi, I'm sure glad I know you."

And when you think about it, you'll probably be in store for some nice gifts yourself on A Person I Know Day. In fact, the more people you know, the more gifts you'll receive. So go for a long walk today and introduce yourself to every person you see. Just walk up and say, "Don't I know you? If not, I'd sure like to." Then give them your address and tell them to send you a gift. You'll make lots and lots of new friends. And you'll be helping the economy.

IF IT AIN'T DIRTY, WHY CLEAN IT?

I've never seen anyone cleaning a church. I've seen many things, but never a cleaning crew working in a church; vacuuming, mopping, dusting the statues and scrubbing the altar. You know why? I figured it out: Churches don't need to be cleaned; God does it. It's one of those miracles. That's how they know it's a church in the first place.

Here's how it works: After a church has been built, the owners wait six months and then look inside. If it's clean, they know it's a church. So they get ready for the grand opening. And from that day on, they never have to clean it. No matter what kind of crud, grime or muck the sinners track in, the place remains spotless. But just between you and me, a little Windex on the stained glass wouldn't hurt once in a while. It would help bring out all those bright, pretty colors they use to show the torture and the bleeding of the saints.

OUR LADY OF THE TV

"Hi. I'm Our Lady of the TV. I'm here to say hello, and to make sure everyone prays real hard for peace. Also, the last time I was here I forgot my sunglasses. Has anyone seen my sunglasses?"

(Stagehand hands her the glasses.)

"Thank you. Hold my purse, would you?"

(She hands him her purse and puts on the sunglasses.)

"I know that many of you lead a pointless existence. You have dead-end jobs, bad marriages and children who hate you because you've ruined their lives. I also know you look to symbols like me to provide solace and hope. Well, here's the deal: I have no solace to offer, and, frankly, there is no hope.

I'm just an illusion; an illusion that means nothing. So work it out for yourselves; if you ask me, you're not trying hard enough. Thank you. I'll be back in a few years. And please stop bothering my son with stupid requests like winning the lottery."

(To the stagehand) "Gimme the purse."

LETTER TO A FRIEND

Dear Trevor,

The reason I'm writing is because I've lost your address and have no way of getting in touch with you. For that reason, chances are you won't receive this, in which case you should not feel obligated to reply. If, however, this letter does reach you and you wish to answer, please enclose your current address so I will know where to send this. By the way, you can ignore the return address on this envelope, as I am moving next week and, although I don't yet have my new address, I will be sending it along as soon as I hear from you.

Should you have any trouble locating me, please be assured I will contact you as soon as I have my new phone, so, by all means, give me a call and let me have your number. If it turns out I'm unable to reach you, please don't hesitate to get in touch, as I always mention it to my friends whenever neither of us hears from the other. Should you encounter any trouble reaching me, please let me know, and I will get back to you at once.

Then again, if you are unable to reach me, perhaps it would be better not to get in touch, because I will most likely be trying to get hold of you. And, of course, if I do reach you please let me know immediately. Con-

versely, if I don't reach you, you will probably hear from me right away.

Well, evening is rolling around, and, as they say in Portugal, "It's time to say goodbye." I hope you receive this before you mail your letter. It's so good to communicate this way.

Sincerely,
Sperla Vaughn

P.S. Should this letter be lost in transit, please disregard.

BITS AND PIECES

TRUE FACT: I saw a guy on the street wearing a T-shirt that said "Couples for Christ." But he was all alone. And I wondered, What would Jesus think?

· What's the difference between a drop and a droplet? After all, if you divide a drop into smaller parts, all you really get is smaller drops. Big or little, a drop is a drop. Same thing with a crumb. But the odd thing about a crumb is that if you cut a crumb in half, you don't get two half-crumbs, you get two crumbs. To me, that sounds like magic. I gotta ask David Copperfield how they do that.

· When it comes to God's existence, I'm not an atheist and I'm not an agnostic. I'm an acrostic. The whole thing puzzles me.

· A saw a homeless guy sitting on the sidewalk, yammering to himself and repeatedly punctuating his remarks with, "You know what I'm sayin'? You know what I'm sayin'?" And I thought, For God's sake, the man is talking to himself! If *he* doesn't know what he's saying, who would?

TRUE FACT: On June 8, 1995, Glacier National Park was closed because of too much snow.

· Colin Powell spent his entire adult life as a soldier, trying to devise the most efficient ways of killing foreigners for his country. Then he became a diplomat, trying to devise the most efficient ways of getting foreigners to cooperate with his country. Tough sell.

· Whenever I hear about parents who have nine or ten children, the only thing I wonder is how they survive the birthday parties.

· I recently learned there are three people still alive who can do the minuet. Unfortunately, only one of them is able to move without a wheelchair.

· I think they should have a hotline that never answers, for people who don't follow advice in the first place.

· I finally figured out what e-mail is for. It's for communicating with people you'd rather not talk to.

· You know what I like most about the NCAA Basketball Tournament? Sixty-three losers.

· The United States most closely resembles a huge, poorly-thought-out sick joke.

· Health tip from the American Medical Association: Never pour corrosive chemicals on your testicles.

· A female teacher seduced a fourteen-year old boy and he turned her in to the police. What was this kid thinking? Was he fuckin' crazy? Or gay? I would have kept that kind of thing real quiet. At least until I graduated.

· Cigarette companies market heavily to young people. They need young customers because their product kills the older ones. It is the only product that, if used as intended, kills the consumer.

· More people write poetry than read it.

· I wish the ecology people would save one species that would make a dramatic comeback and then wipe us all out.

TRUE FACT: There is actually an erotic wrestler.

· When I'm in someone's house and I see something I want that's small and easy to conceal, I steal it. It's my belief that property belongs to the person who wants it most.

· Whatever became of alpha-carotene?

· I wonder what kind of masturbation fantasies Stephen King has.

· I also wonder if anyone has ever masturbated while fantasizing about having sex with a live chicken. Usually, I wonder about these things while I'm masturbating.

· Isaiah said, "They shall beat their swords into ploughshares and their spears into pruning hooks . . ." Let me ask you something. When was the last time you heard of someone who made a fortune selling ploughshares and pruning hooks?

· You're probably thinking to yourselves right now, "I wonder what he thinks I'm thinking right now." Or, you may be thinking, "I wonder when he's going to say, 'You're probably thinking to yourselves right now, I wonder what he thinks I'm thinking right now.'" Or you could be thinking, "I wonder when he's going to wonder when I . . ." Well, maybe not.

· Hey, guys, did you ever get your balls caught in the toaster when it was turned all the way up to dark brown, and your wife was trying to rub butter on your balls, and your pit bull was in the kitchen and he really loves butter? It's an awful feeling.

· When I'm writing, I always like to have the TV playing in the background. I usually try to find a program that's interesting enough to leave on, but stupid enough to ignore.

· I think sometimes the word *overseas* is pluralized unnecessarily. The way I look at it, New York to London is "oversea." After all, there's only one sea in between them.

· This statement is untrue.

· **Regarding astrology:** An obstetrician or a maternity nurse who weighs between one hundred and two hundred pounds actually exerts a greater gravitational force on a baby at the time of its birth than do any of the distant planets that are said to influence a person's personality and destiny. Why aren't these bulky, proximate objects factored into the astrological charts that are so carefully laid out?

· There are caregivers and there are caretakers, and yet the two words are not opposites. Why is this?

· Whenever I hear that someone lives in a gated community I think of places like Auschwitz.

TRUE FACT: There is actually such a thing as the Paralyzed Veterans of America. And I wonder, Who answers the phone?

· Until you're a certain age, you don't have anything to "put behind you." That's what life seems to be: a process of doing things that eventually you just want to put behind you.

· There are now murderous turf-wars going on in which people are being brutally killed over the right to sell a substance called ecstasy.

· You know something you don't see anymore? The sacking of a city. Rome and Constantinople were good examples. Next time we win a war, we ought to sack the capital of the country we defeat. "U.S. TROOPS SACK BAGHDAD." Wouldn't that be good? I guess we do our sacking in subtler ways. Through the business community.

· I think they ought to have really fast escalators that you have to jump on and off, and if you get hurt, too bad.

· When I notice a dead fly on the windowsill—one that wasn't there the day before—I always wonder how he died. I wonder if he had a stroke, or maybe a little fly heart attack. Then I think maybe he's just pretending to be dead so I won't swat him. So I swat him.

· Here's a tip from the power and light company on saving energy: If you have elderly people living with you, cut back on their heat and light. Old people often exaggerate how cold they feel.

NO CHILD LEFT BEHIND

I was thinking the other day that one kid who's really gonna have emotional problems when she grows up is that Jon Benet Ramsey. You know, because of all the media attention, her parents being under suspicion, the speculations about sexual abuse. Jesus, that kind of thing would fuck any kid up. And then I remembered, hey, she was the one who got killed. And I thought, it's a good thing she's dead; at least she won't have to suffer.

TELL PIERRE I SAID HELLO

HANK: I'm going up to San Francisco this weekend.

FRANK: Oh. Well, tell Pierre I said hello.

HANK: Actually, I knew you would say that, so I took the liberty of calling him and telling him you said hello. He said in that case to tell you he also says hello. So, "Hello" from Pierre. And he said to add, "How's it goin'?"

FRANK: Oh, that's great. Well tell him everything's going just fine. And don't forget to say, "How are you?"

HANK: Well, he and I knew you would ask that, and so Pierre has authorized me to say that he's glad you're fine, but that he hasn't been feeling too well lately.

FRANK: Oh. Well, tell him I'm sorry to hear that and I hope it isn't serious.

HANK: He says he knew you would be sorry to hear that, but he thinks it will blow over.

FRANK: Well, tell him if it doesn't I have a great doctor in San Francisco. Ginny and I met him in Hawaii when we were there last year.

HANK: Pierre says he knew you had a great doctor, but he wasn't aware he was located in San Francisco. He also says he didn't know you and Ginny had gone to Hawaii. He thought it was Cancún. And he also says, "How's Ginny?"

FRANK: Tell him Ginny is dead.

HANK: Well, I'm sure he didn't know, but I'm going to go out on a limb here and say that he's real sorry to hear about that, and I'm willing to bet anything he offers his condolences. And, most likely, he'll also say that if there's anything he can do—anything—please don't hesitate to ask.

FRANK: Excuse me, Hank. I'd love to keep talking, but I have to go buy underwear.

HANK: Oh. Well, Pierre says there's a sale at The Gap.

FRANK: Get fucked, Hank.

GUYS WILL BE GUYS

I don't know why people got all excited about that guy Jeffrey Dahmer. Because he broke a few laws? So what? There's nothing wrong with killing twelve people, having sex with their corpses, masturbating on them, eating their flesh and then saving the heads in the refrigerator. What's wrong with that? Nothing. So far, nobody has been able to explain to me what it was Jeffrey Dahmer did that was so wrong.

First of all, let's remember, *wrong* is a relative term. Who's to say what's wrong? Who are we to judge? Put yourself in the other man's shoes. Who among you, under certain circumstances, might not kill twelve people, have sex with their corpses, masturbate on them, eat their flesh and then save the heads in the refrigerator? Not one of you, I suspect. So cut the guy a little slack. Always remember, there, but for the grace of God . . .

YOU'RE NOT FUNNY

Here are some things you should not say if you encounter a comedian. First: If you're with another person at the time, don't say to your friend, "You better watch out, he'll put you in one of his skits." We don't like that. It's not funny. And, by the way, we don't do skits. Second: If you meet him while you're at your job, do not say, "You oughtta work here, you'd get a lot of material." It's not true. Just because you work with a bunch of simpletons, doesn't mean it translates into comedy. Third: If you work at a store and we're shopping there, and some small mix-up occurs that needs to be sorted out, don't say to a co-worker, "He's gonna put this in one of his routines." He's not. One more thing we don't like: When you tell us something that you think is funny and then you say, "You can use that if you want." We don't want to use it. Believe me.

POW! SMACK! BAM!

True: I stopped behind a small, beat-up camper at a red light, and noticed three bumper stickers: DARE TO RESIST DRUGS AND VIOLENCE, THERE'S NO EXCUSE FOR DOMESTIC ABUSE, and STOP SENIOR ABUSE. And I thought, I'm really glad I don't live with those folks. I'd bet anything they were on their way to the hospital emergency room or perhaps intensive psychiatric counseling. If I'd caught up and looked inside the vehicle, I'm sure it would have resembled a Johnson & Johnson showroom.

COUNT TO A BILLION

ANNOUNCER: And now, ladies and gentlemen, direct from Dover, Delaware, Big Earl Stemplemeyer's Television Network presents *Count to a Billion*.

(Applause, lively organ music)

Yes, it's *Count to a Billion*, the show where ordinary people of limited intelligence can win big money by simply counting to a billion. As we like to say, "If you can count at all, and have a reasonable amount of time on your hands, chances are you can count to a billion." So now, here's your host, a man you can count on, that burly guy who's one in a billion, Basil Danderfleck.

(Applause, lively organ music)

BASIL: Thank you, Wynonie Flench. And now, folks, let's meet our two players, Tillie Lipfinder and Zippy Brillnipper, alias Skeezix Pendleton.

(Applause, lively organ music)

BASIL: How about it, folks? Are you two ready to count to a billion?

TILLIE: Yes sir.

ZIPPY: You bet your ass!

(Applause, lively organ music)

BASIL: All right, let's get started. As you know, we have only one rule: No skipping any numbers. Ready, set, go!

(Loud bell, lively organ music, applause, yelps, cheers)

TILLIE: (Incredibly rapid pace) 1, 2, 3, 4, 5, 6, 7, 8, 9, 10, 11, 12, 13, 14, 15, 16, 17, 18, 19, 20, 21, 22, 23, 24, 25, 26, 27, 28, 29, 30, 31, 32, 33 . . .

ZIPPY: (Extremely slowly)   1 . . . 2 . . . 3 . . . 4 . . .

BASIL: Tillie appears to have jumped off to an early lead, but as we know, slow and steady wins the race, so don't count Zippy out yet. By the way, tonight's winner will receive two free meals at Shorty and Bud's Restaurant for the Unclean, featuring their world-famous Chicken in a Shoe. As Shorty and Bud say, "Wouldn't You Like to Eat a Nice Hot Meal Out of Someone Else's Used Footwear?" Well, let's check back in with our two contestants.

TILLIE: (Incredibly rapid pace) 10,366,793, 10,366,794, 10,366,795, 10,366,796 . . .

ZIPPY: (Extremely slowly) 25,853,264 . . . 25,853,265 . . . 25,853,266 . . . 25,853,267 . . . 25,853,268 . . . 25,853,269 . . .

BASIL: Wow! Amazing! In no time at all, Zippy has caught up and pulled ahead. But he'd better not get overconfident, he still has 974 million to go.

    We'll check back in a moment, but first, a reminder that tonight's runner-up will receive a handsome set of matching luggage from America's luggage leader, Packwell and Goforth, now featuring the newest innovation in luggage . . . portable suitcases! That's right, folks, these novel suitcases have actual handles built right into them, so now you can take your luggage with you anywhere you go. Take it on a plane, take it on a boat, you can even put it in your car. No more leaving your bags at home because they're "hard to carry." Take them with you and travel in style! Packwell and Goforth: ahead of their time since 1357.

Let's check in again with Zippy and Tillie.

TILLIE: 536,895,241, 536,895,242, 536,895,243, 536,895,244 . . .

ZIPPY: 67,667,776 . . . 67,667,777 . . . 67,667,778 . . . 67,667,779 . . .

Well, Tillie has come back and taken a big lead, because, unfortunately, Zippy's severe lisp has slowed him down considerably here in this section which includes tho many thicktheth and theventh. I'm sorry . . . so many sixes and sevens. This does not look good for Zippy. But we're about out of time for now . . .

(Groans, hisses, boos, lively organ music)

. . . but join us again next week, as we watch the conclusion of this thrilling match on tape and meet two new contestants, as once again we play America's favorite counting game . . . *Count to a Billion!*

(Cheers, boos, applause, hisses, shouts, threats, curses, audience advancing menacingly toward stage, lively organ music)

ANNOUNCER: (over music and crowd noise)
                  Tonight's guests will stay at the fabulous Fireproof
                  Motel, located between Long John Silver's and the Rub

It and Yank It massage parlor, just outside Dover, Delaware. Dover: "The City That Just Missed the Mark." Don't forget, the Fireproof Motel features superb drinks and finger food in the intimate cocktail lounge, Rita's Box. Drop in and ask Rita for some finger food.

Stay tuned now for a full-length movie on America's favorite new date show, *Dinner, Movie and a Hump*. Tonight, your hosts, Dagwood Parkhaven and Candace Nooch, cook up a delicious whale chowder and breast of hyena on a bed of diced badger as they present an award-winning film about an amnesia victim, *Who the Fuck Am I?*, starring Esther Sylvester, Kermit McDermott, Chi Chi Ameche and Skeeter Van Meter. And introducing Keith Bunghole as the queer.

After the movie and the food, Dagwood and Candace will tear off a lengthy piece of ass on the kitchen table, taking turns being on top, and demonstrating several interesting, new sexual positions, including the Baghdad Twirl and the Bosnian Dick-knot.

Good night everyone, and God bless America!

(Lively organ music, lustful throaty moans and maniacal screaming)

EUPHEMISMS: Death and Dying

Some of our best work with euphemisms involves the subject that makes us the most uncomfortable: death.

Our most common euphemism for death is to say the person *passed away.* Or *passed on.* If you believe in an afterlife, you may prefer *crossed over,* or *crossed over to the other side.* Whenever I hear that someone has crossed over to the other side, I always picture Fifth Avenue.

Then there's the official term for dying, the doctor term. In this case the person simply *expires.* Like a magazine subscription. One month he just doesn't show up. Unfortunately, he can't renew. Or so they say. Better check with the Hindus on that.

Now, continuing. In this current age of specialization—and increasing detachment—if the person in question dies in a hospital, it's called a *terminal episode.* Although the insurance company sees it as *negative patient-care outcome.* That one's actually kinda nice, isn't it? And if the negative patient-care outcome was caused by medical malpractice, then it's referred to it as a *therapeutic misadventure.* Colorful term. No wonder so many doctors are leaving their practices; it's hard to get therapeutic-misadventure insurance.

But by far the most creative terms we've come up with to comfort ourselves about death are the ones that describe the rituals survivors put themselves through. We owe a lot of this softened language to the funeral business. Or, as they prefer to be known, the *death-care industry.* They have completely transformed the language used to describe what happens following a death.

In years past it went like this: "The *old man died,* so the *undertaker* picked up the *body,* brought it to the *funeral home* and put it in a *casket.* People sent *flowers* and held a *wake.* After the *funeral,* they put the *coffin* in a *hearse* and drove it to the *cemetery,* where the *dead man* was *buried* in a *grave.*"

But in these days of heightened sensitivity, the same series of events produces what sounds like a completely different experience: "The *senior citizen passed away,* so the *funeral director* claimed the *remains* of the *decedent,* took them to the *memorial chapel* and placed them in a *burial container. Grieving survivors* sent *floral tributes* to be displayed in the *slumber room,* where the *grief coordinator* conducted the *viewing.* Following the *memorial service,* the *funeral coach* transported the *departed* to the *garden of remembrance* where his *human remains* were *interred* in their *final resting place."*

Huh? What's that? Did someone die or something?

I'VE GOT A TRAIN TO CATCH

This item demonstrates how stupid the average American is. Every ninety minutes someone in this country is hit by a train. A train, okay? Trains are on tracks; they can't come and get you. They can't surprise you when you step off a curb. You have to go to them. Got that?

There are five thousand highway/rail-crossing accidents annually. To counter this problem, the Department of Transportation issued the following rules for people to follow at railroad crossings:

- Don't drive around lowered gates. "Okay, got it."
- Don't cross in front of a train. "Never thought of that."
- Don't walk on the tracks. "Check."
- Be aware that trains can't stop quickly. "Good to know."
- Always expect a train. "This one would probably be tied in to the fact that these are railroad tracks, is that right? Correct me if I'm wrong on this."

- Look for more than one train. "Frankly, this is one I never thought of. Maybe if I remember the others, this one will take care of itself."

GET DOWN!

Here's something to think about: In the course of history's wars, many battles took place in the woods and the countryside. So, sometimes I picture a soldier waking up on a spring morning, wildflowers growing around his tent, birds singing in the trees, perhaps the comforting sound of a brook trickling by in the near distance. And then a ten-pound cannonball hits him in the face. It's an interesting thought, don't you think?

ON MY HONOR

I wanted to be a Boy Scout, but I had all the wrong traits. Apparently, they were looking for kids who were trustworthy, loyal, helpful, friendly, courteous, kind, obedient, cheerful, thrifty, brave, clean and reverent. Unfortunately, at that time, I was devious, fickle, obstructive, hostile, rude, mean, defiant, glum, extravagant, cowardly, dirty and sacrilegious. So I waited a few years and joined the army.

PASS THE MUSTARD

In New York State, the law says that the ingredients of hot dogs can legally include a certain amount or percentage of insect parts and rat droppings. It's permissible by law. So, in New York, when you eat a hot dog, you more or less have to hope that the hot dog you're eating contains only the most nutritious parts of the insects (not just legs and antennae) and that the rats whose feces you're eating were on good, heart-healthy diets.

YOU'VE GOT A NICE VOICE, DO YOU HAVE INSURANCE?

I've been enjoying a new band from England called So Long, Mate! It's a five-man heavy-metal band, and the reason it's called So Long, Mate! is because at the end of each performance the other four members of the band kill the lead singer. As a result, the music has a certain urgency to it. Also, it keeps the tours nice and short; it's basically one night, and then back they go to L.A. to hold auditions. The band plans to have an album ready in the year 2037.

DANNY NEEDS A TORSO

"Hello, this is David Nipplegripper, another insufferable Hollywood movie star who wants you to help some cause or charity merely because I say so. Today, I want to tell you about little Danny Pendejo. Danny needs your help; he was born with no torso. His legs are fine, his arms are fine, and his head is okay except for one really big, caved-in part on top. But he has no torso. Won't you help by being a torso donor? Even a torso that's too big will be better than no torso at all. Thank you. This is David Nipplegripper, reminding you to see my new movie, *Breasts on the Moon*."

NUTS!

Another sign of America's decline: Because a few people are "sensitive to peanuts" and have "allergies" that might "kill them," America's commercial airlines had to stop serving those little bags of peanuts. It wasn't sufficient that the affected people could simply refuse the peanuts when they were offered; the argument was made that the people who did eat the peanuts were putting "peanut dust" in the air, creating a health hazard for the "victims." What a load of shit. If someone is in danger of dying from inhaling peanut dust, why aren't they dead already? Why didn't they die at a baseball game or at the circus? America has gone soft.

INSTRUCTIONS: FOLLOW CAREFULLY

Release the handle by pulling down the strap and tightening the fasteners. Press the button and remove the safety cap, then turn the knob to unleash the spring and wind the excess slack onto the spool. Loosen the screws on the plate lid and insert the tabs into the slots. Rotate the control switch a quarter of a turn before lowering the two levers. Then drop the main crank into a neutral position. Be careful not to unscrew the housing before engaging the catch. Plug in and you're set to go. If smoke fills the room, read the troubleshooting guide at the rear of this manual.

ACTORS, NOT ACTIVISTS

I like the good actors. The real actors. The ones who keep their lives private. Sean Penn, Harvey Keitel, Alan Arkin, Robert Duvall, Al Pacino, Jack Nicholson, Johnny Depp, Robert De Niro, Gary Oldman, William Hurt, Dustin Hoffman, Gene Hackman, Gary Sinise, Christopher Walken, Gary Busey. They keep to themselves. You don't see them appearing all the time on TV. They don't cooperate with *Access Hollywood* and *Entertainment Tonight*. They're actors. Not celebrities. They keep to themselves. That's why their work is so good. Good for them.

DEAR MA

Dear Ma,

Even though you're dead, I wanted you to know I'm doing real well. No thanks to you, I might add. I now have my own TV show and it's getting very high ratings. I play the part of a guy whose mother dies but it doesn't really bother him. I know they don't have good reception where you are, so I'm going to send you a tape. Do you think a tape will be okay in the intense heat?

Love, Dirk

TEAMS SUCK!

I don't like ass kissers, flag wavers or team players. I like people who buck the system. Individualists. I often warn kids: "Somewhere along the way, someone is going to tell you, 'There is no "I" in team.' What you should tell them is, 'Maybe not. But there *is* an "I" in independence, individuality and integrity.' "

Avoid teams at all cost. Keep your circle small. Never join a group that has a name. If they say, "We're the So-and-Sos," take a walk. And if, somehow, you must join, if it's unavoidable, such as a union or a trade association, go ahead and join. But don't participate; it will be your death. And if they tell you you're not a team player, just congratulate them on being so observant.

IN THE GROOVE

You ever run over a guy with your car? And you kind of panic? So you back up? And run over him a second time? And then you realize you have to get the fuck outta there before the police show up? So you put it in drive again and run over him a third time? What the fuck—might as well. What else you gonna do at that point, drive around him? Anyway, as you drive away, did you ever reflect on the fact that each time you ran over him the crunching sound got fainter and fainter? That's because he already had two good, deep grooves pressed into him that you kept driving through.

PRIDE GOETH . . .

Parents are such fuckin' doofuses. I saw a bumper sticker that said "Proud parents of a sailor." What the fuck is so special about being a sailor? How about "Proud parents of a tailor"? Isn't a tailor worthy, too? The whole "proud parent" thing is bullshit. Pretty soon I'm expecting to see "Proud parents of a child." Have a little self-respect, will ya? You never see the children with bumper stickers that say "Proud son of Mr. & Mrs. Klayman." That's because Mr. & Mrs. Klayman are such fuckin' doofuses.

I'M IN THE MORAL MINORITY

I don't think there's really such a thing as morality. I think it's a human construct designed to facilitate the control of people. Values, ethics, legal standards—all of these things are human-generated, and they're lumped under some vague idea called morality. But suppose humans got it wrong? Suppose there's no actual, objective morality? Suppose there's just a natural, worldly, secular, common-sense standard of behavior whose purpose is what's best for getting along and what's best for survival? That would be a good system. Why should a system like that be overlaid with a sense of spooky, mystical, judgmental oversight?

JUST DIE, MOTHERFUCKER

When this Catholic guy, Cardinal Bernardin of Chicago, died, they praised him for accepting death gracefully. Excuse me, but isn't that what you're supposed to do? Accept death gracefully? What's that? You say many people *don't* accept death gracefully? I see. So now we're evaluating people's behavior and praising them based on what other people *don't* do? Wonderful.

I don't think people should ever get credit for doing something they're supposed to do, even if it's rarely done by others. Condemn the ones who don't do it if you like, but don't praise the ones who do it. Only one of the two behaviors is worth commenting on, not both.

TRUE STUFF

You know those broken white lines that separate the lanes on a highway? Have you ever counted them? If you do, you'll find that there are a hundred of them every mile. It's true. Each line is a hundredth of a mile from the next one. Count them for yourself as you track your distance on the odometer. Just count how many there are each tenth of a mile; there should be ten. But while you're counting, don't forget to keep an eye out for that big eighteen-wheeler up ahead, parked sideways in the middle of the road.

CHOW TIME

"Hi, I'm Ferris Banderhead, another bothersome movie star who tells people to support some charity or other in order to make myself appear concerned and to increase my popularity. Not to mention easing the guilt I feel for having much more than I deserve. But enough about me. April is National Hunger Month. In Beverly Hills, we're having our annual Hunger Banquet and Gala called 'Hors d'oeuvres for Ethiopia.' Send in your dollars today and help us feed people around the world who could certainly use a nice hors d'oeuvre. And remember, the sooner we conquer hunger, the sooner we can start working on upset stomach. Thank you. This is Ferris Banderhead, reminding you to see my new spy movie, *The Snotlocker Papers.*"

Mannheim Rehab: Call Today

"I'm Dr. Mannheim of the Mannheim Rehab and Recovery Center. People ask me, 'How can I tell when one of my loved ones needs help with a substance abuse problem?' And I say, 'If you see them lying in a corner, naked, in a puddle of their own filth, it may be time to think about counseling.' Call Mannheim today, and we'll come over and pick them up. But before we get there . . . please clean up the filth."

UNCLE BLITZEN

Uncle Blitzen was a troubled man. As a child, visiting backstage at a concert, he was fondled by a viola player and lived the rest of his days with an unnatural fear of stringed instruments. He was one of the nine hundred people present at the Jonestown Massacre, but he threw away the Kool-Aid and only pretended to be dead. When everyone stopped moving he looted the corpses. Subsequently, he moved to Stockholm, where he became the town scumbag. Years later, he reemerged in England as a self-proclaimed bishop, roaming the Midlands with a band of rogue altar boys, administering forced communion to lapsed Catholics. He died during Hurricane Shlomo in front of an adult sex shop when the store's sign blew down and he was crushed to death by a giant neon dildo.

UNCLE PINOCCHIO

Uncle Pinocchio had twenty-three separate and distinct personalities; unfortunately, all of them were unpleasant. He believed that Porky Pig cartoons represented actual events, and he once stabbed his dog with a ceremonial Japanese saber in a dispute over a lamb bone. He always wore a three-piece suit. It didn't have a vest, the jacket was just torn in half. He drifted from job to job: balloon vendor, freelance daredevil and stoop laborer among them. He finally settled in his basement, where he lost his mind trying to invent a rectal harmonica. After that, the family kept him tied to a linden tree in the backyard, where they fed him with a slingshot. After six years, they released him on Mussolini's birthday, whereupon he married a passive-aggressive librarian who later beat him to death with a dictionary stand.

UNCLE SHADRACK

Uncle Shadrack felt he was special because one of his testicles was shaped like a Brazil nut and the other like a cashew. He loved to run up to women, screaming, "You want some mixed nuts?" He told me that in his younger days he was quite a lover and once fucked a girl so hard her freckles fell off. Alas, he didn't marry well. His wife, Chlorine, looked like something that might be found in the Dumpster behind a cloning center. Her PMS was so bad she had a mood swing installed in her backyard. As a child, while watching a gay pride parade, she was run over by a float full of lesbians, and was eventually found dead in a military barracks, having ingested a load of bad sperm. Shadrack was electrocuted by a RadioShack pacemaker he purchased at a thrift shop.

UNCLE SHEMP

Uncle Shemp was alarmingly unexceptional. He had no detectable lifestyle, and his only accomplishment was the fact that he was a lifelong member of the general public. He started slowly, struggled hard and eventually clawed his way to the back of the pack. Occasionally, he would show a sudden flash of mediocrity, but quickly return to his usual pattern of complete insignificance. He was a man without memories. He didn't have amnesia, he simply had no memories. As he put it, "Nothing big ever really happened." As a result, he wore a Medic-Alert bracelet saying PLEASE LET ME DIE. His only pleasure was his hobby: picking through airline wreckage, looking for children's toys. He died at seventy-five from a head injury suffered as the result of undue glee following a bowel movement.

TUMOR HUMOR: GUYS, GALS & CANCER

WOMEN: THE PRODUCE DEPARTMENT

MAE: I see where Ruthie Garrick went under the knife the other day. She had a tumor on her the size of a grapefruit.

AGNES: Well, that's bigger than Estelle Mealy's tumor. Estelle's was the size of a large navel orange.

PAULA: Yeah, but sometimes a large navel orange can be almost as big as a small grapefruit.

KATE: That's true. Especially one of them small Indian River grapefruits. I don't like them. Too sour.

PAULA: Me either.

MAE: Listen, girls, this wasn't no small Indian River–size tumor. The doctor said this thing was almost the size of a cantaloupe. He claimed if he'd-a left it alone any longer, it probably woulda wound up as big as a casaba melon.

AGNES: Earlene Miller had a tumor the size of a casaba melon. Actually, her sister claimed it was approaching honeydew proportions.

PAULA: Well, I don't know nothin' about no tumors, but when my aunt Ruby died, her liver was the size of a champion watermelon. I got a picture of it somewhere.

KATE: Really? You know, they say that after you die, your liver keeps right on growing.

PAULA: Well, I'm thinkin' Ruby's liver had probably reached its limit. I mean, where do you go from watermelon?

KATE: Beach ball.

MAE: Kate, a beach ball's not a food!

KATE: You want food? I'll give you food. Wait'll you hear this. Ten years ago, when my sister Myra had her gallbladder out, they found twenty gallstones in it. Each one of them was the size—and the shape—of a different type of food: a raisin, a pea, a caper, a grape, a radish, an olive, a pearl onion, a melon ball, a hazelnut, a marshmallow, a Brussels sprout, a bing cherry, a kumquat, a gherkin, a filbert, a small whole boiled potato, a cocktail sausage, a meatball, a lima bean and a dwarf pumpkin.

PAULA: They took all of that out of your aunt?

KATE: They sure did.

PAULA: Jesus! Did she feel any better?

KATE: She said she was hungry.

MEN: THE SPORTS SECTION

JIM: I see where Petey Whelan died the other day. They say he had a tumor on him the size of a beach ball.

ED: No kiddin'? That one under his arm? Jesus, it musta grown fast.

JIM: It sure did. I can remember the day I first saw it; it was small, like a marble. Then almost overnight it looked like a golf ball. I couldn't believe it!

TOM: That was the day he showed it to me. By the time I saw it, it looked more like a slightly enlarged handball, maybe just approaching racquetball size. I spent about an hour with him, and as I was leavin', I glanced at it. The damn thing looked like a tennis ball. I don't mean it had fuzz on it or anything. I just mean it was the size of a tennis ball.

JIM: Yeah. That's when he went to the hospital. He said on the way over in the taxi it went from a baseball to a softball, and then, in the waiting room, it reached the size of a small, regulation volleyball. Finally, when he got into the examining room, the doctors were so alarmed at its growth they smashed it with a big fryin' pan, and it temporarily flattened out into an oval shape.

ED: I remember that. For about an hour it resembled a football.

TOM: Yeah. Then it slowly became round again, but it kept on gettin' bigger. Suddenly, it developed big black spots all over it.

ED: The soccer-ball stage.

TOM: Yeah. Of course, by that time the situation was hopeless. Pretty soon the thing was up to the size of a basketball, and before you knew it, it had gone right past medicine ball and was headin' for beach-ball status. They finally had to move him out of his room and put him in the gymnasium.

ED: Appropriate. How did he die, anyway?

JIM: They tried to operate on him, but as soon as they made an incision all the air rushed out of him. Death by deflation.

TOM: Poor guy.

ED: Yeah.

TOM: Hey, you know what we forgot? Lacrosse and polo.

SOARING AND PLUNGING IN THE MEDIA

One of my pet pursuits is keeping track of how the news media describe those things in the news that increase or decrease. I can generally rely on the fact that the same verbs will be used repeatedly in the same situations.

One of the first things I noticed is that while certain things *skyrocket*, others tend to *mushroom*. Medical costs *skyrocket*. The national debt doesn't do that; it *mushrooms*. And, experts warn, if present trends continue, both of these things will eventually *go through the roof*.

But *mushrooming* is not the only thing the national debt does; it also *balloons*. There aren't too many things that *balloon*. The annual budget deficit used to *balloon*, then for a while it didn't *balloon*, now it *balloons* again. And, by the way, people can *balloon*, as well. I remember reading in the tabloids once that the actress Delta Burke had *ballooned* to some weight that, apparently, the publication found unacceptable.

So, thus far we've *skyrocketed*, *mushroomed* and *ballooned*. But let's not forget *snowballing*. You know what snowballs? An investigation. What happens is, an inquiry becomes an *investigation*, and the investigation begins to *snowball*. And what does it *snowball* into? Right! A *full-blown probe*. And if the probe uncovers enough dirt, it could possibly *mushroom* into a *full-blown scandal*.

Then we have the case of *swelled*. During the 1990s, job rolls *swelled*. By the way, I've often wondered if those job rolls are at all similar to the welfare rolls we used to hear so much about. Just between you and me, I've never actually seen welfare rolls, but I'm sure that with a little margarine or jelly they're quite delicious. And it's certainly heartening to see the food stamp program working so effectively.

Getting back to our subject here, I've found that one of the best places to keep an eye on these "up and down" words is Wall Street. Financial reporting. For purposes of this activity, I'll use hypothetical examples of economic activity that don't actually reflect recent conditions. I can't keep adjusting this material according to the whims of the economy. And besides, this is about language, not finance.

Just to review: We've already skyrocketed, mushroomed, ballooned, snowballed and swelled. Now, as we enter the world of Wall Street, we add a few simpler verbs: *climb, surge* and *jump*. "The stock market *climbed* today as prices *surged* on news that housing starts had *jumped* ten percent." Lots of action.

Another big thing on Wall Street is *soaring*. "Stock prices *soared* today, as reports showed earnings were *up sharply*." Or they may have *shot upward*. At any rate, upward is good. I remember one time hearing Lou Dobbs himself telling me that the Dow Jones Industrials had *vaulted upward* two hundred points. And, on the same day, not to be left too far behind, the long bond *inched higher*.

Then we have the very special case of *spiraling*. The nice thing about *spiraling* is that it can go in either direction. "As medical costs have *spiraled upward*, the quality of medical care has *spiraled downward*." And not only do these two medical numbers *spiral upward* and *downward*, both of them are actually capable of *spiraling out of control*.

Spiraling downward brings us to the verbs for things that are falling. For some reason, downward verbs are more colorful than upward verbs. Downward is where we discover *plunge, plummet* and *nosedive*. You can always tell when a bull market is over, because *housing starts plunge, new-car sales plummet* and *orders for durable goods take a nosedive*. At a time like that, stock prices are usually on the verge of *collapse*.

Or, instead of collapsing, they may simply *tumble, drop sharply* or *go into a tailspin*. And if stock prices are in a *tailspin*, you can be sure it won't be long before they find themselves in *a dizzying free fall*.

Continuing with bear markets, not all days are so dramatic. Occasionally, prices only *dip slightly. Dip slightly* is the opposite of *edge higher*.

And before we leave these words for increasing and decreasing, I would like to make special mention of *beefed up*. I remember reading once that, in anticipation of a visit by Yassir Arafat, security at the United Nations had been *beefed up*.

Arafat being a Muslim, of course, beef would be the preferred meat. You certainly wouldn't want security to be *porked up*. I can think of any number of reasons why we wouldn't want that. And by the way, if you've ever seen some of these security people, you know that the last thing they need is more pork. Or beef. Or food of any kind, for that matter.

Beefed up is one of those terms that has no exact opposite. Nothing ever gets *beefed down*. They never say, "Now that Arafat's visit has concluded, security at the United Nations has been *beefed down*." Doesn't sound right. Instead, they say *scaled back*. Always remember, anything that's been *beefed up* can be *scaled back*. Although occasionally, for variety's sake, rather than *scaled back* the item may be *pared down*.

Hiked and *trimmed* are two more good "up and down" examples. Quite often, during the same session of Congress, defense spending will be *hiked* while education spending is *trimmed*. And sometimes, if Congress is in a really bad mood, education spending is *slashed*, and defense spending *skyrockets*.

Well, we've gone from *sky-high* to *rock bottom* and we seem to be *winding down* now, so let me add one last item: I think I may have figured out the difference between *ramping up* and *ratcheting up*. I'm pretty sure that while *ramping up* takes place on a continuum, *ratcheting up* is more a series of increments. But I do find it interesting that, as with the beef situation, I rarely hear of *ramping* or *ratcheting down*.

As for me, I'm at wit's end.

PROBLEMS AND ISSUES

As you know, people no longer have *problems* in this country, they have *issues*. This shift grows out of our increasingly desperate need to shade the truth and see things as more positive than they really are. Problems sound negative and ordinary; issues sound important, worthy of attention. People are proud to announce them: "I have issues." They feel superior to others who haven't made the switch: "Poor fuck. He has problems. I have . . . issues!" To feel extra superior they may even pair it with some other trendy upgrade: "He has a *drug problem*, I have *chemical dependency issues*."

As with everything in American culture, the use of the word spread indiscriminately to the point where it, of course, lost all its usefulness: During the murder case in San Francisco in 2001 in which two dogs mauled a woman to death, one of the neighbors said, "Everyone knew those dogs had issues with females." Commercials picked it up: L'Oreal says, "Mature skin has issues all its own." An adult diaper commercial informs me that "Many women have bladder-control issues."

So now people have all these issues: trust issues, boundary issues, abandonment issues, personal-space issues. Clearly, I have a problem with this word, but *problem* has lost its power, cheapened by the careless use of expressions like, "What's your problem?" "You got a problem with that," "No prob-lem," and, for those truly in a hurry, "No prob."

I needed a new word, and I refuse to say "issues." So, instead, I turned to that ultimate source of creative language-bending, our nation's capital. I heard a prominent senator, when asked if some issue presented a problem for him, say, "Well, it's not a problem, but it is a *concern.*" And I thought, Wow, another choice for people who refuse to acknowledge problems. I adopted it immedi-ately. But I hope *concern* doesn't catch on to the point where it becomes a prob-lem. After all this trouble, I'd hate to have to deal with concern issues.

THE SECRET NEWS
(News ticker sound effect)

ANNOUNCER: (whispering)
Good evening, ladies and gentlemen, it's time for the Secret News.

(News ticker gets louder.)

ANNOUNCER: Shhhhh!

(Ticker lowers.)

ANNOUNCER:
Here is the Secret News:
All people are afraid.
No one knows what they're doing.
Everything is getting worse.

Some people deserve to die.

Your money is worthless.

No one is properly dressed.

At least one of your children will disappoint you.

The system is rigged.

Your house will never be completely clean.

All teachers are incompetent.

There are people who really dislike you.

Nothing is as good as it seems.

Things don't last.

No one is paying attention.

The country is dying.

God doesn't care.

Shhhhh.

BONUS MATERIAL

SUICIDE: THE OPTION

Part 1: An Introductory Course

THE TIME IS RIPE

Do you realize that right now—right this second—somewhere around the world some guy is gettin' ready to kill himself? Isn't that great? Do you ever stop to think about that kinda shit? I do. It's interesting. It's fun. And it's true! Think about it: Right this second, some guy is gettin' ready to bite the big bazooka! Because statistics show that every year a million people commit suicide. A million! That's 2,800 a day. That's one every thirty seconds. Think about it: Since you've been reading this, another guy has bit the dust.

IT'S A GUY THING

And I say "guy," because men are four times more likely than women to commit suicide—even though women attempt it more. So men are better at it! That's something else you gals'll wanna be workin' on. If you want to be truly equal, you're going to have to start takin' your own lives in greater numbers.

But personally, I just think it's interesting to know that at any moment the odds are good . . . that some guy is draggin' a chair across the garage floor . . . tryin' to get it right underneath that ceiling beam. Wouldn't want to be too far off center. If it's worth doin', it's worth doin' right.

Somewhere else, another guy is goin' over and gettin' a gun out of a dresser drawer. Somebody else is opening up a brand-new package of razor blades—maybe struggling with the packaging a little bit.

"Goddamn plastic! Why do they wrap these things so fuckin' tight? Shit! It's always some fuckin' thing. Nothing ever goes right! Goddamn fuckin' shit prick!"

I just think suicide is interesting as hell. It's probably the most interesting thing you can do with your life. End it!

Part 2: All Suicide, All the Time

IT SURE BEATS GOLF

Suicide is an interesting topic, because it's an inherently interesting decision: to decide voluntarily not to exist anymore. It's profound. You know what it is? It's the ULTIMATE MAKEOVER. That's why I think it belongs on television. In this depraved culture? With the shit that passes for entertainment in this country? Suicide would be a natural on television. People would love it. In fact, I'll bet you could have an all-suicide channel. On cable TV. I'll bet. Shit, they've got all-golf. What the fuck? You ever watch golf? It's like watching flies fuck.

If you can get a bunch of brainless, white male assholes to sit still and waste a Sunday afternoon watchin' that kinda bullshit, you *know* you can get some people to watch suicides. All day long. Twenty-four hours a day, nothing but suicide. Must-die TV!

C'MON DOWN!

You'd get a lot of people watching that kinda shit; you'd get a lot of people volunteering to be *on* there, too. Just so their friends could see them on TV. People are goofy. You'd get a *lot* of volunteers. You'd get all those leftover assholes from *Let's Make a Deal*. They'd be lined up around the block, pushing each other out of the way, putting on funny capes and hats and makeup and calling themselves "Captain Suicide!"

People would be competing for Most Unusual Method: They'd be jumpin' off of barns, lightin' themselves on fire, puttin' rat poison on a taco, drinking Mop & Glo, sticking mothballs up their ass. You'd probably have some weird fuck show up who figured out how to kill himself with a Stinger missile and some dental floss. People are fuckin' goofy!

I'll bet you could find a married couple—in one of them trailer parks or somethin'?—who'd be perfectly willing—perfectly willing!—to sit in a loveseat and blow each other's heads off with shotguns. While a love song is playin'. People are fuckin' nuts!

E PLURIBUS UNUM

This country is full of nitwits and assholes. You ever notice that? Nitwits, assholes, fuckups, scumbags, jerk-offs, and dipshits. And they all vote!

In fact, sometimes you get the impression they're the *only* ones who vote. You can usually tell who's been doin' the voting by lookin' at the election returns. It sure ain't me out there, wastin' my time with a meaningless activity like that.

You know those people on *The Jerry Springer Show?* Those are the average Americans. Oh, yeah, believe me. The below average can't get on the show. The below average are all sittin' home, watchin' that shit on TV. Gettin' ready to go out and vote. Fillin' out their sample ballot.

DUMB-DE-DUMB-DUMB

Americans are dumb. AMERICANS ARE FUCKIN' DUMB!

You can say what you want about this country—and I love it here; I wouldn't live anywhere else:

- I love the freedoms we used to have.

- I loved when it didn't take a natural disaster for us to care for one another longer than five minutes at a time.

- I loved when we weren't on camera all day long, indoors and out, from every conceivable angle.

So, I love this country. I wouldn't live any other place at any other time in history. BUT! BUT! Say what you want about America— Land of the Free, Home of the Brave—we've got some dumb-ass motherfuckers floatin' around this country. Dumb-ass mother-fuckers.

Now, of course, that's just my opinion; you can think what you want about the American people. You can think of them as smart, dumb, naïve, innocent, ignorant, gullible, easily led, blissfully unaware—whatever you like . . .

Part 3: The Pyramid

THE RATINGS GAME

But no matter what you think of the American people, you're gonna have to deal with them, because you're in the television business now. You've got the All-Suicide Channel on cable TV; you need viewers. You have to worry about ratings; you have to worry about . . . sweeps months!

By now, most folks know what sweeps months are—the most important ratings months of the year. When the networks put on all their biggest attractions and hottest stars, trying to pump up the ratings, so their local stations can adjust their advertising rates. So, you're going to have to deal with that competitive television-industry mentality; you're going to have to get out there and compete for viewers.

So I think, during sweeps months . . . on the All-Suicide Channel . . . you're gonna have to go with mass suicides. Huge, public events, on live television, where hundreds of people kill themselves all at the same time.

SOUNDS LIKE A PLAN

Now, the question is: How are you going to do this? How are you going to get large numbers of people to commit suicide all at once, at a time and place of your choosing? In fact, how are you going to get people to commit suicide in the first place? Where will these people come from?

In order to make this whole thing work, you'll need careful planning and organization. You're gonna need a system; you can't just sit around all day, waiting for people to drop by the studio and commit suicide. You need a plan. And folks, today must be your lucky day, because, as it happens, I have just such a plan. Here's what we do:

PYRAMID SCHEME

The first thing we need is to build up a large pool of suicide volunteers—people who can be easily persuaded to kill themselves. Essentially, what we're looking for are people without hope: individuals society has given up on, fate has given up on, or who have completely given up on themselves. Rock-bottom, dead-end, totally fucked-up people with no hope, no future, and no reason to live. A pool of the hopeless, to serve as suicide volunteers. Think of it as a pyramid. That gives us a visual fix. The Pyramid of the Hopeless. So let's get busy and build our Pyramid.

BOTTOMING OUT

Naturally, we have to start at the bottom, and in this lowest layer, I think we oughtta put the homeless people. God knows, we've got enough of them. In fact, we've got so many, we don't know how many there are. Nobody gives a fuck about 'em, nobody wants 'em, nobody's got a plan, nobody's got a program, nobody's got any money. Society doesn't give a fuck about homeless people. They're totally hopeless, so, in the Pyramid they go.

PEN PALS

The next group we're gonna deal with is these people in prison. Especially the ones serving extremely long sentences. And I'll grant you, many of the sentences are deserved. I'm sure as many as half the people in prison are in there for things they really did. And that's not a bad average, one out of two.

But this is obviously another group that nobody gives a shit about. We don't rehabilitate them, because we say rehabilitation doesn't work. And it probably doesn't work because if they do get out of prison, nobody will give 'em a job, anyway. So they're in a hopeless loop of crime and punishment.

And the judges give 'em these extreme, draconian sentences. They get 60-, 70-, 80-, 100-year sentences; life terms, double life terms. One guy recently—and I swear this is true—one guy was given three consecutive life terms—plus two death penalties. Well, how the fuck do you serve that? Even David Copperfield can't do that. You gotta be a Hindu to pull that shit off. Then you've got the people on death row, a couple thousand of them. They ain't goin' anywhere. Boom! In the fuckin' Pyramid they go.

ANOTHER CRAPPY DAY

Now, this next group going into our Pyramid is, more or less, self-selected—and possibly a bit controversial to some folks. These are these people who claim to be depressed. Apparently, in this land of plenty, the richest nation the history of the world (we're so proud of saying that), where some of our supermarkets have over a hundred thousand items on their shelves, we have 19 million Americans who claim to be depressed. And some of them take medicine for it. And, sometimes, the medicine makes them commit suicide, which *really* depresses the shit out of the rest of them. No hope for these folks—in they go!

And let's not forget the ones who only *think* they're depressed. They *think* they're depressed, because they saw the Prozac commercial on television and the doctor looked like a nice guy, the music sounded kind of peppy, and, ". . . what the fuck, some of these pills might just pick me right up." Hopeless mind-set. In the fuckin' Pyramid. Quickly!

CHOOSE YOUR DISEASE CAREFULLY

Now we come to the top of our magnificent structure of despair, and this ultimate space has been reserved for those who are *truly* sick: the terminally ill. No pretenders here. Hundreds of thousands of dead-enders with no hope at all:

- Some of them have something there's no cure for.

- Some of them have something there's no cure for, and nobody's lookin' for a cure, because there ain't enough people sick with what they got, so there ain't no money in the cure.

- Some of them have something there's a cure for, but they haven't got the money for the cure.

- Some of them have something there's a cure for, they've got the money, but they're too far gone.

- Some of them have something there's a cure for, they've got the money, they're not too far gone, but they don't have a ride. And most of those people are too sick to commit suicide. BOOM! In the Pyramid.

TAKING STOCK

Now, let's review and see what we have. Let's put ourselves in the office of vice president of programming at the All-Suicide Channel and analyze what there is to work with. Well, thanks to our carefully thought-out Pyramid of the Hopeless, we find ourselves blessed with an abundance of homeless, imprisoned, condemned, depressed, and terminally ill people—probably millions of them. In other words, we've hit the jackpot. And let's not forget, many of these people more than likely fall into several categories.

JUMPING TO CONCLUSIONS

So, here's my idea, as well as the premise it's based on: I'm convinced that in this depraved culture that so devalues human life and dignity, and where reality television has convinced everyone they belong on national TV, I'm convinced that if you added in the excitement of a brand-new All-Suicide Channel debuting with maximum publicity, you could get five hundred of these hopeless people to hold hands and jump into the Grand Canyon. I'll fuckin' bet you. I'll bet you you could get that done in this country right now.

I'm convinced they would do it. For money! Oh, for money. You gotta give 'em *some*thing. You gotta make it worth their while. After all, they're Americans—they're for sale. Give 'em a little something. Give them a toaster. Americans will do anything, but you gotta give 'em a toaster, don't you?

EYES ON THE PRIZE

So give 'em a little prize—everybody wants a prize. Give 'em some sorta gizmo. Give 'em a cell phone—give 'em a laptop. Give 'em a cell phone that takes a *picture* of a laptop. Give 'em a laptop that takes a picture of a cell phone!

Give 'em an all-terrain vehicle; give 'em a riding lawn mower, a

snowblower, an outdoor barbecue, a Jet Ski. In other words, give
'em one of those things they buy for themselves when they're tryin'
to take their minds off how badly they're gettin' fucked by the system.

Here's an idea: Just before they jump into the canyon, give 'em a
hat with a built-in camera; tell 'em it's Jump-Cam. Tell 'em you'll
send the video home to the family. How about a T-shirt? Who don't
want a T-shirt? Nobody! Give 'em a nice T-shirt:

"I COMMITTED SUICIDE, AND ALL I GOT WAS THIS STU-
PID FUCKIN' SHIRT."

LEAP OF FAITH

And how about this: If you *really* want to raise the profile of this
promotion—if you really want to attract attention—get a bunch of
those evangelical Christians to participate and call it "Jump for Jesus!" They'd go for it in a minute. "Jump for Jesus!"

But let's be fair about these Christians, because they do come in
for a lot of abuse these days. So let's be fair: All Christians really
want out of life is to die—and go see Jesus. So, give them a helping
hand. Be a Good Samaritan, and do the Christian thing. Get 'em to
jump in the canyon.

Tell 'em it's a shortcut to heaven. Mention the word *martyr*. It
works with the Moslems, it works with the Catholics; who knows? It
might even work with these folks. You never know.

Give them a little encouragement. "He's down there. He's at the
bottom of the canyon. Look for the man with the glowing head."

Part 4: Ah, Youth

NETWORKING

You could have a lot of fun with a channel like that. A *lotta* fun. But you know somethin'? You might not want to be on cable. Cable has a limited audience. You might want to get more people lookin' in, and, if so, you're gonna have to go to the broadcast networks; one of the big broadcast networks. Now, I don't know about you, but when I think about suicide and network television, I'm thinkin' FOX! I'm tellin' you, if the people at FOX ain't sittin' around having meetings on an idea like this, they ain't doin' their goddamn jobs over there.

So you put this thing on FOX—and you get Budweiser to sponsor it. Well, Budweiser and a whole bunch of car companies, so people can be thinkin' about drinkin' and drivin' at the same time. Isn't that fun? Isn't it fun to watch the commercials they run during sporting events on TV? "Drink this! Drive that! Fuck you!" They don't care. They don't give a shit about you. And then every now and then they qualify their message. "Don't let your friends drive drunk." Yeah, sure.

GET 'EM WHILE THEY'RE YOUNG

So you put this thing on FOX. And if you do—or if you put it on any broadcast network—you're gonna have to bring in a younger audience. Everybody knows, that's what the advertisers are looking for: eighteen- to twenty-four-year-olds. So you'll have to get young people interested in this, and you know how you do that? You know how you get young people interested in suicide? You don't call it suicide. You call it EXTREME LIVING! They'd eat it up.

Let's face it, young people are attracted to suicide in the first place. Did you know suicide is the third-leading cause of death between fifteen and twenty-four? It's third! It's ninth in the general population. That'll give you an idea of how popular this after-school activity has become . . . among our teenage folks.

BOY'S LIFE

Especially these young boys, these adolescent males. And a lot of them, you know, they kill themselves when they're jerking off. Yeah. They don't mean to. It just happens. You know about that? Jerkin' off and dyin'? Most people never heard of it. It's just one of those things Americans can't handle, so nobody talks about it. It's not on *Larry King Live*, it's not on Barbara Walters, and you're not gonna see it in *People* magazine. But it's out there, folks. And it's extremely common.

You just ask any teenage boy what he knows or what he's heard . . . about cuttin' off your air supply just at the moment you're about to have a sexual release. He'll tell you an interesting story or two. The kids call it scarfing, because some of them use scarves to do it.

DO IT YOURSELF

Or screw the kid, you don't need him. Just get on the Internet and Google in the words *autoerotic asphyxia*. It's the practice of cutting off the oxygen to the brain at the last moment during masturbation, in order to heighten and intensify the orgasm. And when I say common? A thousand kids a year die from this. A thousand of 'em, okay? So if that many kids die, think how many of 'em are tryin' to pull this off. If you'll pardon the pun I threw in there just to lighten the mood.

THE WAY THINGS WORK

But here's the way it works—apparently. Apparently! I mean, I never tried it; it sounded kinda risky to me. Jerkin' off is all I need, you know what I mean? I ain't tryin' to double my money; fuck that shit. Not me. I just jerk off, wipe off my chest, get up, and go to work. Nothin' fancy. Nothin' fancy at our house, we're simple folk.

But here's the way it's *supposed* to work—and this is why it's such a big attraction in the first place: Apparently, it is true, physiologically speaking, that if you cut off your air supply—the oxygen to your brain—just at the moment you're about to have an orgasm, the orgasm is about . . . I don't know, let's say five hundred times better. Somethin' like that—it's incredibly intense. So what you've gotta do is stand up on a chair, or a bucket or something like that, and you put a rope around your neck, and you start jerkin' off.

And while you're pullin' your pud—while you're whalin' away—you have to arrange to almost strangle yourself . . . just before you have an orgasm. And by the way, while all this activity is goin' on, you've gotta maintain a hard-on. Which ain't easy, 'cause you might just be gettin' ready to buy the farm. So you better be fantasizin' about somebody you really like . . . or some*thing* you really like . . . I don't know what it might be. Maybe gettin' fucked in the ass by a game warden, who knows? Hey, I'm not here to judge. We're all different. To each his own.

So let's recap: Standin' on a chair, rope around your neck, peter in your hand. Now you have to time it just right, so that just before you come—you almost die! And sometimes you miscalculate. You don't know if you're comin' or goin'.

BLAME GAME

And the parents of these kids are too embarrassed to tell the police, so they put the kid's dick away and say he had poor grades. Or, "His girlfriend left him." "Well, no wonder, lady. Look at his fuckin' hobbies." And the policeman writes it down as suicide, once again screwing up the statistics.

Then they blame the whole thing on heavy metal music. You know about that? Ever since the incident with Judas Priest about twenty years ago, they blame suicide on heavy metal. If you remember, Judas Priest is a heavy metal band, and in 1985, two kids in Nevada spent all day listening to one of their albums and then they killed themselves. And ever since that time, heavy metal gets blamed for teenage suicide. If it's murder, they tend to blame rap.

DON'T LOOK AT US

But it's never the parents. You ever notice that?

Apparently—if you listen to them—parents bear no responsibility for turnin' out a fucked-up kid; or even a good kid who *gets* fucked up. Parents have to be the most full-of-shit people in the world. Always have been. Top to bottom, front to back—completely full of shit.

But it comes with the job, doesn't it? In fairness, it's really part of the job description. If you want to be a parent, you've gotta be full of shit. At least half the time.

When you think about it; parents have it both ways. If the kid turns out to be a loser, they had nothin' to do with that. "Must be those kids he hangs around with down at the parking lot." But boy, if he's a winner? Got a scholarship or somethin' like that? Man, they're the first ones out there, raisin' their hands, tryin' to take a little credit. It's a nice state of mind . . . if you can talk yourself into believin' it.

THE SENSITIVE PHYSICIAN:
GETTING A LEG UP

Framstein! How's it goin'? Well, I got some bad news for you, plus a little good news that might give you a lift. The bad news is—you're gonna lose that left leg. We gotta cut the fuckin' thing off; it's all rotten at the bottom and frankly, it smells like shit. That's why I'm wearin' this mask. You don't mind if I open the window, do you? Jesus, that's strong!

Okay, listen. Put down the prayer book and listen; prayers ain't gonna help you now. Here's the deal. We're gonna do the operation tomorrow afternoon. We had to wait, because we ran outta that sterile shit they swab you with before the surgery. Plus, we couldn't find the saw. Turns out, the carpenters were usin' it to build a bar in the doctors' lounge, so it's a little bit dull. But we think we can get by with it for just one leg. The bone has kind of rotted away anyhow, so maybe we can just snap it off with our hands and forget the saw altogether.

Another thing. We're runnin' low on anesthetic, so about halfway through you'll probably start to feel a little uncomfortable. If it gets really bad, just take a couple of deep breaths and hang on to the sides of the table—the whole thing shouldn't last more than three or four hours.

What's that? Oh, yeah, the good news. Well, the guy in the next room is your size, and he's gonna lose the opposite leg, so he wants to buy all your left shoes. Plus—and I'll bet you didn't think of this—your sock supply is gonna double overnight. So try to see the bright side.

Now, listen, I'd love to stay and visit, but I gotta take a shit. I ate some tainted fish last night, and I don't feel too good. We ran outta toilet paper, so I gotta go down to the gas station. To be honest? I wish I could crawl into that other bed over there and catch a few z's, but I gotta keep makin' these rounds. Hippocratic oath and all that crap.

By the way, one more piece of good news? By the time this is over, you'll probably drop thirty or forty pounds. Ha ha ha! We call it the Miracle Amputation Diet. Get it? Well, I'll see you tomorrow. And hey! Try to keep a smile on your face, will ya? You're depressing the nurses.

THE SENSITIVE PHYSICIAN:
IT'S A BOY—SORT OF

Hello, Mr. Belden, good to see you again. Have a seat. Listen, I don't know what kind of shit your wife's been eatin' the past nine months, but this kid she dropped in the delivery room this morning is the weirdest fuckin' thing I've ever seen. I've been doin' this shit for thirty-six years now, so, take my word, I've seen my share of edgy-lookin' kids. This one is really strange. Believe it or not, the little booger has an extra head . . . and . . . six hands! *Six!* And, get this, two of them are under his *arms*! I've never seen anything like it. Neither have any of the people on the eighth floor. I kind of showed him around; I hope you don't mind.

Now, in cases like these, Mr. Belden, there's an important question I have to ask. It's just routine, but I really have to ask. Would you mind if I got a couple of pictures of the kid for my website? I kind of keep a digital scrapbook; people get a kick out it. In fact, if it's not askin' too much, I'd like to get a coupla shots of the three of you. Maybe you and your wife holdin' the baby? Just a thought.

And speaking of pictures, I guess you know the *National Enquirer* pays good money for stuff like this. I have some contacts over there, and I'd be glad to split the money with you. One more thing. If I were you, I'd get on the phone with the *Guinness Book of World Records* as soon as possible. It might be a nice way of honoring the kid.

Eventually, of course—let's face it—you're gonna have to decide what to do with him. And I suggest, before you take the easy way out and just have him destroyed, you might wanna think about sellin' him to a European circus. The Europeans aren't as squeamish about this shit as Americans, and they'd pay plenty to put him on display. Anyway, lots of time to think about that. Stay and I'll go get my camera and bring out the kid. Or kids. Depending on how you look at it. Ha-ha-ha!

THE SENSITIVE PHYSICIAN:
IT AIN'T EASY BEIN' A SURGEON

Wake up, Mr. Fleckner. Listen, we brought you out of the anesthesia to explain what's going on. First of all, the transplant is coming along great, so don't be alarmed by all the blood on the windows; things are going to work out fine. But, frankly, we have to take a little break. Most of us were out all night and we're kinda beat. In fact, I fell asleep a couple of times, myself, while the nurses were still prying your chest open.

But here's the most important thing: It's lunchtime, and I've got a chicken sandwich I've been thinkin' about all morning. My wife makes this great chicken; she marinates it in curry sauce, and it's way better than the shit they serve in the cafeteria. So, do you think you could lie real still for about an hour and a half? Just try to lie real still. But remember to keep pressing down on the incision so the bleeding stays at a minimum, okay? We're gonna leave you with a few gauze pads, in case it starts gushing again.

And listen, we're not sure of this, but we think we left a scalpel somewhere next to your intestines. So don't roll over on your left side. Okay? Or maybe it's your right. I forget. Just to be safe, don't roll over at all. And try not to cough. I'd like to get it back, it's my lucky scalpel.

If you have to go to the bathroom, use that sink over in the corner. Or you can just go ahead and do it on the table; we'll clean up after the operation. And don't worry if you pass out; in your condition the sleep will do you good. We'll see you a little later. By the way, is there anything you'd like me to bring you? They've got a vending machine in the staff dining room.

CELEBRITY CRYSTAL BALL

I predict Charles Manson will be released from prison and record another album. This time people will listen.

Hollywood movie stars will continue to adopt Third World children and those children will continue to grow up socially maladjusted.

I predict former president Bill Clinton will be found in bed with a transsexual and claim on national television, "I did not have sex with those people."

I predict that, while taping an AIDS special in Africa, Geraldo Rivera will catch the syph from a native.

Jimmy Hoffa will be found alive, living with a family of gibbons.

Elvis Presley will be seen sneaking into a Swiss Porta-Potty with a suitcase full of cheese burritos.

I predict that, as a practical joke, Henry Kissinger will have his bladder removed and overnighted to Renée Zellweger.

I predict Liza Minnelli will decide never to get married again, although she will continue to get divorced.

During a party at Larry Flynt's house, Gary Coleman will disappear forever inside the vagina of Anna Nicole Smith.

I predict Defense Secretary Donald Rumsfeld will be found unconscious in an Iraqi police barracks with goat semen in his hair.

Britain's playful Prince William will play a royal prank on several members of the Irish press—and get the royal shit beat out of him.

Charles Gibson and Diane Sawyer will resign from ABC News and hitchhike across Canada wearing his and her pirate costumes.

Heidi Fleiss will reveal that during a one-night stand with Don Ho, following each orgasm, they ran around the room screaming, "Heidi Ho!"

Condoleezza Rice will attend a European ministers' conference with five pounds of potato salad stuffed in her brassiere.

The long string of Kennedy-family tragedies will come to an end at a reunion in Massachusetts when all remaining members are wiped out in a hotel fire.

Prince Charles and Camilla Parker Bowles will name their firstborn Eileen the Cocksucker. Other members of the Royal Family will fail to see the humor.

I predict Shirley MacLaine will reveal that in various past lives she has been an explorer, an empress, a priestess, and a Maxi-pad.

I predict Al Roker will sleepwalk into a Dunkin' Donuts and eat six dozen lemon custards. All the staples in his stomach will pop at once and six policemen will be killed.

I predict Bing Crosby will return from the dead and beat the shit out of Joan Crawford's grandchildren.

The Vatican will reveal that in 1996, when John Paul II's plane landed near the South Pole, in keeping with his custom he kissed the tarmac, and his lips stuck to the ground.

While seated on the *Tonight Show* panel, Rudolph Giuliani will fall asleep and have a vigorous wet dream. Jay will go to commercial.

A new biography of Jacqueline Onassis will reveal that as a young woman she fell in love with a poor man, but immediately ended the affair when she realized her mistake.

I predict Chuck Woolery will host a new game show based on guessing the size of a woman's bush.

Sharon Osbourne will claim she can accurately predict stock market trends by analyzing the stains in Ozzy's shorts.

Gary Busey will suffer multiple spine injuries while engaging in rough sex with a family of Montana brown bears.

I predict Rio de Janeiro will rename its main thoroughfare after the Mills Brothers.

I predict that the popular host of *Jeopardy!*, Alex Trebek, will be killed by the Mob because he knows too much.

Hollywood will revive a popular series of 1940s jungle movies when Russell Crowe stars in *Tarzan Fucks a Zebra*.

Connie Chung will reveal that the late Sonny Bono speaks to her in dreams and is relaying accurate tips on Powerball numbers.

I predict that, as a publicity stunt for a new line of human growth hormones, Paul Simon, Tom Cruise, and Paul Anka will be laid end to end and measure just under twelve feet.

The scandals in the Catholic Church will continue as a group of seminarians in Italy are found to be manually pleasuring zoo animals.

Pat Robertson, Jerry Falwell, and Billy Graham will lead a nationwide prayer vigil and ask God to do something about America's moral climate. God will promptly strike all three of them dead.

And finally: Watch for Dom DeLuise to explode fairly soon.

IDEA FLOW: BRAIN TO BRAIN

Here comes an idea; down my arm, through my pen, and into your eye. You want another? Fine. This time we'll take the scenic route:

Driving due south out of the hopeless, urban sprawl of Brain City, our idea squeezes through the Isthmus of Neck and, bearing right, travels swiftly across and over majestic Shoulder Falls. On, quickly, past Bicep Hill (which the locals refer to as Mount Bicep) and suddenly into the tense and busy town of Elbow Junction.

A leisurely lunch, some extended masochism at the souvenir stand, and once again we're moving. Taking a sharp left turn, we embark on the long, boring passage across the plains of Western Forearm. More than halfway home now. Picking up speed, in no time we find ourselves passing through the Straits of Wrist, and then, at seeming long last, our idea comes to rest on the rich delta of The Hand. Here it is loaded aboard the writing implement.

Our job is done; we've gotten the idea into the pen. Captain Paper Mate will take it from here, and, of course, many others will handle it as well, as it makes its way into your eyes and then on to your brain. We wish them well; they have our prayers.

By the way, I wonder if this idea will wind up on an even- or an odd-numbered page?

KEEP IT OFF THE NEWS

One thing that bothers me about television newscasts is the inclusion of stories that aren't really news. For some reason, news producers insist on running these bullshit, feel-good stories that provide no useful information and add nothing to our lives. These are the sort of things I mean, and every item in this piece is something I have actually heard reported.

Some guy's bank makes a mistake and bills him 6 million dollars; a fourth-grade class puts a science experiment involving insects on the space shuttle; a choir of prison inmates sings at a police convention; a fifty-two-year-old man goes back to college and makes the basketball team; a grandmother sets a new speed record for flying a balloon across Lake Michigan; the Winter Carnival begins in St. Paul, and the first event is the ice sculpting championships. Who gives a fuck about these things? They're not news. They're called human-interest stories. Well, I'm human and I'm not interested.

It's Not News

- A friendly bet between two politicians whose teams are in the Super Bowl is not news. The only reason a bet between the mayor of New Orleans, who puts up a pot of filet gumbo, and the mayor of Philadelphia, who puts up a platter of cheese steaks, might someday be considered newsworthy is because of the remoteness of the possibility that the New Orleans Saints will ever be in a Super Bowl.

- A woman whose town tells her she can't keep her pet pig, so she decides to move rather than give up the pig, is not news. It's just stupid.

- Two hundred skydivers holding hands in a big circle as they free-fall is not news. You know what's news? If all two hundred parachutes fail to open. I'd watch that in a minute.

These TV people must think we're morons. Well, actually, we are—no secret there. We must be. Otherwise, why would they send a camera crew out to the clock store to show the man setting all the clocks ahead when daylight saving time changes? They must think someone will find it interesting. It's not. And it's not necessary to show it on the news. Leave the clock man alone.

- A cabdriver dresses up as Elvis Presley to "brighten people's lives after 9/11." It's not news. It's not even news if the cabdriver dresses up as Osama bin Laden to *darken* people's lives after 9/11. A cabdriver is never news, unless he runs over a first-grade class in front of the Museum of Natural History. Then I'm interested.

- And incidentally, when are the media people going to simply stop covering these Elvis impersonators altogether? The only thing it does is encourage these people to continue their disturbing behavior. Maybe if television reduced its coverage these troubled individuals would let the fat junkie rest in peace.

Beat it, Kid!

Most stories about children do not qualify as news, either, and could easily be omitted without anyone noticing or caring. A ten-year-old boy who has compiled a great record choosing stocks is not news. If he's that fucked up when he's ten, I'm not interested in him.

- Spelling bees don't belong on the news, either. No one cares if a twelve-year-old can spell *zoosporangium*. How often does that come up?

- Missing children are not news for the simple reason that there are so many of them. It happens all the time. "News" means new, different, novel—something that stands apart from the ordinary. One more missing kid should not stop the presses. And by the same token, a kid being found is not important, either. If I don't care when a kid gets lost, why should I care when he gets found? Why should anyone care? Except the parents. Was the kid found? Fine. Were the parents happy? Fine. Leave the rest of us out of it.

- Here's another earthshaking event the news cretins never fail to cover: last year's quintuplets celebrating their first birthday. Yeah? So? Why is that special? Because there are five of them? Doesn't impress me. There are five of lots of things.

- A four-year-old calling 911 and saving his mother's life is not news. It's a curiosity. Emergency 911 stories are never news. The emergency operator coaching someone on how to assist in giving birth: big deal. These things are not news because, once again, they happen all the time. News means new, not "Oh, look, it happened again."

- The same thing is true of a baby being left in a 120-degree car on a hot day with all the windows closed, while the mother goes shopping. You hear it three or four times every summer. It's no longer news.

And by the way, considering how often these child-trapped-in-a-car stories have been reported on TV, don't you think by now parents should have gotten the idea? Actually, isn't that one of the more fundamental rules of child rearing? "DON'T BAKE YOUR CHILDREN!" One concession I will make on this: If last year's quintuplets were baked to death in a car on their first birthday, that would probably belong on the news.

On The Medical Front

Under my standards, not every unusual medical story qualifies as news. A guy donating one of his kidneys to his sister is not news. A guy donating *both* of his kidneys to his sister—*that* would be news. A woman in her sixties having a baby is not news, it's narcissism. She's deranged. How would you like to be eighty-two years old the night your kid goes to the prom?

- And someone ought to tell the news geniuses that not every set of surgically separated Siamese twins is worth covering anymore. One story like that was quite enough. Simply separating these people is no longer news. On the other hand, if you gave them two sets of matching breast implants, that might qualify. Or if you sewed them back together because they got lonely, then maybe you've got something. But otherwise, do me a favor and keep that shit off my TV.

- Another medical angle: People with diseases or physical limitations should not automatically be considered news, even if they do something unusual. A paraplegic climbing a mountain; a crippled woman being named Teacher of the Year; a blind couple raising a deaf child. These things belong in *Reader's Digest*, not in a newscast.

- And please, no more stories about athletes who succeed in spite of having cancer. It's just not news; it happens too often. And by the way, why is it that every celebrity who gets cancer always says, "I'm going to lick this thing"? Just once, I'd like to hear some famous person say, "I've got cancer, and this is it. I'll be dead in six months."

The Animal Kingdom

Animal stories should also be excluded. A female cat who's nursing a litter of mouse babies is not news. It's cute, but it's not news. Cute can never be news. Which also explains why a waterskiing dog, a squirrel riding a motorcycle, or a monkey who likes to go horseback riding is not news.

- Nor is it especially noteworthy when a household pet finds its way home to its family from a thousand miles away. You know what would be news? If the pet returned from a thousand miles away, rejected the family, killed their new dog, and went across the street to live with a different family. Then you've got yourself a news story.

- And let's all agree right now to end this nonsense about Groudhog Day. We're living in the digital age; we have nanotechnology; we can clone animals; we've been to the moon; thousands of satellites orbit the earth; doctors can transplant a complete set of heart and lungs at one time . . . and once a year we stop everything to find out whether some groundhog in Pennsylvania will see his shadow? So we'll know whether or not winter will last another six weeks? It's absurd. You say it's harmless fun and no one really takes it seriously anyway? Well, if no one takes it seriously, that's all the more reason not to do it.

Hopscotching the Headlines

Here are some more things that aren't news:

- A convention of people who collect PEZ dispensers. They showed that on TV. It included a guy who covered every wall of his eight-room house with 55,000 PEZ dispensers. A man like that should not be on television, he should be living in one of those big buildings maintained by the state, where attendants come around every now and then to see if you've hung yourself.

- An eighty-six-year-old skydiver is not news; it's a novelty. You wanna know what's news? An eighty-six-year-old skydiver crashing into a monkey who's riding a horse. That's fuckin' news. And I'll be glad to stop whatever I'm doing to watch it on TV.

- The annual fat-guy, swimming-pool, bellyflop-diving contest is not news, either. It's disgusting. Another disgusting thing that shouldn't qualify is any food-eating contest: pies, hot dogs, pizza, brownies. The only news there is that Americans still don't understand how unattractive gluttony is in a country that has so many hungry people. And actually, that's not news, either; Americans don't understand a lot of things.

- I also don't think it's necessary to report on the rescue of people missing for six days following an avalanche, a cave-in, or some other outdoor mishap. People who go into the wilderness and put themselves in harm's way should not even be rescued, much less put on television. My philosophy is, "You takes your hike, you takes your chances." The media should be allowed maybe two of these stories a year, if that. And then only the most dramatic ones. Like if the people were gone so long they resorted to cannibalism.

- Here's something else: A Vietnam veteran with no legs "walking across America" to fight hunger is not news; it's a publicity stunt. You want to fight hunger? Bring canned goods into a poor neighborhood. That's how you fight hunger. You fight hunger by giving people food. It's as simple as that. You don't do it with publicity stunts. You don't do it with Hands Across America, Dicks Across Detroit, or Cunts Across Canada. Those things are not news.

Another good way to fight hunger would be to stop electing rich, conservative criminals who are interested only in fattening their bank accounts at everyone else's expense.

Speaking of such things, here's an item that would be *big* news— if somehow it ever happened: Any member of George Bush's family giving a homeless person ten dollars to buy a meal. Now, *there* would be a reason to interrupt regular programming.

Just to prove my point, try this thought experiment: Imagine yourself showing up at the back door of any one of the many houses owned by the Bush family. Now picture yourself asking them for a sandwich. Do they give you one? Lots of luck. What you *would* get would be a swift kick in the balls and ninety days in jail.

One more thing: I don't want to know about fetal surgery.